READING AND WRITING
IN THE
ACADEMIC COMMUNITY

READING AND WRITING IN THE ACADEMIC COMMUNITY

SECOND EDITION

MARY LYNCH KENNEDY
State University of New York at Cortland

HADLEY M. SMITH
Ithaca College

Prentice
Hall

Upper Saddle River, New Jersey 07458

Library of Congress Cataloging-in-Publication Data

Kennedy, Mary Lynch (date)
  Reading and writing in the academic community / Mary Lynch Kennedy, Hadley M.
Smith—2nd ed.
    p. cm.
    ISBN 0-13-030464-6
    1. English language—Rhetoric. 2. Research—Methodology. 3. Academic writing.
  4. College readers   I. Smith, Hadley M. (date)   II. Title.

PE1478.K395 2000
808′.042—dc21   00-034021

Editor in Chief: Leah Jewell
Acquisitions Editor: Corey Good
Assistant Editor: Vivian Garcia
AVP/Director of Production and Manufacturing: Barbara Kittle
Managing Editor: Mary Rottino
Production Editor: Kathy Sleys
Copyeditor: Bruce Emmer
Prepress and Manufacturing Buyer: Mary Ann Gloriande
Marketing Manager: Brandy Dawson
Cover Designer: Robert Farrar-Wagner
Cover Art: Jane Sterret/SIS, Inc.

This book was set in 10/12 Minion by Lori Clinton
and was printed and bound by R. R. Donnelley & Company.
Covers were printed by Phoenix Color Corp.

© 2001, 1994 by Mary Lynch Kennedy and Hadley M. Smith
Prentice-Hall, Inc./A Division of Pearson Education
Upper Saddle River, New Jersey 07458

Printed in the United States of America

10   9   8   7   6   5   4   3   2   1

ISBN 0-13-045294-7

Prentice-Hall International (UK) Limited, *London*
Prentice-Hall of Australia Pty. Limited, *Sydney*
Prentice-Hall Canada Inc., *Toronto*
Prentice-Hall Hispanoamerica, S. A., *Mexico*
Prentice-Hall of India Private Limited, *New Delhi*
Prentice-Hall of Japan, Inc., *Tokyo*
Pearson Education Asia Pte. Ltd., *Singapore*
Editora Prentice-Hall do Brasil, Ltda., *Rio de Janeiro*

Brief Contents

Contents

Part II

Writing Academic Essays, 81

C H A P T E R   3

RESPONDING TO SOURCES, 82

C H A P T E R   4

COMPARING AND CONTRASTING SOURCES, 141

CHAPTER 8
WRITING RESEARCH PAPERS, 285

Part III

Reading Selections, 331

C H A P T E R 9

GRADES AND LEARNING, 332

C H A P T E R 1 0

TECHNOLOGY AND SOCIETY, 352

C H A P T E R 1 1

TASTES IN POPULAR MUSIC, 378

C H A P T E R 1 2

EUTHANASIA AND PHYSICIAN-ASSISTED SUICIDE, 400

A P P E N D I X   B

WRITING ESSAY EXAMINATIONS, 495

WORKS CITED, 499

INDEX, 501

Preface

TO THE STUDENT

When you come to college, you join a new community. It consists of a group of people who share knowledge, beliefs, and values and operate according to a set of agreed norms. The type of writing done in this community is well established, and it follows certain expectations and conventions. In some ways, it is like high-school writing. You will find yourself writing for similar purposes—to respond, compare and contrast, argue, and analyze. But in other ways, college writing is different.

College writing assignments often have a greater degree of specificity than high-school assignments. Another important difference is that they require you to engage other writers' texts. When you use textual sources, you are expected to do more than simply report to your audience the set of facts or body of material that you have read. You are expected to alter the reading material so that it fits your own writing purpose. For example, a high-school writing assignment might ask you to write an essay on the causes of the growth of poverty in the United States, whereas a comparable college assignment might ask you to evaluate the views of Lester C. Thurow and Barbara Ehrenreich on the feminization of poverty. The college assignment focuses on a particular feature of poverty and requires you to read, analyze, and perhaps compare the texts of two authors and evaluate their positions. You will have to summarize, paraphrase, and quote the reading materials in your essay, and you will also have to keep in mind that your professor is more interested in your appraisal of Thurow's and Ehrenreich's views than in your explanation of them.

Sometimes college students are mystified by academic writing assignments. They find them analytical, abstract, and impersonal and are puzzled by their inability to do well on them. *Reading and Writing in the Academic Community* aims to make academic writing assignments accessible. Our goals are to help you attain the habits of mind needed for academic reading and writing and to give you a ready command of the forms, features, and conventions of academic prose. We take you through the reading and writing process, showing you how to tackle assignments in phases: prewriting, drafting, revising, and editing. We also provide you with many helpful models of other students' work.

Throughout *Reading and Writing in the Academic Community*, our foremost consideration is your purpose for writing academic essays. The book is divided into three parts. Part I, "Reading and Writing Conventions," focuses on your purpose for reading the sources that you will draw on in your essays. Part II, "Writing Academic Essays," is driven by a central question: What do you want to get across to readers in your academic community? At the heart of each essay you write is the particular purpose you want to accomplish. On one occasion you may decide that the best way to get your readers to understand a difficult issue is to compare and contrast two authors' views. Another time your aim is to persuade your readers of your viewpoint. In another paper you may want to analyze and evaluate other writers' views.

Whatever your purpose for writing, you can fulfill it more easily if you know how to organize your essay using patterns that reflect your thinking. In each chapter in Parts I and II, we show you how student writers typically arrange texts for various purposes and we guide you through the process of composing essays of your own.

Since so much of your college writing will require you to draw on sources, a key ability is critical reading. That is why Part I focuses on the reading process. Chapter 1 offers you a set of powerful strategies for assertive reading and shows you how to apply them to your assignments. Chapter 2 introduces you to three basic conventions of academic writing—summarizing, paraphrasing, and quoting—and provides you with extensive practice using these techniques.

Part II is devoted to essay writing. In Chapter 3, we discuss responding to sources, showing you how to compose essays by relating your own knowledge and experience to the material you read. In this chapter, you will find pointers for creating titles and openers; developing a thesis; and crafting paragraphs, including introductions and conclusions. You will also learn a number of useful strategies for revising preliminary drafts of your essays.

In Chapters 4, 5, and 6, we take you through the process of composing essays while engaging multiple reading sources. Chapter 4 explains how to make comparisons and contrasts that draw on textual sources as well as on your own ideas. We pay special attention to assignments that ask you to compare and contrast the views of two or more writers on the same topic. Chapter 5 offers suggestions for writing four types of papers that draw on multiple sources and, in some cases, your own knowledge and experience: a summary of multiple sources, an objective synthesis, an essay written in response to multiple sources, and a synthesis essay written for a specific purpose. The focus of Chapter 6 is developing strong arguments supported by reliable reading sources. We take you through the process of clarifying and refining issues, probing both sides of controversies, composing an arguable thesis, and marshaling a body of solid evidence to make a strong case.

In Chapter 7, we take up analysis and evaluation. We first show you how to write a systematic rhetorical analysis of a reading source. Then we explain how to compose an essay in which you evaluate the strengths and weaknesses of a source according to a set of established criteria. Finally, we take you through the process of writing an essay in which you analyze an issue objectively, "unpacking" it so that your reader can understand its complexities. Chapter 8 sets forth a process for conducting independent library research: posing questions and setting research goals, searching for information in print and electronic sources, and composing a research paper. In this chapter, we make a special effort to explain the use of computerized catalogs and indexes and the Internet so that you will feel confident using these powerful tools to obtain information for your research papers.

You will notice that throughout Parts I and II, we make extensive use of sample student essays. As we analyze these models, we guide you through the process of composing similar essays of your own.

Part III of the book is an anthology of compelling, high-interest reading selections. Chapters 9 to 14 focus on provocative, timely topics: grades in higher education, technology and society, tastes in popular music, euthanasia and physician-assisted suicide, racial profiling, and gender equity in sports. Following Part III, you will find one appendix of updated information on MLA and APA documentation styles and another on writing essay examinations.

As you analyze the reading sources and write essays for the assignments in this book, you will master the basic conventions of academic writing. Eventually, these conventions and processes described in this book will become second nature, and you will be able to execute the processes with very little effort.

TO THE INSTRUCTOR:
HIGHLIGHTS OF THE SECOND EDITION

The second edition of *Reading and Writing in the Academic Community* continues to present a comprehensive rhetoric covering assertive, critical reading and the major types of academic writing students encounter as undergraduates and an anthology of timely, high-interest readings. A distinct strength of the book is that it makes few assumptions about students' prior experience in the academy and provides explicit, step-by-step instruction in paraphrasing, summarizing, quoting, writing essays in response to readings, composing synthesis essays, and using sources to compose comparison-and-contrast essays, argument essays, analysis essays, evaluation essays, and research papers.

The second edition contains many new features that make the book more flexible and enhance its usefulness as a combined rhetoric and reader. The book has been expanded from two parts to three. Instead of combining rhetoric and reader, the reading selections now have a section of their own, Part III.

- Part III contains six entirely new chapters containing twenty-seven new reading selections on provocative topics: grades in higher education, technology and society, tastes in popular music, euthanasia and physician-assisted suicide, racial profiling, and gender equity in sports. We continue to accompany each reading selection with a prereading activity and reading comprehension questions that encourage students to (1) grasp the informational content, (2) decide what form, organization, and expository features the author uses, and (3) analyze rhetorical concerns, such as the context of the piece and the author's purpose with regard to his or her audience. As in the first edition, several writing assignments accompany each reading, and a further selection of writing assignments is presented at the end of each topically related chapter of readings.

- Questions, exercises, and activities give increased attention to group work and collaboration.

- Throughout Parts I and II, many new sample student essays and exercises have been added, and the text has been rewritten to reflect these changes.

- A strengthened presentation of thesis statements appears in Chapter 3, "Responding to Sources."

- Chapter 6, "Drawing on Sources for an Argument Essay," has been greatly expanded to include a detailed discussion of marshaling a body of solid evidence and making a strong case through ethical, emotional, and logical appeals.

- Chapter 7, "Analysis and Evaluation," has been substantially revised. The section on analyzing and evaluating literary works has been deleted, and a new section on writing an exploratory analysis essay has been added.

- Chapter 8, "Writing Research Papers," has changed significantly. It now includes an updated section on electronic resources and electronic and Internet research; new sections on using virtual libraries, locating and evaluating information on the World Wide Web, and collecting information through surveys and interviews; and a new sample research paper.
- Appendix A on MLA and APA documentation styles has been brought up to date.
- A new appendix (Appendix B) presents strategies that will enable students to do well on essay examinations.

ACKNOWLEDGMENTS

We owe special thanks to the students at Cornell University, Ithaca College, and the State University of New York at Cortland who contributed essays to this book. We are greatly indebted to Christina Haas and Linda Flower for the concept of "rhetorical reading," to Marlene Scardamalia and Carl Bereiter for "knowledge-telling" and "knowledge-transforming," to Victoria Stein for "elaboration," and to Linda Flower for "writer-based and reader-based prose." We have also drawn on the work of other researchers and writers, including Edward Corbett, Peter Elbow, Donald Murray, and Mina Shaughnessy.

At Prentice Hall, we have had the privilege of working with an outstanding team: Vivian Garcia, Leah Jewell, Corey Good, Brandy Dawson, and Kathy Sleys.

We are also grateful to our reviewers for their helpful suggestions and insightful analysis: Susan North of the University of Tennessee, Sara McLaughlin of Texas Tech. University, Maryanne Felter of Cayuga Community College, Chris Jennings of Tidewater Community College, Eileen Thompson of Lane Community College, George T. Karnezis of North Central College, Margaret Dawe Baughman of Wichita State University, Lyle W. Morgan of Pittsburgh State University, and Stuart Barbier of Indiana University–Purdue University, Fort Wayne.

Finally, we want to thank Nancy Siegele and Bill Kennedy for their help, humor, and support in getting us through yet another revision of a textbook.

Mary Lynch Kennedy

Hadley M. Smith

READING AND WRITING
IN THE
ACADEMIC COMMUNITY

Introduction

THE ACADEMIC COMMUNITY AND ITS CONVENTIONS

The purpose of *Reading and Writing in the Academic Community* is to help you learn how to communicate successfully among the members of the "academic community," a group that includes teachers, scholars, and artists as well as you and your fellow students. Individuals in the academic community hold widely diverse opinions, but they all share a special interest in language and interact regularly by writing and reading one another's work. Written communication is not identical in all fields of study, but members of the academic community share certain standards and conventions for written expression. When novices and apprentices write for academic audiences, sometimes they become so confused and frustrated that they feel that "academic writing is a trap, not a way of saying something to someone" (Shaughnessy 7). But once they learn the language conventions that govern the academic community, they see that this new way of reading, writing, and thinking is not so difficult to accomplish.

The best way to learn the language conventions of the academic community is to master a variety of strategies for reading and writing. Most important is learning how to comprehend the sources you read and use them in your own compositions. Assume that you are taking a Western civilization course and you have received the following essay assignment:

> Draw on your textbook and related reading to explain why existentialism, Marxism, and Christianity were considered major intellectual trends of the twentieth century.

The task requires you do three things: (1) read complex texts; (2) summarize, paraphrase, and quote various authors; and (3) weave textual material into your essay. But do you think your professor will be satisfied if all your essay does is summarize relevant passages from the textbook and other reading you have done? Probably not. Usually, college professors expect more than report writing. They want students to move beyond *knowledge-telling,* which is simply restating the information in reading sources, to *knowledge-transforming,* which involves using textual information to support one's thesis or point of view (Scardamalia and Bereiter). A student who is transforming knowledge rather than retelling it might write the history essay for the purpose of convincing her audience that Marxism had a greater impact on the twentieth century than existentialism or Christianity. She does more than simply report on existentialism, Marxism, and Christianity as major intellectual trends of the twentieth century. Her goal is more complex. She analyzes and synthesizes the readings for a particular rhetorical purpose: to persuade her readers that one trend had a greater effect on the twentieth century than the others. Expert academic writers make statements that go beyond those in the original texts, and in so doing they transform the sources rather than simply translate them.

A major convention of academic writing is to collect evidence from print sources. Think of how you might do this to write about television in a course on child development. You could use information in your reading to convince your audience that television advertising targeted at children should be banned. In a sociology class, you could summarize articles in order to compare and contrast the level of violence in Japanese and American television programs. In an engineering course, you could draw on reading sources to explain the technical barriers that hinder the development of high-definition television, and as a political science student, you could summarize research to illustrate how televised debates have affected American presidential elections. In each situation, you would write with a different purpose and audience in mind.

The academic community shares certain expectations for the way writers use language and develop ideas. Unless you follow these conventions, readers will not take your writing seriously. To a large extent, your success in college depends on your ability to learn the language that the academic community writes and speaks.

LEARNING THE CONVENTIONS

Unfortunately, some students never internalize the conventions of academic writing. They puzzle over "what the teacher wants" and have difficulty adjusting to the demands of different professors. Since all professors are part of the academic community, their fundamental expectations are similar. Once you master the forms and conventions of academic writing, you should never have to relearn them. What is the best way to do this? The trick is to "overlearn" them to the point where they become automatic. Once you have a ready command of the strategies and they have become habits of mind, you will not have to give them a second thought. You will be free to focus on being imaginative and finely crafting your prose. You will be able to accomplish your goals as an academic writer most effectively when you can execute certain processes without effort.

GOALS OF THIS TEXTBOOK

This book has three objectives:

1. To help you attain the habits of mind needed for the process of academic reading and writing
2. To give you a ready command of the forms, features, and conventions of academic writing
3. To show you that once you have practiced and internalized these forms and conventions, you can use them to communicate your ideas about any topic

Each chapter in Parts I and II focuses on conventions and ways of thinking that are crucial to success in college. The bulk of Chapter 1 explains how to read academic sources, not only for literal content but also for an awareness of the writer's goals and your own goals, that is, how you ultimately intend to use the information the sources provide. Chapter 2 explains the basic strategies—summarizing, paraphrasing, and quoting—you will need when writing about texts, and it stresses how you can use these strategies for your own rhetorical purposes. In Chapter 3, you will learn how to use your own knowledge and experience to comment on, respond to, or extend the ideas in reading sources. You will learn how to draw on sources to write comparison-and-contrast essays in Chapter 4. Synthesis, the process of combining ideas from multiple sources to make your own point, is covered in Chapter 5. In Chapter 6, you will study strategies for developing logical arguments that will sway an academic audience, and in Chapter 7, you will learn how to analyze and evaluate readings. Chapter 8 discusses strategies for conducting library research. The strategies and conventions we cover in these chapters are central to academic writing. They will provide you with a solid base for more specialized work in specific disciplines. Chapters 9 through 14, Part III of the book, constitute an anthology of twenty-eight reading selections that you can draw upon as you work through the assignments in Parts I and II.

Once you master the basic processes and conventions of academic writing, you will be able to use them for more complex purposes. You will move beyond knowledge-telling to knowledge-transforming and using sources more creatively. In the following sample paper, first-year college student Nora Gold uses many of the conventions you will learn in this book. Notice how she synthesizes material from a number of reading sources in order to make a statement about teen curfew laws.

Gold 1

Nora Gold

Professor Smith

Academic Writing I

30 March 2000

Curfew Laws: Demonizing Teens

In the summer of 1996, sixteen-year-old Asha Sidhu was arrested by the San Diego police, taken to the station, interrogated by officers, accused of various offenses, and held for hours, all without her parents' being informed (Allen 4). What crime did she commit? She was out after the 10:00 p.m. curfew. Even though she was only two blocks from her home and was out with her parents' permission, the San Diego curfew law gave the police the right to treat this honor student as if she were a common criminal (4). Teen curfew laws, such as the one enforced in San Diego, are being established in cities across the United States for the alleged purpose of reducing youth crime. These laws will do little to deter those teens who are criminally inclined and are unfair to the millions of young people who have done nothing to deserve being held under house arrest. Enforcing teen curfews amounts to penalizing young people so that adults can enjoy a false sense of security and politicians can give the impression that they are tough on crime.

More and more frequently, American communities are relying on curfews in their efforts to battle youth- and gang-related crime. A recent survey indicated that no fewer than 337 American cities have curfews, a third of which have been imposed since 1995, and thirty-five other cities are considering curfew laws (Powers). Typical curfew hours are

Summary from Allen

Citation of author

Nora's thesis

Paraphrase from Powers

1

2

Gold 2

11:00 p.m. on weeknights and 12:00 p.m. on Fridays and
Saturdays, and these restrictions usually apply to individuals
under eighteen (Powers). Some municipalities have even
established daytime curfews that ban teenagers from the streets
during the hours that school is in session (Davidson). In
addition to curfews passed by city and town governments,
certain privately owned shopping malls have established teen

curfews. A notable example is the Mall of America's 6:00 p.m.
weekend curfew for youths under sixteen who are not accompanied
by an adult (Freeman 483-84). This policy is enforced strictly
by guards stationed at all of the Mall's twenty-three
entrances. The Mall of America, a huge shopping and
entertainment complex located in Bloomington, Minnesota,
instituted the curfew policy following an incident in which a
teen fired a gun on Mall property (483). The combination of
strict public and private sector curfews could essentially
confine teens to home and school unless they are accompanied
by an adult.

From several different perspectives, youth curfews
represent an attack on Americans' civil liberties. The most
obvious constitutional problem is that curfews grant police the
power to detain citizens for nothing more than appearing young

3

(Budd 23). This is blatant age discrimination and also violates
the constitutional principles of reasonable suspicion and
presumption of innocence. Some curfew laws include provisions
that fly in the face of Fourth Amendment protections against
unreasonable search and seizure. For instance, a law passed in

Cicero, Illinois, gives police the right to seize the vehicles
of teenagers who violate the local curfew ("Lights Out"). Since

Gold 3

curfew laws allow the police considerable discretion in how the law is applied, some observers fear that officers will concentrate enforcement efforts on poor and minority teens ("Lights Out"). This policy might intensify our society's problems of racial and class-based discrimination. Another concern is that curfews may violate the First Amendment right of assembly since they allow little opportunity for young people to congregate outside of school (Freeman 482-84). Given the serious constitutional questions that curfews raise, why do they continue? Curfews remain in place because Americans under age eighteen cannot vote and thus lack the political power to resist unfair laws. As Budd points out, "Such a blunt and overreaching crime-fighting technique would clearly be unenforceable against adults" (23).

Some people might argue that it is worth sacrificing the constitutional rights of teenagers in order to protect all Americans, young and old, from crime. There is, however, little evidence that curfews make our country any safer. On the surface, it seems unlikely that curfews would deter anyone with serious criminal intentions. Budd points out that teens who are willing to risk spending years in jail for committing serious crimes, such as burglary or assault, are unlikely to fear the relatively minor penalties for violating curfew laws (22). Crime statistics support this notion. According to Budd, no studies have provided empirical evidence that curfews actually work (22). For example, San Diego officials claim their curfew law helped reduce juvenile crime; Budd points out, however, that the crime rate decline occurred only during hours of the day not covered by the curfew (22-23). In a comprehensive

Summary from Freeman

Quotation from Budd

Paraphrases from Budd

4

Gold 4

study, Dan Macallair and Mike Males, both of the Center on
Juvenile and Criminal Justice, analyzed the impact of
California's curfew laws, and their findings were clear:
curfews did not lower juvenile crime rates (Davidson).
According to Macallair and Males, "This was true for any race
of youth, for any region, for any type of crime" (qtd. in
Davidson).

If curfews appear to violate teens' rights and do not
even accomplish their intended purpose of reducing crime, why
are more and more cities establishing curfews? One reason that
curfews appeal to politicians and adult citizens is that they
give the appearance of attacking crime without asking the
taxpayers to provide much additional funding. According to Rice
University sociologist Steven Kleinberg, "People feel insecure
economically, and so there's resistance to dealing with
delinquency through measures that require an investment. . . . In
this climate of thought, it's a helpful belief to say, 'It's
their [teens'] fault' " (Allen 5). Sociologists have argued
that youth crime can be addressed effectively only through
programs that help teens develop into productive adults, such
as after-school tutoring and sports, rather than laws that
attempt to keep them off the streets (Allen 4-5). Rather than
addressing social problems that affect teens, the focus of
curfew laws is seemingly "to make adults feel better" ("Lights
Out"). Surely, our efforts and money should go into programs
for troubled youth that appear to work rather than senseless
curfew enforcement, which, although inexpensive, does nothing.

"The image of dissolute youth roaming the streets in
search of victims is now a fixture of our political rhetoric,

---

Margin annotations:

Paraphrase from Davidson

Quotation (from Davidson) of Macallair and Males

Quotation (from Allen) of Kleinberg

Paraphrase from Allen

Quotation from unsigned article

Quotation from Budd

5

6

Gold 5

and curfews offer a satisfying and uncomplicated solution"
(Budd 23). A curfew is a simplistic and ineffective response
to teen crime. Until we develop and support effective programs
to address poverty, domestic violence, drug abuse, and a host
of other social problems, teen crime will continue. Harassing
thousands of innocent teenagers, such as Asha Sidhu, will do
nothing to make our streets safer.

Gold 6

Works Cited

Allen, John. "U.S. Teens Face Rash of Get-Tough Actions As
    Nation's Fear Grows." <u>National Catholic Reporter</u> 10 Jan.
    1997: 4-5.

Budd, Jordan C. "Juvenile Curfews: The Rights of Minors vs. the
    Rhetoric of Public Safety." <u>Human Rights</u> Fall 1999: 22-24.

Davidson, Margaret. "Do You Know Where Your Children Are?"
    <u>Reason</u> 31.6 (Nov. 1999). Expanded Academic ASAP 14 Mar.
    2000 <http://web6.infotrac.galegroup.com/itw/infomark/
    859/977/57071541w3/purl=rcl_EAIM_0_A56750029&dyn=
    4!xrn_1_0_A56750029?sw_aep=ithaca_lib>.

Freeman, Alysa B. "Go to the Mall with My Parents? A
    Constitutional Analysis of the Mall of America's Juvenile
    Curfew." <u>Dickinson Law Review</u> 102 (1998): 481-538.

"Lights Out." <u>The Economist</u> 18 Sept. 1999: 30.

Powers, Ron. "More Cities Enact Curfews for Youth." <u>Ithaca
    Journal</u> 28 Feb. 2000: 1B.

Alphabetized
Works Cited
page

Exercise...

Study Nora's essay. Then answer the following questions.

1. What is Nora's overall purpose? What point is she making? How does she get that message across to her readers?

2. What aspects of the essay remind you of things you have been taught in the past about writing?

3. What aspects of the essay are at odds with what you have been told about writing? Can you account for any discrepancy?

4. How does Nora's essay differ from essays you have written in high school?

5. What is the relationship between Nora's ideas and those of the authors of the sources she cites?

6. Which approach is Nora using: knowledge-telling (simply telling her readers the contents of the reading sources) or knowledge-transforming (giving her readers a new understanding of information in the reading sources or using that information as support for her own thesis or point of view)?

. . . .

Part I

READING AND WRITING CONVENTIONS

1

READING ACADEMIC SOURCES

College students sometimes have difficulty comprehending textbooks and other required reading, and even when students understand these works, they find it hard to communicate that understanding in writing. Why do intelligent students who were accomplished readers in high school have problems with reading assignments? We will try to give you some insight into this phenomenon. Read the following two passages for an understanding of the authors' main ideas.

> Man is spirit. But what is spirit? Spirit is the self. But what is the self? The self is a relation which relates itself to its own self, or it is that in the relation [which accounts for it] that the relation relates itself to its own self; the self is not the relation but [consists in the fact] that the relation relates itself to its own self. Man is a synthesis of the infinite and the finite, of the temporal and the eternal, of freedom and necessity, in short it is a synthesis. A synthesis is a relation between two factors. So regarded, man is not yet a self. (Kierkegaard 146)

> One of childhood's saddest figures is the one who hangs around the fringes of every group, walks home alone after school, and sobs in despair, "Nobody wants to play with me." Children can be unpopular for many reasons, sometimes because they are withdrawn or rebellious. They may walk around with a "chip on the shoulder," showing unprovoked aggression and hostility. Or they may act silly and babyish, showing off in immature ways. Or they may be anxious and uncertain, exuding such a pathetic lack of confidence that they repel other children, who don't find them fun to be with. (Papalia and Olds 233)

Most students have difficulty understanding the passage from the Danish philosopher Kierkegaard but no problem with the excerpt by Papalia and Olds. The words Kierkegaard used are no more complex than those of Papalia and Olds. So what accounts for the disparity in comprehensibility? A fundamental difference between the two passages is that Kierkegaard's definition of "self" is theoretical and abstract, whereas Papalia and Olds's description of unpopular children is grounded in everyday experience. Readers comprehend not just by recognizing vocabulary but also by relating the content to things they already know and understand. For example, as you read the textbook excerpt, perhaps the image of an unpopular child with whom you are acquainted came to mind. Because you already have sufficient knowledge to make this image concrete, the text is relatively easy to understand. In contrast, if you have never thought before about the philosophical definition of "self," you may have found the Kierkegaard passage difficult. It does not relate directly to your prior knowledge or experience as the Papalia and Olds excerpt does. Another difference between the two passages concerns their organization. The Papalia and Olds excerpt is easy to understand because it follows a logical, conventional pattern. It starts off with the consequences (effect) of unpopularity—the lonely child—and then goes on to list the reasons (causes) for the problem. But the Kierkegaard passage is difficult to grasp because it does not follow a familiar pattern.

You could make sense of the child passage because you have a working knowledge of the concept of "unpopularity" and of the cause-and-effect pattern. You have stored mental images or representations of these things because you have experienced them repeatedly. You have stored mental images for any number of things: the concept of loneliness, ordering food at a restaurant, writing a thank-you note. When you read, these images help you make sense of the text. Your mind is very active. It does not work like a recording machine, robotically filing away information. It is continually making connections between the words on the page and the ideas in your head. When you have difficulty understanding a text, it is because you lack the appropriate background and cannot make these connections.

E x e r c i s e

Read "From Fine Romance to Good Rockin'—and Beyond: Look What They've Done to My Song" by Michael Budds on pages 391–398. As you read, write "yes" in the margin next to any passages that you can connect with your own experience and "no" next to any passages that seem foreign to your experience. Are the passages marked "yes" easier to understand than those marked "no"? After you have finished, try to estimate the percentage of the selection that seems familiar to you and the percentage that seems foreign.

Now read Jerry Farber's essay "A Young Person's Guide to the Grading System" on pages 333–336, and annotate the margin as you did for the Budds reading. Again estimate the percentage of the selection that seems familiar to you and the percentage that seems foreign. Based on the percentages for Farber and Budds, which selection should be easier to understand? Which do you think you actually did understand better?

A COMPREHENSIVE STRATEGY FOR THE READING PROCESS

We pointed out that it is hard to understand a text if you lack the necessary background knowledge. What can you do to improve your reading skills in preparation for college reading and writing tasks? A powerful strategy is to approach texts from several different perspectives. This will increase your chances of understanding even difficult reading sources. In this section, we will show you how to use each of the following strategic approaches.

COMPREHENSIVE READING STRATEGY

- Grasp the *information*, the main idea, and details.
- Decide how the text functions, what *form, organization, and features* the author uses.
- Consider the *rhetorical concerns,* the context in which the author is writing and the effect he or she is intending to achieve (Haas and Flower).

As you use each of these three approaches to reading, ask yourself the following questions.

STRATEGIC APPROACH	QUESTIONS TO ASK
Reading for information	What has the author written?
	What is the main idea?
	What other content is important?
Reading for form, organization, and features	How has the author written the piece?
	Is the author using an identifiable form?
	How do the different parts function?
	How is the text organized?
	What are the text's distinctive characteristics?
	Does the author use any special conventions?
Reading for rhetorical concerns	What is the context of the piece?
	What is the author's purpose?
	How is the author trying to affect the audience?

When you read for information, function, and rhetorical concerns, you are reading in three different but not necessarily separate ways. All three approaches can be used simultaneously and harmoniously. Skilled readers look at how information; form, organization, and features; and rhetorical elements function together. For the purposes of this discussion, however, we will present the strategic reading approaches one by one.

READING FOR INFORMATION

We often read to obtain information. We scan the front page of the newspaper to find out the latest developments in a current political crisis; we thumb through *Consumer Reports* to locate facts on a car we are interested in buying; we study a textbook to learn details about an important historical event. College students regularly read for information they can recycle into their own writing.

When you read for information, you must be *assertive*. This means reading with a purpose instead of passively processing print. An example of assertive reading is scanning an encyclopedia article in search of facts that are relevant to a topic you are researching. Your purpose is clear: to home in on certain parts of the text. The following techniques will help you be an assertive reader.

STRATEGIES THAT PROMOTE ASSERTIVE READING

- Call up your prior knowledge and feelings about the topic.
- Preview the material, and derive questions that will guide your reading.
- Annotate the material and take notes.

Calling Up Prior Knowledge and Feelings

Recall what we mentioned earlier about bringing prior knowledge and experiences to bear on the text. They enable you to comprehend what you read and in the process integrate what you already know about a topic with the new information in the text. You can interpret a difficult source best if you can relate it to an existing conceptual framework. This is why people who have read extensively in a subject find it easy to understand complex texts written in that area. Prior knowledge prepares them to receive new information. Prior experience may bias you in certain ways; nonetheless, integrating your experiences with the text is exactly what makes comprehension possible. As a process-oriented reader, you can benefit from your prior experience *before* you read, *while* you are reading, and *after* you have completed the text.

USING PRIOR KNOWLEDGE IN THE READING PROCESS

- Call up your prior knowledge *before* you read.
- Probe for links between the content and your prior knowledge *while* you are reading.
- Look for additional links *after* you read through the text.

This process will help you take full advantage of what you already know as you work to understand the text, and at the same time it will make you aware of how your personal experiences influence your reading. Two ways to call up prior experiences are freewriting and brainstorming.

Freewriting involves writing anything that comes to mind about a topic. Write nonstop for ten minutes or so, and do not worry about usage, spelling, or mechanics. Just jot down whatever is in your head. The following is an excerpt from a student's freewriting on why parents and their children typically have different tastes in popular music, an exercise the student completed prior to reading Budds's "From Fine Romance to Good Rockin'—and Beyond: Look What They've Done to My Song."

> There's no question that my parents and I have different tastes in popular music. They dislike a lot of the music that my younger brother and I enjoy, especially techno and rap. And while I don't actually dislike their classic rock, I have to say that I would almost never play those tunes myself. So why are my parents' tastes so different from mine? One reason is that they just haven't heard much new music. My parents say they didn't have as much time to listen to music once they started full-time jobs, so they know a lot about the music that was popular when they were teenagers, like the Beatles and the Rolling Stones, but almost nothing about the music of the past twenty-five years. Believe it or not, they had never heard the Chemical Brothers or Dr. Dre until I started listening to their albums. You can't really enjoy a type of music until you get to know it. To them, all rap "sounds just the same," whereas to me, each rap artist has a distinct style. I don't think I will stop listening to new popular music once I leave college, because music is just too important to me.

Brainstorming uses a process of free association. To begin the process, skim the reading source and come up with key words or phrases that seem pivotal to the assignment. Then list whatever associations come to mind when you think about these target concepts.

Do not bother to write complete sentences; just list words and phrases. Give your imagination free rein. Here is a short excerpt from some brainstorming that a student did after skimming Budds's article. Since the article discusses changes in popular musical tastes, the student decides to describe his own musical tastes as a reference point before he begins to read the Budds selection carefully from beginning to end. He brainstorms a list of words and phrases that explain why he likes rap.

<u>What appeals to me about rap</u>:

urban	club scene
rhythm	innovative
has a message	cutting-edge
tells about reality	creative
no sugar-coating	political
strong bass	radical
danceable	

Freewriting and brainstorming are ways of calling up your prior knowledge about a topic. They will strengthen your understanding of the ideas under discussion and help you read more objectively. You will be more conscious of your opinions and biases, and you won't inadvertently confuse them with those of the author. All the same, you can never be completely objective. Since you comprehend texts by relating known concepts to new ideas, your understanding will always be a function of your prior knowledge. In fact, your reading of a particular text may change as you make fuller use of your background knowledge.

Previewing and Deriving Questions

After you have called up prior knowledge and expressed your feelings about the topic, come up with some goals for what you want to get from the reading source. In textbooks, you can use the reader aids that accompany each chapter: preview outlines, introductory and concluding sections, and review questions. Chapter or section headings may also suggest concepts or issues that the chapter will cover. Use these reader aids to generate your own questions about the chapter content; you will then answer the questions as you read. This tactic works best if you write out the questions and then record the answers as you come to them. If you enter them in a reading journal or log, you can reread the log at a later date to retrieve the content you obtained in your reading. Too often, students spend hours reading information-rich texts only to find several days later that they remember virtually nothing and must reread all the material. The extra time it takes to preview a text and formulate reading questions represents a real savings compared to the extra time needed for rereading texts.

Annotating the Material and Taking Notes

Another technique that promotes active reading is to enter into a dialogue with the author by *annotating* the text as you read. When you annotate, you make marginal notes, underline, or highlight the text in order both to call out the most important concepts and to record your initial brief responses to what the author says. The following example shows a student's annotations of paragraphs 5 and 6 from Michael Budds's essay. The student highlights important concepts in the left margin and uses the right margin for personal reactions.

Annotations

Rock critics are racist and elitist

Much of the negative response to rock and roll by voices in the establishment must be identified as both racist and elitist.[4] The music was roundly condemned by individuals who, with little experience and little understanding of its nature or history, judged it on the basis of what it was not and whose it was. The foreground importance assigned to the sounds of guitars and drums—often raucous, insistent, and amplified to penetrating levels of volume—was in itself perceived as an unabidable physical assault by detractors. In 1956, *Time* magazine, the prominent current events periodical of record for American society, helped set the tone for the national debate in its first report on rock and roll by describing the music in such loaded terms as "jungle," "juvenile delinquency," and "Hitler mass meetings."[5] Rock and roll, moreover, began its life as a symbol of integration, as an interracial music—with the participation of performers and consumers of both races. Although opportunities for African-American musicians were still systematically restricted, this circumstance alone was enough to rally the champions of entrenched segregation and bigotry.

I think some people today hate rap because they are racists

Stereotypes of rock

Rock threatened the traditional pop music establishment (like Sinatra?)

In addition to the perceived threat to the society at large, the threat to the standing popular music industry was undeniable. Entertainment music in America was a highly lucrative business that directly affected the livelihood of countless individuals. Rather suddenly, the musical products of young Southern upstarts flooded the marketplace with stunning success. Serious loss of income and loss of control forced industry executives to adopt a defensive posture. Leaders of the recording industry went so far as to condemn the music of their competitors as socially irresponsible and morally corrupting. The editors of *Billboard* and *Variety,* trade magazines of the profession, called for self-policing and raised the specter of government censorship as the ultimate solution to the dilemma.[6] In a

Money talks

This is totally unfair!

Rock becomes acceptable, little by little, because it makes money

short time, of course, the industry—chastened by reality, bent on surviving, and enticed by obvious financial rewards—embraced the world of rock and roll by buying it up piece by piece. This transaction helped legitimize the music's hold on the American middle class, but it also introduced musical compromises dictated by purely commercial concerns and a sensational approach to merchandising. It also meant that, in the view of many, by the end of the 1950s the industry itself had become part of the problem.

What a sellout!

A useful annotation technique is to draw on prior knowledge to *elaborate* the reading source. *Elaborations* are associations, extensions, illustrations, or evaluations. You can elaborate by suggesting situations the writer has not envisioned and by providing analogies, examples, or counterexamples of ideas (Stein). A student uses several of those strategies to elaborate on the first two paragraphs in the Budds selection.

Elaborations

I've never understood the fear that rock is a threat to society. Rock just expresses the threatening attitudes that are already out there in the society; it doesn't create them.

No musical repertory in Western civilization has aroused more controversy than rock and roll. No musical repertory has attracted so many powerful and self-righteous opponents. No musicians, viewed as a representative group, have taken such self-indulgent and often self-destructive delight in combining the roles of entertainer/artist and social outlaw. One need only invoke characterizations of three identifiable strains of this music—"shock rock," "cock rock," and "schlock rock"—to appreciate its power to send self-proclaimed protectors of American culture into fits of anguish. The implications of this music's underprivileged birthright, the complex temper of American society since its emergence as a mainstream phenomenon in the wake of World War II, its identification with the thought and behavior of teenagers, and its potential as a means for acquiring almost limitless wealth have all contributed to its perceived menace.

Other aspects of the rock "menace" are its link to the drug culture and to violence. Maybe Budds thinks that drugs and violence come under "behavior of teenagers," but I think these are big enough problems to be mentioned separately and involve lots of people well out of their teens.

I think a lot of the rock censorship effort is politically motivated. Rock is an easy target for politicians who want to appear to have strong morals and thus attract mainstream Middle American voters.

As a result, rock and roll has become a prime target for censorship campaigns by a host of special interest lobbies—religious, political, economic, and musical.[3] Such opposition, be it well-intentioned or vested in self-interest, has existed as an almost chronic condition throughout the music's rather short history. It can be argued, however, that the passion and energy expended in attempts to alter or suppress rock and roll expression have only spurred rockers to flaunt or exaggerate the "objectionable" aspects of their music and worldview in a spirit of defiant celebration. Rock fans have affirmed the behavior of musicians with unbridled enthusiasm and, by their adulation, have encouraged them to challenge the status quo.

Sure! I doubt that many teenagers would pay any attention to Marilyn Manson if it wasn't that adults think he is so terrible. Forbidden things attract many teenagers. Why don't adults understand this?

Some students overuse highlighting markers. You may have difficulty deciding what is important as you read through a source for the first time. It may seem that every concept is worthy of special attention. But if you highlight a large percentage of the text, you will have a lot to reread when you study for an exam or look for ideas for a paper. Another problem with highlighting is that it is a passive, mechanical activity that does not engage you with the text. It only gives the illusion that you are reading effectively. There is an advantage to writing out summary statements and reactions as opposed to just highlighting important ideas. Writing comments forces you to process the information, restate it in your own words, and react to it. The ultimate goals of any annotating process are to involve you intellectually with the text and to give you access to it without rereading. Writing out marginal notes is the best way to accomplish this.

When you encounter difficult sources, probably the most successful strategic reading approach is to use a preview-and-question or other note-taking method along with marginal annotations. Under certain circumstances, however, one system may be more practical than the other. Since you cannot annotate books, magazines, and microforms from the library, you must take separate notes. If these sources are easy to read and have straightforward content, you can streamline note-taking and annotating procedures to capture only the most basic ideas. But remember that it is natural to forget much of what you have read; even relatively simple ideas may slip from your memory unless you record them in notes or annotations.

Whether you take separate notes or annotate, it is helpful to write down personal reactions to the text as you read. You might want to designate a notebook as your reading journal or log. Your reactions can include agreements and disagreements, questions you have for the author, and judgments on the text's relevance or acceptability. In general, this process involves relating the author's ideas to your prior knowledge and experiences. Reacting as you read is particularly important if you intend to write a paper that gives your view on the ideas in the source. To get the juices flowing, ask yourself the following questions:

QUESTIONS FOR REACTION

- What do I already know about this topic from books, magazines, television, school or college courses, personal experience, or conversation?
- What is the relationship between my prior knowledge and the information being presented in the text?
- Do I have personal opinions or biases on this topic? With what parts of the author's discussion do I agree or disagree?

Answering these questions will help you link the content of the source to relevant information that you already know.

Notice how the goals of summarizing and reacting are represented in marginal notes and a journal entry for paragraphs 15 and 16 from Budds.

Annotations

Rock provides a record of teens' concerns.

Each generation creates its own rock genres. Rock is diverse.

In spite of the big-business packaging, there is, probably, no better record of what has concerned American teenagers in the second half of the twentieth century than rock and roll. From its commercial beginnings, it remains a music with an attitude, purposefully at odds with authority figures and social prescriptions. And, just as important, these concerns have often been communicated, without apology or embarrassment, in the common language of teenagers intent on carving out a meaningful identity for themselves and their peers. Although still shocking in some quarters, moreover, the casual use of profanities, the graphic references to sexual behaviors and drug use, and the open attacks on other cultural "sacred cows" have not been exclusive to rock and roll.

Because of its essential commercial application in American popular culture as dance-related song (the demand for new product) and because of the need of each new generation of American youth to identify itself musically according to its own terms, the history of rock and roll has unfolded in an often confusing succession of substyles or subgenres that represent a broad range of expression. Although it is useful to appreciate such diversity under the umbrella of rock-related popular music, such subcategories

Elaborations

Is rock a just a "record" of what teens are thinking, or does it actually play a role in creating these attitudes? I've known people who first got into the Grateful Dead and then got into Dead Head culture.

To understand a rock genre, you have to know its roots.

have always represented meaningful distinctions to connoisseurs, and, in fact, a number of them can be described rather discretely in musical and sociological terms. It is important to understand whether a particular "movement" uses the urban blues, the Anglo-American ballad, or the mainstream popular song as its point of departure. Was the music, for example, created by ambitious young Southerners with a first-hand knowledge of minority music, by middle-class African-American talents from Detroit groomed for entertainment glory, by turned-on and tuned-in Bohemians in San Francisco with a Counterculture agenda, or by the rappers of America's inner-cities caught "between the outlaw culture of the streets and the hardcore taste of the music business"?[10] It is, likewise, instructive to construct a profile of representative groups of musicians and to place their accomplishments in context.

Does it really matter if we know the origins of a particular rock genre? My little sister is really into Ben Harper, but she doesn't know anything about the blues tradition that influences Harper. Does that mean that she enjoys the music any less than people who do know about blues?

Journal Notes

Budds seems to imply that you can't truly appreciate a type of rock music without knowing about its origins. That idea really troubles me. I do know about the origins of some of the music I like—ska, for example—but I really don't know much about the origins of techno even though I like it. Does this mean that I would appreciate ska more than techno? Actually, I probably enjoy techno more and know quite a bit about current artists. I don't know where techno came from, but that doesn't affect my enjoyment of it.

Reading assertively by taking notes, annotating, and reacting is important when your ultimate goal is to write about the text. Notes and annotations are the raw material for summaries and paraphrases, two forms of writing we will discuss in Chapter 2. Responses recorded in marginal notes and freewriting are the basis for response essays. In Chapters 3 and 7, we will discuss how you can move from these initial responses to essays of personal reaction and analysis. Assertive reading not only helps you understand the ideas in sources but also sets you well on the way to writing source-based essays.

E x e r c i s e ....

Read Jerry Farber's essay "A Young Person's Guide to the Grading System" on pages 333–336 using the assertive reading techniques described so far. Practice the process approach. First, preview the source and use freewriting to activate your prior knowledge of the topic. Next, read the articles and use the preview-and-question technique to take separate notes. Annotate the source as well. After you have finished reading, freewrite your overall reactions to Farber's argument.

. . . .

READING FOR FORM, ORGANIZATION, AND FEATURES

To become a proficient college reader and writer, you have to pay attention to what authors are *doing* as well as saying. This means that in addition to reading for content, you have to consider form, organizational pattern, and the distinctive features of the text.

Just as you have prior knowledge and experiences that are related to the content you read, you also have expectations about the ways authors set up their texts. Since you have already had at least twelve years of reading practice by the time you enter college, you possess a certain amount of knowledge about the forms, structures, and features of different types of texts. You already know that stories have elements like setting, plot, and theme; business letters contain an inside address and salutation; poems sometimes rhyme and have uneven lines; and newspaper articles are constructed with the most important facts presented in the first paragraph and the less essential information later in the piece. In other words, you have developed conceptual frameworks for these texts. This type of knowledge is crucial to reading comprehension.

Forms of Writing

Each piece of writing belongs to a class or category that can be distinguished by common characteristics. Most likely you would have no difficulty recognizing the characteristics of literary genres like short stories, novels, and poems or nonliterary forms like news articles, editorials, and biographies. As you become more familiar with academic writing, you will see that it has identifiable forms (see Table 1-1). Some of these forms are specialized—for example, the psychological research article, the scientific lab report, and the philosophical essay of reflection. Other forms are more conventional, and you will see that they are commonly used in many different fields.

Readers who know about different types of academic writing have expectations about the organization of the text and the author's intentions. For example, readers familiar with the characteristics of argument have definite expectations about an argument essay. They presume that the writer will lay out both sides of a controversial issue, make some concessions to people who hold an opposing view, and then refute their claims. Knowledge of form is indispensable if you want to read with full comprehension. Make a conscious effort to tap your existing knowledge and to learn about new forms whenever possible. The reading selections in Part III of this book will give you a good start.

E x e r c i s e . . . .

Review the essays by Budds (pages 391–398) and Farber (pages 333–336). Identify the form of each piece, and list the characteristics on which you based your decision.

. . . .

TABLE 1-1 FORMS COMMON IN ACADEMIC WRITING

Essay Type	Characteristics
Response	Includes identification of reading material to which the writer is responding, indication of the focus of the paper, commentary, and reactions.
Comparison and contrast	Presents a thesis based on the elements being compared or contrasted. The essay usually follows one of two patterns of organization: in the *point-by-point* pattern, the writer shifts back and forth between the elements being compared; in the *block* pattern, the writer explains one item completely before turning to the other.
Synthesis	Includes a thesis or unifying theme around which the writer organizes material selected from two or more reading sources. The writer sets the context for the reader by giving appropriate background information on sources. Clear connectives differentiate the writer's ideas from those of the authors of sources.
Argument	Includes an argumentative thesis, background information on the issue, support for the position being argued, mention of positions in opposition to the writer's, and response to opposition.
Analysis	Includes identification of reading material being analyzed, background information, statement of the writer's purpose for writing, summary of main points of the source, and examination of the author's presentation. Shows how the author's technique and various parts of the piece contribute to the theme and the author's purpose.
Evaluation	Includes identification of the material being evaluated, background information, statement of the writer's purpose for writing, summary of the main points of the source, and consideration of the author's presentation. The essay includes comments on the author's success in achieving his or her purpose, usually by reviewing features and techniques. Discusses overall strengths and weaknesses.
Literature review	Identifies trends in current research on a particular topic. Often summarizes key issues and may include analysis or evaluation of trends. Typically involves synthesis of sources but may be a series of free-standing summaries.
Research	Starts with a question or problem that requires collecting facts, opinions, and perspectives from books, magazines, newspapers, or other sources. The author makes sense of information derived from a variety of sources. May include literature review, analysis, or evaluation.

Patterns of Organization and Development

Just as you come to college already knowing something about different forms of writing, you also know about the basic features of texts. You can identify introductions, conclusions, theses or main idea statements, and topic sentences of paragraphs. In your own essays, you've used particular organizational plans, such as cause and effect or comparison and contrast. Writers use a variety of these patterns, depending on their purpose for writing. Table 1-2 identifies the most common patterns and gives a brief description of the purpose for each.

TABLE 1-2 PATTERNS FOR DEVELOPING AND ORGANIZING IDEAS

Pattern	Writer's Purpose
Time order, narration, process	To present ideas or events in a chronological sequence; to tell what happened (narration) or to describe a sequence of actions (process)
Antecedent and consequence, cause and effect	To present causes (antecedents) or examine effects or outcomes (consequences); to reveal the causes of a particular outcome or phenomenon or to explain its consequences, usually by explaining the relationship between the causes and the effects
Description	To present the physical attributes, parts, or setting of the topic, often out of a desire to give a personal impression of the person, place, or thing being described
Statement and response	To present a statement and give a reaction, often in a question-and-answer, problem-and-solution, or remark-and-reply format
Comparison and contrast	To present the similarities or differences between objects, approaches, or viewpoints
Example	To present illustrations or instances that support an idea
Analysis or classification	To divide the topic into parts (analyze) or to group parts or facets of the topic according to some principle or characteristic (classify)
Definition	To explain a word, concept, or principle
Analogy	To show the similarity between things that otherwise bear little or no resemblance; to explain something by comparing it point by point with something similar

Sometimes writers tell their readers how they are going to organize material. When writers explain what they are doing or direct their audience to read in a certain way, readers know what to expect. If the writer has not indicated what he or she is doing, however, you have to determine the pattern of development yourself.

A key to unlocking the meaning of a text is to identify the pattern of organization. A writer may use a single organizational pattern to develop an entire piece of writing, but it is more likely that the piece will consist of many overlapping patterns. An initial, quick reading will often give you a sense of the text's overall organizational pattern. Keep this pattern in mind, and then, when you do a close reading, annotate the places where the author has used other patterns of development. Consider how one of our students annotated paragraph 7 from the Budds selection.

Time order

Example

Cause and effect

> In retrospect, it seems possible to identify a number of factors that help explain this radical change in musical taste. First of all, the popular song tradition of Tin Pan Alley, which had been centered in New York City and had flourished for more than three generations, began to show signs of wear. The search for fresh and compelling expression within the rather well-defined style became increasingly difficult. The traumatic events of World War II, moreover, made the sanitized worldview delivered in the snappy dance songs and dreamy love ballads that were hallmarks of the genre seem inappropriate or irrelevant to the new generation of youngsters. At the same time that Tin Pan Alley was reaching its peak in the songs of Gershwin, Kern, Rodgers, and Porter, two minority song traditions that had evolved from longstanding folk practice—the urban blues of black America and the country and western songs of rural white Southerners—entered the popular arena and reached a larger audience thanks to a process of commercialization that included recordings, radio stations, and more venues for live performance. The inexpensive portable transistor radio, a by-product of wartime technology, enabled young people to acquaint themselves with rhythm and blues as well as country and western music without parental knowledge or supervision.

The general plan for the paragraph is cause and effect; Budds identifies the various causes of a "radical change in musical taste." But within this overall pattern, Budds describes a time-ordered sequence of events and gives examples.

Exercise ....

Identify the patterns of development used by the authors of the following passages. Choose from the nine patterns presented in Table 1-2. Remember that in some instances, different patterns of development may overlap.

1. Page 401, paragraph 2 (Anonymous, "It's Over, Debbie")
2. Page 384, paragraph 3 (Richard Brookhiser, "All Junk, All the Time")
3. Page 354, paragraph 13 (Joshua Quittner, "Invasion of Privacy")
4. Page 360, paragraph 7 (John Leo, "When Life Imitates Video")

Features of Writing

In addition to identifying the form and organizational pattern of a reading source, proficient readers pay attention to its distinctive features. They look for special qualities or distinctive characteristics of the text. To understand more clearly what we mean by "features," take a look at the following passages from Budds and Farber.

Budds (paragraph 5)

Much of the negative response to rock and roll by voices in the establishment must be identified as both racist and elitist.[4] The music was roundly condemned by individuals who, with little experience and little understanding of its nature or history, judged it on the basis of what it was not and whose it was. The foreground importance assigned to the sounds of guitars and drums—often raucous, insistent, and amplified to penetrating levels of volume—was in itself perceived as an unabidable physical assault by detractors. In 1956, *Time* magazine, the prominent current events periodical of record for American society, helped set the tone for the national debate in its first report on rock and roll by describing the music in such loaded terms as "jungle," "juvenile delinquency," and "Hitler mass meetings."[5] Rock and roll, moreover, began its life as a symbol of integration, as an interracial music—with the participation of performers and consumers of both races. Although opportunities for African-American musicians were still systematically restricted, this circumstance alone was enough to rally the champions of entrenched segregation and bigotry.

Farber (paragraph 4)

Learning happens when you *want* to know. Ask yourself: did you need grades to learn how to drive? To learn how to talk? To learn how to play chess—or play the guitar—or dance—or find your way around a new city? Yet these are things we do very well—much better than we handle that French or Spanish that we were graded on for years in high school. Some of us, though, are certain that, while we might learn to drive or play chess without grades, we still need them to force us to learn the things we don't really want to learn—math, for instance. But is that really true? If for any reason you really want or need some math— say, algebra—you can learn it without being graded. And if you don't want it and don't need it, you'll probably never get it straight, grades or not. Just because you pass a subject doesn't mean you've learned it. How much time did you spend on algebra and geometry in high school? Two years? How much do you remember? Or what about grammar? How much did all those years of force-fed grammar do for you? You learn to talk (without being graded) from the people around you, not from gerunds and modifiers. And as for writing— if you ever do learn to write well, you can bet your sweet ass it won't be predicate nominatives that teach you. Perhaps those subjects that we would never study without being graded are the very subjects that we lose hold of as soon as the last test is over.

COMPARISON OF THE FEATURES OF THE TEXTS

Budds	*Farber*
Draws on observations of historical events to verify the author's points.	Asks the reader to draw on his or her own experience to verify the author's points.
Cites other sources and ends with a list of references.	Includes no references to outside sources.
Does not address the reader directly.	Speaks directly to the reader with the pronoun *you*.
Contains relatively long sentences.	Includes sentences as short as two words in length. A number of sentences are four to ten words long.
Uses vocabulary that assumes a sophisticated audience such as "perceived as an unabidable physical assault by detractors."	Uses informal vocabulary such as "bet your sweet ass."

As a college student, you will undoubtedly read many sources that have features like those found in Budds's writing. Scholarly writers often draw extensively on evidence from published sources or original research, and they carefully document all the information that they use. Like Budds, they adopt rather formal voices and use sentences with a number of coordinated and parallel elements. But some academic writers use conversational, less formal styles like Farber's. One style is not necessarily more appropriate or correct than the other.

In your own work, you will learn to write in ways that are appropriate to given situations. For example, your psychology lab reports will be relatively formal, with concise sentences describing procedural matters. By contrast, personal essays will be less formal in tone, and they might even include dialogue. In later chapters, we will include examples of professional and student writing that illustrate a range of styles and techniques.

Of all the conventions we have discussed, the feature that best characterizes academic discourse is the practice of integrating one's own ideas with information from reading sources. Sometimes writers simply refer to the sources, but more often they paraphrase, quote, or summarize them. When they do this, they always cite the author and provide bibliographic information for their readers. Let us illustrate with an example from Douglas Putnam's "Gender Games: What about Men?" (pages 451–453).

It was not until 1991, ten years after it became the governing body for women's college athletics, that the NCAA's members formally adopted gender equity in athletics as a basic principle of the organization (Tarkan 1995: 26). Executive director Cedric Dempsey admits that progress has been slow. "We are trying to change a culture," he says. "It is more difficult than it might appear" (Chambers 1997: C10).

Putnam is referring to ideas published in other sources, so he puts in parentheses the names of the scholars and the dates of their publications. If you are interested in learning more about Tarkan's or Chambers's research, you can consult the alphabetical list of references on the last page of the Putnam selection (see page 453) and then locate the studies in your college library.

Another distinctive feature of academic writing is content endnotes or footnotes. Sometimes academic writers want to give their readers additional information, but they don't want to interrupt the flow of the text. In this case, they provide a reference numeral in the text and include the extra information in a footnote or in a list titled "Notes" at the end of the piece. Here is an example from Budds.

> Song texts of mainstream America had long been influenced by the high culture of Europe, however watered down for middle-class consumption. Romantic love, the subject of the vast majority of all songs, was treated in a highly idealistic, typically sentimental manner. Although rarely profound, the language tended toward the poetic, preferring a high-priced vocabulary filled with euphemism and fully respectful of an unwritten, but widely sanctioned code of public propriety. Songs with texts overstepping this sensibility were banned by radio stations or deleted from the musical scores of Broadway and Hollywood.[7] Early in the nineteenth century, for example, Stephen Foster's Jeanie was "borne like a vapor on the summer air."

> 7. The grand exception appears to be songwriter/composer Cole Porter (1891–1964), whose witty but suggestive lyrics earned for him the nickname "the genteel pornographer" from Cecil Smith in *Musical Comedy in America* (New York: Theatre Arts Books, 1950).

The convention of referring to sources is not confined to academic writing. In fact, when you read the selections in this book, you will discover that writers whose work appears in newspapers or popular magazines (rather than in scholarly journals) regularly cite, paraphrase, quote, and summarize sources. But often these writers do not supply bibliographic information for the reader. A good case in point is "First and Last, Do No Harm," an article by Charles Krauthammer, which was originally published in *Time*. Turn to page 416 and scan the article looking for places where Krauthammer refers to outside sources. Notice that when he includes a quotation, he does not tell his readers its page number in the original source. The convention of meticulously citing sources is not always observed outside the academic community. Magazine writers may even include a fact or concept without explaining where it came from. And depending on their editorial policies, some newspapers publish stories based on the statements of unnamed sources. In Chapter 2, we will discuss in detail how you, as an academic writer, should follow conventions for citing sources.

E x e r c i s e ....

For this exercise, you will look for identifiable features in three articles:

Sidney Hook, "In Defense of Voluntary Euthanasia," pages 403–404

Lori Andrews, "The Sperminator," pages 369–376

Pat Griffin, "Sport: Where Men Are Men and Women Are Trespassers," pages 448–449

As you read each article, record answers to the following questions.

1. Does the author use the first-person *I* or *we* or the second-person *you*? Explain why.
2. Has the writer used primarily long sentences (over twenty-five words), short sentences (under ten words), or varied sentence length? Cite examples.
3. Does the writer support his or her assertions with evidence from published sources? From personal experience? Give examples.
4. Does the writer use any method to cite and document sources?

• • • • • • • • • • • • • • • •

READING FOR RHETORICAL CONCERNS

Skilled readers are interested in rhetorical concerns as well as content and text features. What exactly do we mean by "rhetorical"? The term relates to *rhetoric*. Many people who hear the word *rhetoric* think of affected or pretentious language. "The politician's speech was all rhetoric" means that the politician used a lot of empty or inflated language and either did not say very much or else diverted attention from where it should have been. When we speak of rhetoric in this book, however, we are not referring to pompous language. We mean *an author's attempt to use language to achieve an intended effect on an audience.* An important word here is *intended.* Both writing and reading are intentional. They are deliberate actions, guided by a purpose or goal.

As we wrote this textbook, we had a clear purpose and intention: to show our audience how to become competent readers and writers in the academic community. As you read this book, you also have a clear purpose and intention: to learn how to write papers for college courses. Without intention, the acts of reading and writing are meaningless.

RHETORICAL READING

• Be aware of the author's purpose and intentions for writing the text.
• Be aware of your purpose and intentions for reading the text.

When you think about *rhetorical reading,* keep in mind that two sets of intentions are involved. One pertains to what you perceive to be the intentions of the author of the text, and the other refers to your own intentions as a reader. Thus rhetorical reading has two distinct meanings. The first refers to the goals of the author of the reading source. As you read with an eye to discovering the author's ultimate purpose, ask yourself the following questions.

DETERMINING AN AUTHOR'S RHETORICAL PURPOSE

• What prompted the author to write?
• What audience does the author have in mind?
• What impact does the author want to have on the reader?

- What role does the author assume with regard to the audience, the subject matter, and his or her own voice?
- How does the author view what others have said on the topic?

The answers to these questions help define the author's rhetorical purpose and the rhetorical context of the piece.

The two forms of rhetorical reading are in no way at odds with each other. In fact, good readers are able to separate their own rhetorical goals from those of authors. Even though both forms of rhetorical reading can function simultaneously and harmoniously, for convenience we will discuss them separately.

Author's Rhetorical Goals

To determine an author's rhetorical goals, a key question to ask is *What prompted the author to write?* To answer this question, you have to step inside the author's mind to discover his or her intentions. In some cases, these motives may be obvious. When you receive an advertisement in the mail, you know that the ad writers are trying to convince you to buy something, and they are also attempting to please their employers and earn a paycheck. True, they may have other motives that you cannot easily guess—for instance, striving to win a promotion or an advertising industry award—but at least some of their goals are relatively clear. The goals of academic writers are usually not so obvious as those of advertisers. But if you ask the right questions, you will be able to discover the imperative—the feeling, view, incident, or phenomenon—that inspired the author to write.

Take Farber's essay on pages 333–336. What prompted Farber to write this? Farber's piece is laid out as an argument in which he details what he sees as the problems with the traditional A-through-F grading system. He tries to anticipate the position of people who favor grades and then respond to their points one by one. Overall, his goal is to convince the reader that grades hinder learning and that education happens best in an environment free of grades. Farber has an agenda for educational reform, and in this article, he attempts to generate support for his ideas.

What audience does the author have in mind? This is a crucial question for determining the author's rhetorical goals. A skilled writer develops an argument and organizes material for the needs of a particular group of readers. If you can identify this audience, you will be well on the way to determining what the author is trying to accomplish. One way to determine the audience is to consider the type of publication in which the piece appears. Staff writers for newsmagazines like *Newsweek* or *Time* direct their articles to a general audience, whereas writers for *The National Review* or *The Nation* anticipate readers of a particular political persuasion.

Although Farber mentions reform at all levels of education, most of his comments relate to undergraduate college education. He has two audiences in mind: students and professors or college administrators. Notice that in paragraph 8 he addresses students when he asks, "Do you think you're a lazy student?" At many points, Farber refers to the experience of being a student and to the effects of grades on the individuals who receive them. In other passages, Farber addresses an audience other than students. In his last paragraph, he asks, "But what about the students themselves? Can they live without grades? Can they learn without them?" These questions are addressed to an audience concerned about students, not to the students themselves. Once you identify Farber's two audiences, you will enrich your reading of the article because you will be able to distinguish between the arguments that are meant to appeal to students and those that are intended for college professors and administrators.

What impact does the author want to have on the reader? What does the writer expect the reader to do or think after reading the piece? These questions get to the heart of writers' goals. Some writers want to prompt overt changes in the behavior of readers. For example, the writer of an article on ozone depletion warns readers to reduce their use of air conditioners and aerosol cans. Other authors intend to change opinions rather than behavior. The author of a biography of Mozart might encourage readers to accept a new interpretation of the composer's significance. However, many writers work for more subtle changes in readers' perspectives. For instance, a newspaper writer may provide conflicting information on a Supreme Court decision that the journalist herself believes to be important. Although the news writer may not intend to get readers to either favor or oppose the court decision, she probably believes, in the tradition of news reporting, that providing citizens with accurate and detailed information will help them arrive at sound decisions of their own. Thus the writer's intended impact is to prompt independent and informed thought in the reader. Whether writing is overtly manipulative or not, good writers know how they expect to affect readers.

Farber's intentions are clear. He wants to convince his readers to agree with his position on grades and his broader plan for a society that depends less on what he terms "Mickey-Mouse requirements." In contrast, Budds's essay is not argumentative in tone. Still, Budds does intend to influence his audience. Presumably, he wants his readers to understand a set of factors that may explain why rock and roll has generated such controversy in the society at large. Budds's piece was first published in a collection of essays on music censorship. It is the first selection in the volume, so the editors of the collection must believe that readers need to understand the historical background Budds provides in order to appreciate the subsequent articles on very specific cases of censorship. They placed Budds's essay first in order to have a particular impact on the readers.

What role does the author assume in relation to the subject matter, the audience, and his or her own voice? Skilled writers consciously adopt a tone, voice, attitude, or posture that is appropriate to their audience and subject. Note how Farber directly addresses his readers and bases his appeal on the experience he shares with them. Farber's personal voice comes through in his conversational tone: "Wouldn't it be great to be free to learn?" He identifies with his readers as fellow victims of the destructive grading system. In contrast, Budds speaks to his audience as one professional to another, and his personality is nowhere near as evident as Farber's. In both cases, the authors' stance and voice are appropriate to their rhetorical purposes.

How does the author view what others have said on the topic? As we mentioned earlier, academic writers depend heavily on other sources and typically acknowledge what other individuals have written on the topic. Often they provide readers with background by describing the literature in the field. They may draw on sources to support their positions, or they may argue against the views expressed in other sources. We can categorize the ways authors use sources to build arguments according to the following scheme. A writer constructs a *one-dimensional argument* by presenting a viewpoint and then drawing support from sources that argue a similar viewpoint. The writer creates a *two-dimensional argument* not only by drawing on sources for direct support but also by using them for counterarguments. A two-dimensional argument thus anticipates and deals with opinions that are contrary to those of the writer. Farber makes a two-dimensional argument: he anticipates what supporters of grades might say about his proposal to eliminate grades and responds to their concerns.

Reader's Rhetorical Goals

The second meaning of rhetorical reading pertains to the goals of the reader of the source rather than those of the author. When you read novels and popular magazines, your goal may be pure enjoyment; however, your goal for academic reading is typically more functional. For example, in a college writing course, you are often asked to read sources and then write about them. If your assignment is to summarize the source, you will read with the goal of extracting and rewording the author's main ideas. If your assignment is to respond to the author's ideas, you will read for the purpose of generating reactions to the author's argument. Effective readers tailor their reading goals and strategies to the task at hand.

When you are *reading to write,* reading a source for a writing assignment, you need a clear rhetorical purpose. This purpose should guide your reading as well as your writing. It should help you keep in mind that as you interact with the author of the text, you are assuming two roles: the role of a reader and the role of a writer.

The first step in reading *to write* is making sure that you fully understand the writing assignment. Examine the assignment carefully. Underline key words that are crucial to your aim and purpose in writing. Ask yourself the following questions.

QUESTIONS TO ASK ABOUT ASSIGNMENTS

- What is the topic or issue I will be writing about?
- As I read, can I find key words or phrases that might signal material that is relevant to my topic?
- Who is the audience for my paper, and what are this audience's needs?
- Does the assignment require me to adopt a particular perspective on the issue or to use a particular plan of development?
- Do I already have a particular view on the issue that I intend to develop or defend?

Answering these questions will help you develop a mind-set for the assignment. Then you can fit relevant parts of the source into this mental image as you read.

For example, assume that you are asked to write an essay in which you summarize and respond to Budds's essay on rock music. In this case, you will read with two distinct purposes: to identify Budds's main points and to relate your own knowledge of and opinions about rock music to Budds's discussion. Your notes and annotations will reflect these two reading goals. However, if your assignment is to write an essay explaining the evolution of rock from earlier forms of popular music, your reading will focus on stylistic turning points in the history of popular music. Your reading goals would also change, depending on whether your essay is intended for an audience of professors or for an audience of other students.

When you receive an assignment, try to define a rhetorical purpose that will drive your reading of the text. This purpose will suggest a method of structuring the source information. For example, consider the following rhetorical purposes and the corresponding plans for organizing the material in Budds's essay.

PURPOSE	PLAN
Explain why rock music is controversial	Group by the various aspects of rock that have led to conflict
Argue for or against rock censorship	Group by reasons censorship is either helpful or harmful to society
Explain how African American music affected the development of rock	Group by African American genres or artists
Describe the impact rock music has had on American society	Group by changes in society and corresponding developments in rock music

When you read with the goal of fitting the source information into a specific rhetorical plan, you will read more efficiently and be better able to extract relevant information from complex texts. Indeed, a major advantage of rhetorical reading is that it is an aggressive, engaging approach to a text. If you read just to get through the required number of pages, you will recall little, particularly if the source is challenging. Rhetorical reading is purposeful reading. It increases the likelihood that you will comprehend the material, and it lays the groundwork for writing.

READING AND INTERPRETATION

In this chapter, we have recommended a variety of approaches to strategic reading, some of which depend heavily on your personal knowledge of the topic and goals for reading. As we mentioned earlier, there is more than one way to understand a text. Scholars may argue long and hard about the meaning of a single passage in a text important to their discipline, or they may discover an entirely new interpretation of a text that was long assumed to be adequately understood. It should come as no surprise that when students with different backgrounds and different reading purposes approach the same source, their interpretations may vary. When you read a source with a particular purpose in mind, you may arrive at an interpretation that differs from that of another student or a professor. As a reader, you must be aware that a text may have several possible interpretations, some of which may conflict. Often class discussions center on comparing and possibly linking various interpretations of texts.

Sometimes our students argue that the author's intended message is clearly what the text means, no matter what readers think the author intended. Even if this were true, we cannot contact the author each time we are in doubt about what a text means. Viewing the author as the ultimate judge of debates about meaning does not help us solve the everyday problems of interpretation. Once ideas appear in print, readers usually have to build meanings for them as best they can.

Does all this imply that you are a prisoner of your own past experience and knowledge, doomed to a personal, subjective interpretation of every text you read? Not necessarily. As we mentioned, many texts have relatively unambiguous meanings on which most readers agree. By becoming aware of the factors that influence your personal understanding of texts, you can to some extent see beyond the bounds of your own experiences. For instance, once you recognize your tendency to read Farber's article from a student perspective, you are then free to speculate how professors might react to the article. As you become more aware of the ways in which your personal knowledge affects your understanding, you will become a better reader.

In cases where there is wide disagreement on the meaning of a text, there are still ways to distinguish among interpretations. In the academic community, readers usually favor interpretations that explain a number of texts rather than just one, that are particularly interesting and creative, or that are readily defended on the basis of textual evidence. Thus judgments can be made on the relative strength of interpretations even in the absence of any ultimate authority.

TABLE 1-3 SUMMARY OF THE GUIDELINES FOR THE READING PROCESS

Before You Read

1. Call up your prior knowledge and feelings about the topic (see pages 15–16).
2. Preview the material and derive questions that will guide your close reading (see page 16).

As You Read

1. Annotate the material and take notes (see pages 16–21).
2. Identify the form of the piece. Given the form, what expectations do you have about the way the article will be organized?
3. Identify how the author has organized his ideas. What is the principal pattern of development? Does it overlap with other patterns?
4. Identify specific features of the piece (tone, vocabulary, sentence length, use of outside sources, and so on).

After You Read

Write out answers to the following questions:

1. What prompted the author to write this piece?
2. What audience is the author addressing?
3. What impact does the author want to have on readers?
4. What role does the author assume with regard to the audience, the subject matter, and the author's voice?
5. How does the author view what others have said on the topic?

Exercise ....

The purpose of this exercise is to give you practice using the three strategic approaches: (1) reading for content; (2) reading for form, organization, and features; and (3) reading for rhetorical concerns. Read "The Dignity of Helplessness: What Sort of Society Would Euthanasia Create?" by Rand Richards Cooper on pages 411–415. Approach the reading by following the process described in Table 1-3. Record answers *before* you read, *as* you read, and *after* you have read the article.

Exercise ....

The purpose of this exercise is to give you practice using Cooper's article to write an essay for a particular rhetorical purpose. Select one of the following purposes, or formulate a rhetorical goal of your own.

1. Either agree or disagree with Cooper's assertion that widespread acceptance of euthanasia would damage our society.
2. Explain Cooper's perspective for an audience of first-year nursing students.
3. Weigh the pros and cons of euthanasia for an audience consisting of the family members of the terminally ill or the bedridden elderly.

When you have written a preliminary draft of your essay, exchange papers with a classmate. Use the following questions to direct your reading of your peer's draft. Give complete answers so that the writer can use your comments to revise the paper.

1. Is the writer's rhetorical purpose clear? What point is the writer trying to make, and how is he or she trying to affect or influence the reader?
2. What audience does the writer have in mind?
3. Is the essay well organized? What pattern of development is used?
4. Does the essay hold your attention? Which parts are most interesting to you?
5. What do you like best about this paper?

When you get your paper back from your classmate, use the comments to revise your essay.

....

2

LEARNING THE BASIC CONVENTIONS
Summarizing, Paraphrasing, and Quoting

Since many writing assignments require you to draw on books, articles, lecture notes, and other written material, it's important that you learn how to use reading sources to their best advantage. The ability to take information from reading sources and use it in a composition addressed to one's own audience is useful not only in academic writing but also in business and professional settings. When writers prepare annual reports for stockholders in large corporations, they may summarize hundreds of individual reports, studies, and analyses. They repackage information that was originally produced for accountants, managers, engineers, and other professionals so that the general public can easily understand it. For in-house business documents, writers often take information that was originally intended for one audience, for instance, technical experts, and make it intelligible for another audience, say, the sales staff. Much of the writing that goes on in business, government, and other professions involves reducing, processing, and translating information for a designated audience or purpose.

Writers use three basic techniques to represent information they acquire from sources. First, they *summarize* the information by focusing on key elements and compacting or omitting details. Whether summaries are brief or comprehensive, they are attempts to capture the overall message. Second, they *paraphrase* selected parts of sources by translating the source material into their own words. Finally, they *quote* directly from original sources. Later in this chapter, we will discuss each of these three techniques.

SETTING RHETORICAL GOALS

When you summarize, paraphrase, and quote, even though you are working with another person's ideas, you will still be guided by your own *rhetorical purpose*. Recall from Chapter 1 that *your rhetorical purpose is your reason for writing and the desired effect that you hope to have on your audience.* When you incorporate sources into your writing, you won't be passively transferring them from one document to another. You'll be making many decisions about how to tailor them to your own purpose.

Your rhetorical purpose will dictate the amount of source material you include in your paper and the form this material will take. It will provide you with answers to a number of questions:

- Will you summarize the author's thesis and entire supporting argument or simply summarize the author's main points?
- Will you paraphrase the author's thesis or other important points?
- Will you quote selectively from the information you are borrowing?

Students often think that when they summarize, paraphrase, and quote a text, they have to convey it exactly as it was originally written. Of course, accuracy is important whenever you draw on a source. You cannot distort the message to make it appear that the source states something that its author did not intend. But the way you use the source depends on your own intentions. Two writers can draw on the same source in very different ways.

Consider two assignments. In the first assignment, your psychology professor asks you to write a three-page paper summarizing major theories for the causes of schizophrenia. You scan relevant sections of your assigned readings and class notes and write brief summaries of each theory. Given the page requirement, you make each summary concise, providing only enough information for the reader to understand the broad outlines of the theory. In the second assignment, your professor asks you to write a four-page argument defending what you believe is the most plausible explanation for schizophrenia. For this assignment, you summarize the passages describing the theory you favor and also paraphrase and quote evidence that supports the theory; you may also consider evidence that argues against competing theories. Your essay would contain details that you did not include in the paper that summarized the principal theories. To illustrate, we have taken excerpts from student papers written in response to these two assignments. Student A is summarizing a passage from R. D. Laing's book *The Politics of Experience* as part of a three-page summary of chief theories for the causes of schizophrenia. Student B is writing a four-page defense of Laing's theory.

Student A

R. D. Laing maintains that schizophrenia is not a disease but rather a means to escape or even resolve an impossible situation. According to this view, people become schizophrenic when they are caught in a double bind, usually in a family setting, so that any course of action (or inaction) they take leads to psychic stress. They extract themselves from these unlivable situations by "going crazy." Laing supports his theory by analyzing the families of schizophrenics and attempting to identify the double binds that he believes produced the patients' conditions (100-30).

Student B

In the 1960s, R. D. Laing began to question the traditional assumption that schizophrenia is a physiological illness. Traditional psychiatric practices relied heavily on using drugs that reduce schizophrenic symptoms while largely ignoring the under-

```
lying causes. Laing, however, identified the actual root of the
problem: the family. By analyzing the dynamics of schizophren-
ics' families, he demonstrated that schizophrenia results when a
family creates an environment that places one family member in a
double bind. In this untenable situation, all of the unfortunate
victim's options for acting or thinking lead to emotionally unac-
ceptable consequences, and schizophrenia becomes a refuge from an
impossible life. Laing's theory goes to the heart of the schiz-
ophrenic's problem and thus suggests to the therapist a course
of action, whereas treating the symptoms of schizophrenia with
drugs leaves the basic cause intact (100-30).
```

Both students provide essentially the same information about Laing's theory, but whereas Student A writes an objective summary, Student B reveals that he advocates Laing's views and rejects the medical model for schizophrenia. As this example demonstrates, the task at hand and the writer's rhetorical purpose determine how the source material will be used.

Even though we urge you to let your rhetorical purpose determine the way you draw on sources in your writing, we also have to caution you to take care not to distort sources deliberately. As an academic writer, you have the right to defend your own opinion, but you should not use sources in a way that changes or hides their intended meaning. You may have observed that this is done in advertising. Advertisers sometimes twist the meaning of a source to suit their rhetorical purpose of convincing readers to purchase a product. When ad writers mention experiments that demonstrate a product's usefulness or superiority, sometimes they refer only to the parts of these studies that portray the product in the most favorable light. In contrast, staff writers for *Consumer Reports* might summarize the same studies in their entirety and thereby show the limitations of the product. Or they might compare them with studies that show that other products work as well or better. Academic writers are expected to conform to a standard of objectivity that is more like the one for *Consumer Reports* than the one for advertising. Certainly, scholars often write about matters that are controversial and present source material in ways that best support their personal views, but they are always expected to represent the source material accurately. Make sure that you do not twist the words of authors you use as sources or put your own words into their mouths.

Exercise . . . .

Before class, turn to page 345, read "Inflating the Grades" by Stephen Goode and Timothy Maier, and write out answers to the accompanying questions.

During class, break up into groups of three or four students. Each group will be assigned one of the following rhetorical purposes.

1. Write an essay for teachers suggesting ways they can resist the pressure to inflate grades.
2. Argue that grades should be eliminated in higher education.
3. Explain why grades have risen in recent years on campuses across the nation.
4. Argue that academic standards should be raised on your campus.

Discuss with your group how you would use Goode and Maier's article to write a paper for your assigned rhetorical purpose. Appoint a spokesperson who will report your group's consensus to the class.

. . . .

CONSIDERING YOUR AUDIENCE

As we mentioned, when you summarize, paraphrase, and quote portions of reading sources, you will be tailoring the material for your own audience—readers who may have different needs from the readers of the original source. It is important to envision this audience as you work with the sources.

Before you incorporate sources into your writing, ask yourself the following questions.

QUESTIONS ABOUT AUDIENCE

- Am I writing for my professor or for a broader audience?
- Is my audience in the academic community?
- Am I writing for a general audience or for specialists?
- What will my audience already know about the topic?
- Will I need to explain basic concepts or provide background for the source material to make sense?
- Will my audience be biased either for or against what the source says?
- Can I predict how my audience will react to the source?
- What is the overall impact that I want to have on my audience?
- How will my writing inform, influence, or change my audience?

Answers to these questions will help you clarify your audience's needs so that you can mold the information into a form your readers can comprehend.

To see how considerations of audience affect summarizing, read two passages excerpted from summaries of Goode and Maier's "Inflating the Grades." In the margin of your book, speculate on the audience for whom each passage is intended.

Passage 1

According to Goode and Maier, the use of student evaluations as a measure of teaching success may provide a motive for grade inflation. Students often give good teaching evaluations to teachers who give them good grades on their work. The pressure to inflate grades is particularly strong, Goode and Maier point out, on part-time faculty members, who typically have short-term contracts and no job security. If their student evaluations are not strong, these part-timers may very well lose their jobs, so they may be reluctant to risk the anger of students who are displeased with their grades. Full-time faculty members in permanent, tenure-track positions may, from their position of greater security, resist the pressure for higher grades. They are more willing to take the stance of Professor Mark Edmundson of the University of Virginia: "I do feel a certain amount of pressure. Fending it off is part of the job" (qtd. in Goode and Maier 347).

Passage 2

On the surface, grade inflation might seem like a benefit to students who will get a higher GPA for less effort. But Goode and Maier point out that grade inflation may actually diminish the value of college students' academic achievements. According to Kiki Petrosino, a student at the University of Virginia, "I've got the good grades. But part of me would like so much to have my A stand out. I wish my A would mean more" (qtd. in Goode and Maier 350). Goode and Maier list a number of campuses where the percentage of A's and B's is very high, in some cases over 80%. Under these circumstances, good grades cease to mean very much. But it will be difficult to revive the value of the A unless students are "willing to accept the possibility of a C grade" (Goode and Maier 349).

The first excerpt is intended for a report to college presidents on the causes of grade inflation, while the second is intended for an article in the campus newspaper on the consequences of grade inflation for students. As you read the excerpts, you may have noticed that even though both draw on the same source, their emphasis, tone, form, and content are tailored for the designated audiences.

Sometimes readers have difficulty understanding ideas from sources. If you anticipate this happening, draw on additional sources or your own knowledge in order to provide background, definitions, or other forms of information that will help your readers understand what the source is saying. For example, assume that you are writing a paper about racial profiling, the police practice of targeting nonwhites as potential criminals, which has been the subject of much public discussion. Your primary source is a lengthy article on racial profiling. One section of the article compares racial profiling to the actions of Bernhard Goetz, New York City's famous "subway vigilante," but the article does not bother to review the Goetz incident. If you do not know the details of the Goetz incident yourself, you would have to look for another source that provides this background information. Then you would have to explain to your readers that Goetz was a white civilian who in 1984 shot four African American teenagers who he thought intended to mug him in a New York City subway car.

If you don't have to supply your readers with background information, you can reduce summarizing or paraphrasing to the simple process of transforming material meant for one audience and making it comprehensible to other readers. Later in this chapter, we will describe more detailed procedures for summarizing and paraphrasing, and we will stress the importance of thinking about audience. Whenever you receive a writing assignment, try to identify the audience it specifies. If the audience is not evident, ask the professor for guidance or define an appropriate audience on your own. Avoid writing only to yourself. Egocentric writing does not communicate effectively to anyone else. Egocentric summary writing may become nothing more than a prompt that helps the writer recall the source but is of little help to someone who has not read it. When you draw on source material, always have your audience clearly in mind.

E x e r c i s e ....

Read "Make Mine Hemlock" by Ernest van den Haag on pages 406–409. As you read, look for indications of the audience van den Haag has in mind. Is he writing for a college-educated audience? For religious individuals? For physicians? For people who are ill or elderly? Write a paragraph that describes van den Haag's intended audience. Be sure to defend your answer with references to van den Haag's piece.

• • • • • • • • • • • • • • • •

IDENTIFYING YOUR SOURCES

Perhaps the most basic and universal practice in academic writing is to identify for readers each piece of information that is borrowed from sources. You should strictly observe this convention in all academic disciplines. Failure to adhere to it, even in short pieces of writing, is unacceptable and considered to be plagiarism. Virtually all scholars draw on the work of others, and they always acknowledge their sources.

Often students have trouble adjusting to the academic convention of acknowledging sources because they are accustomed to more popular forms of writing and other media where sources are not cited. Striking examples are the television ads that claim, "Tests show that . . ." without specifying where and by whom these tests were conducted. In addition, as we observed in Chapter 1, sometimes writers of popular magazines and nonfiction books do not acknowledge sources. Thus it is no wonder that students often overlook the importance of identifying sources. In the academic community, however, readers are demanding; they want to know which ideas are original, which ideas are from elsewhere, and exactly where each borrowed idea comes from.

For an example of how academic writing differs from popular writing in its handling of sources, consider the following excerpts from Michael Budds's "From Fine Romance to Good Rockin'—and Beyond: Look What They've Done to My Song" (page 393), a chapter from a scholarly book, and from Philip O'Donnell's "Ours and Theirs: Redefining Japanese Pop Music," a magazine article.

Budds

Serious loss of income and loss of control forced industry executives to adopt a defensive posture. Leaders of the recording industry went so far as to condemn the music of their competitors as socially irresponsible and morally corrupting. The editors of *Billboard* and *Variety*, trade magazines of the profession, called for self-policing and raised the specter of government censorship as the ultimate solution to the dilemma.[6]

O'Donnell

According to the Recording Industry Association of Japan (RIAJ), foreign artists in 1992 had a market share of less than 24 percent. That figure has remained relatively constant for over a decade, and domestic music has been consistently outselling imports for thirty years.

To make this comparison complete, you should know that at the end of his chapter, Budds provides complete bibliographic information for each source, while O'Donnell has no such list. Budds acknowledges his source by name ("the editors of *Billboard* and *Variety*"), and the [6] at the end of Budds's final sentence refers the reader to endnote 6, where the specific sources are detailed. Now look at the excerpt from the magazine. O'Donnell provides statistics from the Recording Industry Association of Japan, but he does not provide complete bibliographic information for this source. We are not criticizing O'Donnell or the magazine that printed his article but simply pointing out that standards for identifying sources are less strict in the popular press than in academic publications. As a student writer, you must adhere to academic standards for citing sources, even though you are continually exposed to less rigorous standards in the magazines and newspapers that you read regularly.

The precise way in which source material is cited varies, depending on the academic discipline, but there are general guidelines that cover most subject areas.

CONVENTIONS FOR CITING SOURCES IN ACADEMIC WRITING

- Cite each source used and each piece or block of information drawn from the source.
- Make documentation clear enough so that the reader can identify where each fact or idea came from and also differentiate the writer's own ideas or assertions from those borrowed from the sources.
- Provide complete citations to sources either in footnotes or endnotes or in a list of works cited at the end of the piece.

These citations enable readers to locate the exact page on which the borrowed fact or idea appears in the original document. The citation should be thorough enough so that if readers have access to an appropriate library, they can locate the original source. Compare the following summaries of David Rothenberg's article "Learning in Finland: No Grades, No Criticism." In the first, the writer fails to acknowledge Rothenberg; in the second, the writer refers to Rothenberg by name and includes a page reference in parentheses.

Without Attribution

In Finland, it is difficult to get admitted to the most prestigious universities, but once students are in, the competition stops. College students' work is never graded, and students can't fail a course, even if they do not submit the "required" work. When students submit work that falls short of expectations, they are rarely criticized or asked to revise. Finnish professors discourage competition among students, and critique is just

not part of the Finnish educational culture. Students ultimately
graduate by completing a final exam or project and may take as
many years as they like to reach this goal.

With Attribution

According to David Rothenberg, who spent a semester as a
visiting professor in Finland, it is difficult to get admitted
to the most prestigious Finnish universities, but once students
are in, the competition stops. College students' work is never
graded, and students can't fail a course, even if they do not
submit the "required" work. Rothenberg notes that when students
submit work that falls short of expectations, they are typically
not criticized or asked to revise. Finnish professors discourage
competition among students, and "critique is just not part of the
Finnish educational culture" (B9). Students ultimately graduate
by completing a final exam or project, and Rothenberg explains
that they may take as many years as they like to reach this goal.

The first passage gives you no indication of the source of the ideas. Any student who used this passage in an essay would be plagiarizing the author, even if Rothenberg's article was included in a list of sources at the end of the essay. Once the author's name, quotation marks, and the page number are added, you know immediately that the writer is summarizing and quoting from Rothenberg. Notice also how the second writer attributes the material to Rothenberg, using words like "According to David Rothenberg," "Rothenberg notes," and "Rothenberg explains." Often citations become quite numerous. If a writer alternates, sentence by sentence, among various sources, every sentence might need a reference. Consider an excerpt adapted from a paper by our student Yesenia Hernandez. Yesenia draws on three readings on rap music.

There is so much controversy surrounding rap and its negative image that the positive aspects of rap are overlooked. For
example, rappers in New York City formed what is called the Stop
the Violence movement to encourage kids to find solutions to
their problems rather than resort to violence, and a similar
effort among Los Angeles rappers was directed at reducing gang
violence (Hackett and Adrianson). Rappers often urge young people
to "get down with the program" and reject drugs, crime, and
racism (Gates 61). As Dyson points out, for inner-city residents,
rap serves as "a form of cultural resistance" (7) and expresses
the problems their communities face. Public Enemy's album <u>Fear
of a Black Planet</u> is a good example of rap that highlights ghetto
problems and promotes community and individual self-help. Rap is
providing a medium where positive attitudes are expressed by
artists.

Needless to say, authors' names and page numbers by themselves do not give readers all the information they need about the sources. At the end of the paper, a "works cited" list, organized alphabetically by authors' last names, provides the complete identification.

Works Cited

Dyson, Michael Eric. "2 Live Crew's Rap: Sex, Race, and
 Class." <u>Christian Century</u> 2-9 Jan. 1991: 7-8.

Gates, David. "Decoding Rap Music." <u>Newsweek</u> 17 Mar. 1990:
 60-63.

Hackett, Darren, and Doug Adrianson. "Rap's Roots Steeped in
 Black Tradition." <u>Miami Herald</u> 17 June 1990: 1.

Public Enemy. <u>Fear of a Black Planet</u>. Audiocassette. CBS,
 1990.

Yesenia uses the Modern Language Association (MLA) documentation style. This is the most commonly used style in the humanities. Other student work in this book also uses the MLA style. We will discuss this style in more detail later in this chapter and give you a comprehensive guide to MLA documentation in Appendix A. We will also cover the style of the American Psychological Association (APA), a style popular with social scientists and educators. If you are writing for an audience in a specialized area, you will probably need to use its documentation style. If this is the case, consult a style manual appropriate for that discipline. Incidentally, the "Hernandez 4" in the upper right corner of the works cited page provides the last name of the writer and the page number in the essay.

You will notice that Budds's essay in Chapter 11 and some other scholarly works included in this textbook do not use the MLA documentation style. Some scholarly journals use their own documentation style, and others use the standard style for their discipline.

AVOIDING PLAGIARISM

Failure to identify the source is a form of *plagiarism*. Over the past decade, accusations of plagiarism for not citing sources damaged the careers of several prominent scholars and politicians. Similarly, student plagiarism can lead to a failing grade or even expulsion. Be sure to consult your writing instructor, college writing center, student handbook, or college catalog for details of how plagiarism cases are handled on your campus.

To avoid plagiarism, you must do more than cite your sources. You must set off direct quotations with quotation marks and entirely reword and document any material you paraphrase or summarize. Be sure the vocabulary and the sentence structure are significantly different from the original. It is not enough to change the words but keep the same sentence structure and order of the ideas. The following examples show adequate and inadequate paraphrases.

Original

The current constitutional debate over heavy metal rock and gangsta rap music is not just about the explicit language but also advocacy, an act of incitement to violence.

Inadequate Paraphrase

Today's constitutional debate about gangsta rap and heavy metal rock is not just about obscene language but also advocacy and incitement of acts of violence.

Adequate Paraphrase

Lyrics in some rap and heavy metal songs that appear to promote violence, along with concerns about obscenity, have generated a constitutional debate over popular music.

The inadequate paraphrase reshuffles the words from the original but retains the vocabulary, sentence structure, and order of ideas. There is no acceptable middle ground between an adequate paraphrase and a direct quotation. You must either reword or quote word for word. An inadequate paraphrase is considered a form of plagiarism since it is interpreted as an attempt to pass off another writer's sentence structure and word choice as your own.

While it is hard to define precisely how much rewording is necessary to avoid plagiarism, the following guidelines will help.

GUIDELINES FOR REWORDING SOURCE MATERIAL

- As a rule of thumb, do not repeat more than three consecutive words from the original without putting them in quotation marks. You may occasionally need to repeat a three-word phrase, but whenever possible, substitute synonyms for the original words.

- Change as best you can the original order in which concepts are presented. For example, if the author you are paraphrasing presents a generalization and then backs it up with an example, try using the example as a lead-in to the generalization. For an individual sentence, try to relocate a phrase from the beginning of the sentence to a position near the end, or vice versa.

In our discussion of paraphrasing later in this chapter, we will provide more specific techniques for rewording source material.

Remember that entirely rewording the material you obtain from a source does not make it yours. You must still cite the source so that the reader will know exactly where the information came from. Failing to document a paraphrase or summary is considered plagiarism.

E x e r c i s e ....

Reread Stephen Goode and Timothy Maier's article "Inflating the Grades" on pages 345–350. As you read, pause at each place where Goode and Maier use a fact or idea that you believe comes from another source. Each time you pause, write "yes" in the margin if you think Goode and Maier provide enough information for you to locate the original source and "no" if they do not. Can you make any generalizations about when Goode and Maier choose to identify sources as opposed to when they do not cite a source? If you were to convert Goode and Maier's article into an academic paper, how many sources would appear in the list of works cited?

• • • • • • • • • • • • • • • •

THE SUMMARIZING PROCESS

The term *summary* covers a wide range of activities. For example, to answer essay exam questions, writers compress ideas that extend over many pages of their textbook. They summarize when they write short papers reviewing the main ideas presented in assigned journal articles. In preparing research papers, writers summarize when they combine ideas from a number of sources to develop a particular perspective on an issue. They also summarize as they take notes on the main points of a class lecture. Summarizing is not a simple or one-dimensional operation. It is a complex, challenging task that requires a full range of academic reading and writing abilities.

As we indicated earlier, your rhetorical purpose has a direct impact on the way you summarize. The first step in any summarizing process is to clarify this rhetorical purpose to make sure you know why you are drawing on the source. To do this, ask yourself how the reading material will fit in with your overall message and how it will be received by your audience.

After you have specified your rhetorical purpose and defined your audience, there are several approaches that you can follow to create a summary. We will discuss three of them.

APPROACHES TO SUMMARIZING

- Creating a graphic overview that you can convert into a summary
- Focusing on main ideas, patterns, and rhetorical situations and compressing information to create a summary
- Creating a sentence outline that you can convert into a summary

CREATING A GRAPHIC OVERVIEW

One way to summarize a complex source is to create a *graphic overview* and use it as the outline for the summary. A graphic overview is a diagram that represents the central ideas in the original source, shows how they are related, and indicates the author's overall purpose. It reflects the three main elements of a text that we discussed in Chapter 1: (1) content; (2) form, organization, and features; and (3) rhetorical goals. You might think of it as a framework for the source's main ideas, similar to the frameworks we discussed on pages 23–24. To construct a graphic overview, write down key words and concepts, and depict the relationships among them by drawing circles and boxes connected by lines and arrows. Use labels to show how the basic ideas are interrelated.

Here is an excerpt from an essay by Carl Sagan called "In Defense of Robots"; a graphic overview of the passage is presented in Figure 2-1.

FIGURE 2-1   GRAPHIC OVERVIEW OF THE EXCERPT FROM "IN DEFENSE OF ROBOTS"

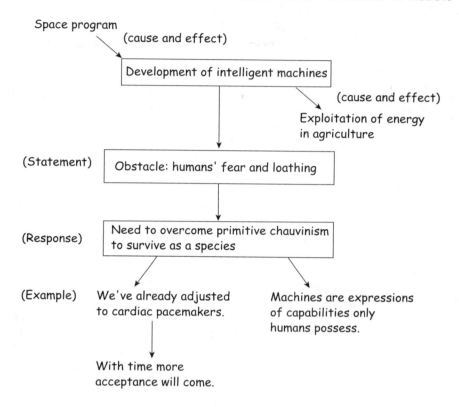

Excerpt from "In Defense of Robots"

We appear to be on the verge of developing a wide variety of intelligent machines capable of performing tasks too dangerous, too expensive, too onerous or too boring for human beings. The development of such machines is, in my mind, one of the few legitimate "spin-offs" of the space program. The efficient exploitation of energy in agriculture—upon which our survival as a species depends—may even be contingent on the development of such machines. The main obstacle seems to be a very human problem, the quiet feeling that comes stealthily and unbidden, and argues that there is something threatening or "inhuman" about machines performing certain tasks as well as or better than human beings; or a sense of loathing for creatures made of silicon and germanium rather than proteins and nucleic acids. But in many respects our survival as a species depends on our transcending such primitive chauvinisms. In part, our adjustment to intelligent machines is a matter of acclimatization. There are already cardiac pacemakers that can sense the beat of the human heart; only when there is the slightest hint of fibrillation does the pacemaker stimulate the heart. This is a mild but very useful sort of machine intelligence. I cannot imagine the wearer of this device resenting its intelligence. I think in a relatively short period of time there will be a very similar sort of acceptance for much more intelligent and sophisticated machines. There is nothing inhuman about an intelligent machine; it is indeed an expression of those superb intellectual capabilities that only human beings, of all the creatures on our planet, now possess. (Sagan 292)

The advantage of the graphic overview is that it forces you to think about the big picture. You can manipulate chunks of information like pieces in a puzzle and determine how they best fit together. Notice that the graphic overview of Sagan's article makes clear that Sagan has three main assertions that are logically connected. It would be easy to summarize this source now that you see all the main ideas diagrammed on a single page.

Of course, creating a graphic overview is a highly individual process. A single, definitive graphic overview does not exist for each text. Variations are possible. Consider the alternative representation of the Sagan text in Figure 2-2.

FIGURE 2-2   ALTERNATIVE GRAPHIC OVERVIEW OF THE EXCERPT FROM "IN DEFENSE OF ROBOTS"

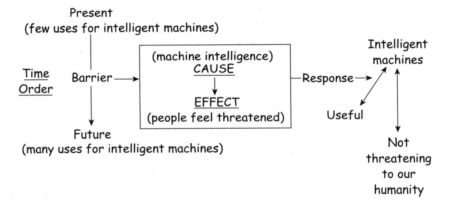

You can make a graphic overview for a source of any length—a single paragraph, a sequence of paragraphs, or a complete article—but the strategy works best if you can fit the diagram on a single page so that you can see it all at once. Of course, this limits the amount of detail the graphic overview can contain. But if you try to cram in lots of details, you will soon lose sight of the big picture. The technique works best for recording the general outlines of an author's argument. When you are working with long or complex sources and want more than a broad outline, you may find the one-page format too restrictive.

You can move directly from the graphic overview to the written summary by following these steps.

CONVERTING A GRAPHIC OVERVIEW TO A WRITTEN SUMMARY

1. Study each main idea in the graphic overview, and in your own words write it out in one or more sentences.

2. Use labeled lines and arrows to show the logical connections among the main ideas, just as in the graphic overview.
3. Write transitional expressions that mean the same as the logical connections.
4. Combine all the sentences into a single summary using transitional expressions and making any necessary adjustments so that the sentences fit together.

Note in Figure 2-3 how these steps are used to create a summary from a graphic overview of the Sagan passage.

FIGURE 2-3   CREATING A SUMMARY FROM A GRAPHIC OVERVIEW

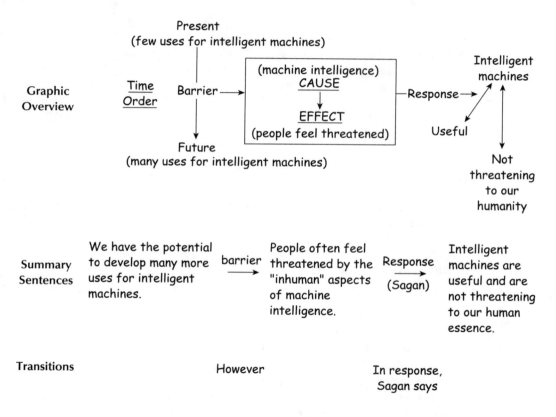

In his essay "In Defense of Robots," Carl Sagan argues that humans must overcome their prejudices against intelligent machines. He explains that we have the potential to develop many more uses for intelligent machines; however, people often feel threatened by the "inhuman" aspects of machine intelligence. In response, Sagan argues that intelligent machines are useful and are not threatening to our human essence.

Depending on the assignment, your summaries will vary widely in length and complexity. For lengthy, more detailed summaries, you may need to go back to the original source for additional information. You might have to expand some of the main ideas in the graphic overview into entire paragraphs and make the transitions more elaborate. Even though the graphic overview does not provide all the raw material for the summary, at the very least it suggests its overall structure.

The beauty of the graphic overview is that it removes you from the author's exact words and thus helps you avoid plagiarizing. Because the graphic overview allows you to visualize relationships among main ideas in a form other than sentences and paragraphs, once you understand the web of meaning, you can express it in your own words. You don't fall back on the author's language as you write your summary.

E x e r c i s e ....

Read "Grades and Money" by Steven Vogel on pages 337–340. Then construct a graphic overview, keeping in mind the three source elements: (1) content; (2) form, organization, and features; and (3) rhetorical goals. Working from this overview, write a summary of about 200 words that captures Vogel's main ideas. Bring both the graphic overview and the summary to class. Working in groups of three or four, compare your overviews and summaries. To what extent do your graphic overviews differ? How do your summaries differ? Do the graphic overviews differ more than the summaries? If so, can you explain why?

COMPRESSING INFORMATION

Another powerful approach to summarizing is to analyze and manipulate the source until you have reduced it to its essentials. This process draws on a variety of summarizing strategies.

SUMMARIZING STRATEGIES

1. Annotate the text, labeling or underlining important material.
2. Delete unimportant detail, examples, and redundancy.
3. Combine ideas in sentences and paragraphs.
4. Compress words in the original text into fewer words, and provide general terms to cover several specific items.
5. Locate and emphasize the thesis and topic sentences. Invent thesis and topic sentences if none are found.
6. Identify and imitate the organizational pattern of the source.
7. Identify and incorporate the rhetorical context and the author's rhetorical purpose.

These strategies need not be applied in any particular order, and you don't have to use all seven of them for each summary you write. Simply choose the strategies that are appropriate for the source you are working with. In some cases, all you need to do to generate a short summary is explain the context and indicate the author's rhetorical purpose. In other cases, you may have to use the full range of strategies.

1. *Annotate, label, or underline important material.* As we explained in Chapter 1, your annotations provide a record of your initial understanding of the material. This record is extremely useful when it comes time to write a summary. Marginal labels, underlining, and other notations may also alert you to ideas that should appear in your work. By paraphrasing those ideas, you will be well on the way to producing a summary.

The next three strategies often work together. We will describe each of them and then show you how they work.

2. *Delete unimportant detail, examples, and redundancy.* Cross out or label as nonessential any material that you think is unimportant for your summary. Also take out information that merely repeats what was said previously. Academic sources are often highly redundant because authors repeat or illustrate complex concepts in order to give the reader more than one chance to understand them.

3. *Compress words in the original text into fewer words, and provide general terms to cover several specific items.* Another strategy you can use, along with deleting unimportant detail, examples, and redundancy, is to compress several words or phrases into fewer words and reduce items in the same class to a single category.

4. *Combine ideas in sentences and paragraphs.* After you delete nonessential material and categorize bits of information, you are often left with disjointed pieces of text. If you want your summary to flow smoothly, you have to rearrange key ideas, make elements parallel, or add logical connectors.

Look at how we performed the operations for strategies 2, 3, and 4 in Figure 2-4. Notice how we deleted the nonessential examples of the three cities; compressed text, for example, substituting "urban" for the phrase "in large cities"; and then combined this reconfigured material into a concise summary.

FIGURE 2-4   Using Summarizing Strategies to Compress Information

Original Sentence from Source

Schools in large cities, such as New York, Boston, and Philadelphia, have been criticized for passing students from grade to grade for demonstrated effort, regular attendance, and good citizenship rather than for adequate academic performance.

Edited Sentence

urban
Schools (in large cities,) ~~such as New York, Boston, and Philadelphia,~~ have been criticized for
promoting
(passing students from grade to grade) for (demonstrated effort, regular attendance, and good
unjustified reasons
citizenship rather than for adequate academic performance.)

Resulting Summary Sentence

Urban schools have been criticized for promoting students for unjustified reasons (Janik 43).

5. *Locate and emphasize the thesis and topic sentence.* You are probably familiar with conventions like thesis statements and topic sentences. The thesis is the focal point of a piece, the author's main point or the claim the author demonstrates or proves. Topic sentences contain the main ideas of paragraphs or other subdivisions of a text. In practice, a thesis or a paragraph's main idea may be expressed in more than one sentence, so do not assume that you should always search for a single sentence. Since thesis statements and topic sentences often include the author's most important ideas, you can build a summary by paraphrasing them and then weaving the paraphrases together into a coherent whole.

Although the topic sentence often comes at the start of a paragraph, this is not always the case. It can appear in the middle or at the end of a paragraph as well. Notice that in Sagan's paragraph (page 47), the topic sentence occurs at the very end. Similarly, although the thesis statement is typically in the first paragraph or another introductory paragraph, it can also appear at the end of the piece. You will find that in some paragraphs, there is no explicit topic sentence; the main idea is implied through an accumulation of details, facts, or examples. When you are summarizing such a paragraph, try to create a topic sentence of your own by combining ideas that will make a unified statement. Here is an example of a paragraph that does not have a distinct topic sentence.

> Buddha is said to have achieved spiritual enlightenment through meditation and fasting. Similar procedures, however, are used to prepare for divine inspiration in religions the world over. This fact has implications for how one might view the development of religion in various cultures. Indeed, this aspect of the religious experience may be a direct response to human physiological characteristics. People the world over share common experiences as a consequence of being members of the same species. It seems reasonable that they might interpret these experiences the same way.

The first sentence tells how Buddha acquired spiritual enlightenment. The remaining sentences, however, suggest that Buddha is used merely as an example because they discuss a larger population—religious people throughout the world. The final sentence is a partial statement of the main idea: people everywhere have the same interpretation of certain experiences. We combine these ideas to arrive at a topic sentence:

> Human beings everywhere share certain experiences that they interpret as having religious significance.

6. *Identify and imitate the organizational pattern.* The author's organizational plan will also help you summarize. A good summary reflects the structural pattern of the source. You may recall that we advised you to change the order of the source when you are paraphrasing. But summarizing follows a different procedure. In fact, once you identify how the author has arranged the piece, you can use this pattern as the skeleton for your summary. Because organization conveys meaning, your reader should be able to follow the train of thought quite easily.

In Table 1-2 in Chapter 1, we described nine organizational plans for academic writing: time order, narration, process; antecedent and consequence or cause and effect; description; response; comparison and contrast; example; analysis or classification; definition; and analogy. Each plan may be used to organize an entire piece of writing or only a small segment of it, and several patterns can be used simultaneously. As you are reading the source you will summarize, make a marginal note about its organizational plan.

To illustrate how to base a summary on the author's organizational plan, reconsider the excerpt from Sagan's "In Defense of Robots" on page 47. Which of the nine plans best describes the excerpt? A strong candidate is the response plan, since Sagan is responding to the critics of machine intelligence. You could construct your summary by first explaining the perspective Sagan is reacting to (the human bias against machines) and then describing Sagan's response. The organizational plan can thus provide the backbone for your summary.

7. *Identify and incorporate the rhetorical context and the author's rhetorical purpose.* In some cases, you will include in your summary the rhetorical context of the source and the author's rhetorical purpose, particularly if you are writing a summary that will stand alone rather than one that will become a part of a longer essay. To determine the rhetorical context, ask yourself the following questions.

QUESTIONS FOR DETERMINING RHETORICAL CONTEXT

- What is the author's background? Is he or she an acceptable, credible authority?
- What feeling, view, incident, or phenomenon brought about the need or motivated the author to write?
- What role does the author assume in relation to the audience?
- In what type of publication does the piece appear? If the publication is a journal, magazine, or newspaper, who are its typical readers?
- When was the piece published? Is it current or out of date?

Purpose is determined by how the author tries to affect or influence the audience. Sometimes the purpose is easily identified because it is a controlling feature of the piece, as is the case in an argumentative text or a highly opinionated editorial. Other times the author's purpose may not be self-evident. (To review the concept of rhetorical purpose, reread pages 29-33.)

The following summary of Vogel's "Grades and Money" (see pages 337–340) illustrates that once you have identified the rhetorical context and determined the author's purpose, you have created a concise, informative summary.

Summary of Vogel's "Grades and Money"

Steven Vogel, a philosophy professor, notes that his students seem much more concerned about grades than he and his peers were as undergraduates in the early 1970s. Vogel's purpose in writing is to explain why the current generation of students is so obsessed with grades. He asserts that his students now view grades as "money" they receive in exchange for the "work" of learning. They have adopted this viewpoint because "money, nowadays, is the only value we know" (340). Vogel addresses his piece to readers in his own generation, particularly academics, who might not understand the motives of today's college students.

As with the graphic overview technique, the seven strategies we have just described can be used to produce detailed or brief summaries of short and long sources. When you have written a draft of your summary, check to see that you have changed the author's wording or else you will run the risk of plagiarizing the source. Also remember to document your summary by providing your readers with information about the author, title, place and date of publication, and pages. (For a more detailed explanation of documentation, see pages 41–44.)

Exercise ···

Use at least two summary strategies to construct a 200-word summary of Lori Andrews's essay "The Sperminator," which begins on page 369. Write for an audience of first-year college students who have not read Andrews's article.

· · · · · · · · · · · · · · · · ·

CREATING A SENTENCE OUTLINE

A sentence outline is especially useful for creating a summary that follows the organizational format and order of the original source. If the source contains an introductory paragraph, five body paragraphs, and a conclusion, the sentence outline will reflect this organizational distribution. You might write a sentence summary of each paragraph and then combine the sentences to form a coherent passage. The resulting summary is actually a miniature version of the original. The sentence summary technique is particularly well suited for long sources that have subdivisions or follow clear-cut organizational plans.

To illustrate the process, imagine that you are summarizing Donald F. Sabo's "Different Stakes: Men's Pursuit of Gender Equity in Sports" (pages 462–468). If you look at the essay, you will see that Sabo uses subtitles and the transitional phrase "In summary" to divide his article into five sections. Your first step is to create a sentence outline by writing a sentence summary for each of the sections. The second step is to merge these sentence summaries into a coherent paragraph.

Sentence Outline of Donald F. Sabo's "Different Stakes: Men's Pursuit of Gender Equity in Sports"

Introduction (unlabeled, precedes the first subheading)

Although most people assume that Title IX benefits only women, it actually helps male athletes as well, particularly those in sports other than football.

The Guises of Sexism in Sports

In the past, male dominance of college athletics was justified by asserting that men were better suited for athletics than women, but this justification has been replaced in recent years by the claim that efforts to achieve gender equity will weaken sports programs overall to the detriment of both male and female athletes.

Men Are Discovering Title IX

Men are becoming more aware of Title IX, and some are beginning to take an active role in promoting gender equity in sports.

Men's Stake in Gender Equity

The end of the male-dominated sports establishment seems appropriate as, in response to feminism, our society redefines what it means to be a man.

Conclusion (signaled by a line of space and the phrase "In summary")

Sexism continues in college sports, particularly within the football hierarchy, but both men and women stand to gain from gender equity.

Summary Created from the Sentence Outline

In "Different Stakes: Men's Pursuit of Gender Equity in Sports," Don Sabo maintains that although most people assume that Title IX benefits only women, it actually helps male athletes as well, particularly those in sports other than football. In the past, male dominance of college athletics was justified by asserting that men were better suited for athletics than women, but according to Sabo, this justification has been replaced in recent years by the claim that efforts to achieve gender equity will weaken sports programs overall to the detriment of both male and female athletes. Men are becoming more aware of Title IX, Sabo notes, and some are beginning to take an active role in promoting gender equity in sports. He believes that the end of the male-dominated sports establishment seems appropriate as, in response to feminism, our society redefines what it means to be a man. Sabo concludes that sexism continues in college sports, particularly within the football hierarchy, but both men and women stand to gain from gender equity.

When you convert a sentence outline to paragraph form, consider making the following additions.

ADDITIONS TO THE SENTENCE SUMMARY OUTLINE

- Identify the author and the title of the reading source.
- Add appropriate transitional words and expressions.
- Supply documentation.
- Add rhetorical context, when necessary.

In the summary of Sabo's article, we have highlighted the writer's additions to the sentence outline. Look especially at the instances of attribution. This is where the writer adds connectives like "according to Sabo" and "Sabo concludes." For summary writing, attribution is an especially effective transitional device. For your summary to make sense, you may also need to add an introductory sentence or two to identify the rhetorical context of the original source. Since you don't want your summary to sound like a set of disconnected ideas, you should double-check that you have added enough context and transitions.

DOCUMENTING SUMMARIES

Remember that you must document all information you obtain from sources. Even if you have summarized the text in your own words, you must make its origin clear to your readers. The sample summaries in this chapter clearly indicate that the writers are borrowing information from sources.

Summarizing a source without proper documentation is considered plagiarism. Always cite the source at the point where you use it in your writing. Also include it in the works cited list at the end of your paper. (We explain how to set up a works cited list on pages 43–44.)

Exercise ....

Make a 250-word sentence summary outline of Jeffrey Goldberg's essay "The Color of Suspicion" (pages 427–441), and then convert the outline into a summary. Make sure that the organization of your summary reflects the plan of Goldberg's article.

. . . .

THE PARAPHRASING PROCESS

Paraphrasing is a powerful operation for academic writing, but students do not use it enough. Too many beginning academic writers rely on direct quoting when they use reading sources. Quotations are necessary only when you have a clear reason for including the precise wording of the original. We will discuss some of the reasons for quoting in the next section of this chapter. A drawback of quoting is that it is a passive process of mechanically copying portions of the text. Paraphrasing is an active process that forces you to grapple with the author's ideas. In this way, paraphrasing promotes comprehension. It is no wonder that many professors ask students to paraphrase rather than quote source material. They know that if students can paraphrase ideas, the students understand the ideas.

Whereas a summary contains only the *most important* information from the source, a paraphrase includes *all* the information. Writers paraphrase to record the total meaning of a passage. Notice the difference between the paraphrase and the summary in the following example, which draws on a sentence from Steven Vogel's "Grades and Money" (page 338).

Vogel's Sentence

Students expect that their grade will indicate the amount of time they have put into the course, as if they were hourly workers, and many faculty agree that it's important to consider "effort" when they "award" grades.

Paraphrase

Professors often reward students' efforts with higher grades, and indeed, most students assume that they should receive grades that reflect how much time they invest in schoolwork, just as if they were being paid by the hour (Vogel 338).

Summary

Students and many professors think grades should reflect effort to some degree (Vogel 338).

To include in your paper only the gist or main idea of a reading source, summarize it. Paraphrase when you want to capture the meaning of the text in its entirety. In general, relatively small sections of the original, often a sentence or two, are paraphrased, while larger chunks of information are summarized.

Begin the paraphrasing process by articulating your rhetorical purpose and defining your audience, as when summarizing. The act of clarifying how you intend to use the paraphrase and the effect you hope it will have on your audience will prepare you to paraphrase effectively.

Earlier in this chapter we discussed how extensively you must alter the wording of the original when you paraphrase. Change both vocabulary and sentence structure, and never repeat more than three consecutive words from the original.

STRATEGIES FOR PARAPHRASING

As with summarizing, you can sometimes paraphrase simply by rewriting the original passage for a new audience. Envision your readers and then change the original text to make it more suitable for them. Suppose that your objective is to paraphrase the following sentence from Budds for middle school students.

> In terms of text, the song traditions of the African-American community and the rural white community reflected a level of realism and honesty that flew in the face of the mainstream's rules of decorum and its penchant for romantic "sweetness."

Because you do not want to talk over the students' heads, you put the sentence into simpler language.

```
The blunt, down-to-earth lyrics of African American and rural
white music clashed with mainstream songwriters' practice of
idealizing romance and avoiding sexual references (Budds 395).
```

You could simply rewrite the original, as here, keeping in mind that the audience might not understand terms like *penchant*. As the example demonstrates, paraphrasing will often require you to express abstract ideas in a more concrete form. For many assignments, however, you will need a more systematic approach to paraphrasing. When a passage includes difficult concepts or complex language, it may be hard to reword it and still preserve the original meaning. In these cases, try the following paraphrasing procedures.

IMPORTANT PARAPHRASING STRATEGIES

- Locate the individual statements or major idea units in the original.
- Change the order of major ideas, maintaining the logical connections among them.
- Substitute synonyms for words in the original, making sure the language in your paraphrase is appropriate for your audience.
- Combine or divide sentences as necessary.
- Compare the paraphrase to the original to ensure that the rewording is sufficient and the meaning has been preserved.
- Weave the paraphrase into your essay in accordance with your rhetorical purpose.
- Document the paraphrase.

Sometimes you may use only some of these seven strategies, and you may apply them in any order. For illustrative purposes, we are going to paraphrase a sentence from John Leo's article, "When Life Imitates Video," using all the strategies in the order listed. Let's assume that we are writing for an audience of first-year college students. The excerpt is taken from page 361 and refers to the possible role that violent video games played in motivating the Columbine High School massacre in Littleton, Colorado.

> If we want to avoid more Littleton-style massacres, we will begin taking the social effects of the killing games more seriously.

Locate individual statements or major idea units.   First, we will determine how many major ideas are presented in the passage. We find two central units of information: (1) avoiding more school massacres and (2) taking seriously the impact of violent video games.

1. If we want to avoid more Littleton-style massacres, . . .
2. we will begin taking the social effects of the killing games more seriously.

Change the order of major ideas maintaining the logical connections among them.
Now we will change the order of the two units of information, placing the second before the first. To accommodate this switch, we substitute "If we begin" for "we will" and "we may" for "If we want to" so that the recommendation to take seriously the social impact of killing games fits at the beginning of the sentence.

1. If we begin taking the social effects of the killing games more seriously, . . .
2. we may avoid more Littleton-style massacres.

E x e r c i s e ....

Change the order of the ideas in each of the following sentences. An example is shown.

> When Boris Pasternak was awarded the Nobel Prize for his novel *Doctor Zhivago*, Soviet authorities pressured him to reject the prize.

```
Soviet authorities pressured Boris Pasternak to reject the Nobel
Prize when he was awarded it for his novel Doctor Zhivago.
```

1. As the Industrial Revolution progressed, exploitation of child labor became a serious social problem.

2. Although there are currently several theories concerning the origin of the universe, the Big Bang theory is the one most widely held.

3. Despite the common belief that the brush is the primary tool of the painter, many well-known paintings were created entirely with pallet knives.

4. Even though the secretary of defense disagreed sharply with the president's foreign policy, she did not resign from office.

• • • • • • • • • • • • • • • • •

Substitute synonyms for words in the original.   At this stage, it is important to think about audience. Leo's original language is relatively easy to understand. If the language of the original source is too formal or sophisticated, you may want to make it more accessible to your readers. In addition, you may need to provide a context for certain types of material that you excerpt from reading sources.

Whenever you replace original text with synonyms, try to come up with synonyms without consulting a dictionary or thesaurus. Many students who have trouble substituting words rush to reference books and copy synonyms without considering how they fit into the general sense of the sentence. This is a mistake. Paraphrases filled with synonyms taken indiscriminately from a dictionary or thesaurus are awkward and confusing. Here is a procedure for finding synonyms on your own.

COMING UP WITH YOUR OWN SYNONYMS

1. Think of a word or phrase in your vocabulary that comes as close as possible to the meaning of the original word.

2. Read the original sentence, substituting your synonym for the original word. Reread the sentence to see if it makes sense. If the new word changes the meaning, come up with another synonym and try the substitution again.

3. Compare the dictionary definitions of the original word and your synonym. If the definitions do not correspond, come up with another synonym and try the substitution again.

When you are paraphrasing a passage that contains a word you don't understand, you will have to supplement these strategies. Before you consult a dictionary or thesaurus, try to figure out the approximate meaning of the unfamiliar word, based on its relationship to the words you already know in the sentence. We call this procedure using *contextual clues* to discover meaning. Use contextual clues to figure out a synonym for the italicized word in the following sentence.

> After meeting someone for the first time, we often retain a *gestalt* of what the person is like but cannot remember specific details such as eye color.

From the sentence, you learn that a *gestalt* is something other than a memory of specific details, so you can infer that it means an overall impression. Check a dictionary to see if the definition we derived from context is appropriate.

Contextual clues will not give you a complete definition of an unknown word, but they will help you unlock enough of the meaning to know what synonym to substitute for it. Always check a synonym that you figure out from contextual clues by substituting it for the word it replaces in the original sentence. If you are not sure the synonym fits, consult a dictionary to check your understanding of the original word. Also, check your synonym against the synonyms listed in the dictionary or thesaurus.

As we mentioned, if you copy a synonym without examining its fit in the original sentence, your paraphrase may not sound right, and it may distort the meaning of the original. As a last resort, consult the dictionary, using the following procedure.

LOCATING SYNONYMS IN A DICTIONARY

1. Read *all* the definitions for the word. (Do not read the synonyms.)
2. When the dictionary lists more than one definition, reread the original sentence to see which definition works best in the context.
3. Try to come up with your own synonym based on the definition.
4. Replace the original word with your synonym. Does the sentence still have its original meaning?
5. If the dictionary gives synonyms for the original word, compare them to your synonym. Do they mean the same thing?

If you are using a thesaurus, make sure that you follow steps 4 and 5 so that you do not pick inappropriate synonyms. Remember that no two words mean exactly the same thing, and a synonym listed in a thesaurus is not necessarily an appropriate substitute for the original word in all contexts. Returning to our example, by substituting synonyms, doing a little more rearranging, and providing context where necessary, we arrive at the following paraphrase:

```
If we consider seriously how violent video games affect society,
we may be able to prevent future Littleton-style tragedies (Leo
361).
```

You do not have to find a substitute for every word in the sentence you are paraphrasing. You can repeat words that are essential to the meaning or have no appropriate synonyms such as the term "Littleton-style" in our example.

E x e r c i s e . . . .

Rewrite the following paragraph from James Monaco's book *How to Read a Film* by substituting synonyms for the underlined words and phrases. Come up with your own synonyms for familiar words. If contextual clues do not unlock the meaning of unfamiliar words, use the procedure for finding synonyms in a dictionary or thesaurus.

> The theoretical <u>interrelationship</u> between painting and film <u>continues to this day</u>. The Italian Futurist movement produced obvious parodies of the motion picture; <u>contemporary</u> photographic hyperrealism continues to comment on the <u>ramifications</u> of the camera esthetic. But the connection between the two arts has never been as <u>sharp</u> and <u>clear</u> as it was during the Cubist Period. The primary <u>response</u> of painting to the <u>challenge</u> of film has been the <u>conceptualism</u> that Cubism first <u>liberated</u> and that is not <u>common</u> to all the arts. The work of <u>mimesis</u> has been left, in the main, to the recording arts. The arts of representation and <u>artifact</u> have moved on to a new, more abstract <u>sphere</u>. The <u>strong challenge</u> film presented to the pictorial arts was certainly a function of

its _mimetic capabilities_, but it was _also due to_ the one factor that made film _radically different_ from painting; film moved. (Monaco 25)

. . . .

Combine or divide sentences as necessary.   Since our paraphrase is well-coordinated, there is no pressing need to divide it; nevertheless, for illustration we will split it into two smaller units.

```
We should consider seriously how violent video games affect soci-
ety. Then we may be able to prevent future Littleton-style
tragedies (Leo 361).
```

Compare the paraphrase to the original.   At this juncture, before we incorporate the paraphrase into our essay, we will compare it to Leo's original sentence and make any revisions that are necessary.

Original

If we want to avoid more Littleton-style massacres, we will begin taking the social effects of the killing games more seriously.

Paraphrase

```
If we consider seriously how violent video games affect society,
we may be able to prevent future Littleton-style tragedies (Leo
361).
```

As you compare your paraphrase to the original, ask yourself the following questions.

QUESTIONS FOR REVISING PARAPHRASES

- Did I leave out important ideas in the original source?
- Did I change the meaning of the original text by adding my own interpretation or superfluous ideas?
- Did I follow the original text too closely by neglecting to rearrange main idea units?
- Did I include too many words from the original text or repeat more than three words in a row?
- Did I substitute inappropriate synonyms that change the original meaning of the text?
- Did I choose words that are inappropriate for my audience?

Exercise . . . .

Here we present a sentence from a textbook and sample student paraphrases. Compare each paraphrase to the original to see if the writer needs to make revisions. Ask yourself the questions for revising paraphrases.

Somatic cells, while tiny compact worlds within themselves, nevertheless do not exist in isolation; instead, cells bond together, according to their special function, and thereby form definite units or structures called tissues. (Luckman and Sorensen 138)

PARAPHRASES

1. A tissue is formed by the bonding of different somatic cells according to their common functions (Luckman and Sorensen 138).

2. Tissues that are definite units or structures are formed by cells that bond together. They bond according to the special functions they have. Somatic cells are an example of small cells that bond together to form a tissue instead of remaining separate (Luckman and Sorensen 138).

3. Somatic cells, like any other cells, do not live alone. They join together with other cells depending on their specific functions and form a substance called tissue (Luckman and Sorensen 138).

4. Tissues are formed when somatic cells collide outside their small worlds. In order for these cells to be bonded, they must match in a certain way (Luckman and Sorensen 138).

5. Tissues are formed by the bonding together of somatic cells according to their special functions (Luckman and Sorensen 138).

* * * * * * * * * * * * * * * *

Weave the paraphrase into your essay.   We are now ready to weave the paraphrase into our essay in a way that helps further our rhetorical purpose. Consider the following example.

Essay Excerpt

So what is causing the current outburst of deadly violence in American public schools? One explanation is that the current school-age generation has been entranced by violent entertainment, including television, films, and video games. In the wake of the massacre at Columbine High School in Littleton, Colorado, John Leo wrote that if we considered seriously how violent video games affect society, we might be able to prevent future Littleton-style tragedies (361). It is hard to imagine that children who spend hours each day "killing" in cyberspace will not be affected by the experience.

We cannot be sure that a paraphrase is successful without seeing it in context. The paraphrase must accurately reword the author's message and also fit smoothly in the passage of the essay for which it was intended. To achieve this fit in our example, we had to identify the overall subject of Leo's piece. We did this by adding "In the wake of the massacre at Columbine High School in Littleton, Colorado, John Leo wrote that . . ." This phrase also attributes the material to Leo.

Document the paraphrase.   Remember that failing to document a paraphrase is considered plagiarism. Always indicate the author of the source, the page numbers of the information you paraphrased, and a complete entry on the works cited page.

In addition to the seven paraphrasing strategies we have discussed, you can use graphic overviews as paraphrasing tools. If you are paraphrasing complex sentences or groups of sentences, construct a graphic overview of the text and then derive your paraphrase from the overview. To review how we created a summary from a graphic overview, see pages 46–50, but keep in mind that a paraphrase includes all the points from the original rather than just the key ideas.

E x e r c i s e ....

For this exercise, we have reproduced two excerpts from student essays that draw on Steven Vogel's "Grades and Money." For each excerpt, convert the quotation to a paraphrase by using the strategies described in the text. Remember that in addition to accurately rewording the author's ideas, you have to make sure the paraphrase fits smoothly into the existing paragraph. If you have not read Vogel's article, it will help to know that Vogel is a college professor of philosophy who claims that students have come to see grades as "money," the currency of higher education. According to Vogel, professors "pay" students for their academic work with grades, and thus grades are valued more than learning.

1.   The tragic aspect of the A-F grading system is that it devalues education. Under this system, students attend college not to learn but rather to accumulate an impressive portfolio of grades. Students see grades, not knowledge, as the payoff for hard academic work. "If grades are money, then learning is a cost--a painful effort one undergoes only for the reward it produces" (Vogel 339). Thus it is not that students need grades to motivate them to learn but rather that achieving the grades has itself become the ultimate goal of higher education.

2.   Most students expect relatively high grades in courses where they work hard. Perhaps the exception is mathematics, where some students readily admit a lack of aptitude, but even students who recognize that they are struggling in a particular subject expect decent grades if they are trying. At the same time, students who are doing well in a subject are often not content with any grades below an A. "These honor students are in some ways the worst in terms of their fixation on grades and their constant and creative search to find ways to manipulate the system: their skill at doing so, after all, has gotten them where they are today" (Vogel 339). Since virtually all students, from the academically talented to the academically challenged, think they deserve higher grades, professors are under constant pressure to compromise their standards.

DIRECT QUOTING

As we mentioned earlier, when you draw on sources, it is usually best to summarize or paraphrase rather than quote directly. As a general rule, repeat sources word for word only when there is an obvious rhetorical advantage to quoting, for example, when rewording the original will weaken your argument or prevent you from including particularly elegant language.

Sometimes students quote for convenience because they think it will be too much trouble to paraphrase the source. But it is to your advantage to negotiate a difficult text and render its meaning in your own words. When you quote excessively, you relinquish rhetorical control and give it to the source author. You can also end up with a series of strung-together quotations in an essay that seems purposeless and disjointed.

REASONS FOR DIRECT QUOTING

Given these admonitions, when is it advisable to quote? We will discuss five common purposes for quoting and give an example of each.

WHEN TO USE DIRECT QUOTATIONS

- To retain the meaning and authenticity of the original source
- To lend support to an analysis or evaluation
- To capture exactly language that supports your point
- To employ a stylistic device
- To capture language that is unusual, well crafted, striking, or memorable

A typical reason for quoting is to retain the meaning or authenticity of the original source. Assume that you are writing about Joshua Quittner's "Invasion of Privacy" (pages 352–358), an article that discusses individuals' constitutional right to privacy. In your essay, you decide to quote directly from relevant parts of the United States Constitution. In this case, it would not be effective to paraphrase the Constitution, since the exact wording is crucial to its interpretation. When precise wording affects your argument, you may need to quote.

Another purpose for quoting involves analysis and evaluation. When you analyze and evaluate texts, you need to identify specific passages that support your position. We will discuss analysis and evaluation essays in Chapter 7. For now, we will illustrate with an excerpt from an essay by Helen Chang analyzing Linda Grant's text, "What Sexual Revolution?"

> Although Grant makes some good points about the significance of the sexual revolution for many women's lives, one flaw in her argument lies in her overly general and sweeping definition of "women." The women Grant refers to are for the most part white and middle-class. A case in point is her statement that prior to the 1960s, women who had jobs were "sexless, repressed--spinsters whom, by implication, no man wanted or loved" (2). Perhaps this was true for the privileged classes, but many poor women did work and also had children and husbands who valued them.

If Helen had paraphrased Grant's words instead of quoting them directly, she would have weakened her point.

A third purpose for quoting is to capture exactly language that supports your point. In his article "From Fine Romance to Good Rockin'—and Beyond: Look What They've Done to My Song," Michael Budds explains that with the advent of rock and roll, popular music lyrics became more sexually explicit. He illustrates this shift by quoting directly from a Tin Pan Alley song and then contrasting it with early rock and roll lyrics. Excerpts from the lyrics Budds quotes make his point quite vividly.

Tin Pan Alley (from "All the Things You Are," lyrics by Jerome Kern)

Some day my happy arms will hold you,
And some day I'll know that moment divine
When all the things you are, are mine.

Rock and Roll (from "Sixty-Minute Man," lyrics by William Ward and Rose Marks)

If your man ain't treatin' you right, come up here and see old Dan.
I rock 'em, roll 'em all night long: I'm a sixty-minute man.

Quoting directly from the lyrics lends a sense of reality to Budds's discussion. The exact language of the lyrics tells the reader much more about the treatment of sexuality in each song than a paraphrase would reveal.

Another reason to use a direct quotation is as a stylistic device. A common technique for opening or closing a paper is to supply a direct quotation. Consider how Charles Krauthammer, author of "First and Last, Do No Harm" (pages 416–418), ends his article with a quotation from the Hippocratic Oath that has for centuries been the pledge doctors take when they enter the profession:

"I will give no deadly medicine to anyone if asked"—The Hippocratic Oath

A final reason for quoting is to capture language that you find especially effective or memorable. Notice how our student Karla Allen employs Charles Dickens's memorable lines.

```
In Charles Dickens's words, "It was the best of times, it was
the worst of times" (3). While big corporations were reaping
larger profits than ever before, many smaller companies and indi-
viduals found themselves out of work.
```

Exercise ....

Explain why students used direct quotations in each of the following examples.

```
1. Computer expert Alan Kay once stated that "although the personal
   computer can be guided in any direction we choose, the real sin would
   be to make it act like a machine" (Frude 24). As Kay indicates, we
   should take advantage of recent advances in artificial intelligence to
   produce a computer that simulates human thinking.
```

2. The Supreme Court's recent decisions on search warrants seem to support the logic that "if you have nothing to hide, you have nothing to fear" (Stephens 22).

3. "I'm going [to the party] because I've been invited. . . . And I've been invited because Luciana is my friend. So there. [Her mother replied], "That one's not your friend. You know what you are to them? The maid's daughter, that's what!" (432). This brief yet dramatic confrontation draws the reader immediately into the theme of Liliana Heker's story "The Stolen Party."

4. One of the physician's most fundamental rights is the right to choose patients. In Section VI of the Code of Ethics, the American Medical Association guarantees that "a physician is free, except in emergencies, to choose whom to serve" (Zuger and Miles 1926).

. . . .

ALTERING QUOTATIONS

There will be times when you wish to alter a direct quotation by omitting or inserting words. These changes are permissible as long as you follow conventions that alert your audience to what you are doing. In the following example, we give a sentence from Michael Moffatt's "College Life: Undergraduate Culture and Higher Education" and an excerpt from a student paper that quotes part of the sentence. The student uses *points of ellipsis,* a set of three spaced periods, to show where words have been omitted. The square brackets around the points of ellipsis show that they were added by the student and distinguish them from any spaced periods that might appear in the original.

Original

As it is elsewhere in American middle-class culture, friendliness is the central code of etiquette in student culture, the expected code of conduct in student collectivities such as dorm-floor groups and fraternities, the one taken-for-granted politesse whose systematic breach almost always generates anger and even outrage in students. (Moffatt 52–53)

Student Essay

While students may tolerate outrageous and idiosyncratic behavior in the residence halls, they will not put up with unfriendliness. According to Moffatt, "As it is elsewhere in American middle-class culture, friendliness is the central code of etiquette in student culture [. . .] whose systematic breach almost always generates anger and even outrage in students" (52-53).

In cases where you need to show omission at the end of quoted material, use a period followed by the three spaced points of ellipsis.

Sometimes, you will find it necessary to insert your own words into a quotation. When you *interpolate* in this way, signal this to your audience by placing your words between brackets. Notice how our student Spencer Levy uses this convention when he quotes the final sentence from Toni Cade Bambara's story "The Lesson."

Original

But ain't nobody gonna beat me at nuthin.

Student Essay

```
At the end of the story, when we hear Sylvia boasting that
"nobody [is] gonna beat me at nuthin," we know that she does not
need our sympathy; she simply deserves our praise.
```

By inserting the verb *is,* Spencer was able to work the quotation into the structure of his sentence. Brackets also enable you to explain or identify quoted material. In the following example, a student uses this technique to provide context for a quotation from Jerry Farber's essay "A Young Person's Guide to the Grading System."

```
Farber points out that "many of us understand all this [that
grades are just a game we play to please teachers] and yet remain
convinced that we need to be graded in order to learn" (333).
```

The student inserts "that grades are just a game we play to please teachers" in order to explain "all this." Remember that the only time it is permissible to change a quotation or interject your own words is when you use ellipsis points or brackets.

DOCUMENTING QUOTATIONS

Enclose short quotations (up to four typed lines) in double quotation marks. Set a longer quotation apart from your text by indenting it ten spaces, as has been done for the following quotation from Rand Cooper's article "The Dignity of Helplessness: What Sort of Society Would Euthanasia Create?"

```
                                                        Jones 4

        At the end of his article, Cooper reminds us that physi-
    cian-assisted suicide may affect not only the individuals who
    choose this option but the rest of society as well:
                A sense of this deep privacy drives the right-to-die
                movement in America today. And yet to step outside the
                rights framework is to ask how institutionalizing
                assisted suicide will affect not only those who die,
                but those who live on; not only individuals, but soci-
                ety. The fact is, our deaths are both solo journeys
                toward an ultimate mystery and strands in the tapes-
                tries of each other's lives. Which side of this real-
                ity will we emphasize? Whose death is it, anyway? The
                debate about assisted suicide should begin at the place
                where that question ceases to be a rhetorical one. (415)
    Cooper is right that most deaths have a strong impact on those
```

> who are left behind. In this sense, we have a responsibility to
> consider others when we make choices about our own deaths. While
> we tend to think of death as a private matter, it most certainly
> does have a public dimension.

Notice that for a long quotation, the parenthetical citation goes outside the final punctuation. For short quotations, place the parenthetical citation between the final quotation marks and the closing punctuation:

> Farber points out that "many of us understand all this
> [that grades are just a game we play to please teachers] and yet
> remain convinced that we need to be graded in order to learn"
> (333).

In the MLA documentation style, the parenthetical citation is an absolute requirement for quotations in academic prose. You must acknowledge the author and provide the page number of the quotation in the original text.

In our example, the phrase "Farber points out" leads in to the quotation and acknowledges the author. Many other verbs can be used to introduce quotations:

acknowledges	describes	proposes
addresses	determines	proves
adds	discovers	questions
admits	emphasizes	rationalizes
agrees (disagrees)	envisions	refers to
analyzes	evaluates	remarks
answers	examines	replies
argues	explores	reports
ascertains	expounds on	reviews
asks	finds	says
assesses	furnishes	shows
believes	identifies	states
categorizes	inquires	stipulates
cites	investigates	stresses
compares (contrasts)	lists	suggests
concludes	makes the case	summarizes
concurs	measures	surveys
considers	notes	synthesizes
critiques	observes	traces
defines	points out	views
delineates	postulates	warns
demonstrates	presents	writes

These verbs can be used as lead-ins to summaries and paraphrases as well as quotations.

WEAVING QUOTATIONS INTO YOUR ESSAY

There are a number of ways to weave a quotation into your writing. You can acknowledge the author in the text itself or place the name in parentheses. When you acknowledge the author in the text, you can cite the name before the quotation, within the quotation, or after it. For example, let's say you are quoting the following sentence from Vogel's article:

> We let grades count as money—we let education count as money—because money, nowadays, is the only value we know.

Here are five options. Option A allows you to insert the quotation without acknowledging the author in the body of the text. Instead, you place the name in parentheses.

A. "We let grades count as money--we let education count as money--because money, nowadays, is the only value we know" (Vogel 340).

When you use option A, remember to connect your own ideas to the quotation. Don't just plop the quotation into your essay. Lead in to it by providing transitions or connecting ideas. Inexperienced writers sprinkle their papers with direct quotations that appear to have little connection with the rest of the text. If you have difficulty coming up with connecting ideas, use option B, C, D, or E. In these options, you acknowledge the author within the text.

B. Vogel argues, "We let grades count as money--we let education count as money--because money, nowadays, is the only value we know" (340).

C. "We let grades count as money--we let education count as money--because," Vogel argues, "money, nowadays, is the only value we know" (340).

D. "We let grades count as money--we let education count as money--because money, nowadays, is the only value we know," Vogel claims (340).

A final option is to introduce a quotation with a complete sentence followed by a colon.

E. Vogel reminds us that the problem with grades in higher education reflects the values of the larger society: "We let grades count as money--we let education count as money--because money, nowadays, is the only value we know" (340).

You will find the following rules about capitalization and punctuation useful when you quote.

Capitalization

1. If the quotation is a complete sentence, begin it with a capital letter.

   According to Leo, "Video games are much more powerful versions of the military's primitive discovery about overcoming the reluctance to shoot" (360).

2. If the quotation is not a complete sentence, begin it with a lowercase letter.

    ```
    Video games that include cops as targets are, according to Leo,
    "exploiting resentments toward law enforcement and making real-
    life shooting of cops more likely" (360).
    ```

3. If the quotation is preceded by the word *that,* omit the comma. If the quoted words become part of the structure of your own sentence, begin the quotation with a lowercase letter.

    ```
    Leo points out that "adolescent feelings of resentment, power-
    lessness, and revenge pour into the killing games" (360).
    ```

4. If you continue a quotation within a sentence, do not capitalize the opening word unless it begins a complete sentence or is a proper noun.

    ```
    "Did the sensibilities created by the modern video kill games,"
    asks Leo, "play a role in the Littleton massacre?" (360).
    ```

Punctuation

1. Set off the quoted material with double quotation marks: "..."
2. Set off quoted material within a quotation with single quotation marks.

    ```
    Leo notes that "psychologist David Grossman of Arkansas State
    University, a retired Army officer, thinks 'point and shoot'
    video games have the same effect as military strategies used to
    break down a soldier's aversion to killing" (360).
    ```

3. Separate the verb of acknowledgment from a short quotation with a comma and from a long quotation with a colon.

    ```
    Many parents assert that their children are aware of the differ-
    ence between video games and real life; however, these games may
    have more impact on children's values than most parents realize.
    Leo points out:
              We are now a society in which the chief form of play
              for millions of youngsters is making large numbers of
              people die. Hurting and maiming others is the central
              fun activity in video games played so addictively by
              the young. A widely cited survey of 900 fourth-through-
              eighth-grade students found that almost half of the
              children said their favorite electronic games involve
              violence. Can it be that all this constant training in
              make-believe killing has no social effects? (360)
    ```

4. Close a quotation by placing the period or comma after the parenthetical documentation of the page number.

    ```
    According to Leo, many Americans believe that video games are
    just a "harmless activity among children who know the difference
    between fantasy and reality" (360).
    ```

5. When you acknowledge a source, set off the title with underlining or quotation marks. Underlining tells your audience that you are quoting from a long source: a book, full-length play, journal, magazine, or long poem. Quotation marks signal a shorter work: a chapter or section in a book, an article in a journal or magazine, a poem, or a short story.

> In his novel *The Stranger,* Albert Camus describes . . .
>
> James Joyce's short story "The Dead" concerns . . .
>
> In Chapter 3, "Responding to Sources," Kennedy and Smith discuss . . .
>
> *Romeo and Juliet,* a play by Shakespeare turned into a film by Zeffirelli, shows how . . .

Exercise

Scan "The Color of Suspicion" by Jeffrey Goldberg (pages 427–441) and "Title IX from Outer Space" by Walter Olsen (pages 458–461) for places where the authors have quoted directly from other sources. Can you make any generalizations about how these authors use direct quotations to build their arguments? Do the authors differ in the way they use quotations?

INCORPORATING SUMMARIES INTO ESSAYS

Usually, when you paraphrase and summarize, your purpose is to do much more than reproduce or reduce the content of a text. Most likely, your rhetorical purpose requires you to incorporate the paraphrase or summary in your essay. For example, instead of simply writing a free-standing summary of Vogel's "Grades and Money," you might include the summary in an essay in which you react to, analyze, or evaluate the article. For the reaction paper, you might take a particular stance—for example, the point of view of a college student, professor, or administrator.

When you incorporate paraphrases or summaries into an essay that has its own purpose, you will find that you have to adapt and transform them so that they are compatible with the rest of the paper. For example, consider the various ways that a summary of the article "It's Over, Debbie" (pages 401–402) might function in an essay written for a specific purpose. It will help to know that the article is a first-person narrative written by a physician in training who describes administering a lethal dose of morphine to a dying patient who is suffering terribly. Your summary could be written from the perspective of the physician, like the original article, and focus on the medical ethics of the situation. You could also shift the perspective of the summary to the patient and focus on an individual's right to decide when it is time to die. To illustrate, look at Elizabeth Goldman's essay, which begins with a short summary of "It's Over, Debbie." We have reproduced Elizabeth's introductory summary, the first sentence or two from each of her body paragraphs, and her conclusion. Notice how her opening summary highlights each of the three perspectives that she develops in her paper.

Goldman 1

Elizabeth Goldman

Professor Smith

Academic Writing I

22 October 1999

When the Time Comes

"Let's get this over with," were only the words spoken by
Debbie, a twenty-year-old terminal cancer patient, to the
physician on call at the hospital. Minutes later, the doctor gave
Debbie a fatal dose of morphine to end her suffering. "It's
Over, Debbie," a narrative of this event, was published
anonymously by the doctor who administered the morphine. The
details are sparse: the physician was awakened at night and told
that a cancer patient was "having difficulty getting rest." The
doctor proceeded to the cancer ward and found a young woman who
was breathing heavily and was vomiting repeatedly as a result of
her medication. An IV and nasal oxygen were helping to keep her
80-lb. body alive, but over the past two days, she hadn't eaten
any food. The doctor made a decision on the spot to honor the
dying woman's request for death. An older woman, very likely the
patient's mother, was also in the room and seemed "relieved" once
the morphine made Debbie relax and then die. Imagine yourself in
the role of Debbie, her mother, or the doctor. What would you
do? When I place myself in any of those roles, I come to the
same conclusion: there comes a time when it is appropriate to
end a painful and hopeless struggle to remain alive, a principle
our society and legal system needs to support.

If I become a doctor, I hope that all the technical
medical training on how to sustain life will not overcome my

common sense and basic compassion for others. It is true that the IV, nasal oxygen, and other forms of treatment were keeping Debbie alive, but what is the value to Debbie of a life that offers nothing but suffering?

. . . .

If I, rather than Debbie, were lying in the hospital bed suffering, I have no question that I would want to die, for my own sake and for the peace of mind of those I love.

. . . .

The mother's perspective is perhaps the most difficult to imagine. I have read that according to therapists, the most devastating trauma of all is being predeceased by a child. But if my child were suffering, I hope I would be able to place her needs ahead of my own.

. . . .

Our society still maintains laws against committing or assisting in suicide, and we have locked away Dr. Jack Kevorkian for his courageous defense of the right to die. We need to acknowledge that our laws against suicide coupled with our advanced medical technology can cruelly condemn the dying to spend their final days in agony. Our society needs to accept, as Debbie, her mother, and her physician did, that death is sometimes the only humane option.

Work Cited

"It's Over, Debbie." <u>Journal of the American Medical Association</u> 259.2 (1998): 272.

THE SUMMARY ESSAY

In college, sometimes you are asked to write a summary for its own sake rather than incorporate it into a piece that you are writing for another rhetorical purpose. You may even be assigned a free-standing paraphrase. For instance, your philosophy professor might ask you to write a paraphrase of an especially demanding passage of text, or your English teacher might tell you to put a poem into your own words. If your professors require you to keep a course journal or reading log, they may ask you to enter paraphrases of selected passages of text.

A more common assignment than a free-standing paraphrase is a free-standing summary. You can write a free-standing summary in an essay format. Typically, a summary essay of a reading source includes the following elements.

ELEMENTS IN A FREE-STANDING SUMMARY ESSAY

Introduction	• Engages the reader with an interesting opening
	• Identifies the source (author, title)
	• Explains the topic of the source
	• Conveys the main perspective or thesis of the source
Body	• Discusses in each paragraph a key element of the source
	• Links material together according to a clear plan, usually reflecting the organizational pattern of the source
Conclusion	• Closes the essay by broadening the focus and placing the source in a larger context

If you wish, you can draw on your knowledge and experience as you compose a free-standing summary. In fact, if you are well versed in the subject matter and feel comfortable and confident working with the source, you should let your voice surface in the summary itself. Your summary will sound less like a straightforward transfer of information and more like a personal, inventive rendition of the source material. Your audience will hear your voice at least as loudly as they hear the information you are summarizing. Of course, when you draw on your knowledge and experience while summarizing, make sure that you do not put words in the author's mouth. Remember that one of the basic rules for summarizing is that you remain faithful to the original source. In the summary of Lee Silver's "Jennifer and Rachel" (362–367) that follows, notice where James Henderson integrates the material he is summarizing with his own knowledge.

James Henderson

Professor Smith

Academic Writing I

28 September 1999

Summary of "Jennifer and Rachel" by Lee M. Silver

How might our society change if individuals began to clone themselves to produce children rather than conceive though sexual relations? This question conjures up images of Aldous Huxley's <u>Brave New World</u>, where hordes of identical children were "hatched" and raised in uniform batches to fulfill specific social needs. According to Lee M. Silver, author of "Jennifer and Rachel," human cloning will happen, but it will not pose the danger to our humanity or our social structure that Huxley predicted. Silver presents his own fictional account of cloning, but in his tale, a single woman named Jennifer clones herself to create a child that is entirely her own. He tells Jennifer's story to illustrate why someone might choose to be cloned, and then, through commentary on the scenario, he explains why we should not fear these products of our own brave new world.

Silver's scenario is set in the year 2049, when human cloning is technically possible but illegal in the United States. Jennifer, a financially secure woman, decides that she wants to give birth to a child and raise it alone. Several options for becoming pregnant are possible for Jennifer, but she chooses cloning because no one else's genetic material will be involved. This technology enables Jennifer to know automatically what her child's traits will be, an idea that appeals to her. After she makes her decision, she travels to

Henderson 2

the Cayman Islands, where the procedure takes place. Nine months later, Jennifer gives birth to her daughter. Rachel grows up very much like other children. Jennifer intends to tell Rachel the full story of her creation and birth as soon as she is old enough to understand the concept. Silver's scenario is certainly plausible; my cousin Louise, a single woman in her thirties, just adopted a child from Honduras, and no one questioned her desire to be a single parent. If cloning were available now, Louise might have used it.

After Silver presents the Jennifer and Rachel scenario, **3** he anticipates and responds to the objections that some people might have to Jennifer's choice to clone herself. One objection is that as a clone of her mother, Rachel is denied the right to grow up and develop her own identity. Since Jennifer and Rachel have the same genes, will Rachel grow up to be just like her mother? Will she have the freedom to develop a personality of her own? According to Silver, the fact that Rachel and Jennifer have the same genetic makeup doesn't mean that their lives will be the same. Rachel's childhood is bound to differ from that of her mother because the environmental influences will not be the same. Mother and daughter will be members of distinct generations and grow up under different social circumstances, as is the case with other children and their parents. And after all, what teenage girl tries to grow up to be just like her mom? While most parents have certain expectations for their children, Silver sees no reason that Jennifer will burden her clone daughter with unreasonable goals. Silver is probably thinking of the many parents like my

own who have their children's lives all plotted out for them.
And I'm most certainly not a clone!

Silver also notes that cloning may be perceived as a   **4**
violation of religious doctrines, and I know that the Vatican
has, in fact, condemned human cloning. In response to this
objection, Silver points out that cloning does not involve
tampering with embryos, as abortion does, but rather involves
only unfertilized eggs and regular body cells that, without the
cloning process, would never develop into embryos. Though some
people feel that the scientists who clone humans are "playing
God," Silver points out that this claim applies equally to all
reproductive technologies, not just to cloning.

But the critics of cloning are not finished by any means;   **5**
they next point out that cloning has the potential to interfere
with evolution and thus affect the future progress of our
species. In response, Silver argues that relatively few people
will find cloning attractive and hence that such a limited use
of the technology is unlikely to affect human evolution. As
for the critics' claim that evolution must be allowed to take
its course, Silver maintains that "unfettered evolution" won't
necessarily guarantee improvement for the species.

The last objection to cloning that Silver addresses is   **6**
that it might create an underground market in designer clones.
The genetic material of famous and talented individuals might
be stolen and cloned, and the resulting embryos could then be
sold to parents who want a child with outstanding
characteristics. Silver agrees that this practice is possible
but maintains that it would most likely be prohibited by law.

He also questions whether many parents would want to raise other people's clones rather than their own biological children. I imagine that it would be very difficult to raise a child whose talents and skills far surpassed my own. Say my son was Michael Jordan's clone. As a nine-year-old, what would little Mike think of my lead feet and pitiful jump shot? In any case, Silver states that those parents who do purchase designer clones may be disappointed since environmental influences will ensure that the clones are significantly different from their biological parents.

Silver envisions a future where cloning will be one of the available reproductive choices, and he suggests that some of us may have good reason to give birth to a cloned child. Though many fear the idea of human cloning, Silver believes that this process poses no significant risks to the clone children or to our society at large. By the time I am ready to have a family, the Jennifer and Rachel scenario may be more than just fiction, and the debate Silver outlines will be more than a hypothetical exercise.

7

Work Cited

Silver, Lee. "Jennifer and Rachel." <u>Remaking Eden: Cloning and Beyond in a Brave New World</u>. New York: Avon, 1997.

We suggest that you use matter-of-fact titles for free-standing summaries. James Henderson's title, "Summary of 'Jennifer and Rachel' by Lee M. Silver," indicates the straightforward goal of his essay. Clever or elaborate titles may seem inappropriate for summary essays.

Drawing on the strategies we have presented in this chapter, we outline the process of summary writing in Table 2-1.

TABLE 2-1 **THE PROCESS OF SUMMARY ESSAY WRITING**

Prewriting: Planning and Preparatory Activities

1. Read the assignment, and formulate your rhetorical goals.
   - Why are you writing the summary, and what desired effect do you hope to have on your audience?
   - How much of the source material should you include in the summary, and what form should this material take?
   - Will your summary be a comprehensive account of the author's thesis and argument, or will it emphasize only the author's central points?

2. Consider your audience.
   - Are you writing for your professor or for a broader audience?
   - Is your audience in the academic community?
   - Are you writing for a general audience or for specialists?
   - What will your audience already know about the topic?
   - Will you need to explain basic concepts or provide background for the source material to make sense?
   - Will your audience be biased either for or against what the source says?
   - Can you predict how your audience will react to the source?
   - What is the overall impact that you want to have on your audience?
   - How will your writing inform, influence, or change your audience?

3. Read the source for content; form, organization, and features; and rhetorical concerns.
   - Reading for content: What is the author's thesis or main point? What are other important points?
   - Reading for form, organization, and features: How does the author get his or her points across? What is the method of presentation? What is the pattern of organization?
   - Reading for rhetorical concerns: What is the author's purpose? How does the author intend to influence the audience? Who is this author and what is his or her background? To whom is the piece addressed? In what type of publication is it published? What is the author's relationship to the audience?

Drafting

1. Arrange summarized material in paragraphs.
2. Identify the source by title and author.
3. Insert transitions and logical connectors.
4. Supply parenthetical documentation.
5. Title your summary.
6. Create a works cited page.

Revising

If possible, have a classmate or friend read your summary and answer the questions on the following checklist. If no one is available, answer the questions yourself.

✓ *Checklist for Revising a Summary Essay*

_____ 1. Have you identified the author and title of the source?
_____ 2. Have you indicated the author's purpose and the point he or she is trying to get across (thesis)?
_____ 3. Have you referred to the rhetorical context (audience and place of publication) if it is discernible?
_____ 4. Are there clear transitions and logical connectors between paragraphs?
_____ 5. Are there clear transitions within paragraphs?
_____ 6. Have you paraphrased instead of following the original word for word?
_____ 7. Have you included too many quotations?
_____ 8. Does the summary include too much detail, redundancy, or examples?
_____ 9. Have you adapted the summary to your audience's needs?
_____ 10. Have you provided parenthetical documentation?
_____ 11. Have you included a works cited page?
_____ 12. Have you corrected sentences that sound stilted or awkward?
_____ 13. Have you corrected errors in usage, punctuation, or mechanics?
_____ 14. Have you corrected typographical errors or misspellings?

Part II

WRITING ACADEMIC

ESSAYS

3

RESPONDING TO SOURCES

In grade school or even in high school, you undoubtedly wrote personal essays drawing on life experiences. You probably wrote on assigned topics such as "An influential person in my life" or "An important lesson I learned" or responded to more open-ended assignments that allowed you to write about relevant personal experiences. Your essays for college applications may have asked you to draw on your personal experience. In all these situations, you composed the essays by searching your memory, recalling previous experiences, and reviewing your prior knowledge of the topics.

In Chapter 1, we explained that reading comprehension occurs when you relate your prior knowledge to the material that you are reading. An important element of the prereading strategy is calling up this knowledge so that you can benefit from it as you read. In fact, your prior knowledge is essential to all your reading.

Nonetheless, college writing assignments seldom ask you to write exclusively about prior knowledge, memories, and personal experiences. As we explained in Chapters 1 and 2, your professors typically expect you to write your papers by drawing on books, articles, and other sources. That is not to say that as an academic writer you will never make references to personal experiences. Occasionally, you will be asked to give personal reactions to readings. Such assignments will extend your understanding of the readings by allowing you to demonstrate their relevance to your life. Consider the following example of an assignment from a psychology class:

> As we have read in our textbook, research suggests that firstborn children experience greater anxiety throughout their lives than later-born children do. In a two-page essay, describe these research findings and test them against your own experience as a member and observer of families.

In response to this assignment, students summarized material from the textbook and linked it to their own lives. Essays that cling to the textbook and make minimal use of students' own ideas will not work here; nor will essays that focus entirely on personal experiences. The assignment asks students to draw on two sources: the text and real life.

RESPONSE ESSAYS: AN INTRODUCTION

The writing tasks that we will focus on in this chapter call for a balance between textual content and the writer's own expression. You are not being asked to offer opinions substantiated only by your own knowledge and experience. Your professors expect you to give an *informed* outlook. They want to hear your point of view on the reading source. You could approach these assignments in an elementary fashion by summarizing the text and tagging on a few sentences of commentary or reaction. But there are much more interesting ways to go about it. To illustrate, let us look at a student essay written in response to the following assignment:

> In his article "Invasions of Privacy," Joshua Quittner explains that he is willing to risk his personal privacy in order to take advantage of electronic technology, such as the Internet. In a brief essay of two to three pages, tell your classmates what you think of Quittner's ideas.

It will be easier to analyze the student essay if you first read Quittner's article on pages 352–358. As you read, think about how you would respond to the above assignment. You can practice the three approaches to strategic reading we discussed in Chapter 1 by recording your answers to the questions accompanying the article.

The student paper reprinted here demonstrates how personal response to a source can form the basis for an essay. Notice that Diane Abramowitz does more than simply summarize the source and add personal reaction. As you read the essay, see if you can identify Diane's purpose.

Abramowitz 1

Diane Abramowitz

Academic Writing I

Professor Smith

27 September 1999

Hackers

Opens with a question

How would you feel if someone read your private mail or journal? Violated? Scared? Two months ago, someone hacked into my AOL account and read all my incoming and saved e-mail messages. Even more frightening, the hacker used my account to send out a chain letter, under my screen name, to over seven hundred people. By getting my password, the hacker had, in effect, stolen my identity, and thus I was blamed for mailing the chain letter, a violation of AOL policy. My e-mail account was suspended, but fortunately AOL accepted my explanation and restored my access with a new password. The hacker, however,

Describes personal experience to introduce topic

1

was still able to break in and send the chain letter to another thousand people. Once again, AOL suspended my account. It was only after I convinced AOL once again that I was not responsible and got them to change both my screen name and password that I managed to escape the hacker.

Introduces Quittner's article

Joshua Quittner went through an experience similar to mine, but instead of his e-mail it was his phone that was attacked. He recalls this event in the article "Invasion of Privacy." Soon after Quittner published a book on computer hackers, someone redirected his incoming phone calls to an answering machine containing an insulting message. The phone company was able to restore the phone service initially, but the hacker struck again. Over the next six months, the hacker interfered with Quittner's phone repeatedly, despite the best efforts of the phone company. Even though Quittner found this incident annoying, he concludes in his article that the usefulness of electronic technologies, such as telephones and the Internet, meant more to him than the privacy he lost by using them. While I agree with Quittner that technology improves our everyday lives significantly, I am not resigned to giving up my privacy in order to enjoy those advantages.

Quittner's main idea

Writer's thesis

Quittner's article describes a wide range of current technologies that have the potential to compromise our privacy. According to Quittner, we leave an electronic record of our whereabouts and activities as we use ATM machines, E-Z Pass lanes, and Web shopping sites and even as we walk down the street past a store that uses video surveillance. Our

2

3

Abramowitz 3

interests, preferences, and purchasing habits are recorded as
we browse the Web or make credit card purchases. A skilled
Internet researcher can, starting with only a name and address,
uncover much of the personal information that has been stored
online. Quittner points out that we can protect ourselves, to
some extent, against invasions of privacy by being more careful
about the personal information we divulge and the technologies
we use. He also suggests that the online business community or
the government do more to protect individual privacy in
cyberspace. In the final analysis, however, Quittner concludes
that he is willing to risk losing some of his privacy in order
to benefit from the power and convenience of technology. He
has "nothing to hide" and just wants some control over who has
access to his personal information.

Quittner does not overstate the advantages of electronic
technology in everyday life. The Internet and e-mail are the
major forms of communication of the 1990s. America Online is
not only a place I do research; it is my way to keep in touch
with my friends all over the United States. Calling people and
carrying on long conversations is expensive, but on AOL, I pay
a flat rate per month to communicate for as long as I want
with as many people as I want at a time. In addition to
accessing e-mail, I use the Internet to search for information.
I can find material on virtually anything that interests me,
from government statistics on the gross domestic product to the
menu of the Italian restaurant down the block. Without a
doubt, Internet access makes my life better.

Margin notes:

Summary of Quittner's article

Draws on personal experience to illustrate one of Quittner's points

4

Abramowitz 4

Since Quittner and I agree that the Internet improves our
lives, it puzzles me that we don't have similar feelings about
online privacy. While Quittner seems resigned to giving up some
of his privacy, I don't think I should have to surrender my
privacy when I go online. You can't be an individual without
having secrets that you share only with those you trust. When

Challenges one of Quittner's claims and gives reasons for her disagreement

someone trespasses into my online time, I feel that my rights
have been violated. I don't want strangers to know what I am
writing to my friends or relatives, and I don't want anyone
looking over my shoulder while I'm surfing the Internet. Even
though I am just "browsing" a Web page, I don't want to be
followed around wherever I go to chat or browse. In legal
terms, following people around is known as stalking. But what
can the authorities do? At this point in time, there are no
Internet authorities to track down the hackers or other
cyberspace violators. Certainly, local, state, and federal
authorities must take immediate steps to ensure that our right
to privacy is protected. We don't have to accept, as Quittner
does, that our privacy rights and modern technology are simply
incompatible.

The movie <u>Hackers</u> illustrates that if we fail to protect
online security, we stand to risk more than just someone
reading our e-mail messages. The film focuses on people who

Reference to a film plot that illustrates a problem associated with Quittner's point of view

possess a certain kind of intelligence and training that allows
them to penetrate the most complex computer systems. Six
teenage hackers foil a plan that would cause an ecological
disaster. Of course, the plan was created by another rebel
hacker. No one else is aware of the plot, and thus the world's

5

6

Abramowitz 5

ecosystem is literally at the mercy of these battling hackers. Luckily, the "good guys" win, but the movie leaves me with an uneasy feeling. Knowing that there are good hackers out there, do I still feel safe?

"The only guys who insist on perfect privacy are hermits like the Unabomber. I don't want to be cut off from the world. I have nothing to hide. I just want some measure of control over what people know about me" (Quittner 35). Although there is no such thing as perfect privacy, that doesn't mean that we don't need and deserve as much privacy as possible. The government must take a much more active role in ensuring that hackers do not threaten either our national or our personal security. In the future, our individual freedom may depend as much on access to cyberspace as it now does on access to the ballot box and the podium.

7

Speculates about the future

Abramowitz 6

Work Cited

Quittner, Joshua. "Invasion of Privacy." Time 25 Aug. 1997: 28-35.

Complete citation for Quittner's article

Diane has a more complex goal than merely summarizing the source and giving a brief personal reaction. Let's zero in on her rhetorical purpose. From her comments, we can assume that she is a frequent user of online communication, and she agrees with Joshua Quittner that this technology improves one's quality of life. But Diane takes issue with Quittner's willingness to surrender a degree of personal privacy in return for the advantages that technology has to offer. Her goal as a writer is to assert that one should be able to benefit from current technology without giving up privacy rights. Notice that Diane supports her position by bringing her own knowledge into play. In the first paragraph, she describes how her own e-mail account was penetrated by a computer hacker who then used the account to send out bogus letters to hundreds of e-mail addresses. Diane uses this personal experience to introduce Quittner's article, which begins with a description of his own experience with a malicious phone hacker. In the fourth paragraph, Diane explains how she relies on the Internet to communicate with friends and do research; these examples demonstrate how important the Internet has become to everyday life. Paragraph 5 includes Diane's personal feeling about having someone read her e-mail or monitor her Web browsing habits. Her goal is to convey the sense of violation one experiences when victimized by electronic eavesdropping.

We have seen that in the first, fourth, and fifth paragraphs, Diane describes experience from her own life and her feelings about those experiences to demonstrate that online privacy violations should be taken seriously. In the sixth paragraph, she uses the film *Hackers* as an example of how computer experts may one day wield tremendous power to affect our personal lives if we fail to institute electronic privacy safeguards. As Diane's essay shows, personal knowledge includes not only things experienced directly but also things read in books or magazines, viewed on film or television, or heard on radio or audio recording. You may draw on a full range of personal knowledge when you write response essays.

Exercise

Reread Diane Abramowitz's essay, listing any changes you think she might make in content, form, organization, or features in order to achieve her rhetorical purpose more successfully. In class, compare your list to those of your classmates. Discuss any differences in perception.

WRITING RESPONSE ESSAYS

Which scenario best describes your past experiences with writing?

A. You receive a writing assignment that is due in two weeks. Not long before the essay is due (sometimes the night before), you read the assigned material, take a few notes, and sit down at the computer to pound out a finished product. If you have time, you read over the essay for typos before handing it in. A week later, maybe longer, the teacher returns your paper. You check out the grade, glance at the teacher's comments, and stash the essay in your notebook.

B. You receive an assignment that directs you to write an essay in stages. The first draft is due in one week, a second draft a week later, and perhaps a final draft a week after that. Before you compose the preliminary draft, you do some prewriting activities, reading the assigned material and responding to it in your course journal. You use these prewriting notes to write your essay. When you bring your essay to class, you give it to a group of peers or to the teacher. These reviewers make suggestions for revision. You rethink the paper, make revisions, and resubmit it. The teacher returns the paper with comments and a grade. You check out the grade; read over the comments, especially those referring to the improvements you made; and store the essay in your notebook.

These scenarios represent two different approaches to writing. Scenario A focuses on the finished product, whereas scenario B values the *process* as much as the product. The product-oriented writer tries to create a perfect polished essay in one try. The process-oriented writer works at assignments in phases: *prewriting, drafting, revising,* and *editing.* Another difference between the two approaches is that for the product-oriented writer, composing is often a solitary activity. But the process-oriented writer engages in collaborative activities, sometimes in prewriting discussions and often in peer review groups.

In this textbook we take a process approach to reading and writing. You may recall that in Chapter 1 we advised you to become a process-oriented reader. We discussed ways to tackle reading assignments in phases, thinking about your prior knowledge and experiences with the subject before you read, then consciously probing for links between the reading material and your prior knowledge and experience while you are reading, and finally looking for additional links after you've read through the text. All of this work is *prewriting.*

Whenever you gather, read, and organize materials for writing, you are engaged in prewriting. Once you begin to compose your paper, you have entered the *drafting* phase. After you have completed a draft and received some feedback from your teacher or peers, you will rework your paper in the *revising* phase. Perhaps you will expand on important points, delete irrelevant material, and clarify any points that confused your readers. Finally, you will move on to *editing.* At this phase, you focus on the surface features of your writing, checking for problems with usage, spelling, punctuation, and mechanics.

We want to emphasize that although we refer to reading, prewriting, drafting, revising, and editing as phases, writers do not necessarily proceed from one stage to the next in a systematic fashion. The process is recursive. The various activities can occur at any point in the process. For example, revising can take place while you are writing out your essay or after you have completed a first draft. As we wrote this textbook, we revised some of it at the drafting stage, most of it at the revision stage as we completed each chapter, and a few parts at a later date after we had completed the entire manuscript.

Though you need not work through the reading and writing process in lockstep fashion, marching methodically from one stage to the next, you should be aware that some types of pacing are more productive than others. When you are drafting your essay, if you stop every few minutes to fret about spelling, punctuation, or correct usage, you may end up with disjointed, disconnected prose. The beauty of the process approach to writing is it allows you to concentrate on generating ideas while you are drafting. Editing comes later.

You should also be aware that writers may use different composing styles, depending on their purposes. A writer completing a complex history assignment may spend much more time on prewriting activities—reading, underlining, and annotating the materials and taking notes—than a writer who is composing an essay drawing on prior knowledge or personal experience.

Prewriting. As a college writer, you will be spending a substantial amount of time prewriting: analyzing your assignments, specifying your purposes for writing, establishing your audience, and reading your sources. As you take up each source and decide what you want to obtain from it, remember to look beyond content. Also consider form, organization, features, and rhetorical context. Then as you underline, annotate, and take notes, plan how you will use the reading source in your essay. You may have to reread part or all of it, reread your notes, record additional notes, and do more planning. Once you have done all this rereading, noting, and planning, you are ready to write your first draft.

Drafting. From what we just described, you can see that throughout the prewriting phase, you will be continually shifting back and forth between your role as reader and your role as writer. As you begin drafting, the writer role will take on more importance, but you will not give up the reader role. Throughout the drafting stage, you may find it necessary to refer to the reading sources to retrieve a quotation, verify a piece of information, or flesh out a note.

Revising. After you have generated a draft, get some feedback from your teacher or peers. If this is not possible, set the draft aside and come back to it in a day or two. Then take the advice of Donald M. Murray (12–14), author of over a dozen books on writing, and reread your draft asking yourself the following questions:

1. Are there any surprises? Do I say anything I hadn't intended to say? If so, is this the direction I want to take?
2. Does everything in the draft lead to one dominant meaning?
3. Will my intended reader understand what I have said?
4. Is the form appropriate, and is the organization supportive?
5. Is the evidence varied, adequate, and appropriate?
6. Can I hear the voice and language of the text?

You may have to reread your draft three or four times, and most likely you will find yourself making many changes.

Editing. When you are satisfied with your work, reread your essay line by line and sentence by sentence, checking for usage, punctuation, spelling, and mechanics. Apply the spell checker. If you have especially weak editing skills, ask your teacher if it would be all right to have a friend read over your work.

E x e r c i s e ....

Write a one-paragraph description of how you wrote essays in high school. Consider the following questions: How did you come up with ideas for your writing? What organizational plans did you use? Did you create outlines? Did you write first drafts without notes? Did you ask friends, family members, or teachers to read your rough drafts? If so, what types of feedback did you receive, and how did you respond? When you proofread, what specific issues of usage, spelling, punctuation, and mechanics did you focus on?

Now consider the overall writing process you have used. Over how many days did the process extend? What were the strengths of your approach to writing assignments? What were your weaknesses? What parts of the process were the easiest for you, and what parts were the hardest? Write another paragraph in response to these questions.

In class, compile a joint list of students' strengths and weaknesses. Discuss why students' responses vary.

• • • • • • • • • • • • • • • • •

PREWRITING

For assignments that require you to use reading sources in your writing, the key to success lies at the *prewriting* stage. This is the period just before you sit down at the computer to type out a complete draft of your paper. It is the time for reading and rereading the text, annotating, taking notes, and planning your essay. You will find that it is far more efficient to select relevant parts of the reading source, bring your prior topic knowledge into play, and organize these ideas at this stage than to rack your brain and refer continually to the reading source *while* you are drafting your essay.

When you receive your assignment, put on your rhetorical glasses and from there on in think in terms of audience and purpose. Keep in mind that a rhetorical situation exists: just as the author of the source you are about to read has written to his or her readers for a reason, you are writing your essay for a reason. You are trying to affect or influence your readers in a certain way.

Do a first reading to get a general impression of the source.

After you have analyzed your assignment and determined that you are being asked to write an essay in response to a reading source, turn your attention to your purpose for reading. You will be reading the text for the purpose of generating reactions to the author's ideas. Review the prereading and close reading strategies we discussed in Chapter 1 (pages 13–33). Your first reading may elicit little more than a general, impressionistic reaction. In the case of Joshua Quittner's article "Invasion of Privacy," our students' initial reactions ranged from "Outrageous! No one should have the right to pry into my personal business" to "Why worry about a technology that makes our lives more convenient and safer?" After this initial reading, freewrite your reactions. Write nonstop for ten minutes or so, jotting down whatever comes to mind about the topic.

Reread and elaborate.

The second reading allows you to probe your memory and make associations between prior knowledge and the propositions in the text. As we explained in Chapter 1 (pages 18–21), this strategy is called *elaboration*. To elaborate, annotate in the margins of the text or take separate notes. Here a reader elaborates on two passages from "Invasion of Privacy."

Text	Elaboration Notes
Losing control of your telephone, of course, is the least of it. After all, most of us voluntarily give out our phone number and address when we allow ourselves to be listed in the White Pages. Most of us go a lot further than that. We register our whereabouts whenever we put a black card in an ATM machine or drive through an E-Z Pass lane on the highway. We submit to being photographed every day—20 times a day on average if you live or work in New York City—by surveillance cameras. We make public our interests and our purchasing habits every time we shop by mail order or visit a commercial Website.	Yes, computer hackers can do more damage than phone hackers. The hacker that seized control of our AOL account tried to give us a bad name with hundreds of people. We can choose to have an unlisted phone number, but we don't have a choice about how information collected by the ATM, the E-Z Pass, or a surveillance camera is used. We should have the same choice of being "unlisted" with those services as we do with phones.

Text	**Elaboration Notes**
I don't know about you, but I do all this willingly because I appreciate what I get in return: the security of a safe parking lot, the convenience of cash when I need it, the improved service of mail-order houses that know me well enough to send me catalogs of stuff that interests me. And while I know we're supposed to feel just awful about giving up our vaunted privacy, I suspect (based on what the pollsters say) that you're as ambivalent about it as I am.	But I don't do so willingly! I have no choice! Yes, along with dozens of other catalogs you don't want at all. I read that one catalog order can generate over 100 solicitations from other companies. I think the majority of undergraduates value their privacy. One of the most controversial issues on campus is the authority the college retains to enter at will the private dorm rooms that we have rented as our living space.

As you reread the source, elaborate as fully as you can. It is useful to summon up a wide range of options even if some of these elaborations will not prove valuable to you in your later writing. You will find it easier to work from a rich pool of resources from which you can easily make selections. Review the examples of elaborating that appear in Chapter 1 (pages 18–21).

You may be asking, "How can I forge connections between information in memory and information in the reading source when I am dealing with a topic that is new to me?" When you don't have a pool of topic-related prior knowledge that you can draw forth readily, it helps to focus on your purpose for elaborating and remind yourself of all the different forms your elaborations can take.

Establish Purposes and Forms of Elaborations.

Researchers who study composition have found that elaborations serve three purposes (Stein 148):

- To produce new ideas
- To develop critical viewpoints
- To develop ideas already stated by the author

Let us illustrate these three functions with another passage from Quittner's article.

Text	Elaboration	Function
"It's a very schizophrenic time," says Sherry Turkle, professor of sociology at the Massachusetts Institute of Technology, who writes books about how computers and online communication are transforming society. She believes our culture is undergoing a kind of mass identity crisis, trying to hang on to a sense of privacy and intimacy in a global village of tens of millions. "We have very unstable notions about the boundaries of the individual," she says.	Our "mass identity crisis" is reflected in youth fashion advertising. Young people are encouraged to develop a particular "look" that the fashion industry wants to sell, but part of the sales pitch is that a standardized "look" worn by thousands of others will highlight the purchaser's individuality.	Develops an idea already stated by the author
	Is it technology or is it our market economy that has created our society's identity crisis?	Develops a critical view
	My guess is that marketplace forces are at the root of the problem but that technology makes these forces even more powerful. "Be all that you can be."	Produces a new idea

Notice the functions the elaboration serves. It extends Turkle's point about the impact of technology by linking it to the market economy; it poses a critical question about Turkle's conclusion; and it develops a new idea using Turkle's idea as a springboard. There are countless ways you can bring your own ideas to bear on the reading source. Some of them are as follows.

STRATEGIES FOR ELABORATING ON READING SOURCES

- Agree or disagree with a statement in the text and give reasons for your agreement or disagreement.
- Compare or contrast your reactions to the topic (for example, "At first I thought . . ., but now I think . . .").
- Extend one of the author's points.
- Draw attention to what the author has neglected to say about the topic.
- Discover an idea implied by the text but not stated by the author.
- Provide additional details by fleshing out a point made by the author.
- Illustrate the text with an example, incident, scenario, or anecdote.
- Embellish the author's point with a vivid image, metaphor, or example.

- Test one of the author's claims.
- Compare one of the author's points with your own prior knowledge of the topic or with your own or others' experiences.
- Interpret the text in the light of your prior topic knowledge or experiences.
- Personalize one of the author's statements.
- Question one of the author's points.
- Speculate about one of the author's points by
  Asking questions about the direct consequences of an idea
  Predicting consequences
  Drawing implications from an idea
  Applying the idea to a hypothetical situation
  Giving a concrete instance of a point made in the text
- Draw comparisons between the text and books, articles, films, or other media.
- Classify items in the text under a superordinate category.
- Discover relationships between ideas in the text that are unstated by the author.
- Validate one of the author's points with an example or prior topic knowledge.
- Criticize a point in the text.
- Create hierarchies of importance among ideas in the text.
- Make a judgment about the relevance of a statement that the author has made.
- Impose a condition on a statement in the text (for example, "If . . ., then . . .").
- Qualify an idea in the text.
- Extend an idea with a personal recollection or reflection.
- Assess the usefulness and applicability of an idea.

E x e r c i s e ....

This exercise will give you practice using different forms of elaboration. Read and reread each of the following passages, elaborate, and record your elaboration notes in a notebook or journal.

1. "A Young Person's Guide to the Grading System" by Jerry Farber, page 333, paragraphs 1–3. Elaborate on Farber's passage in the following ways:
   a. Agree or disagree with a statement in the text and give reasons for your agreement or disagreement.
   b. Extend one of the author's points.
   c. Illustrate a statement with an example, incident, scenario, or anecdote.
   d. Compare one of the author's points with prior topic knowledge or your own or others' experiences.

2. "Jennifer and Rachel" by Lee M. Silver, pages 336-337, paragraphs 29–32. Elaborate on Silver's passage in the following ways:
   a. Discover an idea implied by the text but not stated by the author.

    b. Provide additional details by fleshing out a statement made by the author.

    c. Validate one of the author's points with an example or prior topic knowledge or experience.

3. "It's Over, Debbie," pages 401–402, entire article. Elaborate on the article in the following ways:

    a. Draw attention to what the author has neglected to say about the topic.

    b. Discover relationships between ideas in the text that are unstated by the author.

    c. Speculate about one of the author's points by asking questions about the direct consequences of an idea, predicting consequences, drawing implications from an idea, or applying the idea to a hypothetical situation.

Exercise

Assume that you are working on the following essay assignment.

> In "Jennifer and Rachel," Lee M. Silver attempts to demonstrate that human cloning has legitimate applications and does not pose the threats to society that are alleged by the critics of the technology. In a three-page essay, summarize and respond to Silver's viewpoint.

Turn to "Jennifer and Rachel" (pages 362–367) or another selection of your choice. As you read, elaborate in some of the ways we described on page 93. Jot down your elaborations in a notebook or journal.

Develop a Thesis.

Even more important than generating your own ideas is deciding how you will use them in your essay. If you already know the point you want to make, your rhetorical purpose will allow you to derive a *preliminary thesis* from your elaborations. For example, if you decide to argue that technological advances that make life more convenient should not come at the expense of individual privacy, you can prove your point by selecting elaborations that disagree with Quittner, draw attention to important factors he leaves out, challenge and question his ideas, make relevance judgments, or qualify his ideas and assess their applicability.

    The preliminary or *working thesis* is the central idea that you intend to develop in your paper. You might think of it as a capsule summary of your entire essay. It reflects your rhetorical purpose and the effect you want to have on the audience. It may also indicate your organizational plan. In a response essay, the thesis expresses your general reaction to the source. It may express your level of agreement (or disagreement) with the source or indicate ways you will extend or build on the source. We call the thesis preliminary at the prewriting stage because writers often revise their thesis statements later in the writing process.

    One of the principal characteristics of the academic essay is that it is *thesis-driven*. This means that the thesis is revealed early in the essay and everything that follows serves to support it. You may find this convention unappealing because it forces you to reveal the end before you have told the story and thus may sound like a formula for boredom. All the same, the convention of beginning with a thesis statement is strong in the academic tradition, and your readers will expect you to observe this practice. The thesis for an academic essay should accomplish the following goals.

GOALS OF A THESIS STATEMENT

- Provide a comprehensive statement of the writer's intentions and central idea
- Indicate the complexity of the writer's thinking
- Suggest how the essay will be organized
- Be consistent with the discussion in the body of the essay and with the conclusion

How can you come up with a thesis statement at the outset of the writing process if you are not yet sure about the point you wish to make in your essay? If this is the case, review your elaboration notes as follows.

1. *See if one type of elaboration predominates.* Again, using the Quittner article as an example, perhaps a good portion of your elaborations were drawn from your personal experiences. You could plan an essay in which you show how your experiences either validate or contradict Quittner's claims.

2. *See if a good number of elaborations were triggered by a particular source idea.* Let's say you elaborated at length on one of Quittner's assertions: "Popular culture shines its klieg light on the most intimate corners of our lives, and most of us play right along. If all we really wanted was to be left alone, explain the lasting popularity of Oprah and Sally and Ricki tell-all TV" (paragraph 11). If you wish, you may focus your paper on this single aspect of the topic.

3. *Classify your elaborations.* Select workable categories and discard the rest. You might highlight the elaborations in which you agree or disagree with the author of the source and then work only with these as you draft your essay.

Let us illustrate these procedures. Here we present elaborations on certain paragraphs from Quittner's "Invasion of Privacy." As you study these elaborations, try to decide if one particular type of elaboration predominates. Are a good number of elaborations triggered by a certain idea in the reading source? Do the elaborations fit into any classification scheme?

Text	Elaborations
Paragraph 4	
I should also point out that as news director for Pathfinder, Time Inc.'s mega info mall, and a guy who makes his living on the Web, I know better than most people that we're hurtling toward an even more intrusive world. We're all being watched by computers whenever we visit Websites; by the mere act of "browsing" (it sounds so passive!) we're going	When I first read this paragraph, I didn't like the idea that someone is looking over my shoulder as I browse through Web sites. Since I'm alone when I browse, it feels like it should be private.

public in a way that was unimaginable a decade ago. I know this because I'm a watcher too. When people come to my Website, without ever knowing their names, I can peer over their shoulders, recording what they look at, timing how long they stay on a particular page, following them around Pathfinder's sprawling offerings.

But when I think about it, Web browsing is one of the least private activities because I am linked up to a network of literally millions of people and organizations. And of course, the commercial Web providers have to keep track of the interests of people visiting their sites since they are in business to appeal to customers. Many of the most useful and interesting sites wouldn't even be there if they weren't created and maintained by businesses.

Paragraph 10

I don't know about you, but I do all this willingly because I appreciate what I get in return: the security of a safe parking lot, the convenience of cash when I need it, the improved service of mail-order houses that know me well enough to send me catalogs of stuff that interests me. And while I know we're supposed to feel just awful about giving up our vaunted privacy, I suspect (based on what the pollsters say) that you're as ambivalent about it as I am.

Yes, all the conveniences Quittner values appeal to me as well. I would miss my ATM card and my e-mail more than I miss the privacy that I lose by using these technologies.

Paragraph 11

Popular culture shines its klieg lights on the most intimate corners of our lives, and most of us play right along. If all we really wanted was to be left alone, explain the lasting popularity of Oprah and Sally and Ricki tell-all TV.

It's sad, but I guess I have to agree with Quittner that our society doesn't seem to place a very high value

Memoirs top the best-seller lists, with books about incest and insanity and illness leading the way. Perfect strangers at cocktail parties tell me the most disturbing details of their abusive upbringings. Why?

on privacy. Just look at all the attention given to President Clinton's affair with Monica Lewinsky. The press gave us all the sordid details and we read and discussed them. This didn't happen during Kennedy's presidency in the 1960s even though he also had affairs.

Paragraph 17

It all started in the 1950s, when, in order to administer Social Security funds, the U.S. government began entering records on big mainframe computers, using nine-digit identification numbers as data points. Then, even more than today, the citizenry instinctively loathed the computer and its injunctions against folding, spindling and mutilating. We were not numbers! We were human beings! These fears came to a head in the late 1960s, recalls Alan Westin, a retired Columbia University professor who publishes a quarterly report *Privacy and American Business.* "The techniques of intrusion and data surveillance had overcome the weak law and social mores that we had built up in the pre–World War II era," says Westin.

Without Social Security numbers, I can't imagine how our huge country could run efficiently. For example, you might pay your income taxes and the money would get credited to someone with the same name as you!

Paragraph 23

"Most people would be astounded to know what's out there," says Carole Lane, author of *Naked in Cyberspace: How to Find Personal Information Online.* "In a few hours, sitting at my computer, beginning with no more than your name and address, I can find out what you do for a living, the names and ages of your spouse and children, what kind of car you drive, the value of your house and how much taxes you pay on it."

I don't like the idea that any person who is good with a computer could find out so much about me.

Paragraph 28

The real problem, says Kevin Kelly, executive editor of *Wired* magazine, is that although we say we value our privacy, what we really want is something very different: "We think that privacy is about information, but it's not— it's about relationships." The way Kelly sees it, there was no privacy in the traditional village or small town; everyone knew everyone else's secrets. And that was comfortable. I knew about you, and you knew about me. "There was a symmetry to the knowledge," he says. "What's gone out of whack is we don't know who knows about us anymore. Privacy has become asymmetrical."

Yes! Before there were computers, there were still nosy people who knew everyone else's business. In relation to our friends and families, our individual privacy is not affected that much by technology.

Paragraph 35

"Technology has outpaced law," says Marc Rotenberg, director of the Washington-based Electronic Privacy Information Center. Rotenberg advocates protecting the privacy of E-mail by encrypting it with secret codes so powerful that even the National Security Agency's supercomputers would have a hard time cracking it. Such codes are legal within the U.S. but cannot be used abroad—where terrorists might use them to protect their secrets—without violating U.S. export laws. The battle between the Clinton Administration and the computer industry over encryption export policy has been raging for six years without resolution, a situation that is making it hard to do business on the Net and is clearly starting to fray some nerves. "The future is in electronic commerce," says Ira Magaziner, Clinton's point man on Net issues. All that's holding it up is "this privacy thing."

I'm afraid that the law will never catch up with the technology. The law is changed so slowly and technology advances so rapidly. There will always be new electronic snooping methods, and just as soon as the laws are created to control one method, two more will be invented.

Paragraph 38

I'm with Kelly. The only guys who insist on perfect privacy are hermits like the Unabomber. I don't want to be cut off from the world. I have nothing to hide. I just want some measure of control over what people know about me. I want to have my magic cookie and eat it too.

Yes, I agree with Quittner. I don't believe that we can both have all the technological conveniences that we want and complete privacy. We just need to keep the two in balance.

Notice that the elaborations on these paragraphs express the writer's reluctant acceptance of Quittner's ideas. A viewpoint emerges: although any loss of personal privacy is regrettable, the advantages of the new technology make it worth sacrificing a degree of privacy. The writer also indicates that technology advances with such speed that it will leave in its wake any efforts to protect privacy. From these elaborations the writer derives the following preliminary thesis:

> Quittner's claim that technological advances are having a negative impact on personal privacy is, unfortunately, true. He is also correct that the benefits of the technology are worth the loss of privacy. Even if we wanted to stop the loss of privacy, it would not be possible, given the rapid progress of technology.

You may be surprised that this preliminary thesis statement is three sentences long. You may have been told that a thesis statement should be a single sentence. Thesis statements in academic essays are often two, three, or more sentences. If you have a complex reaction to the reading source, the thesis of your response essay may be lengthy. Consider the thesis statement that took up the entire second paragraph of our student Steven Siegele's essay:

> It is true, as Quittner points out, that Americans don't place a high value on their privacy. While Quittner views this situation as a trade-off between the disadvantage of losing privacy and the advantage of gaining technological conveniences, it may be that declining interest in personal privacy signals a growing awareness that we live in a global society created by electronic communication. In this new society, the quality of our lives depends very directly on our connections to others. Personal space and autonomy are less important than networking and collaboration. This shift will result in stronger, more supportive communities that provide greater security for individuals than communities with traditional privacy rights.

As his thesis indicates, Steven wants his audience to look to the future and visualize how electronic communications will lead to a world in which our traditional notions of personal privacy are not relevant. Overall, Steven's objective is to bring his audience to share his vision of a society that relies more on interconnectedness than on personal autonomy. This is a complicated objective, and it takes an entire paragraph to express it. Still, other reactions to Quittner can be expressed in more compact thesis statements, for example, the following thesis, written by student Colin Smith:

> The benefits of electronic data systems simply do not outweigh the potential damage that will be done to personal privacy rights.

Lisa Rodriguez's thesis is longer than Colin's, but it is still not a separate paragraph:

> Is it worth giving up our personal privacy so that we can enjoy the convenience of ATMs and e-mail? I think not. For two

centuries, Americans struggled to establish and extend personal
rights, and it is a sad commentary on our times that we are willing to sacrifice our liberties in order to avoid standing in line
to cash a check or spending a few cents to send a letter.

As our examples indicate, the length and complexity of the thesis statement depends on the writer's rhetorical purpose.

You may also be surprised that several of these thesis statements contain the first-person pronouns—*our, we, I.* Personal pronouns are appropriate in certain types of academic writing, particularly in response essays. In fact, it is difficult to write from personal experience without using *we, I, my,* or *me.* These pronouns also help writers label their own views so that they will not be confused with those of the source authors. Personal pronouns also appear in respected professional journals, such as *College English.* Nonetheless, they are discouraged in other academic writing contexts. In the sciences, lab reports are generally written to sound very objective and impersonal ("The solution was heated over a Bunsen burner" rather than "I heated the mixture over a Bunsen burner"). Ask your professor if you are unsure about using personal pronouns in your assignment.

We should stress that your preliminary thesis statement is subject to change throughout the writing process. Too often students think that they have to make sense of the topic and come up with a full-blown thesis before they can begin to write the essay. Writing is a creative process that advances your thinking. Often your ideas about a topic will develop as you draft the essay. If you hold tenaciously to your initial thesis, you won't be able to take advantage of the new thinking that the writing process inspires.

We will discuss revising entire essay drafts later in the chapter, but we will briefly touch on thesis revision here because writers typically revisit their thesis statements repeatedly as they work on their initial drafts. One result of in-process revisions is to enrich the thesis and make it more comprehensive. In the following example, notice how the successive revisions of a preliminary thesis statement reflect increasing complexity of thought. The thesis is written in response to Jerry Farber's essay "A Young Person's Guide to the Grading System," which appears on pages 333–336.

Preliminary Thesis	I am against the grading system.
First Revision	I believe the grading system runs counter to the goals of education.
Second Revision	I believe grades are counterproductive because they focus students' attention on scores rather than knowledge.
Third Revision	Even though many students believe that they need grades for motivation, I feel that grades are counterproductive because they distract students from the most important goal of education: gaining knowledge.

The third revision includes an acknowledgment of viewpoints that differ from the writer's. If the essay is structured as a response to ideas the writer disagrees with, it is best to indicate this plan in the thesis statement. In general, it is helpful to readers if your thesis indicates not only your position on the topic but also the approach you will take to develop it. Notice how the intended organization plan for the essay is signaled in each of the following thesis statements. The topic for this example is affirmative action in college admissions.

ORGANIZATIONAL PLAN	THESIS STATEMENT
Time order	During the 1960s and early 1970s, it was widely accepted that affirmative action policies were beneficial, particularly in the college admission process. After the *Baake* decision in 1978, however, arguments against affirmative action grew louder and reached a crescendo in the 1990s.
Comparison and contrast	The supporters and critics of using affirmative action in college admission decisions disagree on a range of social issues. Among them are what constitutes merit, how America should address class-based education deprivation, and which rights are protected by the Fourteenth Amendment.
Case in point	Opponents of affirmative action would argue that my adopted brother from Guatemala and I should receive the same treatment in the college admission process. On the other hand, proponents of affirmative action would maintain that my brother should be given special advantages.

Notice that none of these three thesis statements expresses the writer's viewpoint on affirmative action. Although the term *thesis* is often used to refer to an argumentative position, it has a much broader meaning in the academic community. The thesis statement specifies your *intention* in writing—what you hope to accomplish but not always your opinion. In many cases, your intention in writing will not be to win an argument but rather to present an issue objectively for the benefit of your readers, and that intention would still be labeled your thesis statement.

As you approach the end of the revision process, make sure that your thesis is consistent and comprehensive. It must be consistent with the discussion in the body of your essay and with the perspective that comes through in your conclusion. If the drafting process has altered your perspective on the issue, modify the thesis so that it is consistent with this shift. Read the introduction and then immediately read the conclusion to check for consistency. The thesis should be comprehensive enough that it captures all the major viewpoints the essay presents.

A final piece of advice is to avoid a banal thesis statement that includes an opinion but makes only a superficial attempt to come to grips with the topic. Imagine that you are writing an essay in response to Lee Silver's defense of human cloning in "Jennifer and Rachel." After reading Silver's piece, you decide you are opposed to human cloning and write the following thesis statement:

```
I am opposed to human cloning because it involves asexual repro-
duction of a human being.
```

This statement indicates opposition to human cloning and then provides a brief definition of cloning as if it were a reason to reject the technology. It leaves readers with a question:

why does the writer find "asexual reproduction" troubling? Since there are a number of possible answers to this question, readers can only guess how the writer would answer it.

The next sample thesis includes a reason for the writer's belief but still does not indicate that the writer weighed the evidence or thought about the issue in any depth.

```
I oppose human cloning because it is an unnatural process that
no normal person would be willing to undergo.
```

Notice how the offhand dismissal of cloning proponents as abnormal makes the writer seem immature. You risk losing the respect of your reader at the outset if your thesis indicates a superficial approach to the topic. Take advantage of the thesis statement to indicate the full complexity of your viewpoint, as in the following example:

```
I oppose human cloning for the same reason that I oppose selec-
tive breeding and other eugenic technologies: because it is based
on the assumption that some individuals' genes are better than
those of others. If this assumption becomes widely accepted, it
will jeopardize the basic human rights of those who are judged
genetically inferior.
```

Exercise . . . .

For the exercise on page 95, you jotted down elaborations in response to "Jennifer and Rachel" or another article of your choice. Using these elaborations, derive a preliminary thesis for a response essay. Recall the assignment:

In "Jennifer and Rachel," Lee M. Silver attempts to demonstrate that human cloning has legitimate applications and does not pose the threats to society that are alleged by the critics of the technology. In a three-page essay, summarize and respond to Silver's viewpoint.

As you examine your elaborations, see (1) if any one type of elaboration predominates, (2) if a good number of elaborations were triggered by a particular source idea, or (3) if you can classify the elaborations.

. . . .

Select an Organizational Plan.

After you come up with a preliminary thesis, your next step is to decide which organizational format you will use. First, review the organizational plans for academic writing that we presented in Table 1-2 (page 24). Many of these plans are appropriate for response essays, depending on the sources and your rhetorical purpose. Two additional patterns that are commonly used for response essays are summary and response and point-by-point response. Diane Abramowitz (pages 83–87) uses the summary and response pattern:

Paragraphs 2–3   Summary of Quittner's points
Paragraphs 4–6   Diane's commentary and reaction

Diane could have used the point-by-point response pattern by taking up each of Quittner's main points and responding to them one by one. To do this, Diane would alternate between her own ideas and those expressed by Quittner, perhaps in the following manner:

Paragraph 2   Brief summary and commentary

Paragraphs 3–6   In each paragraph, summary of one of Quittner's points and response to it

Note how we could use the summary and response and point-by-point alternating patterns to organize the elaborations we presented on pages 96–99.

PART OF ESSAY	SUMMARY AND RESPONSE PATTERN	POINT-BY-POINT PATTERN
Introductory paragraphs	Summarize Quittner's claim that we are sacrificing personal privacy in our pursuit of new technologies that make our lives more convenient and his belief that this trade-off is worthwhile. Explain your reluctant acceptance of Quittner's position.	Briefly summarize Quittner's claim that we are sacrificing personal privacy in our pursuit of new technologies that make our lives more convenient and his belief that this trade-off is worthwhile. Present your thesis.
Body paragraphs	Give reasons why the technological advances are worthwhile and why the losses in personal privacy are not that significant.	Alternate between Quittner's statements and your reactions. For example, first summarize the points Quittner makes in paragraphs 10 and 11 and give your reactions; then summarize the points Quittner makes in paragraph 17 and give your reactions; and so on.
Concluding paragraph	See the techniques on page 111.	See the techniques on page 111.

The summary and response and point-by-point patterns are not the only ways to organize response essays. As we mentioned earlier, your rhetorical purpose may provide the blueprint for your essay. Suppose that you disagree with Quittner's willingness to trade personal privacy for high-tech conveniences. You might develop your essay in a comparison-and-contrast format if you have heard about devastating cases of privacy violations that can be contrasted with the milder examples in Quittner's article. Or you might show the negative consequences of allowing convenience to take precedence over personal rights and thereby follow one of the standard formats for a cause-and-effect essay. To give another illustration, you might turn to a well-learned routine that you acquired in high school: the five-paragraph theme.

Introduction	Summarize the points in the article you are responding to and announce your position.
Three body paragraphs	In each paragraph, present a reason why you hold your position.
Conclusion	Sum up your main points, speculate about the implications of what you have just said, or call your readers to action.

The five-paragraph format is appropriate in some cases, but don't rely on it exclusively. One of the principal reasons this format is taught so widely is that it provides a general-purpose organizational plan students can rely on when they are writing under time pressure, especially during standardized tests, and do not have the leisure to think carefully about the organization structure that best fits the situation. The five-paragraph plan may serve as a security blanket when you are under pressure to produce a coherent essay in a very limited time, but it also shackles your writing. Your ideas about the topic should determine how you organize your essay, but your ideas may be distorted if you force them into an inappropriate pattern. In Appendix B, we give some advice on writing in-class exams, and our recommendation is that you approach exams with a handful of writing plans in mind rather than a single all-purpose format.

E x e r c i s e ....

Turn to the elaboration notes on "Jennifer and Rachel," or another article of your choice, that you took for the exercise on page 95. Review the notes; then classify your elaborations and study them to discern patterns for developing and organizing your essay. Next, outline your essay according to the summary and response pattern, the point-by-point pattern, or some other plan. Recall the assignment:

> In "Jennifer and Rachel," Lee M. Silver attempts to demonstrate that human cloning has legitimate applications and does not pose the threats to society that are alleged by the critics of the technology. In a three-page essay, summarize and respond to Silver's viewpoint.

. . . .

DRAFTING

To understand drafting better, think of the types of prior knowledge you have already brought into play. You have tapped your prior knowledge of the topic to produce a pool of elaborations on the reading source, and you have invoked your prior knowledge of organization and structure to discover an organizational plan. At this point, you will summon up two other types of knowledge: (1) knowledge of the basic features of writing—elements like titles, introductions, sentences, paragraphs, transitions and connecting ideas, and conclusions—and (2) knowledge of strategies for summarizing, paraphrasing, and quoting sources.

Here we will draft the essay sequentially, starting with the title and ending with the conclusion. We do not mean to suggest that you will follow this order. The title may be a final addition to the essay, tacked on when you are editing your final copy. You may find it easier to write the introduction after you compose the body, and you may start the body with your reactions rather than the source summary. Whatever you do, don't stare at the blank page waiting for the title or first sentence to come to you. Start wherever you feel ready to write, and return later to the parts that caused initial hesitation.

Title Your Response Essay.

It is usually better to title your essay after you have revised your first draft. That way, if you've changed direction, you will not have to retitle the piece. Your title should express the position you take in the essay or relate to your thesis in some way. In Chapter 2, we recommended that you use matter-of-fact titles for free-standing summaries, for example, "A Summary of Lee Silver's 'Jennifer and Rachel.'" But a straightforward title is not suitable for essays in which you express your own ideas. For these essays, your title should indicate your perspective and, if possible, capture the essence of the issue you are addressing. The title "A Response to Lee Silver's 'Jennifer and Rachel'" doesn't even indicate that the topic of Silver's essay and the student's will be human cloning. Here are some suggestions for creating titles.

TITLING YOUR ESSAY

- Let the title reflect your organizational plan. An essay that develops according to the comparison and contrast pattern might be titled "The Anticloning Lobby: Humanists or Hypocrites?"
- Borrow an apt phrase from the reading source or from your essay. The last sentence of Silver's piece includes the phrase "our brave new reproductive world," which borrows from Aldous Huxley's famous novel *Brave New World*. An essay written in response to Silver might be titled "Our Brave New Reproductive World."
- State the general topic and then, after a colon, your perspective or stance—for example, "Human Cloning: A New Technology Sparking a Bitter Debate."
- Phrase the title as a question—for example, "Will Cloning Solve the Crisis of the American Family?"
- Use another well-known quotation or saying, such as "Cheaper by the Dozen: Cloning and Human Reproduction."

E x e r c i s e ....

Return to the elaboration notes, preliminary thesis, and organizational plan you have developed for the paper on human cloning or another topic of your choice. Use the guidelines we have provided to come up with a preliminary title for the essay. You may want to revise this title after you have completed the first draft.

. . . .

Write Introductions.

Introductions prepare readers for what comes next. The following list contains the primary objectives of introductions.

HOW TO WRITE EFFECTIVE INTRODUCTIONS

- Use an opener that will interest the reader.
- Announce the topic.
- Disclose a thesis or attitude toward the topic.
- Establish your voice.
- Provide the reader with the title, author, and some summary information about the reading source.

Notice that single-source response essays typically provide the reader with the title, author, and summary information from the reading source. Let's see how Jennifer Rowland uses these strategies to develop her introduction in her essay on page 108.

Notice how Jennifer leads the reader smoothly and logically from one idea to the next. She begins by quoting Quittner's description of how exposed we are when we browse the Web and then mentions his other examples of technology that records our activities for others to see. She next explains that Quittner believes it is worth giving up privacy to enjoy the benefits of technology, and then she asks whether this sacrifice is necessary. Finally, she responds with her thesis that if proper controls were placed on the information industry, we should be able to maintain our privacy rights while still enjoying the benefits of technology. The introduction accomplishes several different tasks, and you should guard against confusing or losing the reader as you accomplish them.

The opening sentences of an essay should engage the readers and encourage them to read on. The opening also establishes the writer's voice as formal or informal, academic or conversational. Some forms of academic writing require you to open your paper in a designated way and write in a very professional voice. For instance, research studies often open with a one-paragraph abstract that summarizes the study's principal findings in formal, objective language. Response essays give you much more freedom. If you wish, you can use an informal opening that speaks directly to the reader. If you have difficulty deciding how to begin, use one of the techniques listed on page 109.

Jennifer Rowland

Professor Smith

Academic Writing I

23 September 1999

Protecting Privacy in the Global Village

"By the mere act of browsing . . . we're going public in a way that was unimaginable a decade ago" (Quittner 28). In his article "Invasion of Privacy," Joshua Quittner explains how browsing the Web, using a credit card, driving through the E-Z Pass tollbooth, or even making a telephone call can leave an electronic record of our activities that may later be accessed by complete strangers. Even when we are not connected to the various branches of the information highway, surveillance cameras and other monitoring devices keep track of us. Though Quittner admits readily that our personal privacy is diminishing, he believes that this loss is well worth the advantages that individuals gain by using information technology. Although I share Quittner's enthusiasm for new technology, I question why I must sacrifice my privacy in order to enjoy new innovations. With proper regulation of the communications industry, Americans should be able to benefit from new technologies without giving up their right to privacy.

ESSAY OPENERS

Technique	*Example*
Quotation (from the reading source or elsewhere)	"Human embryos are life-forms, and there is nothing to stop anyone from marketing them now, on the same shelves with Cabbage Patch dolls" (Ehrenreich 86). Perhaps we are headed to a future where, as Ehrenreich suggests in her article "The Economics of Cloning," we will purchase rather than bear our children.
Question	Many parents want their children to have certain family characteristics--their grandfather's hair, their aunt's height, their father's eyes--but would you want a child who was an exact replica, a clone, of you or your spouse?
Anecdote, brief story, or scenario	Imagine you were born a clone, an exact copy of your mother or father, rather than a combination of genetic material from them both.
Fact or statistic	When human embryos were first cloned, President Clinton issued an executive order banning any further human cloning in government-sponsored research.
Generalization	Despite our fascination with genetic technologies, many of us recoil from the idea of cloning human beings.
Contradiction	Although cloning may multiply the odds that infertile couples will conceive, it may also multiply the chances of a genetic disaster.
Thesis statement	Cloning human beings threatens our very future as a species.
Background	Cloning, a biological process that makes it possible to produce an exact replica of a living organism, has been applied to simple life forms for years. Now it is possible to clone complex animals, even humans.

Avoid using paper openers that will bore or turn off your readers. If your opening sentences alienate readers, it will be difficult to win them back in the paragraphs that follow. The following paper openers are used too often and sound trite.

OVERUSED OPENINGS YOU SHOULD AVOID

Opening	*Example*
Clichés or platitudes	As we consider how human cloning might be regulated, we should keep in mind that a stitch in time saves nine.

Dictionary definitions of well-known words	According to <u>Webster's International Dictionary,</u> a <u>clone</u> is . . .
Restatement of the assignment	In "Jennifer and Rachel," Lee Silver argues that the adverse effects . . .
An obvious statement of your purpose	In this essay, I will give my reactions to Lee Silver's defense of human cloning in "Jennifer and Rachel."

Reread the preliminary thesis you wrote at the prewriting stage (page 103) and decide if you want to revise it before incorporating it into your introduction. Make sure that it still captures the principal perspective that you want to develop. The thesis statement is often located at the end of the introduction, following the opening, explanation of the general topic, and identification of the source. But it can occur anywhere within the introduction, even in the very first line. Wherever you place it, be sure to provide your reader with enough context to understand it fully. As we explained, a thesis statement may be several sentences long.

The introduction can include more than one paragraph. Long academic essays often have an introduction that contains many paragraphs. Shorter essays can also have multiparagraph introductions. For lengthy, complex thesis statements, a two-paragraph introduction may work best. Another consideration is that a dramatized scenario or vignette that is used to open a paper may run to several paragraphs. These opening paragraphs would be followed by a paragraph that zeroes in on the topic and presents the thesis.

E x e r c i s e

Return to the elaboration notes, preliminary thesis, organizational plan, and title you have developed for the paper on human cloning or another topic of your choice. Write an introductory paragraph for the paper, making sure that you (1) use a paper opener that will interest the reader, (2) announce the topic, (3) disclose a thesis or attitude toward the topic, (4) establish your voice as a writer, and (5) provide the reader with the title, author, and some summary information about the reading sources.

Write the Body of the Response Essay.

The essay you compose at this stage should be a preliminary draft, not polished, final copy. Think of this first draft as a discovery draft, an opportunity to find out more about what you want to say.

As you draft the body, follow the organizational plan you chose at the prewriting stage—summary and response, point-by-point, or another pattern. Develop sections and paragraphs so they fit into your plan. If your prewriting plan proves unworkable or you discover a new direction for the paper, rethink your organizational strategy.

Summary. The summary is an integral part of the response essay. Keep in mind that the type of summary you write depends on your rhetorical purpose. Ask yourself if your purpose is to provide your readers with a comprehensive summary that covers all the major aspects of the reading source. Or do you want simply to reduce the reading source to a series of gists?

Remember that your objective is to tailor the summary to the reaction. After you organize and classify your ideas and establish your direction, adapt the summary to your purpose. You need not summarize the entire article, only the sections that relate to your purpose. The summary should highlight the passages that prompted your reaction and refer only incidentally to other portions of the text.

Paragraphs.   Develop paragraphs that are unified and coherent. Make sure that each paragraph develops a central idea and that all the sentences contribute to this idea in some way. As you read the following paragraph, notice how each sentence develops the point that our everyday activities are becoming a matter of public record.

> As Quittner points out, we leave electronic trails behind us as we move through our everyday lives. When my computer alarm wakes me up at the preprogrammed time, I register my presence in cyberspace by logging on to my e-mail account to check for any messages and then moving on to a local weather Web site to help me decide what to wear. I'm still barely awake when the cashier swipes my ID at the campus coffee shop. On my way across campus, I stop by an ATM in the student center and get cash to repay a friend from whom I borrowed over the weekend. My first-period course meets in a networked classroom, and the professor asks us to log on to the course Web page to download the next assignment. It's only 9:00 a.m., and I've already created a trail, dropping electronic breadcrumbs at four different locations.

Also strive to make your paragraphs coherent. In a coherent paragraph, repeated words and ideas, rewording of ideas, and transitional expressions (*also, for example, thus, similarly, consequently,* and so on) show the reader the logical links among the sentences. We will give you additional pointers on coherence later in this chapter.

Write the Conclusion.

Write a closing paragraph that does more than summarize your argument or restate your thesis. Use one of the following techniques.

TECHNIQUES FOR WRITING CONCLUDING PARAGRAPHS

- Stress the significance of your thesis rather than simply repeating it. Encourage your readers to look beyond the thesis to an important future goal.
- Predict consequences.
- Call your readers to action.
- Use any of the devices for paper openers (see page 109).

E x e r c i s e ....

Return to the draft you are composing on human cloning or another topic of your choice, and work on the summary, body paragraphs, and conclusion. Make an effort to (1) adapt the summary to your rhetorical purposes, (2) develop unified and coherent paragraphs, and (3) write a conclusion that does more than simply restate the thesis.

. . . .

REVISING

After you have composed a draft of your essay, set it aside and come back to it in a day or two. You will acquire fresh insights in the interim. It is also beneficial to have someone else read your draft and give you feedback. Your teacher may be arranging to have peer review groups in class. If not, if it is all right with your instructor, ask your roommate, a family member, or a friend to review your draft.

The reviewer of your essay will find the following questions helpful.

✓ CHECKLIST FOR REVISING A FIRST DRAFT

_____ Is the writer's rhetorical purpose clear? (How is the writer attempting to influence or affect readers?)

_____ Does everything in the draft lead to or follow from one central thesis? (If not, which ideas appear to be out of place?)

_____ Will the reader understand the essay, and is the writer sensitive to the reader's concerns?

_____ Does the writer provide necessary background information about the source, including author and title?

_____ Is the summary information complete, or does the writer need to add more material?

_____ Throughout the essay, when referring to the source, does the writer supply necessary documentation?

_____ Are there clear transitions or connectives that differentiate the writer's own ideas from those of the source author?

_____ Is the organizational plan or form appropriate for this kind of paper? (If not, can you suggest another format?)

_____ Is the writer's response varied, adequate, and appropriate for this kind of paper? (If not, can you explain why?)

_____ Does the writer provide transitions or connecting ideas between the summary and reaction sections? (If not, where are they needed?)

_____ Do you hear the writer's voice throughout the entire essay? (Can you describe it?)

_____ Does the writer open the paper in a way that catches the reader's attention?

_____ Does the conclusion simply restate the main idea, or does it offer new insights?

_____ Does the essay have an appropriate title?

For purposes of illustration, we will reproduce Jane Wolf's first draft and revision; then we will discuss the changes that she made. Jane wrote this essay for her introductory computer science course. The assignment was to read a book on the social consequences of computers and then submit a short essay of response to the book. Jane selected *The Intimate Machine,* in which Neil Frude argues that humans may one day have fulfilling emotional relationships with intelligent machines.

First Draft

Wolf 1

Jane Wolf

Professor Kennedy

English 131

15 July 1999

<u>Intimate Machine</u> Paper: First Draft

A book titled <u>The Intimate Machine</u> describes a machine
that could be programmed to act like a friend. The machine
would "be programmed to behave in a congenial manner" and "to
be charming, stimulating, and easygoing," to "sometimes take
the initiative," and "to have a personality of its own" (Frude
169). The machine would provide people with many of the
benefits of friendship. It would carry on a conversation and
take an active interest in humans. It could even become
intimate with them. Such an idea is not so far-fetched. People
already use machines for therapeutic purposes, and they play
chess with computers. People may be shocked by the idea of
having a machine as a friend, but they should not condemn
something that could benefit so many lonely people (157-87). I
disagree with Frude, and I worry that machines have already
replaced too many people today. I think it is far better for
people to befriend people than to become intimate with
machines.

1

Machines already function as therapists and teammates. They also teach classes. When my economics professor cannot make the class, he sends us a video lecture to watch in his place. Machines have also replaced bank tellers, telephone operators, and checkout cashiers. If this trend continues, we will soon have robot waiters, nurses, and mechanics, and, finally, machine friends. We will have less and less human contact in our daily lives.

I would argue that it is important to bring more and more people together than to separate them by introducing machines as friends. A lonely person may get some enjoyment from conversing with a "charming, stimulating, and easygoing" machine, but the satisfaction would be much greater if the person had genuine human contact. It is true that the machine would always be available, but the person would know that it had not come of its own free will.

Some people will find the prospect of having a friendly, intimate machine tempting. But I would urge them to reconsider their position. Instead of putting so much research time and money into developing friendly machines, why not study ways to bring people together and enhance human relations? People need spontaneous, human love, not a programmed simulation.

Revised Draft

Wolf 1

Jane Wolf

Professor Kennedy

English 131

15 July 1999

(handwritten bubble note: How do you regard your personal computer, as a "tool," a "colleague" or a "friend"? You might be surprised that anyone would consider a machine a friend, but in)

Do We Want Programmed Friends?

~~Intimate Machine Paper: First Draft~~

~~An book entitled~~ The Intimate Machine ~~describes a~~ machine *Neil Frude explains that* *s*

~~that~~ could be programmed to act like ~~a~~ friend. The machine would

"~~be programmed to~~ behave in a congenial manner" and "~~to~~ be

charming, stimulating, and easygoing/" ~~to~~ "sometimes take the *It would*   *it would*

initiative," and "~~to~~ have a personality of its own" (Freud 169).

Frude claims that   *us*

^The machine would provide ~~people~~ with many of the benefits of

with us

friendship. It would carry on a conversation and take an active

our affairs. We

interest in ~~humans~~. ~~It~~ could even become intimate ~~with them~~.

says Frude.

Such an idea is not so far-fetched, People already use machines

for therapeutic purposes, and they play chess with computers.

Frude points out that we

~~People~~ may be shocked by the idea of having a machine as a

we

friend, but ~~they~~ should not condemn something that could benefit

so many lonely people (157-87). I disagree with Frude. ~~and~~ I

worry that machines have already replaced too many people ~~today~~.

I

~~I think~~ ^It is far better for people to befriend people than to

become intimate with machines.

As Frude points out

^Machines already function as therapists and *partners for games* ~~teammates~~. They

is unable to attend

also teach classes. When my economics professor ~~cannot make the~~

class, he sends ~~us~~ a video lecture to watch in his place.

Machines have also replaced bank tellers, telephone operators,

1

2

and checkout cashiers. If this trend continues, we will soon

have robot waiters, nurses, and mechanics, and, finally, machine

friends. We will have less and less human contact in our daily

lives. and less understanding of each other's wants and needs

~~I would argue that~~ It is important to bring ~~more and more~~
rather
people together than ~~to~~ separate them by introducing machines as
talking to a machine
friends. A lonely person may get some enjoyment ~~from conversing~~
about politics or sharing a secret or juicy piece of gossip
~~with a "charming, stimulating, and easygoing" machine~~, but the
there were
satisfaction would be much greater if ~~the person had~~ genuine
A human friend would respond less predictably and would probably
human contact. It is true that the machine would have more authenitic
stories to tell.
always be available, but the person would know that it had not

come on its own free will. Nor would it be able to turn itself on. It would
be totally dependent on the human user.

Some people will find the prospect of having a friendly,

intimate machine tempting. But I would urge them to reconsider

their position. Instead of putting so much research time and

money into developing friendly machines, why not study ways to

bring people together and enhance human relations? People need

spontaneous, human love, not a programmed simulation.

3

Work Cited

Frude, Neil. <u>The Intimate Machine</u>. New York: New American

Library, 1983.

Revise the Title and Opening.

Starting with the title, let us discuss some of the additions, deletions, and other changes Jane made. As we mentioned earlier, you will probably title your essay after you have revised your preliminary draft. Jane decided to phrase her title as a question: "Do We Want Programmed Friends?" Notice that she did not underline or capitalize the title or place it in quotation marks.

Next, compare the opening sentences of the two drafts.

First Draft

```
A book titled The Intimate Machine describes a machine that could
be programmed to act like a friend.
```

Revised Draft

```
How  do  you  regard  your  personal  computer--as  a  "tool,"  a
"colleague," or a "friend"?
```

The first draft begins with a statement of fact. Although this is an acceptable way to open an essay, Jane thought it was too formal, so she decided to address the reader with a question instead. Notice that the new opening also does a better job of establishing the writer's voice.

Revise the Body Paragraphs.

If you refer to Jane's preliminary draft, you will see that the main way she altered the body paragraphs was by adding details. Paragraph 2 was already adequately developed with examples, but Jane needed to add details in order to flesh out paragraph 3. Both of these body paragraphs follow directly from the introduction. In paragraph 2, Jane develops the statement "I worry that machines have already replaced too many people," and in paragraph 3, she explains why it is "better for people to befriend people than to become intimate with machines."

In a response essay, you can also develop body paragraphs by quoting, paraphrasing, or summarizing pertinent ideas from the source and forging a connection between those ideas and your own thoughts. You may recall that this summary and response method was used in the model student essay on pages 83–87. Also keep in mind that you can use any of the patterns of development (cause and effect, comparison and contrast, example, and so forth; see Table 1-2) to develop your body paragraphs.

Revise the Conclusion.

Jane left her closing paragraph untouched because she was satisfied with its form and content. She brings her essay to a close by acknowledging that some people may not share her view and calling on her readers to change their outlook and set new priorities for the future.

Revise Connective Ideas.

Comparing Jane's two drafts, you can see that in the revised version, she signals her reader each time she presents one of Frude's points. In the first draft, the reader is not

always sure where Frude's ideas end and Jane's begin. The addition of attribution—
"Frude claims that . . .," ". . . says Frude," "Frude points out . . ."—helps the reader make
this differentiation.

Improve Focus and Development.

Well-written papers have a clear, sharply defined focus. When you reread your first draft,
check to see if you present a consistent perspective throughout the entire piece. Make
sure that you have not started off with a thesis that expresses your intention but then
drifted away from it in the subsequent paragraphs. Make sure also that you have not
started off with one intention as expressed in your thesis but then ended up with
another position.

    If you drifted away from your original goal, examine each sentence to determine
how the shift took place. You may need to eliminate whole chunks of irrelevant material, add more content, or rearrange some of the parts. If this is the case, ask yourself
these questions:

- What should I add so that my audience can follow my train of thought more easily?
- What should I eliminate that does not contribute to my central focus?
- What should I move that is out of place or needs to be grouped with material else-
  where in the paper?

After you make these changes, read over your work to make sure that the new version
makes sense, conforms to your organizational plan, and shows improvement.

Improve Cohesion.

When you are satisfied with your focus and development, check that the ideas in the essay
connect with each other. Your readers should be able to follow your train of thought by
referring to preceding sentences, looking ahead to subsequent sentences, and being mindful of transitions and other connective devices. The following are some common connective devices.

CONNECTIVE DEVICES

- Repeating words or parts of words
- Substituting synonyms or related words
- Using personal pronouns and demonstrative pronouns *(this, that)* with easily recog-
  nizable referents
- Using explicit or implied transitions that signal relationships such as addition, exem-
  plification, opposition, similarity, cause, effect, or time order
- Substituting a general term for a more specific term or terms

    Here is a paragraph showing a number of connective devices from an essay written
by Maura Kennedy in response to John Knowles's novel *A Separate Peace*. We have highlighted and labeled some of these devices. See if you can find others.

A Separate Peace shows that sarcasm helps us to escape from stating the truth straightforwardly. Gene, the weaker character, uses sarcasm to express disapproval, whereas Finny, the symbol of strength, blatantly states his disapproval. Gene uses sarcasm because he feels resentment toward Finny. His indignation stems from jealousy. This becomes evident after Finny charms his way out of trouble for wearing the Devon tie as a belt. Gene explains, "He had gotten away with everything. I felt a sudden stab of disappointment." Later, he adds, "That was because I just wanted to see some more excitement; that must have been it" (Knowles 21). Although Gene's jealousy almost causes him to dislike Finny, he cannot admit this painful fact, and he covers it up.

Labels at left: Transition: contrast · Transition: cause · Pronoun · Demonstrative pronoun · Transition: Time · Transition: contrast · General term

Labels at right: Repeats word · Synonym · Repeats word · Synonym · Pronoun · Repeats word · Pronoun

Exercise

Identify the connective devices in the following paragraphs from Maura Kennedy's essay written in response to John Knowles's novel *A Separate Peace.*

```
      I have often tried to cover up the truth as well. I once
had a very close friend, "Sally," whom I gradually came to
despise. I kept telling myself that Sally was conceited and cared
about no one but herself. I later realized that I, being shy,
was jealous of her outgoing personality and her ability to make
people like her. Just as Gene realizes that he and Finny aren't
"competitors," that Finny has always thought of him as his best
friend and would never do anything to hurt him, I realized the
same about my friend. Then I became even more annoyed, because
even though I was rude to Sally, she still thought of me as her
best friend. My annoyance caused a resentment that eventually
ended our friendship. By the time I realized this, we were both
better friends with other people. Gene also realizes too late
that his competition with Finny "was so ludicrous [he] wanted to
cry" (Knowles 58). I too found this out after Sally and I had
stopped being best friends. And like Gene, I still think about
it today, three years later.
```

Gene, meanwhile, fools himself by making up stories. So does Finny. When Gene gets Leper's telegram, he immediately imagines Leper escaping from spies. He lets himself believe this because deep down he knows that whatever has happened to Leper probably isn't as exciting as his imaginative prediction. When Leper's real reason for "escaping" shatters his hopes, Gene must deal with the unpleasant truth that he had been avoiding. Although Finny's character is in many ways stronger than Gene's, Finny also makes up his own stories about the war in order to escape from reality. Finny doesn't want to accept the fact that he won't be fighting in the war. Because he doesn't like this idea, he tries to convince himself and others that there is really no war at all. To him, "the fat old men" in the government have made up the war (Knowles 107). He finally faces the truth about the war when he sees Leper. Knowles shows that even strong people like Finny delude themselves rather than recognize an unpleasant truth.

Exercise..

Return to the draft of the response essay you are revising. (1) Reread the essay to see if you present a consistent perspective. (2) Examine the draft to see if you provide your readers with enough transitional expressions and connecting ideas.

• • • • • • • • • • • • • • •

Improve Style.

The first step in gaining control of your writing style is to understand how you use written language. Consider the effect your language choices have on your audience with respect to:

1. writer-based versus reader-based prose
2. sentence length
3. presence of strong verbs
4. ineffective expressions
5. sexist language
6. voice

Move from writer-based to reader-based prose.   Early in this chapter, we stressed that when you begin to work on an academic writing assignment, you should carefully consider your intended audience. Keep this audience in mind throughout the entire reading and writing process, especially at the revising stage. Making a distinction between writer-based prose and reader-based prose will help you attend to audience needs as you revise (Flower). *Writer-based prose* is egocentric because it records ideas that make sense to the writer with minimal effort to communicate these ideas to someone else. You can compare writer-based prose to a set of personal notes in which the writer puts down information that is meaningful personally but may not make sense to a larger audience. In contrast, *reader-based prose* clearly conveys ideas to other people. The writer does not assume that the reader will understand automatically but rather provides information that will facilitate the reader's comprehension. It is easy to forget about audience amid all the complications of producing the first draft of an academic essay. That's why first drafts are quite often writer-based. An important function of revising is to convert this writer-based prose to something the reader can readily understand.

Read the following excerpt from a rough draft in which a student responds to the views of Bill Joy on technical advancements. As you read, note each sentence that is writer based.

                                                                    Korf 1

Emily Korf

Professor Smith

Academic Writing I

17 April 1999

                        Humans and Technology

    The article deals with the author's ideas about the

interaction between humans and technology in the next

century. Joy backs up his views with numerous examples and

with references to conversations he has had with experts in

the field. After reading his article, I feel that I agree

with many of the points Joy raises, particularly the ethical

issues.

Notice how the student assumes the audience is familiar with both the assignment and the articles on which it is based. For example, the introduction begins "The article deals with . . ." as if the reader knows in advance the article that will be discussed. Also, this first sentence indicates the author has "ideas" about "the interaction between humans and technology." What, exactly, are the author's ideas about this topic? Does the author fear or embrace technology? The introduction provides no answers to these questions. It seems that the student is writing for someone who already knows the author's viewpoint. Similar failures to consider the audience occur throughout the paragraph.

Note how we have transformed the excerpt from writer-based prose to reader-based prose.

```
                                                          Korf 1

Emily Korf

Professor Smith

Academic Writing I

17 April 1999

                        Human Obsolescence

     In "Why the Future Doesn't Need Us," Bill Joy, the

cofounder of Sun Microsystems, expresses his fear that

twentieth-century technology might exterminate the human

species. His particular concern is that the world might be

overrun by genetically engineered life forms capable of

reproduction or self-replicating computerized robots. Since

Joy knows personally many of the world's most important

scientists and is himself a respected computer expert, he is

able to provide strong evidence that those best informed

about advanced technology fear its consequences. I agree

with Joy that researchers must consider carefully how any

technology they produce might affect the larger society.
```

As you revise your first drafts, make sure you have provided the necessary context or background for material from sources. Unless the assignment indicates that the audience has read the sources, do not assume that your readers will share your prior knowledge and experience.

Vary sentence length.   Do you habitually write sentences that are the same length without ever considering that your audience may find this style monotonous? Note the monotony in the following passage, written in response to Jerry Farber's essay "A Young Person's Guide to the Grading System" (pages 333–336), which opposes using traditional letter grades:

```
Another problem with Farber's argument is the lack of sufficient
evidence. Farber uses strictly personal experiences to show that
grades don't work. He could have used examples from other people
```

or from books. Also, he might have cited statistics from research studies and experiments.

When you discover a problem with sentence length, a workable solution is combining or dividing sentences. Working with the Farber example, you could combine the second and third sentences using one of the following techniques.

TECHNIQUES FOR COMBINING SENTENCES

Technique	*Example*
Join independent clauses with a coordinating conjunction (*and, but, for, or, nor, yet,* or *so*)	Farber uses strictly personal experiences to show that grades don't work, but he could have used examples from other people or books.
Join independent clauses with an adverbial conjunction (*however, consequently, thus, furthermore, nevertheless, then, certainly, besides, similarly,* and so on)	Farber uses strictly personal experiences to show that grades don't work; however, he could have used examples from other people or books.
Embed one sentence within another	Farber uses strictly personal experiences, rather than examples from other people or books, to show that grades don't work.
Change an independent clause to a dependent clause and use a subordinator (*since, if, because, unless,* or the like) to relate it to an independent clause	While Farber uses strictly personal experiences to show that grades don't work, he could have used examples from other people or books.

Make sure that all your sentence combinations contribute to clarity and coherence. You need not combine sentences at every sentence boundary: your goal is variety, not consistency.

To break up a long sentence, subdivide it at the clause boundaries. Here are some procedures that will help you with this revision.

TECHNIQUES FOR DIVIDING LONG SENTENCES

- Search for coordinating conjunctions (*and, but, for, or, nor, yet,* and *so*) and for adverbial conjunctions (*however, nevertheless, consequently, thus,* and so on), and try to divide sentences at these points.
- Search for subordinating conjunctions (*if, when, unless, because, although,* and so on), and try to break up the sentence by turning the dependent clause into an independent clause.
- Look for other incidents of *and* or *but* between multiple verbs sharing a subject, and try to divide the sentence by inserting a period before the conjunction and inventing a subject for the second verb.

Consider how our student Carrie Miller used these procedures to revise a paragraph from a paper on acid rain. Here is an excerpt from Carrie's first draft.

Excerpt from First Draft

Miller 3

Acid rain has been with us for longer than most people realize, for the term <u>acid rain</u> was originally coined back in 1872 when British chemist Robert Angus Smith noticed that buildings were being worn away by acid rain falling on industrial England (Begley 9). Acid rain is caused by sulfur emissions from burning soft coal and other fossil fuels. These particles become airborne and eventually settle back to earth via precipitation, which changes the pH of the water and soil. As Smith observed, the acid pits and crumbles buildings. We know that what the acid rain does to lakes and forests is even more harmful because Anne La Bastille, wildlife ecologist and consultant, points out that in the Adirondack area where she lives, "thirty-five percent of the big trees were dead or dying" (96). Another observer complains that the Adirondack region has about 520 lakes that are suffering from rain pollution (La Fave 42). Acid rain leaves a lake crystal clear and devoid of many species of fish. An analogy would be a bottle of vinegar, which has a pH of 5, and much of the rainfall in the eastern United States measures 4.5 on the pH scale, which means that the rainfall is more acid than vinegar. Certainly, the rain is diluted as it soaks into the ground, but the effects are cumulative (Krester, Colquhoun, and Pfeiffer 25).

Carrie broke up the first, fifth, and eighth sentences and combined sentences 3 and 4 and sentences 6 and 7. Compare the revised version to the original.

Excerpt from Revised Draft

Miller 3

Acid rain has been with us for longer than most people realize. The term <u>acid rain</u> was originally coined back in 1872 when British chemist Robert Angus Smith noticed that buildings were being worn away by acid rain falling on industrial England (Begley 9). Acid rain is caused by sulfur emissions from burning soft coal and other fossil fuels. These particles become airborne and eventually settle back to earth via precipitation, which changes the pH of the water and soil; consequently, as Smith observed, the acid pits and crumbles buildings. We know that what the acid rain does to lakes and forests is even more harmful. Anne La Bastille, wildlife ecologist and consultant, points out that in the Adirondack area where she lives, "thirty-five percent of the big trees were dead or dying" (96). Another observer complains that the Adirondack region has about 520 lakes that are suffering from rain pollution (La Fave 42), which leaves them crystal clear and devoid of many species of fish. An analogy would be a bottle of vinegar, which has a pH of 5. Much of the rainfall in the eastern United States measures 4.5 on the pH scale, which means that the rainfall is more acid than vinegar. Certainly, the rain is diluted as it soaks into the ground, but the effects are cumulative (Krester, Colquhoun, and Pfeiffer 25).

Miller 6

Works Cited

Begley, Sharon. "On the Trail of Acid Rain." <u>National Wildlife</u>
    Feb.-Mar. 1987: 8-13.

Krester, Walter A., James R. Colquhoun, and Martin H. Pfeiffer.
    "Acid Rain and the Adirondack Sport Fishery."
    <u>Conservationist</u> Mar.-Apr. 1983: 22-29.

La Bastille, Anne. <u>Beyond Black Bear Lake</u>. New York: Norton,
    1987.

La Fave, Aziel. "Reflections of Terror Lake." <u>Conservationist</u>
    July-Aug. 1983: 38-42.

Stress verbs rather than nouns.   Proficient writers express action with strong verbs. They shy away from empty verbs and avoid using too many nouns. Compare the following sentences. In the first version, the writer uses nouns to get the message across, but in the revised version, the message is conveyed with verbs. We have underlined the nouns and italicized the verbs.

Original

The <u>creation</u> of an overall <u>design</u> for a <u>computer system</u> *is* the <u>responsibility</u> of a <u>systems analyst</u>, whereas the <u>implementation</u> of the <u>design plan</u> *is* often the <u>duty</u> of a <u>computer programmer</u>.

Revision

The <u>systems analyst</u> *designs* the <u>computer system</u>, and the <u>computer programmer</u> *makes* the <u>system</u> *work*.

Notice that the first version contains two occurrences of the verb *is*. All forms of the verb *be (is, are, was, were, be, being, been)* draw their meaning from the nouns preceding and following them. They are weak and lifeless on their own. Sentences structured around *be* verbs depend heavily on nouns to convey their central ideas. Some of those nouns can be cumbersome. *Nominalization* is the practice of making nouns from verbs or adjectives by adding suffixes (*-ance, -ence, -tion, -ment, -sion*). Such nouns are often used in prepositional phrases. Thus an additional sign of nominalization is frequent use of prepositions.

We have underlined the *be* forms, the instances of nomimalization, and the prepositions in the sentence we considered earlier. Notice that the revision does not rely on *be* verbs or nominalization.

Original

The <u>creation</u> of an overall design <u>for</u> a computer system <u>is</u> the responsibility <u>of</u> a systems analyst, whereas the <u>implementation of</u> the design plan <u>is</u> often the duty <u>of</u> a computer programmer.

Revision

The systems analyst designs the computer system, and the computer programmer makes the system work.

We don't mean to suggest that writers should never use *be* verbs or nominalization. Problems in style arise only when these forms are overused. Although there is no absolute rule, you should look closely when you find more than one *be* verb or one nominalization per sentence. You need not analyze the nouns and verbs in every paper you write, but it is a good idea to check periodically the direction in which your style is developing. Over time, you will find that less analysis is necessary because you will tend to use more active verbs and fewer prepositions and nominalizations.

Use words effectively. Clear writing is concise and explicit. It avoids ineffectual expressions and words that do not contribute directly to the meaning of the paper. Study the underlined words and phrases in the following passage:

<u>Basically</u>, those in support of surrogate motherhood claim that this <u>particular</u> method of reproduction has brought happiness to countless infertile couples. It allows a couple to have a child of their own <u>despite the fact that</u> the woman cannot bear children. In addition, it is <u>definitely</u> preferable to waiting for months and sometimes years on <u>really</u> long adoption lists. <u>In my opinion</u>, however, surrogate motherhood exploits the woman and can be <u>especially</u> damaging to the child. <u>Obviously,</u> poor women are affected most. <u>In the event that</u> a poor couple cannot have a child, it is <u>rather</u> unlikely that they will be able to afford the services of a surrogate mother. <u>Actually,</u> it is fertile, poor women who will become "breeders" for the infertile rich. In any case, the child is <u>especially</u> vulnerable. The <u>given</u> baby may become involved in a custody battle between the surrogate mother and the adopting mother. If the <u>individual</u> child is born handicapped, he or she may be <u>utterly</u> rejected by both mothers. <u>Surely,</u> the child's welfare should be <u>first and foremost</u> in everyone's mind.

Notice that these underlined elements are either hackneyed words and phrases or unnecessary qualifiers, intensifiers, or modifiers. None of these words furthers the writer's intentions. They are inherently vague. Use the following list to track down ineffectual expressions in your writing and remove them.

INEFFECTUAL WORDS AND PHRASES

a bit	given *(adjective)*	rather
absolutely	individual *(adjective)*	really
actually	in the event that	simply
a little	in my (personal) opinion	somewhat
awesome	kind of	sort of
basically	merely	specific
certain	most	surely
certainly	obviously	the fact that
definitely	particularly	utterly
especially	pretty	very
generally	quite	

Detect sexist language.   Always reread your drafts to check that you have avoided sexist language. Use the masculine pronouns *he* and *his* and nouns that end in *-man* or *-men* only when they refer to a male or it is important to point out that a group is composed entirely of males. Don't use these forms to refer to women. Instead, use the following techniques.

TECHNIQUES FOR AVOIDING SEXIST LANGUAGE

- Use expressions that recognize both sexes ("his or her," "she or he").
- Use plural pronouns ("they," "their").
- Use nouns that are not gender-specific ("mail carrier," "police officer").
- Revise the sentence to avoid the need for a pronoun entirely.

   Observe how we used these techniques in the following example.

Original Draft with Sexist Language

We are increasingly becoming a self-centered society. This obsession with self explains some of the lawlessness on the nation's
highways. As each <u>man</u> struggles to defend <u>his</u> own turf, <u>he</u>
forgets about sharing the road with <u>his fellow</u> drivers. Impatient, inconsiderate motorists yell, threaten, and physically
attack people. The average <u>man</u> on the street puts <u>his</u> life in
danger every time <u>he</u> crosses an intersection.

Revision of Sexist Language

We are increasingly becoming a self-centered society. This obsession with self explains some of the lawlessness on the nation's
highways. As motorists struggle to defend their own turf, they
forget about sharing the road with other drivers. Impatient,
inconsiderate motorists yell, threaten, and physically attack
people. The average person on the street puts his or her life in
danger merely by crossing an intersection.

Add your own voice.   After you have finished a complete draft with major revisions, read your paper aloud. Better still, ask a friend to read it aloud to you. Does your writing sound like you? Or does it sound stiff, wooden, impersonal, colorless? Would your paper be better if it resonated with some of your personality? How can you revise it to project your own voice? Here are a few suggestions.

HOW TO ADD YOUR OWN VOICE

- If too many of your sentences wind endlessly around themselves without stopping for air, try dividing them into units of varying length.
- Give a rhythm to your prose by alternating short sentences with longer ones, simple sentences with complex ones, statements or assertions with questions or exclamations.
- Bring your readers into the essay by addressing them with questions and commands, expressions of paradox and wonderment, challenge and suspense.

These devices will bring the sound of your voice into otherwise silent writing and liven it considerably. Be careful, though. Some college instructors may not want you to liven up your writing. They prefer a relentlessly neutral style devoid of any subjective personality. Proceed cautiously.

E x e r c i s e ....

Compare the following early draft with its revision. Does the revision resonate with the writer's voice? What aspects of the revision contribute to this effect?

EARLY DRAFT

> Another text that poses a problem with regard to credibility is <u>Tears of the Indians</u>, written by Bartolomé de Las Casas, an eyewitness and authority on the Spaniards' involvement in the New World. Readers must approach Las Casas's firsthand account analytically because the essay is subjective and hyperbolic, especially in the author's description of the Indians as pious and innocent. No one, much less an entire people, could ever fit that idealized description.

REVISION

> The problem of knowing just how much of an author's writing to believe arises again in reading Bartolomé de Las Casas's <u>Tears of the Indians</u>. Las Casas was an eyewitness and therefore an authority on the Spaniards' involvement in the New World. His essay is a firsthand account, but still we must read it with an analytical mind. We can see one good example of his subjectivity in the hyperbole he employs. He describes the Indians as pious and innocent (7). However, it is doubtful that they were ever so completely virtuous.

E x e r c i s e ●●

Either join a small group of classmates or work by yourself to revise the draft of your response essay. Keep in mind the six concerns just covered:

- Moving from writer-based to reader-based prose
- Varying sentence length
- Stressing verbs rather than nouns
- Using words effectively
- Detecting sexist language
- Adding your own voice

Rewrite the essay, making the necessary revisions.

●●●●●●●●●●●●●●●●●

EDITING

When you are satisfied with your revision, read your paper aloud. This will enable you to catch any glaring errors. Then reread the essay line by line and sentence by sentence. Check for correct usage, punctuation, spelling, mechanics, manuscript form, and typographical errors. If you are using a word processing program with a spell checker, run the checker on your essay. If you are especially weak in editing skills, if it is all right with your instructor, try getting a friend to read over your work.

This stage of revision encompasses rules for usage, punctuation, spelling, and mechanics. We cannot begin to review all that material here. Think seriously about purchasing a few good reference books: a good dictionary; a guide to correct usage, punctuation, and mechanics; and a documentation manual like the *MLA Handbook for Writers of Research Papers* or the *Publication Manual of the American Psychological Association.* Your campus bookstore may stock a variety of self-help books for improving spelling, vocabulary, and usage. Browse through them and select the ones that best serve your needs.

Here is a checklist of some features to note as you edit your paper, but remember that you need to adhere to all the rules of standard written English.

✓ CHECKLIST FOR EDITING

_____ Are all your sentences complete?

Original

Computer scientists must develop programs that model human common sense. If they want their machine to think as humans do.

Revision

Computer scientists must devise programs that model human common sense if they want their machine to think as humans do.

_____ Have you avoided run-on sentences, both fused sentences and comma splices?

Original

Artificial intelligence is advancing rapidly, the new supercomputers will accelerate the pace.

Revision

Artificial intelligence is advancing rapidly, and the new supercomputers will accelerate the pace.

_____ Do pronouns have clear referents, and do they agree in number, gender, and case with the words for which they stand?

Original

A computer scientist who works on artificial intelligence should always consider the social consequences of their work.

Revision

A computer scientist who works on artificial intelligence should always consider the social consequences of his or her work.

_____ Do all subjects and verbs agree in person and number?

Original

Not one of the programs designed to simulate the way humans think have shown any evidence of possessing humanlike common sense.

Revision

Not one of the programs designed to simulate the way humans think has shown any evidence of possessing humanlike common sense.

_____ Is the verb tense consistent and correct?

Original

Some scientists claim that only artificial intelligence can provide the answers needed to ensure the survival of the human race. They predicted that by the year 2050, computers would entirely control the allocation of the earth's resources.

Revision

Some scientists claim that only artificial intelligence can provide the answers needed to ensure the survival of the human race. They predict that by the year 2050, computers will entirely control the allocation of the earth's resources.

_____ Have you used modifiers (words, phrases, subordinate clauses) correctly and placed them where they belong?

Original

Currently, computer scientists across the nation work on artificial intelligence programs with enthusiasm.

Revision

Currently, computer scientists across the nation work enthusiastically on artificial intelligence programs.

_____ Have you used matching elements in parallel constructions?

Original

Proposed artificial intelligence projects include creating machines that can arbitrate disputes between humans, developing medical systems capable of diagnosing rare diseases, and programs that will provide expert advice on financial investments.

Revision

Proposed artificial intelligence projects include machines that can arbitrate disputes between humans, computerized medical systems that can diagnose rare diseases, and programs that can provide expert advice on financial investments.

_____ Are punctuation marks used correctly?

Original

The potentially dire social consequences of artificial intelligence, must be examined carefully, before we embrace this powerful new frightening technology.

Revision

The potentially dire social consequences of artificial intelligence must be examined carefully before we embrace this powerful, new, frightening technology.

_____ Are spelling, capitalization, and other mechanics (abbreviations, numbers, italics) correct?

Original

Artificial Intelligence research is funded largely by the Military because the technology plays a crucial roll in many weapons systems.

Revision
- -

Artificial intelligence research is funded largely by the military because the technology plays a crucial role in many weapons systems.

Do not forget to check for proper manuscript form. For this part of the revision process, you need a lot of patience and good eyes. Here is a checklist of features to note.

✓ CHECKLIST FOR MANUSCRIPT PREPARATION

_____ Have you double-spaced and left at least one-inch margins on all sides?

_____ Are all typed words and corrections legible?

_____ Have you included the identifying information your instructor has specified (name, date, course number, and so on)?

_____ Will your audience be able to tell which thoughts are yours and which are derived from sources?

_____ Are all quotations enclosed in quotation marks and properly punctuated? Are long quotations indented ten spaces?

_____ Have you properly documented all quotations, paraphrases, and summaries?

_____ Do you include all sources in a works cited list?

E x e r c i s e . . . .

Edit the revised version of your response essay.

. . . .

EXPANDING YOUR RHETORICAL GOAL

When you write the type of response essay we have been discussing in this chapter, you are meeting the author of the reading source halfway. You are bringing your prior topic knowledge and experiences to bear on the ideas you read, and then as you compose the essay, you are forging connections between your own ideas and those of the author. The reader of your essay is well aware that the reading source has triggered your particular response.

If you have a good deal of knowledge about the topic or if you have generated a rich pool of elaborations, you may be able to compose a different type of response essay. The reading source will still trigger your reaction, but it will serve as a springboard or taking-off point rather than a mine from which you have unearthed a good portion of your material. In other words, the essay will be driven by your own ideas and conception of the topic, and you will take your own angle or approach. The readers of your essay will still be aware that the reading source has provided you with ideas, evidence, or support for your thesis, but they will see that you have taken the initiative and are not simply reacting to another person's ideas. Rather than summarizing and responding to a text (knowledge-telling), you are transforming it for your own design and purpose (knowledge-transforming). The following chart contrasts response essays of both types.

TOPIC: *THE INTIMATE MACHINE*

Stock Summary and Response Essay	*Response Essay with a Self-Directed Purpose*
Source author's conception of the topic is the driving force behind the writer's essay.	The writer's conception of the topic drives the essay.
Writer's ideas are prompted by or derive from the ideas of the author of the reading source.	The writer uses some of the source author's ideas, but the emphasis is on developing the writer's own points.
The writer is engaged in knowledge-telling.	The writer is engaged in knowledge-transforming.

Now let us look at a response essay that is written with a self-directed rhetorical purpose and then discuss its characteristics.

Alsen 1

Bruce Alsen

Professor Kennedy

English 131

15 July 1999

Delivered in a Box: A Future Friend

The Intimate Machine is the first companion machine that will verbally interact with you, making informal conversation. Its comprehensive 50,000-word vocabulary and pleasant, synthesized voice enable it to respond with a wide range of suggestions, information, and opinion that strongly resemble actual human speech. Programmed with a wealth of powerful, well-trained friendship indicators, the machine offers 25 friendship levels, ranging from mere acquaintance to intimate partner. You can select the degree of attachment and intimacy on which you wish to operate. Rated as "an attractive social partner" by the

1

Alsen 2

Board of American Psychologists, the Intimate Machine

offers simulated human friendship at its highest level,

giving better responses than 95% of the friends you

already have. Plastic housing. Runs on AC adaptor

(included) or C-size rechargeable batteries (not

included). 4 1/4" H x 14 1/8" W x 15 1/4" L (24 lbs.).

64335 ....$12,229.00

If you have a Hammacher Schlemmer or Sharper Image

catalog, you've probably seen the advertisement for the

interactive talking chess player. But is it absurd to think

that you will soon see an ad for a machine that can simulate

human friendship? In a book titled <u>The Intimate Machine</u>, Neil

Frude reminds us that "not too long ago it was thought that

the idea of a machine that could play a reasonable game of

chess was equally absurd" (186). The technology for an intimate

machine exists. Are you ready to buy one from your mail-order

catalog?

Who knows? Machines that simulate human behavior are

probably the wave of the future. Computers have already

replaced humans in a number of contexts. We have automatic

bank tellers, computerized telephone operators, and automated

cashiers at the supermarket checkout. Machines have also made

inroads into our private lives. "People willingly talk to

machines about their personal problems, and they often feel

they are helped by therapeutic programs" (Frude 185). Our

children no longer sit at their teachers' feet at storytime;

they sit in front of computer monitors and read video

books.

Picture the twenty-first century when your son is in
college. He's in his dorm room sitting at his personal
computer when his Seiko Talking Watch reminds him of the time.
Using his universal remote control, he activates his
affectionate machine. The machine senses that he is upset
because the paper he is writing is not going well. The machine
is "understanding and good humored," and in order to take
Joey's mind off his paper, it engages him in an "interesting
conversation that . . . [continues] from previous discussions"
(183). The lively interchange is interrupted by a telephone
call. Two of Joey's human friends want him to join them for a
few beers. It's Saturday night. He responds that he's too
busy, brushing aside their complaints that he never wants to
go out anymore. Joey and the machine settle down to another
evening alone in his room. He switches on the answering
machine and closes the blinds. This is the ultimate intimate
relationship. It is all the social contact he needs.

Do you accept this scenario as part of the natural course
of events? Brian Gaines, a specialist in human-machine
interaction, says, "We are clearly beginning to accept the
computer as a 'colleague' rather than a 'tool'" (Frude 187).
Will we soon accept it as a friend and intimate social partner
as well? Frude claims that "we stand on the threshold of a
dramatic extension of the opportunities of social contact." At
least he admits that "the consequences for human relationships
as we know them will be profound" (187).

These consequences should be of the utmost concern to us.
Inanimate objects have already replaced human beings in many

Alsen 4

areas of our lives. Machines supply us with the services we once received from humans. Increasingly, as we go about our day-to-day activities, we do not interact with other people in a meaningful way. Machines have become our chess opponents, our colleagues, and our therapists. Before long, they will become our friends and lovers.

   The effects that this phenomenon will have on human relationships will be devastating. Admittedly, there are many people in this world who need more opportunities for social contact, but this contact should develop between humans. Let us not be lured by the novelty of intimate machines.

5

Alsen 5

Work Cited

Frude, Neil. <u>The Intimate Machine</u>. New York: New American Library, 1983.

In this essay, Bruce moves beyond a simple response to the reading source. One of Frude's claims—that the development of affectionate machines will have profound consequences for human relationships—triggers the essay. But in developing the essay, Bruce has used more of his own knowledge and imagination than information from the reading source. His purpose is to draw attention to what the author has *not* said about the topic rather than to elaborate on the various points that already appear in the text.

   To develop an essay of this type, you can follow the same preparatory procedures as for a stock summary and response essay. The difference lies in the way you use your elaborations. As we saw earlier, elaborations can become the blueprint for the standard response essay. You can often find a paper in your notes. When this does not occur, either of two straightforward patterns (summary and response or point by point; see page 104) can serve as prefabricated plans for the essay. If you have a more personal rhetorical purpose, however, try either of these two approaches:

- Pull back from your elaborations and try to reconceptualize or transform them.
- Write a preliminary draft that takes you in a new direction and triggers new ideas.

Either procedure involves a substantial amount of ruminating, reflecting on the material you have already developed, and deciding how to use and expand it in a more interesting way. The following questions will prove helpful.

QUESTIONS FOR DEVELOPING A RESPONSE ESSAY WITH A SELF-DIRECTED PURPOSE

- How can I make this material more interesting, relevant, eventful, or meaningful?
- What new angle or point of view can I take with regard to this material?
- Can I create a rhetorical situation in which I am writing to move or influence a certain group of readers for a specific reason?
- Can I address a more definite audience?
- How can I better engage the reader?
- Can I fashion a richer rhetorical situation?

After you have come up with a thesis and a fresh approach, be sure to review the source to determine how it will figure in your essay. You won't be able to proceed as you would for a stock summary and response essay because you won't be following a prefabricated plan. You will use your elaboration notes, the source, and perhaps a preliminary draft as the raw materials for your essay.

TABLE 3-1 SUMMARY OF THE GUIDELINES FOR RESPONDING TO SOURCES

Prewriting: Planning and Preparatory Activities

1. Read the assignment, and formulate your rhetorical purpose.
   - Why are you writing the response essay, and what desired effect do you hope to have on your audience?
   - How much of the source should you summarize, and what form will the summary take?

2. Consider your audience.
   - Are you writing for your professor or for a broader audience?
   - Is your audience in the academic community?
   - Are you writing for a general audience or for specialists?
   - What will your audience already know about the topic?
   - Will you need to explain basic concepts or provide background for the source material to make sense?
   - Will your audience be biased either for or against what the source says?

- Can you predict how your audience will react to the source?
- What is the overall impact that you want to have on your audience?
- How will your writing inform, influence, or change your audience?

3. Read the source to get a general impression of the content; form, organization, features; and rhetorical concerns.

- Reading for information: What is the author's thesis or main point? What are other important points?
- Reading for form, organization, and features: How does the author get his or her points across? What is the method of presentation? What is the pattern of organization?
- Reading for rhetorical concerns: What is the author's purpose? How does the author intend to influence the audience? Who is the author, and what is his or her background? To whom is the piece addressed? In what type of publication is it published? What is the author's relationship to the audience?

4. Reread and elaborate.

- Tap your memory, and make associations between your prior knowledge and the ideas in the reading source (see the strategies for elaboration of reading sources on pages 93–94).
- Review your elaborations, and develop your thesis.
    See if one type predominates.
    See if a good number of elaborations were triggered by a particular idea in the reading source.
    Classify them.
- Decide on a suitable organizational format.
    Summarize the relevant parts of the source, and state your position.
    Develop your commentary, or briefly summarize the source and give your view.
    As you develop your position, alternate between the ideas in the reading source and your response, or use an organizational pattern (see page 24) that is appropriate for your rhetorical purpose.

Drafting

1. Write an opening paragraph in which you accomplish these goals:
   - Use an opening that will interest the reader.
   - Announce the topic and disclose a thesis or attitude toward it (the thesis may come later).
   - Indicate the source title and author, and provide some summary information about the source.
   - Establish your own voice.

2. Arrange your elaboration notes in paragraphs, and develop each paragraph to its fullest.

3. Compose a concluding paragraph in which you use one of these techniques:
   - Stress the significance of your thesis rather than simply repeating it. Encourage your readers to look beyond the thesis to an important future goal.
   - Predict consequences.
   - Call your readers to action.
   - Use any of the devices for paper openers (see page 109).

Revising

1. If possible, have a classmate or friend read over your first draft and answer the questions on page 112. If no one is available, leave your work for a day or two and then answer the questions yourself.
2. When you revise, keep the following concerns in mind:
   - Moving from writer-based to reader-based prose
   - Varying sentence length
   - Stressing verbs rather than nouns
   - Using words effectively
   - Detecting sexist language
   - Adding your own voice

Editing

1. When you are satisfied with your revision, read your paper aloud. Then reread it line by line and sentence by sentence. Check for correct usage, punctuation, spelling, mechanics, manuscript form, and typos.
2. If you are using a word processing program with a spell checker, run the checker on your essay.
3. If your editing skills are not strong, have a friend read over your work.

4

COMPARING AND CONTRASTING SOURCES

How many times have you received an essay examination question or a composition topic that began "Compare and contrast . . ."? Your social studies teacher may have asked you to contrast the abolitionists' view of slavery with the pro-slavery view, or your English teacher may have told you to compare two characters in a short story. In primary school, you probably wrote comparison-and-contrast compositions, comparing two types of animals or showing the difference between two countries or states.

We typically use comparison and contrast every day. Asked to describe a new song on the radio, we might say, "It has a rap beat, but the lyrics sound more like pop music." We frequently view things in terms of what they are like and unlike. Writers regularly use comparison and contrast to describe, explain, and argue.

USES OF COMPARISON AND CONTRAST

Leslie Heywood, the author of "Satellite" (pages 454–457), uses comparison in her descriptions. Look for them in the passage quoted here. The setting is the weight room where Heywood works out with the boys on the distance running team. She is describing a confrontation with the coach of the sprinters' team.

> I sit up and there he is: the sprinters' coach. He looks just like—*just like*—Luke Spencer on *General Hospital*, and this is Luke Spencer's year. A few months from now he will rape Laura [and] then marry her, and the whole country will tune in, whether they usually watch the soaps or not, the hype in the papers approaching that reserved for Prince Charles and Princess Di, whose wedding will also happen that month. Like Luke on TV, Coach Luke is gaunt and thin, skin really white, with unruly threads of albino-red hair fanning the air behind him, thinning a bit right on top. He moves quickly, and is sarcastic a lot like he's sarcastic right now, twisting that smile that says he knows it all and knows it right, your place in the universe nothing like his. I look up at him, ready for a fight. He looks at me like you'd look at a rooster who's strutting his stuff just before he's going to get cooked. Not this rooster, mister, not me. I look at him with his own look that says you don't even exist and you'd better get out of my way. His mouth turns up at one corner and he laughs, "Hey, my guys need this bench and you all should go do something else." I don't move. (456)

Did you find the following comparisons?

- The similarities between Coach Luke and Luke Spencer on *General Hospital*
- The similarity between media hype over *General Hospital* and media coverage of the royal wedding
- Heywood comparing herself to a rooster who's strutting his stuff just before he's going to get cooked

The comparisons add depth to Heywood's descriptions and leave the reader with rich, memorable images.

A writer who uses comparison for the purpose of explanation is David Rothenberg in "Learning in Finland: No Grades, No Criticism" (pages 341–344). Here he explains the views of university students in Finland and in the United States:

> The Finnish view is that simply doing the work on one's own time is the point of education. My students always claimed to be too busy, but they rarely seemed stressed or burned out. Students must think, they must write. In Europe, they often save all their thinking for the final project and the final exam at the end of the single course they typically take each semester. In the United States, students and professors communicate all the time—discussing, chatting, bouncing ideas back and forth, at least in small classes. The Finns put more of a boundary between the learned and the learner. Professors are encouraged to pontificate, to put forth information, and the student to sit silently and take it all down. (342)

A writer can also make an argument on the basis of similarity, as Pat Griffin does in "Sport: Where Men Are Men and Women Are Trespassers" (448–449) when she argues that women athletes possess some of the qualities, talents, and characteristics that only male athletes are supposed to have:

> Women's serious participation in sport brings into question the "natural" and mutually exclusive nature of gender and gender roles. If women in sport can be tough minded, competitive, and muscular too, then sport loses its special place in the development of masculinity for men. If women can so easily develop these so-called masculine qualities, then what are the meanings of femininity and masculinity? What does it mean to be a man or a woman? These challenges threaten an acceptance of the traditional order in which men are privileged and women are subordinate. (449)

In "A Young Person's Guide to the Grading System" (333–336), as Jerry Farber argues that students don't need grades even though they may think otherwise, he compares them to addicts:

> We're like those sleeping pill addicts who have reached the point where they need strong artificial inducement to do what comes naturally. We're grade junkies—convinced that we'd never learn without the A's and F's to keep us going. (333)

Notice that all of the quoted passages show writers using comparison and contrast for a precise purpose. Heywood is describing Coach Luke, Rothenberg is explaining the differences between Finnish and American views of higher education, Griffin is making a case for gender equality, and Farber is arguing against grades. Writers use comparison and contrast simply to explore interesting points of similarity between two things or to reveal that grounds for comparison actually exist. But usually they state a particular position on the two subjects they are comparing.

RHETORICAL PURPOSE FOR COMPARISON-AND-CONTRAST ESSAYS

As a college writer, you will often be asked to make comparisons and contrasts that draw on textual sources as well as your own ideas. Occasionally, you will compare your own experience with information from reading sources, but more typically, you will compare and contrast the views of various writers. Take, for example, an assignment based on assisted suicide, the topic of Chapter 12.

> Compare and contrast two authors' views on assisted suicide: those of Ernest van den Haag in "Make Mine Hemlock" and those of Rand Richards Cooper in "The Dignity of Helplessness: What Sort of Society Would Euthanasia Create?"

Since this is a loosely defined assignment, there are a number of ways you can approach it. The most rudimentary approach is simply to list the similarities and differences in the two authors' views and use the list to compose your essay.

SIMILARITIES

- Neither author is questioning assisted suicide per se.
- Both authors offer some of the same examples.

DIFFERENCES

- Van den Haag is in favor of institutionalizing assisted suicide; Cooper is against it.
- Van den Haag bases his argument on the notion of rights; Cooper claims that this notion is too narrow a framework.
- Van den Haag finds fault with the argument that life is a social duty that no one should shirk; Cooper bases his argument on the "texture of civic life."
- Van den Haag discusses abled individuals' right to commit suicide and also goes into detail about assisted suicide for disabled individuals; Cooper focuses on the elderly.
- Van den Haag goes into detail about the competence of individuals who wish to shorten their life; Cooper does not treat this issue.
- Van den Haag goes into detail about safeguarding the disinterestedness of people who assist with suicides; Cooper predicts that people may act out of self-interest.

- Van den Haag dismisses "slippery slope" arguments; Cooper dwells on the long-range negative consequences of euthanasia.
- Van den Haag says that today people hold the view that "individuals collectively own society, rather than vice versa"; Cooper claims that contemporary society is moving toward communitarianism and interest in togetherness rather than separateness.
- Van den Haag thinks Dr. Kevorkian is courageous; Cooper questions everything Kevorkian has done.
- Van den Haag claims that there are safeguards to ensure that no one is pressured to end his or her life; Cooper claims that the elderly do not have "absolute autonomy" in this matter.

We could easily construct an essay from this list by using a block presentational pattern, allocating a small block to similarities and a large one to differences. The resulting essay would be rather flat because it would simply catalog the similarities and differences. There is nothing intrinsically wrong with this goal, but when it is the only end in mind, it is easy to fall into the trap of doing too much summarizing and too little discussion of similarities and differences. We recommend that you take the process a step further. After you identify similarities and differences, step back and ask yourself what they represent, reveal, or demonstrate. Reflect on the list, select from it, shape it, or expand it. Ask yourself the following questions.

QUESTIONS ABOUT SIMILARITIES AND DIFFERENCES

- Can I select from among the similarities and differences and categorize them in a way that will make my paper more interesting, relevant, eventful, or meaningful?
- Is there a new angle or point of view I can take?
- Can I make the essay functional? Can I create a "rhetorical imperative," that is, write to move or influence a certain group of readers for a specific reason?
- Can I address a more definite audience?
- How can I engage the reader best?
- Can I fashion a richer rhetorical situation?

To illustrate, let us examine a student essay written in response to the assignment on page 143.

Robles 1

Anna Robles

Professor Kennedy

Composition 101

5 May 2000

The Controversy over Assisted Suicide

Paper opener: rhetorical questions

Should competent people, particularly those who are terminally ill or handicapped, have the right to end their lives? Or should they be forced to go on living even if they do not wish to do so? What it comes down to is the question of who owns life: God, the individual, or the larger society? Many people believe that suicide is a sin and a transgression against God and nature. End of discussion. But Ernest van den Haag and Rand Richards Cooper wish to pursue the matter

Background, titles, and authors

further. Van den Haag presents his argument in "Make Mine Hemlock," and Cooper makes his case in "The Dignity of Helplessness: What Sort of Society Would Euthanasia Create?" Van den Haag claims that no one "owns" us. We own ourselves and control our own destinies. Therefore, any able-bodied person should be permitted to end his or her life. And disabled people who wish to end their lives should be given assistance. Cooper disagrees. He thinks it is wrong to eliminate the stage of life when people become sick and helpless, and he questions whether we will "be a better, richer, more humane society for having done so" (14). He also warns that widespread practice of assisted suicide will present a dire threat to society. Ernest van den Haag and Rand Richards Cooper have very little in common. They base their

Thesis

arguments on different assumptions, and they have very different views of the consequences of assisted suicide.

Both van den Haag and Cooper agree on one point. Dying patients have the right to refuse treatment, and physicians may choose to respect the decision and even help them die. Van den Haag thinks physicians are obligated to assist terminally ill patients. Cooper does not go that far, but he does accept the idea of physicians' relieving unnecessary pain. He remarks:

Points of similarity

Support from the article: quotation

> In fact, it's not assisted suicide per se I'm questioning, which in other forms has long been practiced unofficially by physicians informing the gravely ill about lethal doses, turning off ventilators to "let nature take its course," and so on. It's the institutionalizing of the practice I'm wondering about, and its effect on our relation to the idea of suffering. (14)

Even though they don't really see eye to eye, this seems to be the only point on which van den Haag and Cooper share any common ground.

First point of difference

Very different assumptions underlie Van den Haag's and Cooper's arguments. Van den Haag bases his argument on individual rights, whereas Cooper maintains that the notion of individual rights is too narrow a framework. Van den Haag says that neither God nor society "owns" people. They "are thought to own themselves" (60). He explains: "Owners can dispose of what they own as they see fit. We thus become entitled to control life, including its duration, to the extent nature

Van den Haag

Support from the article: quotation

permits, provided that this control does not harm others in ways proscribed by law" (60). Van den Haag believes that our obligations to ourselves are more important than our obligations to society. He finds fault with the argument that life is a social duty that no one should shirk.

Cooper

Support from the article: quotation and paraphrase

Cooper moves his argument outside the framework of the "right" to die. He feels that Americans are obsessed with individual rights: "The appeal of rights is so compelling that it leaves scant room for realities and interests not easily expressed as rights" (12). For Cooper, "our deaths are both solo journeys toward an ultimate mystery and strands in the tapestries of each other's lives" (14). We are interconnected, and this connectedness to one another, the effect that each individual has on "the texture of civic life" (13), is more important than individual rights. In other words, our duty to society outweighs our duty to ourselves.

4

Second point of difference

Cooper

Support from the article: quotation and paraphrase

Van den Haag and Cooper also have different opinions about the ramifications of institutionalizing assisted suicide. Cooper points out that if the practice is sanctioned, it will lead unavoidably to undesirable attitudes. He predicts a "creep toward an increased sense of burdensomeness" (12) on the part of the elderly. Viewing themselves as burdens to their loved ones, they will end their lives. Cooper also claims that the ready availability of assisted suicide will transform the way we regard aging. "How often in the assisted-suicide future," he asks, "will someone look at an elderly person and think, consciously or semiconsciously, 'Gee, guess it's about time,

5

huh?' " (13). Cooper sees other negative consequences. He predicts that if we legalize assisted suicide and thus follow what he calls "the quality-of-life, take-me-out-and-shoot-me principle," we will "preempt the infirmities of old age and terminal illness" (13). Eventually, we will look askance at disabled and handicapped people of all ages. We will end up thinking, "as Germany did under the Nazis, . . . of the handicapped as a drain or drag on the healthy body of the rest of us: a pointless deformity; an un-luck; an un-person" (13).

Van den Haag

Van den Haag would accuse Cooper of committing the slippery slope fallacy. Slippery slope arguers predict that one thing will inevitably lead to another more undesirable thing. They also warn of dangerous precedents. Van den Haag says the suggestion that doctors, or anyone else, "would wantonly kill burdensome patients who do not want to die" is unjustified (62). He also thinks the analogy to Nazi Germany is unsound. He argues, "But Nazi practices were imposed on physicians and hospitals by political directives which did not evolve from any prior authority given physicians to assist in suicide. There was no 'slippery slope'" (62). To van den Haag, the slippery slope argument is an "unrealistic nightmare" (62).

Support from the article: quotation

6

Conclusion

Cooper speaks of the importance of accompanying people through terminal illnesses and asks if this is not "one of the core experiences we need to have" (14). Toward the end of his article, he asks, "Whose death is it anyway?" (14), implying that the duty to die, as well as the duty to live, is owed to society. Van den Haag could not disagree more. "Society cannot

7

Robles 5

be shown to have a compelling interest in forcing persons to
live against their will," he says. "Moreover, such an interest
would hardly justify the cruelty involved" (62).

Robles 6

Works Cited

Cooper, Rand Richards. "The Dignity of Helplessness: What Sort
    of Society Would Euthanasia Create?" Commonweal 25 Oct.
    1996: 12-14.

van den Haag, Ernest. "Make Mine Hemlock." National Review 12
    June 1995: 60-62.

Anna does more than list the multitude of differences between van den Haag and
Cooper. She describes one area of agreement, and then she selects two points of difference and makes them the focus of her essay: the different assumptions that underlie each
author's argument and the views each holds about the consequences of permitting
assisted suicide. In paragraph 2, she explains that both van den Haag and Cooper
acknowledge that dying patients have the right to refuse treatment and that physicians
may choose to respect the decision and even help them die. Next, in paragraphs 3 and
4, she investigates the bases of each author's argument: van den Haag's claims about
individual rights and Cooper's claims about civic duty and the needs of society. Then,
in paragraphs 5 and 6, Anna discusses Cooper's predictions about the dangers inherent
in the legalization of assisted suicide and van den Haag's dismissal of this chain of
events.

Exercise

Return to Anna Robles's essay and consider her rhetorical purpose. Break into groups, and
answer the following questions:

1. What do you think prompted Anna to respond to the assignment the way she did?
2. How does Anna view her audience?

3. What impact does she want to have on these readers?

4. What role does Anna assume in relation to the subject matter, the audience, and her own voice?

(For further explanation of these elements, see pages 30–32.)

. . . .

WRITING AN ESSAY THAT COMPARES AND CONTRASTS SOURCES

To write a comparison-and-contrast essay, you will follow the same process we outlined for the response essay in Chapter 3. You will work on your assignment in phases: *prewriting, drafting, revising,* and *editing.*

PREWRITING

Before you sit down to compose a preliminary draft, read and reread the sources, annotate them, take notes, and plan your essay. The effort you put into these prewriting activities will save time and ensure you of more success than if you moved directly from reading the sources to writing your essay. To begin, tailor your reading goal and strategies to the task at hand. For illustration, we will assume you are responding to the same assignment that Anna Robles addressed in the essay you just read:

> Compare and contrast two authors' views on assisted suicide: those of Ernest van den Haag in "Make Mine Hemlock" and those of Rand Richards Cooper in "The Dignity of Helplessness: What Sort of Society Would Euthanasia Create?"

Do a first reading to get a general impression of the source. Since the assignment asks you to compare and contrast van den Haag's and Cooper's views on assisted suicide, read the selections to determine how the two authors' views are similar and how they are different. Van den Haag's article appears on pages 406–409, and Cooper's is on pages 411–415. Start by reading the van den Haag selection. Then when you move on to Cooper, read the selection with two questions in mind:

- How are Cooper's views on assisted suicide similar to van den Haag's?
- How do Cooper's views differ from van den Haag's?

Your first reading of the sources will make you aware of major similarities and differences. Freewrite your reactions. Write nonstop for ten minutes, jotting down whatever comes to your mind.

Reread, elaborate, and map correspondences. Next, reread the two articles. The second reading allows you to do two things:

- Tap your memory and make associations between your previous knowledge and experiences and the reading sources
- Identify and map correspondences between the two sources

As you perform these activities, annotate the texts or take separate notes. As Anna rereads the selection by van den Haag, she elaborates and identifies places where he agrees or disagrees with Cooper.

Van den Haag	Elaboration
Paragraph 11	
It is not clear to whom the duty to live could be owed. Once the government no longer legally recognizes God as the authority to which duties are owed, nature cannot have prescriptive authority to force unwilling persons to live, since such authority would have to come from God. Only society is left as the source of this alleged duty. But society cannot be shown to have a compelling interest in forcing persons to live against their will. Moreover, such an interest would hardly justify the cruelty involved. . . .	Cooper disagrees. He claims that society should have a compelling interest in keeping people alive because we are all interconnected. He doesn't think society is forcing elderly people to stay alive. He claims that they really don't want to die; they consent to assisted suicide because they feel helpless and they are convinced they are a burden to society. I don't know what he'd say about cruelty. He seems to think that it is important for people to suffer.

As you reread the two sources, elaborate fully, and identify as many similarities and differences as you can. A rich store of prewriting notes and annotations will be a great help when you write your comparison-and-contrast essay. If you have difficulty elaborating on the reading sources, refer to the strategies for elaborating on reading sources on pages 193–94. Here are some additional strategies that will help you compare the two reading sources.

ELABORATING TO UNCOVER COMPARISONS AND CONTRASTS

- Identify points where one source author: (1) Agrees or disagrees with the other author, (2) Says something relevant about the topic that the other author has neglected to say, (3) Qualifies ideas stated by the other author, and (4) Extends a proposition made by the other author.
- Validate one author's assertion with information provided by the other author.
- Subsume similarities and differences between the sources under subordinate categories.
- Create hierarchies of importance among ideas that are similar or different.
- Make judgments about the relevance of one author's view in relation to the other's view.

As you identify correspondences between the two reading sources, create a *web* (see Figure 4-1). Webbing enables you to link points of similarity and difference. Identify a

FIGURE 4-1 Beginning of a Web for Comparison and Contrast

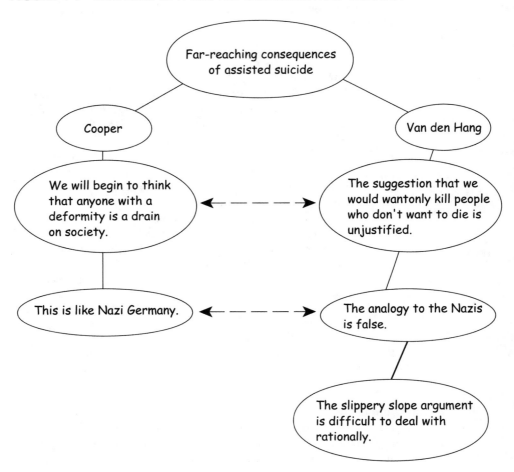

point of similarity or difference, summarize it in a short phrase, and write it in a box on a sheet of paper. Next, spin out the web by placing each author's ideas around this key idea node. Circle each idea, and draw lines connecting it to the key idea. Where appropriate, connect the circles to each other. When you are finished webbing, you will have a visual display of the points of similarity and difference.

Plan your essay. Once you have generated a series of elaborations, you are ready to select and organize your ideas and sketch out a blueprint for your essay. Keep in mind that your purpose is to compare and contrast the views expressed by the two authors. As you review your elaborations, separate the ones dealing with similarities from the ones dealing with differences (see page 143). Mark the text wherever you discover similarities or differences (use symbols: = or √ for similarities, ≠ or × for differences), and create two lists, as we illustrated on page 143.

Next, analyze the similarities and differences to discover the points you will discuss. They can be aspects of the subject, major topics, or prominent themes. Categorize the similarities and differences accordingly. See if you can form one or two generalizations. Even if your generalizations have exceptions, they will still be useful.

Usually, a writer compares reading sources in order to draw certain conclusions and make particular points clearer to the reader. As we said earlier, you could simply catalog all the similarities and differences, but this limited rhetorical purpose leaves little room for you to exercise judgment or analytical skill. A more powerful purpose requires you to select, categorize, and focus.

LIMITED GOAL	**MORE POWERFUL GOAL**
Catalog all the similarities and differences.	Select from among the similarities and differences, categorize them, and focus the essay on generalizations.

Observe how Anna selected from among the long list of differences between van den Haag and Cooper listed on page 143. She pinpoints two major areas of difference: the assumptions underlying their arguments and their views on the consequences of assisted suicide.

ASSUMPTIONS FOR ARGUMENTS

- Van den Haag says that today we believe that "individuals collectively own society, rather than vice versa." He bases his argument on the notion of rights. He finds fault with the argument that life is a social duty that no one should shirk.
- Cooper argues that the notion of individual rights is too narrow a framework. He claims that we're moving toward communitarianism and togetherness rather than separateness. He bases his argument on the "texture of civic life."

VIEWS ON CONSEQUENCES OF ASSISTED SUICIDE

- Cooper emphasizes long-range negative consequences of euthanasia. Van den Haag dismisses Cooper's "slippery slope" arguments.
- Van den Haag claims there are safeguards to ensure that no one is pressured to end his or her life; Cooper contends that the elderly do not have "absolute autonomy" in this matter.

Once you have decided on your areas of focus, return to the reading sources and search for any relevant material you may have overlooked.

Decide on an organizational plan.

Comparison-and-contrast essays are usually organized in one of two formats: point-by-point or block. Point-by-point arrangement identifies key aspects or facets of the subject that is being compared and contrasted. For the assignment we are working on, that means we would move back and forth between van den Haag and Cooper, comparing and contrasting them on the basis of key points or features of their arguments. Block arrangement presents one side at a time. We would discuss everything van den Haag has to say about the topic before moving on to Cooper. To see how professional writers use these arrangements, read the following passages from an article in which Nancy Henley, Mykol Hamilton, and Barrie Thorne discuss sex differences and sexism in communication.

Point-by-Point Arrangement

> There are other sex differences in speech sounds. For boys in our culture, masculinity and toughness are projected by a slightly nasal speech; girls and "gentlemanly" boys have oral, or non-nasal, speech. Males also speak with greater intensity than females. There are differences in the intonation patterns used by each sex: Women have more variable intonations (contrasting levels) than men do; women are said to have more extremes of high and low intonation than men, and to speak with long rapid glides that are absent in men's speech. (174)

Table 4-1 depicts the point-by-point arrangement. Henley, Hamilton, and Thorne explain sex differences in speech sounds by comparing the speech of males and females on the basis of three features: nasality, intensity, and intonation.

TABLE 4-1   POINT-BY-POINT PRESENTATION

Subject	Males	Females	Points of Comparison
Sex differences in speech sounds	Projects masculinity and toughness for boys; oral non-nasal speech for gentlemen	Have oral, non-nasal speech	Nasal quality
	More intensity than females	Less intensity than males	Intensity
	Glides absent	More variable; more extremes of high and low; speak with long, rapid glides	Intonation

Block Arrangement

Self-disclosure is another variable that involves language but goes beyond it. Research studies have found that women disclose more personal information to others than men do. Subordinates (in work situations) are also more likely to self-disclose than superiors. People in positions of power are required to reveal little about themselves, yet typically know much about the lives of others—perhaps the ultimate exemplar of this principle is the fictional Big Brother.

According to the research of Jack Sattel, men exercise and maintain power over women by withholding self-disclosure. An institutional example of this use of power is the psychiatrist (usually male), to whom much is disclosed (by a predominantly female clientele), but who classically maintains a reserved and detached attitude, revealing little or nothing of himself. Nonemotionality is the "cool" of the professional, the executive, the poker player, the street-wise operator. Smart men—those who manipulate others—maintain unruffled exteriors.

Women who obtain authoritative positions may do likewise, but most women have been socialized to display their emotions, thoughts, and ideas. Giving out this information about themselves, especially in a context of inequality, is giving others power over them. Women may not be more emotionally variable than men, but their emotional variability is more visible. This display of emotional variability, like that of variability of intonation, contributes to the stereotype of instability in women. Self-disclosure is not in itself a weakness or negative behavior trait; like other gestures of intimacy, it has positive aspects—such as sharing of oneself and allowing others to open up—when it is voluntary and reciprocal. (176–77)

Table 4-2 depicts the block arrangement. Discussing sex differences in self-disclosure and emotionality. Henley, Hamilton, and Thorne first describe the behavior of males and then describe the behavior of females.

TABLE 4-2   BLOCK PRESENTATION

Sex	Behavior	Points of Comparison
Males	1. Exercise and maintain power over women by withholding personal information. 2. Are "cool," nonemotional, unruffled.	Self-disclosure, emotionality
Females	1. Display personal information to people in power. 2. Appear to be more emotional because they display emotion.	Self-disclosure, emotionality

Notice that Anna Robles organizes the body paragraphs of her essay on pages 145–149 in a point-by-point arrangement. She covers three points: one point on which van den Haag and Cooper agree and two points on which they disagree. You can visualize this arrangement in a chart or tree diagram (see Figure 4-2). It is beneficial to use some type of graphic organizer as a preliminary outline.

FIGURE 4-2   DIAGRAM FOR A POINT-BY-POINT COMPARISON

Subject: Assisted suicide
Sources Being Compared: Van den Haag
                                    Cooper
Points of Comparison: 1. Assisted suicide per se
                                    2. Assumptions underlying argument
                                    3. View of consequences

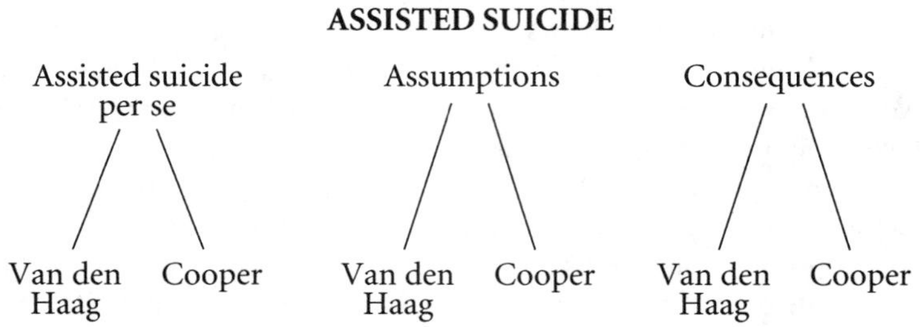

ASSISTED SUICIDE

Assisted suicide per se	Assumptions	Consequences
Van den Haag Cooper	Van den Haag Cooper	Van den Haag Cooper

OUTLINE FOR A COMPARISON ESSAY WRITTEN IN A POINT-BY-POINT ARRANGEMENT

Paragraph 1   Introduction
Paragraph 2   Similarities between the two authors

Underlying Assumptions of Argument (first major difference)

Very different assumptions underlie van den Haag's and Cooper's arguments. Van den Haag bases his argument on individual rights, whereas Cooper maintains that the notion of individual rights is too narrow a framework.

Paragraph 3   Van den Haag's assumptions
Paragraph 4   Cooper's assumptions

Views on Consequences of Assisted Suicide (second major difference)

Van den Haag and Cooper also have different opinions about the ramifications of institutionalizing assisted suicide.

Paragraph 5   Cooper's views
Paragraph 6   Van den Haag's views
Paragraph 7   Conclusion

If Anna had used the block comparison pattern, instead of taking up each of the two points of comparison and alternating between van den Haag and Cooper, she would have presented one side at a time and contrasted the two authors in blocks, one block devoted to van den Haag and the other to Cooper. The pattern is shown in the tree diagram in Figure 4-3.

FIGURE 4-3   Tree Diagram for a Block Comparison

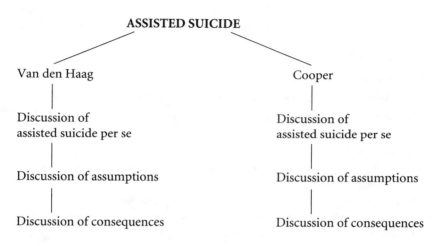

ASSISTED SUICIDE

Van den Haag

Discussion of assisted suicide per se

Discussion of assumptions

Discussion of consequences

Cooper

Discussion of assisted suicide per se

Discussion of assumptions

Discussion of consequences

OUTLINE FOR A COMPARISON ESSAY WRITTEN IN A BLOCK ARRANGEMENT

Paragraphs 1 and 2   Same as for the point-by-point essay.

First Block: Van den Haag

Paragraph 3   Assumptions underlying his argument
Paragraph 4   Views on the consequences of assisted suicide

Second Block: Cooper

Paragraph 5   Assumptions underlying his argument
Paragraph 6   Views on the consequences of assisted suicide
Paragraph 7   Conclusion

Exercise

Rewrite each of the passages on pages 154–155 in the alternative form, that is, recast the point-by-point passage into block format and put the block passage into point-by-point format.

DRAFTING

The next step is to write a preliminary draft of your essay. Remember that this will not be a final, polished draft. You will have an opportunity to change your direction, sharpen your focus, and make other revisions at a later date. As you are drafting, follow your outline and keep the reading sources open in front of you. You will need to consult them often for the quotations, paraphrases, summaries, and other references you will use to support each of your points. There are certain conventions for comparison essays that you should follow.

CONVENTIONS FOR COMPARISON ESSAYS

- Give your readers some background about the topic.
- Identify the sources by title and author.
- Indicate clearly the focus and thesis of your paper.
- Make clear to your readers the points of comparison you will discuss.
- Develop each point of comparison by paraphrasing, summarizing, or quoting relevant points in the readings, or bringing your prior topic knowledge and experience to bear on the text.
- Be sure you discuss the same points for each author. For example, if you discuss assumptions and consequences for van den Haag, discuss the same points for Cooper.
- Use transitions and verbs that signal similarities and differences and help your readers follow your train of thought.

  also, likewise, in the same way, similarly

  on the contrary, in contrast, even so, however, but, although, despite, in spite of, nevertheless, nonetheless

  on the one hand, on the other hand, not only . . . but also

  agree, accede, acknowledge, concur, go along, assent

  disagree, counter, deny, retort, contradict, object

- Differentiate your own ideas from those of the authors of the sources.
- Document source material that is paraphrased, summarized, or quoted.

REVISING

If your teacher agrees, make arrangements to have a classmate or friend review your preliminary draft and give you feedback. If this is not possible, set the paper aside for a few days and then review it yourself. Respond to the following set of questions.

✓ CHECKLIST FOR REVISING THE FIRST DRAFT OF A COMPARISON-AND-CONTRAST ESSAY

_____ Is the writer's rhetorical purpose clear? (How is the writer attempting to influence or affect readers?)

_____ Does the writer simply catalog similarities and contrasts or focus on key points?

_____ Are the key points clearly expressed in the thesis statement?

_____ Does everything in the essay lead to or follow from one central meaning? (If not, which ideas appear to be out of place?)

_____ Will the reader understand the essay, and is the writer sensitive to the reader's concerns?

> _____ Does the writer provide necessary background information about the subject matter, the sources, and their titles and authors? (If not, what is missing?)

> _____ Are there clear transitions or connectives that differentiate the writer's own ideas from the ideas in the sources?

> _____ Does the writer display an awareness of the authors by referring to them by name?

_____ Is the organizational format appropriate for a comparison-and-contrast essay?

_____ Is the writer using a point-by-point or a block arrangement?

_____ Has the writer clearly stated the points of comparison? (Explain how these criteria or bases for comparison are clear or confusing?)

_____ Does the writer provide transitions and connecting ideas when moving from one source to another or from one point of comparison to the next? (If not, where are they needed?)

_____ Do you hear the writer's voice throughout the entire essay? (Can you describe it?)

_____ Does the writer open the paper in a way that catches the reader's attention?

_____ Does the conclusion simply restate the main idea, or does it offer new insights?

_____ Does the essay have an appropriate title?

_____ Do you have other suggestions you can give the writer for improving this draft?

EDITING

When you are satisfied with your revision, read your paper aloud. This will enable you to catch any glaring errors. Then reread the essay line by line and sentence by sentence. Check for grammatical correctness, punctuation, spelling, mechanics, manuscript form, and typographical errors. If you are using a word processing program with a spell checker, run the checker on your essay. If your editing skills are not strong, get a friend to read over your work.

Exercise

Make arrangements to have someone review your preliminary draft or, if this is not possible, review it yourself. Answer the questions on pages 158–159. Then use the feedback you receive to revise and edit your paper.

Table 4-3 summarizes the guidelines for comparing and contrasting sources.

TABLE 4-3   SUMMARY OF THE GUIDELINES FOR COMPARING AND CONTRASTING SOURCES

Prewriting: Planning and Preparatory Activities

1. Read the assignment, and decide on your rhetorical purpose.
   - Why are you writing the comparison essay, and what desired effect do you hope to have on your audience?

2. Consider your audience.
   - Are you writing for your professor or for a broader audience?
   - Is your audience in the academic community?
   - Are you writing for a general audience or for specialists?
   - What will your audience already know about the topic?
   - Will you need to explain basic concepts or provide background for the source material to make sense?
   - Will your audience be biased either for or against what the sources say?
   - Can you predict how your audience will react to the sources?
   - What is the overall impact that you wish to have on your audience?
   - How will your writing inform, influence, or change your audience?

3. Read the sources to get a general impression of the content; form, organization, and features; and rhetorical concerns.
   - Reading for information: What is the author's thesis or main point? What are other important points?
   - Reading for form, organization, and features: How does the author get his or her points across? What is the method of presentation?
   - What is the pattern of organization? Reading for rhetorical concerns: What is the author's purpose? How does the author intend to influence the audience? Who is the author, and what is his or her background? To whom is the piece addressed? In what type of publication is it published? What is the author's relationship to the audience?

4. Read the selections you are comparing for the purpose of determining how they are alike or different.
   - In what ways are the selections similar?
   - In what ways do the views in one selection differ from those expressed in the other selection?

5. Reread and elaborate.
   - Tap your memory, and make associations between your background knowledge and the ideas in the reading sources (see the strategies for elaboration of reading sources on pages 93–94).

- Identify points where one source author agrees or disagrees with the other author, says something relevant about the topic that the other author has neglected to say, qualifies ideas stated by the other author, extends a statement made by the other author.
- Validate one author's point with information provided by the other author.
- Subsume similarities and differences between the sources under subordinate categories.
- Create hierarchies of importance among ideas that are similar and those that are different.
- Make judgments about the relevance of one author's view in relation to the other author's.

6. Use webbing to link points of similarity and difference (see page 152).

7. Plan.
   - Review your elaborations.
   - Identify all those that deal with similarities and differences, and place them in categories.
   - Analyze the similarities and differences, asking yourself, "What do these similarities and differences demonstrate? What do they tell us about each of the sources?"
   - Form some kind of generalization based on the significance of the similarities and differences.
   - Formulate your thesis statement.
   - Return to the sources to verify your conclusions.
   - Select an organizational format: point-by-point or block arrangement.

Drafting

1. Write an opening paragraph in which you accomplish these goals:
   - Use an opening that will interest the reader.
   - Announce the topic and disclose a thesis or attitude toward it (the thesis may come later).
   - Indicate the source titles and authors, and provide some summary information about the sources.
   - Establish your voice.

2. Arrange your elaboration notes in paragraphs, and develop each paragraph to its fullest.

3. Compose a concluding paragraph in which you use one of these techniques:
   - Stress the significance of your thesis rather than simply repeating it. Encourage your readers to look beyond the thesis to an important future goal.
   - Predict consequences.

- Call your readers to action.
- Use any of the devices for paper openers (see page 109).

Revising

1. If possible, have a classmate or friend read over your first draft and answer the questions on pages 158–159. If no one is available, answer the questions yourself.
2. When you revise, keep the following concerns in mind:
   - Moving from writer-based to reader-based prose
   - Varying sentence length
   - Stressing verbs rather than nouns
   - Using words effectively
   - Detecting sexist language
   - Adding your own voice

Editing

1. When you are satisfied with your revision, read your paper aloud. Then reread it line by line and sentence by sentence. Check for correct usage, punctuation, spelling, mechanics, manuscript form, and typos.
2. If you are using a word processing program with a spell checker, run the checker on your essay.
3. If your editing skills are not strong, have a friend read over your work.

Exercise

Read the following essay by Joel Knight. Joel is responding to an assignment that asked him to compare and contrast the views of Laurel Richardson in *The Dynamics of Sex and Gender: A Sociological Perspective* and Eugene R. August in "Real Men Don't: Anti-Male Bias in English," both of which discuss the topic of sexist language. Break into small groups. Divide the questions on pages 158–159 among the groups. Each group should answer its set of questions and report its findings to the rest of the class.

Joel Knight

Professor Kennedy

English 131

12 July 1998

Bias in the English Language: No One Is Exempt

Are you aware of how much sexist language exists in

English? After reading Laurel Richardson's <u>The Dynamics of Sex</u>

<u>and Gender: A Sociological Perspective</u>, you will learn that

English contains a lot of anti-female bias. But this is only

half of the story. If you want to hear the whole story, you

have to read what Eugene August has to say about anti-male

bias in "Real Men Don't: Anti-Male Bias in English." Each

author claims that language is damaging to the members of his

or her own sex. Richardson does acknowledge that language is

negative toward men, but if you want to be aware of all the

forms of anti-male bias, you have to read August's essay.

Richardson makes a strong case that the language that has

negative effects on women has positive or neutral effects on

men. A major example is the use of the pronoun <u>he</u> and the noun

<u>man</u> to represent both sexes. Richardson cites research that

shows that on all occasions when people see or hear these

generic words they visualize men rather than women. This gives

men a feeling of dominance, power, and importance (20).

Richardson goes on to give many examples of words that define

women as "immature, incompetent, and incapable and males as

mature, complete, and competent" (21). She also shows that

"women are defined in terms of their sexual desirability (to men)" (22) and "in terms of their relations to men" (22), whereas "men are defined in terms of their sexual prowess [with women]" (22) and "in terms of their power in the occupational world" (22). In addition, Richardson points out that historically, words referring to women have acquired "obscene and/or debased connotations," but this has not happened to words referring to men.

Does the English language always treat men in a positive way? Richardson admits that even though language is usually more flattering to men than to women, there are times when it harms men. She points out that connotations of men as aggressive, active, and strong can put a strain on them. She also notes that the demands of language can make men "feel competent or anxious, valuable or worthless," depending on the particular context (22). Another problem, says Richardson, is that "rarely does our language legitimize carefreeness for males. Rather, they are expected, linguistically, to adapt to responsibilities of manhood" (21).

But there is much more anti-male bias in English than Richardson mentions in her article. In fact, in August's opinion, it is men who get the bad rap from language, not women. August gives a number of examples that show that the same language that glorifies women is derogatory toward men. He points out that the male is never thought of as the primary parent because language equates "parent" with "mother." Similarly, men are never thought of as victims of rape or abuse because language equates "victim" with "woman" (116).

3

4

August says that language also keeps men "within the confines of a socially prescribed gender role," whereas women are permitted a wide range of roles (117). Last, August discusses at length how crime and evil are usually associated with men, not with women (120-21).

One might argue that August is one-sided because he fails to show that women are harmed by language. When he mentions women, it is either in an indirect way or to show how much better off they are than men. For example, when he discusses words like <u>sissy</u>, he says, "Although the female is being slurred indirectly by these terms, a moment's reflection will show that the primary force of the insult is being directed toward the male, specifically the male who cannot differentiate himself from the feminine" (118). There is no denying that August is preoccupied with anti-male bias in language, but we can't fault him for that. People need to hear that language is offensive to men as well as women.

By itself, neither Richardson's essay or August's gives a complete picture of how language is biased against either sex. To be fully aware of how the English language disparages males as well as females, we need to read both. Once we realize that language can have negative effects on all of us, we can work together to make the necessary changes.

Knight 4

Works Cited

August, Eugene R. "Real Men Don't: Anti-Male Bias in English."
University of Dayton Review. winter/spring 1986-1987:
115-24.

Richardson, Laurel. The Dynamics of Sex and Gender: A
Sociological Perspective. 2nd ed. New York: Harper, 1981.

E x e r c i s e ●

Read Erika Perotte's essay, "Finding Meaning in Memoir," on pages 261–265. Write an essay comparing Erika's essay to the essay by Joel Knight.

● ● ● ● ● ● ● ● ● ● ● ● ● ● ●

5

COMPOSING OTHER TYPES OF MULTIPLE-SOURCE ESSAYS

As a college writer, you will often compose papers that draw on multiple reading sources. For example, you might write a paper based on several journal articles, a chapter from a book, and a piece from a newspaper. The task is complex because you have to note consistencies among the sources and then integrate these bits of relevant information with your own ideas. The amount of information you draw from the sources, as opposed to your personal store of knowledge, will depend on the topic and the assignment. In this chapter, we will show you how to write four types of papers that draw on multiple sources:

- A summary of multiple sources
- An objective synthesis
- An essay written in response to multiple sources
- A synthesis written for a specific purpose

SUMMARY OF MULTIPLE SOURCES

Summarizing involves focusing in on the key elements in the text and compressing other information, such as examples and details. In Chapter 2, we gave you strategies for summarizing sources (see page 46).

You probably won't use all seven strategies at one time. For most assignments, a subset of strategies will suffice.

To illustrate the process of composing a summary of multiple sources, we will examine student writer Jean Szary's summary of three articles on the topic of date rape. Jean was asked to summarize in two to three pages the views expressed by three authors: William Celis III in "Students Trying to Draw the Line between Sex and an Assault," Murray Rothbard in "Date Rape," and Neil Gilbert in "The Phantom Epidemic of Sexual Assault."

Jean's first challenge was to reduce about thirteen pages of source material to a two- to three-page summary. With this goal in mind, she read each article, underlining or highlighting only the most essential information. Then, using the summarizing strategies, she compressed the important information in each article into a single paragraph. Next, she stepped back to look at the larger picture and examine her rhetorical purpose. She asked herself two questions: What is each author's overall purpose? And do these purposes relate to each other in any significant way? Reviewing the articles, she concluded that Celis, writing for the *New York Times*, has a fairly objective purpose of providing his readers with

167

an overview of the issue of date rape on college campuses. Rothbard, however, is very opinionated, and his purpose is to criticize Celis and downplay the seriousness of the problem of date rape. Gilbert takes Rothbard's denunciation a step further and tries to convince his readers that feminists have concocted a false epidemic of sexual assault.

The information about the authors' purposes furnished Jean with a logical order for her summary and provided her with transitions for moving from one source to the next. As she wrote her draft, she made a special effort to attribute source ideas to the authors by occasionally mentioning their names. She also used transitional words and phrases and provided page references for direct quotations. Here is an annotated version of Jean's summary.

Szary 1

Jean Szary

Professor Smith

Academic Writing I

15 April 1991

Summary of Three Articles on Acquaintance Rape

Three articles that treat the controversial topic of acquaintance rape are "Students Trying to Draw Line between Sex and an Assault" by William Celis III, "Date Rape" by Murray Rothbard, and "The Phantom Epidemic of Sexual Assault" by Neil Gilbert. In a special report to the New York Times, William Celis III gives his readers a general overview of the issue of date rape on college campuses. He relates how women students have developed increased awareness but decreased tolerance of rape. The problem, says Celis, is one of perception. Both men and women students question, "When is sex considered sex, and when is it considered rape?" (A1). Because colleges have been reluctant to deal with acquaintance rape, there are now laws requiring them to report crimes on campus. Celis goes on to explain that women's attitudes toward forced sex have changed over the past twenty years and that women complain more about

---

Annotations (left margin):

Straight-forward title

Statement that frames the three summaries and gives titles and authors

Place of publication, audience, statement of author's purpose

Attribution

Parenthetical documentation

Attribution

Right margin: 1

Szary 2

Parenthetical documentation

men's sexual advances. A big part of the problem is that men "have been conditioned to pursue women for sex" (B8) and to believe that when a woman says "no," she really means "yes."

Attribution, transition

The issue here is miscommunication. Celis concludes that colleges have responded to the growing problem of date rape with education programs, discussion groups, and improved counseling.

Publication, author, audience, author's purpose
Attribution

Economist Murray Rothbard criticizes Celis in a brief but provocative article published in a conservative periodical, The National Review. Rothbard ridicules the problem of date

Attribution

rape. In his view, "There is no problem." He says that if either the man or the woman was unwilling to participate in

Attribution

sex, rape took place. Otherwise, there was no rape. Rothbard

Transition, attribution

suggests that feminists want a notarized consent form before sex. Finally, he comes up with a flip solution to the "problem": outlaw all sex.

Transition

Continuing in the same vein as Rothbard, Neil Gilbert

Author, purpose, publication, author's audience

tells readers of his article in The Public Interest that feminists have grossly exaggerated the problem of acquaintance rape and thus concocted a false epidemic. Gilbert compares

Attribution

studies that show high incidences of assault and rape with studies that have lower estimates and criticizes the

Connector

researchers' definitions of rape. He claims that these women researchers seek "to impose new norms governing

Documentation. Transition, attribution

intimacy between the sexes" (61). He also attacks educational programs on sexual assault and date rape, saying that feminists are trying to alter consciousness, not raise it.

2

3

Attribution,
transition

Documenta-
tion

Gilbert concludes that there are very few objections to the feminists because women in general agree "with their feelings of being 'screwed over' by men" (65).

Szary 4

Works Cited

Celis, William, III. "Students Trying to Draw the Line between Sex and an Assault." <u>New York Times</u> 2 Jan. 1991: A1,B8.

Gilbert, Neil. "The Phantom Epidemic of Sexual Assault." <u>Public Interest</u> Spring 1991: 54-65.

Rothbard, Murray. "Date Rape." <u>National Review</u> 25 Feb. 1991: 42.

When you are asked to write a summary of two or more reading sources, you will find it useful to use the following strategies.

STRATEGIES FOR WRITING A SUMMARY OF MULTIPLE SOURCES

- Read each source, annotating it to highlight the important ideas. (If you are writing a short summary, concern yourself with only the most essential information.)
- Reduce each source to its gist by combining important ideas in one or more summary paragraphs (use the summarizing strategies on page 50).
- After you have reduced each source, step back and determine how the authors' purposes relate to one another.
- Decide on your order of presentation.
- Begin with a statement that frames the summary and, if appropriate, gives the titles and authors of the sources.
- As you draft the summary, attribute source ideas to the author.
- Provide transitions in the appropriate places.

- Write a straightforward title.
- Check that you have documented direct quotations and provided a works cited page.

When you are satisfied with your draft, if it is all right with your teacher, give your summary to a classmate or friend and ask that person to use the following checklist to give you some feedback.

✓ CHECKLIST FOR REVISING A MULTIPLE-SOURCE SUMMARY

_____ Has the writer given the piece a straightforward title?

_____ Toward the beginning of the summary, has the writer provided a general statement that provides a framework for the piece?

_____ Has the writer mentioned titles and authors of the sources?

_____ Has the writer explained the author's purpose while summarizing each source?

_____ Has the writer attributed the material to the source author (for example, "Celis goes on to say . . .")?

_____ Has the writer provided appropriate transitions or connecting ideas when moving from one source to the next?

_____ Has the writer cited page numbers for direct quotations?

_____ Has the writer supplied a works cited page?

OBJECTIVE SYNTHESIS

An _objective synthesis_ is a piece of writing created by combining separate units or bits of information from two or more reading sources into a coherent whole. Before you can synthesize sources, you have to analyze them, breaking each one down into separate elements. The next step is to identify common elements and determine the relationships among them. The final step is to recombine the elements into a new composition.

Like a summary, an objective synthesis leaves little room for your own ideas. Your goal is simply to select material from various reading sources and integrate it into a new composition. Writers usually compose objective syntheses when they are engaged in report writing—for example, writing a nonjudgmental survey of sources that address a particular issue. The goal is to repackage information from sources for a new audience.

A psychology professor we know assigns students in his introductory course a series of "microthemes," which are brief overviews of topics of interest to them. Throughout the semester, each student is required to read up on topics and submit twenty-five of these one-page reports, some of which are to be read to the entire class. Let's examine Christopher Bruno's microtheme on the topic of phobias. Christopher synthesized information from four sources: a dictionary, two encyclopedias, and a psychology textbook.

pho•bi•a *n.* **1.** A persistent, abnormal, or illogical fear of a specific thing or situation. **2.** A strong fear, dislike, or aversion. —**phobic** *adj.*

   —**phobia** *suff.* An intense, abnormal, or illogical fear of a specified thing: *xenophobia.*

   —**phobic** *suff.* **1.** Having a fear or an aversion for: *xenophobic.* **2.** Lacking an affinity for: *lyophobic.*

(American Heritage Dictionary)

Phobia, irrational fear that tends to persist despite reassurance or contravening evidence. Psychoanalytic theory suggests that phobias such as fear of high places, closed spaces, infection, etc. are actually symbolic displacements of more basic but repressed fears and impulses.

(Random House Encyclopedia)

Phobic Neurotic Disorders. These neuroses are characterized by an abnormal fear of a specific object or type of situation. The patient may have one phobia or several, and the degree of disturbance varies considerably among the objects of the phobias. It is believed that in a phobic reaction anxiety originally attached to a specific idea, object, or situation is displaced to something symbolic of the idea, such as dirt, or particualar animals, places, or diseases. Phobias are frequent in children as well as adults. The main treatment is psychotherapy.

(Funk & Wagnalls New Encyclopedia)

Phobias

When a person's anxiety is focused irrationally on a particular object or situation, it is called a *phobia.* (The term comes from the Greek word for "fear.") Unlike those with generalized anxiety, people with phobias believe they know what triggers their feeling of dread. The case below is in many ways typical:

> The client was a 30-year old male who reported intense fear of crossing bridges and of heights. The fear had begun 3 years earlier when he was driving over a large suspension bridge while feeling anxious due to marital and career conflicts. Looking over the side he had experienced intense waves of fear. From that time onward his fear of bridges had become progressively more severe. At first, only bridges similar to the original were involved, but slowly the fear generalized to all bridges. Concurrently, he developed a fear of heights. Just before he came for treatment, he had been forced to dine atop a 52-story building. He had developed nausea and diarrhea and had been unable to eat. This had decided him to seek treatment. [Hurley, 1976, p. 295]

A phobia, then, can be extremely disruptive to a person's life. Ironically, the person may recognize that the fear is irrational, yet still be unable to dismiss it. Only avoidance of the feared object relieves the anxiety. Table 15.1 lists some of the phobias clinicians have encountered.

Table 15.1   Common Phobias

Phobia	Feared Object or Situation
Acrophobia	High places
Agoraphobia	Open places
Claustrophobia	Enclosed places
Ergasiophobia	Work
Gamophobia	Marriage
Haphephobia	Being touched
Hematophobia	Blood
Monophobia	Being alone
Ocholophobia	Crowds
Taphophobia	Being buried alive
Xenophobia	Strangers

Psychologists have proposed several theories to account for phobias. Freudians have argued that phobias develop as defense mechanisms against dangerous or unacceptable impulses. A man with a bridge phobia, for instance, may be defending against a suicidal urge to jump from a bridge. Learning theorists, in contrast, believe that phobias may result from classical conditioning. A child stung by a bee, for example, may thereafter fear bees because of their past association with pain. Firsthand contact with the feared object is not even needed for this type of classical conditioning to occur. A person may fear swimming in the ocean, for instance, after watching the movie *Jaws*. Here a previously neutral stimulus (ocean water) is repeatedly paired with a terrifying experience (watching people devoured by a shark) until eventually the water alone is enough to generate fear. Other phobias may be instilled through observational learning (Bootzin and Max, 1980). A girl who hears her mother express a terror of heights, for instance, may express the same fear later, even though heights have never been associated with any real danger to her. (Wortman, Loftus, and Marshall 438–39)

After reading the four sources, Christopher took each one apart in order to characterize the different bits of information that it contains. As he moved from one source to the next, he noted information that was repeated. Then he examined information that was not mentioned in the preceding source. For example, both the *American Heritage Dictionary* and the *Random House Encyclopedia* give definitions of **phobia,** but the encyclopedia also suggests a cause for the condition. The *Funk & Wagnalls New Encyclopedia* includes definition and cause and also describes the characteristics of patients suffering from phobias and comments on their treatment. The psychology text contributes information to the areas already mentioned and provides new information on various types of phobias.

To help in planning his synthesis, Christopher made up a chart to display the relationships among the sources (see Table 5-1).

TABLE 5-1 COMPARISON OF INFORMATION IN SOURCES

	American Heritage Dictionary	*Random House Encyclopedia*	*Funk & Wagnalls New Encyclopedia*	**Psychology Textbook**
Definitions	(1) Fear of a specific thing or situation. Fear is persistent, abnormal, and illogical. (2) Strong fear, dislike, aversion.	Irrational fear that persists despite reassurance or contravening evidence.	Type of neuroses; abnormal fear of a specific object or type of situation.	Anxiety focused irrationally on a particular object or situation. Origin is the Greek word for "fear."
Causes		Psychoanalytical theory suggests that phobias are actually symbolic displacements of more basic but repressed fears and impulses.	Belief that in a phobic reaction anxiety was originally attached to a specific idea, object, or situation, such as dirt or particular animals, places, or diseases.	*Freudians:* Phobias develop as defense mechanisms vs. unacceptable impulses. *Learning theorists:* Phobias result from classical conditioning. Child stung by bee may develop phobia toward bees. Firsthand contact with feared object not necessary. You could fear swimming in ocean after seeing *Jaws.* Phobias can also result from observational learning, e.g., girl fears heights because her mother has fear.

	American Heritage Dictionary	Random House Encyclopedia	Funk & Wagnalls New Encyclopedia	Psychology Textbook
Patients' characteristics			Patient may have one phobia or several. The degree of disturbance varies among the objects of the phobias. Phobias are frequent in children as well as adults.	People know what triggers their feelings of dread. They may recognize the fear as irrational but still be unable to dismiss it. Only avoidance of the feared object relieves anxiety.
Types				Table lists common types of phobias— claustrophobia, xenophobia, acrophobia, etc.
Treatment			Main one is psychotherapy.	
Examples				Story of the man who developed a phobia toward bridges.

After Christopher broke down the sources into parts, identified their common characteristics, and noted other elements, he rearranged these units and integrated them into a single, coherent synthesis. To illustrate, we have annotated the draft of his synthesis.

Christopher Bruno

Professor Mazza

Psychology 101

15 Sept 1999

Phobias Microtheme

Do you feel queasy in high places, uneasy in crowds, or ill at ease in the presence of strangers? If so, you may be acrophobic, claustrophobic, or xenophobic. A <u>phobia</u> (the term is derived from the Greek word for "fear") is a type of neurosis or anxiety. It is an abnormal fear of an object, or situation. The fear is illogical and irrational because it persists even when the patient is reassured or given contravening evidence. People with phobias may know what triggers their feeling of dread and may recognize the fear as irrational, but they are unable to dismiss it. The only way they can relieve their anxiety is to avoid the feared object or situation. Phobias are frequent in children as well as adults, and people can have one or several with varying degrees of disturbance. There are various theories about the causes of phobias. Psychoanalysts suggest that people with phobias have some basic but repressed fears and impulses, but they shift the fears to something symbolic of the idea, such as dirt or particular animals, places, or diseases. In other words, according to these Freudians, phobias develop as defense mechanisms against dangerous or unacceptable impulses. Learning theorists claim that phobias result from classical conditioning. A child stung by a bee, for instance, may develop a phobia toward bees. It isn't even necessary to have

Psychology
textbook

*Funk &
Wagnalls*

*Random
House*

Psychology
textbook

*Funk &
Wagnalls*

*Random
House* and
*Funk &
Wagnalls*

Psychology
textbook

Psychology
textbook

1

*Funk &
Wagnalls*

firsthand contact with the feared object. It would be possible

to develop a fear of swimming in the ocean after seeing Jaws.

Observational learning can also lead to phobias. A child might

be terrified of heights because she observed her mother's fear

of high places. A common treatment for phobias is

psychotherapy.

Christopher's synthesis is much shorter than the combined lengths of the original sources. He was able to compress the original into fewer words because he did not repeat ideas that recurred in two or more sources. To keep the synthesis to the required one- to two-page length, he also deleted details (the table of common phobias) and examples (the case of the man who was afraid of bridges). If his goal had been to create an even tighter synthesis, Christopher would have eliminated more information and included only the key ideas in each text.

The techniques Christopher used to write his microtheme are appropriate for objective synthesis papers of any length. To write an objective synthesis, use the following strategies.

STRATEGIES FOR WRITING AN OBJECTIVE SYNTHESIS OF MULTIPLE SOURCES

- Read all of the sources.
- Reread the first source, taking it apart and identifying the functions of the various units of information (saying, for example, "This is a definition," "These are reasons," "Here are some of the effects").
- As you move from one source to the next, identify common characteristics ("This source also gives a definition").
- After you have analyzed all the sources, study recurring themes and common characteristics, and organize them in new combinations.
- Decide on the order in which you will present your information.
- Begin with a lead and a straightforward statement of the topic.

E x e r c i s e ....

Use the following excerpts to compose an objective synthesis. Assume that your rhetorical goal is to inform your readers that language conveys a negative image of both men and women.

1. Discussion of words like *sissy* as insults have been often one-sided: most commentators are content to argue that the female, not the male, is being insulted by such usage. "The implicit sexism" in such terms, writes one

commentator, "disparages the woman, not the man" (Sorrels 87). Although the female is being slurred indirectly by these terms, a moment's reflection will show that the primary force of the insult is being directed against the male, specifically the male who cannot differentiate himself from the feminine. Ong argues in *Fighting for Life* that most societies place heavy pressure on males to differentiate themselves from females because the prevailing environment of human society is feminine (70–71). In English-speaking societies, terms like *sissy* and *weak sister,* which have been used by both females and males, are usually perceived not as insults to females but as ridicule of males who have allegedly failed to differentiate themselves from the feminine. (August 118)

2. Whether one looks at elite titles, occupational roles, kinship relationships, endearments, or age-sex categorical designations, the pattern is clear. Terms referring to females are pejorated—"become negative in the middle instances and abusive in the extremes" (Schulz, 1975:69). Such semantic derogation, however, is not evidenced for male referents. *Lord, baronet, father, brother, nephew, footman, bowman, boy, lad, fellow, gentleman, man, male,* and so on "have failed to undergo the derogation found in the history of their corre-sponding feminine designations" (67). Interestingly, the male word, rather than undergoing derogation, frequently is replaced by a female referent when the speaker wants to debase a male. A weak man, for example, is referred to as a *sissy* (diminutive of *sister*), and an army recruit during basic training is called a *pussy.* And when one is swearing at a male, he is referred to as a *bastard* or a *son-of-a-bitch*—both appellations that impugn the dignity of a man's mother. (Richardson 25-26)

. . . .

ESSAY WRITTEN IN RESPONSE TO MULTIPLE SOURCES

In Chapter 3, we discussed essays written in response to select ideas from a single reading source. In this chapter, we will discuss the multiple-source response essay. In this type of essay, you react to themes or commonalities that occur in two or more sources. To prepare for an essay of this type, you need to read the sources with a particular objective in mind: to establish bases for relating one source to another. Once you've identified relationships among the sources, you will proceed as you would for any response essay, summarizing the sources and elaborating by bringing your previous knowledge to bear on the texts. To a large extent, the summaries and elaborations will be governed by the controlling idea of your essay.

A response to multiple sources differs from a summary of sources or an objective synthesis because the writer has a more encompassing purpose. In addition to selecting and combining pieces of information from the various texts, the writer is also generating his or her own ideas and incorporating them into the essay. To illustrate how this is done, we have annotated an essay by student Matthew J. Williams. Matthew draws on "Music" by Allan Bloom and "Engaging Students in the Great Conversation" by Neil Postman. He was responding to the following assignment:

After reading Bloom and Postman, write an essay in which you agree or disagree with the position put forth by these professors. Consider your own experience with music and how it corresponds to or contradicts Bloom's and Postman's main points about the effects of popular music. Engage these men, and with your own powerful voice, converse with them.

Matthew J. Williams

Professor Kennedy

Composition 100

3 October 1996

Who Are They to Judge?

A Reaction to Two Pompous Academics

Title reflects writer's stand

Paper opener: quotation

Introduction of sources and authors

Shakespeare writes in <u>The Merchant of Venice,</u> "The man that hath no music in himself, / Nor is not mov'd with concoured of sweet sounds, / Is fit for treasons, stratagems and spoils." Upon concluding Allan Bloom's essay "Music" and Neil Postman's essay "Engaging Students in the Great Conversation," I sat in total disheartenment. Both Bloom and Postman seem to have forgotten what music is all about--the expression of one's soul. So I opened up my desk drawer, picked out a Bob Marley tape, and stuck it in my Walkman. I then had a mild epiphany. I realized that these gentlemen's opinions were not only narrow-minded but also downright erroneous. Both men take an annoyingly pompous position and a highly irritating I-am-better-than-thou attitude. I, for one, have a liking for a wide range of music, from Gregorian chant to common hip-hop. I get the feeling that Bloom and Postman

think that I should be canonized for liking the former and
sent to hell for liking the latter. I find a lot about Bloom
and Postman is wrong: their tone; their disapproval of the
media (particularly television) and the educational system;
their belief that the current generation no longer listens to
classical music and thereby lacks culture, and their
association of popular music with sex.

Tone shows what a person thinks of himself or herself.
Both Bloom and Postman take on an overly pompous elitist tone,
which tells me that neither man cares about being open-minded.
All they care about is their own opinions on music. I tend to
respect people more when they take a more reasonable, double-
sided approach. Bloom and Postman deride modern music without
offering positive remarks. Admittedly, Bloom makes one good
point, saying, "The music of the new votaries . . . knows
neither class nor nation" (132), a sentiment that is completely
true. But he fails to realize that his (and many others')
stuffy attitudes about classical music explain why modern rock
took such a strong hold.

Both Bloom and Postman want to blame the media and the
education system for the rise of popular music. They both
believe that the television industry promotes only contemporary
music and our education system fails to provide culture for
us. For instance, Postman, speaking of classical composers,
states, "Television tries to mute their voices and render their
standards invisible" (2). But what would Christmas be without
the National Broadcasting System's airing of "The Nutcracker
Suite"? I have also seen such highly revered movies as

Margin notes:

Thesis

First point
to which
writer is
reacting

Second
point to
which
writer is
reacting

2

3

Williams 3

<u>Amadeus,</u> depicting Mozart's life, on national television. Yet
Bloom and Postman insinuate that all television is bad, and
channels such as MTV are Lucifer himself. They are so
opinionated that they fail to mention PBS, A&E, or the
Discovery Channel. I think that both men were so busy writing
their essays that they didn't carefully examine television
programming.

Bloom and Postman claim that the education system fails
to teach students "the products of classical art form" (Postman
3). Postman says that schools have only one type of concert:
rock concerts. Apparently neither man has been to a high
school chorus or band concert lately. Perhaps my upstate New
York high school was different from its counterparts across the
nation in teaching students the fine arts, though I doubt it.
In chorus, with approximately 150 members out of 400 high
school students, we sang pieces ranging from fugues of the
Baroque period to a medley of Simon and Garfunkel's greatest
hits. In band we played Handel's "Water Music" and a medley of
Andrew Lloyd Webber's compositions from <u>Phantom of the Opera.</u> A
minimum of two years of the fine arts, with a passing grade,
was required for graduation. We were exposed to a rich music
history but also taught that popular contemporary music is
important too.

Postman's tone makes me believe that he would agree with
Bloom's statement that "classical music is dead among the
young" (132) Both authors think that only a small number, if
any, young people in this generation listen to classical music.
Wrong. I was walking down the hall to a friend's room the

4

5

Third point
to which
writer is
reacting

Williams 4

other day when I heard a Mozart symphony blaring behind his
door. I was a bit surprised, but I didn't have a heart attack.
I enjoy listening to and performing classical music, as well
as popular music, and the majority of my friends share this
attitude. Obviously, Bloom and Postman have never listened to
musical groups such as Enigma, whose use of Gregorian chant in
their upbeat music got me hooked on this medieval art form.

6

Bloom and Postman also complain that our society no
longer provides us with the culture we need. Their assumptions
make young readers like me feel like commoners, who are not
classy enough to fit the classical mold. Bloom and Postman
seem to be saying that we are reverting to barbarism, like the
children in <u>Lord of the Flies,</u> and that the world is going to
hell because we no longer diligently listen to Mozart or Bach.
They are overlooking the fact that society did not always
embrace the classical music they hold so dear.

7

Finally there is Postman's belief that rock music is just
setting the stage for sex and Bloom's statement that "young
Fourth point to which writer is reacting
people know that rock has the beat of sexual intercourse"
(136). When I listen to rock music, I do not have wet dreams.
I listen to music for the musicalness and meaning of the
particular artist's soul, not because it is a turn-on. Was
Fred Small talking about sex when he wrote "The Peace Dragon"?

8

Postman and Bloom don't like popular music, so they find
fault in it. Their numerous personal opinions fail to convince
me of their one-sided view that pop and rock music is bad. I
Conclusion
also get the feeling that neither man actually took the time
to examine rock music. It contains the same elements of

Williams 5

meaning as classical music, despite the different way it is

performed. Perhaps in two or three centuries, the music of

today will be played on public radio stations across the

world, as fine pieces of work. Won't that make Postman and

Bloom blush.

Williams 6

Works Cited

Bloom, Allan. "Music." Speculations: Readings in Culture,

Identity, and Values. Ed. Charles Schuster and William

Van Pelt. Englewood Cliffs: Prentice, 1993. 131-43.

Postman, Neil. "Engaging Students in the Great Conversation."

Reading, Writing, and Thinking. Ed. Isabelle Bradley. New

York: Houghton, 1978. 1-5.

A response essay allows the writer to draw on personal knowledge and express personal views. In this sense, Matthew's essay is different from the summary of multiple sources on pages 168–170. The summary is entirely dependent on the sources, whereas the response essay includes the writer's own ideas about the topic. Matthew views popular music quite differently from Bloom and Postman and takes offense at their tone and the number of the claims they make in their articles: their disapproval of television and the educational system, their assertion that young people do not listen to classical music and thereby lack culture, and their association of popular music with sex.

Matthew opens his essay with a quotation from *The Merchant of Venice*, a lead that is sure to engage his readers. He then introduces the authors and sources and expresses his reaction. Toward the end of the introductory paragraph, he states his thesis. Next, he devotes each of the body paragraphs to one of the points to which he is reacting: paragraph 2 to Bloom and Postman's tone, paragraph 3 to their condemnation of television and schools, paragraph 4 to their claim that young people do not listen to classical music, and paragraph 5 to their association of popular music with sex. Matthew concludes his essay with an interesting speculation.

To write a straightforward essay in response to multiple sources, use the following strategies.

STRATEGIES FOR WRITING A RESPONSE TO MULTIPLE SOURCES

- Read through all the sources to get a general impression of the content.
- Reread each source, looking for themes or characteristics it shares with the other sources.
- Once you have discovered some commonalities among the sources, express the relationships in a general statement.
- Generate your own reactions (use the strategies for elaborating on texts on pages 93–94).
- Zero in on a single controlling idea or thesis that will govern your essay.
- Study the controlling idea, the sources, and your elaborations, and decide how you will organize your essay: summary followed by response or a pattern of alternating summary and response (for a review of these patterns, see pages 103–104).
- Draft the essay, drawing from your knowledge of the basic features of writing: titles, introductions, sentences, paragraphs, transitions, and so on (see pages 107–111).

When you have completed your essay, if your teacher agrees, ask a classmate or friend to read it over and give you some suggestions for revision. Your reviewer will find the following checklist helpful.

✓ CHECKLIST FOR REVISING A MULTIPLE-SOURCE RESPONSE ESSAY

_____ Does the writer begin with a title that reflects an overall reaction or stand?

_____ Does the essay open with a lead that will interest the reader?

_____ Does the writer provide the reader with some background information on the topic?

_____ Is there a controlling idea statement, thesis, or mention of the themes or ideas the sources have in common?

_____ Does the writer identify the authors and titles of the sources?

_____ Does the writer provide sufficient summary information about each source treated in the paper?

_____ When moving from one source to the next, does the writer provide transitions or connecting ideas that indicate the relationships between the sources?

_____ Does the writer provide an appropriate amount of response?

_____ Does the conclusion do more than simply summarize the main points of the paper?

_____ Does the writer include parenthetical documentation where it is necessary?

_____ Is there a works cited page?

WRITING A SYNTHESIS FOR A SPECIFIC PURPOSE

A synthesis for a specific rhetorical purpose achieves a genuine blend of two sets of ideas: information from various reading sources and your own stored knowledge about the topic. Your aim is to draw from different sources the material you need to support *your own* thesis or views. In this type of essay, your aim is not simply to communicate information in the sources, as you would in a summary or an objective synthesis. Nor is it simply to present your general impression of or reaction to the sources. Your goal is to select from the sources information that you can use to develop and support your own thesis.

We will use our student, Jennafer Ross, as an illustration. Jennafer received an assignment that required her to write about the problem of date rape by drawing on three or more sources. As you read Jennafer's essay, observe how she uses the readings. Instead of devoting separate paragraphs to each source, she organizes the paragraphs around her own ideas and draws from the sources only the pieces of information that support the point she is trying to make. In each paragraph, she has a specific purpose, and she draws on the sources only insofar as they enable her to fulfill it.

Ross 1

Jennafer Ross

Academic Writing I

Professor Smith

1 May 1997

Coming to Terms with a Serious Problem

"You're a VIRGIN?" he scoffs, unbelieving. "Man, you're telling me you're nineteen years old and you're still a virgin. What's wrong with you? What are you gay or something?" he asks half-jokingly, but half-seriously. He challenges, "Boy, you gotta get laid." [1]

"What? You're kidding me! She slept with him already?" she exclaims. "I don't believe it," she adds scornfully. "I didn't think she was like that. What a slut." [2]

Surprised by these reactions? Well, these statements were taken from actual conversations between college students. It seems that being a man means that you should have had or should be having sex, while being a woman means you should cross your legs and say "no." Men and women grow up with distorted images of sex and their own sexual roles. They learn [3] that men are supposed to be aggressive; that women are to be passive (Gibbs 54); that when a woman says "no" she really means "yes"; and that a man is entitled to sex if he spends money on a woman. These expectations, although unrealistic, are reflected in our attitudes, our language, and our actions. They reflect a society that for years has overlooked sex crimes, saying, "Boys will be boys" (Jacoby 22), and only recently acknowledged that date rape is a ruthless crime where a victim is sexually assaulted by a familiar person, an acquaintance, or even a friend. Why has it taken us so long to come to terms with date rape?

Many times men and women have very different ideas of what constitutes rape. According to Ellen Goodman, both the man and the woman involved in a case of date rape may easily pass lie detector tests and make convincing witnesses because in reality both believe they are telling the truth. Nancy Gibbs notes:

> Women charge that date rape is the hidden crime: men complain it is hard to prevent a crime they can't define. Women say it isn't taken seriously: men say it is a concept invented by women who like to tease but not take the consequences. Women say the date-rape debate is the first time the nation has talked frankly about sex: men say it is women's unconscious reaction to the excess of the sexual revolution. (48)

And what happens when alcohol is involved in a date rape? One male college student remarked, "Hey, a drunk girl is fair game" (Keegan 92). Others warned a female friend, "Linda, don't

Points that the writer wants to get across to her readers

Paragraph organized around conflicting attitudes

4

get so drunk. . . . People may want to take advantage of you"
(93). In our society, a drunk woman is expected to be
responsible for her actions, while a man who is drunk is not
(Freeman 97). This double standard brings Dean Kilpatrick,
director of the Crime Victim Research and Treatment Center of
the Medical University of South Carolina, to ask, "Why does a
woman's having a drink give a man the right to rape her?"
(Gibbs 50). These conflicting attitudes between men and women
are a product of much social conditioning. This conflict may
result in restricted communication, confusion, and very
different expectations between the sexes.

Paragraph
organized
around the
role of
language

     The notion that men have power over women is reflected in
and reinforced by the verbal language and body language we use
every day. When a couple is married, the woman takes the man's
name, indicating that she now belongs to him (Henley, Hamilton,
and Thorne 170). Inanimate objects that are owned by men often
take on female representation. Ships and boats are almost
always named after women, and "Fill 'er up" means put some gas
in the car (170). Body language also shows that men are in
control. Just as primates express dominance with touching, men
often use this technique with the opposite sex (181). These
instances of language use enforce men's power over women.
According to psychologist Gina Rayfield, since men hold the
power in our country, they are conditioned to view women as
inferior (Gibbs 3). Because of these perceptions, many men
can't take "no" for an answer (Jacoby 22). They may feel that
since they have power, they have the right to decide when to
have sex with women. Jacoby argues that this does not justify

5

date rape. Even the most inexperienced man can tell the
difference between a lackadaisical "no, we shouldn't" and
screams and tears--the difference between reluctance and rape
(24). If this is so, then why do some men persist?

Paragraph
organized
around
historical
perspective
and its
implications

6

One reason is that throughout history, men have taken
advantage of women without much consequence. Many people still
believe the myth that women actually have a desire to be
overpowered. This stereotype of women may influence the
perceptions of men who commit date rape. According to Gibbs,
in early civilizations, raping a virgin was the only sex crime
punishable by law. It was a serious offense only because a
virgin was monetarily valuable; the assailant was required to
reimburse the woman's father. If a married woman was raped,
she was treated as an adulteress and drowned or stoned to
death (51). Goodman remarks that our culture is tied up in the
"<u>Gone with the Wind</u> fantasy" where Scarlett O'Hara is forced
into bed, kicking and fighting, yet wakes up smiling and
laughing. Even worse is the Gothic romance novel, which almost
always depicts a woman struggling fervently against a powerful
man, only to succumb to his passionate advances. Why should we
be surprised that men do not believe their dates' protests
when they are constantly receiving messages from society that
women want to be overpowered and their struggling is only a
form of seduction (Gibbs 54)? These messages also affect
children. In a recent survey of eleven- to fourteen-year-olds,
25% of the boys and about 17% of the girls thought it was OK
for a man to make a woman kiss him or have sex with him if he
had spent money on her. Fully 33% of the children said it

would be all right for a man to rape a woman who has had a prior sexual encounter (Gibbs 54). Obviously, these children are getting the wrong message. What will happen if they carry these ideas through adolescence and adulthood? Will the boys become rapists? Will the girls be easy targets? Will these young people know the difference between sex and rape?

Paragraph discussing legal implications

Perhaps one of the reasons date rape has not been taken seriously is that many date rape cases do not go to trial. If a rapist is convicted, the sentence is usually light. Cornell professor Andrea Parrot notes that in the past, women didn't report a rape because they thought they would make themselves vulnerable to all types of vicious slander (Yaukey 3A). This is still true today. Parrot points out that because taking a rape case through the college system and then to the governmental judicial system is such a long, drawn-out, and painful process, very few women go through the trouble; therefore, very few offenders are convicted (3A). Patricia Freeman lists the sentences of various convicted rapists in her People's Weekly article about date rape on college campuses. One man was sentenced under a lenient law for youths. Instead of rape, he was charged with "first-degree criminal conduct," given three years' probation, and fined $975 in court fees and $200 for compensation to the victim. He was told that if he obeyed, the incident would be erased from his record (102). Another man accused of date rape pleaded guilty to "second-degree sexual assault" and served only twenty days in jail and two years' probation (96). On a more encouraging note, a man involved in a group rape where the woman was highly intoxi-

7

cated pleaded guilty to "felony sexual battery involving
multiple perpetrators" and received 364 days in jail, a harsh
sentence for a date rape case (99). Lieutenant Jack Handly of
Florida State University was pleased. "Years ago, possibly
months ago, the opinion would have been that she drank of her
own accord and was responsible for what happened," he said
(100). Handly went on to note that perhaps now people will
realize the woman was really raped (100). Administrators at
Cornell University report that cases involving rape or sexual
harassment are becoming more numerous. They hope it is because
women have enough confidence in the justice system to step
forward and admit that they have been victimized; they hope to
see more rape cases brought to trial and more offenders
prosecuted (Yaukey 3A). Perhaps if more criminals are reported
and convicted, people, especially men, will begin taking date
rape more seriously.

Paragraph summing up Jennafer's points

It's OK for a man to be a virgin at nineteen, at twenty,   **8**
at forty, at a hundred. It's OK for a woman to sleep with a
man, if it's what they both want. It's not OK for a man to
persuade, manipulate, or force a woman to have sex with him;
it's rape. What causes a man to rape a woman? Many factors are
involved. Men and women often have very different ideas of
what differentiates rape and sex. Because men usually have the
power in our society, they may expect that the same is true in
the bedroom and what they say goes. Our society gives out
messages that women want to be overpowered and that a woman's
reluctance is a form of seduction. Last, men who are convicted
of date rape are usually slapped on the hand and given light

Ross 7

sentences, since for years our society has reasoned that "boys will be boys." This situation has to change if we are to see women get the respect they deserve. Says Corbin Bernsen from the television show <u>L.A. Law</u>, "How we treat each other is the core of all issues, and the relationship between man and woman is the most basic of human relationships. If we don't treat it with respect, I don't think we can solve anything else" (Freeman 99).

Ross 8

Works Cited

Freeman, Patricia. "Silent No More." <u>People's Weekly</u> 17
    Dec.1990: 94-104.

Gibbs, Nancy. "When Is It Rape?" <u>Time</u> 3 June 1991: 48-55.

Goodman, Ellen. "Date Rape: A Gray Area in Assault." <u>Ithaca
    Journal</u> 13 May 1991: 10A.

Henley, Nancy, Mykol Hamilton, and Barrie Thorne. "Womanspeak
    and Manspeak: Sex Differences and Sexism in Communication,
    Verbal and Nonverbal." <u>Beyond Sex Roles</u>. 2nd ed. Alice G.
    Sargent. St Paul: West, 1985: 168-85.

Jacoby, Susan. "Common Decency." <u>New York Times Magazine</u> 19 May
    1991: 221-24.

Keegan, Paul. "Dangerous Parties." <u>New England Monthly</u> Feb.
    1988: 52-57.

Richardson, Laurel. <u>The Dynamics of Sex and Gender: A
    Sociological Perspective</u> 2nd ed. New York: Harper, 1981.

Yaukey, John. "Campus Weak on Rape, Prof Says." <u>Ithaca Journal</u>
    23 May 1991: 3A-4A.

We annotated portions of Jennafer's paper to show you how she integrated her own ideas with paraphrases, quotations, and summaries of the various sources. Notice that she employs the sources to develop her own ideas. The essay is driven by her ideas, not the ideas presented in the sources.

Exercise . . . .

Compare Jennafer's essay to Matthew Williams' essay, a typical response essay in which the writer's primary purpose is to react to ideas presented in the sources.

. . . .

If you receive a loosely defined assignment like "Write about the problem of rape in an essay drawing on three or more outside sources," you will have to read the sources to obtain background information on the topic and identify its dimensions. You will have two goals for the initial reading: to bring your own ideas to bear on the topic by elaborating on and reacting to the material and to identify common elements in the sources.

To achieve the latter goal, read each source searching for the commonalities it shares with the other sources. As you take up each source, ask yourself the following questions.

QUESTIONS FOR IDENTIFYING RELATIONSHIPS AMONG SOURCES

- Does the source give background information or additional information about points that are presented in other sources?
- Does it provide additional details about points made in other sources?
- Does it provide evidence for points made by another author?
- Are there places where this author contradicts or disagrees with the other authors you have read?
- Are there places where the author supports or agrees with other authors?
- Are there cause-and-effect relationships between this source and the other sources?
- Are there time relationships among the sources?
- Does this source contain elements that can be compared or contrasted with those in other sources?
- Are there other common threads running through this source and the other sources?
- Do the authors of the sources use similar key words or phrases?
- Are there any other ways you can categorize the ideas in the sources?

After you have elaborated on the sources and discovered their common elements, determine the points you wish to get across to your readers. Looking back at Jennafer's introductory paragraph, we see that her goal is to explain why people have only recently admitted that date rape is a serious problem. Jennafer accomplishes this goal by making us aware of the conditions that lead to date rape and explaining why we have not taken this crime seriously in the past. She describes men's and women's conflicting attitudes toward rape, the role language plays in empowering men to intimidate women, and historical, cultural, and legal views with regard to rape.

The next step is to locate source information that you can use to develop each of the points you will make in your essay. This will require you to go back to the sources. Reread them, looking for bits of information that relate to your points. Mark this content in the text, or copy it into your notebook. When you have obtained a sufficient amount of relevant information, you can begin to draft your essay, but first decide whether you will paraphrase, quote, or summarize the supporting information. Here is a recap of the entire process.

STRATEGIES FOR WRITING A SYNTHESIS FOR A SPECIFIC PURPOSE

- Read all the sources to get a general impression of the content.
- Reread each source, elaborating on it by bringing your previous knowledge to bear on the text.
- Determine the elements each source has in common with the other sources by asking the questions for identifying relationships among sources (page 192).
- Decide what points of your own you want to get across to your readers.
- Locate in the sources information that you can use to develop each of your points.
- Draft your essay by quoting, paraphrasing, or summarizing relevant supporting information from the sources and by drawing on your knowledge of the basic features of writing: titles, introductions, sentences, paragraphs, transitions, and so on (see pages 107–111).

When you are satisfied with the draft of your essay, if it is all right with your teacher, ask a classmate or friend to give you suggestions for revision by using the following checklist.

✓ CHECKLIST FOR REVISING A SYNTHESIS ESSAY WRITTEN FOR A SPECIFIC PURPOSE

_____ Does the title give you some indication of the writer's attitude toward the topic?

_____ Is there an interesting lead that attracts the reader's attention?

_____ Does the writer give you sufficient background information on the topic?

_____ Does the writer make his or her overall purpose clear to the reader?

_____ Can you identify the writer's thesis or expression of point of view?

_____ As you read each paragraph, are you aware of the purpose that the writer is trying to accomplish?

_____ In each paragraph, does the writer provide sufficient support from the sources?

_____ Does the writer include enough of his or her own commentary in each of the paragraphs?

_____ Does the conclusion do more than simply summarize the main points of the paper?

_____ Does the writer include parenthetical documentation where it is necessary?

_____ Is there a works cited page?

E x e r c i s e . . . .

This assignment asks you to read another synthesis essay written by a student—Christine Widdall's essay "Nature or Nurture?"—and compare it to Jennafer Ross's essay "Coming to Terms with a Serious Problem." Comment on each writer's lead, rhetorical purpose, thesis, use of source information to develop each of her points, and inclusion of paraphrases, summaries, quotations, and conclusion.

. . . .

Christine Widdall

Professor Cannon

Composition 101

27 April 1999

Nature or Nurture?

It was the summer of 1994, and the bleachers were filled
at the Syracuse College Natatorium. Spectators were here to
watch two scholastic water polo teams compete for a qualifying
spot in the Empire State Games finals. Water polo is
considered a tough, competitive sport, played by skilled
swimmers, combining the skills used in soccer, basketball, and
football. Water polo players are never allowed to touch the
bottom, must elevate their bodies hip high when guarding or
throwing, swim several cumulative miles a game, be constantly
aggressive, and at times play for twenty minutes nonstop. As
"The Star-Spangled Banner" finished, the crowd cheered with
anticipation, and the athletes readied themselves for a judges'
inspection. In water polo, fingernails and toenails must be
checked so that players don't scratch their opponents,
accidentally or intentionally. Tonight's inspection lineup
would be different from other Empire State water polo games
because on the Central team would be a teammate who painted
"Go for Gold" on her fingernails. Valerie Widdall would be the
first female athlete to play on the Central Water Polo Squad
and one of only two or three females who have ever
accomplished this feat statewide. After landing a berth, she
told reporters, "I love rough sports. . . . For girls who like
rough stuff I recommend it. The only problem is, I have to cut

1

my nails, and I love my nails" (Grotke). To compensate for her
loss, she painted her fingernails to signify her team's goal,
a gold medal.

Females trying to be part of a man's world is not a new
concept, but the equality of women in sports has not always
been recognized. Women have been accepted as better nurturers
and housekeepers. They are considered fragile and meek, the
gender to be cared for. But there in the middle of an Empire
State water polo match was a fourteen-year-old female who
signified neither fragility nor meekness. She even asked her
coach if she could be placed, "'in the hole,' which is where
the biggest and strongest players plant themselves near the
net" (Kirst). What brought Valerie to this point in her life?
Some would say she was born with hormones different from most
females'. But could it be that she was nurtured in a way that
encouraged her to strive for success in whatever direction she
took in life? Did her caregivers teach her that cultural
socialism should not dictate her achievements in life, but
instead she should control her own destiny?

Researchers for centuries have wondered what controls the
development of a person's cultural character. In the early
1900s, anthropologists like Franz Boas, while studying cultural
diversity, began to recognize that "specific forms of our
actions are culturally determined" (138). My opinion is that
for centuries, female culture has been biologically determined.
I mean that because females menstruate, we are predisposed to
cultural dictation. I am not the only one who believes in this
theory.

Widdall 3

Mary Pipher, a psychologist, counselor, and author of the book, <u>Reviving Ophelia</u>, describes early adolescence as a time when something dramatic happens to girls, "a time when they lose their assertiveness, [and] energetic and 'tomboyish' personalities" (19). She reinforces her theory by reminding her readers that "writers such as Sylvia Plath, Margaret Atwood, and Olive Shreiner have described the wreckage. Diderot, in his writing to young friend Sophie Volland, described his observation harshly: 'You all die at 15.'" (19). Pipher's book is named after the story of Ophelia, from Shakespeare's <u>Hamlet</u>, which she believes reflects on the destructive forces that affect young women (20).

Generally speaking, boys and girls seem to be equal until the onset of puberty or adolescence. Society creates differences at birth by dressing girls in pink and boys in blue. But if we take away the color-coding and gender-acting bias, we could, in theory, have generic children. When children's biological clocks turn them into maturing adults, cultural traditions begin to change them. When caregivers fit children into a mold created by cultural traditions, the children are forced to become creatures created by societal norms. Girls become female clones, women with no individuality and emotionally fearful of never being the perfect female.

I agree with Mary Pipher that American culture has "smacked girls in the head" during early adolescence with girl-hurting "isms," such as sexism, capitalism, and looksism (23). The problem, in my opinion, seems to be that older women are afraid to break the cultural molds and teach their daughters to be who they really want to be. My daughter was lucky because I was lucky. Our family traditions overruled society's traditions. We come from a long line of farmers, and although women did have a housewife role, they were also expected to throw the hay and milk the cows. Even though the farm life stopped, our family's cultural beliefs that women are strong, healthy people did not stop.

The women in my family played football and wore silk. We bore the children and put shingles on the roof. We could put on pants to go hunting and put on a dress to "strut our stuff." We had some cultural dictation, but generally speaking, we were allowed to be who we wanted to be. Biologically, I am a woman, but I am also a person whose gender should not always dictate how my needs and desires are fulfilled. There is no doubt in my mind that I am an androgynous being. Research has shown that since androgynous adults are free to act feminine or masculine, they are the most well-adjusted people (Gurian 18). I believe this holds true for men also.

7

Michael Gurian, who has spent years observing and researching the male culture, believes that "male culture never changes significantly because it is ruled by male biology" (27). Biology is what we are born with, and yes, much of what we will become will be ruled by hormones. Women will be able to give birth because they have uteruses and eggs. Men will be able to impregnate women because they have sperm. But do these facts direct how we should act or who we should become? Men, like women, should be able to choose. If they enjoy staying home and taking care of the children while their wives go

8

out to work, let them. Men are still men even if they enjoy
wearing aprons, puttering in the kitchen, and shopping for
groceries. I believe men should have the same rights as women
and should be allowed to live an androgynous lifestyle too.

Yes, it was my daughter on that male water polo squad,
and when my son asked if he could go out for field hockey
(which is a female sport in America), I said, "Go for it." I
have raised four sons and two daughters, and I feel that I
have given to each of them a sense of free will. I want them
to strive for personal achievement, not social achievement.
This way of thinking didn't happen overnight. It was passed on
little by little from my grandmother to her daughter to me,
and slowly each generation's freedoms increased.

As Valerie played in the pool below, her great-
grandmother watched from the stands and after the game told a
reporter, "I have to laugh at the way things have changed.
When I was a child in the Great Depression, little boys played
ball. Little girls were supposed to think about getting
married. And here I sit watching my great-granddaughter do just
fine on an all-boys team--while her dad has stayed home to
watch the three youngest children" (Kirst). Times have changed,
and, more important, cultural traditions are beginning to
change. As Sean Kirst wrote at the end of his interview with
Valerie's family, "Girls playing ball? Dads watching kids? In
the space of a half-century, the world became a different
place."

We are undoubtedly born biologically predisposed, but we
don't have to become cultural clones. I believe that cultural

traditions are changing, and as that happens, people will be able to settle down and become who they want to be. I am a woman because I was born that gender, but I am happiest when I'm allowed to be human. This is what I wanted my children to learn and understand. I believe I gave this wisdom to them, and I can already see that they are passing it on to their children. My daughter did not have an unusual set of hormones. She had caregivers who believed she should become who she wanted to be and allowed her to strive toward that goal, even if it meant swimming with the big boys.

Works Cited

Boas, Franz. "Stability of Culture." <u>Anthropology and Modern Life.</u> 1928. New York: Norton, 1962. 132-67.

Grotke, Ron. "Big Splash for Whitney Point Girl." <u>Press and Sun Bulletin</u> 2 Aug. 1994: C5.

Gurian, Michael. <u>The Wonder of Boys</u>. New York: Penguin, 1997.

Kirst, Sean. "Sparkplug in the Water." <u>Post Standard</u> 6 Aug. 1994: A1.

Pipher, Mary. <u>Reviving Ophelia</u>. New York: Ballantine, 1994.

6

DRAWING ON SOURCES FOR AN ARGUMENT ESSAY

Think about the last time you had an argument.

With whom were you arguing?

What was the quarrel about?

What was your position?

What was the other person's point of view?

Did you come to any type of resolution?

Take a few minutes to answer these questions in your notebook or journal. After you have finished, compare your experiences with those of your classmates. You will discover one essential similarity: all the arguments involved a disagreement, a division of opinion, or a dispute.

When academic writers "argue," they never pick a fight or hurl accusations at each other. "To argue" in academic writing means to sort out, investigate, and express an attitude or opinion on a certain topic. In this broad sense, every college paper that expresses a thesis is an argument because the writer's goal is to get the reader to accept his or her perspective, position, or point of view. Even if you are summarizing material or presenting an objective synthesis or comparison and contrast, you are hoping that your reader will accept *your* version of the given information. In most college papers, you will be attempting to influence your reader in a more direct way. Take the three types of academic writing we have discussed in this book: the response essay, in which you explain how you agree or disagree with an author (Chapter 3); the comparison essay, in which you show the similarities or differences between two sets of views (Chapter 4); and the synthesis essay, in which you draw on different source materials to support your thesis (Chapter 5). Each essay entails an argument of some sort because you are attempting to demonstrate or prove the validity of your view. Writers also use the word *argument* in a more specialized sense, which is in keeping with historical rhetorical tradition.

In Chapter 1, we mentioned that *rhetoric* has a number of different connotations. In common parlance, it often means pretentious, empty, or inflated language. In this book, we have defined *rhetoric* broadly as a writer's use of language to achieve an intended effect on an audience. In this chapter, we focus on a particular intended effect: to *persuade* or *convince* your readers of your position. Many of the principles and strategies we discuss are the same ones that ancient rhetoricians used to argue cases, resolve conflicts, and move people to action.

If you were a student living in ancient Greece more than two thousand years ago, instead of taking general education courses, electives, and courses in your major, you would have devoted all your time to rhetoric, a subject that would have prepared you to present eloquent, persuasive arguments. Unlike the academic subjects with which you are familiar, rhetoric is not a content area that deals with a defined body of knowledge. It is a discipline that studies how people consciously and intentionally use written and oral verbal expression to affect an audience. Today, rhetoric examines a wide range of objectives—to inform, motivate, entertain, persuade—but in ancient times, its focus was the strategies and resources needed to convince an audience.

In ancient Greece, knowledge of rhetoric was especially valuable for a young man entering the Greek political assembly, where, because there were no lawyers, each man had to present his own case (women did not participate in the political process, nor did they attend school). A knowledge of rhetoric also enabled young men to become advocates for others, judicial orators, or professional speech writers. Skill in this type of persuasive argument is not as crucial today as it was two millennia ago; nonetheless, the ability to present a clear, logical, compelling defense of your position is important for most college courses.

The difference between written argument in the broad sense of getting your reader to see your perspective, position, or point of view and argument in the narrower sense of persuading your readers that your position is better than another position is illustrated in the following pair of thesis statements. The writers' topic is the difficulty Asian American students encounter when they try to get parental support for participation in sports.

Thesis A: Argument in the Broad Sense

Asian American parents are much more supportive of their children's academic pursuits than of their participation in high school sports programs.

Thesis B: Argument in the Specialized Sense

It is not insensitivity, lack of interest, or ignorance of American sports that make Asian American parents much more supportive of their children's academic pursuits than of their participation in high school sports programs; it is the parents' value orientation and cultural conditioning.

Writer A's purpose is to make her readers aware of the problem, whereas Writer B's objective is to persuade her readers that certain explanations of the parents' attitudes carry more weight than others. Writer B's thesis has more of an argumentative edge. She makes a claim. She asserts that two factors account for the parents' reluctance to support sports: their value orientation and their cultural conditioning. She is aware that some people have alternative explanations, namely, that the Asian American parents are lacking sensitivity, interest, and knowledge. She acknowledges these opposing views in her thesis when she says, "It is not insensitivity, lack of interest, or ignorance of American sports . . ." Later, in the body of her essay, she will persuade her readers that her explanations—that the parents' value orientation and cultural conditioning account for their lack of support—are more convincing than other interpretations of the problem.

Writer A has no opposition to worry about. Her objective is to inform her readers about a particular phenomenon and offer explanations for it, not to persuade them that one set of explanations is superior to another. Writer A's thesis is not necessarily arguable. She will develop it by offering reasons why the parents encourage their children to pursue academics but not sports; she will not argue that some reasons are more valid than others. For Writer B, the topic—that Asian American parents support their children's academic pursuits rather than their participation in sports—has become an arguable issue. Writer B has taken the topic to another level. Now it involves a debate: which reasons have more explanatory power, the parents' value orientation and cultural conditioning or their insensitivity, lack of interest, and ignorance of American sports?

ARGUMENT IN THE BROAD SENSE

- Your thesis is not necessarily issue-centered, arguable, or debatable.
- You do not acknowledge explicitly your audience's (conflicting) view.
- Your purpose is usually to explain or present your position. You are not intent on persuading your readers.

ARGUMENT IN THE SPECIALIZED SENSE

- Your thesis is issue-centered, arguable, and debatable.
- You anticipate and acknowledge conflicting views.
- Your purpose is to convince your readers to accept and agree with your position.

The word *argue* derives from a Greek word related to *argent*, "silver or white," denoting brilliance or clarity (which explains why Ag is the chemical abbreviation for silver). From this same word came the name of Argos, the mythological demigod with a hundred eyes. The word implies that a speaker or writer has seized upon an idea, clarified its point, and made its meaning strikingly visible. The goal of the writer of persuasive arguments is to move audiences to thought or action through the clarity of his or her reasoning process.

To develop a strong argument, you must impart breadth and depth to its focus. Try to make the argument two-dimensional. Such an argument will not hammer away at one central idea until it has exhausted all available evidence and concluded by restating the original proposition:

> The nuclear family consisting of a mother, father, and children is the most appropriate structure for contemporary society. . . . Thus we see that the nuclear family is the most appropriate structure for modern society.

Instead it will pursue a rounder, perhaps more oblique path if it recognizes its own limitations. It will explicitly acknowledge competing hypotheses, alternative explanations, and even outright contradictions:

> The nuclear family consisting of a mother, father, and children is the most appropriate structure for contemporary society, even though it does not serve the needs of every family.

The value of this approach is that it avoids the "tunnel vision" of repeating one and only one proposition. It implies that you have explored competing hypotheses and have weighed the evidence for and against each. Your readers may or may not agree with your conclusion, but they will certainly respect your effort to set it in a broader context.

Exercise

To develop full, rich, round arguments requires some practice. One can often get this practice by playing with controversial ideas in a creative and free-spirited way. Take an idea, any idea, no matter how preposterous or absurd—for example, "Homelessness is a desirable way of life," "The government should allow all immigrants to enter this country," "Drugs should be freely available to anyone who wants them," "Communities should have the right to prohibit stores from selling questionable types of rock music," "Public schools and colleges should enforce strict dress codes." First, state the idea in your own words. Next, articulate the opposition. Then brainstorm for possible reasons to explain the first idea. After that, brainstorm for possible reasons to explain the second idea. Decide which reasons are most convincing for each position. Rank them in order of strength or importance. Decide which position is most convincing. State that position as the main clause of a sentence. Recast the other position as a subordinate clause linked to the main clause by *because, although, despite,* or some other connective. Finally, try to express the relationship between both clauses: What is the link that brings them together?

THE ARGUMENT ESSAY

Before proceeding further, we would like you to take a look at an argument essay written by a college student, examine its features, and familiarize yourself with this particular type of writing. Later in the chapter, we will discuss the characteristics of an argument essay in more detail. Erica Mazor was asked to write an argumentative essay on a topic that would be of interest to other students in her composition class. She selected as her topic homelessness and the severely mentally ill. As you read the essay, take note of the impact Erica has on you as a reader, and jot down your responses. Does she convince you of her position on the issue? Why or why not? Which features of the essay account for its impact?

Erica Mazor

Professor Kennedy

Composition 101-094

14 April 1998

The Severely Mentally Ill Should Be Cared

For--Voluntarily or Involuntarily

A couple rummaging for food in a trash can, a young man sleeping on a park bench, an elderly woman screaming at an invisible enemy--the hunger and desperation of the homeless have become common features of our nation's major cities. Tamar Lewin, reviewing E. Fuller Torrey's book <u>Nowhere to Go: The Tragic Odyssey of the Homeless Mentally Ill</u>, tells us that estimates of our nation's homeless range from 350,000 to one million. Psychiatrist Nancy Wolff and her colleagues report that most studies show that one-third of these homeless are mentally ill (341). Although many people believe that the estimated number of the mentally ill homeless is exaggerated, strong evidence points to the contrary. Eighty percent of mentally ill patients were discharged from mental institutions over the past thirty years (Lewin). Many of the patients who suffer from major mental illnesses like schizophrenia ended up on the streets. Deinstitutionalization has contributed greatly to the homeless population. Opponents of involuntary hospitalization argue that it violates rights, but just as severely physically ill people should be hospitalized, so should the severely mentally ill, whether it be voluntarily or involuntarily.

Straight-forward title

Paper opener: examples

Background

Thesis

Mazor 2

Scenarios

Consider the following scenarios:

- An elderly man rushes across the avenue and is hit by a bus and seriously injured. He pleads with the police to take him home instead of to the hospital. The police call an ambulance, and the man is quickly transported to a nearby emergency room.

Arguing from examples

- A young woman with chronic asthma has an attack on a crowded city street. A passerby offers to assist, but she refuses his help. Worried that she is seriously ill, the man hails a cab and escorts the woman to the nearest hospital.

- A middle-aged woman, ravaged by paranoid schizophrenia, lies in the fetal position on a blanket on a subway platform. Commuters walk past her day after day. Finally, some people speak to her and offer to call the police. The woman yells at them to leave her alone. They walk away.

Is the third individual less seriously ill than the other two? If she wants to remain untreated, should she be permitted to do so?

E. Fuller Torrey, a psychiatrist who has written extensively on mental illness, points out that the original plans for deinstitutionalization were based on ideology. Liberals found civil rights activists' demands for mental

Opposing argument

patients' freedom compelling, and conservatives were glad to cut mental health budgets by shutting down state hospitals. Torrey notes that advocates of deinstitutionalization based their opinions on studies such as Erving Goffman's <u>Asylums</u>, which argue that psychiatric patients' abnormal behavior is mostly a consequence of hospitalization, not of mental illness. Torrey explains that supporters of deinstitutionalization assumed that mentally ill individuals would voluntarily seek treatment if they needed it. These supporters wanted society to recognize patients' rights to live in the community, and they also sold deinstitutionalization as a cost-cutting strategy (Torrey). Lewin reminds us that community programs were supposed to solve the problems of the mentally ill. They were to have allowed the severely mentally ill to avoid extended confinement in huge, sterile mental institutions located far away from their homes. Local communities were to provide treatment, housing, and other aid to discharged patients. Most important, the patients would not be locked up against their will.

Refutation, response to opposing views

But deinstitutionalization did not work out as planned. Torrey says that patients are worse off now than if they had stayed in the hospital. Only a few of them receive proper aftercare (Torrey). Most do not. Furthermore, research has shown that Goffman's claim that mental patients are psychotic because of hospitalization is grossly false. As one expert says, schizophrenia and manic depressive illnesses are physical disorders of the brain, and many of the mentally ill homeless suffer from these two diseases. Patients with these illnesses need well-supervised treatment (Lewin). It is important to point out that biological brain disorders can be controlled with drugs, and this allows thousands of people diagnosed with

4

Mazor 4

mental illness to lead very productive lives. But some individuals who are mentally ill do not believe that they are ill; therefore, they will not voluntarily seek out or accept treatment. If the community programs had actually materialized as they should have, the only patients to be helped would have been the ones who admitted they were ill. Another factor that hampered the effectiveness of the programs was that psychiatrists began to treat patients who were less ill but could pay more. Thus the programs did not even fulfill their responsibilities.

Overall, deinstitutionalization has caused a dramatic downward slump in the quality of life of the homeless. Members of communities fear the mentally ill homeless and fight for ways to rid their neighborhoods of street people. This antagonism does not alleviate the situation of the mentally ill. Community members want them moved to another location, and not entirely without reason: untreated mentally ill constitute a population that commits violent acts (Lewin). Before deinstitutionalization, mentally ill people had lower arrest rates than the general population. A study in the 1970s revealed that the likelihood of released patients to commit violent crimes had risen dramatically. They were twice as likely to commit murder, five times as likely to commit aggravated assault, and seven times more likely to commit rape than the general population (Lewin). Elliot Liebow, an anthropologist, asserts in his book, <u>Tell Them Who I Am: The Lives of Homeless Women</u>, that the abysmal conditions associated with homelessness tend to aggravate mental health

Support for thesis

5

problems (42). However, with treatment, the individual's disorder can be controlled, and he or she can begin to fit into the general population.

Support for thesis

Not only should we worry about the untreated homeless mentally ill harming others, but we should also be concerned about them harming themselves. In many states, patients cannot be committed if it cannot be shown that they pose a danger to themselves or others. In Lewin's review of Torrey's book, we are shown incidents that should make us question this policy. In Wisconsin, a judge ruled that a man who barricaded himself in his house and sat with a "rifle in his lap muttering 'kill, kill, kill'" did not show enough violence to qualify for hospitalization (Lewin). Lars Eighner, a homeless man who wrote a book called Travels with Lizbeth: Three Years on the Road and on the Streets, tells us about a mentally ill woman with whom he was acquainted. On medication, she was intelligent and mentally stable. On the streets, she acted violently, talked nonsense, and literally threw her Social Security check away (170). Only when she was extremely physically violent was she committed involuntarily. Her medication worked so well that she would cease to be violent almost as soon as she took her first dose. As a result, she was immediately discharged from the hospital (171). Surely, if she was in an extended, supervised treatment program, she could have lived a more satisfying life in the community.

Not all members of the medical community think the mentally ill should be treated involuntarily. Douglas Mossman, a psychiatrist at Wright State School of Medicine in Dayton,

Mazor 6

Opposing
view

Ohio, argues that the mentally ill are better off now that
they are free to make their own decisions about their
lifestyles and free to display obvious signs of illness without
fear of involuntary hospitalization (76). John Martin, a
sufferer of schizo-affective condition, disagrees. Martin is

Response to
opposing
view

active in the community and holds a full-time job. Yet he
feels that the quality of life of the mentally ill was
significantly better in institutions. He reflects that "in
terms of meaningful activities and personal relationships, I
had lived better when I was a patient" (3). In the hospital,
an attendant made sure he took proper care of himself. Martin
also took part in social activities with other patients and
had active treatment. He feels that for many of the seriously
mentally ill, life is better in hospitals. Martin asserts that
many of the mentally ill need the "protective and sheltered
artificial community that can be created in a hospital
environment" (6). Admittedly, community programs benefit
patients who are highly motivated, but effective
institutionalization is more able to meet the needs of the
chronically ill, those who are not highly motivated and end up
homeless. As the evidence reveals, the quality of life of the
homeless mentally ill plummeted with deinstitutionalization.

Opposing
view

Dr. Mossman also argues that deinstitutionalization is not
the cause of the problems faced by the majority of the
homeless mentally ill population. He claims that those who
believe the problems could have been solved, had it not been
for deinstitutionalization, are believing a myth. Mossman
claims that the "abandonment thesis"--the belief that American

8

psychiatrists have abandoned the mentally ill--allows Americans
to deal more comfortably with the problems of homelessness
(71). Those who claim that deinstitutionalization contributed
greatly to homelessness merely ignore the fact that mentally
ill people do not necessarily want to be confined in
hospitals. Furthermore, Mossman asserts that homelessness
fluctuates in response to economic factors (73).

Response to opposing view

To be sure, unemployment, cuts in welfare benefits, and
the loss of low-cost housing do contribute to the overall
problem of homelessness; nonetheless, we cannot deny that when
thousands of severely mentally ill patients were released into
the community, only a small portion were able to succeed in
independent living situations. Granted, many people with mental
illnesses have homes and hold steady jobs, but the severely
mentally ill have difficulties dealing with the normal duties
and routines of daily life. And granted, people who are
mentally ill and have homes are more likely to stay in one
place long enough to benefit from a treatment program (Liebow
231). But until we solve the problem of the lack of affordable
housing for the poor, the majority of the homeless mentally ill
will continue to roam the streets, unassisted and untreated.

9

Conclusion

Liebow's and Mossman's points are well taken:
unemployment, decreases in welfare benefits, and the dearth of
low-cost housing cause homelessness. We cannot deny, however,
that failure to treat the nation's severely mentally ill has
also contributed to a rise in the homeless population. The
severely mentally ill require and deserve proper treatment.
Without it, they are doomed. It is incumbent on us to save

10

them from the degradation of homelessness. By allowing them to remain in an unstable environment, we are not fulfilling our responsibilities. We should demand that they be taken off the streets and given the medical treatment they deserve.

Works Cited

Eighner, Lars. <u>Travels with Lizbeth: Three Years on the Road and on the Streets</u>. New York: Fawcett-Columbine, 1993.

Lewin, Tamar. Rev. of <u>Nowhere to Go: The Tragic Odyssey of the Homeless Mentally Ill</u>, by E. Fuller Torrey. <u>New York Times</u> Book Review 18 Dec. 1988: 14.

Liebow, Elliot. <u>Tell Them Who I Am: The Lives of Homeless Women</u>. New York: Penguin, 1993.

Martin, John. "Deinstitutionalization: What Will It Really Cost?" <u>Schizophrenia Digest</u> Apr. 1995. <u>Internet Mental Health.</u> 22 Mar. 1998 <http://www.mentalhealth.com/mag1/p51-sc02.html>.

Mossman, Douglas. "Deinstitutionalization, Homelessness, and the Myth of Psychiatric Abandonment: A Structural Anthropology Perspective." <u>Social Science and Medicine</u> 44 (1997): 71-83.

Torrey, E. Fuller. "Stop the Madness." <u>Wall Street Journal</u> 18 July 1997: A14.

Wolff, Nancy, et al. "Cost Effectiveness Evaluation of Three Approaches to Case Management for Homeless Mentally Ill Clients." <u>American Journal of Psychiatry</u> 154 (1997): 341-48.

Exercise..

Break into small groups, and select a recorder and a reporter. Each member reads to the group his or her answers to the following questions: Does the writer convince you of her position on the issue? Why or why not? Which features of the essay account for its impact? Come up with a group response, and report it to the rest of the class.

* * * * * * * * * * * * * * * *

Erica opens the paper with a lead—three vivid examples of homeless people—that captures the reader's attention. She then supplies figures to inform the reader of the severity of the problem: there are between 350,000 and a million homeless in the United States, a third of whom are mentally ill. Erica attributes the problem to deinstitutionalization. She argues that many of the severely mentally ill patients who have been discharged from mental hospitals have ended up on the streets. Thus deinstitutionalization has resulted in homelessness. Erica contends that to solve the problem of homelessness, severely ill people—whether they are physically or mentally ill—should be hospitalized, and this hospitalization should take place involuntarily, if necessary. This is her *central assertion* or *claim*. She knows that her claim will occasion a challenge from others. Many people oppose involuntary hospitalization on the grounds that it violates the rights of the individual. Notice that Erica's thesis is issue-centered, arguable, and debatable, and it acknowledges the opposing view.

```
Opponents of involuntary hospitalization argue that it violates
rights, but just as severely physically ill people should be
hospitalized, so should the severely mentally ill, whether it be
voluntarily or involuntarily.
```

In paragraph 2, Erica presents three scenarios, the first two depicting physically ill individuals who are escorted to hospitals despite their pleas to the contrary and the third portraying a mentally ill woman for whom hospital treatment is not deemed necessary. Erica ends the paragraph by asking the reader two questions: "Is the third individual less seriously ill than the other two? If she wants to remain untreated, should she be allowed to do so?" Erica is doing two things here: arguing from examples and appealing to the reader's emotions.

In paragraphs 3 and 4, as Erica presents the views of supporters of deinstitutionalization and shows the holes in their argument, she accomplishes two goals. She provides the reader with background about deinstitutionalization of the severely mentally ill and in so doing bolsters her argument by showing how much stronger the views of detractors are than those of supporters.

Opposing View

```
Involuntary hospitalization violates patients' rights. It is
preferable to house the severely mentally ill in community
programs that respect their rights and also have a number of
other advantages.
```

Response to Opposition

```
Community programs did not materialize as they should have. Nor
are they necessarily accommodating all of the severely mentally
ill.
```

Such a response is called a *refutation* or *rebuttal*.

In paragraphs 5 and 6, Erica offers additional persuasive reasons why severely mentally ill individuals should be in hospitals rather than living in the streets.

Reasons for Erica's Position

```
Deinstitutionalization has caused a dramatic downward slump in
the quality of life of the mentally ill homeless. The mentally
ill homeless pose a danger to themselves.
```

She continues to address readers who find her position unacceptable, presenting their counterarguments and explaining why the arguments are ineffective.

Reasons for the Opposing Position

```
The mentally ill are better off making decisions about their own
lifestyles and being free to display obvious signs of illness
without fear of involuntary hospitalization. Deinstitutionaliza-
tion does not cause homelessness.
```

Erica's concluding strategy is to exhort her readers to accept the responsibility of ensuring that the severely mentally ill homeless are taken off the streets and given proper treatment. Notice that her tone becomes urgent. She is compelled to appeal to her reader's sense of civic responsibility. Keep in mind that in the conclusion of an argument essay, in addition to recapping your argument, you can use any of the techniques described in Chapter 3—stressing the significance of your thesis, predicting consequences, or calling your readers to action. You can also use any of the devices for paper openers (see pages 109–110).

All written arguments have basically the same components as Erica's essay.

COMPONENTS OF ARGUMENT ESSAYS

- Introductory section containing a lead, definition of the issue or problem, and thesis statement
- Section of background information
- Section containing reasons and evidence to support the thesis statement
- Section mentioning opposing views and providing a rebuttal
- Conclusion

FINDING AN ISSUE AND STAKING OUT YOUR POSITION

An argument must treat an issue, problem, or question that evokes debate. It begins with a controversial topic and then focuses on aspects of the topic that are open to question. If it begins with the topic of abortion, it might zero in on the issue of whether or not women should have free choice in the matter of abortion. The topic and issue must be genuinely debatable. They cannot be based on subjective opinions, personal preferences, or beliefs on which everyone agrees. Nor should they involve disagreements that are of no practical importance or are not open to legitimate debate. Whether Cherry Garcia ice cream is tastier than caramel crunch would not be a suitable topic for an argument essay because ice-cream flavor is a matter of personal preference. Whether or not air pollution is hazardous to health is unacceptable because no one would argue otherwise. Your topic and issue should be arguable and worth arguing about.

In some courses, your professors will stipulate the issues they want you to discuss. For example, in a course on public health and welfare, you might be asked to give your views on whether doctors are obligated to treat patients who have tested positive for HIV. Other professors allow students to select their own topics. If this is the case, you must convert your topic into an arguable statement or issue. One way to do this is to ask, "What is currently controversial? What do people argue about?" Take genetic engineering. If you know something about the topic, you may be aware that although some forms of genetic engineering are beneficial, the prospect of genetically engineering humans is quite scary. If you know very little about the topic, you will have to read up on it to find where the major controversies lie. Once you have discovered the controversial aspects of your topic, convert this information into an issue: whether scientists should use genetic engineering procedures on humans. If you prefer, state your issue as a question: Should scientists use genetic engineering procedures on humans?

CONVERTING A TOPIC INTO DEBATABLE QUESTIONS OR ISSUES

1. Identify a suitable topic.
2. Ask, "What is controversial about the topic? What do people argue about?"
3. Convert the controversial aspects of the topic into a question or issue.
4. Double-check that the topic and issue are genuinely debatable and worth arguing about.

Once you have identified an issue, do extensive reading to learn as much as you can about its complexities. Investigate its history, the context in which it is couched, and the arguments on both sides of the controversy.

Keep in mind as you read that you may have only scratched the surface of the conflict. You may find so much information on your issue that you will have to do a considerable amount of redefining and narrowing.

Be sure to probe both sides of the issue and read with an open mind (even if you have already taken a stand). A useful exercise at this point is what Peter Elbow calls the "believing game." As you encounter various views on the issue, try to see them through the holder's eyes. Even if someone's views are absurd or directly opposite to yours, put yourself in that person's place. As Elbow points out, "To do this requires great energy, attention, and even a kind of inner commitment. It helps to think of it as trying to get inside the head of someone who saw things this way—perhaps even constructing such a person for yourself. Try to have the experience of someone who made the assertion" (149).

FORMULATING A THESIS

After you have learned about the issue you are engaging and examined the reasons why people on both sides of the debate hold particular views, you are ready to take a position. When we speak of argument essays, we call this *making a claim*. A *claim* is an assertion that can be disputed by others.

Write a clear-cut statement of your central claim on the issue and then a statement of the opposition's primary claim:

Writer's Claim

```
The government should impose strict guidelines on genetic engi-
neering of humans because it will have disastrous consequences
for the human species and it meddles with evolution.
```

Opposition's Claim

```
Genetic engineering allows scientists to improve on the human
species and prevent its extinction.
```

You can express your thesis in either of two ways:

- As a statement of your central claim:

  ```
  The government should impose strict guidelines on genetic
  engineering of humans because it will have disastrous
  consequences for the human species and it meddles with
  evolution.
  ```

- As a statement that incorporates both your claim and the opposition's:

  ```
  Although genetic engineering allows scientists to improve on
  humans and prevent their extinction, the government should
  impose strict guidelines because genetic engineering will
  have disastrous consequences for the human species and it
  meddles with evolution.
  ```

Regardless of the option you choose, you will discuss opposing viewpoints in the body of your paper.

SUPPORTING YOUR THESIS

To defend your claim and disprove your opponent's position, you need to make a compelling case supported by convincing reasons. You may have had strong opinions on the issue from the outset ("No, it is immoral to interfere with nature"; "Yes, genetic engineering will prevent people from inheriting deadly diseases"), but opinions are not enough.

An *opinion* is a belief that is not substantiated with evidence or proof. Writing "In my personal opinion" is redundant because by their definition, opinions are personal. Consider the following opinions:

```
The school year should be shortened because young kids usually
waste their summers anyway.
```

```
From the time I was thirteen, I worked hard at a job all summer
long. Kids should work during the summer and not go to school.
```

Both statements express personal views, but neither gives firm grounds of support for the view.

A *reason* carries with it the weight of evidence. Read this example:

> Because our school year is 180 days long but Japan's and
> Germany's has from 226 to 243 school days, Japanese and German
> children devote more time to learning science and math. A length-
> ened school year would allow our students to spend as much class-
> room time on science and math as students in other industrialized
> countries, and that will help them catch up with the competition.

The student who wrote this has provided grounds of support for her view. To make a strong argument, you need to support your views with substantial reasons and ground each of these reasons in solid evidence. We will explain how to do this later in the chapter.

Exercise ....

In your journal or notebook, make a claim for one of the following issues or another issue of your choice:

- Whether we should buy American-made goods rather than imports
- Whether rap or heavy metal music promotes violence
- Whether television damages family life
- Whether the United States should extend the school year
- Whether cosmetics firms should be allowed to experiment on animals

Next, state the major reason why you hold your position. Ask yourself two questions: (1) What underlying fact or cause is the basis for my view? (2) Based on this reason, would someone agree or disagree with my position? Now break into small groups and share your positions and reasons with your classmates. As each student explains the issue and gives his or her position and reason for holding it, the other group members should assume a noncommittal position. In other words, if a student in your group explains why she is in favor of lengthening the school year, pretend that you have no opinion on the issue. From your neutral stance, evaluate your classmate's argument. Have you been persuaded to accept his or her view?

· · · · · · · · · · · · · · · · ·

Marshaling Solid Evidence and Making a Strong Case

As we mentioned earlier, rhetoric, the "art of persuasion," was the most important subject in the Greek curriculum over two thousand years ago. At that time, there were no attorneys, and people usually argued their own cases in courts of law. As you can imagine, private citizens were very interested in learning how to present an effective argument that would enable them to win a case. One of the most influential handbooks explaining how to formulate and present arguments was written by the Greek philosopher Aristotle in the fourth century BCE. Much of what Aristotle proposed in his *Rhetoric* is still applicable today. He taught that there are three appeals a person who is arguing a position can make to his or her audience:

The first kind depends on the personal character of the speaker [*ethos*]; the second on putting the audience into a certain frame of mind [*pathos*]; the third on the proof [*logos*]. (1.2.1356)

When we speak of *ethos* today, we mean the way the writer conveys a favorable or creditable impression of himself or herself to the reader. By *pathos* we mean the way the writer takes into account the interests and needs of the reader, and by *logos* we mean the way the writer provides the audience with solid reasons arranged in a logical sequence.

Let's go back to Erica's essay on pages 204–211 to look at how she establishes her credibility, interests her audience, and presents a well-reasoned, compelling case.

Make Ethical Appeals.

To be ethical is to conduct oneself in accordance with the principles of right and wrong, to make appropriate moral choices, and to have sound fundamental values. These traits make writers creditable to their audiences. Readers also expect a writer who is trying to persuade them of something to possess authority, honesty, respect, and competence. There are a number of ways to project a favorable image of oneself and thus make ethical appeals.

WAYS TO MAKE ETHICAL APPEALS

- Establish your authority by exhibiting in-depth knowledge of the subject and drawing on the expert judgments of others.
- Be fair, honest, and accurate.
- Show respect for your audience by using an appropriate tone.
- Divulge your character by drawing on personal experiences that directly support your points.
- Demonstrate competence with correct usage, punctuation, and mechanics.

Establish your authority.   Since you will not be an expert on the issue on which you will write, you will need to learn about it by reading as much as you can. Explore various aspects of the issue, the context in which it is embedded, its history, and the positions held by people on both sides of the debate. One way to write with authority is to draw on respected researchers and reputable experts in the field.

Erica does an exemplary job of establishing her credibility right at the start of her essay. In the opening paragraph, she projects the image of a writer who is able to capture the interest of her readers and inform them of the seriousness of the issue and her particular position. Then in paragraphs 3 and 4, she demonstrates that she is knowledgeable about the subject and can speak with a sense of authority. Notice how she bolsters her authority with quotations and paraphrases from psychiatrist E. Torrey Fuller and other sources of expert information. Erica maintains this positive image in the remainder of the essay by following a well-developed line of reasoning that takes into account other people's views as well as her own.

Be fair, honest, and accurate.   It is much easier to write a one-sided argument than to examine the issue from the point of view of someone who does not agree with you. But how persuasive is an argument that presents only half of the debate? How convincing would

Erica's argument have been if it omitted the objections of those who are opposed to involuntary hospitalization? Erica makes her own position more reasonable by taking into account the beliefs and values of those who think differently.

When you are making an argument, winning isn't everything. Don't stoop so low that you would tamper with the evidence, withhold it, take it out of context, or ignore it (especially if it strengthens the case of your opposition). Nor should you bring in irrelevant data or examples or quote a person who has no expertise on the subject under discussion.

Show respect for your audience. The tone a writer uses in an argument essay reveals his or her attitude toward the subject, people who might not agree with the thesis, and the audience reading the piece. Tone is created with a number of stylistic features, among them choice of vocabulary and level of formality, the inclusion of questions, and the use of first-person *(I, my, mine, we, our)* and second-person *(you, your)* pronouns.

Consider the opening paragraph of Michael Messner's essay, "When Bodies Are Weapons," on the social role that violence plays in constructing masculinity.

> In many of our most popular spectator sports, winning depends on the use of violence. To score and win, the human body is routinely turned into a weapon to be used against other bodies, causing pain, serious injury and death. How do we interpret the social meaning of this violence? Is it socially learned behavior that serves to legitimize masculine power over women? Commentators—both apologists and critics—have made sweeping statements about sports and violence, but their analyses rarely take into account the meanings of violence in sports to athletes themselves. We can begin to understand the broader social meanings of violence in sports by listening to the words of former athletes. (89)

Messner has a reasonable, familiar tone. It is neither overly formal nor uniformly colloquial. Notice how he establishes a relationship with his audience by referring to "*our* most popular sports" in the opening sentence. As he continues, he pulls the readers further into the discussion by asking them questions—"How do we interpret the social meaning of this violence? Is it socially learned behavior that serves to legitimize masculine power over women?"—and by continuing to use the first-person pronoun.

In the following paragraphs from the beginning of William Raspberry's essay, "Racism in the Criminal Justice System Is Exaggerated," the tone is more aggressive.

> There are not more college-age black men in jail than in college. I suspect that old canard was launched when someone said (presumably accurately) that more college-age black men are in jail than in college *dormitories*—a statistic that would leave out off-campus students and almost all technical school and community college enrollees.
>
> So what's the truth? The Justice Department's Bureau of Justice Statistics says that in 1993 approximately 157,000 black males aged 18 to 24 were in local jails and state and federal prisons.
>
> During that same period, according to the education branch of the Census Bureau, 379,000 males in the same age group were in post-secondary education—better than 2 to 1 in favor of college.

The number of incarcerated black men has increased since that period, and I wouldn't be shocked to learn that the number of black college students has gone down. Still, we're not close to having more in jail than in college.

But it isn't just the accuracy of that much-cited statistic that bothers me; it's the *uselessness* of it.

Raspberry's tone is more informal than Messner's. Like Messner, he uses first-person pronouns and directs questions to the reader, but he also uses contractions *(we're, it's, isn't)*. Raspberry reveals more of his attitude. Consider how emphatic he is in the first sentence—"There are not more college-age black men in jail than in college"—and notice how he expresses his feelings by using italics to accentuate words.

We should alert you that some professors may object to first-person pronouns and contractions in academic writing, so before you make these stylistic choices, check with your teacher. To be on the safe side, write in a calm, cool, reasonable tone. Avoid sounding alarmed, aggressive, or abusive. Never use inflammatory language or demeaning words, such as *idiotic, stupid,* or *ridiculous,* when presenting opposing views, and when you respond to the opposition, be conciliatory rather than combative or condescending.

Read paragraph 7 of Erica's essay, and notice how she responds to Dr. Mossman's views by first conceding that he has made a valid point.

> <u>Admittedly</u>, community programs benefit patients who are highly motivated, <u>but</u> effective institutionalization is more able to meet the needs of the chronically ill, those who are not highly motivated and end up homeless.

Notice that she does this again throughout paragraph 9 and at the beginning of paragraph 10.

> <u>To be sure</u>, unemployment, cuts in welfare benefits, and the loss of low-cost housing do contribute to the overall problem of homelessness; <u>nonetheless, we cannot deny</u> that when thousands of severely mentally ill patients were released into the community, only a small portion were able to succeed in independent living situations. <u>Granted</u>, many people with mental illnesses have homes and hold steady jobs, <u>but</u> the severely mentally ill have difficulties dealing with the normal duties and routines of daily life. <u>And granted</u>, people who are mentally ill and have homes are more likely to stay in one place long enough to benefit from a treatment program (Liebow 231). <u>But</u> until we solve the problem of lack of affordable housing for the poor, the majority of the homeless mentally ill will continue to roam the streets, unassisted and untreated.
>
> Liebow's and Mossman's <u>points are well taken</u>: unemployment, decreases in welfare benefits, and the dearth of low-cost housing cause homelessness. <u>We cannot deny, however</u>, that failure to treat the nation's severely mentally ill has also contributed to a rise in the homeless population.

We have underlined the words and phrases that contribute to Erica's conciliatory tone. Think of how her readers would have reacted if she had responded to Liebow and Mossman as follows:

> <u>Nonsense</u>, unemployment, cuts in welfare benefits, and the loss of low-cost housing are not as important as the fact that when thousands of the severely mentally ill were released into the community, only a small portion were able to succeed in independent living situations. <u>It's ridiculous</u> to talk about people with mental illness having homes and holding steady jobs, because the severely mentally ill have difficulties dealing with the normal duties and routines of daily life. <u>And it's beside the point to say</u> that people who are mentally ill and have homes are more likely to stay in one place long enough to benefit from a treatment program (Liebow 231).

This insulting and condescending tone would have alienated Erica's readers and done little to persuade them of the validity of her argument.

Divulge your character.   Another way to project a favorable image of oneself is to use as evidence a personal experience that strengthens your argument and substantiates your claims.

Consider a paragraph from an essay in which student Patti Sergent argues that cultural factors limit women's potential and restrict their professional opportunities.

> I got through most of high school with my academic potential intact. For me, the adverse cultural impact occurred in my senior year during a college advisement session with my guidance counselor. In my hand, I had transcripts with A's and SAT scores of 1350, and in my heart I had a serious interest in chemistry. Mr. Duel informed me that "girls should start at a community college because many drop out of school to get married within the first two years." Though I lost a little of my confidence, I ignored my adviser and attended a four-year college, but even there I was constantly reminded that "girls," a term I find offensive, make better teachers than researchers.

This story tells the readers that the writer is strong, ambitious, and intent on accomplishing her goals. Her experience is credible evidence because it relates directly to the topic at hand.

Demonstrate competence.   Readers are more likely to be persuaded by an error-free text than by one that is marred by problems with spelling, punctuation, paragraphing, documentation format, capitalization, and pagination. Before you go public with your paper, read it aloud to another person and then proofread it line by line and word by word.

Limit Emotional Appeals.

Writers use emotional appeals to provoke, entice, or arouse the reader and to establish empathy. Though it is important to establish rapport with one's readers, be careful not to exploit their emotions. A good piece of advice is to use emotional appeals only as supplements to ethical and logical appeals, not as substitutes for them.

WAYS TO MAKE EMOTIONAL APPEALS

- Draw on firsthand experiences.
- Use concrete examples, anecdotes, stories, comparisons, and contrasts the reader can identify with.
- Use metaphors, similes, and words that bring to mind particular images and connotations.
- Tie the issue in with the reader's sense of responsibility, civic duty, patriotism, values system, or beliefs.

Draw on firsthand experiences. A personal experience can function both as an ethical appeal that creates a favorable image of the writer and as an emotional appeal that stirs the reader. The example of writer Patti Sergent's encounter with her high school guidance counselor reveals traits about Patti's character and at the same time creates a sense of indignation in the readers. We are appalled by the fact that such a bright young woman was discouraged from pursuing serious study in science.

Use concrete examples. Erica Mazor opens her essay with examples—"a couple rummaging for food in a trash can, a young man sleeping on a park bench, an elderly woman screaming at an invisible enemy"—that are commonplace in our large cities. Readers can identify with these scenes as well as with the hypothetical situations Erica describes in paragraph 2.

Exercise . . . .

Look for other examples, anecdotes, stories, or comparisons and contrasts in Erica's essay. In your journal, describe the effect that these devices have on you as a reader. Share your findings with the class.

• • • • • • • • • • • • • • • •

Use metaphors, similes, and evocative language. Metaphors and similes are comparisons. In a metaphor, the comparison is implicit, and in a simile, it is spelled out. Jeffrey Goldberg opens the article on page 427 with a metaphor, along with other words that evoke vivid images:

> Sgt. Mike Lewis of the Maryland State Police is a bull-necked, megaphone-voiced, highly caffeinated drug warrior who, on this shiny May morning outside Annapolis, is conceding defeat.

In paragraph 45, he employs a simile and a sharp comparison:

> The suspects are wearing backward baseball caps and low-slung pants; the woman with them is dressed like a stripper.
>
> "Is this racial profiling?" Jones asks. A cynical half-smile shows on his face.

The four buyers are white. Jones and Robinson are black, veterans of the streets who know that white people in a black neighborhood will be stopped. Automatically. Faster than a Rastafarian in Scarsdale.

Writers use metaphorical language to enable readers to establish connections that will create clear-cut pictures in their minds.

Exercise ....

Explain the impact each of the following descriptions has on you as a reader.

1. Sgt. Mike Lewis of the Maryland State Police is a thick-necked, loud-spoken police officer who drinks a lot of coffee.
2. "Sgt. Mike Lewis of the Maryland State Police is a bull-necked, megaphone-voiced, highly caffeinated drug warrior."
3. Her clothes were very provocative.
4. She was dressed like a stripper.
5. White people in a black neighborhood will be stopped just as quickly as black people in a wealthy white neighborhood.
6. "White people in a black neighborhood will be stopped. Automatically. Faster than a Rastafarian in Scarsdale."

• • • • • • • • • • • • • • •

Appeal to the reader's sense of responsibility, civic duty, patriotism, values system, or beliefs. This is an effective technique for closing an argument paper. Erica uses it in her concluding paragraph.

```
The severely mentally ill require and deserve proper treatment.
Without it, they are doomed. It is incumbent on us to save them
from the degradation of homelessness. By allowing them to remain
in an unstable environment, we are not fulfilling our responsi-
bilities. We should demand that they be taken off the streets and
given the medical treatment they deserve.
```

Present Logical Appeals.

With logical appeals, you call on your readers' reason and logic. Logical appeals are the linchpins of effective argument essays. Without solid reasons and evidence, the argument falls apart. Four components are central to a logical argument:

- The writer's primary claim, assertion, or thesis
- Reasons that support the central claim
- Assumptions that link the reasons with the central claim
- Evidence that supports the reasons

Erica Mazor's primary claim is "homeless individuals who are severely mentally ill should be hospitalized, whether it be voluntarily or involuntarily." Two of the reasons she gives are that deinstitutionalization has caused a dramatic downward slump in the quality of life of the mentally ill homeless and that mentally ill homeless individuals who are violent pose a danger to others as well as to themselves. These reasons are based on assumptions that Erica believes her readers share: first, that quality of life in the hospital is better than the quality of life on the streets, and second, that people who pose a danger to themselves or others should not be allowed to roam the streets. If Erica's readers do not share her assumptions, the argument will collapse.

Two other components important to an argument are these:

- Consideration of objections raised by people who disagree with the writer's claim and evidence offered in support of these objections
- The writer's refutation of the objections, including reasons why the objections do not undermine the writer's argument

The following are some possible objections to Erica's thesis that homeless individuals who are severely mentally ill should be hospitalized voluntarily or involuntarily:

- Involuntary hospitalization violates patients' rights. It is preferable to house the severely mentally ill in community programs that respect their rights and also have a number of other advantages.
- The mentally ill are better off making decisions about their own lifestyles and being free to display obvious signs of illness without fear of involuntary hospitalization.
- Deinstitutionalization does not cause homelessness.

Let us examine the evidence Erica offers in support of the reasons for her position and also the evidence she offers as she presents and refutes the opposition. The main types of evidence writers use are *facts; statistics; examples;* and *expert testimony, statements, or other relevant information from acknowledged authorities.* Reread paragraph 5 of Erica's essay. Examine the various types of evidence she offers in support of her claim that "deinstitutionalization has caused a dramatic downward slump in the quality of life of the homeless."

- She presents relevant information from a reviewer: Tamar Lewin.
- She cites statistics about the likelihood of released patients committing violent crimes.
- She presents testimony by an authority: anthropologist Elliot Liebow.

Examine the evidence Erica offers in paragraph 6 in support of her claim that "not only should we worry about untreated homeless mentally ill harming others, but we should also be concerned with them harming themselves." She uses fact, an example based on the fact, and an example based on the published experiences of Lars Eighner. Now study the evidence she offers as she presents and refutes the opposition in paragraphs 3, 4, 7, 8, and 9.

PARAGRAPH 3

Opposing View

- Background information on opposing view from psychiatrist E. Fuller Torrey
- Additional information from Lewin

PARAGRAPH 4

- Fact given by psychiatrist E. Fuller Torrey
- Fact provided by Lewin

PARAGRAPH 7

Opposing View

- Statement by authority: psychiatrist Douglass Mossman

Refutation

- Testimony and specific case of John Martin

PARAGRAPH 8

Opposing View

- Statements by authority: psychiatrist Douglass Mossman

PARAGRAPH 9

Refutation

- Fact presented by Liebow

In addition to using the types of support Erica has employed, you could also supply a personal narrative that relates to the issue at hand. Consider an example from a student who is giving his views on the issue of whether children should receive monolingual or bilingual education. Jim Li supplies a personal example to support his point that monolingual education retards immigrant children's educational progress.

> An immigrant child should not have his educational progress retarded because of his lack of proficiency in English. Due to monolingual education, I wasted two years not acquiring any new knowledge except for math, which required very little English. While the other kids in Mr. Baranello's fifth-grade class were busily working on social studies and science assignments, I sat in the far corner of the room engrossed in a thick novel. It was not in English, however. It was in my native language. Except for participating in a one-hour ESL lesson every other day and a daily math lesson, I spent my first year and a half in an American school hardly communicating with anyone. Bilingual education would have served as a transitional device for me because for several years I would have received the larger part of instruction in my home language. As Porter points out, this would have led to "better learning of English, better learning of subject matter, and better self-concept" (152).

When you include personal experiences in your argument essays, be sure they relate directly to the reason you are developing.

EVIDENCE TO SUPPORT YOUR REASONS

- Examples based on a similarity to something that happened in the past, a similar case, a hypothetical situation, or relevant experience
- Relevant information: facts, statistics, points of interest
- Statements, testimony, or other relevant information from acknowledged authorities
- Your own personal narrative

E x e r c i s e

Read the selection by Don Sabo on pages 462–468. Identify the types of evidence Sabo uses, and evaluate the effectiveness of each type.

In addition to offering evidence when presenting their major assertions and the views of their opposition, writers of argument essays may use examples, facts, expert testimony, and other types of evidence in other parts of their essays, especially when giving background information. It is always important to provide context for the issue you are debating. You will have to explain the context in more detail in some cases than in others. The amount of background you provide depends on your audience's familiarity with the subject.

E x e r c i s e

Reread Erica Mazor's introductory paragraph and identify the types of evidence she provides.

CONSIDERING YOUR AUDIENCE AND IDENTIFYING YOUR READERS' NEEDS

It is important to consider the audience for any essay, but this step is especially critical for an argument. Before sitting down to write, ask yourself the following questions.

QUESTIONS ABOUT AUDIENCE FOR AN ARGUMENT ESSAY

- Am I writing for my professor, my classmates, a broader audience, or a specific group of readers?
- What do my readers already know about the issue? Will I have to explain basic concepts and provide background information for my point of view to make sense?
- How do I want to come across to my audience—as an objective, scholarly authority or also as someone who identifies with my readers and shares their concerns?
- Is my audience noncommittal, or have my readers already taken a stand on the issue I am discussing?

Answers to these questions tell writers a number of things:

- How much effort to expend to attract their readers' attention with the lead sentence and introduction
- How much background information to provide so that readers will thoroughly understand the issue
- How to address readers (objectively or using pronouns like *I, you,* or *we*)
- How to organize their presentation and how much space to devote to opposing views

Erica made a conscious decision to address her peers rather than the teacher. She decided to open the essay with a few salient examples that would grab readers' attention and then give them background information on homelessness and the severely mentally ill. Because of the nature of her audience, she made the tone of the paper friendly and accessible.

The point at which you decide to take up the views of your opponents will depend on your audience and the nature of the opposing argument. If you know your readers have good reason to disagree with you, you may want to devote a good portion of your essay to answering each of their objections point by point. Later in this chapter, we will provide a sample argument essay of this type. If you think it will be easy to influence your readers to accept your point of view or if you think their arguments are especially weak, you can dismiss your opposition summarily and get on with discussing your position. Notice that Erica's thesis statement reflects her order of presentation: "Opponents of involuntary hospitalization argue that it violates rights, but just as severely physically ill people should be hospitalized, so should the severely mentally ill, whether it be voluntarily or involuntarily." Let the pattern of your thesis statement reflect the overall arrangement of your essay.

ORGANIZING AND ARRANGING THE ARGUMENT ESSAY

As we mentioned earlier, some of the principles of argument that were taught in ancient times have been adapted for writers today. *Ad Herennium,* a Latin treatise on Greek rhetorical theory, divides arguments into six parts (Corbett 25):

- Introduction *(exordium)*
- Statement or exposition of the case under discussion *(narratio)*
- Outline of the points or steps in the argument *(divisio)*
- Proof of the case *(confirmatio)*
- Refutation of the opposing arguments *(confutatio)*
- Conclusion *(peroratio)*

Today's principles of organization are not so different. Most modern writers of arguments use some variation of the following divisions:

- Opening
- Explanation of the issue and background

- Writer's thesis
- Presentation of and response to opposing views
- Reasons supporting thesis
- Conclusion

Whether you choose to acknowledge and respond to opposing views before you give reasons for your own position, after you present your case, or both before and after, as Erica has done, depends on the situation and the nature of your audience. There is no rule that says that you must arrange your essay in one particular way or another.

TYPICAL ARRANGEMENT OF AN ARGUMENT ESSAY

Title

- -

Introduction

- -

    Opener: Introduce the topic, and interest your reader.

    Issue: Familiarize your reader with the controversy, and give background information the reader needs to know to understand the issue at hand.

    Thesis: Give your stand on the issue and perhaps the view of the opposition.

Body Paragraphs

- -

VARIATION A	VARIATION B
Give opposing views and your refutation.	Present reasons and evidence for your thesis.
Present reasons and evidence for your thesis.	Give opposing views and your refutation.

Conclusion

- -

    Recap argument.

    Make final appeal to readers.

As we pointed out earlier, there may be times when your opponents' objections are numerous, weighty, or substantial. In these cases, you may want to arrange the body of your essay in a different way. Instead of presenting the conflicting view and your position in separate, self-contained sections, you can respond to the objections in a point-by-point fashion. In the exercise on page 228, we reproduce a student essay that is organized in this way. The writer's issue is whether physicians have a right to refuse to treat patients who are HIV-positive. Her position is that doctors have an obligation to treat all people. Since physicians have a number of persuasive reasons for declining treatment, the writer decided to take up and refute their claims one at a time. You will see that as she does this, she also offers reasons in defense of her own position. Here is an outline of this alternative arrangement.

ALTERNATIVE ARRANGEMENT FOR AN ARGUMENT ESSAY

Title

Introduction

    Opener: Introduce the topic, and interest your reader.

    Issue: Familiarize your reader with the controversy, and give background information the reader needs to know to understand the issue at hand.

    Thesis: Give your stand on the issue and perhaps the view of the opposition.

Body Paragraphs

State a conflicting view.

Refute that view.

State another conflicting view.

Refute that view.

State another conflicting view.

Refute that view.

(Continue in this manner as necessary.)

Conclusion

Recap argument.

Make final appeal to readers.

E x e r c i s e

Read Jackie Weichert's essay. Then answer the questions.

1. For whom do you think Jackie is writing this essay: for her professor, her classmates, a broader audience, or a specialized group of readers? How did you come to this conclusion?

2. Does Jackie tell her audience enough about the topic so that her essay will make sense? What makes you say so?

3. Do you think Jackie views her audience as noncommittal or as strongly opinionated about the issue? Why do you say this?

4. What impression do you have of Jackie? Does she come across as a scholarly, objective authority or as someone who identifies with the readers and shares their concerns?

5. How does Jackie handle opposing views?

6. What reasons does Jackie give to support her position? If you can, cite instances of her use of examples, relevant information from sources, statements or testimony from acknowledged authorities, and personal experience.

7. How does Jackie order her reasons, from weak to strong or strong to weak? What effect does she achieve by this order?

8. Write an essay in which you compare Jackie Weichert's essay to Erica Mazor's essay on pages 204–211.

* * * * * * * * * * * * * * * *

Weichert 1

Jackie Weichert

Professor Kennedy

English 131

14 August 1992

Aid for AIDS Victims

Opener: dramatic scenario

Those who know the most about AIDS are among those most afraid of the disease. Imagine going into your family doctor's office complaining of fatigue. The doctor conducts some blood tests to see what the problem is. After the results come back, he tells you he will not treat you anymore, but he won't say why. When you see the test results, you find out that you have contracted AIDS. Your mind immediately goes back to an operation you had ten years before and the blood transfusion you had. Why won't your doctor treat you? AIDS can be contracted only from an exchange of body fluids. You try to find a new doctor, but nobody will take you. You're alone, you're going to die, and you can't find a doctor who will help you.

In the early 1980s, few people had heard of acquired immune deficiency syndrome (AIDS). Today, we know many things about the human immunodeficiency virus (HIV) that causes AIDS. We know how HIV carriers infect others, and we also know how

Weichert 2

Identifica-
tion of
issue
to prevent infection. Nevertheless, there is still a lot of fear surrounding HIV and AIDS. Surprisingly, much of the fear comes from the medical community. It arises from not being able to stop AIDS. As of yet, there is no cure and no vaccine to prevent its spread. Because of this, some doctors will no longer treat people who have tested HIV-positive. Whether or not health care professionals must treat patients with AIDS or HIV infection is currently a topic under heavy debate in both professional and private communities. Although one can understand why physicians are reluctant to treat patients who are HIV-positive, they should be obligated to do so.

Thesis

Background
Health care workers who are against treating AIDS patients cite Principle VI of the 1980 Principles of Medical Ethics of the American Medical Association (AMA), which first appeared in 1912. Principle VI says: "A physician shall, in the provision of appropriate patient care, except in emergencies, be free to choose whom to serve" (Zuger and Miles 1926). Physicians claim that according to this code, they can reject anybody whom they feel, even for some unexpressed reason, they cannot treat. They say Principle VI is clearly stated so there can be no debate; a doctor does not have to treat all patients who request his or her care.

Opposition's
first
argument

Response to
opposition's
first
argument
The doctors' points are well taken. However, others question their interpretation of Principle VI. Accordingly, the Council on Ethical and Judicial Affairs of the AMA issued a report called "Issues Involved in the Growing AIDS Crisis" in December 1987. The report refers to the tradition of the AMA (since its organization in 1847) that "when an epidemic

prevails, a physician must continue his labors without regard to his own health" (Benesch and Homisak 24). This more recent statement seems to contradict Principle VI. If we view AIDS as an epidemic, doctors cannot refuse to treat AIDS patients. The Council on Judicial and Ethical Affairs addresses Principle VI directly when it explains:

Authority

> Principle VI of the 1980 Principles of Ethics states
> that a physician shall . . ., except in emergencies,
> be free to choose whom to serve, with whom to
> associate and the environment in which to provide
> medical services. The Council has always interpreted
> this Principle as not supporting illegal or
> invidious discrimination against a patient based
> solely on his or her seropositivity. (Benesch and
> Homisak 25)

It should be obvious to doctors that using Principle VI to explain their unwillingness to treat AIDS victims is not enough justification.

Opposition's second argument

Another argument doctors use for not treating HIV-positive patients is that there is no infallible protection from cuts and needle pricks. AIDS can be contracted if the body fluids of an HIV-positive patient come in contact with those of the doctor. Health care professionals claim that they are in great risk of contracting the disease through a cut while operating or from a prick from a needle that has been used to inject an infected patient. Dr. Mark S. Litwin of Brigham and Women's Hospital expresses this concern: "Every so often you take off your gloves after an eight-hour case and your middle finger is

5

covered with blood. You cringe and a wave of nausea hits you. Should you get tested? Is it safe to have sex with your wife?" (Rosenthal 32). This is surely a fear that health care workers must deal with every day.

But as real as doctors' fear of contracting AIDS is, can it be exaggerated? "Data show that doctors and health-care workers who follow safety precautions for treating AIDS patients . . . are protected" (Benesch and Homisak 25). Moreover, "disease-control centers have advised health workers to use precautions . . . to avoid contact with all patients' blood" (Rosenthal 33). Are doctors who don't want to treat AIDS patients taking every possible precaution? A further question involves the AIDS incubation period of six months. Is it safe for physicians to assume that any patient is AIDS-free? Doctors' arguments that protection isn't enough lack justification. It has been proven that protection will safeguard doctors from contracting HIV. Furthermore, doctors are advised to avoid contact with all patients' blood since they don't know who may or may not be HIV-positive. Yet many doctors do not take precautions at all times. This may be because they think they are safe if the patient has not been identified as having AIDS or because they do not like wearing the protection. In this case, health care workers are allowing themselves to become vulnerable to infection, and they should not blame their patients.

The doctors also claim that "obligations to self and family override obligations to patients [with AIDS]" and that "physicians who contract AIDS are permanently lost to society

Response to opposition's second argument

Opposition's third argument

6

7

Weichert 5

and their patients" (Pellegrino 1940). These doctors argue that because AIDS is a communicable disease, a physician who contracts it becomes a danger to his or her patients and family.

Response to opposition's third argument

To be sure, AIDS is a communicable disease, but when compared with other communicable diseases, AIDS is not highly contagious. If doctors treat patients with other communicable diseases, why do they claim the right to reject AIDS patients? Hepatitis B is a highly communicable and fairly dangerous disease, yet doctors treat it all the time. Granted, there are measures that can prevent hepatitis (Dan), but hepatitis B is not an easily detected disease. By the time a patient is found to have it, the people close to him may have already contracted it. Yet doctors work with hepatitis cases fairly frequently, exposing themselves, their families, and their other patients to risk. In this sense, it may be safer to treat AIDS than some other highly communicable diseases.

8

Opposition's fourth argument

Yet another argument physicians use to justify their refusal to treat AIDS patients is that the disease is incurable. Doctors point out that treatment will only "postpone the inevitable" (Teich 22). Should a doctor be required to operate on a person in the last stages of AIDS when surgery may add only days to the patient's life?

9

Response to opposition's fourth argument

The doctors are absolutely correct. There is no question that AIDS patients will die. Nevertheless, they have as much right to have their pain lessened as anyone else. People with leukemia have little chance of surviving, yet doctors fight to save leukemia patients. AIDS patients are no different. They

10

have little hope of living, but they deserve to be able to
fight for what's left of their lives. By not helping them in
this struggle, doctors are turning their backs on fellow human
beings. Doctors have no right to decide who will be given a
chance at life, however slim, and who should die without
treatment.

Conclusion

Nobody questions that AIDS victims are human. We are
constantly told that we can be friends with them, we can touch
them, and we can hug them. But when a doctor won't help such
people, we begin to think that there is something the doctors
aren't telling us about AIDS--perhaps HIV-infected people are
more dangerous than we originally thought--and we become
scared. We fear for ourselves, worrying how we would be
treated if we became infected with the deadly virus. If nobody
will help you, not even your doctor, you can lose all sense of
being and all will to live. The moral thing to do is to make
sure all AIDS victims get the medical attention they need.
Whether a doctor wants to treat AIDS patients or not, he or
she has a moral obligation to do so, and this obligation
should be enforced.

11

Weichert 7

Works Cited

Benesch, Katherine, and Theresa Homisak. "The Duty to Treat
    AIDS Patients." Trial May 1988: 22-25.

Dan, Bruce B. "Patients without Physicians: The New Risk of
    AIDS." Journal of the American Medical Association 258
    (1987): 1940.

Pellegrino, Edmund D. "Altruism, Self-Interest, and Medical
    Ethics." Journal of the American Medical Association 258
    (1987): 1939-40.

Rosenthal, Elisabeth. "Risk of Contracting AIDS Virus Is
    Changing Practices in Medicine." New York Times 11 Nov.
    1990: 1, 32+.

Teich, Mark. "The Untouchables?" Omni June 1988: 22-23.

Zuger, Abigail, and Steven H. Miles. "Physicians, AIDS, and
    Occupational Risk: Historic Traditions and Ethical
    Obligations." Journal of the American Medical Association
    258 (1987): 1924-28.

WRITING AN ARGUMENT ESSAY

Now that you have studied and analyzed two argument essays, you are ready to write one of your own. Select a controversial topic that interests you. Here is a recap of the process we described in this chapter.

PREWRITING

Clarify and refine the issue you will write about.   If you plan to write on a controversial subject that you already know a lot about, you will have no trouble delving beneath the surface and discovering a number of underlying conflicts. Let's say you've read up on the controversy involving the labeling and censoring of certain types of music. Ostensibly, the issue is whether music should be censored. But you perceive a deeper issue. You believe that groups advocating censorship have goals other than protecting youths from "dangerous" lyrics. You think these groups want to suppress all mention of social conditions—drug use, racism, homosexuality, sexual violence—that diverge from the purported norm. Your background knowledge enables you to refine the issue and thus come up with a more innovative slant on the topic.

If you have not read widely or had experience with the subject, however, you will have to learn more about it by carefully reading the sources your professor recommends. If your professor has not provided a reading list, you will have to locate relevant sources in the library. Chapter 8 will give you useful advice about how to conduct library searches. When you first approach the reading sources, read for answers to the questions "What is controversial about this subject?" and "What do people argue about?"

Let's say your topic is the annual holiday commemorating Christopher Columbus's discovery of America. You are aware that various groups—Native Americans, Italians, Hispanics—have different views on the appropriateness of parades and other festivities, but you're unsure of the details surrounding the controversy. As you read through the sources, ask yourself, "What is so controversial about celebrating Columbus Day? What are these groups arguing about?" Your initial reading reveals a major controversy on whether Columbus's conquests should be celebrated or condemned.

After you have clarified the issue, continue reading the sources, but keep in mind that now your goal is to investigate various aspects of the broad issue so that you can delve beneath the surface and obtain a fresh perspective. For example, if your assignment is to write an essay on gun control, after your initial reading of the sources, you might move from a broad issue like whether handguns should be banned to a more pointed controversy, such as whether law-abiding members of violent communities should be allowed to purchase handguns for self-defense.

Probe both sides of the controversy.   As you read through the sources, do your best to understand different positions on the issue. We suggested earlier that you play the "believing game." Take Peter Elbow's advice and get inside the heads of the people who hold views different from your own. Take, for example, the experience of our student Eileen Laureano. Eileen had taken a firm stand on the issue of whether Columbus Day should be celebrated. She felt strongly that since so many Native Americans had perished in the aftermath of Columbus's explorations, Columbus Day should be a time of grief rather than celebration. As Eileen read through her sources, however, she tried to keep an open mind. She pretended that she was a patriotic American who believes that Columbus's contributions should be revered and recognized, and she also tried to see things through the eyes of Italian Americans who believe that by denouncing the celebration, we are depreciating the heritage of their people.

Write out clear-cut statements of your own position and the position of anyone objecting to your view.   Here is an example.

Issue: Whether rap music has redeeming qualities

Writer's position: Rap music lyrics are a reflection of urban realities.

Opposing view: Rap music lyrics are radical, extremist, and dangerous to our youth.

Compose a thesis that expresses your position as well as the position of those who disagree with you.   You can express your thesis in either of two ways:

- As a statement of your central claim:

  Rap music lyrics are a reflection of urban realities: drug use, crime, violence toward women.

- As a statement that incorporates both your claim and the opposition's:

  Rather than being radical, extremist, and dangerous to youth, rap music lyrics are a reflection of urban realities: drug use, crime, violence toward women.

The reason for including the opposing view in your thesis is to let your reader know from the start that your argument will be two-dimensional, not one-sided.

If you have difficulty expressing a lot of information in one sentence, use two or three sentences for your thesis:

  People who claim that rap music lyrics are radical, extremist, and dangerous to youth are seriously mistaken. The lyrics are a reflection of urban realities: drug use, crime, violence toward women.

To sum up, make sure that your thesis is issue-centered, arguable, and debatable.

- Be sure to anticipate and acknowledge conflicting views.
- Your purpose is to convince your readers to accept and agree with your position.

Reread the sources, formulate reasons that back up your thesis and explain your opponents' views, and then locate various types of evidence in support of the reasons.   *Record all this information in your notebook or journal.* A reason carries the weight of evidence. Be sure that each of your reasons is grounded in facts, statistics, examples, expert testimony, statements, or other relevant information from acknowledged authorities. To see how material from reading sources is eventually incorporated in argument essays, take a look at two excerpts from student papers.

The first is a paragraph in which Eileen Laureano uses facts, statistics, and other relevant information to argue against celebrating Columbus Day.

> Native Americans, in contrast, view the Columbus Day holiday as an insult to their struggles and persecution. The people brought to the "New World" by Columbus's expedition succeeded in exterminating the original inhabitants of the Americas. Many aboriginal nations perished at the hands of the Dutch, English, French, and Spanish. The Tawantinsuyu of the Inca empire were destroyed soon after Columbus's arrival. Theirs was once a civilized nation that ruled over 20 million people and had reached a high level of social, military, agricultural, and handicraft development (Llosa 48). The West Indian population also decreased from 50 million in the fifteenth century to 4 million in the seventeenth century (New Encyclopaedia Britannica 883). If conquest and exploration brought only bloodshed and extermination, then we should have no pride in celebrating this holiday.

In the second excerpt, Jim Li relies on an authority on bilingual education to support his argument that children should receive instruction in their native language as well as in English.

> Rosalie P. Porter, the director of English as a second language and bilingual programs for the Newton, Massachusetts, public schools, points out in her article "The Newton Alternative to Bilingual Education" that second-language learning occurs at varying rates in different individuals. "The ultimate goal is that all students who arrive knowing a language other than English will become bilingual and fully capable of using the second language--English--for social and academic purposes" (150). By combining the mother tongue with English and flexibly catering to the individual's progress, language learning can become most effective.

Use ethical, emotional, and logical appeals to establish credibility, interest your audience, and present a well-reasoned, compelling case.   Make ethical appeals by exhibiting in-depth knowledge of the subject and drawing on the expert judgments of others; being fair, honest, and accurate; and showing respect for your audience by using an appropriate tone. Divulge your character by drawing on personal experiences that directly support your points, and demonstrate competence with correct usage, punctuation, and mechanics. Make emotional appeals by drawing on firsthand experiences and concrete examples, anecdotes, stories, comparisons, and contrasts the reader can identify with. Also use metaphors, similes, and evocative words that bring to mind particular images and connotations or relate the issue to the reader's sense of responsibility, civic duty, patriotism, values, or beliefs. Make logical appeals with solid reasons and evidence.

DRAFTING

Arrange solid reasons in a logical sequence. After you have selected information from the reading sources that supports your own reasons and those of your opposition, you need to arrange this material to form the body paragraphs of your essay. There are three common arrangements for argument essays:

1. Writer presents the opposition first, dismisses it, and then gives reasons for his or her own view.
2. Writer first gives reasons for own view and then presents the opposition and refutation.
3. Writer alternates between the views of the opposition and rebuttal and his or her own views.

All three of these arrangements are effective, but there are reasons why you might choose one pattern over another. Arrangement 1 works well if the objections you are counteracting are weak and insubstantial. You can respond to them right off and dismiss them summarily. You might also use this arrangement if you intend to work your essay up to a climax, moving from the opposition's views to your refutation, then to your weaker reasons, and finally to your strongest points. If you are addressing a friendly, easily persuadable audience, try arrangement 2. Readers who are predisposed to your position or already on your side will have a vested interest in your views and only a passing interest in the views of the opposition. Arrangement 3 works well when your opponents have a substantial, extended argument that is not easily dismissed. As you take up and challenge the opposition's claims point by point, you can also weave in support for your own views.

Take your readers' level of interest and background knowledge into account.   If your readers already have a stake in the issue, they will be eager to hear what you have to say. Suppose that you are a campus leader writing to persuade students to go along with a proposed increase in the student activity fee. Before voting for or against the increase, students who wish to be informed will be interested in your views. If you don't think your readers are intrinsically interested in the issue, however, open your essay with a lead and an introductory paragraph that will motivate them to read on.

The amount of background you provide also depends on your audience. If you know your readers are knowledgeable about the subject and familiar with the controversy surrounding it, you will not have to do a lot of explaining, defining, or narrating of past events. The topic of record labeling is a good example. If you are writing an argument essay to your classmates about the censorship of song lyrics, you can assume that most of them know a fair amount about the controversy. Conversely, if your purpose is to convince your classmates that history justifies Irish Americans' financial support of the Irish Republican Army, you will have to supply historical information and explanations that place the controversy in a contemporary context.

Decide how you want to come across to your audience.   Undoubtedly, you want your audience to view you as someone who is knowledgeable and believable. The best way to establish your credibility is to provide your readers with a two-dimensional argument that rests on solid reasons and is documented with reliable sources. If you simply offer opinions or unsubstantiated reasons, your readers will feel no compulsion to accept your view.

Whether you write in a professional or a personal voice depends on the context of the situation. Some teachers require that their students submit impersonal third-person writing; others allow the use of *I, we,* and *you.* Some arguments lend themselves to scholarly, objective prose; others work better when the writer uses *I, we,* and *you* to identify personally with the issue and pull the readers into the controversy.

REVISING

If it is all right with your instructor, have a classmate or friend read over your first draft and answer the questions listed on page 240. If no one is available, answer the questions yourself. Keep in mind the following concerns:

- Moving from writer-based to reader-based prose
- Varying sentence length
- Stressing verbs rather than nouns
- Using words effectively
- Detecting sexist language
- Adding your own voice

After you have produced a first draft of your essay, use the following checklist to revise your work.

✓ CHECKLIST FOR REVISING AN ARGUMENT ESSAY

_____ Does the writer organize the discussion around the discernible purpose of persuading or convincing an audience?

_____ Does the writer move beyond the purpose of simply synthesizing or comparing and contrasting opposing views?

_____ Is the argument two-dimensional, taking into account both sides of the issue, or is it one-sided?

_____ Does the writer use the conventions (not necessarily in this order) that the reader expects to find in an argument essay:

_____ Explanation of the issue

_____ Arguable thesis

_____ Background information

_____ Support for the position being argued

_____ Mention of the conflicting position

_____ Writer's response to the opposition

_____ Conclusion

_____ Does the writer present reasons rather than opinions?

_____ Are the reasons supported with evidence?

_____ Does the writer draw on reliable sources?

_____ Does the writer make a favorable, creditable impression?

_____ Does the writer display an awareness of the audience's needs by setting a context for the reader in the following ways?

_____ Giving appropriate background information

_____ Mentioning authors and titles of sources when necessary

_____ Supplying necessary documentation for sources

_____ Providing clear connectives that differentiate his or her ideas from those of the writers of the sources?

EDITING

When you are satisfied with your revision, read your paper aloud. Then reread it line by line and sentence by sentence. Check for correct usage, punctuation, spelling, mechanics, manuscript form, and typographical errors. If you are using a word processing program with a spell checker, run the checker on your essay. If your editing skills are not strong, get a friend to read over your work.

ANALYSIS AND EVALUATION

The reason we analyze things is to help us understand them better. Let's say you're working hard at a part-time job, but you don't seem to be saving much money. You investigate the causes of your problem by itemizing your weekly purchases. This systematic analysis of your spending habits reveals that a surprising portion of your paycheck is being spent on the take-out dinners you buy every night on your way home from work. Analysis serves many purposes. It enables you to identify and solve problems, examine how things work, and inquire into the complexities of various phenomena.

In college, you will be asked to write analyses of issues and texts. The procedure is the same. You break the subject up into elements, facets, or parts. For this process, you will use the critical thinking and reading strategies that we have presented throughout this book: examination of content; form, organization, features; and rhetorical situation.

In this chapter, we will focus on three types of essays:

- Rhetorical analysis
- Evaluation
- Exploratory analysis

RHETORICAL ANALYSIS AND EVALUATION AS OPPOSED TO RESPONSE

Professors ask students to write analysis essays because they want to hear students' *own* interpretations of what they read. That's why it's important to come to your own conclusions rather than parrot back the interpretations you hear in class lectures and discussions. Keep in mind that your professors expect you to base your interpretation on a systematic examination of the material, not on personal opinions or reactions. A reaction or response essay is different from an analysis essay. As you saw in Chapter 3, the response essay is based on your previous knowledge of and experiences with the topic. *Response essays focus on your reaction to content, whereas analysis essays focus on how that content is conveyed.*

The *evaluation essay,* also referred to as a *critique, critical essay,* or *review,* is similar to an analysis in that it requires you to do a systematic examination of the reading source. The primary difference is that the evaluation essay judges the strengths and weaknesses of the source according to established criteria. The analysis essay offers an interpretation; it does not assess the source's quality or worth. For example, if you were to *analyze* Patricia J. Williams's article "Road Rage" (pages 424–425), your goal would be to interpret the article by showing how the various rhetorical techniques that Williams uses contribute to her thesis. If you were to *evaluate* "Road Rage," your goal would be to measure *how well* Williams conveys her thesis. You would base this judgment on a set of clear-cut criteria.

Another difference between the two types of essay is that the evaluation essay has more of a persuasive edge than the analysis essay. For the evaluation, your aim is to get your reader to agree with you and, in some cases, for instance, when you write a book review, to affect your reader's actions. The review may determine whether or not your readers actually read the book.

The distinctions among essays of response, analysis, and evaluation are extremely important. Unless your assignment specifically calls for it, personal reaction is inappropriate in analyses and reviews.

ESSAY TYPE	STRATEGY	GOAL
Response essay (subjective)	Obtain ideas from your personal knowledge and experience and apply them to the reading material	Express informed opinions about the subject matter
Analysis essay (objective)	Obtain ideas from your examination of the various elements of the reading source	Interpret how the writer's techniques convey meaning
Evaluation essay (objective)	Obtain ideas from your examination of the various elements of the reading source and judge them according to a set of established criteria	Show the relative strengths and weaknesses of the work

As the chart illustrates, response essays are *subjective* and essays of analysis and evaluation are *objective*. When you analyze and evaluate, you do not rely on personal reactions. You base your conclusions on a reasoned examination of standards that are acceptable to your readers. You already know many of these standards—you have been using them throughout this book. In this chapter, we will discuss additional criteria that are commonly used in English and composition courses. You should keep in mind, however, that various academic fields have their own standards for analyzing and evaluating written work. When you take courses in the social sciences, you will see that the criteria in those fields differ somewhat from the criteria used in the humanities. Make a point to learn the criteria for quality writing in the various academic fields, and refer to them when you read and write in each area.

RHETORICAL ANALYSIS

Before we describe the process for composing a rhetorical analysis, we want you to take a look at an essay of this type. The essay was written in response to the following assignment:

> Write a systematic analysis of a reading selection of your choice. As you interpret the text, comment on the author's rhetorical strategies.

Steve Stout wrote his essay on "Skills and Pills," written by physician Kate Scannell when she was clinical director of AIDS services at a county hospital in San Francisco. Scannell explains that when she started working at the hospital, she treated her terminally ill patients the only way she knew how, with impersonal, aggressive medical service. She relates in detail her efforts to help Raphael, a young man who was near death. Each time Raphael asked Scannell for help, she responded with her "skills and pills." She was unaware that Raphael was not asking her to treat his disease but to put him out of his suffering. One night when Scannell was off duty, another physician granted Raphael his wish. After Raphael's death, Scannell was better able to communicate with her patients. She learned to practice medicine more compassionately, with her heart as well as her skills and pills.

Stout 1

Steve Stout

Professor Kennedy

English 223

6 November 1998

The Role of Imagery in "Skills and Pills"

In her article "Skills and Pills," Kate Scannell describes the process she went through as a physician learning how to administer effectively to AIDS patients. Throughout the article, she uses a series of images that serve to emphasize and illuminate the transformation she experienced, from a devotee of medical technology to a compassionate caregiver who is aware of the limitations of medical science.

Scannell, who is now clinical director of services for AIDS patients at a county hospital in San Francisco, began working in the AIDS ward right after medical school. Her initial response to AIDS was to give each patient full, aggressive treatment. Describing herself as an "ever-ready gunfighter," she says, "I stalked the hallways ready for surprise developments and acute medical problems to present

Title (focus of essay)

Paper opener giving author, title, and topic

Initial identification of author by full name

Thesis

Later identification of author by last name only

Summary

Textual evidence supporting thesis

1

2

Stout 2

themselves. [When they did,] I would shoot them down with my
skills and pills" (102). Scannell explains that she was
listening to the voices of her old teachers in medical school,
who had told her to use every intervention possible to keep
her patients alive.

For months Scannell persisted in offering her brand of
intensive, exhaustive medical service. Then one day she
encountered Raphael. Raphael was a twenty-two-year-old AIDS
patient, "a large, bloated, purple, knobby mass with eyes so
swollen shut that he could not see" (103). When Raphael asked
Scannell to help him, she put her "diagnostic sharpshooting
abilities" to work. Each time Raphael asked for more help,
Scannell responded with more medical procedures. She said that
when she left the hospital that evening, she knew that she had
done everything conceivable to help her patient.

That night Raphael again asked for help. The attending
physician responded very differently from Scannell, however.
Instead of giving Raphael skills and pills, he disconnected
Raphael's intravenous and blood transfusions and gave him some
morphine. "Raphael smiled and thanked the doctor for helping
him, and then expired later that evening" (104).

Raphael's death changed the way Scannell practiced
medicine. She describes her transformation in terms of a
clothing image:

> Like the vision of Raphael's spirit rising free from
> his disease-racked corpse in death, the clothing
> fashioned for me by years of traditional Western

Side annotations:

Use of present tense to explain how writer uses techniques

Summary paragraph

Summary paragraph

Margin numbers: 3, 4, 5

Block format for long quotation

> medical training fell off me like tattered rags. I
> began to hear my own voices and compassionate
> sensibilities once again, louder and clearer than
> the chorus of voices of my old mentors. (104)

Scannell compares her self-discovery to an archaeological expedition. She says, "I got crushed under mounds of rubble that collected over the years of my intense and all-consuming medical training" (104). She describes this rubble as consisting of increased medical technology, the dictum that physicians must save lives at all costs, and the taboos against doctors using intuition or compassion (104).

Paragraph with textual evidence supporting thesis

Conclusion

Now transformed, Dr. Scannell no longer listens to the voices of her old teachers, and she is no longer a sharpshooter. She listens instead to the people behind the disease. She no longer offers these patients skills and pills; instead, she gives them conversation and compassion.

6

Work Cited

Scannell, Kate. "Skills and Pills." <u>AIDS: The Women</u>. Ed. Ines
    Rieder and Patricia Ruppett. San Francisco: Cleis, 1988.
    102-05.

In this essay, Steve's aim is to show his readers how one of Scannell's rhetorical strategies, her use of imagery, operates in the article. His title indicates that he will focus on "the role of imagery," and his thesis reveals that he will explain how the imagery functions. The introductory paragraph reveals that he will show how Scannell's images serve to emphasize and illuminate the transformation she experienced. In paragraphs 2, 4, and 5, he describes how Scannell uses particular images, backing up his points with quotations from the article. The main purpose of paragraph 3 is to summarize relevant parts of the article. Note that Steve does not summarize the entire article. He gives only the background information readers need to comprehend the analysis.

WRITING A RHETORICAL ANALYSIS ESSAY

Now that you have read a model analysis essay, you can practice writing one of your own. In the next section, we will take you through the process Steve experienced as he wrote his analysis. The process we describe is applicable to any assignment that requires you to write a rhetorical analysis of nonfiction.

PREWRITING

Successful analysis requires careful planning. Assignments that direct you to analyze or evaluate a text are typically harder than assignments that ask you to react, compare and contrast, or argue because they require a more detailed examination of the reading source and a deeper knowledge of the author's writing techniques. Without sufficient initial planning, you may become lost or turn out an extended summary or reaction instead of an analysis. Without extensive preparation, it is almost impossible to write a satisfactory analytical piece.

Clarify the Assignment, Set Your Rhetorical Goal, and Consider Your Audience.

When you receive your assignment, pay attention to what it asks you to do. Some assignments, like the one our student Steve received, are open-ended and allow the writer to determine the aspects of the reading source that will be examined. Other assignments may stipulate the parts of the text on which you should focus. For example, a professor might ask you to discuss the role of language in a particular piece or to comment on the structure of a work and explain why it is organized as it is. If you have questions about the type of analysis the assignment calls for, be sure to ask your professor before you proceed.

After you have clarified the assignment, decide on your rhetorical purpose by asking yourself, "Why am I writing this analysis essay? What desired effect do I hope to have on my audience?" Your fundamental purpose is to give your readers your interpretation of the reading source and in so doing explain how one or more characteristics of the text contribute to its meaning. Looking back at Steve's essay, you can see that his objective is to demonstrate how various images in Scannell's "Skills and Pills" help the author convey that she has experienced a dramatic transformation.

The next decisions concern your audience. Ask yourself:

- What will my readers already know about the source?
- How much of the source should I summarize, and what form will the summary take?

- Will I need to explain basic concepts and provide background for the material to make sense?
- What overall impact do I hope to have on my readers?

If your audience is familiar with the piece you are analyzing, supply only a minimal amount of background information. If your audience has not read the piece, as was the case with Steve, give some general background and summarize the parts of the source that are crucial to your analysis. It isn't necessary to summarize the entire text, only enough to persuade your readers that you have a valid, reasonable interpretation.

Do a First Reading to Get a General Impression of the Source.

Your first reading may leave you with little more than a general impression of the reading source. You will get an overall sense of the subject, the author's approach, and the central point, but you probably won't pay much attention to other characteristics of the text unless they are very conspicuous. At this stage, you may want to freewrite your reactions, especially if the text evokes a strong response. A reader's first reaction to Scannell's "Skills and Pills" might have been, "Wow, that doctor certainly did an about-face!" The reader might also have been unsettled by Scannell's graphic description of Raphael's ravaged body.

Reread and Ask Analysis Questions.

Analyzing a reading source is largely a matter of asking the right questions about it. The second reading allows you to ask questions, annotate the text, and take analysis notes. Essentially, you will work with the same questions concerning content; form, organization, and features; and rhetorical concerns that you have been using throughout this book. But you will add to them and make them more probing and more detailed. Your objective is to delve deeper into the material. Don't trust your memory. Write the answers to the analysis questions in your journal or notebook. The answers to these questions will serve as the basis for your analysis essay.

Examine content.   Start by examining the content. Locate the thesis or central point the author is making about the topic and identify other important points. Ask yourself, "Which aspects of the topic are emphasized and which are downplayed or ignored?" Next, examine the types of evidence the author uses, estimate whether they are sufficient, and determine whether they lead logically to the conclusions. (For a review of various types of evidence, see pages 222–225.) Finally, ask whether the author acknowledges and refutes the views of individuals who might oppose his or her argument.

Determine form, organization, and features.   Identify the form of the text. In this book, you have already examined certain essay types: response, comparison and contrast, and argument. Other recognizable forms of nonfiction are editorials, news stories, feature articles, biographies, memoirs, autobiographies, and letters to the editor. Ask, "How does the form contribute to the piece?"

Then determine the organizational pattern. Is it chronological order or narrative; cause and effect; comparison and contrast, either point-by-point or block; argument, including position, reasons, opposition, and refutation; problem and solution; statement and response; question and answer; or classification? How does the organizational pattern contribute to the meaning of the piece? Would the meaning change if the parts were arranged differently, for example, if the narrative progressed from past to present instead of present to past; if the consequences were explained before the causes; or if reasons were ordered from least important to most important instead of vice versa?

Finally, zero in on the features of the text, asking yourself how they help convey the author's points. Search for memorable or significant devices that enable you to see the subject in a new perspective. You will want to look closely at features like language, sentence elements, images and scenes, and references and allusions.

Look to see if the language serves to heighten and illuminate the topic. Does the author use precise wording, vivid details, words that appeal to the senses, and words with emotional intensity? Is figurative language (similes and metaphors) used? A *simile* occurs when the write draws a comparison, using *like* or *as* to show the two elements that are being compared. Kate Scannell uses simile when she writes:

> Like a very weary but ever-ready gunfighter, I stalked the hallways ready for surprise developments and acute medical problems to present themselves. (102)

A *metaphor* is an implicit comparison because the *like* or *as* is not mentioned. Scannell uses metaphor when she writes:

> The clothing fashioned for me by years of traditional medical training fell off me. (104)

Here she likens the treatments, cures, and procedures that she learned in medical school to clothing. For another example, read how Jeffrey Goldberg describes Sergeant Mike Lewis:

> He can smell crack cocaine inside a closed automobile. He's a human drug dog, a walking polygraph machine. (427)

Next, examine sentence elements. Are you struck by rhythmic, balanced, symmetrical, and graceful sentences? Look for these characteristics in the following excerpt from an essay written by Gore Vidal about the "inventors" of the Constitution:

> But the Inventors were practical men and the federal constitution that they assembled in in 1787 was an exquisite machine that, with a repair here and a twist there, has gone on protecting the property of the worthy for two hundred years while protecting in the Bill of Rights (that sublime afterthought) certain freedoms of speech and assembly which are still unknown even now to that irritable fount of America's political and actual being, old Europe. (Vidal 153)

How do these sentences help convey the meaning of the text?

Also take stock of the author's use of images and scenes. *Images* are mental pictures. Recall the images Steve Stout examines in "Skills and Pills":

> Like the vision of Raphael's spirit rising free from his disease-racked corpse in death, the clothing fashioned for me by years of traditional Western medical training fell off me like tattered rags. I began to hear my own voices and compassionate sensibilities once again, louder and clearer than the chorus of voices of my old mentors. (104)

I got crushed under mounds of rubble that collected over the years of my intense and all-consuming medical training. (104).

Scenes are also mental pictures, but they have enough detail in them that they could be acted out. To illustrate her point that physically ill individuals are escorted to hospitals involuntarily whereas mentally ill people are not, Erica Mazor depicts three scenes:

- An elderly man rushes across the avenue and is hit by a bus and seriously injured. He pleads with the police to take him home instead of to the hospital. The police call an ambulance, and the man is quickly transported to a nearby emergency room.
- A young woman with chronic asthma has an attack on a crowded city street. A passerby offers to assist, but she refuses his help. Worried that she is seriously ill, the man hails a cab and escorts the woman to the nearest hospital.
- A middle-aged woman, ravaged by paranoid schizophrenia, lies in the fetal position on a blanket on a subway platform. Commuters walk past her day after day. Finally, some people speak to her and offer to call the police. The woman yells at them to leave her alone. They walk away. (205)

Each vignette enables the reader to visualize the characters and action, and, in so doing, it drives home Erica's point. As you examine the text, ask yourself, "Does the writer create memorable images and scenes that contribute to the meaning?"

Finally, examine the author's references and allusions to determine if they illuminate or add significantly to the subject matter. Take account of the writer's formal references to other written sources as well as other types of references and allusions. An *allusion* is a reference to some other parallel concept. Describing the patients on her AIDS ward, Scannell writes:

Some patients were so emaciated by profound wasting that I could not shake disquieting memories of photographs I had seen as a little girl which depicted Auschwitz and Buchenwald prisoners. (103)

Scannell's reference to prisoners of concentration camps intensifies her description of the patients' sad state. Notice Jeffrey Goldberg's allusion in the following description:

The four buyers are white. Jones and Robinson are black, veterans of the street who know that white people in a black neighborhood will be stopped. Automatically. Faster than a Rastafarian in Scarsdale. (431)

Define rhetorical concerns. As we explained in Chapter 1, skilled writers consciously adopt an attitude or rhetorical posture that is appropriate to their audience and subject. As you read the text, ask yourself, "What is the writer's persona or stance, and how does this stance contribute to his or her point?" Notice how Leslie Heywood narrates "Satellite" (pages 454–457) from the point of view of a teenage girl. This stance enables her to address her readers on a very personal level. Also consider how the writer's voice contributes to the piece. While Heywood adopts a personal voice, on the topic of gender equality in sport, Douglas T. Putnam (pages 451–453) keeps himself at a distance as he explains the effect that Title IX has had on male players.

For a summary of the analysis questions, see questions for analysis and evaluation on pages 267–269.

Exercise ....

Apply the analysis questions to Leslie Heywood's memoir, "Satellite," on pages 454–457. Write a one-page explanation of how the analysis process affected your understanding of the reading selection.

• • • • • • • • • • • • • • • •

Review Your Answers to the Analysis Questions.

Soon after you have finished rereading and responding to the analysis questions, pause to organize your thoughts. It is best to do this while the answers are still fresh in your mind. Planning at this stage will save time because you won't have to do extensive rereading of the source later on while you are drafting. First, reexamine your rhetorical purpose. Keep in mind that your objective is to show your readers how the author of the source has used specific rhetorical techniques to get his or her points across. Review your notes on the analysis questions as follows.

Look to see if a particular question produced a lengthy, substantive response. If this is the case, go for depth rather than breadth, and focus your analysis on a single, prominent feature. For example, reading "Satellite," you may have been so struck by Leslie Heywood's tone that you wrote extensive notes in response to questions about rhetorical concerns, especially those with reference to the author's stance and voice. These notes may supply you with enough material for your analysis.

See if you are able to group answers that pertain to similar categories. This is the approach our student Steve used in his essay on pages 243–245. When Steve reviewed his analysis notes, he discovered that his most promising insights were about Kate Scannell's descriptive and figurative language, particularly her imagery. Since all of the images he was considering were evoked by figurative language, he decided to subsume language under the category of imagery. As you may recall, Steve does not refer specifically to metaphors and similes; instead, he describes the images that these devices call up.

Steve also took copious notes on Scannell's moving descriptions of the AIDS patients, but he decided against including them in his essay. As you review your analysis notes, you will find that you have collected much more information than you can possibly include in your paper.

Select two or more elements for your focus. Instead of zeroing in on a single, substantive response or categorizing related responses, focus on two or more areas. If Steve had decided to fashion his essay in this way, he might have selected four characteristics of Scannell's article: descriptive language, figurative language, images, and scenes.

Return to the relevant parts of the text to check for supporting material. In your essay, each time you make a point about the textual features you are analyzing, you will provide textual evidence in the form of a quotation, paraphrase, or summary. At this juncture, go back to the reading source and mark all the passages that you might use to support your points. If you cannot find enough textual evidence, think about changing your focus. Decide on an organizational plan.

You can organize your analysis essay in any number of ways. The important thing is your rhetorical purpose. Your goal is to reveal to your readers how certain characteristics of the reading source contribute to its meaning. We will present three typical patterns of organization and skeletal outlines of each.

Show cause and effect. Here you show the effects of the writer's techniques (causes).

Thesis

In "Skills and Pills," the imagery and descriptive language reinforce Scannell's depiction of her transformation from an impersonal physician to a compassionate companion to her patients.

Essay Structure

- Introductory paragraph(s)
- One to two paragraphs explaining how imagery reinforces the transformation
- One to two paragraphs explaining how figurative language reinforces the transformation
- Concluding paragraph

Present your argument. Another possibility is to structure your analysis along the lines of the unidimensional argument that we discussed on page 202. Your goal is to persuade your readers that your interpretation is valid. State your position, and then give three or four reasons for your stand.

Thesis

Scannell's description and figurative language contribute significantly to her text.

Essay Structure

- Introductory paragraph(s)
- One to two paragraphs giving reasons why the description is significant
- One to two paragraphs giving reasons why the figurative language is significant
- Concluding paragraph

Structure the reading source. A third possibility is to follow the order of the reading source. Take up each feature in the order in which it is presented in the text. Our student Steve operated in this way. Guided by the chronological order of "Skills and Pills," he discussed the imagery at the beginning, middle, and end of the piece.

Thesis

```
Throughout "Skills and Pills," Kate Scannell uses a series of
images that serve to emphasize and illuminate the transformation
she experienced.
```

Essay Structure

- Introductory paragraph(s)
- Paragraph developing imagery at the beginning of the piece
- Paragraph developing imagery in the middle of the piece
- Paragraph developing imagery at the end of the piece

DRAFTING

Now you are ready to compose a preliminary draft of your analysis essay. Remember that this will not be a final, polished draft. You will have an opportunity to revise it at a later date. Before you begin writing, decide how you want to come across to your readers. Will you offer a personal interpretation, using first-person pronouns, or write in a more formal tone? The degree of formality may be dictated by the assignment. If you are unsure about taking a particular stance, ask your professor for advice.

As you draft your essay, you may want to consult the sections on paper openers, introductions, and conclusions in Chapter 3, pages 107–111.

After you have arranged the notes that you took on the analysis questions, convert them into body paragraphs in accordance with your organizational plan. As you develop each paragraph, support your points with evidence (quotations, paraphrases, or summaries) from the reading source.

A further consideration is to adhere to the special conventions that academic writers follow when composing analysis essays.

SPECIAL CONVENTIONS FOR ANALYSIS ESSAYS

- Use the present tense when explaining how the author uses particular procedures and writing techniques.

   ```
   Raphael's death changed the way Scannell practiced medicine. She
   describes her transformation in terms of a clothing image. . . .
   Scannell compares her self-discovery to an archaeological expe-
   dition.
   ```

   Notice that Steve writes in the past tense when he is explaining what happened to Scannell, the narrator ("Raphael's death *changed* the way Scannell *practiced* medicine"), but he switches to the present tense when he explains how Scannell, the writer, uses certain techniques ("She *describes*," "Scannell *compares*").

- Identify the author of the source by first and last name initially and thereafter only by last name.
- Indent long quotations (four or more lines) in block format.

REVISING

If your instructor agrees, make arrangements to have a classmate or friend review your preliminary draft and give you feedback. If this is not possible, set the paper aside for a few days and then review it yourself. Respond to the following questions.

✓ CHECKLIST FOR REVISING A RHETORICAL ANALYSIS ESSAY

_____ Can you identify the writer's rhetorical purpose? Is the writer giving you an interpretation of the source and in so doing explaining how certain characteristics contribute to its meaning?

_____ Does everything in the draft lead to or follow from one central meaning? If not, which ideas seem to be out of place?

_____ Do you understand the analysis, and is the writer sensitive to your concerns?

_____ Does the writer provide necessary background information about the subject and enough summary of the source as well as its title and author? If not, what is missing?

_____ When referring to the source, does the writer supply the necessary documentation?

_____ Does the writer provide clear transitions and connecting ideas that differentiate his or her own ideas from those of the author?

_____ Does the writer refer to the author by name?

_____ Which organizational format does the writer use: cause and effect, argument, or order of the source? If another pattern is used, is it appropriate for an analysis essay?

_____ Has the writer made you aware of the bases for the analysis? Which characteristics of the source provide focus? If the bases for the analysis are unclear, explain your confusion.

_____ Does the writer support each point with direct evidence (quotations, paraphrases, summaries) from the source? If not, where is evidence needed?

_____ Does the writer provide smooth transitions and connecting ideas as he or she moves from one point of analysis to another? If not, where are they needed?

_____ Do you hear the writer's voice throughout the essay? Describe it.

_____ What type of lead does the writer use to open the paper? Is it effective? If not, why not?

_____ Does the paper have an appropriate conclusion? Can you suggest an alternative way of ending the essay?

_____ Is the title suitable for the piece? Can you suggest an alternative?

_____ Has the writer followed academic writing conventions, such as writing in the present tense when explaining how the author uses particular procedures and techniques, identifying the author initially by first name and last name and thereafter only by last name, and indenting long quotations in block format?

EDITING

When you are satisfied with your revision, read your paper aloud. Then reread it line by line and sentence by sentence. Check for correct usage, punctuation, spelling, mechanics, manuscript form, and typographical errors. If you are using a word processing program with a spell checker, run the checker on your essay. If your editing skills are not strong, get a friend to read over your work.

EVALUATION

When you evaluate a reading source, you move beyond interpretation into the realm of judgment. Your purpose is to give your readers your estimation of the quality or worth of the piece. Always base your judgment on accepted criteria. For example, rather than simply showing that a writer's evidence supports his or her argument, explain *how well* the evidence serves the writer's purpose. Rather than simply explaining how descriptive language contributes to a theme, appraise the language. In addition to describing the text's strong qualities, you can also point out its weaknesses.

You can't make a valid value judgment about a reading source unless you comprehend it thoroughly. For that reason, you have to analyze the text before you evaluate it. The analysis will also enable you to demonstrate that you are knowledgeable about the topic. Your readers will take your evaluation seriously only if you have established this credibility.

To acquaint you with the characteristics of evaluation essays, let's look at two sample student essays. The first is Helen Chang's evaluation of an argument presented by Linda Grant in the first chapter of her book *Sexing the Millennium: Women and the Sexual Revolution*. Grant asks whether birth control technology has enabled a sexual revolution and whether future generations can deploy that technology to further the cause of human liberation.

E x e r c i s e ....

Read Helen Chang's essay to yourself. Then break the class into five groups. Assign each group a paragraph from Helen's essay, beginning with paragraph 5 and ending with paragraph 10. For each paragraph, assess the quality of Helen's evaluation. Reconvene the entire class. The recorder for each group should report the group's findings.

• • • • • • • • • • • • • • • •

Helen Chang

Professor Smith

Academic Writing II

24 February 2000

Sexual Revolution: Different Meanings for Different Women

In "What Sexual Revolution?" Linda Grant examines the
effects that the sexual revolution has had on women's lives
since the 1960s. Grant recalls the optimism that she and many
of her peers in the 1960s had in hopes that sexual liberation
held the key to greater freedom and was a step toward the
resolution of other forms of social oppression. However, one
can see that perhaps because of their narrow view of sexual
liberation, the sexual revolution failed in the aims that Grant
expected from it.

Grant begins by documenting the surprised reaction many
of her peers had when learning that she was writing a book
about the sexual revolution:

> And then it would come--archly, provocatively, sadly,
> or with a world-weary moue of disillusion, "Really?
> Has there <u>been</u> a sexual revolution?" . . . I could be
> standing there talking to a thirty-eight-year-old
> lawyer who had lived with her partner for ten years
> and was just about to have her first child (with the
> benefit of nanny, cleaning lady, and nursery), and
> she would still say, "Has there <u>been</u> a sexual
> revolution?" (1)

Even though this woman, like many middle-class women, benefits
from the social progress women made in the 1960s and '70s, she

still expresses disbelief that an actual revolution in women's status took place.

Grant explains this logic. After all, women still live in fear of rape. Violent sexual crimes against women are more frequent than ever. Pornography, no longer an underground phenomenon, often depicts women in degrading and dehumanizing positions and is readily available in a variety of forms. Even after women achieved a higher level of freedom of sexual expression in the 1960s, Grant reminds us that teenage girls who sleep with their boyfriends are still called sluts by their friends (2). So has there been a sexual revolution at all? And if so, what were its implications on the lives of women?

Grant does a good job of demonstrating the significant freedoms women have gained since the sexual revolution. Today, women do not have to choose between a career and marriage; many women have both. Mostly due to the invention of the pill in the 1960s, women enjoy a relative amount of reproductive freedom in the form of legal and fairly accessible birth control. Grant points out that it is socially acceptable for women to have sexual relationships with men who are not their husbands. Lesbians have gained a significant amount of visibility, and although they have a way to go toward sharing the privileges that heterosexuals enjoy, gay women have organized politically and socially to create a community and space that is not totally in the closet and underground anymore.

Grant's points are well taken, and she organizes her argument effectively by comparing and contrasting older arguments with current ones. She also provides many interesting details about modern women's sex lives. It is true that women today enjoy significant freedoms that women in generations past did not share. However, does sexual freedom to any extent hold the key to liberation in other walks of life? Will sexual freedom for women alleviate the other problems and oppressions that all women face? Will domestic violence end when women have achieved sexual freedom? Will women be paid wages equal to those of men? Will forms of oppression separate but interconnected with sexism, such as racism and class oppression, be alleviated through the sexual liberation of the human species?

One problem with Grant's thesis is her unclear definition of <u>women</u>. Of which women, exactly, does she speak? Is it true that all women shared the same form of sexual repression before the 1960s? Were all women equally protected by codes of morality? Or was this a privilege of sorts reserved only for a certain segment of the population?

Although Grant makes some good points about the significance of the sexual revolution on many women's lives, one flaw in her argument lies in her overgeneral, sweeping definition of <u>women</u>. The women whom Grant refers to are for the most part white and middle-class. A case in point is her statement about women choosing between a career or marriage: "Women married or had a career, but if they did the latter they would be sexually repressed spinsters whom, by implication, no man wanted or loved" (2). This is a dilemma only middle- and upper-class women faced before the 1960s. For all of history, there was no question that working-class women would work, because they had to. Working-class women who held jobs outside the home were not thought of as sexually undesirable. In fact, the better a woman's ability to work, the better her prospects for marriage may have been, since throughout most of history marriage was more of an economic arrangement than a union based on romantic attraction.

Grant also mentions that recent codes of morality carefully guarded women's sexuality to ensure virginity and fidelity. This is also something that has varied for different women throughout history. Although the untouchable, sexually pure woman was held up as an ideal for all women in the past two centuries, the main function of this view was to bolster the hegemony of the white middle class in England and America, the two countries on which Grant bases her analysis. These codes of morality were not imposed on women of other races and classes, at least not in the same way. The strict controls of white and upper-class women's sexuality ensured paternity and regulated the inheritance of property. Because of the middle class's interest in these matters, and because they were (and are) the ruling class in these countries, all women were not seen as equals.

A good example of this occurred in the American South during the nineteenth century. The disparity between the way white women and African American women are regarded sexually is quite significant. All women were definitely not regarded or treated as equal. Women who were slaves and their descendants were not subject to the same sexual protections that white

8

9

women were. During slavery, black women frequently became white

men's concubines, both by choice and by force. In fact, many

African American women were sold to white men expressly for

sexual purposes, even though most of the men were married to

white women. The purpose of such arrangements was to give

white men a sexual outlet without impregnating their wives,

since birth control was very unreliable at that time. It also

upheld the racial and sexual power structures. By stripping

black women of control over their sexuality, it kept them down

both racially and sexually. By rendering black men powerless to

protect their wives, sisters, and friends, it upheld the power

of white men over black men by not allowing blacks to live up

to the white middle-class society's standards of masculinity.

The system of slavery and racial oppression in the South also

degraded black women into sexual objects, a stereotype that

lingers today.

This is but one example of how women from different

racial, ethnic, and class backgrounds came into the sexual

revolution in the 1960s. Although many of the points Grant

touches on, such as rape, pornography, and reproductive

freedom, affect all women to a certain extent, these issues

have different ramifications for women of varying backgrounds.

Grant makes some effective points about the ways in which men

controlled women's sexuality before and even after the sexual

revolution, but her analysis would benefit from considering the

roles of other factors, such as race and class. The meaning,

significance, and benefits of "sexual liberation" will be

10

Chang 6

different for different women. Other oppressions must also be
fought on the same front that sexual oppression is. The
different manifestations of sexual oppression that women face
must be challenged so that they will not continue to hurt all
women. If a movement is designed to benefit only a few women,
that movement ceases to be revolutionary, and broader social
change will not be possible.

Chang 7

Work Cited

Grant, Linda. "What Sexual Revolution?" <u>Sexing the Millennium:</u>
<u>Women and the Sexual Revolution</u>. New York: Grove, 1994.
1-18.

Helen begins her essay by summarizing Grant's major thesis and supporting some of its claims. In paragraph 4, she commends Grant, pointing out that Grant "does a good job demonstrating the significant freedoms women have gained since the sexual revolution," and in paragraph 5, she praises Grant's organization and use of detail. Then she raises some problems with Grant's thesis and critically examines her sweeping use of the word *women*, especially her emphasis on middle- and upper-class women and her exclusion of women who are working-class. Helen evokes nuances that Grant ignores. She then modifies Grant's totalizing view of history by adducing differences between English and American history that Grant passes over (paragraphs 8 and 9). Finally, Helen concludes by citing a widely known example from American history that Grant has not mentioned, the difference in sexual protections afforded to white women and African American women during the nineteenth century in the American South.

Despite the fact that Helen's overall evaluation of Linda Grant's argument is negative, she discusses the strengths of Grant's piece as well as its weaknesses. Notice Helen's language:

STRENGTHS

Grant does a good job of . . .

Grant's points are well taken . . .

WEAKNESSES

One problem with Grant's thesis is . . .

Although Grant makes some good points
. . . , one flaw in her argument lies in . . .

Whenever you write a negative review of a text, be fair to the author. Do your best to mention a few positive qualities.

Before we outline the process for writing an evaluation essay, let's examine an essay that judges the effectiveness of two reading sources. In the second evaluation essay, Erika Perrotte evaluates two memoirs, "Seven Years Ago I Raped a Woman" by Jack M. and "Notes from a Fragmented Daughter" by Elena Tajima.

Perrotte 1

Erika Perrotte

Professor Kennedy

Composition 101-301

27 April 1999

Finding Meaning in Memoir

Both "Seven Years Ago I Raped a Woman" by Jack M. and 1

"Notes from a Fragmented Daughter" by Elena Tajima are

effective memoirs, but for different reasons. Each possesses

its own particular strengths. Jack M.'s memoir is strong

because the author is excruciatingly honest and open to the

reader about rape and his feelings about it, while Tajima's

piece offers bold descriptions as its greatest strengths.

Jack M. does not hold back and is very straightforward 2

with his audience. His honesty starts right in the title of

his memoir, where he admits, "I raped a woman." He is not

proud of what he has done and makes no excuses for himself. In

this memoir, Jack does not try to rationalize his behavior or

make himself look innocent. Looking back on his life "seven

years ago," he admits his guilt not only for the rape incident but also for the way he treated <u>all</u> the women with whom he had sexual relations in his period of heavy drinking and "slutting" (111). He candidly states, "I was often cruel to these women" (111). Furthermore, Jack bears out his poor treatment of women when he explains that he acted only in ways that would help him ultimately achieve sexual favors. He tells us how he manipulated one of his many pick-ups: "I would do everything I could to make her go to bed with me" (111). Jack admits his shameful behavior, saying, "I would use empathy, understanding, humor, even my deepest secrets to get them on my side" (114). He continues to show his honesty by including statements such as "If the sex was good, I might see them again, but I would quickly get bored . . . and I would abruptly blow them off" (111). Jack is honest at all costs, and his absolute truthfulness serves as the cornerstone of his memoir. He gains his readers' trust by sharing his private memories. Jack is willing to sacrifice his image as a "good guy" as he writes his memoir, thereby creating a very strong and engaging impression as a storyteller.

Jack M.'s honesty with himself and his audience creates an especially interesting element of positive personal development. The author shows how his growth as a man has made him realize the harm and pain he inflicted on his victims. And as a result of this realization, Jack also emphasizes his feelings of remorse. He is deeply ashamed of what he did, and he is taking responsibility for his actions. This former rapist convinces his readers that he has truly changed for the

Perrotte 3

better: he regrets his past actions and hopes that his story will instruct others not to take his path.

While Jack M. centers his memoir on one specific event in his life, Elena Tajima writes about a number of incidents. Nonetheless, all of the memories that Tajima shares deal with one aspect of her life, her heritage. In "Notes from a Fragmented Daughter," she tells of her experience growing up with a mixed American and Japanese heritage. She adds positive energy to her memoir by using bold descriptions when discussing the situations that she has encountered. Tajima is descriptive throughout the memoir, painting vivid pictures of every situation. She adds details about hairstyles, car models, brand names, skin tones, and movie titles. Instead of saying a car, she says "a Volkswagen"; instead of a camera, "a Kodak Instamatic" (82). At first, the specific examples may seem like only a small part of Tajima's memoir, but I believe they are what make it so effective.

Tajima, like Jack M., does not hold back. She gets right to the point and cites various events as support. She also uses many examples to serve as justification for her feelings. For instance, she tells of the time she visited an Asian American exhibit featuring Oriental food. She was asked if she had cooked any of the dishes, simply because she "looked kinda Asian" (82). She goes on to point out that as Americans, we live "in a culture that can't tell Chinese apart from Japanese" (82). Tajima's details and descriptions effectively allow her readers to see what she has dealt with due to her Asian ethnicity, and as a result the audience tends to empathize powerfully with her. "Notes from a Fragmented Daughter" contains bold descriptions of racist stereotypes, including terms such as "flat-faced Chinaman" and "slant-eyed face," descriptions used by others to describe Tajima, not to mention people the author refers to as "idiot," "hillbilly," and "bub," and the sexist attitude she describes as "touch-me-feel-you" (82). Tajima's word choice includes these and a number of other controversial terms. They are not infamously known "bad words," but they are shocking and daring enough to catch our attention. These words are meant to make the reader stop and think twice about how they are being used. Without her word choice, Tajima's memoir would lose a substantial amount of power and feeling.

The most powerful point of Tajima's memoir comes at the end when she gives a lengthy, bold, detailed description of herself:

> A half-Japanese postmodernist Gemini feminist,
> existentialist would-be writer of bad one-act comedy
> revues, avid cat trainer, and closet reader of
> <u>mademoiselle</u>, <u>cosmo</u>, <u>signs</u>, <u>diacritics</u>, <u>elle</u>, <u>tv</u>
> <u>guide</u>, <u>architectural digest</u>, <u>country living</u>, <u>cat</u>
> <u>fancy</u>, <u>bird talk</u>, <u>mother jones</u>, <u>covert action</u>,
> <u>vogue</u>, <u>glamour</u>, <u>the new yorker</u>, <u>l.a. times</u>, <u>l.a.</u>
> <u>weekly</u>, and sometimes <u>penthouse forum</u>. (83)

This quotation is not only proof of the author's bold descriptions but also evidence of the transition that takes place. Tajima breaks rules. Notice that she does not capitalize

6

the titles of the publications she reads. No longer is she sitting back and listening to what others have to say; she is now silencing the oppressive white culture with her newfound spirit. Not only is she speaking up, but she is also talking back to everyone who has hurt her throughout her life. Tajima's memoir begins with her being ashamed of her true identity and ends with her bursting out with an extremely detailed and powerful description of exactly who she is. Readers have to admire her strength of character.

Both "Seven Years Ago I Raped a Woman" and "Notes from a Fragmented Daughter" satisfy my requirements for an effective memoir in that they are honest, descriptive, interesting, and filled with feeling. The authors open themselves up to their readers and use distinctive techniques for getting their points across in bold and powerful ways.

7

Works Cited

M., Jack. "Seven Years Ago I Raped a Woman." <u>Glamour</u> Jan. 1992: 111-15.

Tajima, Elena. "Notes from a Fragmented Daughter." <u>Making Face, Making Soul: Creative and Critical Perspectives by Women of Color</u>. Ed. Gloria Anzaldua. San Francisco: Aunt Lute, 1990. 82-83.

In the opening paragraph, Erika introduces the two reading selections and states her thesis. In her judgment, both selections are effective memoirs because of particular strengths: the honesty and openness of Jack M.'s memoir and the bold descriptions of Tajima's. In paragraphs 2 and 3, Erika discusses the straightforward, honest nature of Jack M.'s piece, backing up each of her points with details and quotations from the text. Paragraphs 4, 5, and 6 focus on "Notes from a Fragmented Daughter." In each paragraph, Erika shows how a certain writing technique contributes to the memoir's effectiveness: in paragraph 4, Tajima's use of details; in paragraph 5, her use of examples and her word choice; and in paragraph 6, her detailed powerful description. Paragraph 7 concludes the essay.

Both Helen and Erika communicate clearly that they are doing more than simply interpreting the reading sources. They are using established criteria to evaluate the texts. Helen evaluates both the strengths and weaknesses of Linda Grant's argument, and her essay is much more pointed and pronounced than Erika's. Helen exposes one flaw after another and takes Grant to task on a number of points. Erika's entire review is complimentary.

E x e r c i s e ....

Reread the essays by Helen Chang and Erika Perrotte. Which do you find more convincing? What accounts for its relative effectiveness? What are the shortcomings of the essay that you do not find as effective?

....

WRITING AN EVALUATION ESSAY

Now that you have studied two evaluation essays, you can practice writing one of your own, beginning the process with prewriting and then proceeding through drafting, revising, and editing.

PREWRITING

As always, your first act is to set your rhetorical goal. Do this by asking yourself, "Why am I writing this evaluation?" and "What desired effect do I hope to have on my audience?" Your central goal is to use carefully selected criteria to persuade your readers of the reading source's quality, importance, or worth. Looking back at the student essays, you can see that Helen's goal is to persuade the reader that Grant has fashioned a rather weak argument, whereas Erika's objective is to convince her audience that Jack M. and Elena Tajima have created interesting, well-crafted memoirs.

Your next decision concerns your audience. Ask yourself these questions:

- Are my readers already familiar with the reading source?
- How much of the source should I summarize? What form should the summary take?
- Do I need to explain basic concepts and provide background for the material to make sense?

As we mentioned earlier, the assignment will signal how much summarizing you need to do. If you are evaluating a reading selection of your own choice or a text that has not been covered in class, give your readers general background information and summarize the parts of the source that they need to understand in order to profit from your evaluation.

Exercise..

Take a few minutes to compare Helen's and Erika's summaries of the reading sources. You haven't read these texts, but do you think these student writers did an adequate job? Do their evaluations leave you with unanswered questions? What additional background information about the sources do you need to know?

• • • • • • • • • • • • • • • • •

Read, Reread, and Analyze the Reading Source.

Do a first reading to get an overall sense of the text, and then freewrite your general impressions. The purpose of the second reading is to ask a series of analysis and evaluation questions. These questions serve two functions. They help you break down the text into its major components, and they eventually become the basis for your paper. With a few additions, the questions are the same as the ones for examining a source for an analysis essay. The major difference is that some of the questions are phrased in a way that encourages evaluation as well as interpretation. Record your answers to these questions in your journal or notebook.

QUESTIONS FOR ANALYSIS AND EVALUATION

Questions about Content

- Is the author's thesis realistic?
- Do the other important points follow logically from the thesis?
- Is the author emphasizing appropriate aspects of the topic? Does the author disregard important aspects or put too much emphasis on certain points?
- Does the author acknowledge and refute the views of individuals who might oppose his or her argument?
- Does the author use a sufficient amount of evidence to support his or her points? Which points need more support or explanation? (For a review of the various types of evidence, see pages 222–225.)
- Do the author's conclusions follow logically from the evidence, or are there places where the reader has difficulty seeing the connection?
- Are the conclusions accurate? Do they have direct implications for readers, or do they have limited applicability and usefulness?

Questions about Form, Organization, and Features

FORM

- Is the form appropriate for the content? Would the writer have been better able to convey his or her message in another form?

ORGANIZATION

- Is the organizational pattern clear and well conceived?
- Would the meaning be better represented if the parts were arranged differently—for example, if the thesis was disclosed in the introduction instead of the conclusion; if the narrative progressed from past to present instead of present to past; if reasons were ordered from most important to least important instead of vice versa?

FEATURES

Language

- Does the author's language serve to heighten and illuminate the topic, or is it merely adequate?
- Does the author use precise wording, vivid details, words that appeal to the senses, and words with emotional intensity?
- If the author uses figurative language, are the similes and metaphors appropriate, or are they confusing, inexact, or misleading?
- Is the author's vocabulary unnecessarily formal or pompous? Does the author use big words where common ones would do?

Sentence Elements

- Are the sentences balanced and symmetrical or disorganized and awkward?
- Is the author concise, or does he or she try to pack too many ideas into long, sprawling sentences?

Images and Scenes

- If the author creates images and describes scenes, do they vivify the text, or are they superfluous?
- What would be gained if the author included more images?
- What would be lost if images were left out?

References and Allusions

- Do the author's allusions illuminate or add significantly to the subject matter?
- What would be lost if they were left out?
- Are the references to other written sources welcome additions to the text, or do they seem superfluous?
- Are the other sources timely, or does the author rely on outdated information?

Questions about Rhetorical Concerns

- Is the author's persona or stance suitable, or does it detract from the piece?
- Are the voice and tone appropriate or unnecessarily pompous or formal?
- Does the author come across as authoritative, creditable, and reliable, or are you left with questions about his or her background, prestige, political or religious orientation, or overall reputation?
- Is the author impartial or biased?
- Does the author supply sufficient background information, or does he or she make erroneous assumptions about the reader's previous knowledge?

Review Your Answers to the Analysis and Evaluation Questions.

After you have recorded your answers to the analysis and evaluation questions, gather your notes to decide which elements to focus on in your essay. As you are sorting and organizing your material, bear in mind that your rhetorical purpose is to judge the strengths and weaknesses of the reading source according to a set of carefully selected criteria. These criteria will emerge if you follow the same procedures that we outlined for the analysis essay.

1. Look to see if a particular question produced a lengthy, substantive response.
2. See if you are able to group answers that pertain to similar categories.
3. Select two or more elements for your focus.
4. Return to the relevant parts of the text to check for supporting material.

For a detailed explanation of each procedure, reread pages 250–251.

Decide on an Organizational Plan.

To organize your evaluation essay, you can use any of the plans we suggested for the analysis essay:

- Cause and effect
- Argument
- Structure of the reading source

See pages 251–252 for an explanation and brief outline of each pattern. By far the most typical structure for an evaluation is some variation of the format used for an argument essay. You can write a unidimensional argument following this format:

- State your thesis—your judgment based on three or four criteria that you will use to evaluate the source.
- Allocate one or more body paragraphs to each criterion, developing each with specific evidence from the source.

Another possibility is to construct a two-dimensional argument for the purpose of assessing the source's weaknesses as well as its strengths:

- State your thesis—your evaluation and the criteria for strengths and weaknesses. For example, "Despite the fact that Carmichael uses convincing evidence to support his position, he weakens his argument by failing to acknowledge the opposition and making overly broad generalizations."
- Allocate a paragraph or two acknowledging the source's strengths, substantiating your claims with evidence.
- Allocate paragraphs to discussing the weaknesses.

DRAFTING

Before you begin writing your preliminary draft, consult the sections on openers, introductions, and conclusions on pages 107–111. Introductory paragraphs of evaluation essays typically include an interest-catching opening sentence, mention of the title and author of the reading source, a thesis disclosing the writer's judgment, mention of the criteria for evaluation, and as much summary of the source as the audience will expect.

Follow your organizational plan as you move into the body of your essay. Be sure to keep your criteria in the forefront as you flesh out your body paragraphs with evidence (quotations, paraphrases, and summaries) from the reading source. Finally, check that you are observing the academic writing conventions (described on page 252).

REVISING

Make arrangements to have a classmate or friend review your preliminary draft and give you feedback. If this is not possible, set the essay aside for a few days and then review it yourself. Respond to the following set of questions.

✓ CHECKLIST FOR REVISING AN EVALUATION ESSAY

_____ Can you identify the writer's rhetorical purpose? Is the writer evaluating the reading source in terms of established criteria?

_____ Does everything in the draft lead to or follow from one central meaning? If not, which ideas seem out of place?

_____ Has the writer provided all the information you need to understand the essay?

_____ Do you have enough background about the source, including the title, author, and relevant summary? If not, where do you need more information?

_____ When referring to the source, does the writer supply the necessary documentation?

_____ Are you always able to differentiate the writer's words from those of the author of the reading source? If not, where is there a need for connecting ideas and transitions?

_____ Is the organizational plan appropriate for an evaluation essay? If not, what other organizational pattern do you suggest?

_____ Has the writer made the standards or criteria of evaluation clear to you? If the criteria are unclear, explain your confusion.

_____ When discussing each criterion, does the writer give evidence for the judgment by quoting, paraphrasing, or summarizing relevant parts of the text? Are there any places where additional evidence is needed?

_____ When moving from one evaluative criterion to another, does the writer provide smooth transitions and connecting ideas? If not, where are they needed?

_____ Is the writer's voice appropriate for this type of essay? Why or why not?

_____ Is the opening satisfactory? Why or why not?

_____ Does the essay have an appropriate conclusion?

_____ Is the title suitable for the piece?

_____ Has the writer observed academic writing conventions of using the present tense when explaining how the author uses various techniques and procedures, identifying the author initially by full name and thereafter only by last name, and indenting long quotations in block format?

EDITING

When you are satisfied with your revision, read your paper aloud. Then reread it line by line and sentence by sentence. Check for correct usage, punctuation, spelling, mechanics, manuscript form, and typographical errors. If you are using a word processing program with a spell checker, run the checker on your essay. If your editing skills are not strong, get a friend to read over your work.

EXPLORATORY ANALYSIS

In addition to interpreting the text and discussing the author's rhetorical strategies, as one does in a rhetorical analysis, writers also use their analytical skills to explore a topic, problem, or issue. The goal of an exploratory analysis essay is to "unpack" the issue so that your readers will be able to understand its complexities. In an essay of this type, you are not advancing a particular position or arguing a point of view. Your rhetorical purpose is informative; it might be any of the following:

- To present a number of facets of the topic, problem, or issue
- To uncover its various dimensions
- To ask questions about it
- To examine it from several angles
- To get your readers beneath the surface
- To shed some light on a controversy
- To get to the base of a problem

It is sometimes more difficult to analyze an issue objectively and withhold your opinion than it is to argue a point. As an academic writer, you need the ability to remain objective when necessary.

Before we take you through the process for writing an exploratory analysis, we would like you to read a sample student essay by Kimberley De Santis, "Deinstitutionalization: The Past Idea with the Present Misfortunes." You will notice that the essay by Erica Mazor on pages 204–211 treats the same topic. We purposely selected two essays on deinstitutionalization of the mentally ill so that you would clearly see the difference between defending one's position on this topic, as Erica is doing in her argument essay, and investigating the complexities of the topic, as Kimberley is doing in her exploratory analysis essay.

Exercise ....

Read Kimberley De Santis's exploratory analysis essay, "Deinstitutionalization: The Past Idea with the Present Misfortunes." Then reread Erica Mazor's argument essay, "The Severely Mentally Ill Should Be Cared For—Voluntarily or Involuntarily," on pages 204–211. Write a short essay in which you compare the two essays.

. . . .

De Santis 1

Kimberley De Santis

Professor Kennedy

Composition 101

24 April 1998

Deinstitutionalization:

The Past Idea with the Present Misfortunes

They embellish the streets night and day, harmless to   1

society, their pain self-evident. Confused by their

environment, they walk without any destination. They are the

mentally ill homeless, and they reside on the streets of our

cities. Why are these sick people on the streets instead of

in hospitals? Are there too many occupants in psychiatric

wards and not enough vacancies? Are there any vacancies at

all? There is much debate about why the homeless mentally

ill are in such large numbers on the streets. Many citizens

blame the government for the ingenious proposal of

De Santis 2

deinstitutionalization: the release of mentally ill patients into the community. Beginning in the 1960s, the mentally ill were dismissed from the institutional life and initiated into an innovative lifestyle that they had previously been denied. If deinstitutionalization had been a complete success, the mentally ill would be living in community apartments or houses and not sleeping on park benches.

In the past, hospitals housed both borderline and severely mentally ill persons. The inhabitants had conditions such as schizophrenia, manic depressive disorder, autism, panic disorder, and obsessive-compulsive disorder (Torrey 10). Out of those formally committed, 50% to 60% were schizophrenic, 10% to 15% were manic depressive, another 10% to 15% had organic brain diseases such as epilepsy or Alzheimer's, and the remaining few had mental retardation (10). The mentally ill led a life surrounded by other sick persons. Their diseases were not uncommon, but they were placed in the psychiatric hospitals to avoid disruptions that they might cause to mainstream society.

Although there was some concern about disengaging mentally ill patients from institutions, the idea became intriguing. Throughout the 1960s, many people felt that the institutionalization of mentally ill patients was morally wrong (Torrey 143). The government's idea of deinstitutionalization was welcomed. It allowed the mentally ill patients to be free of state hospitals and receive care in community-based living centers (143). President Jimmy Carter and his Commission of Mental Health defined deinstitutionalization as "the objective of maintaining the greatest degree of freedom, self-determination, autonomy, dignity and integrity of mind, and spirit for the individual while he or she participates in treatment or receives services" (11). Prior to 1964, mentally ill patients were placed in state hospitals on the assumption that they were in need of psychiatric treatment. Their mental well-being was determined by psychiatrists or psychologists, and sometimes the treatment was completely involuntary to individuals (143). Deinstitutionalization allowed those patients who were capable of an independent lifestyle to pursue residence within the community.

Nineteen sixty-four was a fruitful year for the mentally ill population. That year the federal Civil Rights Law was passed, stating that only patients who were a danger to themselves or others could be committed to institutions (Torrey 143). The placement of the individuals into the community ensured freedom that had been previously limited. Communal living allowed the mentally ill to have a sense of belonging and a feeling of acceptance in the public realm. For the first time, they could function as if they were part of the traditional society.

Deinstitutionalization was considerably less expensive than institutional living. Community-based clinics averaged about $50 a day, as opposed to psychiatric hospital costs of at least $200 a day (Jaroszewski). As former residents were socialized into the community, they needed to learn to adjust to diverse lifestyles. Lifestyle stability was provided by several outpatient programs. Daily activities were monitored,

and staff assisted the patients as much as needed
(Jaroszewski). Everyday activities such as shopping, cooking,
hygiene, the search for employment, paying rent, and cashing
checks had to be taught so that the mentally ill would be
successful living in the community (Long). These reforms
benefited the mentally ill by giving them a sense of security
within the society. Society at large had always ignored the
state hospitals and the "crazy" patients who occupied them.
Deinstitutionalization allowed the patients to become part of
the prevalent population. Mental illness was no longer taboo,
nor were its victims.

  Thorazine, the first antipsychotic medicine, allowed many
mentally ill people to function as if they had no disease at
all. Thorazine and other antipsychotic drugs introduced later
did not cure the ailments, but they helped control the
symptoms (Torrey 8). As a result, government and health
officials felt it was safe to discharge patients into the
community. It had been said that medicines and other treatments
would be accessible to the needy persons who had been
deinstitutionalized. However, what was not taken into
consideration was how the released patients would actually
receive the medication, rehabilitation, and counseling (8). Few
services were available to the mentally ill, and hence many
persons went untreated. According to psychiatrist E. Fuller
Torrey, "Deinstitutionalization helped create the mental
illness crisis: discharging people from psychiatric hospitals
without ensuring they receive medication and rehabilitation for
survival in the community" (8). Thousands of mentally ill

6

people were without treatment and unable to function
appropriately in society.

Many of the patients who were discharged receive
inadequate care. A 1985 study of 132 patients with
schizophrenia, mood disorders, and personality disorders proved
that to be true. Thirty-three people were placed with
irresponsible families or discharged to public shelters and
addresses that turned out to be abandoned buildings or vacant
lots. Thirty-four were homeless after one month, forty-four
were homeless after three months, and thirty-two remained
homeless after six months. Most were able to cash Social
Security checks or veterans' benefits, but many had no income
and lived on handouts. Many homeless individuals used illegal
drugs and alcohol, and some were arrested for bizarre,
threatening, or offensive behavior, as well as shoplifting,
prostitution, and trespassing (Long). Inadequate government
care can be blamed for the misfortunes that the mentally ill
individuals experienced.

It is often thought that deinstitutionalization was
brought about so that the state no longer had to care directly
for the mentally ill. As documented by the U.S. Department of
Health and Human Services, programs such as Medicaid, the
federal Supplemental Security Income program (SSI), and the
Supplemental Security Disability Insurance program (SSDI)
provide direct entitlements to mentally ill disabled
individuals who live in the community (15). Although these
programs provide assistance, many mentally ill homeless live on
the streets, and their numbers continue to rise. Therefore, one

De Santis 6

question to ask the government is, what can be done to reduce the mentally ill homeless population?

Within the past few years, changes have been made to make the governmental system more rational, systematic, and integrated. "Despite the efforts, the system remains a 'patchwork of settings,' providers, policies, administrative sponsors and founders" (U.S. 17). Services as such are dispersed through a variety of public and private agencies. These include mental hospitals, general hospitals, veterans' hospitals, community mental health centers, residential treatment centers, nursing homes, halfway houses, day treatment centers, board-and-care homes, outpatient clinics, office-based private practitioners (including psychologists, psychiatrists, and social workers), psychosocial rehabilitation programs, clubhouses, and self-help groups (17). Despite the number of care providers, there are still the problems of availability, accessibility, and appropriateness (17). Abolishing the needs of the mentally ill will be a difficult process. Aid, programs, and communal services provide some assistance, but a solution to remove the mentally ill from the streets is a long-term goal that has so far not been accomplished.

Deinstitutionalization marked a new beginning for the mentally ill. They were no longer involuntarily committed and hidden away in hospitals. People believed deinstitutionalization would benefit mentally ill patients by allowing them to function as part of the mainstream. Today, thousands of mentally ill persons struggle to live on their own on the streets of America. With the proposed care

overlooked, the homeless mentally ill now encounter problems
that they are incapable of solving. Lloyd M. Siegel stated in
1981, "Patients wander our streets, lost in time, as if in a
medieval city. We are protecting their civil liberties much
more adequately than we are protecting their minds and their
lives" (Torrey 142). Solutions such as shelters can accommodate
only a fortunate few, forcing many others to find shelter
anywhere and by any means. Government programs do not assist
the entire mentally ill population. Often the process is too
difficult or time-consuming for the individual to pursue or
comprehend. The necessities of the mentally ill were forgotten
when deinstitutionalization was established. Many lost what had
made their lifestyle secure and stable: a home, medical care,
and communal life. Without psychiatric hospitals or
arrangements for monitored community living, they are left with
only the freedom to survive in an ever-changing, hectic world.
The homeless population and their needs are pushed aside just
like the garbage and debris they lie next to.

De Santis 8

Works Cited

Jaroszewski, Lea. "Causes of Homelessness: Mental Health
     Issues." Spare Change 1996: n. pag. 8 Mar. 1998.
     <http://www.way.net/hep/causes4.html>.

Long, Phillip W. "Mental Illness and Homelessness." Harvard
     Mental Health Letter July and Aug. 1990. Internet Mental
     Health. 8 Mar. 1998 <http://mentalhealth.com/magl/
     p5h-hom4.html>.

Torrey, E. Fuller. Out of the Shadows: Confronting America's
     Mental Illness Crisis. New York: Wiley, 1997.

United States. Dept. of Health and Human Services. National
     Institute of Mental Health. Outcasts on Main Street:
     Report of the Federal Task Force on Homelessness and
     Severe Mental Illness. Washington: GPO, 1992.

An in-depth analysis will often require you to marshal information from several reading sources. Kimberley uses four sources to get to the base of the problem. Begin your examination of the reading sources by asking the journalists' questions: Who? What? When? Where? Why? and How? Notice how Kimberley answers these questions in the introduction; then throughout the essay, she covers them in certain paragraphs:

Who?	Paragraphs 1 and 2
What?	Paragraph 1 and throughout the essay
When?	Chronology in paragraphs 3–6 (the past) and paragraphs 7–10 (the present)
Where?	Paragraphs 1, 2, 5, 7
Why?	Paragraphs 3, 4, 8
How?	Paragraphs 5, 6, 7, 9

To open the essay and hook her readers, Kimberley describes the population under discussion without divulging its identity. She immediately whets her readers' interest by raising challenging questions that curious readers will want answered; then she introduces and defines the topic, provides a little background, and states the issue. Next, she describes how the mentally ill were treated in the past, identifies them, and explains why they were placed in psychiatric hospitals. In paragraphs 3 through 6, she investigates the causes of the problem, and in the remainder of the essay, she discusses the effects.

Notice that Kimberley's goal is to enlighten her readers. She wants to bring them to a better understanding of why deinstitutionalization of the mentally ill has not been a complete success. She is not defending a particular position. Compare Kimberley's thesis to Erica Mazor's.

Kimberley's Thesis

If deinstitutionalization had been a complete success, the mentally ill would be living in community apartments or houses and not sleeping on park benches.

Erica's Thesis

Deinstitutionalization has contributed greatly to the homeless population. Opponents of involuntary hospitalization argue that it violates rights, but just as severely physically ill people should be hospitalized, so should the severely mentally ill, whether it be voluntarily or involuntarily.

It is incumbent on Kimberley to explain thoroughly why deinstitutionalization has been unsuccessful, but it is not necessary for her to argue her position. In contrast, Erica must convince her readers that her position—that severely mentally ill people should be hospitalized involuntarily—has more worth than the position of the people who disagree with her.

WRITING AN EXPLORATORY ANALYSIS ESSAY

Now we will take you through the process of writing an exploratory analysis. Before you sit down to draft your essay, you will engage in serious intellectual inquiry, examining reading sources with a view toward explaining the topic, problem, or issue.

PREWRITING

Before you start reading, examine your assignment, set your rhetorical goal, and consider your audience. When you receive the assignment, double-check that it calls for an exploratory analysis rather than the defense of a position. If your professor gives you a lot of latitude, be sure to inquire about what the assignment calls for before you proceed. For example, if the assignment asks you to analyze your tastes in popular music, verify that the intention is an *objective* analysis of your musical preferences, not a justification for them.

Set your rhetorical goal by asking yourself, "Why am I writing this exploratory analysis? What effect do I hope to have on my audience?" Your primary purpose is to explore the topic, problem, or issue so that your readers will be better able to understand its complexities.

For an exploratory analysis essay, it is very important to size up your audience. Be sure you know who your readers are and how much they already know about the topic. Then adjust your plans accordingly. If your readers have little knowledge of the topic, be prepared to give definitions, explain basic concepts, and provide a rich context. If they already know a lot about the topic, you will not have to tell them as much. You can concentrate on finer points and skip over the obvious. In either case, keep in mind that their reason for reading is to obtain better understanding.

Inquire into the Reading Sources.

Do a first reading to acquire baseline information about the topic. As you read each source, look for answers to the six journalists' questions: Who? What? When? Where? Why? and How? Then summarize your findings in notes or on a chart.

QUESTIONS FOR EXPLORATORY ANALYSIS

- Who?
- What?
- When?
- Where?
- Why?
- How?

If you are dealing with a problem or issue, probe further. Ask the following questions:

- Why is this a problem?
- How has it been identified?
- Where did it come from?
- Over time, how has it developed?
- What are its effects, results, consequences?
- Is there anything that sheds more light on it?

Record Answers in Your Notebook.

Reread the sources, delving deeper into the material. Find answers to the next set of questions. Underline and annotate the texts, and take detailed notes.

ADDITIONAL QUESTIONS FOR AN EXPLORATORY ANALYSIS ESSAY

- What things, people, and events are most important to consider?
- What are all the facets of the topic? What strands or facets are mentioned in most or all of the reading sources?
- Are all these facets equally important?
- Are any of these facets related? How?
- Are any of these facets in conflict? How?
- What are various individuals' views, positions, and concerns?
- Are any of these positions contradictory or in conflict?
- Can any of them be grouped?
- Are some more important than others?
- What are their implications?
- What will they lead to?

E x e r c i s e ....

Select either taste in music, the topic of Chapter 11, or racial profiling, the topic of Chapter 13. Read the selections in the chapter. In your notebook, record answers to the questions on both lists of exploratory analysis questions.

. . . .

Review and Categorize Your Answers to the Analysis Questions.

Reread the questions and answers while the reading sources are still fresh in your mind. Reexamine your rhetorical purpose, keeping in mind that your goal is to explore the complexities of the topic in order to make it more understandable to your readers. Group answers into categories. Use the journalists' questions as a base.

WHO?

- What things, people, and events are most important to consider?
- What are various individuals' views, positions, and concerns?
- Are any of these positions contradictory or in conflict?
- Can any of them be grouped?
- Are some more important than others?

WHAT?

- What are all the facets of the topic?
- What strands or facets are mentioned in most or all of the reading sources?
- Are any of these facets related? How?
- Are any of these facets in conflict? How?
- What are the effects, results, consequences?
- Is there anything that sheds more light on the matter?

WHEN?

- Over time, how has it developed?
- What are its effects, results, consequences?

WHERE?

- Where did it come from?

WHY?

- Why is this a problem?

HOW?

- How has it been identified?

Then group the remaining questions and answers.

- What are the implications of the problem?
- What will it lead to?

After you have categorized the questions and answers, return to the relevant parts of the texts for supporting material. Mark passages that you will summarize, paraphrase, and quote.

DRAFTING

Our suggestions for drafting a rhetorical analysis essay apply to exploratory analysis essays as well. Consult page 252.

Decide on an Organizational Plan, and Draft Your Essay.

Review the organizational plans on pages 246–254. Arrangements that lend themselves to analysis essays are time order (chronology), cause and effect, statement and response, and classification. If you look back at Kimberley's essay, you will see that she uses overlapping organizational patterns: time order and cause and effect.

REVISING

If your instructor agrees, make arrangements to have a classmate or friend review your preliminary draft and give you feedback. If this is not possible, set the paper aside for a few days and then review it yourself. Answer the following questions.

✓ CHECKLIST FOR REVISING AN EXPLORATORY ANALYSIS ESSAY

_____ Can you identify the writer's rhetorical purpose? Is the writer "unpacking" the issue so that readers will be able to understand its complexities?

_____ Does everything in the draft lead to or follow from one central meaning? If not, which ideas seem to be out of place?

_____ Do you understand the analysis, and is the writer sensitive to your concerns?

_____ Does the writer provide necessary background information about the subject and enough summary of the source as well its title and author? If not, what is missing?

_____ When referring to the source, does the writer supply the necessary documentation?

_____ Does the writer provide clear transitions and connecting ideas that differentiate his or her own ideas from those of the author?

_____ Does the writer refer to the author by name?

_____ Is the organizational format appropriate for an exploratory analysis essay?

_____ Has the writer made you aware of the complexities of the topic?

_____ Is the basis for the analysis clear? If not, explain your confusion.

_____ Does the writer support each point with direct evidence (quotations, paraphrases, summaries) from the source? If not, where are they needed?

_____ When moving from one point of analysis to another, does the writer provide smooth transitions and connecting ideas? If not, where are they needed?

_____ Do you hear the writer's voice throughout the essay? Describe it.

_____ What type of lead does the writer use to open the paper? Is it effective? If not, why not?

_____ Does the paper have an appropriate conclusion? Can you suggest an alternative way of ending the essay?

_____ Is the title suitable for the piece? Can you suggest an alternative?

_____ Has the writer followed academic writing conventions, such as writing in present tense when explaining how the author uses particular procedures and techniques, identifying the author initially by full name and thereafter only by last name, and indenting long quotations in block format?

EDITING

When you are satisfied with your revision, read your paper aloud. Then reread it line by line and sentence by sentence. Check for correct usage, punctuation, spelling, mechanics, manuscript form, and typographical errors. If you are using a word processing program with a spell checker, run the checker on your essay. If your editing skills are not strong, get a friend to read over your work.

Exercise . . . .

Write an exploratory analysis essay in response to one of the following writing assignments.

1. *Tastes in popular music.* For this assignment you will draw on two sets of sources: the assigned readings in Chapter 2 of this book and the lyrics of your favorite songs. Making reference to both sets of sources, analyze objectively your own tastes in popular music. This assignment does not ask you to defend your tastes. Your goal is to account for your musical tastes, not to convince the reader to adopt your perspective.

2. *Racial profiling.* Drawing on one or more of the articles in Chapter 13, write an exploratory analysis essay on race and the criminal justice system. You may focus on whatever aspect of the topic interests you, but whatever your particular focus, your overall goal should be to shed some light on the controversy rather than just to sustain your own opinion. Your analysis must be substantiated with sound reasoning and convincing examples, and you must make substantial use of source material. Use an organizational plan of your choice, but the paper must have an introduction with a clear thesis statement, well-developed body paragraphs that fit together logically, and a conclusion.

. . . .

8

WRITING RESEARCH PAPERS

To this point in the textbook, you may have been writing essays by drawing on the reprinted sources in Part III. Many of your professors will ask you to write about specified materials, such as textbooks, reserve readings, handouts, or class readings, but they will also ask you to conduct independent research. These research-based assignments may be as short as a one-page critique of an article of your choice, involving under an hour of library research, or as long as a thirty-page term paper requiring a minimum of twenty sources, involving many trips to the library over a period of weeks. Whatever the paper length or time commitment, the success of the entire project depends on the skills of information retrieval you will learn in this chapter.

EXAMPLES OF WRITING TASKS THAT MAY REQUIRE RESEARCH

- Reviews of books that you choose yourself
- Summaries or critiques of journal articles that you have to find yourself
- Short reports on issues currently in the news
- Essays analyzing literature that draw on published literary criticism
- Reviews of the literature in particular topic areas
- Term papers

Although you will find the techniques covered in this chapter useful for *any* assignment that involves research, our examples will focus on a research assignment that has three specific characteristics.

- It allows the student to choose a topic.
- It involves using a range of information sources.
- It requires sustained effort over a period of weeks.

These features call for special skills, as well as the skills you have already learned in this book. Depending on the specific research assignment, you may need any or all of the writing processes discussed in Chapters 1 through 7. The approach to reading academic sources presented in Chapter 1 is crucial to library research, as are summarizing, paraphrasing, and quoting, covered in Chapter 2. In addition, the ability to respond to sources (Chapter 3), synthesize ideas from a variety of sources (Chapters 4 and 5), develop arguments (Chapter 6), and analyze and evaluate sources (Chapter 7) will help you with research-based writing projects. Indeed, if you have mastered the skills in Chapters 1 through 7, you will be well on the way to writing good research papers.

Exercise ●

The exercises in this chapter assume that you are working on a research assignment specified by your instructor. If you do not have an assignment, you will need to come up with a topic to complete the exercises. You might consider a topic of special interest or one that is an extension of the readings in Part III. Do one page of freewriting about your research interests.

● ● ● ● ● ● ● ● ● ● ● ● ● ● ● ●

RESEARCH AS PROCESS

Research is an intellectually complex activity that goes beyond knowing how to "look things up" using indexes and search engines. Good research involves careful thought and creativity as well as the ability to locate information. Let us demonstrate how research functions as part of the overall writing process.

RESEARCH AND THE WRITING PROCESS

Prewriting

- Set a schedule.
- Select a topic.
- Develop a research strategy.
- Use electronic retrieval systems.
- Choose where to do research.
- Locate information in an academic library.
- Locate information on the World Wide Web.
- Collect information through surveys and interviews.
- Evaluate information sources.
- Excerpt relevant information from sources.

Drafting

- Synthesize sources.
- Argue, analyze, and evaluate.
- Draft a thesis.
- Derive a plan.
- Create an outline.
- Write from your outline.

Revising

- Use correct manuscript form.
- Revise based on readers' comments.

Editing

Exercise ....

Speculate on how you can make sense of your research topic. What are the areas of confusion, ambiguity, disagreement, or uncertainty? What information might you collect that would help clarify the issues and contribute to sense-making? Freewrite one page in response to these questions.

. . . .

PREWRITING

SETTING A SCHEDULE

Short assignments based on research may not require a special allocation of time, but assignments that ask students to locate a number of sources call for special planning. A major pitfall of research is failing to allow enough time. You must always allow for the unexpected in research assignments. Even the most knowledgeable researchers can encounter hitches that require more time than they had anticipated. Topics that initially seem promising may prove impossible to research; the sources that you need may be unavailable; preliminary research may show you that your initial research question is naive and must be modified; or you may have the required number of sources on the topic but find they don't fit together in a coherent argument. When students use the World Wide Web for research, they tend to allot less time for the research process because the Web seems to provide immediate, almost effortless access to source material. As we will explain later in this chapter, attempting to use the Web as a means of circumventing library-based research is usually a mistake because it is difficult, and sometimes impossible, to conduct effective Web searches in a range of academic subject areas. Careful research takes time, and there are no reliable shortcuts.

The following chart provides general advice on the time required for research.

ASSIGNMENT	TIME TO COMPLETE RESEARCH AND WRITING	LIBRARY VISITS
Single source, topic specified by assignment	1 week	1
Single source, student's choice of topic	1 week	2
Up to five sources, topic specified by assignment	2 weeks	3
Up to five sources, student's choice of topic	2 weeks	4
Up to ten sources, topic specified by assignment	3 weeks	6
Up to ten sources, student's choice of topic	3 weeks	7
More than ten sources	4 weeks	8

You may be surprised by the number of library visits that we recommend. Remember that we are allowing for the unexpected challenges that often arise in the research process. If you set aside the time we have suggested, you will avoid getting caught short even if things do not go smoothly.

Once you estimate how much time your research project will take, make yourself a schedule. We will illustrate with our student Kristen. Kristen received the following assignment in her composition course:

> Write an eight- to ten-page research paper that addresses an issue related to a specific academic discipline that would be of interest to other first-year college students. Use at least ten sources of information.

Using our calculations as a guide, Kristen estimated that she would need at least four weeks for this assignment. She then created a schedule by specifying the work to be done and the corresponding deadlines:

Research Paper Deadlines

April 3	Settle on preliminary topic
April 5	Attend library orientation tour (10:30 a.m.)
April 6	Write a list of questions I want my research to answer, and brainstorm a list of key terms that pertain to my topic
April 10–14	Locate information (allow time for library visits each evening)
April 16	Outline the paper
April 17–21	Write the first draft, and if necessary, return to the library to fill in any missing information
April 24–26	Revise draft
April 27–31	Edit draft
May 1	Turn in final draft

Exercise

Establish a schedule for your research paper assignment. First, decide which tasks you have to do. Then create a time line that specifies the date by which you will complete each task. Make sure you allot enough time for library research following the guidelines on page 287.

SELECTING A TOPIC

Your instructor may provide you with a specific topic that provides a focus for your research. In a history course, you might be presented with the following assignment: "Working from press releases published within a month of the atomic bomb blasts at Hiroshima and Nagasaki, discuss how the American government justified its use of nuclear weapons to end World War II." This assignment tells you that you need to consult newspapers published in the late summer of 1945 and look for articles that contain government statements on A-bomb explosions over Japan. If you receive an open-ended assignment like

Kristen's, however, you won't know where to begin the search for information. You will first have to narrow and focus the topic. Kristen turns to the following strategies.

STRATEGIES FOR GENERATING TOPICS

- *Freewrite in response to the assignment.* Write nonstop for ten minutes, using any cues in the assignment to generate ideas. Then search your freewriting for useful ideas.

- *Brainstorm.* Create a list of words and phrases in response to the assignment. Then read over the list and look for similarities, patterns, and connections.

- *Use research tools.* Consult general subject headings in indexes, either electronic or paper, to narrow the topic.

- *Consult with your professor.* Ask your professor to suggest topics in his or her discipline.

Kristen begins her topic search by freewriting:

This assignment asks me to write about an academic topic that other first-year students would find interesting. What would that be? The course I am taking this semester that interests me most is sociology. Many of the issues that come up in that course would interest a wide range of people, not just social science scholars, since they pertain to how our society functions. It might be interesting to research how our society will change in the twenty-first century. I guess I could write about the impact of technology, like how the Internet and e-mail will affect interpersonal relationships and workplace interactions. Another issue we discussed in sociology class was how the traditional nuclear family is being replaced by new family structures, including single-parent and gay-parent families. Class members disagreed on whether this change in family structure is positive or negative for children, parents, and society as a whole. Perhaps I could collect more information on how the American family is changing and what the impact of the changes will be.

As you narrow your topic and begin your search for information, also think about your purpose. One purpose could be to provide the reader with a survey of perspectives on a topic; another could be to argue a particular point of view. If you are researching a topic on which you already have definite opinions, you may have a thesis in mind before you consult the information sources. But if you are investigating a new area, you should start thinking about your purpose as soon as you start working with the sources.

When Kristen begins her research, she is not sure what point she wants to prove, but she knows her audience. She narrows her topic and collects information that will appeal to first-year students and make sense to them. Her readers will not have the benefit of her hours of research, so they may need careful explanations of ideas that are self-evident to Kristen herself.

Kristen's general topic, changes in American family structure, is still too broad to research efficiently. The following strategies will help her refine her research goals.

STRATEGIES FOR FOCUSING YOUR RESEARCH GOALS

- *What do you already know about the topic?* In what ways could you expand on this knowledge by turning to sources? What uncertainties do you have about the topic that might be answered in sources?
- *What are your personal feelings on the topic?* What are your values and beliefs on this topic? How might you find sources that support or contradict your views, values, or beliefs?
- *From what perspectives can you view the topic?* What are common beliefs on the subject? What do experts on the topic believe? What do those most directly affected by the topic believe?
- *What might your own audience need to know about the topic?*

As you work to focus your topic, it may be helpful to visit the library. Reference librarians can evaluate your topic and give you specific suggestions for narrowing it. When Kristen asks a reference librarian for help in narrowing her topic, he demonstrates how to use a computerized index to current magazines and journals to browse through subject headings related to the American family. (Later in this chapter, we will discuss computerized indexes and subject headings in detail.) The librarian explains that by looking up a major subject heading related to her topic and then examining its subheadings, Kristen may discover ways to narrow her focus. He also suggests that she scan the titles of magazine articles that are listed under a promising subheading to get a sense of how other writers have narrowed the topic. Finally, he suggests that she locate and look through several articles whose titles indicate that they will provide a survey of information or opinions related to her topic.

Kristen first tries the subject heading "Family" and finds that it has a long list of subdivisions. She scans through the list and notes that several of its subdivisions, such as "Family leave" and "Family values," are terms used by politicians campaigning for office. With this in mind, she returns to the reference desk and asks the librarian how she can find articles on what the candidates currently campaigning for the nation's presidency have said about family values. He shows Kristen how to use a computerized newspaper index to search for articles that focus on two topics: presidential candidates and family values. (Later in the chapter, we will explain how to search simultaneously for two subjects.) She leaves the library with copies of several relevant articles. Though her topic is not yet precisely defined, she thinks that she will link the political rhetoric on family values with the more research-oriented material she studied in her sociology class. She decides that on her next trip to the library, she will focus on sociological studies of the family. Kristen now has a sense of direction and is ready to investigate her topic in more depth.

Even though you may begin with a clear sense of direction, you may shift emphasis or narrow or expand your topic as your research continues. Don't be so committed to your initial topic that you ignore information indicating that a different focus might be more appropriate or more interesting. If you have a thesis in mind, regard it as a first attempt to make sense of the issue without the benefit of all the relevant information. As you collect information, you may find that your preliminary thesis does not fit with all the facts and may need to be altered or even abandoned entirely. Thesis statements may be subject to revision as you research and write. If you cling to your initial thesis in spite of the information you collect, you may produce a paper that is inconsistent, illogical, or confusing.

Since you may have to shift direction, it is important to gather and evaluate information well in advance of your project's due date. Leave yourself enough time to shift emphasis and look for other information sources. With complex topics, you may need to make several shifts before you arrive at an approach that you can sustain throughout a lengthy paper.

Exercise

In one page of freewriting, analyze your research goals and objectives. Do you know where to begin? To what extent have you narrowed your topic? Do you have a preliminary thesis? Have you located some information on your topic? Do you have to alter your focus in response to this information? What will you need to do before you move on to the next stage?

DEVELOPING A RESEARCH STRATEGY

Once you have defined your topic, you need a plan of attack that will guide your search for information. We call this plan your *research strategy*. Think about the types and kinds of sources that will meet your needs.

Whatever research strategy you devise, it should be flexible enough to accommodate the unexpected. As we mentioned earlier, you may need to change your goals during the research process. We wish we could give you an orderly sequence of research activities that would work for any assignment, but in practice, research often does not proceed as planned, and even the elaborate strategies described in textbooks may not lead you to the information you need. Flexibility is the most basic principle of library research.

The following questions will help you derive your research strategy.

QUESTIONS TO CONSIDER WHEN DETERMINING YOUR RESEARCH STRATEGY

- What are the assignment specifications?
- Who is your audience?
- What level of complexity or scope of coverage do you intend to achieve?
- What indexing terms (search vocabulary) will provide access to the information you want?

Assignment Specifications

Your research strategy may be determined largely by the demands of the assignment. Research assignments sometimes specify the types of sources that should be used. An assignment on the contemporary American family might call for "current articles from at least three periodicals," "both books and periodicals," "sources that focus on parenting," "sources written by conservatives as well as liberals," or "evidence from sociological research studies." Each of these directives calls for a particular research strategy. Kristen's assignment specifies a required number of sources but allows her to choose which types.

Audience

Remember that your readers must be able to grasp your ideas, so you need to draw on sources that are appropriate for them. Since Kristen's audience is first-year students, she decides to look for sources meant for a general audience of educated readers.

Level of Complexity or Scope of Coverage

Another part of your research strategy is to consider the variety of perspectives on your topic and decide which ones you will investigate. A major function of research is to explore the full complexity of an issue by examining a range of different opinions. For instance, if you were writing a research paper on trade protectionism for an economics class, you would try to locate sources that are critical of protectionism as well as supportive of it. For her research on changes in family structure, Kristen will look for the perspectives of those who defend the traditional nuclear family as well as those who champion alternative family structures. Your research strategy should include making a list of the differing perspectives you hope to find. Add to this list any new perspectives you encounter as you read the various sources.

Indexing Terms (Search Vocabulary)

To complete your research strategy, produce a list of words or phrases associated with your topic. Anticipate the words that might be used to describe or categorize the subject. These are the terms you will use to look up your topic in catalogs and indexes or on the World Wide Web. For her paper on the American family, Kristen compiles the following search vocabulary list.

Search Vocabulary

    families (or family)
    American families (or family)
    family values
    nuclear families (or family)
    single mothers (or mother)
    single fathers (or father)
    single-parent families (or family)
    families and politics
    family policy
    family structure
    gay families (or family)
    lesbian families (or family)

Variations in spelling and punctuation as well as the differences between singular and plural forms may affect your search results, particularly if you are using an electronic index or search engine. Note that Kristen's list reminds her to check both the singular and the plural of her search terms. She might also try both "single-parent families" and "single parent families." Slight differences such as these can determine whether or not a search is successful.

Be expansive, and list as many terms as you can. Then add to your list when you locate sources that suggest additional terms. You need a rich list of search terms since it is often hard to guess which ones will give you access to the information you want.

Exercise

Outline a strategy for obtaining information for your research topic that takes into consideration the assignment specifications, your intended audience, and the level of complexity or scope of coverage. Then derive a list of search terms that you think will provide access to relevant information on your topic.

EXPLORING VIRTUAL LIBRARIES

Ten years ago, students and scholars working on research papers spent many hours in academic libraries tracking down and reading source material. Libraries housed all of the books, periodicals, and other sources of information that they needed as well as the indexes and catalogs that helped them locate these sources. Advances in electronic information technology over the past decade have made it possible for students and scholars to conduct much of their research without actually going to a library. Using networked computers in their dorm rooms or offices, researchers can connect to their academic libraries' electronic catalogs and to commercial periodical indexes to which their libraries subscribe. Thus without ever entering a library, researchers can compile lists of books, periodical articles, and other sources relevant to almost any topic. In some cases, online systems provide the complete texts of sources, so students may find that they can complete all the research for relatively short projects without traveling to the library at all. As full-text periodical access grows and more book-length works become available online, it will undoubtedly become possible to conduct more extensive research from homes and offices.

The explosive growth of the World Wide Web has also affected how students and scholars conduct research. This vast collection of electronic texts, graphics, and sounds covers every imaginable topic. Most academic libraries now provide World Wide Web access, and many sources that are appropriate for academic research are available in full-text versions on the Web.

USING ELECTRONIC RETRIEVAL SYSTEMS

Whether you are searching your college library's online catalog, an electronic version of a periodical index, or the World Wide Web, you will need to understand certain principles of online searching. Database software often gives users the impression that electronic searching is simple: type in words or phrases that describe the topic, and the software will provide lists of information sources. Despite this impression of simplicity, researchers who want to take maximum advantage of online information systems need to know how search software operates.

How Computerized Information Retrieval Systems Function

You begin searching an electronic database by typing in a "query," which is typically several words that are related to your topic of interest. In response, the retrieval system attempts to match the query with relevant information sources in the system's database. Though systems vary in their precise search strategies, most compare the specific words in queries to indexes or word lists compiled from all the information sources. Some indexes are created by subject-area professionals who read sources and then assign indexing terms that describe their contents; others are merely lists of all the words that occur in the text of the source, often ranked by frequency.

In addition to subject indexes, systems may include indexes based on a variety of bibliographic elements. Author, title, and subject are the standard indexes available for searching library catalogs, but many systems index other items, such as publication date, language, personal name, geographic name, and source type (book, video, sound recording, and so forth). Often you can examine several indexes with a single query; for example, you could search for sources on single-parent families that were published since 1995. In databases that provide the full text of magazine, journal, or newspaper articles, the words used in each article may be indexed so that you can actually search the articles' contents.

You can narrow a search by specifying a particular index, or you can broaden the search by choosing the "key word," "free text," or "all fields" options, which instruct the system to examine all available indexes for matches to the query. In many information systems, key word searching is the default mode that is automatically offered to users, and in these cases, you must select "expert," "advanced," or "power" search options if you want to limit searches to particular indexes.

Each item in a retrieval system index points to one or more electronic "records" for individual sources that are related to the index item. A record contains a description of a source and an indication of where it can be found. In some cases—for instance, when searching the World Wide Web—the record may provide a direct electronic link to the complete version of the source (see Figure 8-1).

It is important to understand that computerized retrieval systems do not, for the most part, possess artificial intelligence. They are merely word-matching tools and cannot make even the simplest inferences about your intentions. Don't expect the system to do any of your thinking for you. In addition, most retrieval systems cannot correct for misspelling or adjust for variations in spelling. Distinctions that may seem insignificant to you, such as the difference between "first" and "1st," may be crucial when using a computerized system.

Recall versus Relevancy

The terms *recall* and *relevancy* are used to describe how information retrieval systems respond to queries. If a system provided perfect recall, it would respond to a query by retrieving from the system's database every source that was related to the specified topic. If a system provided perfect relevancy, it would retrieve only sources containing precisely the type of information specified in the query. Typically, an information search involves a trade-off between recall and relevancy. Maximizing recall will help ensure that relevant sources are not overlooked but may retrieve irrelevant material as well. Maximizing relevancy will help ensure that the sources retrieved are useful but may pass over other sources that would also be of interest to the researcher.

FIGURE 8-1 HOW AN INFORMATION RETRIEVAL SYSTEM WORKS

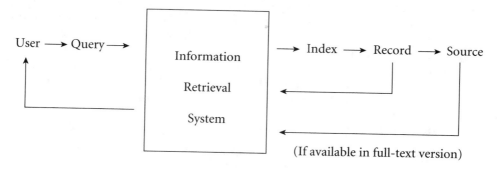

(If available in full-text version)

Balancing recall and relevancy becomes particularly difficult when you are working with a very large database, such as the World Wide Web. A broad search that maximizes recall will retrieve thousands of sources, far more than you can carefully review, but searching for very specific terms may fail to retrieve the material in the database that would best serve your purposes. For example, imagine that you are writing a research paper on whether human cloning should be legal in the United States. If you use the expression "human cloning" to search the World Wide Web, you will retrieve thousands of information sources, only some of which will be relevant to your topic. If you use a more exclusive query such as "human cloning regulation," you will probably retrieve useful sources concerning legal restrictions on cloning, but you may not obtain more philosophical pieces on the wisdom of allowing human cloning.

Key Word Searching

Key word searching typically expands recall at the expense of relevancy. For instance, a key word title search for "Grateful Dead" would retrieve the article titled "Anti-Union Bill Dead in Committee: Autoworkers Grateful for Senator's Pivotal Vote." Many retrieval systems, however, allow you to search for a particular sequence of adjacent words. For example, a search for "Grateful ADJ Dead" would only retrieve items that actually included the phrase "Grateful Dead." The ADJ code functions as an *adjacency operator* on many retrieval systems; on other systems, enclosing the query in quotation marks indicates that the words in the query should be searched as a unit rather than individually.

With large databases, perhaps the best strategy is to conduct four or five relatively narrow searches, trying out a range of search terms. This technique will enable you to zero in on relevant sources and expand recall beyond what would be achieved with a single query.

Truncation

Computerized retrieval systems often allow you to truncate or shorten search terms. The symbols ? and * are commonly used to aid in truncation. Instead of typing in the search statement "politically correct movement," you might enter "political? correct?" This query would retrieve "politically correct movement," "political correctness," and other variations on this terminology. It is often wise to truncate words in search statements, particularly when you are unsure of the precise indexing terms used in the database.

Boolean Searching

By using the Boolean operators AND, OR, and NOT, you can create a very specific search request that takes full advantage of electronic searching. For example, we mentioned earlier that you can restrict a search to a particular publication year. To limit a search by subject and by year, use the Boolean operator AND in your search statement. Let's assume that you want information on the national debate over welfare reform that occurred in 1996. If you enter the subject heading (SH) "welfare reform," the Boolean operator AND, and the publication year (PY) "1996," the computer will respond as follows.

WHAT THE RESEARCHER TYPES

```
(SH = welfare reform) AND (PY = 1996)
```

HOW THE COMPUTER RESPONDS TO THE QUERY

1. Creates a list of all items that have a subject heading (SH) "welfare reform"
2. Creates a list of all items that have a publication year (PY) of 1996
3. Compares list 1 and list 2 and creates a new list of all items that have "welfare reform" as a subject heading *and* were published in 1996
4. Returns to the researcher the total number of items in list 3 and, if requested, the reference for each item in list 3

The Boolean AND sometimes confuses researchers who associate the word *and* with addition and hence think that the operation will increase the number of sources retrieved. The Boolean AND actually places more restrictions on searches and usually cuts down on the number of hits. The Boolean operator that increases the number of sources retrieved is OR. The expression "(SH = welfare reform) AND (SH = occupational training)" retrieves only articles that covered both welfare reform and job training efforts. By contrast, the expression "(SH = welfare reform) OR (SH = occupational training)" locates three types of articles: those that focus exclusively on welfare reform, those that focus exclusively on job training, and those that cover both topics.

The Boolean operator NOT excludes specific items from the retrieval process. For example, the expression "(SH = welfare reform) NOT (SH = occupational training)" identifies articles on welfare reform but excludes articles that concern job training.

You can use Boolean operators in algebraic expressions to piece together complex search statements such as the following:

```
((SH = welfare reform) OR (SH = occupational training)) AND
(PY = 1996)
```

CHOOSING WHERE TO DO RESEARCH

The growth of the World Wide Web has made it easier to locate certain types of information. A guitar player can, within minutes, find Web sites with product information on new and used guitars, chords for the latest songs, and discographies for famous guitarists. This information would take hours to collect without the Web. The Web works well in this case for several reasons. Since thousands of amateur musicians and music fans use the Web to share information, its popular music resources are vast and probably cover any guitar, song, or guitarist. Also, search queries about guitars, guitar music, and guitarists are relatively easy to formulate since they are based on straightforward names (Fender, "Purple Haze," Jimi Hendrix) rather than descriptions of content. Finally, an amateur guitarist is looking for information that is interesting or useful but may not be concerned with precise accuracy. For example, the amateur is satisfied with playable chord progressions that sound acceptably close to the original songs and won't insist on completely authentic musical transcriptions.

Unfortunately, the World Wide Web does not work as well for academic researchers as it does for hobbyists. One difficulty is that books and academic journals remain the standard vehicles for scholarly communication, and these publications are not necessarily available on the Web. Thus there is no guarantee that the Web will provide access to important scholarly resources on your topic. Another problem is that academic research usually involves searching by subject matter rather than by proper name, and the Web is not arranged for efficient subject searching. Given its huge size, haphazard organization, and poor indexing, you may have difficulty locating material on your subject even when it is available on the Web.

A final difficulty is that academic researchers care very much about reliability and accuracy, but the Web has no effective quality control. Anyone can establish a Web page and disseminate any information; thus the Web has expanded tremendously the opportunity for publishing material that has no basis in fact. Some Web pages use graphics that appear very professional, but the content on those pages is merely uninformed opinion. You must be careful because subject searches often direct researchers to Web sites that do not provide reliable information. The issues of reliability and objectivity are further complicated by the commercial nature of many Web sites. For instance, if Kristen used the query "family," she might be directed to Web pages of divorce lawyers and family therapists advertising their services. Commercial Web pages, usually indicated by Web addresses that end in ".com," are often specifically designed to attract Web search engines so that the service or product they are displaying gets maximum exposure. Some commercial sites will provide information useful to researchers, but others are biased and manipulative.

In contrast to the World Wide Web, a college library collection is developed specifically to serve the needs of academic researchers. Books, periodicals, and other materials are chosen either by librarians who specialize in collection development or faculty experts in particular fields of study. Because the collection is built systematically, an academic library collection is much more likely to include the important works in a particular discipline, whereas the Web does not discriminate between expert and uninformed opinion. Your library may also include special collections for programs of study that are highlighted at your college. Currently, relatively few books are available in full-text online versions; thus with the exception of periodicals, most of the scholarly sources in your college library's collection are probably not available online.

Another advantage of conducting research in your college library is that you can get help from reference librarians, whose major responsibility is to help students and faculty members with research. Reference librarians can show you how to use the library's collection and also how to access sources available online from remote sites, including material on the World Wide Web. A few minutes spent discussing your research needs with a reference librarian will be more productive than hours surfing the Web.

A final advantage of academic libraries is that they provide the sophisticated searching tools you need to conduct scholarly research. In your college library, you will find a catalog of the library's holdings, which will likely be available on a computerized system. In some cases, the catalog will provide electronic links to other libraries from which you can obtain material via interlibrary loan. Your library will also have electronic and print versions of periodical indexes that will help you locate information in journals, magazines, and newspapers. These catalogs and indexes allow you to conduct far more precise searches than are possible with the access tools available on the World Wide Web.

While we have stressed the advantages of using your college library and beginning your research there, we do recognize the importance of the Web. Many sources available in academic libraries can be accessed in electronic form over the Web, and some sources are available only online. The Web is particularly useful for locating a specific source you have identified in an index but cannot find in your own library. If you know exactly what source you are looking for, the Web may provide convenient and free access.

ADVANTAGES OF THE WORLD WIDE WEB FOR RESEARCHERS

- Uninterrupted availability
- Continuous updating
- Vast resources
- Coverage of virtually all topics
- Convenience, "one-stop shopping"

ADVANTAGES OF ACADEMIC LIBRARIES FOR RESEARCHERS

- Expert collection development and quality control
- Systematic organization
- Careful indexing
- Expert staff of reference librarians
- Extensive collections of book-length sources

E x e r c i s e

Write a 250-word discussion of the relative merits of a library catalog and the World Wide Web for conducting research on your particular topic.

FINDING INFORMATION IN AN ACADEMIC LIBRARY

If you intend to use an academic library to do research, you must first familiarize yourself with the facility. Libraries vary dramatically in how they organize their collections and how they provide access to materials. Before you attempt to do any research, get a guide or a map that shows how your campus library is organized. Make sure you know where the reference desk is located. Do not confuse it with the circulation desk, the place where items are checked out. The librarians at the reference desk will provide one-on-one research assistance. Your library reference department may also offer library orientation sessions, reference skills workshops, and credit-bearing courses on information resources. Take advantage of opportunities to learn about your library early in your academic career.

Exercise

Take a self-guided tour of your college library. Start by locating the reference desk. Find out what days and hours reference librarians are available and what services they provide. Find out how the collection is organized. Does your library use the Library of Congress or the Dewey Decimal Classification system? Are periodicals shelved with books or separately? Are other formats (recordings, microfilms, and so on) shelved separately? Are there any subject-specific (music, science, and so forth) libraries on your campus? You should be able to answer these questions on the basis of materials that you can get at the reference desk. Now tour the library and make sure you can find the principal elements of the collection.

Library Catalog

The library catalog contains a description of each item in the collection and indexes items by subject, title, and author. Catalogs typically list not only books but also periodicals (magazines, journals, and newspapers), pamphlets, sound recordings (reel-to-reel and cassette tapes, LPs, and CDs), sheet music, microforms (microfilm, microfiche, and microcards), motion pictures, video recordings, computer data files, images (graphics and photos), three-dimensional artifacts, and maps. Note that the central library catalog provides the titles of periodicals (*New York Times, College English, Newsweek,* and so forth) and date range of holdings for periodicals but does not describe individual articles. On pages 301–305, we will explain how to find particular periodical articles on a given subject.

In most academic libraries, the catalog is computerized and can be searched by subject, title, or author according to the principles described on pages 293–296. Your library houses computer workstations linked to the online catalog, but the catalog may also be accessible from other computer workrooms across campus or even from your dorm room or home.

Figure 8-2 depicts a computer catalog entry that Kristen located in her research on contemporary family structure. Notice that the sample entry includes a "call number" for the item: HQ756.P65 1996. This number indicates the item's subject area and its shelving location. You are probably familiar with the Dewey Decimal call numbers used in most primary and secondary schools. College libraries typically use the Library of Congress system rather than the Dewey Decimal system, and the call number in Figure 8-2 is based on the Library of Congress system.

The initial parts of either Library of Congress or Dewey call numbers indicate the general subject area. The following chart lists the basic Library of Congress subject areas and the corresponding Dewey subject headings.

LIBRARY OF CONGRESS	**DEWEY**
A—General Works	000—Generalities
B—Philosophy; Psychology; Religion	100—Philosophy and related disciplines
C—Auxiliary Sciences of History	200—Religion
D—General and Old World History	900—History; Geography
E, F—American History	
G—Geography; Maps; Recreation; Anthropology	
H—Social Sciences (Economics; Sociology)	300—Social Sciences
J—Political Science	
K—Law	
L—Education	
M—Music	700—The Arts
N—Fine Arts	
P—Linguistics; Languages; Literature	400—Language
	800—Literature
Q—Science	500—Pure Science
R—Medicine	600—Applied Science; Technology
S—Agriculture	
T—Technology	
U—Military Science	
V—Naval Science	
Z—Bibliography; Library Science	

Books and other materials are shelved systematically by call numbers. As an example, let's consider the parts of the call number for David Popenoe's *Life without Father*: HQ 756. P65 1996. On the library shelves, books are alphabetized according to the letters indicating the general topic area—HQ in our example. Within each general topic area, items are arranged in ascending numerical order according to the topic subdivision, in this case 756. For books, items within the subdivision are arranged alphabetically by the first letter of the author's last name and then numerically by an additional filing number to ensure that each book in the collection will have a unique call number. In our example, P is the first letter of Popenoe's name and 65 is the additional filing number. Finally, 1996 is the book's date of publication. Call numbers can get more complex than our example indicates, but the same filing and shelving principles apply. Call numbers not only provide a shelving address for an information source but also ensure that items on the same topic will be stored together. Thus if you locate one item on your subject, you may find others in the immediate vicinity.

Periodical Indexes

As we noted, the central library catalog lists titles of periodical holdings but does not provide information on the articles that these periodicals contain. The tools used to access periodical articles are developed by commercial companies that sell their indexes to academic libraries.

FIGURE 8-2   SAMPLE COMPUTER CATALOG ENTRY

Life without father

Author:

- Popenoe, David, 1932-

Title:

- Life without father: compelling new evidence that
  fatherhood and marriage are indispensable for the good of
  children and society / David Popenoe.

Physical description:

- viii, 275 p.; 25 cm.

Publisher:

- New York: Martin Kessler Books, c1996.

Subjects:

- Fatherless families—United States.
- Fatherhood—United States.
- Fathers—United States.
- Paternal deprivation—United States.
- Children of single parents—United States.

Subject, geograhic name:

- United States—Social conditions.

Notes:

- Includes bibiographical references (p. 229-264) and index.

OCLC number:

- 33359622

ISBN:

- 0684822970

System ID no:

- AVC-2851

Holdings:

- LOCATION: General Stacks—CALL NUMBER HQ756 P65 1996

You are probably familiar with the *Readers' Guide to Periodical Literature,* an index that is often available in high school and public libraries in either print or electronic form. The *Readers' Guide* surveys more than two hundred popular magazines as well as a selection of specialized journals and assigns each article to one or more subject areas. Articles are also indexed by the authors' names. The *Readers' Guide* is a good index for college researchers who want nonscholarly articles on topics of general interest. InfoTrac's *Expanded Academic Index,* an electronic retrieval tool, is another general-interest index that is commonly available in college libraries. The *Expanded Academic Index* provides access to articles in over one thousand magazines and journals and covers many of the periodicals available through the *Readers' Guide.*

Using the *Expanded Academic Index,* Kristen enters the search term "family," and as Figure 8-3 shows, she discovers that a number of subject headings contain the word *family.* Kristen notes that the subject heading containing the single word *family* has subdivisions, so she chooses the "narrow" option in order to browse through them. Figure 8-4 shows the first screen of "family" subdivisions. From this and subsequent screens, Kristen chooses the subdivisions "analysis," "political aspects," and "social aspects," which seem closest to her topic. Figure 8-5 (page 304) shows one computer screen of references listed under the "political aspects" subheading. Kristen peruses the lists of sources under each of the relevant subject headings and subheadings. For titles that look promising, she views the complete records for the articles, which include publication information and in some cases the full text.

There are scores of different periodical indexes, available in both paper and electronic forms, that vary widely in topic area and organizational structure. Whereas the *Expanded Academic Index* covers a vast range of subject areas, *Social Science Abstract,* another database Kristen consults in her research on contemporary family structure, focuses on literature in sociology and related disciplines. Some indexes, such as the *Readers' Guide,* are relatively straightforward and self-explanatory, but others, such as the print version of the *MLA Inter-*

FIGURE 8-3   Results of *Expanded Academic Index* Search on "Family"

```
            Expanded Academic ASAP
   ─────────────────────────────────────────────

  Subjects containing the words: family


  Family
       View 3673 articles or Narrow by subdivision
       See also related subjects
  Family (Religious group)
       View 1 article
  Family Adventure Films
       View 1 article
  Family Airlines Inc.
       View 3 articles
  Family Allowances (Inheritance and succession)
       See Spouse's Share
  Family Allowances (Welfare)
       View 56 articles or Narrow by subdivision
       See also related subjects
  Family Amusement Corp.
       View 3 articles
  Family and Alcoholism
       See Family - Effect of Alcoholism on
  Family and Medical Leave Act (Draft)
       View 1 article
  Family and Medical Leave Act of 1987 (Draft)
```

FIGURE 8-4   FIRST SCREEN OF "FAMILY" SUBDIVISIONS

```
                    Expanded Academic ASAP
───────────────────────────────────────────────────────────────

Subdivisions of: family



16th century
    View 2 articles
1890-1899
    View 1 article
18th century
    View 2 articles
1998
    View 1 article
19th century
    View 3 articles
achievements and awards
    View 2 article
addresses, essays, lectures
    View 12 articles
africa
    View 2 articles
africa, southern
    View 1 article
alcohol use
    View 2 articles
analysis
    View 90 articles
anecdotes, cartoons, satire, etc.
    View 33 articles
appreciation
    View 33 articles
```

Expanded Academic Index™ © 2000 Information Access Company.

national Bibliography, can be baffling to the novice. You may need the help of a reference librarian the first time you attempt to use a specialized index. Other examples of periodical indexes are *Book Review Digest, Business Index, ERIC* (Educational Resource Information Center), *Film Literature Index, General Science Abstracts, GPO Monthly Catalog* (federal publications), *Humanities Abstracts, Index to Legal Periodicals, Medline* (health and medicine), *Music Index, National Newspaper Index, PAIS International* (Public Affairs Information Service), *Social Science Citation Index, SportDiscus* (athletics), and *Women's Studies Index.*

Often periodical indexes provide abstracts of articles, which are short summaries of the articles' contents. Keep in mind that abstracts are intended only to help researchers decide which articles are most relevant to their interests; they are not meant to circumvent careful reading of the entire article. Do not rely on abstracts as information sources; they are only access tools. It is considered academically dishonest to cite an article in a research paper if you read only the abstract and not the full text.

FIGURE 8-5 RESULTS WHEN SEARCH IS NARROWED TO "POLITICAL ASPECTS" OF "FAMILY"

Expanded Academic ASAP

Subject: family **Subdivision:** political aspects

Citations 1 to 20 (of 62)

☐ **Children and Families.** Maria Stainer.
Mark   *World and I* Oct 1999 v14 i10 p82
View text and retrieval choices

☐ **Nashville Diarist.** (Al Gore and family values)(Column) Anne Peretz.
Mark   *The New Republic* July 19, 1999 p50 Mag.Coll.: 99D0549.
View text and retrieval choices

☐ **10 reasons why the Religious Right is not pro-family: a tradition**
Mark **of harm.** (Family Values)(includes related article on the 'Pro-Family' rhetoric) Rob Boston.
    Free Inquiry Winter 1998 v19 i1 p21(4)
View text and retrieval choices

☐ **the rhetoric of <family values>: scapegoating, utopia, and the**
Mark **privatization of social responsibility.** Dana L. Cloud.
    Western Journal of Communications Fall 1998 v62 i4 p387(3)
View abstract and retrieval choices

☐ **Building homes, building citizens: housing reform and nation**
Mark **formation in Canada, 1900-20.** Sean Purdy.
    Canadian Historical Review Sept 1998 v79 n3 p492(32) Mag.
Coll.: 95M3147.
View abstract and retrieval choices

Expanded Academic Index™ © 2000 Information Access Company.

    Academic libraries often provide electronic versions of periodical indexes. A major advantage of electronic indexes is that they often cover more than one year of publication. With one command to the computer, a researcher can find references to articles on a particular subject that span several years. With paper indexes, the same search would involve looking up the topic in index volumes for each of the desired years. Your library may devote specific computer workstations to one or several selected electronic periodical indexes or may link all its electronic indexes together so that they can all be accessed, along with the library's online catalog, from each library workstation. These services may be accessible from computer workrooms outside the library or even from your dorm room, depending on the characteristics of your college's computer system.

    As more periodicals are becoming available in electronic form, many academic libraries are cutting back on the number of paper or microform versions in their collections and instead providing online access to periodicals. Your library may have computer work-stations where you can locate, read, and print out full-text versions of the articles you need.

Exercise ....

Select a topic, or use one assigned by your professor. Go to the library, and find two books and two periodical articles on your topic. Use a computerized access tool, either an online library catalog or a periodical database, to find at least one of these sources, and if possible, have the computer print out the record for the source. Photocopy the table of contents of the book or periodical, and on the photocopy, circle the chapter or article that is relevant to your topic. Submit the computer printout and the photocopies to your instructor.

....

FINDING INFORMATION ON THE WORLD WIDE WEB

We have already explained some of the limitations of the World Wide Web as a research tool. Generally, we suggest that you begin your research at the library rather than on the World Wide Web. Once you have conducted preliminary research in the library, you will be able to use the Web to better advantage.

When using the World Wide Web as a primary research tool, you can minimize its problematic aspects by observing several principles:

1. Read all the help screens or searching tips that accompany the particular search engine you are using. Each search engine has unique characteristics that you must understand if you are to take full advantage of its potential.

2. Familiarize yourself with the "expert" or "advanced" searching options. When you start up most search engines, they are configured for simple key word searches of all available indexes. All too often, these key word searches will yield thousands of hits, most of which are not useful. To refine your search and take advantage of features such as Boolean operators, you may need to shift to advanced searching mode.

3. Try your query on several different search engines. Given that the Web search engines are not precise research tools, it often helps to experiment with several and find which responds best to your particular query.

4. Look for electronic sources that have comparable print versions, and steer away from sources that have no print equivalents. Unsubstantiated opinion does sometimes appear in print, but as a general principle, information that finds its way into print is more reliable than information that is available only on the Web.

5. Evaluate the reliability of Web sources. Researchers should always question the reliability of sources, even if they come from an academic library. It is very important to evaluate Web-based sources. With the computer tools currently available, anyone can create a professional-looking Web page and stock it with content that is completely absurd. Ask yourself the following questions about Web sites:

   - What is the overall goal of the Web site? Do the authors of the Web site have motives other than presenting the objective truth? For instance, does the site advocate for a particular political agenda or sell a product?

- Is the site produced by a reputable organization? Does it provide a mailing address and phone number? Does it invite inquiries?
- Do the authors of the Web site identify themselves? Do they provide any evidence of their expertise or credibility? For example, do they possess training or experience in the topic area covered by their site? Do they demonstrate that they are aware of the standard scholarly or professional literature in the topic area?
- Do the authors distinguish between opinion and fact? Do they provide nonanecdotal evidence to substantiate their conclusions? Do they cite published sources?
- When was the site created? How often is it updated? When was it last updated?

COLLECTING INFORMATION THROUGH SURVEYS AND INTERVIEWS

In most cases, the bulk of the material you use in research papers will come from published sources; however, depending on your topic and assignment, it might be appropriate to use information collected through informal interviews and surveys. For example, imagine you are writing a research paper for a psychology class on how birth order (only child, first born, middle child, last born, and so on) affects personality. The psychological literature contains numerous studies on this topic, but you might also interview students in your dorm who represent each of the birth order positions and use these "cases in point" as concrete illustrations of the conclusions reached in the psychological studies. You might also survey twenty or thirty students representing a range of birth orders to see if their perceptions of the relationship between birth order and personality match the research findings.

Informal interviews and surveys provide only anecdotal information and are not a reliable basis for firm conclusions. Still, anecdotes are often useful for explaining a concept or framing an interesting introduction or closing for a research paper. Informal surveys may help you sharpen your research question or identify trends that warrant more careful investigation. Although an informal survey is not sufficient to challenge the conclusions of published studies, it may be useful to note a significant difference between informal and published research results. For instance, imagine that a student researcher conducts an informal survey in a college dorm on the interaction between birth order and personality. If the results of this informal survey differ from published conclusions, the student might suggest in his or her paper that additional formal research should be conducted to see if the published conclusions still hold for the current college-age population.

A final advantage of conducting informal surveys and interviews is that they get you directly involved with the topic. This hands-on approach helps increase your interest, particularly for topics that are rather dry if research is restricted to published sources alone. Even if you do not end up using the anecdotal information you collect, the experience of getting actively involved with the topic will lead to a better final product.

Whenever you conduct informal interviews or surveys, keep in mind the following principles:

1. Make sure you comply with college regulations concerning the use of human subjects. These regulations are typically applied in more formal research studies, but your college may have guidelines even for informal interviews and surveys. Check with your instructor if you are unsure of your college's human subject policies.

2. Whatever your college's policies are, make sure you respect the privacy of your interview or survey subjects. Do not repeat their responses in casual conversation, and do not use subjects' actual names in your research paper unless there is a clear reason to do so and you have obtained their permission.

3. Establish clear goals for your questions. Interview or survey questions should be intended strictly to establish facts, record beliefs about what is fact, or record personal feelings or values.

4. Try asking the same question worded in several different ways. Sometimes a slight change in wording will prompt a different response from a subject. It is often difficult to predict the precise wording that will convey your question most effectively.

5. Don't ask questions that betray a bias. Say you are surveying or interviewing last-born children to research a possible link between birth order and personality. You would indicate a bias if you asked, "In what ways did your parents and older siblings spoil you?" A more neutral question would be "How did your parents and older siblings treat you? Did they treat other family members in the same way or differently?"

6. Do not press anyone who seems reluctant to consent to an interview or complete a survey. Many people prefer not to discuss their personal lives, particularly when someone is taking notes on what they say.

EVALUATING INFORMATION SOURCES

As you search for source material, you are constantly judging whether it has direct relevance to your topic. Don't excerpt information that is only remotely related. If you collect a lot of information without exercising judgment, you may get a false sense of how well your research is proceeding. You could have a large number of sources and still not have the information needed to develop the paper in the direction you intend. As you locate and work with sources, ask yourself how they fit in with your overall goals for the research paper. To what parts of the topic do the sources pertain? Do they support your preliminary thesis? What perspectives on the topic do they represent? Make sense of the sources as you examine each one. Don't wait until you have completed your research.

By urging you to exercise judgment in choosing sources, we are not suggesting that you ignore ideas that conflict with your own. Remember that your thesis is preliminary and subject to change. You may shift your point of view after you read some of the arguments presented in the sources.

In addition to evaluating the sources' relevance to your topic, you should also judge their comparative quality and credibility. Don't think you can have complete confidence in a source simply because you found it in a library. Libraries include wildly opinionated, even bizarre sources along with those that are logical and objective. There is nothing wrong with an author expressing a strong opinion, but it is a mistake for researchers to view all opinions as equally valid. Since research is a quest for understanding, researchers must work with the sources that are most helpful in making sense of the issue.

As you analyze sources, it is always helpful to speculate on the author's rhetorical purpose, as we described in Chapter 1 (pages 30–32). What are the author's reasons for writing? Who is the author's intended audience? How does the author want to influence this audience? The answers to these questions will help you understand the source better and figure out whether it is appropriate for your paper. For instance, if you are writing for a public health course on the impact that smoking in public places has on nonsmokers, you may be skeptical of information from the Tobacco Institute, an organization that represents the interests of the tobacco industry. If you are writing on spending priorities for public education, you may find useful information in a teachers' union publication, but you should keep in mind the union's desire to increase teachers' salaries and benefits. If you think about writers' motives, you will be able to put their ideas in proper perspective.

E x e r c i s e ....

Locate two sources that pertain to your research topic but clearly differ in perspective, authoritativeness, or credibility. Write a one-page paper that compares the usefulness of these sources for your research purposes.

· · · · · · · · · · · · · · · · ·

EXCERPTING RELEVANT INFORMATION FROM SOURCES

The basic skills for excerpting information from library sources—paraphrasing, summarizing, and quoting—are covered in Chapter 2 of this book. Here we will discuss the special problems associated with the sheer number of sources you are working with for a research paper. A common problem is that a researcher loses track of the exact source for an important piece of information. Each time you excerpt a passage from a source, whether you hand-copy, reword, or photocopy, be sure you carefully record a complete citation to the source. Record the exact page numbers where specific pieces of text are located. When you draft your paper, you will cite the source as well as the page for each paraphrase, summary, and quotation. We give citation formats in Appendix A. The following chart summarizes the bibliographic information that you need to record.

INFORMATION YOU NEED FOR YOUR CITATION

Book

Author(s), title, publisher, city of publication, date of publication, pages where the information you excerpted is located

Magazine

Author(s), title of article, name of magazine, date (day, month, year), inclusive pages for entire article, pages where the information you excerpted is located

Scholarly Journal

Author(s), title of article, name of journal, volume number, year of publication, inclusive pages for entire article, pages where the information you excerpted is located

Newspaper

Author(s), title of article, name of newspaper, date (day, month, year), inclusive pages for entire article, pages where the information you excerpted is located

Web Site

Author(s), title of document, Web site name, date of electronic publication, organization associated with the site, date that you (the researcher) accessed the site, electronic address (URL) of the site

Web-Based Version of Source That Is Also Available in Print

Complete information for the Web site, as well as complete publication information for the print version.

Another common difficulty is failing to distinguish adequately between paraphrases and quotations in research notes and thus including in the research paper an author's exact words without indicating that fact. This is an unintentional but serious form of plagiarism. Be very meticulous about your use of quotation marks as you take notes. Reread our discussion of plagiarism on pages 44–45.

There is also a danger of excerpting too much information. Some students compulsively collect every scrap of information that is remotely related to their topic, thinking that they will make sense of it all at their leisure. Don't bury yourself with paper, whether it is note cards, pages of notes, or photocopies of sources. Excerpt only what you think you might use. As we stressed earlier, research is a sense-making process. It is hard to make sense of something when you are overwhelmed with information. In the next section, we will discuss how to judge the usefulness of sources as you locate them.

Much has been written on how you should record information that you excerpt from sources. Some textbooks strongly recommend index cards for research notes because cards can be grouped and rearranged easily. You can cut up pages from your research notebook or photocopies of sources and group these pieces just as you can note cards. Another alternative is to record your research notes on a computer and use word processing or outlining programs to organize the information. We recommend that you try various methods of recording excerpts and decide what works best for you.

In addition to notes that record specific pieces of information from the sources, you should keep a separate set of notes for preliminary thesis statements, organizational plans, or other important ideas that occur to you during the process of research.

Exercise

Read Kristen's paper on pages 320–330, taking note of the ways in which she excerpted information from sources. What method of excerpting predominates? Approximately what percentage of the paper is made up of source excerpts as opposed to the student's own ideas? Do you think this relative proportion is appropriate?

DRAFTING

SYNTHESIZING SOURCES

The research paper is, by its very nature, a synthesis. The power of research is its ability to bring together information from various sources to illuminate an issue, possibly in ways that the source authors did not anticipate. The researcher can be creative at all stages of the research process, but it is the act of synthesis that offers special opportunities for originality. You may be able to make connections among sources that have previously gone unnoticed or to structure information in new ways. Through synthesis, you give shape to the information. This is the ultimate goal of the research process.

In Chapter 5, we discussed four types of syntheses: a summary of multiple sources, an objective synthesis, an essay written in response or reaction to multiple sources, and a synthesis with a specific purpose. For a quick review, see the strategies for synthesizing on pages 170, 177, 184, and 193. You may use any of these approaches in research papers, depending on the assignment specifications and your goals.

ARGUING, ANALYZING, AND EVALUATING

It is common for long research papers to include more than one type of synthesis. Argument (Chapter 6), analysis (Chapter 7), and evaluation (Chapter 7) may also be important elements in a research paper. Reread Kristen's research paper on pages 320–330, paying special attention to the annotations in the margin indicating where she uses argument, analysis, and evaluation.

DRAFTING A THESIS

We mentioned earlier in this chapter that you may have a working thesis in mind when you begin researching. If not, one may emerge as you collect information. The following procedure will help you generate a working thesis from your research notes.

GENERATING A THESIS

1. Scan your research notes quickly, noting any general trends, main concepts, or overall patterns.
2. Freewrite for ten minutes on what you think your research might tell your reader.
3. Reduce your freewriting to several sentences that explain what you want to say to your reader.

After scanning her research notes, Kristen freewrites the following paragraph:

From the sources I read, it seems as if a lot of the current attention to the American family comes from political debates about "family values." One thing that the politicians seem to agree on is that the traditional nuclear family is declining. Some politicians think that this change means that family values are also declining, but others think that a new set of family values is developing that is positive in its own way. Whatever their viewpoint, politicians often use the expression "family values" in a vague way. It's hard to pin down what they have in mind. However, the articles I read that were written by sociologists were much clearer on exactly how family values are changing and what the advantages and disadvantages of those changes might be. I can use the observations of the sociologists to make better sense of what the politicians are talking about in the political debate over family values.

Kristen rereads her freewriting and condenses it into a preliminary thesis:

The political debate over family values has to do with the fact that the traditional nuclear family is declining. But the politicians use expressions like "family values" in a vague way and do not always explain exactly what they are thinking. The writings of sociologists on the family are more objective; the issues are clearer. I will try to use sociology to explain the issues that are at the base of politicians' positions on family values.

This is still a preliminary thesis. Compare it with the thesis excerpted from the final version of Kristen's research paper:

```
To a large extent, the debate over family values revolves around
whether this transformation represents the decline of the Amer-
ican family or an opportunity to strengthen and improve families.
The sociological literature on the evolution and current status
of the American family helps clarify the issues that are at the
core of this political debate. I will use the findings of soci-
ologists who study the American family to analyze issues that lie
at the core of the political controversy over family values.
```

Notice that Kristen's final thesis is refined, more fully developed, and more coherent. The main purpose of a preliminary thesis is to focus your research activities, but sometimes you may need to depart from the initial thesis as you understand more about the topic.

Exercise

Draft a preliminary thesis statement for your own research paper. Ask a classmate to read your thesis statement and orally paraphrase it. Did your intentions come through?

DERIVING A PLAN

A research paper can follow one organizational plan or a combination of the plans we have discussed in this book. Review the major organizational plans presented on page 23.

A plan may occur to you as you conduct research. You may see that the information you collect from various sources fits into an obvious pattern, or you may borrow a plan from one of your sources. You might also consider how you might use the source information to support your thesis.

If no obvious pattern emerges from the information you collected, systematically examine your research notes. Derive one or more possible plans by categorizing the notes.

If you use note cards, sort them into piles, grouping related information, to see what patterns appear. Try several grouping schemes to find what works best.

As Kristen sorts her note cards into piles, she fits them into three main categories:

1. Facts about how the traditional American nuclear family is fading and the new structures that are taking its place
2. Fears of political conservatives about changes in the structure of the American family
3. Reasons that liberals think the new family structures that are evolving will improve our society

Kristen thinks about these three categories, reconsiders her preliminary thesis, and comes up with the following plan.

> —Thesis: The political debate over family values has to do with the fact that the traditional nuclear family is declining. But the politicians use expressions like "family values" in a vague way and do not always explain exactly what they are thinking. The writings of sociologists on the family are more objective; the issues are clearer. I will try to use sociology to explain the issues that are at the base of politicians' positions on family values.

> —First, I need to explain how the American family has changed over time. In particular, I need to trace the decline of the traditional nuclear family and the rise of alternative family structures.

> —Next, I will explain why political conservatives think that the decline of the traditional nuclear family is a threat to family values and to our society.

> —Then I will explain why political liberals see advantages in the new family structures that are emerging.

> —Finally, I will contrast liberal and conservative viewpoints on three specific new family structures: single-parent families, gay-parent families, and couples without children.

CREATING AN OUTLINE

Throughout this book, we have discussed working from organizational plans as you draft essays. We have described these plans as outlines that do not include much detail. Detailed outlines are required for research projects. Because research writers must juggle many sources and deal with issues in depth, they need an outline that will keep them on task and provide a unifying framework for information from various sources. A pitfall of research paper writing is becoming bogged down in the details from sources and failing to clarify the relationships among ideas. If you draft your research paper working from a detailed outline, it will be easier to write, and in the end, your train of thought will be more evident to your audience.

Some instructors call for a traditional outline based on the following structure. Note that such an outline requires at least two entries at each successive level.

I.

  A.

    1.

      a.

        i.

        ii.

      b.

    2.

  B.

II.

The formal outline provides a clear hierarchical structure that is useful for imposing order on a complicated topic with a number of discrete subtopics. Here is a portion of a formal outline for a paper on contemporary family structure.

IV. Advantages of families in which both parents work
  A. Financial security
    1. The majority of families need two incomes to survive.
    2. Welfare reform is based on the premise that both parents are capable of earning money.
    3. Children derive significant benefits from the family's financial security.
  B. Gender role equality
    1. Home responsibilities are shared.
      a. Housecleaning and maintenance
      b. Food preparation
      c. Child rearing
    2. Men and women retain economic autonomy.
    3. Men and women hold equal authority over and responsibility for the fate of the family.
V. Disadvantages of having two working parents

With some topics or certain collections of sources, however, you may feel constrained if you have to force the material into this hierarchy. In these cases, free-form outlining, which allows the writer to determine his or her own structure, may come closer to reflecting your actual thinking. Here is a draft of Kristen's free-form outline based on the organization plan shown earlier. Notice that she expands on the organizational plan as she begins to plug in ideas from some of her sources.

– Thesis: The political debate over family values has to do with the fact that the traditional nuclear family is declining. But the politicians use expressions like "family values" in a vague way and do not always explain exactly what they are thinking. The writings of sociologists on the family are more objective; the issues are clearer. I will try to use sociology to explain the issues that are at the base of politicians' positions on family values.

- Evolution of the American family
  - Rise of the traditional nuclear family (Popenoe 81–91; Scherer 4–6)
  - 20th-century challenges to the traditional nuclear family (Magnet 42; Popenoe 39–42, 204–06; Scherer 4–6)
  - Rise of the postmodern family and alternative family structures (Cherry and Matsumura; Goldschneider and Waite 192–209)
- Political conservatives believe that the decline of the traditional nuclear family threatens both the family and the larger society.
  - Negative effects of divorce on children (Popenoe 20–25, 52–78)
  - Widespread acceptance of divorce weakens commitment to marriage (Gill 86)
  - Negative effects on children of nontraditional family structure (Fagan 157–58; Popenoe 52–78; Goldschneider and Waite 201–02; Magnet 42)
  - Negative effects on women of nontraditional family structure (Griswold 257–60)
  - Negative effects on men of nontraditional family structure (Griswold 257–60).
- Political liberals see advantages in the new family structures that are emerging.
  - Postmodern family is flexible and responsive to social change (Scherer 4–6)
  - Having mothers at home is no longer economically possible (Goldschneider and Waite 203–05)
  - Nonnuclear families of the poor are fragile but can be supported through public assistance programs (Rubin 246)
  - Men are taking more responsibility for the children and the home, which is to their benefit (Goldschneider and Waite 203–05; Johnson 251–52)
  - Nontraditional families can provide a good environment for children (Cherry and Matsumura 25; Ehrenreich 80)
- Debate over homosexual families
  - Conservatives generally attack the concept of homosexual families while liberals generally support it
  - Research shows that gay fathers are effective parents (Barret and Robinson 157–70)
- Debate over childless families
  - Men need the responsibility of children to keep their aggression in check (Griswold 258–60)
  - Childless couples are a viable family structure (Cherry and Matsumura 25)
- Conclusion: Comment on current election year and the continuing family values debate

Exercise ....

Create an outline for your research paper. Ask a classmate to read the outline and answer the following questions: (1) What is the overall plan for the paper? (2) Does each point in the outline relate clearly to the overall goal? Revise your outline in response to your classmate's comments.

. . . .

WRITING FROM YOUR OUTLINE

Use your outline as a guide for drafting. Group your notes or note cards according to the points in your outline, and draft the essay paragraph by paragraph. Keep in mind our advice on developing paragraphs (pages 110–111), introductions (pages 107–110), and conclusions (pages 111–112). Be sure to include complete references for all source information. It is easy to lose track of where information came from if you do not record this information in the first draft.

As you draft your essay, you may find that you need to depart from your outline. The outline is intended to serve as a guide, not a straitjacket. If you discover new patterns or ideas in the process of writing, don't hesitate to include them in your essay.

E x e r c i s e

As you reread Kristen's essay on pages 320–330, compare her outline to her final draft. Where did she expand on the outline as she wrote her draft? Note in the margin the types of synthesis that she uses to develop her paper. Then explain how you will use synthesis strategies in your own research process.

E x e r c i s e

Based on your outline, write a first draft of your research paper. Don't hesitate to include new ideas or patterns you discover as you write.

REVISING

USING CORRECT MANUSCRIPT FORM

Throughout this book, we have provided examples of student papers written in correct MLA manuscript form. Often manuscript form is taught in the context of a research paper assignment. Here is a summary of the MLA rules for manuscript preparation. Following the summary is an illustration using sample pages from Kristen's research paper. We rely on the *MLA Handbook for Writers of Research Papers,* edited by Joseph Gibaldi, as our source.

MLA RULES FOR MANUSCRIPT FORM

- Use 8 1/2-by-11-inch paper.
- Double-space all text.
- Leave a 1-inch margin at right and left, top and bottom.
- In the top margin, 1/2 inch from the top of the page, type your last name and the page number flush right.
- Center the title. Do not use any extra space above or below it.
- Indent the first line of each paragraph 1/2 inch (or five character spaces).
- Indent a displayed (block) quotation 1 inch (or ten character spaces).
- Center the title "Works Cited" at the top of the list of sources.
- Start each bibliographic entry flush left; indent each successive line 1/2 inch (five character spaces).

Use 8½-by-11-inch paper for each page.

One-
half
inch
margin

One inch
margin

Lester 1

Kristen Lester

Professor Smith

Academic Writing I

24 April 2000

What "Family Values"?

Indent one-
half inch
or 5 spaces

It seems that each election year, conservative, moderate,

and liberal candidates go to considerable lengths to express

their strong support for "family values." The assumption

underneath this debate is that the American family is

endangered and needs reinforcement. Unfortunately, the

political rhetoric around family values often degenerates to

posturing that lacks precision and clarity. What exactly are

One inch
margin
(left and
right)

"family values," and how are they in peril? Without a doubt,

American families have changed significantly in recent years.

The traditional nuclear family, with a breadwinner father,

homemaker mother, and children, has been on the decline, and

it is being replaced by what sociologist David Elkind calls

the "postmodern family," a term that encompasses various types

of domestic units such as single-parent families, dual-income

families, and remarried families (Scherer 4). To a large

extent, the debate over family values revolves around

whether this transformation represents the decline of the

American family or an opportunity to strengthen and improve

families. The sociological literature on the evolution and

current status of the American family helps clarify the

issues that are at the core of this political debate. I

One
inch
margin

Use double spaces between all lines, including heading and title.

Lester 6

however, blind to the problems posed by these economic factors, particularly for working-class families.

> It's true that the social and cultural changes we've witnessed have created families that, in some ways, are more responsive to the needs of their members, more democratic than any we have known before. But it's also true that without economic stability, even the most positive changes will not be enough to hold families together. (Rubin 246)

The liberal agenda typically includes social welfare programs that support families at the lower end of the economic spectrum.

Although conservatives claim that two-income families just mean that women will have the double burden of homemaking and employment, liberals respond that men can take on responsibilities in the home. Both liberals and conservatives recognize that women who stay at home to raise children are at a great disadvantage when they later try to enter the work force, and many return to their jobs too quickly because they cannot afford to take time off. However, the shift in values that started in the 1960s includes a recognition that men can and should help with child rearing and household tasks (Goldschneider and Waite 203-05). More men are expressing an interest in helping their wives with the workload and are discovering that a step down from absolute patriarchy often helps in strengthening their relationships with their wives and children (205). Men may find that both personal growth and family happiness are enhanced when gender roles are

One-
half
inch
margin

Double space all lines in the works cited list.

One inch
margin

Lester 4

Works Cited

Barret, Robert L., and Bryan E. Robinson. "Gay Dads."

Indent
one-half
inch or
5 spaces

  Redefining Families: Implications for Children's

  Development. Eds. Adele Eskeles Gottfried and Allen W.

  Gottfried. New York: Plenum, 1994. 157-70.

Cherry, Matt, and Molleen Matsumura. "A Vision of Families for

  the Twenty-First Century: A Declaration of Secular Family

  Values." Free Inquiry Winter 1998: 25-26.

Ehrenreich, Barbara. "In Defense of Splitting Up: The Growing

  Anti-Divorce Movement Is Blind to the Costs of Bad

  Marriage." Time 8 Apr. 1996: 80.

One inch
margin
(left and
right)

Fagan, Patrick. "The Real Root Cause of Violent Crime: The

  Breakdown of the Family." Vital Speeches of the Day 15

  Dec. 1995: 157-58. Expanded Academic ASAP. InfoTrac.

  Ithaca Coll. Lib., Ithaca, NY. 2 April 2000.

  <http://web4.infotrac.galegroup.com>.

Gill, Richard T. "Family Breakdown as Family Policy." Public

  Interest Winter 1993: 84-91.

Goldschneider, Frances K., and Linda J. Waite. New Families, No

  Families? Demographic Change and the Transformation of the

  American Home. Berkeley: U of California P, 1991.

Griswold, Robert L. Fatherhood in America. New York: Harper, 1993.

Johnson, Allan G. The Gender Knot: Unraveling Our Patriarchal

  Legacy. Philadelphia: Temple UP, 1997.

Magnet, Myron. "The American Family, 1992." Fortune 10 Aug.

  1992: 42-47.

One inch margin

REVISING ON THE BASIS OF READER COMMENTS

One result of going through the research process is that you become engrossed in the material; that makes it difficult for you to view your writing objectively. It is important to get feedback on your draft to see if your message gets through to the audience. You may ask your reader to use the following checklist as a feedback guide, or you may work alone and apply the checklist to the draft yourself.

✓ CHECKLIST FOR REVISING A RESEARCH PAPER

_____ Is the paper written on a sufficiently narrow topic?

_____ Can you understand the writer's research goals?

_____ Does the writer present a clear thesis?

_____ Does the writer make sense of the information from sources?

_____ Can you discern the research paper's form (multisource comparison and contrast, summary of multiple sources, objective synthesis, essay of response to multiple sources, synthesis with a specific purpose, argument, analysis, or evaluation)?

_____ Is the information from sources organized according to a clear plan?

_____ Does the writer use information from sources convincingly?

_____ Are the writer's assertions substantiated with material from sources?

_____ Does the writer provide transitions among sources and among pieces of information?

_____ Is the writer's voice appropriate for this type of essay? Why or why not?

_____ Is the opening satisfactory? Why or why not?

_____ Does the essay have an appropriate conclusion?

_____ Is the title suitable for the piece?

_____ Can you identify the source for each piece of information?

_____ Does the paper end with a list of works cited that includes all sources referred to in the text of the paper?

Exercise

If your teacher agrees, have a classmate or friend review your preliminary draft and give you feedback. If this is not possible, set the essay aside for a few days and then review it yourself. Use the checklist for revising a research paper.

EDITING

When you are satisfied with your revision, read your paper aloud. Then reread it line by line and sentence by sentence. Check for correct usage, punctuation, spelling, mechanics, manuscript form, and typographical errors. If you are using a word processing program with a spell checker, run the checker on your essay. If your editing skills are not strong, get a friend to read over your work. Keep in mind the following concerns:

✓ CHECKLIST FOR EDITING A RESEARCH PAPER

_____ Are all your sentences complete?

_____ Have you avoided run-on sentences, both fused sentences and comma splices?

_____ Do pronouns have clear antecedents, and do they agree in number, gender, and case with the words for which they stand?

_____ Do all subjects and verbs agree in person and number?

_____ Is the verb tense consistent and correct?

_____ Have you used modifiers (words, phrases, subordinate clauses) correctly and placed them where they belong?

_____ Have you used matching elements in parallel constructions?

_____ Are punctuation marks used correctly?

_____ Are spelling, capitalization, and other mechanics (abbreviations, numbers, italics) correct?

E x e r c i s e ....

Use the editing checklist as you work to complete your research paper.

● ● ● ● ● ● ● ● ● ● ● ● ● ● ● ●

Lester 1

Kristen Lester

Professor Smith

Academic Writing I

24 April 2000

What "Family Values"?

Opening: relevance of issue to current election

    It seems that each election year, conservative, moderate, and liberal candidates go to considerable lengths to express their strong support for "family values." The assumption underneath this debate is that the American family is endangered and needs reinforcement. Unfortunately, the political rhetoric around family values often degenerates to posturing that lacks precision and clarity. What exactly are

1

"family values," and how are they in peril? Without a doubt,
American families have changed significantly in recent years.
The traditional nuclear family, with a breadwinner father,
homemaker mother, and children, has been on the decline, and
it is being replaced by what sociologist David Elkind calls
the "postmodern family," a term that encompasses various types
of domestic units such as single-parent families, dual-income
families, and remarried families (Scherer 4). To a large
extent, the debate over family values revolves around whether
this transformation represents the decline of the American
family or an opportunity to strengthen and improve families.
The sociological literature on the evolution and current status
of the American family helps clarify the issues that are at
the core of this political debate. I will use the findings of
sociologists who study the American family to analyze issues
that lie at the core of the political controversy over family
values.

This transformation of the traditional nuclear family to
postmodern families was not the first change in family makeup
that America has seen. In the preindustrial era, family life
focused almost entirely on economic survival, and child rearing
was always secondary to this primary task (Popenoe 81-91).
However, the transition to the traditional nuclear family began
in the early 1800s, as industrialization took the edge off the
struggle for economic survival. In the nuclear family, Elkind
explains, the home was the primary focus of life rather than
mere survival, and the care and nurturing of children received

Analytical thesis (margin note)

Objective synthesis to provide background (margin note)

2

much more attention (Scherer 4). The typical picture was of
the husband away at work and the wife taking care of the home
and their two or three children, with the family held together
by strong bonds of romantic and maternal love (4). According
to Elkind, togetherness became a primary family value, and the
family itself was considered more important than any one
member's personal needs or happiness (4). By the 1960s,
however, American culture had changed, and the focus on family
life was replaced with Americans' "quest for personal
liberation and gratification," particularly among the young
(Magnet 45). At the same time, the sexual revolution undermined
the idea that sex should take place only within a marriage and
glorified the joy of sexual adventure, including premarital sex
(Popenoe 39-42, 204-06). In addition, the women's movement
identified the constraints of traditional family life as a form
of oppression (131-32). These new trends weakened Americans'
commitment to the values of the traditional nuclear family.
Those values were, according to Elkind, seen as "overly
idealized and blind to the dark side of human behavior" and
were replaced with a new set of family values that included
acceptance of temporary consensual love and emphasis on
individual autonomy, rather than togetherness (Scherer 6).
Along with those changes in values came a change in family
structure. Postmodern variations on the traditional nuclear
family included single-parent families, gay and lesbian
families, childless families, adoptive families, remarried
families, and families with both parents working (Cherry and
Matsumura; Goldschneider and Waite 192-209).

Lester 4

Summary:
views of
conserva-
tives

Changes in both family structure and family values are particularly feared by political conservatives. One focus of their concern is the high rate of divorce and the effects on children when traditional families break up. The rate of divorce, currently exceeding 50%, is a result of several factors (Popenoe 20-23). First of all, the new emphasis on adult psychological well-being and self-development means that children's needs are no longer considered more important than those of adults. This shift from collectivism to individualism does allow for more free and independent persons, but it decreases social order and leads to higher rates of deviance, juvenile delinquency, crime, loneliness, depression, suicide, and social alienation (24-25, 52-78). Second, the adoption of the no-fault divorce law has numbed society to the enormous impact of divorce (29-30). Conservatives feel as though divorce has become so widely accepted that even stable couples are affected negatively because they are less likely to make the effort to see that their marriages continue to work. Richard T. Gill states that "the omnipresence of divorce makes it harder for couples to commit themselves wholeheartedly to the marital union and, indeed, encourages and really requires them to take protective steps that often undermine the quality of the union" (86). Conservatives fear that as the traditional family declines, American society as a whole will become less stable.

As family values have changed, so has family structure, and conservatives fear that nontraditional family structures that are becoming more common will damage the development of future generations. Children raised in weak or broken families are more likely to fall into patterns that include rejecting

family and school, identifying with youth gangs, and committing

serious crimes (Fagan). They are also more likely to become

involved with suicide, substance abuse, eating disorders,

births outside of marriage, psychological stress, anxiety, and

unipolar depression (Popenoe 52-78). Mother-only families are a

particular concern of those who favor a return to traditional

nuclear families. Children raised without fathers, especially

boys, lack experience with "real" men with whom they may have

a close relationship as opposed to celebrity role models

(Goldschneider and Waite 201-02). The parents in these

situations suffer too. Women carry the double burden of work

and home, and men's position as the family provider often

deteriorates (Griswold 257-60). As a result, many fear that

society will largely consist of irresponsible men without women

to control their sexual behavior and competitive aggression

(257-60). When mothers are working and fathers are absent,

children grow up with less parental participation in the

development of their intellectual, emotional, and moral

education. Thus many conservatives argue that our society's

investment in tomorrow's generation has diminished because our

sense of individualism has advanced too far. Mary Ann Glendon

raises the question, "When parents put personal goals ahead of

family goals, how will kids learn the opposite?" (qtd. in

Magnet 42). It is obviously difficult for a society to promote

aggressively the full development of each individual and still

stay committed to the traditional family structure.

  While conservatives may fear the transformation to

Synthesis summary: views of conservatives

Indication of quotation found in secondary source

5

Transition
to views of
liberals

postmodern families, a common liberal viewpoint is that the
shift in both family structure and family values will serve
Americans well in the years to come. Thus a frequent goal of
the liberal political agenda is to find ways of supporting
postmodern families that may be marginalized or attacked by
traditionalists. Those who value postmodern families point to
the new economic, technological, and cultural changes facing
American families today. We are presented with new challenges
and opportunities to which postmodern families are highly
responsive. David Elkind says that the postmodern family "is

Synthesis
summary:
views of
liberals

more fluid and more flexible. . . . It mirrors the openness,
complexity, and diversity of our contemporary lifestyle"
(Scherer 4). One of those changes involves the role of women
in society. Many observers argue that traditional nuclear
families unfairly restrain women. In this day and age,
demographic and economic changes make it unnecessary and
impractical for homemaking to be a "lifetime career"
(Goldschneider and Waite 203-05). When both parents work, the
economic pressures on the family lessen. Just as the rise of
the traditional nuclear family was a response to
industrialization, the current shift away from the traditional
family has the same driving force: a changing economic reality.
Liberals are not, however, blind to the problems posed by these
economic factors, particularly for working-class families.

Block
quotation

> It's true that the social and cultural changes we've
> witnessed have created families that, in some ways,
> are more responsive to the needs of their members,
> more democratic than any we have known before. But

> it's also true that without economic stability, even
> the most positive changes will not be enough to hold
> families together. (Rubin 246)

The liberal agenda typically includes social welfare programs
that support families at the lower end of the economic spectrum.

Although conservatives claim that two-income families just
mean that women will have the double burden of homemaking and
employment, liberals respond that men can take on
responsibilities in the home. Both liberals and conservatives
recognize that women who stay at home to raise children are at
a great disadvantage when they later try to enter the work
force, and many return to their jobs too quickly because they
cannot afford to take time off. However, the shift in values
that started in the 1960s includes a recognition that men can
and should help with child rearing and household tasks
(Goldschneider and Waite 203-05). More men are expressing an
interest in helping their wives with the workload and are
discovering that a step down from absolute patriarchy often
helps in strengthening their relationships with their wives and
children (205). Men may find that both personal growth and
family happiness are enhanced when gender roles are less
strictly defined (Johnson 251-52).

Many liberals would claim that virtually any family
structure is valid, provided that family members receive ample
"love, fulfillment, and empowerment" (Cherry and Matsumura 25).
According to this view, it would be unjust to judge single-
parent families, same-sex partnerships, extended families, or
any other family form as inherently inadequate. Conservatives

6

7

Synthesis
summary:
views of
liberals

often condemn single-parent families as unacceptable structures
in which to raise children. However, liberals maintain that the
breakup of a marriage does not stop effective parenting and
that effects of divorce on children are often exaggerated. A
study by California therapist Judith Wallerstein is most
commonly cited when measuring these effects (Ehrenreich).
Wallerstein found that 41% of children whose parents are
divorced are "doing poorly, worried, underachieving,
deprecating, and often angry" years after the split.
Ehrenreich, however, points out that this report lacks
credibility because it focused on just sixty couples. More
important, two-thirds of them were without "adequate
psychological functioning" previous to the divorce. Divorce is
typically portrayed on television and in films as devastating
for all involved, but "just as there are bad divorces, there
are good divorces too," Constance Ahron points out
(Ehrenreich). Both parents do, in many cases, remain
financially and emotionally responsible for their children. The
situation after divorce sometimes even improves when families
are relieved of constant fighting and abuse. As divorce has
become more acceptable, its effects have become less harsh.

Two specific family values issues that clearly divide
conservatives and liberals are homosexual parenting and
childless families. The debate over gay and lesbian families
with children has generated much political heat. Currently,
states and municipalities recognize the rights of same-sex
couples to varying degrees, with liberals generally supporting
those rights and conservatives challenging them. Of all the

Synthesis summary: views of liberals

Comparison
and
contrast:
conservative
and liberal
views on a
specific
issue

political debates over the American family, this one is perhaps

the least informed by sociological research. However, such

research does exist. Barret and Robinson reviewed the

sociological literature on gay male parenting and concluded

that children of gay fathers are not significantly different

from their peers raised by straight parents. Some of these

children do have difficulty coming to grips with their fathers'

sexual orientation, but others not only accept their gay

parents but also develop closer relationships with them than is

typical in straight families. Sexual abuse of children is rare

in gay families, and the sons of gay fathers apparently do not

acquire homosexuality from their nontraditional family

lifestyle (Barret and Robinson). Some liberals vigorously

defend the right of homosexual couples to raise children,

including the right to adopt (Cherry and Matsumura).

While the debate over family values often centers on

children, the growing number of childless couples is also a

cause of concern for defenders of the traditional nuclear

family. According to George Gilder, the responsibility of

providing for a wife and children serves to rein in men's

Comparison
and
contrast:
conservative
and liberal
views on a
specific
issue

basic aggressive and violent nature. According to this

argument, the nuclear family helps ensure that men will

contribute to society rather than disrupt it (Griswold 258-60).

Liberals, however, argue that a childless couple is a viable

family and deserves the support of society as much as any

other family (Cherry and Matsumura 25).

As the current election year unfolds, we will undoubtedly

witness more political battles over what is best for the

9

10

Lester 10

American family: a return to traditional family values and structures or an effort to improve the success of the various postmodern family forms. What is the reality beneath the political rhetoric? Are we weakening the most basic social element of our society, or are we gaining a flexibility that the family will need to survive in the twenty-first century? The sociological literature does not provide definite answers to these questions even though it may clarify the underlying issues. When seeking answers to these questions, it is essential to consider which structure is most suitable for raising children so that they grow up to be both autonomous and socially responsible. Children must feel like an important part of their parents' lives and need to be embraced with love, care, and guidance. When these qualities are provided, both individual happiness and social harmony will follow.

Conclusion: return to opening example and look to the future

Lester 11

Works Cited

Barret, Robert L., and Bryan E. Robinson. "Gay Dads."

> Redefining Families: Implications for Children's

> Development. Ed. Adele Eskeles Gottfried and Allen W.

> Gottfried. New York: Plenum, 1994. 157-70.

Cherry, Matt, and Molleen Matsumura. "A Vision of Families for

> the Twenty-First Century: A Declaration of Secular Family

> Values." Free Inquiry Winter 1998: 25-26.

Lester 12

Ehrenreich, Barbara. "In Defense of Splitting Up: The Growing
    Anti-Divorce Movement Is Blind to the Costs of Bad
    Marriage." Time 8 Apr. 1996: 80.

Fagan, Patrick. "The Real Root Cause of Violent Crime: The
    Breakdown of the Family." Vital Speeches of the Day 15
    Dec. 1995: 157-58. Expanded Academic ASAP. InfoTrac.
    Ithaca Coll. Lib., Ithaca, NY. 2 Apr. 2000.
    <http://web4.infotrac.galegroup.com>.

Gill, Richard T. "Family Breakdown as Family Policy." Public
    Interest Winter 1993: 84-91.

Goldschneider, Frances K., and Linda J. Waite. New Families, No
    Families? Demographic Change and the Transformation of the
    American Home. Berkeley: U of California P, 1991.

Griswold, Robert L. Fatherhood in America. New York: Harper, 1993.

Johnson, Allan G. The Gender Knot: Unraveling Our Patriarchal
    Legacy. Philadelphia: Temple UP, 1997.

Magnet, Myron. "The American Family, 1992." Fortune 10 Aug.
    1992: 42-47.

Popenoe, David. Life without Father. New York: Free, 1996.

Rubin, Lillian B. Families on the Fault Line. New York:
    Harper, 1994.

Scherer, Marge. "On Our Changing Family Values: A Conversation
    with David Elkind." Educational Leadership 53 (1996): 4-9.

Part III

READING SELECTIONS

9

GRADES AND LEARNING

In our hometown of Ithaca, New York, the Alternative Community School offers all courses on credit/no-credit basis rather than assigning A–F grades. In lieu of grades, teachers provide end-of-semester assessments, typically several paragraphs for each student, that describe what students learned and indicate the quality of their work. During the four years of high school, each student compiles a portfolio that includes examples of his or her strongest work on essays, exams, lab reports, and other projects. The completed portfolio is the primary requirement for high school graduation.

One of the goals of the credit system used at the Alternative Community School is to help students focus on learning rather than grades. A common critique of A–F grading is that it encourages students to think of the grade itself as the primary purpose of education and makes instructors "teach to the test" rather than attend to the individual needs of each student. At the same time, however, there is a growing movement in America for raising educational standards, a component of which is a call for tougher grading, to motivate higher levels of achievement. Grade inflation is often cited for undermining the integrity of our educational system and devaluing high school and college diplomas.

The readings in this chapter analyze the relationship between grades and learning. Jerry Farber, author of "A Young Person's Guide to the Grading System," argues that the A–F grading system has all but destroyed students' motivation to learn and that learning is meaningful only when students have a genuine desire for intellectual growth. In "Grades and Money," Steven Vogel suggests that the current generation of college students sees grades, rather than knowledge and understanding, as the reward for the effort they invest in academic work and that our society encourages this perception. The motivational value of grades and constructive criticism is stressed in David Rothenberg's "Learning in Finland: No Grades, No Criticism." Finally, Stephen Goode and Timothy W. Maier describe how grades have risen at colleges across the nation and discuss efforts to combat grade inflation in their article "Inflating the Grades."

A Young Person's Guide to the Grading System

Jerry Farber

Jerry Farber, a professor of English at the University of California at San Diego, is the author of many books and articles of social and literary criticism. His work was particularly influential on the student movement of the late 1960s and early 1970s. The following essay was written during that period.

Prereading ·

In the first paragraph of his essay, Farber asks the reader to consider what grades do for learning. Freewrite for ten minutes in response to this prompt.

· · · · · · · · · · · · · · · ·

There's no question that the grading system is effective in training people to do what they're told. The question is: what does it do for learning?   1

Grades focus our attention. But on what? On the test. Academic success, as everyone knows, is something that we measure not in knowledge but in grade points. What we get on the final is all-important; what we retain after the final is irrelevant. Grades don't make us want to enrich our minds; they make us want to please our teachers (or at least put them on). Grades are a game. When the term is over, you shuffle the deck and begin a new round. Who reads his textbooks after the grades are in? What's the point? It doesn't go on your score.   2

Oddly enough, many of us understand all of this and yet remain convinced that we need to be graded in order to learn. When we get to college, twelve years of slave work have very likely convinced us that learning is dull, plodding and unpalatable. We may think we need to be graded: we assume that without the grades we'd never go through all that misery voluntarily. But, in fact, we've been had. We've been prodded with phony motivations so long that we've become insensitive to the true ones. We're like those sleeping pill addicts who have reached the point where they need strong artificial inducement to do what comes naturally. We're grade junkies—convinced that we'd never learn without the A's and F's to keep us going. Grades have prevented us from growing up. No matter how old a person is—when he attends school, he's still a child, tempted with lollipops and threatened with spankings.   3

Learning happens when you *want* to know. Ask yourself: did you need grades to learn how to drive? To learn how to talk? To learn how to play chess—or play the guitar—or dance—or find your way around a new city? Yet these are things we do very well—much better than we handle that French or Spanish that we were graded on for years in high school. Some of us, though, are certain that, while we might learn to drive or play chess without grades, we still need them to force us to learn the things we don't really want to learn— math, for instance. But is that really true? If for any reason you really want or need some math—say, algebra—you can learn it without being graded. And if you don't want it and don't need it, you'll probably never get it straight, grades or not. Just because you pass a   4

Jerry Farber. "A Young Person's Guide to the Grading System." *The Student as Nigger.* New York: Pocket, 1970. 67–72.

subject doesn't mean you've learned it. How much time did you spend on algebra and geometry in high school? Two years? How much do you remember? Or what about grammar? How much did all those years of force-fed grammar do for you? You learn to talk (without being graded) from the people around you, not from gerunds and modifiers. And as for writing—if you ever do learn to write well, you can bet your sweet ass it won't be predicate nominatives that teach you. Perhaps those subjects that we would never study without being graded are the very subjects that we lose hold of as soon as the last test is over.

Still, some of us maintain that we need grades to give us self-discipline. But do you want to see real self-discipline? Look at some kid working on his car all weekend long. His parents even have to drag him in for dinner. And yet, if that kid had been compelled to work on cars all his life and had been continually graded on it, then he'd swear up and down that he needed those grades to give him self-discipline.   5

It is only recently—and out of school—that I have begun to understand self-discipline in writing. It grows out of freedom, not out of coercion. Self-discipline isn't staying up all night to finish a term paper; that's slave work. Self-discipline is revising one paragraph fanatically for weeks—for no other reason than that you yourself aren't happy with it. Self-discipline is following a problem through tedious, repetitive laboratory experiments, because there's no other way of finding out what you want to know. Or it can be surfing all day long every single day for an entire summer until you are good at it. Self-discipline is nothing more than a certain way of pleasing yourself, and it is the last thing anyone is likely to learn for a grade.   6

Coercion inside school probably leads many of us to develop our self-discipline in areas untouched by the classroom. Who knows? If movie-going, dancing and surfing were the only required subjects, there might well be a poetic renaissance. I suspect that most kids fool around with writing on their own at some point—diaries, poetry, whatever—but this interest rarely survives school. When you learn that writing is intellectual slave work, it's all over.   7

Do you think you're a lazy student? No wonder! Slaves are almost always lazy.   8

Suppose I go to college; I want to be a chemist or a high school teacher or an accountant. Are grades really my only reason for learning the field? Is getting graded going to turn me on to my subject? Or is it more likely to turn me off? How sad this is. History is so engrossing. Literature is so beautiful. And school is likely to turn them dull or even ugly. Can you imagine what would happen if they graded you on sex? The race would die out.   9

Wouldn't it be great to be free to learn? Without penalties and threats, without having to play childish competitive games for gold and silver stars? Can you even imagine what the freedom to learn might be like?   10

Perhaps this kind of freedom sounds attractive to you but you're convinced that it isn't suited to our society. Even if the grading system can be shown to work against learning, you may assume that grades are still necessary to *evaluate* people—to screen people for various kinds of work.   11

But think about it. Do you really believe that the best way to determine someone's qualifications is to grade him—A, B, C, D, F—week by week, day by day, in everything he studies for sixteen years of school? Is this monstrous rigmarole honestly necessary in order to determine who gets which jobs?   12

There are far better ways to determine a person's qualifications. Many fields already do their own screening by examination; the bar exam is one instance. In some areas—journalism, for example—supervised on-the-job experience would probably be the most   13 effective screening and qualifying technique. Other fields might call for a combination of methods. Engineers, for example, could be qualified through apprenticeship plus a demonstration of reasonable competency on exams at various levels—exams on which they would, of course, get an unlimited number of tries.

In a great many fields, no screening technique is necessary at all. Countless employers, public and private, require a college degree for no really good reason, simply because it enables their personnel departments to avoid making any meaningful individual evaluation and because it indicates some degree of standardization. There is no reason why a person should be forced to spend four years of his life in college just to get a decent job and then discover that he would have been much better off working in the field itself for four years and pursuing his own learning interests on a less rigid and formal basis.

Still it might be argued that eliminating grades entirely would require too sudden a shift in our society. I would maintain that the sudden shift is desirable. In any case, though, society is not likely to face the simultaneous abandonment of grading by every school in the country. Furthermore, on a campus where there is enormous resistance to abolishing grades, one could put forth a fairly good half-way compromise—the Credit system—which is, from my point of view, worth trying even though it falls short of what should be the real goal: no grades at all.

Under this system, some courses could be made totally free of grading: basic algebra, say, or drawing or poetry writing. The rest would be run on a Credit basis. If you meet the minimum requirements of a course, you get credit for it. No A's or C's or silver stars. Just credit. And if you don't meet the requirements, nothing happens. You don't lose anything or get penalized; you just don't get credit for that course. This is NOT the Pass-Fail System. Pass-Fail is a drag; if you don't pass a course, you get hurt. Under the Credit system you simply either get credit or you don't. All that your record shows is the courses you've earned credit for (not the ones you've attempted). And when you get credit for enough courses, you can get some kind of certification or credential, if you want one, according to the number and type of courses you've taken. And there should be not just a few assembly-line four-year degrees: AB, BS, and so on; there should be scores of more meaningful and varied certifications and degrees. Or maybe there should be none at all, just a list of the courses for which you have credit.

What's wrong with that? College becomes something more like a place for learning and growth, not fear and anxiety. It becomes a learning community, not a gladiatorial arena where you're pitted in daily battle against your fellow students. In elementary and secondary schools, of course, there is an even weaker pretext for grading and even more to be gained by its abolishment.

And we mustn't be too quick to assume that abolishing A's and F's would make our colleges still more overcrowded. If we eliminate the pointless Mickey-Mouse requirements that are foisted on everyone, if we eliminate the gold-star games and all the administrative paperwork and class busywork that go along with them, if we reduce the overwhelming pressure for a meaningless, standardized degree, then perhaps we'll end up with learning facilities that can accommodate even more students than the number that get processed in the factories that we currently operate.

And if an employer wants not just degrees but grade-point averages too, the colleges will explain that that's not what they are there for. Graduate schools, for their part, will

14

15

16

17

18

19

probably not present a serious problem. They already put heavy emphasis on criteria other than GPA's. They stress interviews, personal recommendations: most of them already give their own entrance exams anyway. Besides, the best graduate schools will probably be delighted to get some *live* students for a change.

But what about the students themselves? Can they live without grades? Can they learn   20
without them? Perhaps we should be asking ourselves: can they really learn *with* them?

READING FOR INFORMATION

1. In what sense, according to Farber, are grades a game?
2. What does Farber mean when he says we are "grade junkies"?
3. Paraphrase Farber's definition of self-discipline.
4. According to Farber, how do grades affect self-discipline?
5. If grades were eliminated, how does Farber suggest we might judge the qualifications of college graduates?
6. How does Farber's Credit system differ from Pass-Fail?
7. What improvements in higher education would, according to Farber, result from the elimination of grades?

READING FOR FORM, ORGANIZATION, AND FEATURES

1. Characterize Farber's tone and level of formality. Why did Farber choose that tone? Is the choice a good one?
2. Why does Farber use examples from everyday life to illustrate his points about how students learn?
3. What is Farber's organizational plan?
4. In what ways does Farber try to establish a "conversation" with his readers?

READING FOR RHETORICAL CONCERNS

1. Who is Farber's intended audience? Explain your answer.
2. Why does Farber wait until the end of his essay to explain his Credit system?
3. In which paragraphs does Farber attempt to address the concerns of those who believe grades are necessary? How successfully does he respond to those concerns?

WRITING ASSIGNMENTS

1. In a 1,000-word essay, compare and contrast your own definition of self-discipline with Farber's definition.
2. Write a 1,000-word essay that attacks or defends Farber's Credit system.
3. Use information and examples from Farber's article to analyze how the grading system has affected your own education. Write at least 750 words.

• • • • • • • • • • • • • • • •

Grades and Money

Steven Vogel

Steven Vogel is a professor of philosophy at Denison University.

P r e r e a d i n g ....

The title of Vogel's article suggests that there is a relationship between grades and money. What do you anticipate that relationship might be? Freewrite for ten minutes in response to this question.

. . . .

When I was a college student, back in the early seventies, people I knew made it a point not to talk about their grades. To this day, I have no idea how my friends did in college—they all graduated, which I guess means they did well enough. Today some are lawyers, doctors, businesspeople, software designers, bed-and-breakfast hosts, and so forth, but I'd be hard-pressed to guess who were the straight-A students among them and who barely squeaked through.

    Me, I'm a college professor, teaching philosophy at a small private liberal-arts college in the Midwest. And what strikes me today is how different my students are: they talk about their grades *all the time*. They argue and gossip about them, complain to me and my colleagues about them, orient their whole college lives, as far as I can tell, around them. I say this not to sound self-righteous or holier than they—openness about grades is probably healthier than the kind of highfalutin' squeamishness we exhibited—but rather to explain the difficulty I feel in really *understanding* grades, in grasping what exactly they are and what they're for. My students are much better at it than I am. When they come into my office to ask (usually in despair or anger) why they got the grade they did in my class, I'm always a little confused, and a little embarrassed, for them and for me: *why* exactly are we talking about this? I always think. Of course it's particularly embarrassing because I've been teaching, and assigning grades, for twelve years, and I guess from my students' point of view it's the most important thing I do. (As far as I'm concerned, it's just a twice-yearly annoyance, and furthermore an impossibility: what exactly *is* the difference between a B– and a C+? Damned if I know.)

    No, I don't understand grades that well. But when I read last winter that President Clinton was proposing to grant tax deductions for tuition to all college students who maintain B averages, something about it felt wrong to me, and I started to wonder why.

    Everybody in the world of higher education, and most people outside, too, pays lip service to the idea that the point of education is, well, to *get educated*. It's the learning that's the goal, we say, not the grade; we want our students to learn about history and philosophy and literature and science and art and mathematics because doing so will make them better people, better citizens of a democracy. The point is to develop talents, attitudes, habits of mind that are good in themselves, that will improve their lives (and the lives of their fellow citizens); we say that education itself is such a good. If this is true, then grades

1

2

3

4

Steven Vogel. "Grades and Money." *Dissent* Fall 1997: 102–04.

must play a secondary role; they can serve a motivating function, but ought never to be mistaken for the goal of the process as such.

This is what we *say*, but it is not the way we act, and it is certainly not the way most of our students see the situation. For them the goal of going to class, writing papers, taking exams, and so on, is simply the grade itself. When I ask a student why a higher grade in a course is so important, I'm often told it's because it will increase the grade point average (GPA); when I ask why the GPA is important, I'm told that it's necessary for getting into a good postgraduate school, which is in turn important for getting a good job, which is important for making lots of money. Everything is important *for* something else, in this litany; nothing is important for itself. Except, of course, money.

It's money that's the crux of it. An important part of what we're teaching in college— not what we intend to teach, but what we do teach nonetheless—is how to think about money, what its relation is to value and effort and self-worth. Anyone entering this society surely needs to know all this; it's arguably the most important skill our culture demands. But of course we don't use real money to teach this skill—that would be too expensive and risky. Instead, we use grades. In my college, like most others, grades *are* money. They're the currency around which everything revolves.

What grades *ought* to be is a report, nothing more: how did the student do, how much did he or she learn, how much were his or her skills and critical self-consciousness and knowledge of the world expanded? A serious student might indeed want to know that at the end of the course—might want it to check his or her work, might even want to use it as a carrot or a stick. But we don't use grades as a report; we use them, in myriad ways, as money. We talk about "docking" students' grades for turning in papers late or missing classes, like finance companies assessing a late fee; we offer "contracts," whereby students are promised certain grades for doing a certain amount of work. My dean tells me that the syllabus I give to students at the beginning of the semester *is*, legally speaking, a contract, and has been interpreted by the courts as such—it must specify how I will calculate grades at the end of the term, and woe to me if I say that the final exam will count 30 percent and later change my mind and make it 35 percent. Students expect that their grade will indicate the amount of time they have put into the course, as if they were hourly workers, and many faculty agree that it's important to consider "effort" when they "award" grades.

The relationship between me and the students is really an exchange relationship: they provide me with work of a certain quality and I reward it—pay for it—by giving them a certain grade. This all seems so obvious to everyone that it's never even remarked upon, even though it is entirely different from, and even incompatible with, what we normally say about the relationship in the classroom—which is that it's one where I'm a teacher helping my students learn. Their learning isn't something they "give" me, not something I'm supposed to pay them for. Nothing real is exchanged in the classroom, and so the model of money is out of place there. But we're all so used to it everywhere else that we don't even notice. Yet applying it in the classroom produces perverse results.

If grades are money, and if the product for which they pay is learning, then it's perfectly rational for students to try to minimize that learning while maximizing their "return," and looking for loopholes or strategies that will produce the best possible grade for the least possible effort. And they do: I'm constantly amazed by the mathematically

5

6

7

8

9

sophisticated understanding students instantly develop of whatever new grading scheme I announce, and by their ability to find ambiguities and possible avenues for creative interpretation in it. Their incentive is thus *not* to learn, or to learn as little as possible while maintaining a good GPA—while I am placed in the position of having to figure out new ways to trick them into learning by designing ingenious new ways to grade.

On the faculty side, the situation is more pleasant, if no less perverse. If grades are money, for us they are funny money, Monopoly money, because it costs us nothing to give them out—and no more, except in terms of our self-image, to give out an A than a C. Thus we get to play out our own fantasies about money—we can be skinflints, stingily giving out one or two A's a year, or spendthrifts, spreading high grades everywhere, or, like that guy on the show about the millionaire, looking for needy cases (troubled students, applicants to tough graduate programs) upon whom to generously bestow our wealth. Since we all want to be loved, and since the students seem to care so damned much, the misers are few. The result, as any economist will tell you, is inflation; in many of the best colleges the average grade is around A–.

10

If grades are money, then learning is a cost—a painful effort one undergoes only for the reward it produces. That the learning or the effort might itself be the reward—which is what we *say* about education—makes no sense or is sentimental rubbish. The effect of turning grades into money is to commodify learning, making it appear as something that is painful in itself and useful only for what it can buy. This is exactly the opposite of what education ought to be about.

11

I point all this out to my students when I can, often giving a heartfelt speech on the first day of the course about what I think grades are and how they ought not to be taken so seriously. The students look at me as though I'm crazy.

12

In the last few years, my college has begun to offer merit scholarships, which is to say financial aid to very good students without requiring them to prove financial need; this is one of the ways we have helped to build up an excellent honors program that has been a real boon to the institution. But one characteristic of these scholarships is that to keep them students must maintain a certain GPA—generally a B average and sometimes even higher. Here the analogy between money and grades is not merely an analogy: a B can now literally be worth thousands of dollars. One day a student came to me for advice on her course schedule and informed me that, although she'd like to try a philosophy course sometime, she couldn't risk it because she wasn't sure what her grade would be. When I tried out one of my lines about how "the important thing is learning, not grades," she looked back at me fiercely and explained that if her GPA dropped even a little bit she would lose her scholarship, worth ten thousand dollars; how dare I tell her grades aren't important? I had no response. She was right. She kept the scholarship, and never learned philosophy.

13

By tying grades to money, we give students incentives not to take risks. Very good and well-prepared first-year students often come to me to explain that they would rather take Calculus One than Calculus Two, even though they have already taken calculus in high school—or rather, *because* they have; that way they are guaranteed a good grade. These honors students are in some ways the worst in terms of their fixation on grades and their constant and creative search to find ways to manipulate the system; their skill at doing so, after all, has gotten them where they are today.

14

When I heard that President Clinton was offering tax deductions for B's, I imagined   *15*
my own college's program turned into national policy, and I blanched. Did we really want
to write the current grading system into tax law?

As it turned out, that aspect of the proposal disappeared in the final tax bill. Every-   *16*
body seemed a little dubious about the idea of turning college professors into agents of
national tax policy. But the deeper questions were never asked: about why we so easily
accept the equation between grades and money that the proposal implied, about what
grades really are for and why we take them for granted. What was wrong with Clinton's
well-meaning proposal was that it sent the wrong message. Few noticed because we are all
so in thrall to instrumentalism and commodification—and because we no longer feel sure
what education is for or why we value it. We let grades count as money—we let education
count as money—because money, nowadays, is the only value we know.

READING FOR INFORMATION

1. How do the attitudes of current students toward grades differ from those of Vogel
   and his classmates when they were undergraduates in the early 1970s?
2. What is Vogel's present attitude toward grades? How does it differ from that of his
   students?
3. What was President Clinton's proposal to link college grades to income taxes?
4. In what ways does Vogel see grades as "currency" of higher education? What do
   grades pay for?
5. Why, according to Vogel, do students feel that they should be rewarded for effort as
   well as performance?
6. According to Vogel, what has been the effect of merit-based scholarship?

READING FOR FORM, ORGANIZATION, AND FEATURES

1. Describe Vogel's opening strategy.
2. What form of evidence does Vogel provide to support his point of view?
3. Explain how Vogel's essay is an extended analogy.
4. Why does Vogel, at the beginning of the third paragraph, state that he doesn't understand grades even though he is writing an analytical essay about grades?

READING FOR RHETORICAL CONCERNS

1. Who is Vogel's intended audience? Is the piece offensive to a student audience?
2. How might a professor who takes grades seriously respond to Vogel's piece?
3. Is Vogel attempting to change the behavior of his audience? Explain your
   answer.

WRITING ASSIGNMENTS

1. Write a 250-word summary of the parallel Vogel draws between grades and
   money.

2. Draw on Vogel's article to write a 1,250-word essay that weighs the pros and cons of merit-based financial aid programs for college students.

3. Write a 1,000-word essay in response to Vogel's final statement: "We let grades count as money—we let education count as money—because money, nowadays, is the only value we know."

. . . .

Learning in Finland: No Grades, No Criticism

David Rothenberg

David Rothenberg teaches philosophy at the New Jersey Institute of Technology. He edits the journal Terra Nova: Nature and Culture.

P r e r e a d i n g . . . .

Rothenberg's subtitle suggests an educational system in which students' work is not criticized. Do you think it is possible to learn without constructive criticism from teachers? Freewrite for ten minutes in response to this question.

. . . .

What's it like to teach in a country where there are no grades, no one is allowed to fail, you can stay in school as many years as you like, and students are actually paid to be there?   *1*

Not like home.   *2*

During my semester as a Fulbright scholar at Helsinki's University of Art and Design, teaching philosophy and music, I once met one of my students in the hall and asked her whether she would be turning in her paper on Monday, the day it was due.   *3*

"Perhaps," she said. "If I have time."   *4*

When I ran into another student who was rushing out of the building, I asked, "Have you got your project ready for us for class today?"   *5*

"Sorry, no," he blurted out, as he hurried off. "I've been too busy."   *6*

Welcome to higher education in Finland. Students do their work only when they want to, and they never get grades. No professor can fail a student for not completing work. Students graduate on their own schedule, whenever they've completed their thesis or exam. The more prestigious universities and art schools, such as the one where I taught, are very hard to get into, but once you're in, you're in. And of course, students do not have to pay to go to school—what a vulgar idea! Instead, the government gives each student a small stipend. Although the money is certainly not enough to live on, it does send a specific message: Education is both a right and a privilege.   *7*

Finnish colleges and universities frown on competition. For example, all students who submit work to an art exhibition must be accepted into the show. Everyone must have   *8*

David Rothenberg. "Learning in Finland: No Grades, No Criticism." *Chronicle of Higher Education* 45.9 (23 Oct. 1998): B9+.

an opportunity to present his or her work, no matter how preliminary it may be. The Finns particularly discourage criticism, a main activity in U.S. art schools. Although students listen to the professor's lectures, they tend to work independently and then present their art or other work to the class. No discussion, no revision.

A month before my students' final projects—interactive multimedia works with an emphasis on sound—were due, a handful of students had some work done that they were willing to present in class. We listened to their work, and then talked about it. One student took detailed notes of my critiques, with a rather astonished look on his face, as if he found the whole process most unusual. Some time later, I asked him how his revisions were coming.

"Oh," he said, "I didn't have any time to do any more with it." I was shocked, but critique is just not part of the Finnish educational culture. Just what were these students so busy doing? I was never quite sure, but since they were all in the new-media field, it was easy for them to get outside work that paid better than their student stipends.

Doesn't this lack of attention to criticism lead to a lot of bad art? Yes, but there is always a lot of bad art, in and out of art schools. The same could be said of much academic work produced by teachers as well as students. A lack of quality control is common in academe around the world, as students and professors alike produce reams of material that is rarely criticized, rarely refined, and even more rarely read.

Professors at other Finnish institutions had similar stories.

One architecture professor told me that a few years back, his university had invited a famous American expert on the Finnish architectural hero Alvar Aalto to teach a studio course. The visitor gave a series of lectures and assigned a difficult studio problem to his students. He was shocked that not even one student turned in a final project.

"They did do the projects," said my colleague. "But about a year later, long after the foreign professor was gone. You see, here in Finland, we like to take time with things, to really get them right."

Of course, by then the disgusted foreigner had gone home.

The Finnish view is that simply doing the work on one's own time is the point of education. My students always claimed to be too busy, but they rarely seemed stressed or burned out. Students must think, they must write. In Europe, they often save all their thinking for the final project and the final exam at the end of the single course they typically take each semester. In the United States, students and professors communicate all the time—discussing, chatting, bouncing ideas back and forth, at least in small classes. The Finns put more of a boundary between the learned and the learner. Professors are encouraged to pontificate, to put forth information, and the student to sit silently and take it all down.

Fully aware of this tradition, I wrote out my first two lectures for my course on nature and technology, and I more or less read the lectures to the class. That seemed to be what was expected of me. Afterward, however, I took the risk of asking the students how much they remembered of what I had said. They had absorbed almost nothing. After that, I reverted to my usual, somewhat Socratic method—asking serious, complex questions and trying to get the students to discuss possible solutions, listening to everyone's point of view, working hard to keep the conversation going.

My colleagues said it couldn't be done, that Finnish students are silent, uninterested,

9

10

11

12

13

14

15

16

17

18

and above all not used to open dialogue in the classroom. But, I'm happy to say, it worked fine. Once I pressed them to participate, more and more students became active and engaged in the process of tackling the tough questions I raised.

Students should want to work hard, to improve their work, to make it as good as it can be. Particularly in an art school, and particularly in the nebulous kind of art I was working with—multimedia art using computers and other emerging technologies—a culture of critique is important. Students and professors shouldn't be afraid to ask what is good art and to try to develop it. *19*

Not all my colleagues at the University of Art and Design agreed with me. Said one of the brightest, who runs a research program on how new technology can change education and who writes a weekly on-line column about cyberbusiness: "You Americans are obsessed with competition, while we believe in opportunity. Consider my own case. I am from the working class. I came from a terrible high school. Many of my friends from those days are now criminals. I had terrible grades and would never have been accepted by an American university. Here they had no choice. Once in the system, I could develop my talents, at my own pace, without having to compete with others. In time, I learned how to do well." *20*

"Ah," I said, "but you did learn to do well. There is certainly excellence in your work." *21*

"Not necessarily. I just do it. No one is criticizing me. No one tells me what to do." *22*

In that sense, Finns do resemble Americans—both groups want to be left alone to do their own things in their own way. However, in the United States, almost all activity, even intellectual activity, is evaluated; it is subject to fierce competition for attention and support. In Finland, the state largely replaces the market, and it makes room for all. *23*

A small country aspires to take care of its own. The population of Finland is not much more than that of Connecticut, yet the country has at least four symphony orchestras, four television stations, and scores of newspapers and magazines oriented just to its five and a half million people. Finland is a manageable size, with almost enough opportunities for all. Although unemployment exists, and the economy rises and falls, the country generally remains self-contained. *24*

Is the Finnish system of higher education successful? Certainly, good work does come out of it. And the structure produces less pressure, more time for reflection. Scholars typically get a Ph.D. in the middle of their careers. *25*

Education is clearly respected in Finland, for what degree you have directly affects the amount you earn in a particular job. In the United States, that link seems to apply only in academe: in other sectors of the economy, it's up to the job applicant to convince the employer how much he or she knows and can do. *26*

The Finns seem suspicious of the American penchant for competition, but they realize that their country needs to improve its position in the global economy. Finland for years existed in the shadow of the Soviet Union. Now it's part of the European Union and must compete to become more independent and better known. Finns want to expand their economy beyond their current strengths in manufacturing, production of forest products, and Nokia cellular phones. Some Finns believe that their educational system needs to include more criticism and competition; however, belief in equal opportunity is still stronger in Finland than belief in the responsibility of the individual student. *27*

I admire the Finns for the value they place on education, and for their insistence that *28* education is a right and must remain accessible to all. I even agree that it is a noble goal to free education from the competition for grades and the constraint of time, and to make it a personal journey of self-discovery that can and ought to take years. However, the need for its citizens to compete successfully in trade, manufacturing, and other areas may make this leisurely path toward education a luxury that the nation can no longer afford, at least for all its students. So I tried to foster a spirit of critique among my Finnish students and colleagues, encouraging them not to be afraid to compete and to excel.

READING FOR INFORMATION

1. Without course grades, how do Finnish college students qualify for graduation?
2. In what ways do Finnish universities discourage competition?
3. What is the typical relationship between Finnish professors and their students?
4. Why does Rothenberg believe criticism is essential in education?
5. Why does Rothenberg stop delivering formal lectures to his Finnish students and instead devote classes to discussion?
6. How, according to Rothenberg, does Finland's small size help explain its approach to higher education?
7. What does Rothenberg say about the Finnish economy? How does he link the economy to his discussion of grades?

READING FOR FORM, ORGANIZATION, AND FEATURES

1. Why does Rothenberg open with a question? Why does he immediately provide an answer to the opening question?
2. Why does Rothenberg quote directly from the remarks of his Finnish students?
3. To what extent does Rothenberg attempt to present a balanced appraisal of the pros and cons of the Finnish educational system?
4. What is Rothenberg's overall organizational plan?

READING FOR RHETORICAL CONCERNS

1. Does Rothenberg intend that Finnish professors or students will read his essay? Explain your answer.
2. What is Rothenberg's intention in writing? Does he achieve his purpose?
3. At the end of the article, do you identify more with Rothenberg or with his Finnish students? Explain your answer.
4. Is Rothenberg fair in his presentation of Finnish higher education? Explain your answer.

WRITING ASSIGNMENTS

1. In a 1,000-word essay, argue either for or against the Finnish belief that education should not be competitive.

2. For an audience of American students who have not read Rothenberg's essay, write a 750-word essay that compares and contrasts higher education in Finland and America.

3. Write a 1,000-word essay of personal response in which you summarize the Finnish approach to higher education and then speculate on results if this system were adopted on your own campus.

• • • • • • • • • • • • • • • •

Inflating the Grades

Stephen Goode and Timothy W. Maier

Stephen Goode and Timothy W. Maier are journalists on the staff of Insight on the News.

P r e r e a d i n g •

Freewrite for ten minutes in response to the opening sentence of Goode and Maier's article.

• • • • • • • • • • • • • • • •

Critics of college grading practices say it's time to bring academic rigor and high standards back to campuses where mediocrity has become the accepted norm.   *1*

If a modern-day Rip Van Winkle suddenly awoke after slumbering for two or three decades on an American college campus he'd probably think he had found himself in Garrison Keillor's legendary Minnesota town of Lake Wobegon, where all the students are "above average." Or maybe he'd conclude that they were all just plain brilliant.   *2*

Gone is the "gentleman's C," once regarded as a perfectly acceptable and respectable grade by generations of Americans. Students today regard C's as loathsome and a sign of failure. Instead, at many if not most of contemporary colleges and universities they get A's and B's. Indeed, they get lots of A's and B's.   *3*

The trend is widespread. At Duquesne University in Pittsburgh, for example, three-quarters of the more than 20,000 grades given out to undergraduates in the spring semester a year ago were A's and B's, and at Carnegie-Mellon University in the same city, the A's and B's accounted for nearly two-thirds of the grades.   *4*

Halfway across the country, at the three campuses of the University of Nebraska—Omaha, Lincoln and Kearney—the trend, though not so pronounced as in Pittsburgh, was similar.   *5*

The biggest culprits are the so-called elite schools, which tend to create the fads taken up by the rest of the nation's colleges and universities. Eighty percent of students at prestigious Dartmouth College in New Hampshire received A's and B's. And at Stanford University in California and Princeton University in New Jersey, schools with magical, potent   *6* names, the figures for A's and B's stand at 80 percent (Stanford) and 83.3 percent (Princeton), all according to the *New York Times*.

So pronounced has the increase in grades become that some schools now take pride in bucking the trend. At highly respected Swarthmore College near Philadelphia, students now wear T-shirts boasting, "Anywhere Else It Could Have Been an 'A,'" Swarthmore spokesman Tom Krattenmaker tells *Insight*. Far from succumbing to grade inflation, Krattenmaker says that Swarthmore has tightened standards for students at the small liberal-arts college. To ensure objectivity, Swarthmore brings in outside scholars to judge student performance on the oral and written examinations required by the school's honors program, says Craig Williamson, the English professor who heads the program.   7

Do high grades almost everywhere else mean that today's college students are the brightest and best-prepared students ever, the spin made by some commentators on the phenomenon?   8

No, says Melvyn Leffler, dean of the College of Arts and Sciences at the University of Virginia, or UVA. Leffler first encountered grade inflation when he was chairman of UVA's history department, and as dean he last year commissioned a study of grades at the university which found that grades had increased—particularly during the last decade—from a grade-point mean 10 years ago of 3.05 to 3.15 today, which means that many students are getting A's and B's. (The biggest grade inflation at Virginia took place in humanities courses, and the lowest in science courses, which is true of most universities.)   9

Says Leffler, "We considered the possibility that the rise in grades was due to better students, and rejected that explanation. It just didn't work." Leffler's not sure what explanation to give to the grade rise, except to respond that he wants it to stop.   10

In late March, UVA held a conference on grade inflation, sponsored by the university's Echols Scholars, a group of highly gifted undergraduates, and the subject has been widely discussed at UVA by students, faculty and administrators since that time.   11

The rise in grades also has been an issue of concern at the three campuses of the University of Nebraska, and at such schools as Dartmouth, Princeton, Indiana University in Bloomington and elsewhere—and understandably so. What is at stake is a school's reputation and prestige, the quality of education it provides its students and, therefore, the value of the diplomas the institution awards its seniors. After all, if almost everyone gets mostly A's and B's, just what does a college degree mean?   12

Not very much, maybe, and certainly not as much as it once did. Corporations and employers complain regularly about the low quality of graduates who apply for jobs, whatever the grades they've made in college. "Their eyes glaze over when it comes to lists of A's and B's," says one educator who asked to remain anonymous. Graduate-school admission offices now regularly discount grades of applicants with A's and B's, hoping to put the student's ability into more accurate focus. For conservative critics of higher education such as Charles Sykes, this concern is long overdue—and perhaps a bit suspect.   13

A decade ago, Sykes published *ProfScam*, a book that took American colleges and universities—and particularly the professoriate—to task for lowering education standards, ignoring the needs of students for rigorous training and pandering to such left-leaning notions as "diversity," multiculturalism and sensitivity training.   14

About grade inflation, Sykes tells *Insight*, "The impressive grades don't mean they have done outstanding work for four or five years. All it means is that they paid tuition and got bad parking"—an allusion to the parking problems on many U.S. campuses.   15

For Sykes, "The diplomas from far too many colleges and universities are the academic equivalent of the junk bond. The diploma is not for what you learned and accomplished." 16

This is strong stuff, but just how right the distinguished critic is can be seen by the concern grade inflation has evoked on campuses. In January, for example, University of Nebraska at Lincoln Chancellor James Moesser made an almost unprecedented public announcement questioning whether professors were being demanding enough in their classes. Moesser was careful to add that he didn't want the teachers at UNL to start flunking students right and left, but he was clear that he wanted the academic rigor at the university to increase. 17

Seconding the chancellor, UNL faculty senate president James Ford, a professor of English, added publicly that the university knew its reputation was at issue because graduate schools UNL students apply to—he named Ohio State University—systematically lower UNL grades a notch, B's becoming C's, for example, when they consider UNL graduates for admission. 18

How did we get to where we are? Students blame the need to win admission to graduate school and get good jobs. "Students feel grades are what they're going to be judged by. Dean's lists and grades," Kiki Petrosino, a junior English major at UVA, tells *Insight*. "We don't expect bad grades. I notice when comments on my work aren't good. I always want to hear positive things. I'm not expecting anything lower than an A or a B," says Petrosino, who writes a weekly column in the UVA student newspaper, *The Cavalier Daily*. 19

Professors tend to blame students for putting subtle—and sometimes not so subtle—pressure on them to raise grades to make student futures seem brighter. Some professors don't succumb: "I do feel a certain amount of pressure. Fending it off is part of the job," says Mark Edmundson, UVA professor of English. 20

Many others, however, do give in, and the most vulnerable—and perhaps most likely to submit to student demands—are adjunct professors, the part-time teachers who now make up more than 50 percent of the faculty at many universities. In a recent issue of the journal *Academe*, for example, two adjunct professors argue that their students habitually demand good grades from the part-timers, using as ammo the threat to complain about the quality of teaching, a complaint that puts the adjuncts, who never have tenure and whose jobs already are tenuous, in even greater jeopardy. 21

But for critics such as Sykes, blame for grade inflation should be shared equally by students and professors. Grade inflation, he says, "is the unspoken two-way deal, in which you [the student] don't ask much of me [the professor] and we don't expect you to do much work." Students ask for good grades and don't demand rigor; a professor's free to pursue his research interests—and to fill his classes with students expecting A's and B's who will give the professor good evaluations when evaluation time comes. 22

Sykes sees another explanation for grade inflation in higher education: It already exists in elementary, middle and high schools, so why not college, too? "From the beginning we lull students and their parents into false grades. Why should they expect anything else? They've come to believe they're entitled to them." Proof of Sykes' assertion comes from the College Board, which reports that 37 percent of high-school graduates in 1997 had averages of A– or better, up from the 28 percent of high-school graduates a decade ago who had such high averages. 23

But, at whatever level of education, grade inflation didn't happen overnight. Not surprisingly, critics date its origins to the 1960s, during "the flower-children generation 24 where the 'philosophy' was 'You can't concentrate on punishing people because you will hurt their self-esteem,'" Pery Zirkel, Iacocca Professor of Education at Lehigh University in Bethlehem, Pa., tells *Insight*. "So we pursued this positive approach."

The Vietnam War provided another impetus, with sympathetic professors giving students high grades whether they deserved them or not to keep them in college and away from the draft, observers say. A significant contribution, too, was made by the 1960s student demands for greater "say" and participation in university and college affairs: the "right" to have student representatives on trustee boards, for example, or the "right" to do regular evaluations of teachers, a power that armed students with a new tool assuring that many professors would behave just as the students want them to behave or risk bad reviews.

What's been called "affirmative grading" also began in the 1960s—a response, according to economist Thomas Sowell, to affirmative-action programs that brought often ill-prepared minority students to American campuses where sympathetic professors graded with lenience, hoping to encourage them and make them feel comfortable. Affirmative grading added to grade inflation, observers say.

The stage was set for the 1970s when the abolition of the draft and a number of other factors made college less attractive to many students, sending administrators into a panic at many schools. Among the harder hit were public universities, whose state-legislature-supplied budgets depended on the numbers of students enrolled and taking courses.

"With thousands of dollars at stake, the attitude became: We want to please the customer," says Lehigh's Zirkel. Necessity was the mother of invention, and one of the solutions invented to please the customers—the students—and keep them attending was making it easier to drop classes without getting an F. At one time, students had four or maybe six weeks to drop a course. Now they could wait almost to the final moment of the last class.

The elimination of minus grades (A–, B–) was another sop to the customer, who then no longer had to face report cards suggesting they'd done "minus," or negative-sounding, work. And another sop, according to Zirkel, is those easier grades. "Parents feel better. The idea is that a happy consumer dictates supply and demand," he says, and above all else students had to be kept happy so they'd stay around and take up class space.

What helped to spur the recent debate about grade inflation at the University of Virginia was an article by English Professor Edmundson in the September 1997 issue of *Harper's* magazine, says UVA student Petrosino. "We all internalized it a little bit," she says.

The Edmundson article is beautifully written, entertaining—and devastating. The UVA critic sets himself the question "What are the uses of a liberal education?" and answers that what liberal education is at the University of Virginia and elsewhere these days is "lite entertainment for bored college students."

University culture, Edmundson writes, is "ever more devoted to consumption and entertainment, to the using and using up of goods and images."

Students want to be entertained, expect entertainment from professors and judge their teachers on whether they've delivered that entertainment. Entertainment by definition excludes academic rigor. As far as grades are concerned, no student looks for a C from a course where he or she expects to be entertained.

What to do about grade inflation? Dartmouth College has started placing median class scores next to letter grades on transcripts. That helps anyone interested to determine how the student stood relative to others in a class.

Indiana University has come up with a new transcript that will add even more data   *35*
to a student's grade record. Grades in every course will include not only the median grade,
but also the student's rank in class, and the average GPA of the students in that class.

Students don't care much for the extra information. "The more they add, the less   *36*
[graduate schools and potential employers] are going to look at it," contends Petrosino.

At the University of Nebraska at Lincoln, English Professor Robert Brooke has   *37*
proposed what he calls a portfolio solution to grade inflation. He wants portfolios kept of
the work done by English students during four years which will be judged by a faculty
committee. The department will set the standards students are expected to achieve, including competency in language and writing, and the portfolios will be judged by those standards. Students whose portfolios don't reveal the expected growth and development won't
pass, and the English department can show that the students it graduates have attained a
level of achievement worthy of a diploma.

Dean Leffler of UVA admits, "We haven't been making the kinds of tough decisions   *38*
we should be making." It "simply takes more effort, discipline, time, thought and energy
to assign an A grade rather than a B+, a C rather than a B." It takes more effort, he says,
"because it demands that we have the measure of integrity [necessary] to impose tougher
requirements on students who are not accustomed to having average grades." And a
measure of integrity on the part of students, too, he agrees, who must be willing to accept
the possibility of a C grade.

Indeed, getting students to accept changes may be the hardest part. Duke University   *39*
statistics Professor Valen Johnson, for example, earned the enmity of many faculty and
students alike by coming up with a grading system that would give rigorously graded
courses heavier weight and students who took them more credits than for weakly graded
courses. Johnson's proposal lost at Duke, and the measure of the controversy it has aroused
is revealed by the fact that professors at other universities who are considering the Johnson plan keep their interest a secret.

Stanford University, after dropping the F grade several years ago so students wouldn't   *40*
have to face the word "failed," picked it up again recently, only to drop it again for the
bland NP, or no pass, after students (and some faculty) protested. When the University of
Nebraska at Lincoln announced it was bringing back "minus" grades, the student protest
bordered on a rebellion, according to a story in the *Omaha World-Herald* in February.

Zirkel says would-be reformers must look at the relationship between a professor's   *41*
popularity ratings on student evaluations and the GPA average for his class. Zirkel assures
Insight that almost invariably a professor's high popularity correlates directly with a high
GPA in his classes. Zirkel also urges greater discussion of the problem of grade inflation.
On most campuses, a "conspiracy of silence" reigns about this subject, he says.

An exception is UVA's chemistry department, which decided internally to publish   *42*
grade distributions for each class offered by the department, Petrosino reports. It's a way
of weeding out professors who tend to inflate grades by airing their grade lists publicly.

Meanwhile, we probably can expect business as usual, at least for a while. Last Novem-   *43*
ber, when the annual study of freshmen at American colleges and universities by the Higher
Education Research Institute at the University of California at Los Angeles was released,
more freshmen than ever before in the survey said there was a "very good chance" they'd
make "at least a B average." Record numbers said they expected to win election to academic

honor societies and to rate themselves "above average" or "in the highest category" of writing, artistic, public-speaking, leadership and academic abilities.

Of course it's not fair to blame today's students for a grading system they've been   *44*
caught up in and which was well on its way before they were born. At the root of their sometimes hysterical concern about grades is probably a sneaky suspicion that the good grades they've received for so long bear no relation to their real abilities and when reality hits—reality being that first job—they may not be nearly as good as the grades imply.

Says UVA student Petrosino, "I've always done well. I'm doing all this work. I've got   *45*
the good grades. But part of me would like so much to have my A stand out. I wish my A would mean more."

READING FOR INFORMATION

1. What was the "gentleman's C" mentioned in the third paragraph?
2. Summarize briefly the evidence of grade inflation that Goode and Maier provide.
3. Why are college administrators concerned about grade inflation?
4. What are the responses of employers to grade inflation?
5. Why, according to Charles Sykes, have students come to expect high grades?
6. What are adjunct professors, and why do Goode and Maier believe that adjunct professors are more likely to give high grades?
7. According to Goode and Maier, what influences in the 1960s helped start the process of grade inflation? What factors accelerated grade inflation in the 1970s?
8. How does Edmundson characterize the current state of higher education?
9. Describe some of the efforts colleges are making to combat grade inflation.

READING FOR FORM, ORGANIZATION, AND FEATURES

1. Is Goode and Maier's piece an academic or a journalistic article? Explain your answer.
2. Do Goode and Maier provide an adequate range of examples of grade inflation? Explain your answer.
3. Why do you think Goode and Maier provide historical background on grade inflation halfway through the article rather than at the beginning? Do you agree with their choice? Explain your answer.
4. Why do you think Goode and Maier chose the particular quotation they use to close their article?

READING FOR RHETORICAL CONCERNS

1. Do Goode and Maier agree with the critics of grade inflation? What passages support your opinion?
2. Is Goode and Maier's piece argumentative or objective? Explain your answer.
3. Is the article intended for college administrators? College professors? College students? The parents of college students? Would any of those groups be offended by the piece? Explain your answers.

WRITING ASSIGNMENTS

1. Draw on the information Goode and Maier provide to write a 1,250-word essay that explains the problem of grade inflation and considers possible solutions.
2. Write a 1,000-word analytical essay that explains the origins of grade inflation.
3. Write a 1,000-word argument essay that either attacks or defends the proposition that grades should be systematically lowered on your campus as an antidote to grade inflation.

. . . .

WRITING ASSIGNMENTS FOR CHAPTER 9

1. Draw on all four of the essays in this chapter to write a 1,250-word essay that outlines the pros and cons of the A–F grading system. Keep the essay objective rather than argumentative.
2. In a 1,000-word essay, defend your own opinion on the role grades should play in higher education. Draw on an least two of the reading selections in this chapter.
3. Write a 1,000-word essay that explores the relationship between grades and motivation. Draw on at least two of the selections in this chapter.
4. In a 1,250-word essay, analyze the effect of the A–F grading system on higher education. Draw on all four essays in this chapter.
5. Write a 1,000-word personal narrative of your own experiences with grades that responds to the ideas presented in one of the readings in this chapter.
6. Write a 1,000-word essay that compares and contrasts the approach to higher education in Finland, which is described in Rothenberg's article, with the American system. Draw on at least one of the essays in this chapter in addition to Rothenberg.
7. Write an argument for or against grades in the form of a letter to your parents.

10

TECHNOLOGY AND SOCIETY

In the following passage, Joseph Weizenbaum, one of the foremost computer scientists in the United States, describes his fear that technology poses a threat to human society and individuality.

> We must . . . admit that we are intoxicated with science and technology, that we are deeply committed to a Faustian bargain that is rapidly killing us spiritually and will soon kill us physically. . . . We must live one day at a time in the real world peopled by genuine human beings, not images, a world in which word and deed are inherently valued, not the engineered applause of some abstract audience. (Weizenbaum 11)

Similar fears have been expressed by a wide range of social commentators in the past half century. Nevertheless, technology continues to advance, and it has improved our quality of life. Lifesaving medical advancements are the most frequently cited examples of beneficial technology, but each day Americans rely on such innovations as cellular phones, cable and satellite television, music and video CDs, and the World Wide Web—so much so that it is now hard to imagine doing without this technology.

The readings in Chapter 10 focus on the costs and benefits of technological development. Joshua Quittner, author of "Invasion of Privacy," maintains that the benefit of modern electronic technology, such as the Internet, is worth the reduction of individual privacy that comes with it. The potentially dangerous influence of violent games that young Americans play on the Internet is the focus of John Leo's article "When Life Imitates Video." In "Jennifer and Rachel," biologist Lee M. Silver suggests that human cloning may have legitimate uses and counters the arguments of opponents of cloning. Finally, Lori B. Andrews points out the legal and ethical pitfalls of modern reproductive technology in "The Sperminator."

Invasion of Privacy

Joshua Quittner

Joshua Quittner, a journalist, is a frequent contributor to Newsday *and* Wired. *Among the books he has written with Michelle Slatalla are* Masters of Deception: The Gang That Ruled Cyberspace, Flame War, *and* Speeding the Net: The Inside Story of Netscape, How It Challenged Microsoft and Changed the World.

Prereading ....

Considering your own experience and that of your family and friends, are you confident in the safety of credit cards, ATM cards, phone cards, and other electronic records that control "private" business? Is the convenience of these computerized transactions worth any potential for loss or invasion of privacy?

. . . .

For the longest time, I couldn't get worked up about privacy: my right to it; how it's dying; how we're headed for an even more wired, underregulated, overintrusive, privacy-deprived planet.   *1*

I mean, I probably have more reason to think about this stuff than the average John Q. All Too Public. A few years ago, for instance, after I applied for a credit card at a consumer-electronics store, somebody got hold of my name and vital numbers and used them to get a duplicate card. That somebody ran up a $3,000 bill, but the nice lady from the fraud division of the credit-card company took care of it with steely digital dispatch. (I filed a short report over the phone. I never lost a cent. The end.)   *2*

I also hang out online a lot, and now and then on the Net someone will imperson- ate me, spoofing my E-mail address or posting stupid stuff to bulletin boards or behaving in a frightfully un-Quittner-like manner in chat parlors from here to Bianca's Smut Shack. It's annoying, I suppose. But in the end, the faux Quittners get bored and disappear. My reputation, such as it is, survives.   *3*

I should also point out that as news director for Pathfinder, Time Inc.'s mega info mall, and a guy who makes his living on the Web, I know better than most people that we're hurtling toward an even more intrusive world. We're all being watched by computers when- ever we visit Websites; by the mere act of "browsing" (it sounds so passive!) we're going public in a way that was unimaginable a decade ago. I know this because I'm a watcher too. When people come to my Website, without ever knowing their names, I can peer over their shoulders, recording what they look at, timing how long they stay on a particular page, following them around Pathfinder's sprawling offerings.   *4*

None of this would bother me in the least, I suspect, if a few years ago, my phone, like Marley's ghost, hadn't given me a glimpse of the nightmares to come. On Thanksgiving week- end in 1995, someone (presumably a critic of a book my wife and I had just written about computer hackers) forwarded my home telephone number to an out-of-state answering machine, where unsuspecting callers trying to reach me heard a male voice identify himself as me and say some extremely rude things. Then, with typical hacker aplomb, the prankster asked people to leave their messages (which to my surprise many callers, including my mother, did). This went on for several days until my wife and I figured out that something was wrong ("Hey . . . why hasn't the phone rung since Wednesday?") and got our phone service restored.   *5*

It seemed funny at first, and it gave us a swell story to tell on our book tour. But the interloper who seized our telephone line continued to hit us even after the tour ended. And hit us again and again for the next six months. The phone company seemed power- less. Its security folks moved us to one unlisted number after another, half a dozen times. They put special PIN codes in place. They put traces on the line. But the troublemaker kept breaking through.   *6*

If our hacker had been truly evil and omnipotent as only fictional movie hackers are, there would probably have been even worse ways he could have threatened my privacy. He could have sabotaged my credit rating. He could have eavesdropped on my telephone conversations or siphoned off my E-mail. He could have called in my mortgage, discontinued my health insurance or obliterated my Social Security number. Like Sandra Bullock in *The Net*, I could have been a digital untouchable, wandering the planet without a connection to the rest of humanity. (Although if I didn't have to pay back school loans, it might be worth it. Just a thought.)

Still, I remember feeling violated at the time and as powerless as a minnow in a flash flood. Someone was invading my private space—my family's private space—and there was nothing I or the authorities could do. It was as close to a technological epiphany as I have ever been. And as I watched my personal digital hell unfold, it struck me that our privacy—mine and yours—has already disappeared, not in one Big Brotherly blitzkrieg but in Little Brotherly moments, bit by bit.

Losing control of your telephone, of course, is the least of it. After all, most of us voluntarily give out our phone number and address when we allow ourselves to be listed in the White Pages. Most of us go a lot further than that. We register our whereabouts whenever we put a bank card in an ATM machine or drive through an E-Z Pass lane on the highway. We submit to being photographed every day—20 times a day on average if you live or work in New York City—by surveillance cameras. We make public our interests and our purchasing habits every time we shop by mail order or visit a commercial Website.

I don't know about you, but I do all this willingly because I appreciate what I get in return: the security of a safe parking lot, the convenience of cash when I need it, the improved service of mail-order houses that know me well enough to send me catalogs of stuff that interests me. And while I know we're supposed to feel just awful about giving up our vaunted privacy, I suspect (based on what the pollsters say) that you're as ambivalent about it as I am.

Popular culture shines its klieg lights on the most intimate corners of our lives, and most of us play right along. If all we really wanted was to be left alone, explain the lasting popularity of Oprah and Sally and Ricki tell-all TV. Memoirs top the best-seller lists, with books about incest and insanity and illness leading the way. Perfect strangers at cocktail parties tell me the most disturbing details of their abusive upbringings. Why?

"It's a very schizophrenic time," says Sherry Turkle, professor of sociology at the Massachusetts Institute of Technology, who writes books about how computers and online communication are transforming society. She believes our culture is undergoing a kind of mass identity crisis, trying to hang on to a sense of privacy and intimacy in a global village of tens of millions. "We have very unstable notions about the boundaries of the individual," she says.

If things seem crazy now, think how much crazier they will be when everybody is as wired as I am. We're in the midst of a global interconnection that is happening much faster than electrification did a century ago and is expected to have consequences at least as profound. What would happen if all the information stored on the world's computers were accessible via the Internet to anyone? Who would own it? Who would control it? Who would protect it from abuse?

Small-scale privacy atrocities take place every day. Ask Dr. Denise Nagel, executive director of the National Coalition for Patient Rights, about medical privacy, for example, and she rattles off a list of abuses that would make Big Brother blush. She talks about how

7

8

9

10

11

12

13

14

two years ago, a convicted child rapist working as a technician in a Boston hospital riffled through 1,000 computerized records looking for potential victims (and was caught when the father of a nine-year-old girl used caller ID to trace the call back to the hospital). How a banker on Maryland's state health commission pulled up a list of cancer patients, cross-checked it against the names of his bank's customers and revoked the loans of the matches. How Sara Lee bakeries planned to collaborate with Lovelace Health Systems, a subsidiary of Cigna, to match employee health records with work-performance reports to find workers who might benefit from antidepressants.

Not to pick on Sara Lee. At least a third of all FORTUNE 500 companies regularly review health information before making hiring decisions. And that's nothing compared with what awaits us when employees and insurance companies start testing our DNA for possible imperfections. Farfetched? More than 200 subjects in a case study published last January in the journal *Science and Engineering Ethics* reported that they had been discriminated against as a result of genetic testing. None of them were actually sick, but DNA analysis suggested that they might become sick someday. "The technology is getting ahead of our ethics," says Nagel, and the Clinton Administration clearly agrees. It is about to propose a federal law that would protect medical and health-insurance records from such abuses.   *15*

But how did we arrive at this point, where so much about what we do and own and think is an open book?   *16*

It all started in the 1950s, when, in order to administer Social Security funds, the U.S. government began entering records on big mainframe computers, using nine-digit identification numbers as data points. Then, even more than today, the citizenry instinctively loathed the computer and its injunctions against folding, spindling and mutilating. We were not numbers! We were human beings! These fears came to a head in the late 1960s, recalls Alan Westin, a retired Columbia University professor who publishes a quarterly report *Privacy and American Business*. "The techniques of intrusion and data surveillance had overcome the weak law and social mores that we had built up in the pre–World War II era," says Westin.   *17*

The public rebelled, and Congress took up the question of how much the government and private companies should be permitted to know about us. A privacy bill of rights was drafted. "What we did," says Westin, "was to basically redefine what we meant by 'reasonable expectations of privacy'"—a guarantee, by the way, that comes from the Supreme Court and not from any constitutional "right to privacy."   *18*

The result was a flurry of new legislation that clarified and defined consumer and citizen rights. The First Fair Credit Reporting Act, passed in 1970, overhauled what had once been a secret, unregulated industry with no provisions for due process. The new law gave consumers the right to know what was in their credit files and to demand corrections. Other financial and health privacy acts followed, although to this day no federal law protects the confidentiality of medical records.   *19*

As Westin sees it, the public and private sectors took two very different approaches. Congress passed legislation requiring that the government tell citizens what records it keeps on them while insisting that the information itself not be released unless required by law. The private sector responded by letting each industry—credit-card companies, banking, insurance, marketing, advertising—create its own guidelines.   *20*

That approach worked—to a point. And that point came when mainframes started giving way to desktop computers. In the old days, information stored in government data-   *21* bases was relatively inaccessible. Now, however, with PCs on every desktop linked to office networks and then to the Internet, data that were once carefully hidden may be only a few keystrokes away.

Suddenly someone could run motor-vehicle-registration records against voting registrations to find 6-ft.-tall Republicans who were arrested during the past year for drunk driving—and who own a gun. The genie was not only out of the bottle, he was also peering into everyone's bedroom window. (Except the windows of the very rich, who can afford to screen themselves.)

"Most people would be astounded to know what's out there," says Carole Lane, author of *Naked in Cyberspace: How to Find Personal Information Online.* "In a few hours, sitting at my computer, beginning with no more than your name and address, I can find out what you do for a living, the names and ages of your spouse and children, what kind of car you drive, the value of your house and how much taxes you pay on it."

Lane is a member of a new trade: paid Internet searcher, which already has its own professional group, the Association of Independent Information Professionals. Her career has given her a fresh appreciation for what's going on. "Real privacy as we've known it," she says, "is fleeting."

Now, there are plenty of things you could do to protect yourself. You could get an unlisted telephone number, as I was forced to do. You could cut up your credit card and pay cash for everything. You could rip your E-Z Pass off the windshield and use quarters at tolls. You could refuse to divulge your Social Security number except for Social Security purposes, which is all that the law requires. You'd be surprised how often you're asked to provide it by people who have no right to see it.

That might make your life a bit less comfortable, of course. As in the case of Bob Bruen, who went into a barbershop in Watertown, Mass., recently. "When I was asked for my phone number, I refused to give them the last four digits," Bruen says. "I was also asked for my name, and I also refused. The girl at the counter called her supervisor, who told me I could not get a haircut in their shop." Why? the barbership uses a computer to record all transactions. Bruen went elsewhere to get his locks shorn.

But can we do that all the time? Only the Unabomber would seriously suggest that we cut all ties to the wired world. The computer and its spreading networks convey status and bring opportunity. They empower us. They allow an information economy to thrive and grow. They make life easier. Hence the dilemma.

The real problem, says Kevin Kelly, executive editor of *Wired* magazine, is that although we say we value our privacy, what we really want is something very different: "We think that privacy is about information, but it's not—it's about relationships." The way Kelly sees it, there was no privacy in the traditional village or small town; everyone knew everyone else's secrets. And that was comfortable. I knew about you, and you knew about me. "There was a symmetry to the knowledge," he says. "What's gone out of whack is we don't know who knows about us anymore. Privacy has become asymmetrical."

The trick, says Kelly, is to restore that balance. And not surprisingly, he and others point out that what technology has taken, technology can restore. Take the problem of "magic cookies"—those little bits of code most Websites use to track visitors. We set up a system at Pathfinder in which, when you visit our site, we drop a cookie into the basket of your browser that tags you like a rare bird. We use that cookie in place of your name,

22

23

24

25

26

27

28

29

which, needless to say, we never know. If you look up a weather report by keying in a ZIP code, we note that (it tells us where you live or maybe where you wish you lived). We'll mark down whether you look up stock quotes (though we draw the line at capturing the symbols of the specific stocks you follow). If you come to the *Netly News*, we'll record your interest in technology. Then, the next time you visit, we might serve up an ad for a modem or an online brokerage firm or a restaurant in Akron, Ohio, depending on what we've managed to glean about you.

Some people find the whole process offensive. "Cookies represent a way of watching   30
consumers without their consent, and that is a fairly frightening phenomenon," says Nick Grouf, CEO of Firefly, a Boston company that makes software offering an alternative approach to profiling, known as "intelligent agents."

Privacy advocates like Grouf—as well as the two companies that control the online   31
browser market, Microsoft and Netscape—say the answer to the cookie monster is something they call the Open Profiling Standard. The idea is to allow the computer user to create an electronic "passport" that identifies him to online marketers without revealing his name. The user tailors the passport to his own interests, so if he is passionate about flyfishing and is cruising through L. L. Bean's Website, the passport will steer the electronic-catalog copy toward fishing gear instead of, say, Rollerblades.

The advantage to computer users is that they can decide how much information they   32
want to reveal while limiting their exposure to intrusive marketing techniques. The advantage to Website entrepreneurs is that they learn about their customers' tastes without intruding on their privacy.

Many online consumers, however, are skittish about leaving any footprints in cyber-   33
space. Susan Scott, executive director of TRUSTe, a firm based in Palo Alto, Calif., that rates Websites according to the level of privacy they afford, says a survey her company sponsored found that 41% of respondents would quit a Web page rather than reveal any personal information about themselves. About 25% said when they do volunteer information, they lie. "The users want access, but they don't want to get correspondence back," she says.

But worse things may already be happening to their E-mail. Many office electronic-   34
mail systems warn users that the employer reserves the right to monitor their E-mail. In October software will be available to Wall Street firms that can automatically monitor correspondence between brokers and clients through an artificial-intelligence program that scans for evidence of securities violations.

"Technology has outpaced law," says Marc Rotenberg, director of the Washington-   35
based Electronic Privacy Information Center. Rotenberg advocates protecting the privacy of E-mail by encrypting it with secret codes so powerful that even the National Security Agency's supercomputers would have a hard time cracking it. Such codes are legal within the U.S. but cannot be used abroad—where terrorists might use them to protect their secrets—without violating U.S. export laws. The battle between the Clinton Administration and the computer industry over encryption export policy has been raging for six years without resolution, a situation that is making it hard to do business on the Net and is clearly starting to fray some nerves. "The future is in electronic commerce," says Ira Magaziner, Clinton's point man on Net issues. All that's holding it up is "this privacy thing."

Rotenberg thinks we need a new government agency—a privacy agency—to sort out   36
the issues. "We need new legal protections," he says, "to enforce the privacy act, to keep

federal agencies in line, to act as a spokesperson for the Federal Government and to act on behalf of privacy interests."

Wired's Kelly disagrees. "A federal privacy agency would be disastrous! The answer to   *37* the whole privacy question is more knowledge," he says. "More knowledge about who's watching you. More knowledge about the information that flows between us—particularly the meta information about who knows what and where it's going."

I'm with Kelly. The only guys who insist on perfect privacy are hermits like the   *38* Unabomber. I don't want to be cut off from the world. I have nothing to hide. I just want some measure of control over what people know about me. I want to have my magic cookie and eat it too.

READING FOR INFORMATION

1. According to Quittner, what are some of the ways (name at least five) that we regularly surrender our privacy?

2. What examples does Quittner provide of potentially dangerous invasions of privacy?

3. What evidence does Quittner give to support his assertion that Americans don't really want to be left alone?

4. Why did some Americans react negatively to the storing of personal information on computers according to Social Security number, which began in the 1950s?

5. How, according to Quittner, has the shift from large mainframe computers to desktop PCs affected privacy?

6. In response to the computer revolution, what steps did the federal government take to protect citizens' privacy? What steps did the private sector take?

7. According to Lane, what information can you locate on the Web about a given individual, beginning with only a name and address?

8. What are "magic cookies"?

9. Explain the controversy over encryption technology.

READING FOR FORM, ORGANIZATION, AND FEATURES

1. Quittner begins with a series of anecdotes. How do these anecdotes work together as an opening to his piece?

2. Based on the first ten paragraphs of the article, how would you characterize Quittner's writing style? Is this style appropriate given the nature of the piece he is writing?

3. Describe Quittner's organizational plan.

READING FOR RHETORICAL CONCERNS

1. What in the article indicates Quittner's intended audience?

2. Identify the two sections of the essay where Quittner states his own opinion.

3. Paraphrase Quittner's proposal for balancing privacy concerns and access to technology.

4. In what way is Quittner's article confessional?

WRITING ASSIGNMENTS

1. Write a 1,000-word essay that objectively describes how modern technology has eroded personal privacy. Draw on Quittner's article for examples.

2. In paragraph 10, Quittner asserts:

   > I do all this [surrender privacy] willingly because I appreciate what I get in return: the security of a safe parking lot, the convenience of cash when I need it, the improved service of mail-order houses that know me well enough to send me catalogs of stuff that interests me. And while I know we're supposed to feel just awful about giving up our vaunted privacy, I suspect (based on what the pollsters say) that you're as ambivalent about it as I am.

   In a 1,000-word essay, explain Quittner's assertion and respond to it, based on your own views.

3. Do you think Quittner's views are consistent with constitutional guarantees of civil liberties? Defend your view in a 1,000- to 1,250-word essay.

• • • • • • • • • • • • • •

When Life Imitates Video

John Leo

John Leo is a journalist on the staff of U.S. News and World Report.

P r e r e a d i n g •

Think of the most violent video game you have either played or watched others play. What aspects of the game made it particularly violent? As you played or viewed this game, did it raise your overall level of aggression? Do you think that long-term exposure to this game would have any impact on you? Do you think that young children should have access to this game? Freewrite for ten minutes in response to these questions.

• • • • • • • • • • • • • •

Was it real life or an acted-out video game?   *1*

Marching through a large building using various bombs and guns to pick off victims   *2*
is a conventional video-game scenario. In the Colorado massacre [at Littleton], Dylan Klebold and Eric Harris used pistol-grip shotguns, as in some video-arcade games. The pools of blood, screams of agony, and pleas for mercy must have been familiar—they are featured in some of the newer and more realistic kill-for-kicks games. "With each kill," the *Los Angeles Times* reported, "the teens cackled and shouted as though playing one of the morbid video games they loved." And they ended their spree by shooting themselves in the head, the final act in the game Postal, and, in fact, the only way to end it.

Did the sensibilities created by the modern video kill games play a role in the Little-   *3*
ton massacre? Apparently so. Note the cool and casual cruelty, the outlandish arsenal of
weapons, the cheering and laughing while hunting down victims one by one. All of this
seems to reflect the style and feel of the video killing games they played so often.

No, there isn't any direct connection between most murderous games and most   *4*
murders. And yes, the primary responsibility for protecting children from dangerous games
lies with their parents, many of whom like to blame the entertainment industry for their
own failings.

But there is a cultural problem here: We are now a society in which the chief form   *5*
of play for millions of youngsters is making large numbers of people die. Hurting and
maiming others is the central fun activity in video games played so addictively by the
young. A widely cited survey of 900 fourth-through-eighth-grade students found that
almost half of the children said their favorite electronic games involve violence. Can it be
that all this constant training in make-believe killing has no social effects?

The conventional argument is that this is a harmless activity among children who   *6*
know the difference between fantasy and reality. But the games are often played by unstable youngsters unsure about the difference. Many of these have been maltreated or rejected
and left alone most of the time (a precondition for playing the games obsessively). Adolescent feelings of resentment, powerlessness, and revenge pour into the killing games. In
these children, the games can become a dress rehearsal for the real thing.

Psychologist David Grossman of Arkansas State University, a retired Army officer,   *7*
thinks "point and shoot" video games have the same effect as military strategies used to
break down a soldier's aversion to killing. During World War II only 15 to 20 percent of all
American soldiers fired their weapon in battle. Shooting games in which the target is a man-
shaped outline, the Army found, made recruits more willing to "make killing a reflex action."

Video games are much more powerful versions of the military's primitive discovery   *8*
about overcoming the reluctance to shoot. Grossman says Michael Carneal, the schoolboy
shooter in Paducah, Ky., showed the effects of video-game lessons in killing. Carneal coolly
shot nine times, hitting eight people, five of them in the head or neck. Head shots pay a
bonus in many video games. Now the Marine Corps is adapting a version of Doom, the
hyperviolent game played by one of the Littleton killers, for its own training purposes.

More realistic touches in video games help blur the boundary between fantasy and real-   *9*
ity—guns carefully modeled on real ones, accurate-looking wounds, screams, and other sound
effects, even the recoil of a heavy rifle. Some newer games seem intent on erasing children's
empathy and concern for others. Once the intended victims of video slaughter were mostly
gangsters or aliens. Now some games invite players to blow away ordinary people who have
done nothing wrong—pedestrians, marching bands, an elderly woman with a walker. In these
games, the shooter is not a hero, just a violent sociopath. One ad for a Sony game says: "Get
in touch with your gun-toting, testosterone-pumping, cold-blooded murdering side."

These killings are supposed to be taken as harmless over-the-top jokes. But the   *10*
bottom line is that the young are being invited to enjoy the killing of vulnerable people
picked at random. This looks like the final lesson in a course to eliminate any lingering resistance to killing.

SWAT teams and cops now turn up as the intended victims of some video-game   *11*
killings. This has the effect of exploiting resentments toward law enforcement and making
real-life shooting of cops more likely. This sensibility turns up in the hit movie *Matrix:* world-

saving hero Keanu Reeves, in a mandatory Goth-style, long black coat packed with countless heavy-duty guns, is forced to blow away huge numbers of uniformed law-enforcement people.

"We have to start worrying about what we are putting into the minds of our young," says Grossman. "Pilots train on flight simulators, drivers on driving simulators, and now we have our children on murder simulators." If we want to avoid more Littleton-style massacres, we will begin taking the social effects of the killing games more seriously.

12

READING FOR INFORMATION

1. Describe briefly what you recall from the news coverage of the high school massacre at Columbine High School in Littleton, Colorado.
2. In what ways did Klebold and Harris model their attack on violent video games?
3. Paraphrase Leo's explanation of how violent video games might lead to real-world violence.
4. What strategies has the U.S. military used to make soldiers more willing to shoot the enemy?
5. What changes have taken place in the profile of the human targets in video games?
6. What personality characteristics are encouraged by violent video games?

READING FOR FORM, ORGANIZATION, AND FEATURES

1. Describe Leo's opening strategy. How does Leo attempt to engage the reader?
2. Why does Leo answer two unstated questions in the fourth paragraph? What is the effect of not actually stating the questions?
3. Characterize Leo's use of language. Is it academic or conversational? Give examples of phrases Leo uses that support your judgment.
4. Does Leo have a thesis statement? If so, where is it?

READING FOR RHETORICAL CONCERNS

1. Is Leo's article an argument or a news analysis piece? Explain your answer.
2. Is Leo writing to the young people who play video games or to their parents? What aspects of the article indicate the intended audience?
3. Is Leo sympathetic to the police? To the military? Explain your answers.

WRITING ASSIGNMENTS

1. In a 250- to 750-word paper, attack or defend Leo's claim that video games helped instigate the Columbine High School massacre.
2. Write a 1,000-word essay in which you compare and contrast your own video game experiences with those described in Leo's article. Does your own experience support the assertions Leo makes?
3. Assume that you are a child psychologist in a large public school district. Write a 750-word letter to parents that describes the dangers of violent video games and how parents might respond to those dangers.

. . . .

"Jennifer and Rachel"

Lee M. Silver

Lee M. Silver is a professor at Princeton University who holds appointments in the departments of Molecular Biology, Ecology, and Evolutionary Biology. He is a fellow of the American Association for the Advancement of Science and an expert on the social impact of reproductive technology. This article is excerpted from his book Remaking Eden: Cloning and Beyond in a Brave New World.

P r e r e a d i n g

What have you previously read or seen in the news media concerning cloning? Brainstorm a list of specifics. Now read through your list. Based on the items on your list, would you say the news media present cloning in a positive, negative, or objective light? Do they sensationalize cloning, or do they provide balanced reporting?

Jennifer is a self-sufficient single woman who lives by herself in a stylish apartment on Manhattan's Upper West Side. She has focused almost all her energies on her career since graduating from Columbia University, fourteen years earlier, and has moved steadily upward in the business world. In financial terms, she is now quite well off. In social terms, she is happy being single. Jennifer has had various relationships with men over the years, but none was serious enough to make her consider giving up her single lifestyle.   1

And then on April 14, 2049, the morning of her thirty-fifth birthday, Jennifer wakes up alone, in her quiet room, before the break of dawn, before her alarm is set to go off, and she begins to wonder. With her new age—thirty-five—bouncing around in her mind, a single thought comes to the fore. "It's getting late," she tells herself.   2

It is not marriage or a permanent relationship that she feels is missing, it is something else. It is a child. Not any child, but a child of her own to hold and to love, to watch and to nurture. Jennifer knows that she can afford to raise a child by herself, and she also knows that the firm she works for is generous in giving women the flexibility required to maintain both a family and a career. And now she feels, for the first time, that she will soon be too old to begin motherhood.   3

Jennifer is a decisive woman, and by the end of that day she decides to become a single mother. It is the same positive decision that hundreds of thousands of other woman have made before her. But unlike twentieth-century women, Jennifer knows there is no longer any reason to incorporate a sperm donor into the process. An anonymous sperm cell could introduce all sorts of unknown, undesirable traits into her child, and Jennifer is not one to gamble. Instead, she makes the decision to use one of her own cells to create a new life.   4

Jennifer is well aware that federal law makes cloning illegal in the United States except in cases of untreatable infertility. She realizes that she could get around the law through a marriage of convenience with a gay friend, who would then be declared infertile by a   5 sympathetic physician. But she decides to do what increasing numbers of other women in her situation have done recently—take an extended vacation in the Cayman Islands.

On Grand Cayman Island, there is a large reprogenetic clinic that specializes in cloning. The young physicians and biologists who work at this clinic do not ask questions of their clients. They will retrieve cells from any willing adult, prepare those cells for fusion to unfertilized eggs recovered from any willing woman, and then introduce the embryos that develop successfully into the uterus of the same, or another, willing woman. The cost of the procedure is $80,000 for the initial cell cloning and embryo transfer, and $20,000 for each subsequent attempt at pregnancy if earlier embryos fail to implant. When the clinic first opened, the fees were twice as high, but they dropped in response to competition from newly opened clinics in Jamaica and Grenada.

Since Jennifer is a healthy fertile woman, she has no need for other biological participants in the cloning process. A dozen unfertilized eggs are recovered from her ovaries and made nucleus-free. One-by-one, each is fused with a donor cell obtained from the inside of her mouth. After a period of incubation, healthy-looking embryos are observed under a microscope, and two of these are introduced into her uterus at the proper time of her menstrual cycle. (The introduction of two embryos increases the probability of a successful implantation.) After the procedure, Jennifer stays on the island three more days to rest, then flies back to New York.

A week later, Jennifer is thrilled by the positive blue + symbol that appears on her home pregnancy test. She waits another two weeks to confirm that the pregnancy has taken with another test, and then schedules an appointment with Dr. Steven Glassman, her gynecologist and obstetrician. Dr. Glassman knows that Jennifer is a single woman, and he doesn't ask—and Jennifer doesn't tell—how her pregnancy began. The following eight and a half months pass by uneventfully, with monthly, then weekly, visits to the doctor's office. Ultrasound indicates the presence of a single normal fetus, and amniocentesis confirms the absence of any known genetic problem. Finally, on March 15, 2050, a baby girl is born. Jennifer names her Rachel. To the nurses and doctors who work in the delivery room, Rachel is one more newborn baby, just like all the other newborn babies they've seen in their lives.

Jennifer, holding Rachel in her arms, is taken to a room in the maternity ward, and shortly thereafter, the nurse on duty brings by the form to fill out for the birth certificate. Without a word, she enters Jennifer's name into the space for "the mother." She then asks Jennifer for the name of the father. "Unknown," Jennifer replies, and this is duly recorded. A day later, Jennifer is released from the hospital with her new baby girl.

Rachel will grow up in the same way as all other children her age. Occasionally, people will comment on the striking similarity that exists between the child and her mother. Jennifer will smile at them and say, "Yes. She does have my facial features." And she'll leave it at that.

From time to time, Jennifer will let Rachel know that she is a "special" child, without going into further detail. Then one day, when her daughter has grown old enough to understand, Jennifer will reveal the truth. And just like other children conceived with the help of reprogenetic protocols, Rachel will feel . . . special. Some day in the more distant future, when cloning becomes just another means of alternative reproduction, accepted by society, the need for secrecy will disappear.

Who is Rachel, and who really are her parents? There is no question that Jennifer is Rachel's birth mother, since Rachel was born out of her body. But, Jennifer is not Rachel's genetic mother, based on the traditional meanings of mother and father. In genetic terms, Jennifer and Rachel are twin sisters. As a result, Rachel will constantly behold a glimpse of her future simply by looking at her mother's photo album and her mother herself. She will also understand that her single set of grandparents are actually her genetic parents as well. And when Rachel grows up and has children of her own, her children will also be her mother's children. Thus, with a single act of cloning, we are forced to reconsider the meaning of parents, children, and siblings, and how they relate to one another.

Is Cloning Wrong?

Is there anything wrong with what Jennifer has done? The most logical way to approach this question is through a consideration of whether anyone, or anything, has been harmed by the birth of Rachel. Clearly no harm has been done to Jennifer. She got the baby girl she wanted and she will raise her with the same sorts of hopes and aspirations that most normal parents have for their children. 13

But what about Rachel? Has she been harmed in some way so detrimental that it would have been better had she not been born? Daniel Callahan, the Director of the Hastings Center (a bioethics think tank near New York City), argues that "engineering someone's entire genetic makeup would compromise his or her right to a unique identity." But no such "right" has been granted by nature—identical twins are born every day as natural clones of each other. Dr. Callahan would have to concede this fact, but he might still argue that just because twins occur naturally does not mean we should create them on purpose. 14

Dr. Callahan might argue that Rachel is harmed by the knowledge of her future condition. He might say that it is unfair for Rachel to go through her childhood knowing what she will look like as an adult, or being forced to consider future medical ailments that might befall her. But even in the absence of cloning, many children have some sense of the future possibilities encoded in the genes they got from their parents. In my own case, I knew as a teenager that I had a good chance of inheriting the pattern baldness that my maternal grandfather expressed so thoroughly. Furthermore, genetic screening already provides people with the ability to learn about hundreds of disease predispositions. And as genetic knowledge and technology become more and more sophisticated, it will become possible for any human being to learn even more about their genetic future than Rachel can learn from Jennifer's past. In American society, it is generally accepted that parents are ultimately responsible for deciding what their children should, or should not, be exposed to. And there's no reason to expect that someone like Jennifer would tell Rachel something that was not in her best interest to know. 15

Just because Rachel has the same genes as Jennifer does not mean that her life will turn out the same way. On the contrary, Rachel is sure to have a different upbringing in a world that has changed significantly since her mother's time. And there is no reason why she can't chart her own unique path through life. Furthermore, when it comes to genetic predispositions, they are just that and nothing more. Although their genetically determined inclinations may be the same, mother and daughter may choose to follow those inclinations in different ways, or not at all. 16

It might also be argued that Rachel is harmed by having to live up to the unrealistic expectations that her mother will place on her. But there is no reason to believe that 17

Jennifer's expectations will be any more unreasonable than those of many other parents who expect their children to accomplish in their lives what the parents were unable to accomplish in their own. No one would argue that parents with such tendencies should be prohibited from having children. Besides, there's no reason to assume that Jennifer's expectations will be unreasonable. Indeed, there is every reason to believe Rachel will be loved by her mother no matter what she chooses to do, as most mothers love their children.

But let's grant that among the many Rachels brought into this world, some *will* feel bad that their genetic constitution is not unique. Is this alone a strong enough reason to ban the practice of cloning? Before answering this question, ask yourself another: Is a child having knowledge of an older twin worse off than a child born into poverty? If we ban the former, shouldn't we ban the latter? Why is it that so many politicians seem to care so much about cloning but so little about the welfare of children in general? *18*

Some object to cloning because of the process that it entails. The view of the Vatican, in particular, is that human embryos should be treated like human beings and should not be tampered with in any way. However, the cloning protocol does *not* tamper with embryos, it tampers only with *unfertilized* eggs and adult cells like those we scratch off our arms without a second thought. Only after the fact does an embryo emerge (which could be treated with the utmost respect if one so chooses). *19*

There is a sense among some who are religious that cloning leaves God out of the process of human creation, and that man is venturing into places he does not belong. This same concern has been, and will continue to be, raised as each new reprogenetic technology is incorporated into our culture, from in vitro fertilization twenty years ago to genetic engineering of embryos—sure to happen in the near future. It is impossible to counter this theological claim with scientific arguments. We will come back to God's domain in the last part of this book. *20*

Finally, there are those who argue against cloning based on the perception that it will harm society at large in some way. The *New York Times* columnist William Safire expresses the opinion of many others when he says, "Cloning's identicality would restrict evolution." This is bad, he argues, because "the continued interplay of genes . . . is central to humankind's progress." But Mr. Safire is wrong on both practical and theoretical grounds. On practical grounds, even if human cloning became efficient, legal, and popular among those in the moneyed classes (which is itself highly unlikely), it would still only account for a fraction of a percent of all the children born onto this earth. Furthermore, each of the children born by cloning to different families would be different from one another, so where does the identicality come from? *21*

On theoretical grounds, Safire is wrong because humankind's progress has nothing to do with unfettered evolution, which is always unpredictable and not necessarily upward bound. H. G. Wells recognized this principle in his 1895 novel *The Time Machine*, which portrays the natural evolution of humankind into weak and dimwitted, but cuddly little creatures. And Kurt Vonnegut follows this same theme in *Galápagos*, where he suggests that our "big brains" will be the cause of our downfall, and future humans with smaller brains and powerful flippers will be the only remnants of a once great species, a million years hence. *22*

Although most politicians professed outrage at the prospect of human cloning when Dolly [the first cloned sheep] was first announced, Senator Tom Harkin of Iowa was the one lone voice in opposition. "What nonsense, what utter utter nonsense, to think that we *23* can hold up our hands and say, 'Stop,' " Mr. Harkin said. "Human cloning will take place, and it will take place in my lifetime. I don't fear it at all. I welcome it."

As the story of Jennifer and Rachel is meant to suggest, those who want to clone themselves or their children will not be impeded by governmental laws or regulations. The marketplace—not government or society—will control cloning. And if cloning is banned in one place, it will be made available somewhere else—perhaps on an underdeveloped island country happy to receive the tax revenue. Indeed, within two weeks of Dolly's announcement, a group of investors formed a Bahamas-based company called Clonaid (under the direction of a French scientist named Dr. Brigitte Boisselier) with the intention of building a clinic where cloning services would be offered to individuals for a fee of $200,000. According to the description provided on their web page (http://www.clonaid.com), they plan to offer "a fantastic opportunity to parents with fertility problems or homosexual couples to have a child cloned from one of them."

Irrespective of whether this particular venture actually succeeds, others will certainly follow. For in the end, international borders can do little to impede the reproductive practices of couples and individuals.

Surreptitious Cloning

In democratic societies, people have the right to reproduce and the right to *not* reproduce. This last "right" means that men and women cannot be forced to conceive a child against their will. Until now, it has been possible to exercise this particular right by choosing not to engage in sexual intercourse, and not to provide sperm or eggs for use in artificial insemination or IVF [in vitro fertilization]. But suddenly, human cloning opens up frightening new vistas in the realm of reproductive choice, or lack thereof. Suddenly, it becomes possible to use the genetic material of others without their knowledge or consent.

Let's reconsider the Jennifer and Rachel scenario in the light of reproductive choice. At first glance, it might seem that nothing is amiss here because Jennifer obviously gave her consent to be cloned. But reproductive choice has been interpreted traditionally to mean that people have the right not to be genetic parents against their will. Does this mean that Jennifer should have asked her own parents for permission to create a clone—her identical twin and their child—before proceeding? Actually, all of *your* genes, as well, came from *your* mother and father. Does this mean that your parents have the right to tell you how to use them?

At least Jennifer gave her consent to be cloned. But what are we to make of a situation in which someone is cloned without his or her knowledge, let alone consent? It takes only a single living cell to start the cloning procedure, and that cell can probably be obtained from almost any living part of the human body. There are various ways in which cells could be stolen from a person. I will illustrate one here with what I will call the Michael Jordan scenario.

Let's move to the near future. The year is 2009, and Jordan has now retired as a professional basketball player. He goes into his doctor's office for his annual checkup, during which a blood sample is taken into a standard tube. Jordan's sample, along with others, is given over to a medical technician, who has been waiting for this moment since Jordan scheduled his appointment a month before. After closing the lab door behind her, she opens the tube of Jordan's blood and removes a tiny portion, which is transferred to a fresh tube that is quickly hidden in her pocket. The original tube is resealed, and no one will ever know that it has been tampered with.

At the start of her lunch break, the technician rushes the tube of blood to her friend at a private IVF clinic on the other side of town. The small sample is emptied into a laboratory dish, and there Jordan's white blood cells are bathed in nutrients and factors that will allow them to grow and multiply into millions of identical cells, each one ready for cloning. The cells are divided up into many portions, which are frozen in individual tubes for later use. *30*

And then the word goes out on the street. For a $200,000 fee, you can have your very own Michael Jordan child. Would anyone buy? If not a Michael Jordan child, would they be interested in a Tom Cruise, a Bill Clinton, or a Madonna (the singer not the saint)? *31*

It's important to understand that what most people want more than anything else is to have their *own* child, not someone else's child, no matter who that someone else might be. And if cloning someone else is an option, then cloning oneself is also an option. So what possible reason could exist for choosing a genetically unrelated child? *32*

Perhaps heartless mothers will want a clone of someone famous in the belief that they will prosper on the income that a clone could make, or the fame that he would bring. But it would require an enormous investment in time and money to raise a child over many years before there was even a chance of a payback. Clones of Michael Jordan would likely be born with the potential to become outstanding athletes, and clones of Tom Cruise or Madonna might have the same artistic talent as their progenitors. But the original Jordan, Cruise, and Madonna owe their success even more to hard work than genetic potential. *33*

Clones might not have the same incentive to train and exert themselves even if—and perhaps because—unscrupulous parents and promoters try to force them in a specified direction against their will. And while one Madonna clone might attract fame and attention, the next dozen will almost certainly be ignored. It is hard to imagine that many potential parents would be willing to take this gamble, with the wait being so long, and the chances of success so small. *34*

There will probably always be some infertile couples or individuals who will want to clone simply for the opportunity to raise a child who is likely to be beautiful or bright, without any desire to profit from the situation themselves. These people will be able to reach their reproductive goals by cloning someone—who is not famous—*with* their consent. In the future, cell donors could be chosen from a catalog in the same way that sperm and egg donors are chosen today. *35*

In contrast, cloning surreptitiously will almost certainly be frowned upon even by those who accept other uses of the cloning technology. And those who participate will run the risk of serious litigation on the basis of infringing upon someone else's reproductive rights. This is not to say, however, that surreptitious cloning will never occur. On the contrary, if something becomes possible in our brave new reproductive world, someone will probably do it, somewhere, sometime. *36*

READING FOR INFORMATION

1. What factors led Jennifer to decide to have herself cloned?
2. Why must Jennifer travel to the Cayman Islands for the cloning procedure?

3. Paraphrase Silver's description of the cloning process that Jennifer undergoes.

4. What is the biological relationship between Jennifer and Rachel? Between Rachel and Jennifer's parents?

5. In what ways will Rachel's and Jennifer's lives differ, even though the two individuals are genetically identical?

6. What might be the motive for "surreptitious cloning"?

7. Why does Silver think that relatively few people will want to raise clones of famous, talented individuals?

READING FOR FORM, ORGANIZATION, AND FEATURES

1. Why does Silver begin his piece with an extended scenario?

2. Where does Silver respond to the views of those who oppose human cloning? Is that response successful?

3. Why does Silver choose to discuss "surreptitious cloning" at the end of the piece?

4. Would you characterize this as a piece of academic writing? Why or why not? What types of sources and authorities does Silver cite?

READING FOR RHETORICAL CONCERNS

1. How do Silver's credentials affect your reading of his essay?

2. What assumptions does Silver make about the general public's response to cloning? What is his attitude toward his readers?

3. What is Silver's rhetorical purpose? Why has he written this piece, and what does he want to get across to his readers?

4. Where does Silver suggest his own attitude toward Jennifer's decision to use cloning technology?

WRITING ASSIGNMENTS

1. In a 250- to 750-word essay, summarize the potential benefits and dangers of human cloning that are discussed in Silver's article. Write for an audience of nonscientists.

2. Write a 750- to 1,000-word essay that attacks or defends Silver's suggestion that Jennifer's decision to use cloning technology is reasonable.

3. Using Silver's article as a springboard, discuss the extent to which various segments of our society (scientists, the general public, elected officials, and so forth) should be involved in decisions about human cloning. Write 750 to 1,000 words.

● ● ● ● ● ● ● ● ● ● ● ● ● ● ● ●

The Sperminator

Lori B. Andrews

Lori B. Andrews is an attorney who is internationally recognized for her expertise in legal and ethical issues connected to reproductive technology.

Prereading ·

Read the first paragraph of Andrews's essay. For ten minutes, freewrite your response to the question that closes the paragraph.

· · · · · · · · · · · · · · ·

A few years ago, an elite Midwest teaching hospital called me with an unusual question: "We have six men in comas whose wives, girlfriends, or parents want their sperm. What do we do?"

Boarding the plane to the hospital, I thought about John Irving's novel *The World According to Garp,* in which the central character was the product of a liaison between a nurse and a comatose patient. The nurse in that case knew exactly what she wanted. But I was skeptical that the six women involved with this Midwest hospital had—independently—come to the conclusion that they wanted their loved one's sperm. I suspected that, lurking in the background, I would find an andrologist (a specialist in male infertility) who saw a medical journal article waiting to happen.

As anticipated, the physician in question already had his slides prepared for the talks he would give at medical meetings once he got the go-ahead to do the procedure.

This midwestern andrologist proposed to collect sperm from comatose men in the same way it is collected from paraplegic men—through a technique called electroejaculation. An instrument that looked like a cattle prod would be inserted into the man's rectum. An electric shock would then cause an involuntary orgasm.

The andrologist then went on to tell me about his "patients." One was a twenty-five-year-old man who had been trying to father a child before a car accident put him in a coma with a poor prognosis for recovery. His wife wanted his sperm extracted.

Another was a forty-year-old man who also had sustained a severe head injury, also from a car crash. He had a child from a previous marriage, but none with his second wife, a woman in her midtwenties. He had told friends that he did not want to have additional children. The wife claimed that, in the week before the man's accident, he had changed his mind.

Although conception by men in comas was a new wrinkle in reproductive technology, I was already familiar with the idea of posthumous pregnancy. In 1983, I interviewed Kim Casali, the cartoonist who draws the syndicated "Love Is" cartoons. When her husband, Roberto, underwent chemotherapy for cancer, he froze sperm so that he could father a child if he recovered—or allow his wife to create a sibling for their existing infant if he died. After Roberto passed away, Kim successfully used the sperm. The birth announcement listed the parents as "Kim and Roberto (posthumously)."

From *The Clone Age: Adventures in the New World of Reproductive Technology.* by Lori B. Andrews. © 1999. Reprinted by permission of Henry Holt & Co., LLC.

In 1991, William Kane, a Yale-trained lawyer, froze fifteen vials of sperm specifically intending that his girlfriend, Deborah Hecht, be inseminated after he committed suicide. They chose a name for the baby, Wyatt, and William wrote a letter to the unborn child: "I have loved you in my dreams, even though I never got to see you born." Then he wrote a will giving the sperm to his girlfriend and saying about his impending suicide, "I'd rather end it like I lived it—on my time, when and where I will, and while my life is still an object of self-sculpture—a personal creation with which I am still proud. In truth, death for me is not the opposite of life; it is a form of life's punctuation." He took his life in October 1991 after bequeathing "all right, title and interest" in his sperm to Deborah, saying she should use it to become pregnant.

His two adult children by a previous marriage were not at all thrilled with the possibility of a baby brother or sister. Even though Deborah signed a release saying that neither she nor the resulting offspring would make an inheritance claim against the estate, the existing children—arguing through their attorney/mom, Kane's ex-wife—sued to have the sperm destroyed. The children, whose parents had divorced twenty-five years earlier, characterized their father's desire to create children after his death as "egotistic and irresponsible." They said destroying the sperm would "prevent the disruption of existing families by after-born children" and prevent "emotional, psychological and financial stress on those family members already in existence."

It seemed to me the argument proved too much. If accepted, it would mean that any firstborn, such as myself, could sue her parents if they depleted her resources (or future inheritance) by having another child.

The judge, though, accepted the kids' plea. Perhaps he was troubled by such an untraditional family. The mere fact that Kane requested this bizarre approach to baby-making seemed to indicate that he was not of sound mind. So the judge ordered the sperm destroyed.

Deborah Hecht appealed the decision—and won. The appellate court scolded the trial judge for his precipitous decision, saying that Kane "had an interest, in the nature of ownership to the extent that he had decision-making authority as to the sperm within the scope of policy set by law."

The appellate court asked the trial judge to reconsider the case. Since Deborah had inherited 20 percent of the estate, the trial judge gave her 20 percent of the sperm—3 vials.

Deborah was inseminated with William's sperm, to no avail. She sued again, and in 1997, when she turned forty-two, she won the rest of the sperm. As of late 1998, she was trying once more to get pregnant. Meanwhile, William's existing children have sued her again, this time for emotional distress.

Hecht was actually an easy case. William Kane clearly intended the posthumous use of his sperm in precisely the manner in which Deborah Hecht intended to use it.

A case in France was slightly more difficult. In that case, Corinne Parpalaix, joined by her in-laws, sued a sperm bank for access to sperm that her late husband, Alain, had frozen prior to cancer treatment. She said the sperm should pass to her as part of the estate, but the bank countered that "sperm is an indivisible part of the body, much like a limb or organ and is therefore not inheritable absent express instructions."

In the French decision, the court characterized sperm not as property or part of the person but as "the seed of life . . . tied to the fundamental liberty of a human being to conceive or not to conceive." The court focused its analysis on whether Alain "unequivo-cally" intended Corinne to bear his child. The court held that the evidence established his "deep desire" to make his wife "the mother of a common child."

Back at the Midwest hospital, the comatose men did not have wills stating they *18* wanted to have children via electroejaculation. Nor was it likely that any had talked to their friends about that possibility.

In the first case the andrologist told me about—involving the twenty-five-year-old— *19* there *was* evidence that the man and his wife had been trying to have children in the months preceding the accident. However, I had trouble imagining that a man's wishing to have children whom he would actually raise necessarily indicates consent to have children whom he will never see, touch, or interact with. In the second case, the man had told people that he didn't want children with his second wife at all.

The law is clear that if a woman wants an abortion, her husband can't force her to *20* have a child. Why should she be able to force her husband to give her one? Some men in comas do wake up, after all. How would such a man feel to learn he had become a father through no effort of his own, while comatose?

The andrologist argued that doctors had been harvesting sperm from dead men for *21* years. Dr. Cappy Rothman did so as early as 1978, retrieving sperm from an unmarried nineteen-year-old, for the benefit of his parents, who wanted to continue their lineage.

A 1997 survey found that fourteen clinics in eleven states had honored requests for *22* sperm collection from the dead. Requests came from wives, girlfriends, and parents. The men, as old as sixty and as young as fifteen, had died of automobile or motorcycle acci-dents, lightning strikes, construction or farming accidents, or falls. The process was suffi-ciently commonplace that the America Society of Reproductive Medicine had a protocol, "Posthumous Reproduction," for dealing with it. Yet even though infertility doctors have been collecting and storing dead men's sperm for decades, few women were actually using it to procreate. It wasn't until May 1998 that a woman used sperm collected *after* her husband's death to get pregnant, in contrast to the more common use of sperm that the dead husband had frozen prior to his death.

California is the epicenter of dead men procreating, owing largely to Cappy Roth- *23* man. It's actually a sideline of his. As a urologist and andrologist, he has a one-third inter-est in the for-profit California Cryobank, which distributes 2,000 ampules of donor sperm a month to impregnate women whose husbands are infertile. In 1997, Rothman's donor sperm was used by women in forty-five different countries.

On Rothman's Web site, www.cryobank.com, you can search for a donor using cate- *24* gories such as religion, ethnic group, height, weight, whether there has been a reported pregnancy, eye color, hair color, hair type, blood type, occupation, and years of education. You can also pay $25 each to hear donors on audiotape.

Rothman also distributes T-shirts with attractive turquoise pictures of sperm on *25* them and the words (in English or Japanese) *Future People*. It makes feminists furious, seemingly harkening back to Aristotle's idea that reproduction occurred when men deposited homunculi—the miniature essence of a human—into women, who contributed nothing but the flowerpot in which the seed could grow.

In October 1997, Rothman and I testified in a New York Legislature hearing where *26* the question on the table was: Should a dead man's sperm be used without his previous consent? Rothman claimed there is less grief for the wife and other family members if some of the dead man's sperm is saved. He told legislators, "In one case where a man died by gunshot and I collected his sperm, his family followed me to the sperm bank and were consoled by seeing mobile sperm under the microscope. To console families in that way at a time of grief and tragedy is clearly part of my responsibility as a healer."

Yet different family members grieve in different ways. As the Kane case showed, some family members might not be pleased by the idea of fathering from the grave. And sperm wasn't the only source of dispute. A wealthy California couple, Mario and Elsa Rios, died in a plane crash with two embryos frozen in an IVF program in Australia and a multimillion-dollar estate. Would the embryos inherit the estate, or would the estate inherit the embryos? The answer to that question would make a world of difference. If the embryos were just property of the estate, the *existing* Rios children might choose never to implant them in order not to share the wealth.   27

On the off chance that the embryos might be beneficiaries, though, women began lining up in Australia to carry them. An Australian advisory committee recommended destruction of any embryos (including the Rios') where there was no advance directive about what should be done after the parents died. Right-to-life protests about "killing" the Rios' embryos, though, led to a reprieve. The Victoria, Australia, legislature enacted a law preserving the Rios' embryos for implantation. But since a California court ruled that the embryos would not inherit, far fewer women have been willing to act as the surrogate.   28

Cappy Rothman doesn't have a process for negotiating such disputes. What if the *wife* didn't want to use her dead husband's sperm, but the man's *parents* did, suggesting they would hire a surrogate mother?   29

"Deciding whose right to sperm should prevail is not my role," Dr. Rothman says.   30

But he also denies that role to bioethicists. "What makes an ethicist know what the rest of us should or shouldn't do?" he asks.   31

Existing law doesn't provide much guidance either. Under the Uniform Anatomical Gift Act—the organ donor law in each state—a wife or other relative can donate the deceased's organs or tissue, and can choose the recipient. Technically, then, the wife could donate the sperm to herself.   32

Or could she? The law covers transplantation, but using sperm to create a child doesn't quite fit that description. And wouldn't the wife have a conflict of interest? The law allows the wife to donate organs to further her husband's wishes, since it is unlikely that she would, say, need a kidney at the exact moment the man died. To remove the incentive for the wife to go against her husband's desires, payment for organs is not allowed.   33

But if she wanted a child and he didn't, the existing law wouldn't protect his desires after death. Claims of conflict of interest already are being leveled about fetal tissue transplantation. A federal advisory panel specifically recommended that a woman aborting a fetus *not* be able to designate a recipient even though she technically may do so as its next of kin under the organ donor law. The concern is that women will conceive and abort just to try to help out relatives, by providing fetal tissue, for instance, for treatment of Alzheimer's disease. Isn't donating sperm to herself just as bad? And why should a man's *parents* (the next in line under organ donor laws) have control of his reproductive capacity? There is no "right" to carry on one's lineage; if the son was competent and healthy, for example, his folks could not force him to have a child.   34

Even if the woman does not have the authority to direct the electroejaculation as a surrogate decision maker for the husband, can she make an even bolder claim and argue that his sperm is somehow *her* property (or at least their joint property)? A 1954 Illinois court case banned artificial insemination by donor on the grounds that it was adultery. The underlying theory was that each spouse has a claim to the other's reproductive capacity.

35

Although more recent court cases are uncomfortable with categorizing a man's sperm as his wife's property, another case, *Brotherton* v. *Cleveland,* held that a wife had a property interest in her husband's corneas. In that case, the wife had refused to donate organs or tissue from her dead husband because of his aversion to such a possibility. Nevertheless, the coroner retrieved Brotherton's corneas for donation. The wife successfully sued for damages. In that case, though, giving the wife a property interest was a way to effectuate the husband's prior wishes. In the coma cases, there is no evidence about what the men would do in these circumstances.

36

And unlike the French case where the sperm existed on its own, the coma cases would require andrologists to invade men's bodies to get it. (There is some appeal on equity grounds to seeing men as sperm containers, given that women in recent years have been treated increasingly like fetal containers in court decisions in which women are forced to have cesarean sections or other procedures for the benefit of the fetus.) However, with the sperm still in the men, rather than in the bank, courts are likely to find that electroejaculation violates their liberty interest in bodily integrity. The U.S. Supreme Court believes that a person in a coma or a persistent vegetative state continues to have such a right.

37

Once comatose men are turned into objects from which tissue can be harvested by their wives, what's to keep men from arguing for equal rights? If the wife were comatose, could her husband ask for eggs to be retrieved? Could he argue he had a constitutional right to impregnate her and keep her alive on a respirator for nine months until the child could be delivered by cesarean section?

38

In one case, a comatose twenty-eight-year-old woman was raped by an attendant at her nursing home. When nurses noticed that the woman's stomach was swollen, they gave her three pregnancy tests before telling her parents the truth. Her Roman Catholic parents refused to authorize an abortion. A son was born prematurely, weighing less than three pounds, and the nursing home paid the parents over $6 million to avert a lawsuit. The young woman died shortly before the boy's first birthday, but the child has survived.

39

Although couples can't force their children to give them a grandchild, new reproductive technologies allow them to take matters into their own hands. A twenty-three-year-old man who was planning to attend medical school was involved in a motor vehicle accident that left him in a vegetative state. The patient's father asked about acquiring sperm for the purpose of inseminating the patient's fiancée. The father went so far as to masturbate the son to obtain sperm for a semen analysis, which showed that the son had a normal sperm count and normal mobility.

40

In another case, an eighteen-year-old only child sustained a severe head injury and was declared brain dead within forty-eight hours. The father, who had undergone a vasectomy but who now wished to preserve the family lineage, requested the son's sperm be preserved for future insemination of a surrogate. The electroejaculation was performed, but it turned out that the patient was infertile and no viable sperm were obtained. The father decided to reverse his vasectomy in order to have a child via surrogate motherhood.

41

In Milwaukee, a man froze sperm before undergoing chemotherapy for cancer that   *42*
would render him sterile. His plan was to have a child once his health was restored, but the
cancer treatment was unsuccessful. After his death, his parents got a call from the hospital, asking what they wanted done with their dead son's sperm.

The couple began searching for a woman who would bear their son's child and let   *43*
them act as grandparents. They found such a woman, but two insemination attempts failed.
To increase their odds, they subsequently established a post office box (BABY, P.O. Box
10936 . . .) and began to offer the sperm to single women and married couples to create
as many children as possible.

But is it really feasible that their son would have wanted to spread his seed across   *44*
Wisconsin?

In a similar case, a young woman named Julie Garber, about to undergo cancer treat-   *45*
ment, got an IVF clinic to fertilize her eggs with a donor's sperm and freeze the twelve
resulting embryos. Her plan: to bear and raise her children after her recovery.

She died, though, and her parents laid claim to the embryos. "She passed away six   *46*
months before, and I was in the same room, six feet away from her living cells," says Jean
Garber. "There was something very special."

The Garbers began interviewing the eighty women who applied for the $15,000 job   *47*
as a surrogate mother. One applicant said, "I enjoy so much being a mother I want to give
Julie that chance."

Give Julie the chance to be a *mother*? Julie was *dead*.   *48*

The Garbers found an appropriate candidate, a postal carrier, and transferred the   *49*
embryos into her womb. They arranged to appear on the *Today Show* with her—a family unit
for the 1990s. When she miscarried the day before the show, they didn't divulge that fact to
the producers. Julie's father, Howard, an ophthalmologist turned cable television host, said
they wanted to let other women know about their chance to become mothers from the grave.

The new technologies are broadening the divide between the reproductive haves and   *50*
have-nots. At the same time that the wealthy Howard Garber was attempting to implant his
dead daughter's embryo in a surrogate, he was lobbying against the poor having children.

"Thoughtless, careless and irresponsible people are perpetuating their cycle of poverty   *51*
by having children they can't afford," he told the *Orange County Reporter*. "If you can't feed
'em, don't breed 'em."

Reproductive technologies are being marketed with short-term gains in mind, with-   *52*
out any analysis of the long-term psychological or social impacts. A wife offered the opportunity to save sperm from a beloved husband who has just died may be grateful for the
chance to feel as if she is keeping him alive just a little longer. But the net effect may be
simply to prolong the grieving process. What happens to the wife who remarries and
decides to have a child? Will she feel guilty if she doesn't use sperm from her dead husband?

Already, a New York man has requested that he be given the embryo he and his wife   *53*
froze before her death—so that his *new* wife could carry it to term. In Tennessee, a man
wanted his divorced wife's embryo implanted in his second wife. To my mind, it's bad
enough that wife number two has to live in the same house the first wife did and sometimes wear some of her clothes. But to carry her embryo as well?

In Italy, baby Elisabetta was born in December 1994. Her mother had died in a car   *54*
crash, leaving a frozen embryo that her paternal aunt carried to term. The aunt and her

husband are raising her in the same home with her biological father. So the child's birth mother is also her aunt, while her genetic father is also her uncle.

As a result of Elisabetta's case, the Italian Parliament is considering a law banning surrogate motherhood and postmortem pregnancies. Says a representative of the Guild of Catholic Doctors, "Although we would say these embryos are life, doctors are not bound to go to extraordinary lengths to find a host to carry them." *55*

The problem is mushrooming as a result of a growing trend where women store embryos before cancer therapy that will make them sterile. At Bourn Hall, Robert Edwards's former facility, the new director, Peter Brinsden, says he has frozen embryos from thirty such women. Now four British widowers are seeking surrogates to carry babies from their dead wives' frozen embryos. *56*

A Houston company, Cryogenic Solutions, is capitalizing on the baby boomers' tendency to not want to close off any option. It offers women undergoing abortions the chance to freeze their fetuses, with the thought that, if technology is later developed to (in the company's words) "reanimate" the fetus, the woman can undo her abortion decision and raise that same child at a more convenient time. The service, "pregnancy suspension," costs $356. The company, which trades on the NASDAQ Stock Exchange, is in the process of patenting the procedure. *57*

Geneticist Angus Clarke is frustrated with the fact that reproductive and genetic technologies tend "to be adopted as a matter of course once they become technically feasible, without a careful assessment of the ethical issues involved." He faults the medical profession for claiming that "the ethical questions are faced, and answered, by the families who consult us: it is their decision and we wash our hands of any responsibility." *58*

At the Midwest hospital with the six comatose men, I tried to discourage the doctor from electroejaculating his charges. If men do want to give their wives such a right, they can fill out a donation card, as they do to donate organs. When I later mentioned this in my law school class, several female students got their husbands to give them power of attorney over their sperm. *59*

Because I believed that collecting sperm after death was akin to rape, I urged legislators not to allow it. New York state representative John Goodman introduced a bill now pending in the New York legislature, banning posthumous sperm collection unless the man had previously consented. Already, such a law is in effect in England and is being widely enforced after a case in which a woman, Diane Blood, was impregnated with sperm from her comatose husband. *60*

The incentives for disturbing the comatose—or the dead—are high. Doctors are always looking for new technical challenges, and the financial opportunities for wives who create children after their spouse's death can be quite compelling. After her husband's death, Nancy Hart used his previously frozen sperm to create daughter Judith, then sued the Social Security Administration for death benefits for the little girl. The media put pressure on the agency (a typical article read, " 'Miracle' Baby Denied Death Benefits"), and SSA head Shirley Chater ultimately agreed to pay the girl $700 a month. *61*

Legally, the SSA was not obligated. The law requires that children be compensated to replace support that their father gave them while he was alive, but this father had *never* supported Judith. Yet the fascination with reproductive technologies enchanted even the stodgy Social Security Administration into paying for their use. *62*

Nancy Hart subsequently entered law school, with an express interest in the contin- 63
uing evolution of reproductive technologies and their social implications. "Figuring out
the inheritance rights of a cloned child will make our case seem simple," she says.

In time, perhaps she too will be fielding calls like the one I got from a lawyer in the 64
middle of the night. A man had been fatally victimized by the police, and his wife had
convinced the coroner to save some sperm. Now her lawyer was calling me to see whether,
with sperm on hand, he now had *two* wrongful death claims against the cops, a prospective child's as well as the wife's. I explained, much to his disappointment, that unless the
sperm was turned immediately into progeny, he would not be able to double his financial
recovery.

READING FOR INFORMATION

1. Describe Kim Casali's use of reproductive technology.
2. What legal issues arose from Deborah Hecht's attempt to gain possession of William
   Kane's frozen sperm? What was the final resolution of those issues?
3. Explain the circumstances surrounding Corinne Parpalaix's law suit.
4. What is an andrologist?
5. Describe how Cappy Rothman's sperm bank operates.
6. Explain some of the inheritance complications that can result from artificial insemination.
7. When sperm is removed from a dead or comatose man, how might the procedure
   violate his legal rights?
8. What are some of the legal complications created by storing frozen embryos?

READING FOR FORM, ORGANIZATION, AND FEATURES

1. Does anything about Andrews's tone or style indicate her training as a lawyer?
   Explain your answer.
2. Comment on Andrews's opening strategy.
3. In terms of the way sources are handled, is Andrews's article an example of academic
   writing? Explain your answer.

READING FOR RHETORICAL CONCERNS

1. Explain Andrews's title.
2. What is Andrews's goal in writing? At what point does this goal become clear?
3. How do the issues connected to reproductive technology that Andrews, a lawyer,
   addresses differ from those on which Silver, a scientist, focuses?
4. Reread the final paragraph. What point is Andrews trying to get across?

WRITING ASSIGNMENTS

1. Select one of the cases described in Andrews's essay. In a 500-word essay of your
   own, explain the case and argue a position in response to it.

2. In a 750-word essay, weigh the pros and cons of allowing women to become pregnant from the sperm of a deceased man.

3. In a 750-word essay, summarize the legal issues that arise from sperm extraction and sperm freezing.

. . . .

WRITING ASSIGNMENTS FOR CHAPTER 10

1. Write a 1,000-word essay of personal response that engages the ideas presented in one of the reading selections in this chapter. Describe your own use of technology in detail.

2. Write a 1,250-word essay that summarizes objectively the dangers that modern technology poses for our society. Synthesize material from all four readings in this chapter.

3. In a 1,000-word essay, weigh the pros and cons of one type of technology examined in one or more of the readings in this chapter.

4. Use two or more of the readings in this chapter to help answer the following question: When does our private use of technology intrude on the lives of others to the extent that it should be regulated? Write at least 1,000 words.

5. Synthesize ideas from at least three of the readings in this chapter to explain how one can take advantage of modern technology and still avoid its drawbacks. Write at least 1,250 words.

6. Rent and view a science fiction video, such as *The Net, Hackers, The Terminator, Total Recall, The Boys from Brazil,* or *2001: A Space Odyssey,* that focuses on how technology might affect society. Then write a 1,250-word essay in which you use at least two of the readings in this chapter to analyze the portrayal of technology in the science fiction video.

7. In a 1,000-word essay, explain how two or more of the readings in this chapter have affected your viewpoint on technology.

11

TASTES IN POPULAR MUSIC

One of the most common sources of disagreement among college roommates is conflicting tastes in popular music. It is obvious that many students identify strongly with their own tastes in music but are annoyed or repelled by the genres or artists favored by their roommates. Even though opinions about popular music generate strong feelings, most of us are unaware of how our tastes in music develop, of why we are enthralled with songs of our favorite artists but can't bear to remain in the room with those of artists we dislike. We tend to think of our tastes as a given, like eye color or shoe size, and we rarely analyze their development or evolution. When other people attempt to evaluate or criticize our music tastes, we often become defensive, as if those attempts call our character and identity into question.

The readings in this chapter are attempts to account for tastes in popular music. The introductory chapter from *Dave Barry's Book of Bad Songs*, by humor writer Dave Barry, explains that our musical tastes are defined by the songs we don't like as well as by the songs that appeal to us. Richard Brookhiser's "All Junk, All the Time" maintains that rock is by definition bad music and that people who like it have unrefined tastes and are therefore incapable of appreciating good music. Songwriter and performer David Byrne discusses how the pop music industry attempts to channel our tastes in order to mass-market pop artists, causing us to overlook a wide range of excellent music that is being produced around the globe. His ironic title is "I Hate World Music." Finally, musicologist Michael J. Budds analyzes how the pop music tastes of American youth shifted from Tin Pan Alley to rock and roll while the older generation was so repulsed by rock that they turned to music censorship.

Bad Songs

Dave Barry

Dave Barry is a syndicated journalist whose humorous columns appear in newspapers across the country. He is the author of numerous books, including Dave Barry Turns 40 *and* Dave Barry Talks Back.

Prewriting ●

You are probably familiar with Dave Barry's satirical columns on American culture. Can journalists use humor to analyze serious issues, or does the humor undercut serious discussion? Freewrite for ten minutes in response to this question.

● ● ● ● ● ● ● ● ● ● ● ●

Dave Barry. *Dave Barry's Book of Bad Songs.* Kansas City: Andrews, 1997. 2–12.

This book, like so many of the unpleasant things that we encounter as we go through life, is Neil Diamond's fault. Here's what happened:

One day back in 1992, I was doing what I am almost always doing, namely, trying to write a newspaper column despite the fact that I have nothing important, or even necessarily true, to say.

In this particular column, I was complaining about the fact that they never play any good songs on the radio. When I say "good songs," I of course mean "songs that I personally like." For example, I happen to love "Twist and Shout" as performed by the Isley Brothers. As far as I am concerned, oldies-format radio stations should be required by federal law to play this song at least once per hour.

But they hardly ever play it. Instead, they play "Love Child" as performed by Diana Ross and the Supremes, which is a song that you can listen to only so many times. And when I say "only so many times," I mean "once." And if they ever do play "Twist and Shout," for some bizarre reason they play the Beatles' version, which, according to mathematical calculations performed by powerful university computers, is only $1/10,000$ as good as the Isley Brothers' version.

So anyway, in this column I was ranting about songs that I don't particularly care for, and I happened to bring up Neil Diamond. I didn't say I hate *all* Neil Diamond songs; I actually like some of them.[1] Here's exactly what I wrote:

> It would not trouble me if the radio totally ceased playing ballad-style songs by Neil Diamond. I realize that many of you are huge Neil Diamond fans, so let me stress that, in matters of musical taste, everybody is entitled to an opinion, and yours is wrong. Consider the song "I Am, I Said," wherein Neil, with great emotion, sings:
>
> *I am, I said*
> *To no one there*
> *And no one heard at all*
> *Not even the chair.*
>
> What kind of line is that? Is Neil telling us he's *surprised* that the chair didn't hear him? Maybe he expected the chair to say, "Whoa, I heard THAT." My guess is that Neil was really desperate to come up with something to rhyme with "there," and he had already rejected "So I ate a pear," "Like Smokey the Bear," and "There were nits in my hair."

So that was what I wrote: A restrained, fair, and totally unbiased analysis of this song. Who could possibly be offended?

Well. You think Salman Rushdie got into trouble. It turns out that Neil Diamond has a great many *serious* fans out there, and virtually every one of them took the time to send me an extremely hostile, spittle-flecked letter. In a subsequent column, I combined the key elements of these letters into one all-purpose irate–Neil Diamond–fan letter, as follows:

[1]*For example, I really like "Play Me," especially the part where Neil sings, "Song she sang to me, song she brang to me."*

Dear Pukenose:

Just who the hell do you think you are to blah blah a great artist like Neil blah more than twenty gold records blah blah how many gold records do YOU have, you scumsucking wad of blah I personally have attended 1,794 of Neil's concerts blah blah What about "Love on the Rocks," huh? What about "Cracklin' Rosie"? blah blah If you had ONE-TENTH of Neil's talent blah blah so I listened to "Heart Light" forty times in a row and the next day the cyst was GONE and the doctor said he had never seen such a rapid blah blah What about "Play Me"? What about "Song Sung Blah"? Cancel my subscription, if I have one.

The thing is, I got at least as many letters, just as strongly worded, *attacking* Neil Diamond. But that was just the beginning: I got a whole lot *more* letters from people who wanted to complain about other songs that they hated to hear on the radio. And these people were *angry*. These people were advocating the use of tactical nuclear weapons against the next radio station to play, for example, "American Pie."

8

I have, in my twenty years as a newspaper columnist, written about many vitally important issues—politics, the economy, foreign policy, mutant constipated worms, etc.—and none of these topics has ever stirred up so much passion in the readers as the issue of bad songs. People were stopping me on the street, grabbing me by the shirt, and, with cold fury in their eyes, saying things like: "You know that song about the piña coladas? I HATE THAT SONG! I HATE IT!!"

9

So I realized that I had tapped into a throbbing artery of emotion. I realized that Americans—who are so often accused of not being interested in or informed about the issues—care very deeply about song badness. I also realized that, by probing deeper into this subject, I had a chance to do something that could provide a truly significant benefit to the human race; namely, I could get an easy column out of it.

10

And thus I decided to conduct the Bad Song Survey. I asked my readers to vote for what they considered to be the worst songs, the songs that cause them to poke finger holes in their car radios in their desperate haste to change the station.

11

The response was unbelievable. I think more people voted in the Bad Song Survey than in the presidential election. Certainly the Bad Song voters were more enthusiastic. Here are some typical quotes from the voters:

12

- "The number one worst piece of pus-oozing, vomit-inducing, camel-spitting, cow-phlegm song EVER in the history of the SOLAR system is 'Dreams of the Everyday Housewife.'"

- "I'd rather chew a jumbo roll of tinfoil than hear 'Hey Paula' by Paul and Paula."

- "Whenever I heard the Four Seasons' 'Walk Like a Man,' I want to scream, 'Frankie, SING like a man!'"

- "I wholeheartedly believe that 'Ballerina Girl' is responsible for 90 percent of the violent crimes in North America today."

- "I nominate every song ever sung by the Doobie Brothers. Future ones also."

- "Have you noticed how the hole in the ozone layer has grown progressively larger since rap got popular?"

- "I nominate 'Cat's in the Cradle' by Harry Chapin. Harry's dead, of course, so we'll never have to worry about hearing it performed live again, but darn it, Dave, the next disc jockey here in K.C. that plays that song is going to get smacked across the head with a tube sock full of wood screws."

I ended up writing *two* columns on the results of the Bad Song Survey. These columns generated still *more* mail, some from people who wanted to cast additional votes ("I can't BELIEVE you left out 'Eve of Destruction!' I HATE THAT SONG!"); some from people who were very upset about certain songs that were voted as bad ("Perhaps your readers are not aware that 'The Lion Sleeps Tonight' is a very fine traditional . . ."). And I heard from some people whose lives had actually been changed by the survey. Here's one of my favorite letters:

> Dear Dave,
>
> Your articles on Bad Songs were wonderful. I laughed 'til I cried. However, when I tried to read it to my boyfriend, much to my dismay he knew the words to all of the songs and *likes* them. I had to repeatedly stop reading so he could sing each one, and then listen to his exclamations of "What's wrong with THAT one!?" and "He doesn't like 'Honey'?!!!" etc. I knew he was a sentimental fool, but had no idea how bad his taste was. Now I'm afraid we're too incompatible to continue the relationship.
> Thanks a lot, Dave.
>
> > Susan Bolton
> > "Alone again, naturally"

And that was not the end of it. I don't think there will *ever* be an end to it. We've had an entire presidential administration[2] since the Bad Song Survey, and I am *still* getting mail about it from people wishing to vote for songs they hate, as well as from fans whom I have offended.

Special Note to Neil Diamond Fans

Please stop writing! You have convinced me! Neil is a music god! I worship Neil on a daily basis at a tasteful shrine to him erected in my living room! I love *all* the songs Neil sang to us! Not to mention all the songs he brang to us!

Why do people feel so passionate about this subject? Because music is *personal*. The songs we hear a lot—particularly the ones we hear when we're young—soak into our psyche, so that forever after, when we hear certain songs, we experience sudden and uncontrollable memory spasms taking us back to specific times—some good, some bad—in our lives.

For example, I cannot hear a Beach Boys car song without being immediately transported back to the summers of 1962 through 1965. These were good summers for me—I was in high school and had never heard of gum disease—and Beach Boys car songs got played on the radio all the time, and I have loved them uncritically ever since. To this day, when I'm alone in my car, if the radio plays "Shut Down," a song about two guys drag racing—one driving a Corvette Stingray and the other driving a Dodge with a 413 engine[3]—I'll crank the volume all the way up and sing along:

Pedal's to the floor, hear his dual quads drink
And now the 413's lead is startin' to shrink

---

[2]*If you want to call it that.*
[3]*Whatever the hell* that *means.*

13

14

15

16

17

On a technical level, I have no idea what the Beach Boys mean by the term *dual*   *18*
quads. I'm not a car guy. I'm the kind of guy who, if there's a warning light on my dash-
board that won't go away, will repair it by putting a piece of duct tape over it.

But that doesn't matter. What matters is that when I'm singing along to "Shut Down,"   *19*
I'm no longer a middle-aged guy driving to the laundry to pick up my shirts; I'm seven-
teen, and it's a summer night with tantalizing possibilities of adventure and romance hanging semipalpably in the humid air, and I'm cruising the roads around Armonk, New York,
and even though the vehicle I'm cruising in is my mom's Plymouth Valiant station wagon,
which boasts the performance characteristics and sex appeal of a forklift, I am feeling *good*,
and I am stomping on the gas pedal (not that this has any measurable effect on my mom's
Valiant) and imagining that I'm at the wheel of a Stingray, singing triumphantly along with
the Beach Boys as we roar past the Dodge 413:

> *He's hot with ram induction, but it's understood*
> *I got a fuel-injected engine sittin' under my hood*
> *Shut it off, shut it off*
> *Buddy now I SHUT YOU DOWN!*

So I don't care how many times I hear "Shut Down," or "Little Deuce Coupe," or   *20*
"Fun, Fun, Fun." They're always welcome on my radio; I'll go back to that summer night
any time. On the other hand, I've always had a violent hatred for "I Got You Babe" because
when it came out back in 1965 it was presented as some kind of anthem that spoke for
America's youth; whereas in fact it was a flagrantly inane song ("So put your little hand in
mine; there ain't no hill or mountain we can't climb"), on top of which, as an American
youth, I did not wish to be spoken for by a whining little puke like Sonny Bono.

So songs evoke powerful emotions, both positive and negative. I think the negative   *21*
ones tend to be stronger because, as I noted in the preintroduction warning to this book,
your brain, as part of its lifelong effort to drive you insane, insists on remembering the
songs you hate and playing them over and over and over.

That's why people still write and talk to me about the Bad Song Survey. They seem   *22*
to have this powerful need to get their feelings about certain songs out into the open; somehow, this makes them feel better. It's kind of like psychotherapy, where the goal is to get
patients to probe their subconscious minds, deeper and deeper, until they finally realize that
the root of all their emotional problems is the fact that, during early childhood, they were
exposed to the hit song "The Name Game" by Shirley Ellis ("Shirley Shirley bo Birley, bo
nana fana fo Firley, fee fie mo Mirley, Shirley!").

READING FOR INFORMATION

1. What does Barry object to in Neil Diamond's music?
2. Who is Salman Rushdie?
3. Describe the response to Barry's original column criticizing Neil Diamond.
4. What does Barry conclude from the response to his series of columns on bad songs?
5. Why does Barry think that many Americans have strong feelings about popular music?
6. What characterizes the songs that Barry likes?

READING FOR FORM, ORGANIZATION, AND FEATURES

1. How is Barry's piece organized?
2. Comment on the effectiveness of Barry's use of examples.
3. How does Barry attempt to make the reader laugh?

READING FOR RHETORICAL CONCERNS

1. Who is Barry's intended audience?
2. What effect does Barry want to have on his audience?
3. Identify the sentences that state Barry's main points about Americans' tastes in popular music.
4. Given the humorous tone of the piece, are you able to take seriously the points Barry raises about musical tastes? Explain your answer.

WRITING ASSIGNMENTS

1. Choose two songs, one you like and one you can't stand. In a 750-word essay, compare and contrast the features of these two songs.
2. Listen to at least one of the songs that Barry's readers hated. Write a 500-word response to this song that identifies your own tastes in music.
3. Write a 750-word essay in response to Barry's claim that we take popular music seriously because it is closely linked with significant experiences in our lives.

· · · · · · · · · · · · · · · ·

All Junk, All the Time

Richard Brookhiser

Richard Brookhiser is a senior editor of the National Review *and also writes a column for the* New York Observer. *He has published numerous articles and books, including* The Way of the WASP: How It Made America and How It Can Save It, So to Speak *and* Founding Father: Rediscovering George Washington.

Prereading ·

The title of the article refers to rock music. Write your reaction. Is there any rock music you would call "junk"? Why or why not? Why do you suppose Brookhiser considers rock worthless?

· · · · · · · · · · · · · · · ·

Like a turtle egg buried on the beach, the thought warmed, out of sight, all summer. The   *1*
Olympics and the political conventions helped it grow, but the key stimulus was a passing

sentence in a *New York Times Magazine* article on megachurches, which are evangelical churches that number their congregations in the thousands. The article was discussing the music used in the services, and said something to the effect that the megachurches favored rock. Just like the conventions. Just like the Olympics. Just like everyone everywhere.

Megachurches keep their eye on eternity. In the here and now, rock is triumphant and universal. Its empire will only expand, ferreting out the few nooks it does not yet command, and filling them. Francis Fukuyama alerted us (wrongly) to the End of History. But rock has ended the history of music. There are no ideological, religious, or ethnic redoubts. I once read a profile of the commander of a Salvadoran death squad. He was a Deadhead. Iranian mullahs, Chinese Communists, skinheads, rabbis expecting the return of Menachem Schneerson, Papuan savages dressed only in penis wrappers, all listen, openly or in secret, or their children will.   2

What is rock? A certain set of musicians—drums, guitars, a voice or two. A beat that well, rocks. Lyrics. Pare down the music until it almost vanishes, as in rap; soften the beat until it becomes easy listening; give the songwriter the equipment and the ambitions of Brian Wilson: but the form never quite disappears. It hasn't changed for forty years, and it never will, because it is so easy to do well enough.   3

Consider the elements.   4

Music. The guitar is the ultimate E-Z-2-Play instrument. Why else was it the lyre of the American peasantry? If rock depended on some instrument—trumpet, clarinet, fiddle, piano—that required some tone of the lips or lightness of the fingers to play even barely competently, its pool of potential performers would have shrunk by 90 percent. There is only one instrument easier to fake: drums. The low standards also apply to rock vocalists. Remember Mick Jagger when he was in his prime? Heard him now, when he sounds like a voice on the subway PA system? Mr. Jagger could actually move his notes around, but they were always harsh and homely notes. That's OK—they were good enough for rock.   5

Words. The rock critic Elizabeth Wurtzel, reviewing an album of covers of Cole Porter songs by rock musicians, hoped the experience might inspire rock songwriters to be a little more careful of their rhyme schemes. Wrong! The whole point is not to have to worry about rhyme schemes. If you start worrying, not everyone will be able to do it. So rock will keep on rhyming "pain" and "shame," and "stop" and "stuck."   6

Dancing. I was in fifth and sixth grade just after kids stopped taking solemn little lessons, in gym class or after school, in the box step and the cha-cha. Those who still dance these, and all the other dances of mankind, do it, like fox hunters or Greek scholars, as a passion or a hobby. To fulfill the necessities of social intercourse, it will never be necessary to take a dance lesson again. Slow dancing to rock is what you hope to be doing horizontally with your clothes off afterward. Fast dancing is—well, look at it, at any wedding or bar mitzvah, where even the grown-ups shake their aged hams. The abolition of dance steps was a great relief to the awkward, especially the men, who once had to lead—no more visualizing the points of the compass, no more shame when you crunched the foot you were supposed to be guiding.   7

Entrepreneurs. There is a final way in which rock is easy, which impels the other three. It is easy to make a buck selling it. Because the product is so generic, primitive, and witless, the distributors and marketers can know nothing, ingest huge quantities of drugs, and still   8 not be too addled to make millions. The fields I know best are journalism, publishing, and politics, and so I do know something about laziness and empty pretensions. But if there were ever a land of opportunity for the feckless, the modern music industry is it.

Rock is a form of popular culture that aims downward in terms of class and age, instead of aiming up. Rather than aspiring, it *despires*. Astronomers speak of the red shift, the change in the spectrum of the light of receding galaxies. Rock is redneck shift. The preceding phase of popular music, encompassing jazz, dance bands, and show tunes, was urban and adult. Rock is kids channeling the rhythms of bumpkins.

But the worst thing about rock is not that it fails the culture, but that it fails on its own terms. Popular music is a marker and a memory aid. Most of the important events in life—romance, courtship, celebration—are accompanied by it. We remember them because of their importance to us, no matter what was on the radio. But if the music is crude and blank, does not some of its crudity and blankness infect the experience, and the memory?

And while popular music mostly amplifies pre-existing emotions, at its best it can tug us, tease us, make us grow. Not rock. For all its supposedly revolutionary ethos, rock is a binary switch of angst and hormones—Kafka without humor, or centerfolds in notes. The emotions that unsettle, like stones under a sleeping bag—hope, regret—are beyond its ken. And they are beyond our ken, to the extent rock stuffs our ears.

It's Bottom 40, all junk, all the time. And it's here to stay.

READING FOR INFORMATION

1. Explain the point Brookhiser makes in his first two paragraphs.
2. How does Brookhiser define rock music?
3. Summarize the four elements Brookhiser identifies in rock music.
4. How, according to Brookhiser, does rock music differ from the popular music that preceded it?
5. How does Brookhiser believe that rock music affects our memory for life experiences?
6. Paraphrase paragraph 11.

READING FOR FORM, ORGANIZATION, AND FEATURES

1. What is the function of paragraphs 1 and 2? How do they relate to the rest of the article?
2. What devices or aids pull readers into the conversation and help them follow Brookhiser's argument?
3. Do you think Brookhiser gives sufficient weight to opposing views? Why or why not?

READING FOR RHETORICAL CONCERNS

1. What incidents motivated Brookhiser to write the piece?
2. How do you think Brookhiser's *National Review* readers reacted to his position?
3. How would you characterize Brookhiser's tone of voice? Is it appropriate for his rhetorical purpose?

WRITING ASSIGNMENTS

1. Write a 750-word essay in which you respond to Brookhiser's claim that rock is "all junk."
2. In a 750-word essay, draw on examples from at least four rock songs to comment on the four elements that Brookhiser identifies in rock music.
3. Write a 750-word essay analyzing and evaluating Brookhiser's argument.

· · · · · · · · · · · · · · · · ·

"I Hate World Music"

David Byrne

As the songwriter and lead singer of the Talking Heads, David Byrne played a key role in shaping popular music.

Prereading ·

What does the term *world music* mean to you? Freewrite for ten minutes in response to this question.

· · · · · · · · · · · · · · · · ·

I hate world music. That's probably one of the perverse reasons I have been asked to write   *1*
about it. The term is a catchall that commonly refers to non-Western music of any and all sorts, popular music, traditional music and even classical music. It's a marketing as well as a pseudomusical term—and a name for a bin in the record store signifying stuff that doesn't belong anywhere else in the store. What's in that bin ranges from the most blatantly commercial music produced by a country, like Hindi film music (the signer Asha Bhosle being the best well known example), to the ultra-sophisticated, super-cosmopolitan art-pop of Brazil (Caetano Veloso, Tom Zé, Carlinhos Brown); from the somewhat bizarre and surreal concept of a former Bulgarian state-run folkloric choir being arranged by classically trained, Soviet-era composers (Le Mystère des Voix Bulgares) to Norteño songs from Texas and northern Mexico glorifying the exploits of drug dealers (Los Tigres del Norte). Albums by Selena, Ricky Martin and Los Del Rio (the Macarena kings), artists who sell millions of records in the United States alone, are racked next to field recordings of Thai hill tribes. Equating apples and oranges indeed. So, from a purely democratic standpoint, one in which all music is equal, regardless of sales and slickness of production, this is a musical utopia.

So Why Am I Complaining?

In my experience, the use of the term *world music* is a way of dismissing artists or their   *2*
music as irrelevant to one's own life. It's a way of relegating this "thing" into the realm of something exotic and therefore cute, weird but safe, because exotica is beautiful but irrele-

David Byrne. "'I Hate World Music.'" *New York Times* 3 Oct. 1999. 2.1.

vant; they are, by definition, not like us. Maybe that's why I hate the term. It groups everything and anything that isn't "us" into "them." This grouping is a convenient way of not seeing a band or artist as a creative individual, albeit from a culture somewhat different from that seen on American television. It's a label for anything at all that is not sung in English or anything that doesn't fit into the Anglo-Western pop universe this year. (So Ricky Martin is allowed out of the world music ghetto—for a while, anyway. Next year, who knows? If he makes a plena record, he might have to go back to the salsa bins and the Latin mom and pop record stores.) It's a none too subtle way of reasserting the hegemony of Western pop culture. It ghettoizes most of the world's music. A bold and audacious move, White Man!

There is some terrific music being made all over the world. In fact, there is more   *3* music, in sheer quantity, currently defined as world music than any other kind. Not just kinds of music, but volume of recordings as well. When we talk about world music we find ourselves talking about 99 percent of the music on this planet. It would be strange to imagine, as many multinational corporations seem to, that Western pop holds the copyright on musical creativity.

No, the fact is, Western pop is the fast food of music, and there is more exciting   *4* creative music making going on outside the western pop tradition than inside it. There is so much incredible noise happening that we'll never exhaust it. For example, there are guitar bands in Africa that can be, if you let them, as inspiring and transporting as any kind of rock, pop, soul, funk or disco you grew up with. And what is exciting for me is that they have taken elements of global (Western?) music apart, examined the pieces to see what might be of use and then re-invented and reassembled the parts to their own ends. Thus creating something entirely new. (Femi Kuti gave a great show the other night that was part Coltrane, part James Brown and all African, just like his daddy, Fela Kuti, the great Nigerian musical mastermind.)

To restrict your listening to English-language pop is like deciding to eat the same   *5* meal for the rest of your life. The "no-surprise surprise," as the Holiday Inn advertisement claims, is reassuring, I guess, but lacks kick. As ridiculous as they often sound, the conservative critics of rock-and-roll, and more recently of techno and rave, are not far off the mark. For at its best, music truly is subversive and dangerous. Thank the gods.

Hearing the right piece of music at the right time of your life can inspire a radical   *6* change, destructive personal behavior or even fascist politics. Sometimes all at the same time.

On the other hand, music can inspire love, religious ecstasy, cathartic release, social   *7* bonding and a glimpse of another dimension. A sense that there is another time, another space and another, better universe. It can heal a broken heart, offer a shoulder to cry on and a friend when no one else understands. There are times when you want to be transported, to get your mind around some stuff it never encountered before. And what if the thing transporting you doesn't come from your neighborhood?

Why Bother?

This interest in music not like that made in our own little villages (Dumbarton, Scotland,   *8* and Arbutus, Md., in my own case) is not, as it's often claimed, cultural tourism, because once you've let something in, let it grab hold of you, you're forever changed. Of course, you can also listen and remain completely unaffected and unmoved—like a tourist. Your loss. The fact is, after listening to some of this music for a while, it probably won't seem exotic any more, even if you still don't understand all the words. Thinking of things as exotic is only cool when it's your sister, your co-worker or wife; it's sometimes beneficial to exoticize that which has become overly familiar. But in other circumstances, viewing people and cultures as exotic is a distancing mechanism that too often allows for exploitation and racism.

Maybe it's naive, but I would love to believe that once you grow to love some aspect of a culture—its music, for instance—you can never again think of the people of that culture as less than yourself. I would like to believe that if I am deeply moved by a song originating from someplace other than my own hometown, then I have in some way shared an experience with the people of that culture. I have been pleasantly contaminated. I can identify in some small way with it and its people. Not that I will ever experience music exactly the same way as those who make it. I am not Hank Williams, or even Hank Jr., but I can still love his music and be moved by it. Doesn't mean I have to live like him. Or take as many drugs as he did, or, for that matter, as much as the great flamenco singer Cameron de la Isla did.

That's what art does; it communicates the vibe, the feeling, the attitude toward our lives, in a way that is personal and universal at the same time. And we don't have to go through all the personal torment that the artist went through to get it. I would like to think that if you love a piece of music, how can you help but love, or at least respect, the producers of it? On the other hand, I know plenty of racists who love "soul" music, rap and rhythm-and-blues, so dream on, Dave.

The Myth of the Authentic

The issue of "authenticity" is such a weird can of worms. Westerners get obsessed with it. They agonize over which is the "true" music, the real deal. I question the authenticity of some of the new-age ethnofusion music that's out there, but I also know that to rule out everything I personally abhor would be to rule out the possibility of a future miracle. Everybody knows the world has two types of music—my kind and everyone else's. And even my kind ain't always so great.

What is considered authentic today was probably some kind of bastard fusion a few years ago. An all-Japanese salsa orchestra's record (Orquesta de la Luz) was No. 1 on the salsa charts in the United States not long ago. Did the New York salseros care? No, most loved the songs and were frankly amazed. African guitar bands were doing their level best to copy Cuban rumbas, and in their twisted failure they came up with something new. So let's not make any rules about who can make a specific style of music.

Mr. Juju himself, King Sunny Adé, name-checks the country and western crooner Jim Reeves as an influence. True. Rumor has it that the famous Balinese monkey chant was coordinated and choreographed by a German! The first South African pop record I bought was all tunes with American car race themes—the Indy 500 and the like. With sound effects, too! So let's forget about this authenticity bugaboo. If you are transported by the music, then knowing that the creators had open ears can only add to the enjoyment.

White folks needed to see Leadbelly in prison garb to feel they were getting the real thing. They need to be assured that rappers are "keeping it real," they need their Cuban musicians old and sweet, their Eastern and Asian artists "spiritual." The myths and clichés of national and cultural traits flourish in the marketing of music. There is the myth of the untutored, innocent savant whose rhymes contain funky Zen-like pearls of wisdom—the myth that exotic "traditional" music is more honest, more soulful and more in touch with a people's real and true feelings than the kid wearing jeans and the latest sports gear on Mexican television.

There is a perverse need to see foreign performers in their native dress rather than in the T-shirts and baggies that they usually wear off stage. We don't want them looking too much like us, because then we assume that their music is calculated, marketed, impure. Heaven forbid they should be at least as aware of the larger world as we are. All of which might be true, but more important, their larger awareness might also be relevant to their music, which in turn might connect it to our own lives and situations. Heaven forbid. *15*

La Nueva Generación

In the last couple of years, there have been any number of articles in newspapers and magazines about how Latin music in particular was finally going to become hugely popular in the U.S. of A. Half—yes, half—of the current top 10 singles in Britain, that hot and sweaty country, are sort of Latin, if you count Geri Halliwell's "Mi Chico Latino," and why not? The others are watered-down remakes of Perez Prado's hits from the 50's and 60's. The Buena Vista Social Club record is the No. 1 selling record, in any category, in funky Germany. Les Nubians, a French-African group, is getting played on urban (translate as "black") radio in America. So is this a trend or what? Are these more than summer novelty tunes for anglos? Are we really going to learn to dance, or is this some kind of aberration? *16*

But what about the alterna-Latino bands that are touring the United States and Europe in increasing numbers? The Colombian band Bloque (which, I confess, is on my label) was named best band of the year by a Chicago critic; Los Fabulosos Cadillacs won a Grammy last year. Both bands, and many, many others, mix the grooves of their neighborhoods with the sounds and attitudes of the North American tunes they also grew up with. They are a generation with a double heritage, and their music expresses it. *17*

It's tough for this bunch to crack the American market: they're not always cute, safe or exotic. Their music is often more innovative than that of their northern counterparts, which is intimidating. And as cool as they are, they insist on singing in their own language, to an audience that identifies completely with them, thereby making it more difficult to gain a foothold in the States. *18*

These bands are the musical equivalent of a generation of Latin American writers, including Gabriel García Marquez, Isabel Allende, José Amado and Mario Vargas Llosa, that was referred to as the Boom. These musicians are defining their generation, finding a unique voice, and will influence countless others outside their home countries. Here, I believe, is where change will happen. Although they don't sell very many records yet, these and others (for things analogous to this are happening everywhere, in Africa, in Morocco, in Turkey) will plant the seeds, and while I enjoy hearing Ricky Martin's merengue on the radio, these others will change my life. *19*

READING FOR INFORMATION

1. According to Byrne, what is world music?
2. According to Byrne, how is the term *world music* used to undermine non-Western music?
3. How does Byrne characterize Western pop music?
4. In what ways does Byrne think that music can change our lives?
5. Explain how Byrne believes that music can lead to better understanding across cultures.
6. Why does Byrne believe that authenticity is a "myth"?
7. Describe the new wave of Latin music that is gaining popularity worldwide.

READING FOR FORM, ORGANIZATION, AND FEATURES

1. Comment on the ironic title of Byrne's article.
2. Comment on Byrne's use of subheadings.
3. Characterize Byrne's tone. What is your response to that tone?

READING FOR RHETORICAL CONCERNS

1. How does Byrne hope to affect his audience?
2. How does Byrne's status as a pop music star affect your perception of the article?
3. Is Byrne likely to alienate fans of Western pop music?

WRITING ASSIGNMENTS

1. Write a 750-word essay in response to Byrne's claim that music can literally change a person's life.
2. Write a 750-word summary of Byrne's article for an audience of other students who may be unaware of world music.
3. Write a 750-word essay in which you draw on Byrne's article and a sampling of music you selected on your own to compare and contrast the features of Western and non-Western popular music.

● ● ● ● ● ● ● ● ● ● ● ● ● ● ● ●

From Fine Romance to Good Rockin'—and Beyond: Look What They've Done to My Song

Michael J. Budds

Michael J. Budds is a musicologist who teaches at the University of Missouri-Columbia. Among his publications are the books Jazz in the Sixties *and* Rock Recall.

P r e r e a d i n g ....

Budds is a musicologist, a university-trained expert in analyzing music. Do you think that it is useful to analyze rock music, to study its origins, structure, and social importance? Does this type of analysis have any bearing on the enjoyment of the music? Freewrite for ten minutes in response to these questions.

* * * * * * * * * * * * * *

You want to know what I think of that abomination, rock 'n' roll? I think it is a disgrace. Poison put to sound! When I hear it I feel very sad not only for music but for the people who are addicted to it. I am also very sorry for America—that such a great country should have nothing better to pour into the expectant ear of mankind than this raucous distillation of the ugliness of our times, performed by juveniles for juveniles. It is a terrible and sardonic trick of fate that the children of the present century should have to grow up with their bodies under continual bombardment from atomic fall-out and their souls exposed to rock 'n' roll.[1]

—Pablo Casals, 1961

Rock and roll fans, if even a portion of what the critics have said was true, by now would be stone deaf, with their minds burnt out by drugs, and their bodies wasted by excessive fornication. That none of this is true has never bothered rock opponents or caused them to pause in their attacks. Rock-bashing has remained constant since the mid-1950s both in content and style.[2]

—Linda Martin and Kerry Segrave, 1993

No musical repertory in Western civilization has aroused more controversy than rock and roll. No musical repertory has attracted so many powerful and self-righteous oppo-

1

---

[1]*Pablo Casals, "A Disgrace to Music," Music Journal XIX:1 (Jan. 1961), 18. The Spanish-born Casals (1876–1973) enjoyed an international career as a violoncello virtuoso and conductor and was revered as one of the finest musicians of his time. His harsh assessment of rock and roll must be understood as the perception of one whose life was devoted to European fine-art music.*
[2]*Linda Martin and Kerry Segrave,* Anti-Rock: The Opposition to Rock 'n' Roll *(Hamden, CT: Archon Books, 1988; reprinted New York: Da Capo Press, 1993), vii. Although some commentators are willing to attribute the sordid lifestyles of various rock musicians as well as the deaths of several others to the music itself, it seems clear that many other factors must be considered.*

nents. No musicians, viewed as a representative group, have taken such self-indulgent and often self-destructive delight in combining the roles of entertainer/artist and social outlaw. One need only invoke characterizations of three identifiable strains of this music—"shock rock," "cock rock," and "schlock rock"—to appreciate its power to send self-proclaimed protectors of American culture into fits of anguish. The implications of this music's under-privileged birthright, the complex temper of American society since its emergence as a mainstream phenomenon in the wake of World War II, its identification with the thought and behavior of teenagers, and its potential as a means for acquiring almost limitless wealth have all contributed to its perceived menace.

As a result, rock and roll has become a prime target for censorship campaigns by a host of special interest lobbies—religious, political, economic, and musical.[3] Such opposition, be it well-intentioned or vested in self-interest, has existed as an almost chronic condition through-out the music's rather short history. It can be argued, however, that the passion and energy expended in attempts to alter or suppress rock and roll expression have only spurred rockers to flaunt or exaggerate the "objectionable" aspects of their music and worldview in a spirit of defiant celebration. Rock fans have affirmed the behavior of musicians with unbridled enthu-siasm and, by their adulation, have encouraged them to challenge the status quo.

At the heart of the issue is the mainstreaming of attitudes and practices, musical and otherwise, that represent fundamental departures from those institutionalized by the power culture since the colonization of the United States. This change in taste was even more dramatic—in fact, revolutionary—because it symbolized broad acceptance of the musical customs of black America and rural white America, sectors of society with little prestige and long dismissed as irrelevant to national standards and priorities. The actual musical language of rock and roll had long flourished, primarily in the South, without the sanc-tion of upper- and middle-class white Americans who acknowledged the music of these outsiders begrudgingly as "race music" and "hillbilly music," respectively. What *was* new in the 1950s was an enthusiastic audience of middle-class teenagers from white America and a new designation "rock 'n' roll," which ironically is derived from blues imagery for sexual intercourse. These young people with their new fascination for minority music—with no malice aforethought, initially at least—proved to be an irrepressible force in reshaping many social patterns in American society during the second half of the twentieth century.

What made this transformation of American popular music the source of such violent debate is the very fact that it was generated and sustained by the youth of the power culture without the blessing of their parents. Few other musical movements have been defined so emphatically in terms of age. A house divided by rejection of parental prefer-ences and the attending perception of betrayal and even subversion set the stage for a power struggle that marked the early years of rock and roll. Once the music established itself as more than an irritating fad and then quickly achieved status as the social emblem of rebel-lious youth, initial skirmishes faded as opponents regrouped to wage what has proved to be an ongoing war, one in which calls for censorship were raised as periodic battle cries and attempts at control took various forms.

2

3

4

---

[3]*The most comprehensive and systematic study of this phenomenon is probably Martin and Segrave's* Anti-Rock: The Opposition to Rock 'n' Roll, *as cited above. Another significant study addressing this issue in British society is Martin Cloonan,* Banned! Censorship of Popular Music in Britain, 1967–1992 *(Aldershot, Hampshire: Arena, 1996); see especially Chapter 2, "Censorship: Some Characteristics of the Debate."*

Much of the negative response to rock and roll by voices in the establishment must be identified as both racist and elitist.[4] The music was roundly condemned by individuals who, with little experience and little understanding of its nature or history, judged it on the basis of what it was not and whose it was. The foreground importance assigned to the sounds of guitars and drums—often raucous, insistent, and amplified to penetrating levels of volume—was in itself perceived as an unabidable physical assault by detractors. In 1956, *Time* magazine, the prominent current events periodical of record for American society, helped set the tone for the national debate in its first report on rock and roll by describing the music in such loaded terms as "jungle," "juvenile delinquency," and "Hitler mass meetings."[5] Rock and roll, moreover, began its life as a symbol of integration, as an interracial music—with the participation of performers and consumers of both races. Although opportunities for African-American musicians were still systematically restricted, this circumstance alone was enough to rally the champions of entrenched segregation and bigotry.

In addition to the perceived threat to the society at large, the threat to the standing popular music industry was undeniable. Entertainment music in America was a highly lucrative business that directly affected the livelihood of countless individuals. Rather suddenly, the musical products of young Southern upstarts flooded the marketplace with stunning success. Serious loss of income and loss of control forced industry executives to adopt a defensive posture. Leaders of the recording industry went so far as to condemn the music of their competitors as socially irresponsible and morally corrupting. The editors of *Billboard* and *Variety*, trade magazines of the profession, called for self-policing and raised the specter of government censorship as the ultimate solution to the dilemma.[6] In a short time, of course, the industry—chastened by reality, bent on surviving, and enticed by obvious financial rewards—embraced the world of rock and roll by buying it up piece by piece. This transaction helped legitimize the music's hold on the American middle class, but it also introduced musical compromises dictated by purely commercial concerns and a sensational approach to merchandising. It also meant that, in the view of many, by the end of the 1950s the industry itself had become part of the problem.

In retrospect, it seems possible to identify a number of factors that help explain this radical change in musical taste. First of all, the popular song tradition of Tin Pan Alley, which had been centered in New York City and had flourished for more than three generations, began to show signs of wear. The search for fresh and compelling expression within the rather well-defined style became increasingly difficult. The traumatic events of World War II, moreover, made the sanitized worldview delivered in the snappy dance songs and dreamy love ballads that were hallmarks of the genre seem inappropriate or irrelevant to the new generation of youngsters. At the same time that Tin Pan Alley was reaching its peak in the songs of Gershwin, Kern, Rodgers, and Porter, two minority song traditions that had evolved from longstanding folk practice—the urban blues of black America and the country and western songs of rural white Southerners—entered the popular arena and reached a larger audience thanks to a process of commercialization that included record-

---

[4]"*Elitist*" *is used here to designate an attitude of perceived superiority or privilege.*
[5]"*Yeh-Heh-Heh-Hes, Baby,*" Time LXVII:25 (18 June 1956), 54.
[6]See the editorials "Control the Dim-Wits," Billboard LXVI (25 Sept. 1954); and Abel [Green], "A Warning to the Music Business," Variety CXCVII:12 (23 Feb. 1955), 2.

ings, radio stations, and more venues for live performance. The inexpensive portable tran-
sistor radio, a by-product of wartime technology, enabled young people to acquaint themselves with rhythm and blues as well as country and western music without parental
knowledge or supervision.

The appeal of these new options can be directly related to perceived virtues not to be   8
found in the typical Tin Pan Alley product: an obvious spontaneity and informality in terms
of musical process, an emphatic approach to rhythm that satisfied the important desire to
dance, an intense and sometimes extravagant display of emotion, and the unapologetic treatment of subjects considered taboo as well as traditional subjects treated in a more realistic
manner. The latter aspect became a special focus for guardians of public morals because of
the sexual content of many songs, couched in blunt everyday speech or in suggestive double
entendres inherited from the blues. The much bally-hooed breakdown in reticence about
sexual matters during the early years was, of course, but a prelude to the free speech aesthetic
that came to characterize the rock and roll repertory as the decades passed.

The most conspicuous target for the would-be censor has always been the lyrics of rock   9
and roll songs, which have been labeled from the very beginning as trivial, sexually suggestive, or even obscene. The difference in the nature of song texts, however, must be related
to the traditions from which they spring. Song texts of mainstream America had long been
influenced by the high culture of Europe, however watered down for middle-class consumption. Romantic love, the subject of the vast majority of all songs, was treated in a highly ideal-
istic, typically sentimental manner. Although rarely profound, the language tended toward
the poetic, preferring a high-priced vocabulary filled with euphemism and fully respectful
of an unwritten, but widely sanctioned code of public propriety. Songs with texts overstep-
ping this sensibility were banned by radio stations or deleted from the musical scores of
Broadway and Hollywood.[7] Early in the nineteenth century, for example, Stephen Foster's
Jeanie was "borne like a vapor on the summer air." In time, the popular song industry was
infused with a generous helping of what has been identified as the Jewish-American immigrant's dream, the point of view of so many of its creators. Although the genteel character
of song texts was updated to fit the times, the general approach remained unchanged.

Considering the lyrics of two well-known and fairly representative songs provides   10
convincing evidence of the existence of strikingly different attitudes toward popular song
in twentieth-century American society. The words of Jerome Kern's evergreen classic "All
the Things You Are" (1939), written by Oscar Hammerstein II, stand as a model of Tin Pan
Alley restraint and "prettification":

> *You are the promised kiss of springtime*
> *That makes the lonely winter seem long.*
> *You are the breathless hush of evening*
> *That trembles on the brink of a lovely song.*
> *You are the angel glow that lights a star,*
> *The dearest things I know are what you are.*
> *Some day my happy arms will hold you,*

---

[7]*The grand exception appears to be songwriter/composer Cole Porter (1891–1964), whose witty but suggestive lyrics earned for him the nickname "the genteel pornographer" from Cecil Smith in* Musical Comedy in
America *(New York: Theatre Arts Books, 1950).*

And some day I'll know that moment divine
When all the things you are, are mine.

Such lyrics were valued for their sophistication, their cleverness, their calculated substance. They clearly address sexual issues—in this instance a yearning for a consummated love relationship—but unfold in a perfectly indirect manner, without any trace of vulgarity. The world they represent, it might be noted, is not necessarily the world as it ever was or is, but a world conceived in a delightful or bittersweet fantasy. After all, Tin Pan Alley songs were frequently generated for the escapist entertainment of the Broadway stage or the Hollywood film.

In terms of text, the song traditions of the African-American community and the rural white community reflected a level of realism and honesty that flew in face of the mainstream's rules of decorum and its penchant for romantic "sweetness." Not only were such songs cast in the unvarnished language of colloquial speech, they were often based on the life experience of the music's creators. In comparison to the Tin Pan Alley product, the earthy text of "Sixty-Minute Man" (1951), a rhythm and blues cross-over hit created by William Ward and Rose Marks and popularized by the Dominoes in the early 1950s, leaves little to the imagination.

11

Looka here, girls, I'm telling you now they call me lovin' Dan.
I rock 'em, roll 'em all night long: I'm a sixty-minute man.
If you don't believe I'm all I say, come up here and take my hand.
When I let you go, you'll cry, "Oh, yes, he's a sixty-minute man."
There'll be fifteen minutes of kissin', then you'll holler, "Please, don't stop."
There'll be fifteen minutes of teasin' and fifteen minutes of pleasin',
And fifteen minutes of blowin' my top.
If your man ain't treatin' you right, come up here and see old Dan.
I rock 'em, roll 'em all night long: I'm a sixty-minute man.

The words of this song are overtly sexual. They testify to an easy-going pride in the manly art of seduction with an explicitness judged as disarming and risqué in some quarters but normal and refreshing in others. One might easily argue that, in substance, the themes of these two songs share pronounced similarities. Yet in manner, they must be perceived and, in fact, were perceived as worlds apart. It is a matter of historical record that a majority of young people in the United States indicated their preference for the more realistic approach by their grand-scale enthusiasm for rock and roll during the second half of the twentieth century.

What has been impossible for the critics to accept or appreciate, I suspect, is that this institutionalization of rock and roll by young Americans effected a rather dramatic change in the function of popular music in the greater society after the mid-twentieth century. It can be argued that, in general, Western societies have embraced popular music for its ability to entertain across age groups, typically in the spirit of light-hearted diversion and good humor. Even plaintive love songs contributed to a corporate "feel good" sensibility concerning the universal anguish of lost or doomed romance. When political topics were addressed, social conditions mitigated dissent as eccentric; any perception of insensitivity among those who lacked power was ignored. For members of the mainstream culture, this music was tuneful and often animated; it could typically be described as "pretty" or "nice"; the tone of the text was rarely confrontational or provocative.

12

The birthright of rock and roll, in contrast, demanded that this traditional function   13
be redefined as American youth "fell into" power and began to exert influence on society,
largely because of their number and their middle-class purchasing privileges. For, in addition to its entertainment value, rock and roll also must be judged as political and social to
an unprecedented degree. Its point of view was conditioned initially by adolescent frus-
tration and soon after by youthful cynicism, on the one hand, and idealism, on the other.
This redefinition of popular song included forays into subjects and moods foreign to the
mainstream's entertainment experience. Thanks mainly to the champions of the folk revival
of the 1960s and the dynamic African-American musicians leading the Civil Rights Movement, serious—and highly volatile—problems such as social injustice, hypocrisy, war-
mongering, and the destruction of the environment entered the rock and roll sensibility.
Just as great a departure from custom was the introduction of song texts openly dealing
with the darker sides of human nature. Such themes had been grist for various forms of
fine art (literature, music, painting) since the earliest days of the century and certainly had
found expression in the blues and folk song since their beginnings, but such grim preoc-
cupations had never before entered the realm of the mainstream's commercial song until
the Counterculture forced the issue during the 1960s. (A similar phenomenon must be
observed in the subjects and nature of films directed to the American public during the
same period.) The threat was undeniable and uncomfortable to many adults; the fact that
teenagers were making it was radical, a cause for much handwringing by those threatened.

In a very real sense, then, rock and roll culture has come to accept a premise already   14
in force in folk music and fine-art music, that the subject of music is the entire range of
human experience. Whereas many advocates welcomed this openness in the spirit of uncen-
sored expression and as evidence of the music's "coming of age," opponents redoubled
their efforts and publicized their genuine horror, all the while repeating their time-honored
battle cry that the personal and public behavior of young Americans is influenced directly
and in the most negative way by experiencing this repertory of song. Much criticism, ranging from thoughtful to hysterical, has been focused on a cult of violence initially associated with the 1970s subcategories of punk and heavy metal and more recently with gangsta
rap[8] and the "hate" rock of white supremacist groups. For decades, feminists have been
especially outspoken in condemning misogynist words, images, and actions that have found
a home in the male-dominated world of rock and roll.[9] It is, of course, impossible to defend
a music that serves as an intentional vehicle of evil and hatred, but it also seems reasonable to believe that popular music can reflect as a faithful mirror not only the flaws of
human nature but also socially constructed racism, fascism, sexism, anti-Semitism, elit-
ism, and other plagues at work in contemporary culture.

In spite of the big-business packaging, there is, probably, no better record of what has   15
concerned American teenagers in the second half of the twentieth century than rock and
roll. From its commercial beginnings, it remains a music with an attitude, purposefully at
odds with authority figures and social prescriptions. And, just as important, these concerns

---

[8]*See, for example, Ronin Ro,* Gangsta: Merchandising the Rhymes of Violence *(New York: St. Martin's Press,
1996).*
[9]*An early example is Marion Meade, "Does Rock Degrade Women?"* New York Times II *(14 Mar. 1971), 13,
22.*

have often been communicated, without apology or embarrassment, in the common language of teenagers intent on carving out a meaningful identity for themselves and their peers. Although still shocking in some quarters, moreover, the casual use of profanities, the graphic references to sexual behaviors and drug use, and the open attacks on other cultural "sacred cows" have not been exclusive to rock and roll.

Because of its essential commercial application in American popular culture as dance-related song (the demand for new product) and because of the need of each new generation of American youth to identify itself musically according to its own terms, the history of rock and roll has unfolded in an often confusing succession of substyles or subgenres that represent a broad range of expression. Although it is useful to appreciate such diversity under the umbrella of rock-related popular music, such subcategories have always represented meaningful distinctions to connoisseurs, and, in fact, a number of them can be described rather discretely in musical and sociological terms. It is important to understand whether a particular "movement" uses the urban blues, the Anglo-American ballad, or the mainstream popular song as its point of departure. Was the music, for example, created by ambitious young Southerners with a first-hand knowledge of minority music, by middle-class African-American talents from Detroit groomed for entertainment glory, by turned-on and tuned-in Bohemians in San Francisco with a Counterculture agenda, or by the rappers of America's inner-cities caught "between the outlaw culture of the streets and the hardcore taste of the music business"?[10] It is, likewise, instructive to construct a profile of representative groups of musicians and to place their accomplishments in context.

The contributions of African-American musicians have always represented a vital force in this music's history. From the time of slavery, musical expression has served an especially significant purpose in black America as a means of communicating, preserving, and renewing a cultural identity under miserable social conditions. It is surely no coincidence that the most far-reaching influences of African-American music-making—in the form of rock and roll—occurred in American society at the same time that the greatest strides were being made in the energizing struggle for civil rights. African-American musicians such as Chuck Berry, Little Richard, Fats Domino, and Bo Diddley defined the early rock and roll style of the 1950s, just as their successors carried their community's musical banner forward to create soul of the 1960s, funk of the 1970s, and hip-hop of the 1980s. The power of such music attracted many white listeners as well. It also provided compelling models for both exploitation and genuine imitation by legions of white musicians. The careers of Elvis Presley, Janis Joplin, and the Rolling Stones, to cite a few of the most obvious, would be unthinkable without the examples of African-American musicians.

As the twentieth century reaches its end, the circumstances surrounding rock and roll are more complicated than ever and as controversial as ever. The tradition appears more fragmented than before because of the preservation of historical styles alongside interest in newer ones and because of the participation of various constituencies of performers and listeners representing various ages and lifestyles. There is one aspect of the tradition, however, that remains unchanged: the music created by young Americans for young Americans

16

17

18

---

[10]Martha Bayles, Hole in Our Soul: The Loss of Beauty and Meaning in American Popular Music (New York: Free Press, 1994; reprinted Chicago: University of Chicago Press, 1996), 355.

continues to alarm, shock, and challenge the social code; its opponents are just as prepared as ever to voice their own outrage, to wage their holy war, and to fight for censorship.

READING FOR INFORMATION

1. Who is Pablo Casals, the source of the quotation that begins Budds's piece?
2. According to Budds, how do generational differences influence perceptions of rock and roll?
3. According to Budds, how did class differences influence perceptions of rock and roll?
4. In the 1950s, why was rock and roll perceived as a threat?
5. What factors explain the "radical change in musical taste" (paragraph 7) that expanded the audience for rock and roll?
6. What is Tin Pan Alley?
7. How does Budds contrast the lyrics of Tin Pan Alley songs with rock and roll lyrics?
8. What does Budds mean when he says in paragraph 14 that "the subject of music is the entire range of human experience"? How does this position differ from that of Tin Pan Alley lyricists?
9. Why does Budds feel that rock music is important to the study of history?

READING FOR FORM, ORGANIZATION, AND FEATURES

1. How do the two opening quotations work together to introduce Budds's topic?
2. Although Budds is writing about popular culture, what aspects of his essay suggest that it is written for an academic audience?
3. What characteristics of Budds's piece might make it difficult reading for people without an education in music?

READING FOR RHETORICAL CONCERNS

1. What is Budds's attitude toward rock music? Would you say he is a rock fan? Explain your answer.
2. Do you think Budds cares whether or not his audience likes rock music? Explain your answer.
3. What impact does Budds intend to have on his reader?
4. Budds's essay was originally published in an anthology that focused on censorship of rock and rap. How do you think Budds would stand on pop music censorship? Explain your answer.

WRITING ASSIGNMENTS

1. Use Budds's essay to help you analyze the differences between your own musical tastes and those of a parent or another person who is much older than you are. Write a 750-word essay.

2. Summarize in 500 words Budds's explanation of why rock and roll is controversial. Write for an audience that may not appreciate rock and roll.

3. Summarize in 750 words Budds's account of how musical tastes of young Americans evolved in the second half of the twentieth century. Write for an audience that is not knowledgeable about pop music.

. . . .

WRITING ASSIGNMENTS FOR CHAPTER 11

1. Synthesize material from the readings in this chapter, and include references to specific songs as you analyze objectively your own tastes in popular music. This assignment does not ask you to defend your tastes. Your goal is to account for your musical tastes, not to convince the reader to adopt your perspective. Write an essay of around 1,250 words.

2. Write a 1,250-word essay that analyzes the extent to which our musical tastes are personal choices and the extend to which they are shaped by society. Draw on at least three of the reading selections in this chapter.

3. Write a 1,000-word essay that compares and contrasts popular music you like with popular music you can't stand. Draw on at least three of the readings in this chapter as you identify the aspects of music that you either like or dislike.

4. Draw on at least three readings in this chapter as you describe and account for the musical tastes of your parent or parents. Write an essay of at least 1,000 words.

5. To what extent are musical tastes a part of our personal identities? Answer this question in an essay of 1,000 words that draws on at least two of the chapter readings.

6. Use at least two of the readings in this chapter to explain how your own musical tastes have changed over time. Write an essay of at least 1,000 words.

7. Are efforts to restrict rock music that is obscene or contains antisocial messages legitimate, or are they an attempt to impose the tastes of the older generation on young people? Write a 1,250-word essay that answers this question and draws on at least two of the readings in this chapter.

12

EUTHANASIA AND PHYSICIAN-ASSISTED SUICIDE

The World War II movie *Saving Private Ryan* contains a graphic scene in which a severely wounded soldier is given a lethal dose of morphine to end his suffering. That scene illustrates that the practice of euthanasia, or mercy killing, has over the years been accepted in certain contexts as preferable to a painful death. These mercy killings, whether they occurred on the battlefield or in a hospital ward, were usually kept quiet by witnesses, families, and physicians and were for the most part ignored by law enforcement officials and the courts. However, Dr. Jack Kevorkian, who assisted in numerous patient suicides during the 1990s and publicized each one, forced Americans to face the issue head on and ended the silence surrounding mercy killing. In 1997, the Supreme Court ruled that Americans did not have a constitutional right to assisted suicide, and in March 1999, Dr. Kevorkian was convicted of second-degree murder for helping a patient die. Kevorkian was subsequently sentenced to ten to twenty-five years in prison.

Though recent court decisions have gone against euthanasia and physician-assisted suicide, the debate over the issue, which is actually centuries old, continues. The readings in this chapter illustrate the wide range of viewpoints on this matter. "It's Over, Debbie," which was published anonymously in the *Journal of the American Medical Association*, describes an allegedly true incident in which a doctor intentionally ended the life of a young patient who was suffering horribly with terminal cancer. In his article "In Defense of Voluntary Euthanasia," Sidney Hook, a stroke survivor, explains why he should have been allowed to die as he wished to rather than undergo a painful recovery that was burdensome to others. Ernest van den Haag argues in "Make Mine Hemlock" that neither physicians nor the government should be allowed to interfere in a patient's decision to die. The potential dangers of legalizing mercy killing are pointed out in Rand Richards Cooper's "The Dignity of Helplessness: What Sort of Society Would Euthanasia Create?" Cooper believes that if we accept mercy killing as a solution to suffering, we may begin to dehumanize the sick and the handicapped. Finally, Charles Krauthammer, in "First and Last, Do No Harm," maintains that physicians who assist in suicides violate the most basic value of their profession, that of preserving life.

It's Over, Debbie

Anonymous

This article was published anonymously in the Journal of the American Medical Association.

P r e r e a d i n g ....

Think of a time that you were face to face with a person who was either very ill or disabled. If you traded places with that individual, would your live be worthwhile? Freewrite for ten minutes in response to this question.

• • • • • • • • • • • • • • •

The call came in the middle of the night. As a gynecology resident rotating through a large, private hospital, I had come to detest telephone calls, because invariably I would be up for several hours and would not feel good the next day. However, duty called, so I answered the phone. A nurse informed me that a patient was having difficulty getting rest, could I please see her. She was on 3 North. That was the gynecologic oncology unit, not my usual duty station. As I trudged along, bumping sleepily against walls and corners and not believing I was up again, I tried to imagine what I might find at the end of my walk. Maybe an elderly woman with an anxiety reaction, or perhaps something particularly horrible.

I grabbed the chart from the nurses' station on my way to the patient's room, and the nurse gave me some hurried details: a 20-year-old girl named Debbie was dying of ovarian cancer. She was having unrelenting vomiting apparently as the result of an alcohol drip administered for sedation. Hmmm, I thought. Very sad. As I approached the room I could hear loud, labored breathing. I entered and saw an emaciated, dark-haired woman who appeared much older than 20. She was receiving nasal oxygen, had an IV, and was sitting in bed suffering from what was obviously severe air hunger. The chart noted her weight at 80 pounds. A second woman, also dark-haired but of middle age, stood at her right, holding her hand. Both looked up as I entered. The room seemed filled with the patient's desperate effort to survive. Her eyes were hollow, and she had suprasternal and intercostal retractions with her rapid inspirations. She had not eaten or slept in two days. She had not responded to chemotherapy and was being given supportive care only. It was a gallows scene, a cruel mockery of her youth and unfulfilled potential. Her only words to me were, "Let's get this over with."

I retreated with my thoughts to the nurses' station. The patient was tired and needed rest. I could not give her health, but I could give her rest. I asked the nurse to draw 20 mg of morphine sulfate into a syringe. Enough, I thought, to do the job. I took the syringe into the room and told the two women I was going to give Debbie something that would let her rest and to say good-bye. Debbie looked at the syringe, then laid her head in the pillow with her eyes open, watching what was left of the world. I injected the morphine intravenously and watched to see if my calculations on its effects would be correct. Within seconds her breathing slowed to a normal rate, her eyes closed, and her features softened as she seemed restful at last. The older woman stroked the hair of the now-sleeping patient. I waited for the inevitable next effect of depressing the respiratory drive. With clocklike certainty, within four minutes the breathing rate slowed even more, then became irregular, then ceased. The dark-haired woman stood erect and seemed relieved.

It's over, Debbie.   4

READING FOR INFORMATION

1. The author identifies herself or himself as a "gynecology resident" in a hospital. What, exactly, is a resident in that context?
2. Describe the young patient's medical condition.
3. What does the patient request?
4. In the third paragraph, what does the physician mean by the phrase "Enough, I thought, to do the job"?
5. What is the effect of the morphine sulfate on the patient?

READING FOR FORM, ORGANIZATION, AND FEATURES

1. How does the idea of sleep or rest unify the piece?
2. What is the effect of the phrase "Hmmm, I thought. Very sad," which appears in the second paragraph?
3. Why doesn't the author identify the "second woman" in the hospital room?
4. What is the effect of the final sentence in the piece?

READING FOR RHETORICAL CONCERNS

1. How does the fact that the piece is published anonymously affect your response to it?
2. What do you think the author intends to accomplish?
3. The *Journal of the American Medical Association* is intended for an audience of physicians. How do you think medical doctors would respond to the article?

WRITING ASSIGNMENTS

1. In a 750-word essay, argue for or against the physician's choice to administer a lethal dose of morphine to the patient.
2. Write a 250-word summary of the article for an audience of students who have not read the original piece.
3. In a 750-word essay, analyze the ethical dimensions of the situation described in the article. Make sure you consider the role of the physician, the patient, and the unidentified "second woman."

• • • • • • • • • • • • • • • • •

In Defense of Voluntary Euthanasia

Sidney Hook

Sidney Hook was a philosophy professor at New York University and published widely on a range of social issues. Among his books are Academic Freedom and Academic Anarchy, Common Sense and the Fifth Amendment, From Hegel to Marx, *and* The Paradoxes of Freedom.

Prereading ··

What does the expression "voluntary euthanasia" mean to you? Freewrite for ten minutes in response to this question.

· · · · · · · · · · · · · · · ·

A few short years ago, I lay at the point of death. A congestive heart failure was treated for diagnostic purposes by an angiogram that triggered a stroke. Violent and painful hiccups, uninterrupted for several days and nights, prevented the ingestion of food. My left side and one of my vocal cords became paralyzed. Some form of pleurisy set in, and I felt I was drowning in a sea of slime. At one point, my heart stopped beating; just as I lost consciousness, it was thumped back into action again. In one of my lucid intervals during those days of agony, I asked my physician to discontinue all life-supporting services or show me how to do it. He refused and predicted that some day I would appreciate the unwisdom of my request.   *1*

A month later, I was discharged from the hospital. In six months, I regained the use of my limbs, and although my voice still lacks its old resonance and carrying power I no longer croak like a frog. There remain some minor disabilities and I am restricted to a rigorous, low-sodium diet. I have resumed my writing and research.   *2*

My experience can be and has been cited as an argument against honoring requests of stricken patients to be gently eased out of their pain and life. I cannot agree. There are two main reasons. As an octogenarian, there is a reasonable likelihood that I may suffer another "cardiovascular accident" or worse. I may not even be in a position to ask for the surcease of pain. It seems to me that I have already paid my dues to death—indeed, although time has softened my memories they are vivid enough to justify my saying that I suffered enough to warrant dying several times over. Why run the risk of more?   *3*

Secondly, I dread imposing on my family and friends another grim round of misery similar to the one my first attack occasioned.   *4*

My wife and children endured enough for one lifetime. I know that for them the long days and nights of waiting, the disruption of their professional duties and their own familiar responsibilities counted for nothing in their anxiety for me. In their joy at my recovery they have been forgotten. Nonetheless, to visit another prolonged spell of help-less suffering on them as my life ebbs away, or even worse, if I linger on into a comatose senility, seems altogether gratuitous.   *5*

But what, it may be asked, of the joy and satisfaction of living, of basking in the sunshine, listening to music, watching one's grandchildren growing into adolescence,   *6* following the news about the fate of freedom in a troubled world, playing with ideas, writing one's testament of wisdom and folly for posterity? Is not all that one endured, together with the risk of its recurrence, an acceptable price for the multiple satisfactions that are still open even to a person of advanced years?

Apparently those who cling to life no matter what think so. I do not.   7

The zest and intensity of these experiences are no longer what they used to be. I am   8
not vain enough to delude myself that I can in the few remaining years make an important discovery useful for mankind or can lead a social movement or do anything that will be historically eventful, no less event-making. My autobiography, which describes a record of intellectual and political experiences of some historical value, already much too long, could be posthumously published. I have had my fill of joys and sorrows and am not greedy for more life. I have always thought that a test of whether one had found happiness in one's life is whether one would be willing to relive it—whether, if it were possible, one would accept the opportunity to be born again.

Having lived a full and relatively happy life, I would cheerfully accept the chance to   9
be reborn, but certainly not to be reborn again as an infirm octogenarian. To some extent, my views reflect what I have seen happen to the aged and stricken who have been so unfortunate as to survive crippling paralysis. They suffer, and impose suffering on others, unable even to make a request that their torment be ended.

I am mindful too of the burdens placed upon the community, with its rapidly diminishing resources, to provide the adequate and costly services necessary to sustain the lives   10
of those whose days and nights are spent on mattress graves of pain. A better use could be made of these resources to increase the opportunities and qualities of life for the young. I am not denying the moral obligation the community has to look after its disabled and aged. There are times, however, when an individual may find it pointless to insist on the fulfillment of a legal and moral right.

What is required is no great revolution in morals but an enlargement of imagination   11
and an intelligent evaluation of alternative uses of community resources.

Long ago, Seneca observed that "the wise man will live as long as he ought, not as   12
long as he can." One can envisage hypothetical circumstances in which one has a duty to prolong one's life despite its costs for the sake of others, but such circumstances are far removed from the ordinary prospects we are considering. If wisdom is rooted in knowledge of the alternatives of choice, it must be reliably informed of the state one is in and its likely outcome. Scientific medicine is not infallible, but it is the best we have. Should a rational person be willing to endure acute suffering merely on the chance that a miraculous cure might presently be at hand? Each one should be permitted to make his own choice—especially when no one else is harmed by it.

The responsibility for the decision, whether deemed wise or foolish, must be with the   13
chooser.

READING FOR INFORMATION

1. Describe the initial effects of Hook's stroke.
2. How does Hook view his physician's refusal to stop life support in the wake of Hook's stroke?

3. What factors lead Hook to the conclusion that the costs of surviving a severe stroke do not outweigh the benefits?
4. How does Hook view the possibility of rebirth?
5. According to Hook, what is society's obligation to the disabled or dying?
6. According to Hook, does a suffering person have any obligation to live? What is Hook's rationale for this position?
7. Who is Seneca, whom Hook refers to in paragraph 12?

READING FOR FORM, ORGANIZATION, AND FEATURES

1. Explain Hook's opening strategy.
2. Why do you think Hook chose to separate rather than merge paragraphs 4 and 5?
3. Comment on Hook's choice to end his essay with a one-sentence paragraph.

READING FOR RHETORICAL CONCERNS

1. How does Hook's status as a stroke victim affect the credibility of his article?
2. How might each of the following audiences respond to Hook's argument: elderly people; young, disabled individuals; the grown children of elderly people; the parents of disabled infants; and physicians who care for disabled or elderly patients?
3. Is Hook writing primarily to justify his own opinion or to encourage others to adopt his viewpoint? Explain your answer.

WRITING ASSIGNMENTS

1. Hook closes his piece with the following statement: "The responsibility for the decision, whether deemed wise or foolish, must be with the chooser." Write a 750-word essay in response to this statement that focuses on moral and ethical issues.
2. Write a 750-word analysis of Hook's position from the perspective of the physician who refused to stop life support for Hook.
3. Write a 500-word summary of Hook's article that emphasizes the moral and ethical dimensions of his position.

Make Mine Hemlock

Ernest van den Haag

Ernest van den Haag has been a professor of economics at New York University and a professor of law at Fordham University. Among his books are The Death Penalty: A Debate, Passion and Social Constraint, Political Violence and Civil Disobedience, *and* Punishing Criminals: A Very Old and Painful Question.

Prereading ....

Throughout van den Haag's essay, he discusses religious prohibitions against suicide. For ten minutes, freewrite about your prior knowledge of how religions view suicide.

• • • • • • • • • • • • • • • •

Before Christianity, governments were unconcerned with suicide, which was thought expedient in some circumstances and required by honor in others. However, with the coming of Christianity suicide became a sin, a violation of God's commandments. As unrepentant sinners, suicides were denied burial in consecrated ground and expected to end in Hell. Life was thought to be a gift from God, Who ordained its beginning and end. We possessed the life created by Him, but He owned it. Our possession could not license us to destroy what did not belong to us.

As the grip of Christianity weakened, this part of religion was secularized, as were many others. Suicide became a transgression against nature, not God, usually explained by mental derangement. Absent derangement, suicide was considered a crime against society, thought to own individuals more or less as God had been thought to before. Only in our time has it come to be believed that individuals collectively own society, rather than vice versa. They also are thought to own themselves. Without God (or slavery) no one else really could. Owners can dispose of what they own as they see fit. We thus each become entitled to control our life, including its duration, to the extent nature permits, provided that this control does not harm others in ways proscribed by law.

Very few people are inclined to commit suicide. But this hardly seems a good reason to prevent it, although sometimes it is asserted or implied that the unpopularity of suicide argues for its immorality and for preventing it. Yet, those who do not wish, or do not feel they have the moral right to, end their life can easily refrain. It is not clear on what grounds a government, or anyone else, could be entitled to prevent a competent person from controlling the duration of his or her life.

Although the foregoing view seems irrefutable, not everyone accepts it. It is contrary to tradition, wherefore many obstacles remain in the way of people who try to shorten their life. These obstacles can be nearly insurmountable for those who most wish to do so because of a disabling disease. They may be forced to go on living against their will. Even some healthy persons find the obstacles quite forbidding. They may have to jump out of windows, or use drugs which are difficult to obtain and of the specific effects of which they are not fully

1

2

3

4

Ernest van den Haag. "Make Mine Hemlock." *National Review* 12 June 1995: 60–62. © 1995 by National Review, Inc., *www.nationalreview.com*. Reprinted by permission.

informed. Physicians and other experts, who do know the proper combination and quantities of drugs needed, usually refuse help, either because of moral objections or in fear of legal liabilities. They impose their own socially supported moral beliefs on patients who do not share them, but cannot act unaided. Dr. Jack Kevorkian is a rare and courageous exception.

To be sure, compassionate physicians may feel that terminal patients in extreme pain should be helped to end such pain. They may discreetly prescribe anesthetics which end suffering by ending life. There have been no successful prosecutions for this quasi-legal practice, although some unsuccessful ones have been brought and physicians who prescribe painkillers in the required quantities assume some risk. Physicians also may withhold life-prolonging treatment at the directions of patients or of legal guardians. Patients do have a legal right to refuse any treatment—though the extent of that right is not well defined. However, merely withholding treatment still may lead to an unnecessarily prolonged, stressful, and perhaps painful way of dying.

Even physicians such as Dr. Kevorkian, willing to take major legal risks, have helped only patients who were incurable and, in most cases, had reached a terminal stage. This takes the decision on whether to end life out of the hands of a mentally competent patient and places it into the hands of a physician, who must decide that the patient is terminal enough, or has suffered enough, before helping him to die. He may also refuse to help at all.

Giving physicians (or any other persons) the authority to veto a patient's decision seems unwarranted. Physicians are trained in how to treat diseases so as to prolong life. They are not experts on whether or not to prolong it. There is no training for making such a decision. Indeed, physicians are taught (*primum non laedere*) always to prolong life. No respect is instilled for the patient's wishes, if he prefers to shorten his life. Yet, whether and when to end a person's life is a moral, not a medical, decision, for the patient to make, not the doctor. The physician's task is to inform the patient of his prognosis, perhaps to advise him, and, above all, to help him carry out his decision.

Imagine a 20-year-old patient hospitalized for a condition which, although incurable, is neither terminal nor acutely painful. In the patient's rational, carefully considered view his condition denies him the pleasures of life. He wants to die, but needs assistance. Since he is neither terminal nor suffering unbearable pain, most physicians would be unwilling to help and would run a major legal risk if they did. Again, imagine a 90-year-old who feels that life is of no further interest to him, although he is neither terminal nor in pain. He too will find it hard to persuade a physician to help him die if he cannot do so by himself.

For good or bad reasons, people commit suicide every day. Since many would-be suicides act on impulses which may turn out to be temporary, forcing a moderate delay seems in their interest and legitimate—but is not to be confused with preclusion. Imagine now a healthy young man who, perhaps influenced by Arthur Schopenhauer's philosophy, has decided to commit suicide. Before he has a chance to kill himself, a traffic accident leaves him paralyzed and hospitalized, incurable but not terminal. He now has additional reasons to end his life but is less able, perhaps altogether unable, to do so unless aided. Although we do not make it easy, we cannot prevent an able person from ending his life anytime he wants to. But we can prevent a disabled person from doing the same. Thus we add to the disability nature or accident has inflicted.

This seems odd because our compassionate society usually goes out of its way to help the disabled overcome whatever handicaps are in the way of their desires. Employers are legally compelled to hire disabled persons, schools to make special arrangements to teach them. Public buildings and transportation are made accessible to the wheelchair-bound. Yet, when it comes to suicide, we refuse to allow any assistance to the disabled. We exploit their disability to prevent them from doing what able-bodied persons can do. On all other occasions we try to compensate for the disadvantages nature inflicts on some. Yet when assistance is essential to enable the disabled to commit suicide, we threaten to prosecute anyone who helps them.

Despite the receding influence of religious ideas and our official unwillingness to impose them, and despite the precariousness of the notion that society has a compelling interest in preventing suicide, we continue to treat life as a social duty that individuals, however disabled, should not be helped to shirk. It is not clear to whom the duty to live could be owed. Once the government no longer legally recognizes God as the authority to which duties are owed, nature cannot have prescriptive authority to force unwilling persons to live, since such authority would have to come from God. Only society is left as the source of this alleged duty. But society cannot be shown to have a compelling interest in forcing persons to live against their will. Moreover, such an interest would hardly justify the cruelty involved. To be sure, the great majority has an instinctive wish to live. But why should we enforce the gratification of this wish on those who, for whatever reason, decide not to gratify it?   *11*

A Right to Die?

Since, from a secular viewpoint, the moral right to die can hardly be less fundamental than the moral right to live, our non-recognition of the former must flow from unacknowledged residual theological notions which we have officially renounced imposing on non-believers. Dimly realizing as much, most persons opposed to assistance in suicide tend to avoid moral arguments in favor of prudential arguments. These are of two kinds. The first questions the mental competence of individuals who want to hasten their death. The second questions the disinterestedness of persons willing to help them. We must also deal with questions about ending the life of persons who are in a terminal phase of disease, but not mentally competent to make decisions, and of persons in a permanent coma. These are particularly sticky questions, since ending the life of these two classes of patients would be homicide, justifiable or not, rather than suicide, since, by definition, the patients do not make the decision themselves.   *12*

How can we assess the mental competence of a physically disabled person who decides on suicide? The task is daunting but not impossible. First of all, prejudicial notions must be discarded. A patient who wants his life ended need not be mentally sick, clinically depressed, or temporarily deranged. The idea that he must be mentally sick merely justifies a conclusion foreordained by circular reasoning. Having discarded prejudicial notions, psychiatrists, using their customary methods, can ascertain whether the patient knows who and where he is, and whether his mental processes are realistic and logical to the normal degree. A conversation about what led to his decision is apposite as well. Reasonable opponents of suicide, religious or not, may be invited to participate where feasible. (The whole process could be videotaped if the patient's competence is controversial.) Beyond the judgment of the psychiatrist, based on these data, nothing is needed. The patient's decision should be accepted.   *13*

Intellectual competence is to be investigated, not what is sometimes referred to as   *14* emotional health. "Emotional health" is not a clinical concept, but a moral concept quite amorphous and subject to fashion. It allows the imposition of moral views on a patient who may be diagnosed as emotionally ill if he does not share them.

How can we make sure that no one will be pressed to end his or her life by self-interested relatives, friends, enemies, or caretakers? What about undue influence? Safeguards have long been developed to make sure that a patient's decisions about his last will are uncontaminated. These safeguards can be used as well to ensure that his decision about assisted suicide is independent. Where there are problems with the medical prognosis on which the patient's decision may depend, these must be dealt with by means of second or third opinions.   15

As for the terminal patient who is incompetent or unconscious, if he has provided instructions while competent, they should be followed. If he has not, the decision of relatives and legal guardians must be followed, unless there is evidence to make them suspect. If the situation is cloudy (or if the patient has no relatives) the hospital could name someone, preferably a physician familiar with the patient's syndrome, but practicing elsewhere, to make the decision. If his prognosis and decision agree with those of the treating physician there is no problem. If not, the two physicians will have to ask a third physician willing to decide within 36 hours. Decisions should be independent of the views of hospital administrators and allow ending life when there is no chance of regaining consciousness.   16

Sometimes an analogy between assisted suicide and abortion is suggested. Indeed, opponents of one usually oppose the other as well; in both cases the opposition may ultimately rest on traditional religious ideas even if the opponents are not religious. But the analogy is misleading. Abortion destroys a fetus with the consent of the mother and usually reflects her interests. The fetus does not make the decision and cannot be consulted. Conceivably the fetus could have an interest in survival. If allowed to develop, the fetus may be expected to desire and enjoy life. In contrast, assisted suicide shortens the life of a patient who has decided himself that prolongation does not serve his interests. Surely, the normal fetus could not be assumed to have an interest in self-destruction. The suicidal patient does. (Conflicts about abortion usually are about alleged fetal [versus] alleged maternal rights, with some denying fetal rights. But no one would deny that suicide patients are persons who have rights.)   17

Most arguments about assisted suicide can be dealt with in a reasonable, if not perfect, way. However, the "slippery slope" argument, though influential, is hard to deal with rationally. It suggests that, once we allow doctors to shorten the life of patients who request it, doctors could and would wantonly kill burdensome patients who do not want to die. This suggestion is not justified. The specter of Nazi practices is usually raised to make it credible. But Nazi practices were imposed on physicians and hospitals by political directives which did not evolve from any prior authority given physicians to assist in suicide. There was no "slippery slope." Nor can it be found elsewhere in medical practice. Physicians often prescribe drugs which, in doses greater than prescribed, would kill the patient. No one fears that the actual doses prescribed will lead to the use of lethal doses. No one objects to such prescriptions in fear of a "slippery slope." The "slippery slope" idea seems fortunately to be an unrealistic nightmare. Authorizing physicians to assist in shortening the life of patients who request this assistance no more implies authority to shorten the life of patients who want to prolong it, than authority for surgery to remove the gall bladder implies authority to remove the patient's heart.   18

READING FOR INFORMATION

1. According to van den Haag, how did the spread of Christianity affect the way governments viewed suicide?

2. Explain how religious prohibitions against suicide were, according to van den Haag, eventually "secularized."

3. Who is Dr. Jack Kevorkian?

4. What social pressures does van den Haag believe keep physicians from assisting in suicides?

5. According to van den Haag, why is it inappropriate to give physicians the power to determine whether or not to prolong life?

6. For what reasons does van den Haag claim that prohibiting suicide is discriminatory against the disabled?

7. How does van den Haag respond to the notion that patients who choose to die are, by definition, mentally ill?

8. How does van den Haag suggest that decisions about ending or prolonging life should be made for patients who are incapable of judgment?

9. Why does van den Haag think assisted suicide is fundamentally different from abortion?

READING FOR FORM, ORGANIZATION, AND FEATURES

1. What is the function of the historical background information that van den Haag provides at the beginning of his article?

2. What type of evidence does van den Haag provide to support his argument?

3. Why does van den Haag use a subheading after paragraph 11?

4. Comment on van den Haag's closing paragraph.

READING FOR RHETORICAL CONCERNS

1. How do you think religious Christians would respond to the first two paragraphs of van den Haag's article? Does van den Haag take this potential response into account?

2. Imagine that you are a medical doctor who has just read van den Haag's article. Are you offended that he wants to strip away some of your authority to decide what is best for your patients, or are you pleased that he wants to relieve you of the moral responsibility for difficult decisions?

3. To what extent does van den Haag engage the viewpoints of those who favor prohibition on suicide?

WRITING ASSIGNMENTS

1. Write a 750-word essay in response to the following statement taken from the third paragraph of van den Haag's article: "It is not clear on what grounds a government, or anyone else, could be entitled to prevent a competent person from controlling the duration of his or her life."

2. Write a 750-word argument essay that either supports or refutes van den Haag's implication that suicide should be prohibited by law or by the medical community.

3. Assume the role of a lawyer who represents the American Medical Association. Draw on van den Haag's article to write a 750-word proposal that outlines the position you believe the AMA should take on physician-assisted suicide.

● ● ● ● ● ● ● ● ● ● ● ● ● ● ●

The Dignity of Helplessness:
What Sort of Society Would Euthanasia Create?

Rand Richards Cooper

Rand Richards Cooper is the author of two novels, The Last to Go *and* As Big as Life, *as well as numerous pieces for national magazines.*

P r e r e a d i n g ●

As the first paragraph of his article indicates, Cooper is writing prior to Dr. Kevorkian's conviction and imprisonment in 1999 for injecting lethal drugs into a disabled man who asked to die. Do you think Dr. Kevorkian deserved to go to prison? Freewrite in response to this question for ten minutes.

● ● ● ● ● ● ● ● ● ● ● ● ● ● ●

I'm looking for an argument with Jack Kevorkian; or rather, for one against him. Life for   *1*
Kevorkian lately has come laden with satisfying vindications. Weary prosecutors, having failed to convince three Michigan juries that Kevorkian's eagerness in assisting suicide is a crime, now seem ready to toss in their cards and go home. Once dubbed "Dr. Death" by medical school classmates for his unseemly obsession with terminal illness, the ex-pathologist stands redeemed and embraced as a pioneering American hero. "Jack's doing something that is right," says his lawyer, Geoffrey Fieger. "Everyone instinctively understands that—that's why we're winning."

Whatever you may feel about Kevorkian personally—and I admit to finding him an   *2*
unlikely standard-bearer, with his smug and aggressive looniness, for a human dignity movement—you have to admire how deftly he has taken the pulse of the nation's moral reasoning. Kevorkian has put our agonized ambivalence about life-prolonging medical technologies into the rights-based framework of our political discourse, producing a case for assisted suicide that seems unassailable. Its logic goes like this: If I am afflicted, say, with inoperable cancer, and if after discussions with loved ones I decide I would rather die now, in dignity, than a year from now, why shouldn't I have this right? How does my exercising it conceivably impair the rights of any other person?

It doesn't, say the juries who keep acquitting Kevorkian; that's why the government   *3*
should butt out. Whose death is it, anyway?

Rand Richards Cooper. "The Dignity of Helplessness: What Sort of Society Would Euthanasia Create?" *Commonweal* 25 Oct. 1996: 12–15.

As a means of sparing loved ones suffering, assisted suicide expresses our most compassionate urges and motives. Nevertheless, I believe the notion of a "right" to die provides far too narrow a framework for discussing the widespread institutionalization of the practice. Talk about rights resonates deeply with Americans. It is our strongest political instinct; our melody and our beat. Other societies stress sacrifice or obedience, glory or passion or style or work, but we always come back to rights. And therein lies the rub. The appeal of rights is so compelling that it leaves scant room for realities and interests not easily expressed as rights. And with assisted suicide that means leaving out way too much.   4

Consider the predicament of the elderly. Kevorkian pledges himself to "the absolute autonomy of the individual," and insists that practitioners of "obitiatry" (as he proposed calling the new medical specialty) would administer only to those who truly want to die. But what exactly is the "absolute autonomy" of an elderly, ailing person convinced he or she is a burden to everyone? I remember how my grandmother, who died a few years ago at ninety-seven, used to lament being a "burden" on the rest of us. "I don't know why I'm still alive," she'd say, sighing. She didn't really mean it; but there's no doubt in my mind that the obitiatric option, had it existed, would have added an extra tinge of guilt to her last couple of years—particularly after she entered a nursing home whose costs began to eat up the savings she and my grandfather had accumulated over decades of thrift. Do we want to do that to our elderly and infirm? How will we prevent the creep toward an increased sense of burdensomeness that the very availability of assisted suicide is likely to cause?   5

Next, what about creeping changes in the rest of us? In a society in which assisted suicide is a ready option, how will we view those who don't choose it? I'm imagining Ben Jonson's grim sixteenth-century farce *Volpone*, updated for our time, a circle of heirs crowding round the bedside, impatient for the obitioner. But I'm also thinking about something far subtler, that gradual habituation of mind Tocqueville called the "slow action of society upon itself." Much as we like to imagine otherwise, the truth is that our inventions and our beliefs are implacably dynamic. The things we make turn around and remake us; and just as the Pill helped transform our ideas about sexual freedom, so will the obitioner change the way we regard aging. How often in the assisted-suicide future will someone look at an elderly person and think, consciously or semiconsciously, "Gee, guess it's about time, huh?"   6

And do we want that?   7

Such questions find scant place in a discussion that focuses solely on the "autonomous" individual and his "right" to die. That's why I want to take Kevorkianism out of the discussion of individual rights and put it into a discussion of something I'll call, for want of a better phrase, the texture of civic life. By this I mean simply the thoughts we have in our heads about ourselves and one another; the shape and feel of our daily, moment-to-moment relations. Will institutionalizing assisted suicide equip us to be better human beings for each other, or will it unequip us?   8

When I was twenty I lived for a time in Kenya. One hot afternoon found me at a grade school in Nairobi, helping out at a fair for handicapped children. The event was under-staffed, and when after games and lunch the children started having to go to the bathroom, things got hectic. A clamorous line of kids in leg braces and primitive wheelchairs formed outside the single outhouse. They needed help getting in, help going and cleaning up afterward. I did what I could, but I was young and singularly unschooled in this kind of neediness. Vividly I recall a boy of ten who walked with two crutches, dragging useless legs behind   9 him. During the long wait he had defecated in his pants, and as I helped him to the outhouse door I retched, despite myself, at the stench and the stifling heat. Seeing my distress, another organizer, a thirtyish guy named Dennis, picked up the boy and swiftly carried him into the outhouse. I followed, watching as Dennis squatted before the boy, cleaning him with a towel, the boy looking up with a calm and patient expression.

That memory comes back to me whenever an acquaintance of mine—a man in his mid-sixties and in good health—outlines his game plan for old age. For him, goal number one is never, ever to become a helpless burden. "Once I start shitting my pants," he says, "that's it. Take me out and shoot me." I share his dread of becoming vulnerable, dependent, smelly; who doesn't? Yet at the same time I find myself looking back to that moment in the outhouse in Kenya, years ago. Helplessness was there, of course, and burden too, but beauty as well, so much so that I have never forgotten it—the helper and the helped joined in a mutual courage I could only hope some day to possess. *10*

My point is that we experience a profound aspect of our humanity precisely in our intimate and awful knowledge of each other's physical neediness; and further, that what we draw from this knowledge constitutes not only a spiritual good but a social good. If, following the quality-of-life, take-me-out-and-shoot-me principle, we end up using assisted suicide to preempt the infirmities of old age and terminal illness, how well equipped will we be to encounter infirmity elsewhere? How to become fluent in help if we have banished helplessness from our vocabulary? I'm thinking of the way we treat people in wheelchairs, people who can't feed themselves, whose bodies don't look or work "right." Taken together with prenatal genetic testing and selective abortion, might not assisted suicide further a gradual drift toward functionalism in our attitude to life? Societies that drift in this direction, as Germany did under the Nazis, instill in their citizens a visceral sense of the handicapped as a drain or drag on the healthy body of the rest of us: a pointless deformity; an un-luck; an un-person. Such attitudes are not spontaneous manifestations of evil. You have to train people to feel this way; but if you do, they will. *11*

A few years ago, my mother's lifelong best friend died at sixty of lung cancer. The last phase of Gretchen's life involved multiple surgeries, long hospital stays that sapped the will, and the disorienting pressures of pain and medication. For my mother, there was the anguish of watching a person she loved being overwhelmed by illness—an especially hard kind of sorrow. ("She's not there anymore," my mother would say after a bad visit.) But then came moments of joy—a visit or a phone call or a handwritten note in which, suddenly, Gretchen was there again, emerging by some grace from the fog of her illness to share with my mother an affirmation of how much they had loved and enjoyed each other through the decades of their friendship. *12*

My mother has a bulletin board in her kitchen where she tacks up cards, favorite maxims, snapshots, and the like. But she doesn't display the last few notes she got from Gretchen. Instead, she keeps them taped to the inside of a cabinet high over the stove. I suspect they are still too highly charged for her; too much suffering and beauty attach to them. *13*

Gretchen's illness is the kind on which Kevorkianism makes its core appeal—a remorseless, irreversible disease that steals a person from us bit by bit. Assisted suicide offers a way, in effect, to manage death so that it arrives before this insidious larceny has begun. As such it is an attempt to do people dignity—and our memories of them, too—by enabling them to go out whole. It's an option I imagine Gretchen might well have availed *14* herself of; my mother, for her part, came away from her friend's death with a firm belief in the rightness of assisted suicide.

And yet I think about those notes in her cabinet. It's hard to say this, but I believe that part of what makes them so profoundly meaningful to my mother is that they came from such a dark and pressured place, where Gretchen was not always the "same" Gretchen she had known. Finding her way back from that place to write those notes fashioned an understanding of courage which my mother carries with her today: the last of Gretchen's many gifts to her.   15

One needs to tread very softly here. Taken to extremes, the notion of a vested interest in each other's suffering becomes barbaric; and I don't want anyone to think I'm questioning the correctness of relieving misery and pain. In fact, it's not assisted suicide per se I'm questioning, which in other forms has long been practiced unofficially by physicians informing the gravely ill about lethal doses, turning off ventilators to "let nature take its course," and so on. It's the institutionalizing of the practice I'm wondering about, and its effect on our relation to the idea of suffering. If we make assisted suicide widely available, will we end up virtually eliminating that phase of life in which people are not whole, "not there"? If so, will we be a better, richer, more humane society for having done so?   16

I'm aware many will consider this a pernicious basis for discussing the legality of assisted suicide. The notion that our laws should promote virtues as well as protect rights is anathema to modern American political thought. But the idea of rights alone can't capture the complexity of our connectedness to one another, and anyone who insists exclusively on them can end up sounding weirdly hollow. It is the hollowness, in fact, of Jack Kevorkian himself. I watched him not long ago on "60 Minutes." Asked by Mike Wallace to discuss the ethics of abortion—he is vehemently prochoice—Kevorkian mulled it over for a moment, then responded in this way: "The autonomy of the fetus can never supersede the autonomy of the mother." Whatever you may think of Kevorkian, or of abortion, I think you'll agree that these are exceptionally arid terms with which to encounter complex human dilemmas. But in purest form they are the terms of rights.   17

Current debates about welfare reform, about drug policy, violence on TV, the legality of youth curfews and school uniforms: all suggest a growing urge in America, across the political spectrum, to move beyond laissez-faire liberalism—what political theorist Michael J. Sandel has called our modern "aspiration to neutrality"—toward some vision of the good. Whether you call this impulse communitarianism, republicanism, statecraft as soulcraft, or a concern for civic texture, what it means is making connections not only between laws and rights, but between laws and character—the kind and quality of citizen laws inevitably help produce. Where does assisted suicide fit in? Is it possible that accompanying and consoling those we love through grievous terminal illness constitutes one of the core experiences we need to have? That part of us, some quality of pity and compassion and terror and love, is reachable only by taking that awful journey? And if so, does the law have a role to play? Should laws, can laws, have a stake in our complexity—in the quality of our togetherness as well as the fact of our separateness?   18

For the last few months of her very long life, my grandmother lay in a nursing home, floating in and out of consciousness, largely unable to eat. She wasn't in pain, but clearly she no longer possessed the active, vigorous perception which I believe institutionalizing assisted suicide may ultimately lead us to establish as the bottom-line criterion for meaningful life among the aged and the ill. For my part, I'd been fearing my visits to her, worry-   19 ing that these last images of her diminished and helpless would later greedily elbow out other, happier memories. But this fear proved groundless. As it turns out, even those deeply unsettling moments when she looked more dead than alive and I barely recognized her, or when she unexpectedly squeezed my hand, as if sending a last, bodily message from some strange place between being and not-being—all of that forms part of the story of my grandmother that I carry with me; and I feel I am the richer for all of it, endowed with a more expansive vocabulary of body and spirit; and also a more intimate acquaintance with death, in all its mystery and terribleness.

Anyone who has accompanied someone through a terminal illness knows the solitariness of mortality—"the unknown," wrote English poet Edward Thomas shortly before his own death in World War I, "I must enter, and leave, alone." A sense of this deep privacy drives the right-to-die movement in America today. And yet to step outside the rights framework is to ask how institutionalizing assisted suicide will affect not only those who die, but those who live on; not only individuals, but society. The fact is, our deaths are both solo journeys toward an ultimate mystery and strands in the tapestries of each other's lives. Which side of this reality will we emphasize? Whose death is it, anyway? The debate about assisted suicide should begin at the place where that question ceases to be a rhetorical one.

20

READING FOR INFORMATION

1. How does Cooper characterize Kevorkian in paragraph 2?
2. According to Cooper, what is the logic behind Kevorkian's advocacy for the right to die?
3. In Cooper's opinion, what is unique about the American view of rights?
4. From Cooper's viewpoint, how will the acceptance of assisted suicide affect the way that old age is perceived in our society?
5. Summarize the lesson Cooper learned from the disabled boy in Kenya.
6. Summarize the lesson Cooper learned from the death of his mother's friend Gretchen.
7. In what ways does Cooper feel that the experience of death is not entirely private?
8. What does Cooper want to convey about his grandmother's death?

READING FOR FORM, ORGANIZATION, AND FEATURES

1. Why does Cooper open his article by explaining Kevorkian's success to date in advancing the case for assisted suicide?
2. What is the function of paragraphs 3 and 7?
3. How does Cooper use the idea of engaging in an "argument with Jack Kevorkian" to unify his essay?
4. Why does Cooper use examples from his personal experience to illustrate his point rather than references to published sources?

READING FOR RHETORICAL CONCERNS

1. Are you more affected by Cooper's examples from personal experience, such as the experience outlined in paragraph 9, or by his logical analysis, such as the point developed in paragraph 18?

2. Which of Cooper's examples do you respond to most strongly? Why?

3. How do you think Cooper wants his audience to respond to the last two sentences of his essay?

WRITING ASSIGNMENTS

1. Write a 500-word summary of Cooper's article for an audience of pre-med students.

2. Write a 500-word response to the following question that Cooper poses in paragraph 11: "If, following the quality-of-life, take-me-out-and-shoot-me principle, we end up using assisted suicide to preempt the infirmities of old age and terminal illness, how well equipped will we be to encounter infirmity elsewhere?"

3. Write a 500-word essay that contrasts Cooper's viewpoint with that of Kevorkian.

· · · · · · · · · · · · · · ·

First and Last, Do No Harm

Charles Krauthammer

Charles Krauthammer is a journalist on the staff of Time.

Prereading ·

Doctors are trained to heal and save life. Do doctors violate those fundamental responsibilities when they assist in a suicide? Freewrite in response to this question for ten minutes.

· · · · · · · · · · · · · · ·

"**D**id you ask for your hemlock?" Thanks to appeals-court judges in New York and California, this question will now be in your future.   *1*

You will be old, infirm and, inevitably at some point, near death. You may or may   *2*
not be in physical distress, but in an age of crushing health-care costs, you will be a burden to your loved ones, to say nothing of society. And thanks to courts that back in 1996 legalized doctor-assisted suicide for the first time in American history, all around you thousands of your aging contemporaries will be taking their life.

You may want to live those last few remaining weeks or months. You may have no   *3*
intention of shortening your life. But now the question that before 1996 rarely arose—and when it did arise, only in the most hushed and guilty tones—will be raised routinely: Others are letting go; others are giving way; should not you too?

Of course, the judges who plumbed the depths of the Constitution to find the "right"   *4*
to physician-assisted suicide—a right unfindable for 200 years—deny the possibility to such a nightmare scenario. Psychological pressure on the elderly and infirm to take drugs to hasten death? Why, "there should be none," breezily decrees the Second Circuit Court of Appeals.

King Canute had a better grip on reality. This nightmare scenario is not a hypothesis; it has been tested in Holland and proved a fact. Holland is the only jurisdiction in the Western world that heretofore permitted physician-assisted suicide. The practice is now widespread (perhaps 2,000 to 3,000 cases a year; the U.S. equivalent would be 40,000 to 60,000) and abused. Indeed, legalization has resulted in so much abuse—not just psychological pressure but a shocking number of cases of out-and-out involuntary euthanasia, inconvenient and defenseless patients simply put to death without their consent—that last year the Dutch government was forced to change its euthanasia laws.

Judge Roger Miner, writing for the Second Circuit, uncomprehendingly admits the reality of the nightmare: "It seems clear that some physicians [in the Netherlands] practice nonvoluntary euthanasia, although it is not legal to do so." Well, why would such things occur in the Netherlands? Are the people there morally inferior to Americans? Are the doctors somehow crueler and more uncaring?

Of course not. The obvious reason is that doctors there were relieved of the constraint of the law. The absolute ethical norm established since the time of Hippocrates—that doctors must not kill—was removed in the name of compassion, and the inevitable happened. Good, ordinary doctors, in their zeal to be ever more compassionate in terminating useless and suffering life, began killing people who did not even ask for it. Once given power heretofore reserved to God, some exceeded their narrow mandate and acted like God. Surprise.

In America the great moral barrier protecting us from such monstrous God-doctoring is the one separating passive from active euthanasia. Pulling the plug for the dying is permitted. Prescribing death-dealing drugs to those who are quite self-sustaining is not. It is this distinction that the judges are intent on destroying.

"Physicians do not fulfill the role of 'killer' by prescribing drugs to hasten death any more than they do by disconnecting life-support systems," writes Judge Miner. This pernicious nonsense. There is a great difference between, say, not resuscitating a stopped heart— allowing nature to take its course—and actively killing someone. In the first case the person is dead. In the second he only wishes to be dead. And in the case of life sustained by artificial hydration or ventilation, pulling the plug simply prevents an artificial prolongation of the dying process. Prescribing hemlock initiates it.

The distinction is not just practical. It is also psychological. Killing is hard to do. The whole purpose of this case is to make it easier. How? By giving doctors who actively assist in suicide the blessing of the law and society.

After all, why did we need this ruling in the first place? In New York State, where this case was brought, not a single physician has been penalized for aiding a suicide since 1919. For 77 years, one can assume, some doctors have been quietly helping patients die. Why then the need for a legal ruling to make that official, a ruling that erases a fundamental ethical line and opens medical practice to unconscionable abuse?

The need comes from the modern craving for "authenticity." If you are going to do it, do it openly, proudly, unashamedly. But as a society, do we not want this most fearful act—killing—to be done fearfully? If it must be done at all—and in the most extreme and pitiable circumstances it will—let it be done with trembling, in shadow, in whispered acknowledgment that some fundamental norm is being violated, even if for the most compassionate of reasons.

No more. These judges have now liberated us from the hypocrisy of the unenforced   *13*
law. Damn them. Lack of enforcement is an expression of compassion, but the law is the
last barrier to arrogance. And God knows that in this age of all-powerful medicine, arrogance is the greater danger. Every grandparent will soon know that too.

"I will give no deadly medicine to anyone if asked."—The Hippocratic Oath   *14*

READING FOR INFORMATION

1. What is hemlock?
2. What legal event is Krauthammer writing in response to?
3. Who was King Canute?
4. According to Krauthammer, how has legalized euthanasia worked in the
   Netherlands?
5. Why, according to Krauthammer, did doctors in the Netherlands come to violate the
   "absolute ethical norm . . . that doctors must not kill"?
6. What is the difference between active euthanasia and passive euthanasia?
7. Why does Krauthammer prefer maintaining a law against active euthanasia that is
   rarely enforced rather than removing the law altogether?
8. What is the Hippocratic Oath?

READING FOR FORM, ORGANIZATION, AND FEATURES

1. Explain the function of Krauthammer's first paragraph.
2. Describe Krauthammer's tone. Do you find his tone appealing? Explain your answer.
3. Is Krauthammer's piece argumentative or analytical? Explain your answer.

READING FOR RHETORICAL CONCERNS

1. Does Krauthammer's opening scenario speak to virtually all his potential readers or
   to particular subpopulations?
2. What does Krauthammer want his audience to do or think after reading his article?
3. How does Krauthammer position himself in relationship to the judges whose verdicts
   he is discussing? In relationship to physicians?

WRITING ASSIGNMENTS

1. Is Krauthammer correct that doctors violate the most basic ethics of their profession
   when they intentionally take lives? Develop your answer in a 750-word essay.
2. Read an encyclopedia account of the death of Socrates. Was Socrates' decision to
   drink hemlock morally correct? Defend your answer in a 750-word essay.
3. In a 750-word essay, describe the ideal physician. Include a discussion of this ideal
   physician's stance on mercy killing.

• • • • • • • • • • • • • • • •

WRITING ASSIGNMENTS FOR CHAPTER 12

1. View the video of *Saving Private Ryan*. In a 1,000-word essay, draw on readings in this chapter to analyze the scene in which a severely wounded soldier is given a lethal dose of morphine to end his suffering. Is that action justified?

2. Write a 1,250-word essay that draws on at least three of the readings in this chapter to analyze euthanasia from the perspectives of each of the following groups: elderly people; young, disabled individuals; the grown children of elderly people; the parents of disabled infants; and physicians who care for disabled or elderly patients.

3. Is suicide in essence a private decision, or does it have social consequences? Answer this question in a 1,000-word essay that draws on at least three readings in this chapter.

4. Conduct brief research on the 1999 conviction and imprisonment of Dr. Jack Kevorkian. Draw on at least three of the readings in this chapter to argue whether Dr. Kevorkian is a hero or a murderer. Write a essay of around 1,250 words.

5. In a 1,000-word essay, respond to the scenario presented in the first three paragraphs of Krauthammer's article. Draw on at least two other reading selections in the chapter.

6. Write a 1,000-word "living will" that outlines what you would want your family and your physicians to do if you were no longer able to direct your own medical care. Draw on at least two of the readings in this chapter.

7. In a 1,250-word essay, explain why euthanasia and physician-assisted suicide are complex moral and ethical issues. Remain objective, and draw on at least three of the readings in this chapter.

CHAPTER

13

RACIAL PROFILING

Racial profiling is the police practice of using race as a factor in identifying individuals who might be criminals and hence should be detained and investigated. Some police officers defend racial profiling as a legitimate law enforcement tool, and many of the nation's police departments claim that there is little evidence of racial bias among their members. The average citizen thinks otherwise. A Gallup poll conducted in 1999 found that the majority of people in the United States are convinced that the police engage in racial profiling. To assure people that the practice is not widespread, some police departments have begun to monitor their officers by requiring them to report the race of all drivers they stop.

Civil liberties advocates say that race-based decisions made by law enforcement agencies and the courts have led to high incarceration rates for people of color. In paragraph 5 of "The Color of Justice," law professor David Cole points out that 74 percent of those incarcerated for drug possession are black but only 13 percent of the nation's drug users are black. Racial profiling is only one of several issues that raises the questions about racial bias in our legal system.

In the opening article, "Ragtime, My Time," Alton Fitzgerald White shows that no black man, not even a successful Broadway actor, can escape being stereotyped as a member of the criminal population. In the next selection, "Road Rage," Patricia Williams heightens our awareness of racial profiling and warns of the dire consequences of this practice. In "The Color of Suspicion," Jeffrey Goldberg interviews a number of law enforcement officers and presents their views on profiling and racial bias. In the final selection, David Cole argues that the courts are protecting racial profiling by police officers, rather than helping end it.

Ragtime, My Time

Alton Fitzgerald White

Alton Fitzgerald White starred in the Broadway productions of Smokey Joe's Cafe, The Who's Tommy, Miss Saigon, *and* Ragtime *(in which he plays the leading role of Coalhouse Walker Jr.). White's latest CD is* Ecstasis.

Alton Fitzgerald White. "Ragtime." Reprinted with permission from the October 11, 1999 issue of *The Nation.*

Prereading ....

Read the first paragraph of the selection, and write your reaction. Is everyone entitled to respect? Do honesty, courtesy, and polite behavior guarantee respect? Have you or someone you know experienced lack of respect? Describe the situation.

. . . .

As the youngest of five girls and two boys growing up in Cincinnati, Ohio, I was raised to believe that if I worked hard, was a good person and always told the truth, the world would be my oyster. I was taught to be courteous and polite. I was raised a gentleman and learned that these fine qualities would bring me one very important, hard-earned human quality: Respect!   *1*

While respect is indeed something one has to earn, consideration is something owed to every human being, even total strangers. On Friday, June 16, 1999, when I was wrongfully arrested while trying to leave my building in Harlem, my perception of everything I had learned as a young man was forever changed—not only because of the fact that I wasn't given even a second to use any of the wonderful manners and skills my parents had taught me as a child, but mostly because the police, who I'd always naïvely thought were supposed to serve and protect me, were actually hunting me.   *2*

I had planned the day to be a pleasant one. The night before was not only payday but also I received a rousing standing ovation after portraying the starring role of Coalhouse Walker Jr. in *Ragtime* on Broadway. It is a role I've worked very hard for professionally, and emotionally as well. A role that requires not only talent but also an honest emotional investment, including the morals and lessons I learned as a child.   *3*

Coalhouse Walker Jr. is a victim (an often misused word but in this case the true definition) of overt racism. His story is every black man's nightmare. He is hard-working, successful, talented, charismatic, friendly and polite. Perfect prey for someone with authority and not even a fraction of those qualities. The fictional character I portrayed on Thursday night became a part of my reality on Friday afternoon. Nothing in the world could have prepared me for it. Nothing I had seen on television. Not even stories told to me by other black men who had suffered similar injustices.   *4*

Most Fridays for me mean a trip to the bank, errands, the gym, dinner and then to the theater. On this particular day, I decided to break my usual pattern of getting up and running right out of the house. Instead, I took my time, slowed down my pace and splurged by making myself some homemade strawberry pancakes. It was a way of spoiling myself in preparation for my demanding, upcoming four-show weekend. Before I knew it, it was 2:45, and my bank closes at 3:30, leaving me less than forty-five minutes to get to midtown on the train. I was pressed for time but in a relaxed, blessed state of mind. When I walked through the lobby of my building, I noticed two light-skinned Hispanic men I'd never seen before. Not thinking much of it, I continued on to the vestibule, which is separated from the lobby by a locked door.   *5*

As I approached the exit, I saw people in uniforms rushing toward the door. I sped up to open it for them, especially after noticing that the first of them was a woman. My first thought was that they were paramedics, seeing as many of the building's occupants are retired and/or elderly. It wasn't until I had opened the door and greeted the woman that I   *6* recognized that they were the police. Within seconds I was told to "hold it" because they had received a call about young Hispanics with guns. I was told to get against the wall. I was searched, stripped of my backpack (which was searched repeatedly), put on my knees, handcuffed and told to be quiet when I tried to ask any questions.

With me were three other innocent black men. They had been on their way to their U-Haul, parked on the side of the building. They were moving into the apartment beneath me and were still glowing from the tour I'd given them of the beautiful historic landmark building. I had just bragged to them about how safe it was and how proud I was to have been living there for over five years. And now here the four of us were being told to get on our knees, handcuffed and not allowed to say a word in our defense. As a matter of fact, it was one of these gentlemen who got off his knees, still handcuffed, and unlocked the door for the policemen to get into the lobby where the two strangers were. Instead of being thanked or even acknowledged, we were led out the door past our neighbors, who were all but begging the police in our defense.

We were put into cars with the two strangers and taken to the 33rd Precinct at 165th and Amsterdam. The police automatically linked us to them with no questions and no regard for our character or our lives. No consideration was given to where we were going or what we were in need of doing before they came into our building. Suppose I had an ailing relative upstairs in my apartment waiting for me to return with her emergency remedy? Or young children who were told Daddy is running to the corner store for milk and will be right back? These three gentlemen weren't even allowed to lock their apartment or check on the U-Haul full of their personal belongings.

After we were lined up in the station, the younger of the two Hispanic men was immediately identified as an experienced criminal, and drug residue was found in a pocket of the other. I now realize how naïve I was to think the police would then uncuff me, apologize for their terrible mistake and let me go. Instead, they continued to search my backpack repeatedly, questioned me and put me in jail with the criminals.

The rest of the nearly five-hour ordeal was like a horrible dream, putting me in a surreal state of shock. Everything from being handcuffed, strip-searched, taken in and out for questioning, to being told that they knew exactly who I was and my responsibility to the show and that in fact they knew they already had whom they wanted, left me in absolute disbelief.

When I asked how they could keep me there, or have brought me there in the first place with nothing found and a clean record, I was told it was standard procedure. As if the average law-abiding citizen knows what that is and can dispute it. From what I now know, "standard procedure" is something that every citizen, black and white, needs to learn, and fast. Even though they knew I was innocent, they made me feel completely powerless. All for one reason. Why do you think? Here I was, young, pleasant and successful, in good physical shape, dressed in clean athletic attire. I was carrying a backpack, containing a substantial paycheck and deposit slip, on my way to the bank and to enjoy a well-deserved great day. Yet after hours and hours I was sitting at a desk with two officers who not only couldn't tell me why I was there but seemed determined to find something on me, to the point of making me miss my performance.

It was because I am a black man!

I sat in that cell crying silent tears of disappointment and injustice with the realization of how many innocent black men are convicted for no reason. When I was handcuffed, my first instinct had been to pull away out of pure insult and violation as a human being. Thank God I was calm enough to do what they said. When I was thrown in jail with the criminals and strip-searched, I somehow knew to put my pride aside, be quiet and do exactly what I was told, hating it but coming to terms with the fact that in this situation I was powerless. I was a victim. They had guns!

Before I was finally let go, exhausted, humiliated, embarrassed and still in shock, I   *14*
was led to a room and given a pseudo-apology. I was told that I was at the wrong place at the wrong time. My reply? "I was where I live."

As a result, what I learned growing up in Cincinnati has been shattered. Life will   *15*
never be the same.

READING FOR INFORMATION

1. What parallels does White draw between his own experiences and the experiences of the character he portrays in the play?
2. List examples of White's and his neighbors' gentlemanly behavior, and compare their conduct to the actions of the police.
3. Explain in your own words the injustice White suffered at the hands of the police, and give your interpretation of the events.

READING FOR FORM, ORGANIZATION, AND FEATURES

1. What different functions do the first and last paragraphs serve?
2. What organizational plan does White use?

READING FOR RHETORICAL CONCERNS

1. What is White's purpose in writing this autobiographical piece?
2. How does White's tone express his purpose, sense of audience, and attitude toward the subject?

WRITING ASSIGNMENTS

1. Write a 500-word summary for classmates who have not read White's article.
2. Do you think White's experience is commonplace? Are black males more likely to be arrested than white males? What accounts for this phenomenon? Write a 750-word response to the article in which you answer these questions.
3. This writing assignment requires you to do some research. Synthesize information from White's article with statistics acquired from the Bureau of Justice or a comparable database, as well as from other selections in this chapter. Your essay should be around 750 words long.

• • • • • • • • • • • • • • • •

Road Rage

Patricia J. Williams

Patricia J. Williams is a professor of law at Columbia Law School and author of The Alchemy of Race and Rights. *She writes the column "Diary of a Mad Law Professor" for* The Nation.

Prereading ···•

Have you ever experienced road rage? How would you define road rage? Write your response. After you have read the article, compare your definition to Patricia Williams's.

············•

The Black Ministers Council of New Jersey has been waging a longstanding battle against   1
what it alleges is a practice by state troopers of stopping cars based on race-based "suspect profiling." While ostensibly denying there was any such policy, the head of the New Jersey State Police, Col. Carl Williams, nevertheless described President Clinton's recent discussion with Mexican leaders about their alleged harboring of identified drug traffickers in the following terms: "He didn't go to Ireland. He didn't go to England. Today with this drug problem . . . it is most likely a minority group that's involved." Williams, who was fired for the comments, went on to peg heroin trafficking as a "more or less Jamaican" thing and the methamphetamine market as "basically predominantly white."

Statistics indisputably show that most of those convicted of drug-related offenses are   2
white, yet assumptions to the contrary abound. Georgetown law professor David Cole's important study *No Equal Justice* provides a sampling: "None of the three judges who arraigned felony cases in New York County could recall a single Port Authority drug interdiction case where the defendant was not black or Hispanic. A police officer working at the Memphis International Airport testified that at least 75 percent of those followed and questioned at the airport were black. A Lexis review of all federal court decisions from January 1, 1990, to August 2, 1995, in which drug-courier profiles were used and the race of the suspect was discernible revealed that of sixty-three such cases, all but three suspects were minorities."

At its best, a "suspect profile," even when backed by solid forensic expertise and   3
data, is a composite providing clues, not a guarantee. At worst, profiling may be little more than an individual officer's "hunch." Many agencies misunderstand or misuse even legitimate data about suspect behavior. If, for example, there was a pattern of documented criminality among Canadian women from an extended family in Saskatoon, all of whom had hidden contraband in their backpacks, this might justify bringing out a drug-sniffing dog in encountering another such woman. It would not, however, justify using this information to strip-search every woman who looks like she might be Canadian. Yet, if you change "Canadian" to "Jamaican," that is precisely the logic by which specific features get stretched into broad ethnic assumptions and nationality gets stretched into race.

The black ministers' complaint has been lent particular urgency since last April, when troopers shot eleven rounds into a van of unarmed black and Latino college students after pulling them over for reasons that remain unclear. Yet asserting claims of racism is a complicated matter in today's world. Recently, for example, New York City Police Commissioner Howard Safir exhorted black community leaders not to "play the race card" in addressing the question of police-citizen distrust. The Diallo shooting [in which white police officers fired forty-one bullets into an unarmed black man], he insisted, was a tragic mistake but it was not about race, he insisted. Yet Safir himself then went on to discuss how the Street Crimes Unit has reduced the murder rate in black neighborhoods significantly—simultaneously conceding and skirting the fact that African-American and Latino communities have been targeted for greater police presence because of higher crime rates, and dismissing the harassment complaints of minority citizens with a can't-have-an-omelet-without-breaking-eggs type of argument.

But is it playing the race card to speak of this directly? In the New York and New Jersey area, the crime rate for certain categories of offense is higher in African-American and Latino neighborhoods than in white ones. But national statistics also show that in areas where there are significant numbers of poor whites, the crime rate is virtually the same as for poor communities of color. In New York and New Jersey, however, as in many places in the United States, white communities tend to be much wealthier than communities of color. Thus, the relationship of crime to poverty is obscured, since economic status itself has long been affected by the ongoing legacy of segregation.

These higher *rates* of crime are then miscast in an unfortunate cliché—i.e., blacks just "commit more crime" than whites. There is a great deal one could say about the accuracy of this perception—particularly as it is used to imply that blacks (young men in particular) are innately more crime-prone than whites. If blacks are stopped at rates that are shockingly disproportionate to any other group in the population (as every study thus far documents), then it should not be a surprise that they are subsequently arrested, prosecuted and convicted more frequently than whites, and are incarcerated for longer terms than their white counterparts convicted of similar crimes.

But even that reality, about a minuscule minority of mostly poor, mostly young black men—one in three of whom, according to the Sentencing Project, is in prison or jail, on probation or parole, often for offenses related to the desperate industry of self-medication by, yes, crack cocaine—becomes exaggerated far beyond itself. In any given year in the United States, Cole points out, 98 percent of blacks and 99.5 percent of whites are not arrested for any crime. Yet in many people's minds the statement "Blacks commit *relatively* more crime" becomes twisted into "Blacks commit most of the crime" or, most insidiously, "Most blacks are criminals." In a society where such thinking is pervasive, it is only a short, seemingly logical leap into the habit of viewing all blacks as suspect.

The alleged practices of the New Jersey state troopers, like the Diallo killing, will be investigated and, one can only hope, resolved over time. But the questions that such investigations raise are not for police departments alone. What happens to the democratic promise of our system of justice when, for some, the presumption of innocence until proven guilty becomes nothing more than a quaint fiction for the courtroom? What happens to us all when we become a citizenry so thoughtlessly divided against itself—"safe" on one side, "sorry," like a knell, on the other?

READING FOR INFORMATION

1. What is Williams implying about the relationship among crime, poverty, and race? Do you agree?
2. How do people arrive at the conclusion that "most blacks are criminals"? Paraphrase Williams's explanation.
3. Explain what Williams means when she says " 'safe' on one side; 'sorry,' like a knell, on the other."

READING FOR FORM, ORGANIZATION, AND FEATURES

1. What is the function of paragraph 5?
2. List the types of evidence Williams uses to develop and support her arguments, and give an example of each.
3. What is Williams's closing strategy?

READING FOR RHETORICAL CONCERNS

1. What prompted Williams to write this article?
2. What impact does Williams want to have on her readers?

WRITING ASSIGNMENTS

1. Select a topic that stems from Williams's essay, and develop a 750-word essay of your own. Include a summary of Williams's treatment of the topic.
2. Use the *New York Times Index* or Excite's InfoTracker (http://nt.excite.com) to locate newspaper articles on the young African immigrant, Amadou Diallo, who was shot and killed in New York City in February 1999. Synthesize your findings in a 500-word report to the class. Discuss the circumstances of Diallo's death, the Albany trial and acquittal of the four officers, and the reaction of the public, particularly the African American community.
3. Write a 500-word evaluation of Williams's argument.
4. After reading Alton Fitzgerald White's selection, "Ragtime, My Time," and Patricia Williams's essay, write a 750-word response essay in which you agree or disagree with the positions put forth by these two authors.

. . . .

The Color of Suspicion

Jeffrey Goldberg

Jeffrey Goldberg is a contributing writer for the New York Times Magazine.

Prereading ··

Speculate about the meaning of Goldberg's title by writing responses to the following questions: How would you define the word *suspicion*? What does it mean to display "suspicious" behavior or give a "suspicious" look? What color do you associate with suspicion? Why?

· · · · · · · · · · · · · · · · ·

Sgt. Mike Lewis of the Maryland State Police is a bull-necked, megaphone-voiced, highly caffeinated drug warrior who, on this shiny May morning outside of Annapolis, is conceding defeat. The drug war is over, the good guys have lost and he has been cast as a racist. "This is the end, buddy," he says. "I can read the writing on the wall." Lewis is driving his unmarked Crown Victoria down the fast lane of Route 50, looking for bad guys. The back of his neck is burnt by the sun, and he wears his hair flat and short under his regulation Stetson.

"They're going to let the N.A.A.C.P. tell us how to do traffic stops," he says. "That's what's happening. There may be a few troopers who make stops solely based on race, but this—they're going to let these people tell us how to run our department. I say, to hell with it all. I don't care if the drugs go through. I don't."

He does, of course. Mike Lewis was born to seize crack. He grew up in Salisbury on the Eastern Shore—Jimmy Buffett country—and he watched his friends become stoners and acid freaks. Not his scene. He buzz-cut his hair away and joined the state troopers when he was 19. He's a star, the hard-charger who made one of the nation's largest seizures of crack cocaine out on Route 13. He's a national expert on hidden compartments. He can tell if a man's lying, he says, by watching the pulsing of the carotid artery in his neck. He can smell crack cocaine inside a closed automobile. He's a human drug dog, a walking polygraph machine. "I have the unique ability to distinguish between a law-abiding person and an up-to-no-good person," he says. "Black or white." All these skills, though, he's ready to chuck. The lawsuits accusing the Maryland State Police of harassing black drivers, the public excoriation—and most of all, the Governor of New Jersey saying that her state police profiled drivers based on race, and were wrong to do so—have twisted him up inside. "Three of my men have put in for transfers," he says. "My wife wants me to get out. I'm depressed."

What depresses Mike Lewis is that he believes he is in possession of a truth polite society is too cowardly to accept. He says that when someone tells this particular truth, his head is handed to him. "The superintendent of the New Jersey State Police told the truth and he got fired for it," Lewis says.

This is what Carl Williams said, fueling a national debate about racial profiling in law enforcement: "Today with this drug problem, the drug problem is cocaine or marijuana. It is most likely a minority group that's involved with that." Gov. Christine Todd Whitman fired Williams, and the news ricocheted through police departments everywhere, especially those, like the Maryland State Police, already accused of racial profiling—the stopping and searching of blacks because they are black.

The way cops perceive blacks—and how those perceptions shape and misshape crime fighting—is now the most charged racial issue in America. The systematic harassment of black drivers in New Jersey, the shooting of Amadou Diallo, an unarmed African immigrant, by New York City police officers earlier this year, and other incidents in other states have brought the relationship between blacks and cops to a level of seemingly irreversible toxicity. *6*

Neither side understands the other. The innocent black man, jacked-up and humiliated during a stop-and-frisk or a pretext car stop, asks: Whatever happened to the Fourth Amendment? It is no wonder, blacks say, that the police are so wildly mistrusted. *7*

And then there's the cop, who says: Why shouldn't I look at race when I'm looking for crime? It is no state secret that blacks commit a disproportionate amount of crime, so "racial profiling" is simply good police work. *8*

Mike Lewis wishes that all this talk of racial profiling would simply stop. *9*

As we drive, Lewis watches a van come up on his right and pass him. A young black man is at the wheel, his left leg hanging out the window. The blood races up Lewis's face: "Look at that! That's a violation! You can't drive like that! But I'm not going to stop him. No, sir. If I do, he's just going to call me a racist." *10*

Then Lewis notices that the van is a state government vehicle. "This is ridiculous," he says. Lewis hits his lights. The driver stops. Lewis issues him a warning and sends him on his way. The driver says nothing. *11*

"He didn't call me a racist," Lewis says, pulling into traffic, "but I know what he was thinking." Lewis does not think of himself as a racist. "I know how to treat people," he says. "I've never had a complaint based on a race-based stop. I've got that supercharged knowledge of the Constitution that allows me to do this right." *12*

In the old days, when he was patrolling the Eastern Shore, it was white people he arrested. "Ninety-five percent of my drug arrests were dirt-ball-type whites—marijuana, heroin, possession-weight. Then I moved to the highway, I start taking off two, three kilograms of coke, instead of two or three grams. Black guys. Suddenly I'm not the greatest trooper in the world. I'm a racist. I'm locking up blacks, but I can't help it." *13*

His eyes gleam: "Ask me how many white people I've ever arrested for cocaine smuggling—ask me!" *14*

I ask. *15*

"None! Zero! I debrief hundreds of black smugglers, and I ask them, 'Why don't you hire white guys to deliver your drugs?' They just laugh at me. 'We ain't gonna trust our drugs with white boys.' That's what they say." *16*

Mike Lewis's dream: "I dream at night about arresting white people for cocaine. I do. I try to think of innovative ways to arrest white males. But the reality is different." *17*

A big part of Lewis's reality is a black man named Keith Hill. Lewis killed Keith Hill three years ago. Hill was speeding down Route 13 when Lewis pulled him over. He approached the car, Hill rolled down the window and Lewis smelled burning marijuana. He ordered Hill out of the car, began to search him and came up with thousands of dollars of cash and packets of marijuana. Hill suddenly resisted. What flashed through Lewis's mind was his friend Edward Plank, a trooper killed by a coke runner on this same highway a few months before. *18*

They fought, Hill knocking Lewis into a ravine. They wrestled, and Hill went for Lewis's gun. "We were in a clinch, just breathing heavy," Lewis recalls, "and I said, 'Man, it's just pot, it's not worth it.' " But Hill kept going for the gun, Lewis tells me. He couldn't get it, and ran. He looped through a housing development and back to his car. Hill gunned the engine just as Lewis got himself in front of the car. Lewis drew his weapon and fired, striking Hill twice in the chest.   *19*

Lewis speaks often of the shooting, and of Eddie Plank's death. One day, he collects for me old newspaper stories of trooper shootouts. I'm reading them when we pass two members of his interdiction squad parked on the median of Route 13. They've stopped two cars with New York license plates filled with young black men. "What's up?" Lewis asks Gary Bromwell, a bulky, sullen trooper.   *20*

The two cars were pulled over for speeding and weaving, but that was a pretext. The goal of Lewis's unit, the criminal-interdiction unit, is to find drugs, guns and untaxed cigarettes in the cars of smugglers. However, in order to stop a suspected gunrunner or drug mule, troopers first have to find a reason in the state's traffic laws.   *21*

Bromwell issues written warnings and sends them on their way. I ask Bromwell, who is white, why he didn't ask the young men their consent to search the cars. Reasonable suspicion—anything the trooper can articulate before a judge—is enough to justify a consent search. "They're decent people," Bromwell says.   *22*

How can you tell?   *23*

"They looked me in the eye, and the driver's hand didn't shake when he handed me his license—."   *24*

Lewis interrupts: "No visible sign of contraband, no overwhelming odor of air fresheners emanating from the vehicle, no signs of hard driving"—that is, driving long hours without making stops. He is listing Drug Enforcement Administration–endorsed indicators of drug smuggling. Smugglers use air fresheners to fool drug-sniffing dogs. Signs of hard driving— "these guys drive straight through because they don't want to leave their drugs alone," Lewis says—include loose-fitting clothing, day-old beards and food wrappers on the floor. These signs, though, can also indicate the presence of college students—which is, in fact, the case here.   *25*

Did you stop them because they were black men from New York? I ask.   *26*

"Tell you the truth," Bromwell says, "we couldn't see who was driving these cars. They were speeding."   *27*

After the New York cars pull into traffic, Lewis shows Bromwell and his partner, Rob Penny, the newspaper clippings, hoping they will back him up. "Eddie Plank," he says. "Killed by a black male. My shooting—a black. Robbie Bishop, down in Georgia, killed by a black. North Carolina trooper, killed by a black."   *28*

Bromwell looks uneasy. I ask him if he believes in a connection between the race of the shooters and the crimes they commit.   *29*

"People might think it," Bromwell says, walking away, "but they don't say it." He flashes Lewis a look that says, Shut up, and quick.   *30*

Why a Cop Profiles

This is what a cop might tell you in a moment of reckless candor: in crime fighting, race matters. When asked, most cops will declare themselves color blind. But watch them on   *31* the job for several months, and get them talking about the way policing is really done, and the truth will emerge, the truth being that cops, white and black, profile. Here's why, they say. African-Americans commit a disproportionate percentage of the types of crimes that draw the attention of the police. Blacks make up 12 percent of the population, but accounted for 58 percent of all carjackers between 1992 and 1996. (Whites accounted for 19 percent.) Victim surveys—and most victims of black criminals are black—indicate that blacks commit almost 50 percent of all robberies. Blacks and Hispanics are widely believed to be the blue-collar backbone of the country's heroin- and cocaine-distribution networks. Black males between the ages of 14 and 24 make up 1.1 percent of the country's population, yet commit more than 28 percent of its homicides. Reason, not racism, cops say, directs their attention.

Cops, white and black, know one other thing: they're not the only ones who profile. Civilians profile all the time—when they buy a house, or pick a school district, or walk down the street. Even civil rights leaders profile. "There is nothing more painful for me at this stage in my life," Jesse Jackson said several years ago, "than to walk down the street and hear footsteps and start thinking about robbery—and then look around and see somebody white and feel relieved." Jackson now says his quotation was "taken out of context." The context, he said, is that violence is the inevitable by-product of poor education and health care. But no amount of "context" matters when you fear that you are about to be mugged. 32

At a closed-door summit in Washington between police chiefs and black community leaders recently, the black chief of police of Charleston, S.C., Reuben Greenberg, argued that the problem facing black America is not racial profiling, but precisely the sort of black-on-black crime Jackson was talking about. "I told them that the greatest problem in the black community is the tolerance for high levels of criminality," he recalled. "Fifty percent of homicide victims are African-Americans. I asked what this meant about the value of life in this community." 33

The police chief in Los Angeles, Bernard Parks, who is black, argues that racial profiling is rooted in statistical reality, not racism. "It's not the fault of the police when they stop minority males or put them in jail," Parks told me. "It's the fault of the minority males for committing the crime. In my mind it is not a great revelation that if officers are looking for criminal activity, they're going to look at the kind of people who are listed on crime reports." 34

Chief Parks defends vigorously the idea that police can legitimately factor in race when building a profile of a criminal suspect. 35

"We have an issue of violent crime against jewelry salespeople," Parks says. "The predominant suspects are Colombians. We don't find Mexican-Americans, or blacks or other immigrants. It's a collection of several hundred Colombians who commit this crime. If you see six in a car in front of the Jewelry Mart, and they're waiting and watching people with briefcases, should we play the percentages and follow them? It's common sense." 36

What if you follow the wrong Colombian, or track an Ecuadorean by mistake? "We're not using just race," he says. "It's got to be race, plus other indicators, so that won't happen." 37

I asked Parks to comment on the 3-out-of-10 hypothetical. In Maryland, the state police, as part of a settlement of an American Civil Liberties Union lawsuit, reported that 38 on a particular stretch of highway, the police came up with drugs in 3 out of every 10 consent searches. This was deemed unacceptable by the A.C.L.U. "Three out of 10?" Parks said. "That would get you into the Hall of Fame. That's a success story." He continued: "At some point, someone figured out that the drugs are being delivered by males of this color driving these kinds of vehicles at this time of night. This isn't brain surgery. The profile didn't get invented for nothing."

Profiling in Black and White

"Some blacks, I just get the sense off them that they're wild," Mark Robinson says. "I mean, you can tell. I have what you might call a profile. I pull up alongside a car with black males in it. Something doesn't match—maybe the style of the car with the guys in it. I start talking to them, you know, 'nice car,' that kind of thing, and if it doesn't seem right, I say, 'All right, let's pull it over to the side,' and we go from there."   *39*

He is quiet and self-critical, and the words sat in the mouth a while before he let them out. "I'm guilty of it, I guess."   *40*

Guilty of what?   *41*

"Racial profiling."   *42*

His partner, Gene Jones, says: "Mark is good at finding stolen cars on the street. Real good."   *43*

We are driving late one sticky Saturday night through the beat-down neighborhood of Logan, in the northern reaches of Philadelphia. The nighttime commerce is lively, lookouts holding down their corners, sellers ready to serve the addict traffic. It's a smorgasbord for the two plainclothes officers, but their attention is soon focused on a single cluster of people, four presumptive buyers who are hurrying inside a store the officers know is hot with drugs.   *44*

The officers pull to the curb, slide out and duck behind a corner, watching the scene unfold. The suspects are wearing backward baseball caps and low-slung pants; the woman with them is dressed like a stripper.   *45*

"Is this racial profiling?" Jones asks. A cynical half-smile shows on his face.   *46*

The four buyers are white. Jones and Robinson are black, veterans of the street who know that white people in a black neighborhood will be stopped. Automatically. Faster than a Rastafarian in Scarsdale.   *47*

"No reason for them to be around here at this time of night, nope," Jones says.   *48*

Is it possible that they're visiting college friends? I ask.   *49*

Jones and Robinson, whose intuition is informed by experience, don't know quite what to make of my suggestion.   *50*

"It could be," Jones says, indulgently. "But, uhhhh, no way."   *51*

Are you going to stop them?   *52*

"I don't know what for yet, but I'm going to stop them."   *53*

The whites step out of the building, separate and dissolve into the night before Jones gets to make his stop. Jones is unhappy; he's proud of his tracking skills. "They're hard to see in the dark, I guess," he says, smiling.   *54*

So, race is a legitimate proxy for criminality?   *55*

"No," Jones says. Few cops ever answer yes at the outset. "But it depends. I mean, you're a cop. You know who's committing the crimes. It's your neighborhood. That's how it works."

Jones and Robinson are assigned to Philadelphia's 35th Police District, one of the more drug-ridden districts in a drug-ridden city. Certain sections of Philadelphia are still very much lawless. Last year, the city hired John Timoney, who served as first deputy commissioner under William Bratton in New York City, to revive a police department that had become tragically inept. Timoney, by all accounts, has done a remarkable job reforming the department, and letting the criminal underclass know that their actions will bring consequences.

But Philadelphia is not quite Rudolph Giuliani's New York. Jones and Robinson are surprised to hear, for instance, that the smoking of marijuana in public places is actively discouraged by New York police. They express this surprise after they try to clear a drug corner of young men who continue smoking fat blunts even after Robinson and Jones alert them to the fact that they are in the presence of law-enforcement officers.

"You know, the city is cracking down on marijuana smoking," Jones tells the men. They stub out their joints—but not before one man takes one last, deep drag—and move across the street.

Jones shakes his head and says, "It's like there aren't any laws out here."

Like many black cops, Jones and Robinson have more in common with their white colleagues than they do with, say, the Rev. Al Sharpton. "The problem with black politicians is that they think the cop is automatically guilty," Jones says.

One day, while driving through a particularly rank stretch of their police district, Jones decides that I should interview drug dealers on the subject of police harassment and racial profiling. The point he hopes to make is that the complaints of racial harassment are illegitimate. Jones approaches one group of dealers, heavy-lidded young men drinking 40-ounce bottles of malt liquor. One dealer, who gives his name as Si-Bee, is asked by Jones whether the police are harassing young blacks or simply enforcing the law.

"Why can't I just sit on my corner?" Si-Bee says in response. "Unless you've got probable cause, you can't come and harass me." To which Jones replied: "Whoa. Probable cause. Big word."

"Cops come busting on us for no reason," a young man named Mustafa says. "It's just plain and simple harassment. Just messing with us."

"Which are worse?" Jones asks. "White cops or black cops?"

"Black," comes the reply, virtually in unison.

We return to the car, and Jones laughs: "That one," he says, pointing out the window, "I arrested for dealing. That one we got in a stolen car. That one, the one who wouldn't talk to me, I arrested two months ago. I'm going to court soon to testify against him."

We stop at another corner, another group of feckless youth. Same questions, same responses. I decide to switch subjects. Instead of talking about Philadelphia, I want to know what happens when they drive the New Jersey Turnpike.

"That's the worst," one young man says. "I never ride the turnpike."

I turn to Jones, waiting for a smirk.

It never comes.

"I'm going to have to agree with the brother on that one," he says.

What?

Jones, it turns out, is a staff sergeant in the New Jersey National Guard. "Yeah, when *74*
I go to Jersey for Guard weekends, I take the back roads," he says. "I won't get on the turnpike. I won't mess with those troopers."

"Driving While Black," and Other Exaggerations

Here's the heart of the matter, as Chief Greenberg of Charleston sees it: "You got white cops *75*
who are so dumb that they can't make a distinction between a middle-class black and an
underclass black, between someone breaking the law and someone just walking down the
street. Black cops too. The middle class says, 'Wait a minute. I've done everything right, I
pushed all the right buttons, went to all the right schools, and they're jacking me up anyway.'
That's how this starts."

So is racism or stupidity the root cause of racial profiling? *76*

Governor Whitman, it seems, would rather vote for stupidity. *77*

"You don't have to be racist to engage in racial profiling," she says. We are sitting in *78*
her office in the State House in Trenton. She still seems a bit astonished that her state has
become the Mississippi of racial profiling.

Whitman, though burned by the behavior of her state troopers, is offering them a *79*
generous dispensation, given her definition of racial profiling. "Profiling means a police officer using cumulative knowledge and training to identify certain indicators of possible criminal activity," she told me. "Race may be one of those factors, but it cannot stand alone."

"Racial profiling," she continues, "is when race is the only factor. There's no other *80*
probable cause."

Her narrow, even myopic, definition suggests that only stone racists practice racial *81*
profiling. But the mere sight of black skin alone is not enough to spin most cops into a
frenzy. "Police chiefs use that word 'solely' all the time, and it's such a red herring," says
Randall Kennedy, Harvard Law professor and author of the book *Race, Crime and the Law.*
"Even Mark Fuhrman doesn't act solely on the basis of race."

The real question about racial profiling is this: Is it ever permissible for a law-enforce- *82*
ment officer to use race as one of even 5, or 10, or 20, indicators of possible criminality?

In other words, can the color of a man's skin help make him a criminal suspect? *83*

Yes, Whitman says. She suggests she doesn't have a problem with the use of race as *84*
one of several proxies for potential criminality. "I look at Barry McCaffrey's Web site," she
says, referring to the Clinton Administration's drug czar, "and it says certain ethnic groups
are more likely to engage in drug smuggling."

It is true. Despite President Clinton's recent declaration that racial profiling is *85*
"morally indefensible," the Office of National Drug Control Policy's Web site helpfully lists
which racial groups sell which drugs in different cities. In Denver, McCaffrey's Web site says,
it is "minorities, Mexican nationals" who sell heroin. In Trenton, "crack dealers are predominantly African-American males, powdered cocaine dealers are predominantly Latino."

The link between racial minorities and drug-selling is exactly what Whitman's former *86*
police superintendent, Carl Williams, was talking about. So was Williams wrong?

"His comments indicated a lack of sensitivity to the seriousness of the problem." *87*

But was he wrong on the merits? *88*

"If he said, 'You should never use this solely; race could be a partial indicator, taken   *89*
in concert with other factors' "—she pauses, sees the road down which she's heading, and
puts it in reverse—"but you can't be that broad-brushed."

"Racial profiling," is a street term, not a textbook concept. No one teaches racial   *90*
profiling. "Profiling," of course, is taught. It first came to the public's notice by way of the
Federal Bureau of Investigation's behavioral-science unit, which developed the most famous
criminal profile of all, one that did, in fact, have a racial component—the profile of serial
killers as predominantly white, male loners.

It is the Drug Enforcement Administration, however, that is at the center of the racial-   *91*
profiling controversy, accused of encouraging state law-enforcement officials to build
profiles of drug couriers. The D.E.A., through its 15-year-old "Operation Pipeline," finances
state training programs to interdict drugs on the highway. Civil rights leaders blame the
department for the burst of race-based stops, but the D.E.A. says it discourages use of race
as an indicator. "It's a fear of ours, that people will use race," says Greg Williams, the D.E.A.'s
operations chief.

Cops use race because it's easy, says John Crew, the A.C.L.U.'s point man on racial   *92*
profiling. "The D.E.A. says the best profile for drug interdiction is no profile," he says.
"They say it's a mistake to look for a certain race of drivers. That's their public line. But
privately, they say, 'God knows what these people from these state and local agencies do
in the field.' "

The A.C.L.U. sees an epidemic of race-based profiling. Anecdotes are plentiful, but   *93*
hard numbers are scarce. Many police officials see the "racial profiling" crisis as hype. "Not
to say that it doesn't happen, but it's clearly not as serious or widespread as the publicity
suggests," says Chief Charles Ramsey of Washington. "I get so tired of hearing that 'Driving
While Black' stuff. It's just used to the point where it has no meaning. I drive while black—
I'm black. I sleep while black too. It's victimology. Black people commit traffic violations.
What are we supposed to say? People get a free pass because they're black?"

How to Jack Up a Black Man: A Primer

"You know, the black people out here are different," Girolamo Renzulli says. He is formerly   *94*
of New York, now serving as a Los Angeles County deputy sheriff. We are standing in the
parking lot of the Lennox sheriff's station on the edge of South Central Los Angeles.
Renzulli speaks in low tones.

"How so?"   *95*

"They're just, I don't know, different."   *96*

Like how?   *97*

"Wild," he says. "You'll see."   *98*

The Los Angeles Sheriff's Department does not look at black men differently than it   *99*
looks at white men; it is heinous to even suggest it, the Sheriff himself, Leroy Baca, says.
He has 8,000 sworn officers under his command; the Sheriff's Department polices unin-
corporated areas of Los Angeles County and 40 different towns.

"It's happened before," Baca will acknowledge. "When I was a lieutenant, I knew a   *100*
deputy who stopped interracial couples. We removed him from the field, disciplined him
and transferred him out."

Today, though, it just doesn't happen. Baca reads to me from his "Core Values" state-   *101*
ment, which, among other items, promises that sheriff's deputies will have the "courage"
to stand up to "racism, sexism, anti-Semitism and homophobia."

"Even criminals have dignity as human beings that must be honored," Baca says.   *102*

This is not necessarily an opinion shared by his men. Bobby Harris is a senior deputy   *103*
at the Lennox station, who, with four other deputies, shot and killed one man this year, and,
Harris says, "the year ain't over yet." Deputy Harris not shy about sharing his position on
profiling, which does not dovetail with Sheriff Baca's—at least as Baca described his position to me.

"Racial profiling is a tool we use, and don't let anyone say otherwise," Harris says.   *104*
"Like up in the valley," he continues, referring to the San Fernando Valley, "I knew who all
the crack sellers were—they look like Hispanics who should be cutting your lawn. They
were driving cars like this one"—he points to an aging Chevy parked in the station's lot—
"and all the cars had DARE stickers on them. That's just the way it is."

If it is unclear whether Sheriff Baca is sincerely oblivious to the goings-on at the   *105*
Lennox station, many chiefs, I've found, are not terribly interested in knowing too much
about the tactics their subordinates use to bring down the crime numbers—crime reductions that, in this performance-driven era of policing, are key to job preservation. In Baltimore, for instance, rank-and-file officers know full well who a multi-agency drug
interdiction team that operates at the city's train station is looking for.

"Everyone knows they're looking for 'Yo girls,'" says Craig Singleterry, a black Balti-   *106*
more police officer. "Yo girls," Singleterry explains, are young black women with long nails
and hair weaves who carry such accouterments as Fendi bags and who deliver drugs and
money for dealers in New York.

"Of course we do racial profiling at the train station," says Gary McLhinney, the pres-   *107*
ident of the Baltimore Fraternal Order of Police. "If 20 people get off the train and 19 are
white guys in suits and one is a black female, guess who gets followed? If racial profiling is
intuition and experience, I guess we all racial-profile."

Here is Baltimore's Police Commissioner, Thomas Frazier, on racial profiling: "To   *108*
say that being of any particular race makes you a suspect in a particular type of crime is
just wrong, and it's not done in Baltimore."

Roll call in Los Angeles, and the subject is an upcoming demonstration protesting   *109*
the police killing last December of a 19-year-old woman in neighboring Riverside County.
Tyisha Miller is the West Coast's Amadou Diallo. She was shot to death while slumped in
her car with a gun on her lap. The police officers say they opened fire when she reached
for the gun.

"I heard Al Sharpton is coming out for this," one deputy says.   *110*

"Can you believe it? They're going to turn this thing into another goddamn O.J.,"   *111*
another responds.

"And Jesse Jackson is coming."   *112*

"Oh, for Chrissakes."   *113*

All but two of the deputies are white. One is Hispanic, and he hangs with the whites.   *114*
The other deputy is black, and he does not participate in the conversation. He instead stares
at a fixed point on the wall in front of him. All of the white men in the room wear their hair
in crew cuts. Many of them are ex-marines. Many also wear a tattoo of the Grim Reaper on

their ankles. Deputies assigned to hard-core gang areas often tattoo themselves identically, very much like the gangs they fight. It is the white deputies who do this, in the main, and civil rights activists have loudly accused the Sheriff's Department of harboring racist gangs, identifiable by the tattoos they wear. Because of the criticism, deputies keep their tattoos a secret, even though they see nothing wrong with them. "If it was a picture of a black man hanging from a tree, I could see people getting upset," one deputy, Jeffrey Coates, told me.

Coates is perhaps the hardest-charging deputy at Lennox. He is a heavily muscled white man, a power lifter who usually wears a mustache but shaved it off for SWAT tryouts. SWAT culture frowns on facial hair.   *115*

The first time I met Coates, he was training a new deputy, a black woman named Angela Walton. Walton and Coates seemed to work well together. It can be unpleasant to be a black female deputy in Los Angeles, and Coates would rise to her defense. Once, he recalled, a suspect taunted Walton, saying, " 'I bet yo' training officer treats you real good.' "   *116*

"I wanted to beat his [expletive] face in," Coates remembered. "I told him to shut up, just shut up. Then he called me a nigger. I mean, what's that about? How am I a nigger?"   *117*

Coates was reared in Iowa, but he has an expert feel for the streets of South Central. He also seems to attract gunfire. Not long after I rode with him, he and his partner were shot at by a man with a revolver, who missed. Last year, Coates and a partner killed a man who opened fire on them from seven feet away. After the shooting, Coates paid a mandatory visit to the department psychiatrist. "He asked me how I felt. I said, 'I feel, [expletive] him.'   *118*

"Afterward, the black newspaper wrote, 'Deputies kill another black man,' " Coates said. "But if this guy dumped me, they wouldn't have said anything." Coates doesn't have much patience for those who protest the killing of Tyisha Miller, or those who complain about racial profiling: "I say, get your own house in order. Stop the black-on-black homicide."   *119*

On one of the days we rode together, Coates and his partner for the day, Andy Ruiz, responded to a domestic call that involved an angry young black man with a tire iron. They pulled up just as the young man walked into the street. Coates grabbed the tire iron. Ruiz pulled out his 9-millimeter pistol. He later said, "I was ready to shoot him, really."   *120*

Inside the apartment the young man with the tire iron was trying to destroy, there were empty bottles of malt liquor on the television console. Coates: "You ever hear Chris Rock? He does this thing: 'Guy says, I got a job, man! Like he's proud. Well, [expletive], you supposed to have a job.' " This is an inexact recollection of a Chris Rock routine in which he delineates the differences between "blacks" and "niggers." Rock is very popular with white cops.   *121*

Coates spent one day giving me what might be called a master class in the art of the pretext stop—pulling over blacks and Hispanics, hoping to come up with dope, or guns, or information. "There's a law against almost everything as it relates to a vehicle," Coates said. Coates knows the law, and uses it.   *122*

For example, Coates spotted a type of car, a Monte Carlo, which is known to be favored by gangsters, moving along in traffic. He pulled in behind the car and studied it for a moment.   *123*

"No mud flaps," Coates said, turning on his lights.   *124*

They pulled the car over, and asked the three teenagers, shaven-headed Hispanics, to step outside. They patted them down and looked through the vehicle. The teen-agers freely admitted to being members of the South Los gang.   *125*

"Now the reason we stopped you was that you have no mud flaps on your rear tires," Coates said. "But the real reason we stopped you is because we saw that you're rolling out of your area. Why don't you turn it around and go home." *126*

The men argued: "We're just going to Costco." *127*

For what? *128*

"Pet food." *129*

"Pit bull?" Coates asked. *130*

"Two," one of the men answered. *131*

Coates, same day, different vehicle, a purple Buick Regal with a bumper sticker that reads, "Don't you wish you were a pimp." Coates knows the owner of the car—he put him in jail. Behind the wheel is his wife. "There's got to be some violations on that car," Coates said. *132*

There were two women in the car, smoking, and three very small children. Not one was in a car seat. "There's something hanging from your mirror, ma'am," Coates said, covering his bases. "Now, you've got to have the baby in a car seat, O.K.?" *133*

The Regal pulled off, and Coates shook his head. "I should take her to jail just for the secondhand smoke," he said. "Smoking inside a car with little babies? Can you believe that? This place is crazy." *134*

Coates doesn't believe that everyone in his patrol sector is guilty of something. He told me he believes that slightly less than half are guilty of something. He has a good hit rate—most of the drivers he stops are driving without licenses or registration. *135*

But sometimes, in his sweep of the neighborhood, he makes a wrong call. One day, while patrolling with Walton on a bleak street of boarded-up bungalows and dead-eyed black men, he stopped a car without license plates. An obvious stop, but it's what happened after the car was stopped that warrants notice. Every male Coates stops he asks to step to the police cruiser and place his hands on the hood. Coates will then pat him down for a weapon. *136*

The man driving this particular car acceded readily to this, but he was agitated. "This is my neighborhood," he said. He was a black man in his 30's. He seemed terribly embarrassed. *137*

Coates knew something was off when the man produced his license, registration and insurance card, the trifecta of responsibility. *138*

"I'm sorry. I was just taking the car from the garage back home," the man said. "I should have plates, you're right." *139*

He explained why he was nervous: "I work at Northrop. I don't want anybody to see me like this." He had his palms flat on the hood of Coates's cruiser as he was talking. Walton was standing nearby, her hand near her weapon. *140*

Coates dismissed him without writing a citation. The man thanked the deputy profusely, and took off. *141*

It was a troubling moment, and I asked Coates if it's his policy to remove every male from any car he stops, no matter what the cause for the stop. *142*

"Yes. Officer safety." *143*

"Would you do that in a different part of the country?" *144*

"I wouldn't do it in Santa Clarita," he said, pausing—realizing, perhaps, what that sounded like. "I mean, it all depends." *145*

Do you recognize that you might have just created an enemy on this traffic stop? *146*

"I was polite," he responded. "I always treat people with respect." This is true—he is *147*
generally respectful, even affable. But good manners do not necessarily neutralize humili-
ations.

As I was leaving, I asked Coates if he wore the Grim Reaper tattoo on his ankle. *148*

"I haven't lied to you yet," he said. "So I'm going to have to take the Fifth on that one." *149*

Playing the Percentages

The sheriff's station in Santa Clarita is located on a street named after a nearby amusement *150*
park, Magic Mountain. Santa Clarita is part of Los Angeles County, but it is geographically
and culturally close to Simi Valley—and a world away from the ghettoes of South Central.
Not a lot happens out in Santa Clarita, which is why sheriff's deputies patrol in single-offi-
cer cars. Deputy Sam Soehnel is assigned to patrol the middle-class and white Valencia
area, as well as the small, rundown Mexican section known as Old Newhall. Most of his
problems are in Old Newhall.

"A lot of Hispanics are heavy drinkers," he says. "It's cultural." If pretext stops happen *151*
at all, they happen in Old Newhall.

A typical Saturday, a typical call. Someone has found a bank door ajar. Soehnel comes *152*
to talk to the semi-hysterical woman who discovered the open door. "Do you think someone is locked in the vault?" she asks. The manager comes, and closes up.

"People have very active imaginations here," Deputy Soehnel says. *153*

Imaginations run wild, for instance, when residents see a black man or a Hispanic *154*
man someplace he "shouldn't be."

"If you're in a nice area," Soehnel explains, "and you see a Hispanic guy, he just sticks *155*
out, if he's just walking around, hanging out. People will call 911. If it's off a citizen's call,
I can make contact with the individual. Ascertain what they're doing in the area."

I ask if it's his policy to pull people out of their cars during traffic stops. *156*

"It depends. A nice area, a guy in Valencia, no. But if it's somebody you're not used *157*
to seeing, unfamiliar, yes. On this job, you learn that it's the nice guys that get killed."

Recently, there was a home-invasion robbery on his beat. A black suspect. "We get a *158*
lot of 911 calls," Soehnel says. "I got a call, 'There's a black guy walking around on people's
lawns.' I get there, he's wearing an electric-company uniform. This woman sees a black guy
walking on her lawn and goes ballistic."

Soehnel is sympathetic to the woman. *159*

"You play the percentages," he says. "That's the way it works. People see a black guy, *160*
they think: 'carjacker.' "

Or rapist. *161*

Getting Profiled to Death

"Amadou Diallo was profiled to death," says Ben Ward, New York City's first black police *162*
commissioner. The night Diallo was killed—the night Rudolph Giuliani's experiment in
"zero tolerance" came to an end—the Street Crime Unit that fired the famous 41 shots
was on the hunt for a black rapist.

Ward is no Sharptonite; he was one of the first black police officials to talk openly *163* about what he called the "the dirty little secret" of black-on-black crime. Yet he believes, he says, that most police officers are spectacularly unqualified to discern the difference between lawbreakers and honest citizens.

"The demonstrable evidence shows that they stink at identifying criminals," he says, *164* noting that the Street Crime Unit of the N.Y.P.D. reported that its officers stopped 45,000 people in 1997 and 1998, and arrested only 9,500.

The sociologist Jerome Skolnick once wrote that police officers keep in their minds *165* a picture of the "symbolic assailant." In his work, Skolnick identified that "symbolic assailant" as a young black man.

It's not only white cops who keep that symbolic assailant in mind when they're out *166* on patrol.

"Sometimes, I hate the young black males because of what they do to their commu- *167* nity," Mark Buchanan, a black antigang officer in Boston, told me. "But then I think to myself, 'If this is the way I feel, and I'm black, what must white officers think about blacks?'"

I took this question to Mike Lewis, the Maryland state trooper who thinks often— *168* very often—about race. We were driving through a black ghetto on the backside of Salisbury. It is, he says, a pit stop on the crack highway.

Has this job made you prejudiced? I ask. *169*

He turned his head in surprise. It looked as if he wanted to say something, but noth- *170* ing came out.

Finally, he says: "Let me tell you something. We respond to calls here, and let's say *171* it's a domestic. We get there, 3, 4 in the morning, and the parents are cracked out, and the kids are up watching TV and eating popcorn, and the place is crawling with roaches. When I go home, the first thing I do is take a shower."

So are you prejudiced? *172*

This is how he answers: "We arrested a Salisbury police sergeant a few months ago, *173* for drugs. We knew he was involved with drugs. For years. He was black."

Black, black, black, black. It is what Mike Lewis sees. It is what Jeffrey Coates sees. It *174* is tunnel vision. They understand half the equation—blacks commit more of certain types of crimes than whites. But what they don't understand is, just because blacks commit more crimes than whites doesn't mean that most blacks commit crimes.

"I see a 16-year-old white boy in a Benz, I think, 'Damn, that boy's daddy is rich.' I *175* see a 16-year-old black, I think, 'That boy's slinging drugs,'" says Robert Richards, a black police sergeant in Baltimore who admits that tunnel vision is a hazard of the job. But like many black cops, he sees nuance where white cops see, well, black and white. "When I start thinking that way, I try to catch myself. If I'm walking down the street and I pass a black male, I realize that, chances are, he's not a criminal."

It is, in some respects, nearly impossible to sit in judgment of a Mike Lewis or a *176* Jeffrey Coates. If Coates says he must pull black men out of their cars and search them on traffic stops, well, Coates has been shot at before, and most critics of the Sheriff's Department have not. But if Coates—and his department, by extension—believe that it is permissible to conduct pretext stops in South Central but impermissible to do so in Santa Clarita, then there's a problem.

The numbers cops cite to justify aggressive policing in black neighborhoods and on *177* the highways tell only part of the story—an important part, but only part. For one thing, blacks make up only 13 percent of the country's illicit drug users, but 74 percent of people who are sentenced to prison for drug possession, according to David Cole, a law professor at Georgetown University and the author of *No Equal Justice.*

Common sense, then, dictates that if the police conducted pretext stops on the campus of U.C.L.A. with the same frequency as they do in South Central, a lot of whites would be arrested for drug possession, too.   *178*

Of course, this doesn't happen, because no white community is getting to let the police throw a net over its children.   *179*

What Gets Talked About, and What Doesn't

Bob Mulholland is the sort of white cop who scares even white people. He is tall and thick and his eyes are hard. He works Philadelphia's 35th Police District with Gene Jones and Mark Robinson.   *180*

The three men meet up one afternoon on a drug corner.   *181*

Jones had been talking about the unequal application of the law. He is a mash of contradictions. One moment, he will speak of the need to "fry" black drug dealers. The next, he will talk about the absurd double standard in law enforcement—the way in which white drug users know with near 100-percent certainty that they will never go to jail for marijuana possession. How they know that they will never be jacked up during a pretext stop. How white cops cut white kids a break.   *182*

"We were doing a drunk-driving checkpoint one night," he said. "And I began to notice that when the cops caught a white kid drunk, they would say things like: 'I'm going to call your father. You're in big trouble.' With black guys, they'd just arrest them. Well, I mean, black kids got fathers, too."   *183*

Jones and Robinson like Mulholland. They told me he was fair. So I asked him if he ever sees a double standard in law enforcement, if the ghetto is policed one way and a white neighborhood another.   *184*

"My job is to clear this corner of [expletives]," he says. "That's what I do."   *185*

Do you ever cut anyone slack? Maybe a student who's waiting for a bus?   *186*

"My job is to clear this corner of [expletives]," he says, again.   *187*

But would you do that equally? If this wasn't the ghetto, but a university campus, would you clear the corner of white kids drinking beer?   *188*

"I don't give a [expletive] who's on the corner. My job is to clear the corner of [expletives]."   *189*

Jones and Robinson return to their car and sit in silence.   *190*

"Well," Jones says.   *191*

"That's what you call a back-in-the-day kind of attitude," Robinson says. The "day" being the time when white cops didn't have to worry about repercussions. I ask them if they believe Mulholland would in fact apply his corner-clearing skills with equal vigor in a white neighborhood.   *192*

"No," Jones says.   *193*

"No," Robinson says.   *194*

"Sometimes, white guys come from white neighborhoods to this job," Jones says. "They don't know a lot of black people, except what they see on TV. So they think they've got to act all hard. They get scared easy."   *195*

"Bob's a good guy, though," he continues. "He's a good cop. He's not a racist." Jones   *196*
and Robinson are truly perplexed. White cops are impossible to understand sometimes.
Sometimes they're your friends. And sometimes. . . .

"You won't believe this," Robinson tells me one day. "I got stopped."   *197*
Really?   *198*
"Yeah, in Abington." Abington is a white suburb over the Philadelphia city line. "It   *199*
was weird. I was stopped at a light, and this police officer behind me puts his lights on, so
I pull it to the side, thinking he's going to pass me. I was thinking like a cop. And then
another car comes. The first cop comes over to my window and says he stopped me because
my inspection sticker was placed abnormally high on the windshield."

Gene Jones begins to laugh.   *200*
"I thought they were going to pull out rulers," Robinson continues. "I mean, inspec-   *201*
tion sticker too high on the windshield?"

I ask Robinson what he was wearing. "What I've got on now," a denim shirt and a   *202*
baseball cap.

"Then he sees the police emblem on my car, and he says, 'Oh, you're a cop?' I said,   *203*
Yeah."

Why do you think he pulled you over in Abington? I ask.   *204*
"I don't know. Maybe because my car is kind of old."   *205*
He doesn't believe this even as he says it.   *206*
"Maybe it was that other thing," he continues. "The thing we were talking about."   *207*
Mark Robinson, the cop who profiles, was just profiled, and he can't even call it by   *208*
name.

READING FOR INFORMATION

1. What legal actions and proclamations have prompted Sergeant Mike Lewis to announce that he is giving up his fight against drugs?
2. Summarize the reasons Los Angeles Police Chief Bernard Parks gives for racial profiling.
3. Explain what Goldberg's interview with the Philadelphia drug dealers revealed about police harassment and racial profiling.
4. After reading the article, how would you answer the question Goldberg poses in paragraph 82: "Is it ever permissible for a law-enforcement officer to use race as one of even 5, or 10, or 20, indicators of possible criminality?"
5. Explain the significance of the Grim Reaper tattoo the law enforcement officers wear on their ankles.
6. Explain what Goldberg means in paragraph 179 when he says that "no white community is going to let the police throw a net over its children."

READING FOR FORM, ORGANIZATION, AND FEATURES

1. How does Goldberg use the opening section to inform his readers of the direction he will take in the article?
2. What is the function of paragraphs 6–8?
3. Explain the types of evidence Goldberg uses to develop and support his position.

READING FOR RHETORICAL CONCERNS

1. What prompted Goldberg to write this article?
2. How did Goldberg obtain data for the article?
3. Explain Goldberg's rhetorical purpose. Why has he written this article, and what impact does he hope to have on his readers?

WRITING ASSIGNMENTS

1. To what extent do you engage in profiling? Write a 750-word essay in response to Goldberg's claim that "civilians profile all the time" (paragraph 32).
2. This is a collaborative writing assignment. Break the class into five groups, and assign each group one of the following individuals:
   - Sgt. Mike Lewis (paragraphs 1–30)
   - Police Chief Bernard Parks (paragraphs 34–38)
   - Officers Mark Robinson and Gene Jones (paragraphs 39–74) and Bob Mulholland (paragraphs 180–196)
   - Deputy Jeffrey Coates (paragraphs 114–149)
   - Deputy Sam Soehnel (paragraphs 150–161)

   Summarize the description of the individuals, and explain how the individuals illustrate Goldberg's point that police officers are not color blind and that they do, indeed, use racial profiling. Each group reports to the class.
3. Drawing on Goldberg's article, write a 750-word essay in which you compare and contrast the views of the police and the views of blacks on the topic of racial profiling.
4. For an audience who has not read Goldberg's article, write a 750-word essay in which you discuss the range of people's views about excessive policing of black neighborhoods and racial profiling.

. . . .

The Color of Justice

David Cole

David Cole is a professor at Georgetown University Law Center, a leading scholar on constitutional law, and an attorney with the Center for Constitutional Rights. He is the author of No Equal Justice: Race and Class in the American Criminal Justice System.

Prereading . . . .

Read the opening sentence of the article, and write your reaction. Do you agree?

. . . .

David Cole. "The Color of Justice." Reprinted with permission from the October 11, 1999 issue of *The Nation*.

It's no mean feat to find an issue on which President Bill Clinton, the Rev. Al Sharpton, Attorney General Janet Reno, many of the nation's police chiefs and NAACP president Kweisi Mfume agree, but at a Washington conference in June, they all expressed the view that racial profiling—the practice of targeting citizens for police encounters on the basis of race—needs to end. Clinton proclaimed profiling "wrong" and "destructive," and ordered federal agencies to gather data on the demographics of their law enforcement patterns. The consensus on profiling was underscored in August, when the National Association of Police Organizations, which staged a debate on the subject at its annual meeting in Denver, had to rely on a white separatist, Jared Taylor, to defend the practice.

Given the mountain of evidence that has piled up recently on racial profiling, the consensus is not surprising. Studies in Maryland, New Jersey, Illinois, Florida, Ohio, Houston and Philadelphia have confirmed that minorities are disproportionately targeted by police. On April 20 the New Jersey Attorney General's office issued a 112-page *mea culpa* admitting that its state troopers had engaged in racial profiling, offering statistics to support the claim and advancing a sophisticated analysis of the nature and scope of the problem. The next day North Carolina—yes, North Carolina—became the first state to pass a law requiring troopers to record and make public the racial patterns of their traffic stops. Connecticut followed suit with its own reporting law in June, and most recently, Florida Governor Jeb Bush has directed the Florida Highway Patrol to begin collecting similar data on January 1, 2000.

The press has covered the subject widely, recounting tales of black professionals stopped for petty traffic violations and investigating the arrest patterns of offending cops. While police departments are obviously at the heart of the problem, the crucial role that courts have played in protecting and sustaining widespread racial profiling has been overlooked. The courts have not only failed to recognize that racial profiling is unconstitutional, but they have effectively insulated it from legal challenge. Where lawsuits challenging profiling have succeeded, it is only because political pressures compelled the police to settle.

The legal case against profiling should be easy to make. Defenders of the practice argue that it makes sense to target minorities because they are more likely than whites to commit crime. But the Constitution forbids reliance on racial generalizations unless they are the only way to achieve a "compelling purpose." Law enforcement is undoubtedly compelling, but racial stereotypes are hardly the only way to go about it. In fact, race is a particularly bad basis for suspicion, since most black people, like most whites, don't commit any crime. Annually at least 90 percent of African-Americans are not arrested for anything. On any given day, the percentage of innocent African-Americans is even higher. Thus, racial profiles necessarily sweep in a large number of innocents. In addition, when officers target minorities they miss white criminals. One need only recall the *Saturday Night Live* skit in which the black actor Garrett Morris and the white actor Chevy Chase walk through Customs. Morris, carrying nothing, is immediately surrounded by multiple Customs agents, while Chase pushes through an open wheelbarrow full of powder cocaine without a hitch.

Yet the Supreme Court has all but invited racial profiling. In 1996 the Court upheld the practice of "pretextual traffic stops," in which police officers use the excuse of a traffic violation to stop motorists when they are investigating some other crime. The same year, the Court allowed the police to use the coercive setting of a traffic stop to obtain consent to search. Together, these rules allow the police to stop and search whomever they please

1

2

3

4

5

on the roads, without having to demonstrate probable cause. And where the police are freed from the need to justify their actions, they appear to fall back on racial stereotypes. In Maryland, for example, blacks were 70 percent of those stopped and searched by Maryland State Police from January 1995 through December 1997, on a road where 17.5 percent of the drivers and speeders were black. New Jersey reported that 77 percent of those stopped and searched on its highways were black or Hispanic, even though only 13.5 percent of the drivers were black or Hispanic.

At the same time, the Court has erected major barriers to lawsuits challenging profiling as racial discrimination. Dismissive of statistical evidence, the Court requires proof that individual officers acted out of racist motives in each case. Thus, the array of recent studies showing that minorities are disproportionately targeted do not establish a violation of the Constitution's equal protection guarantee. In fact, unless the police admit to racial profiling, the Court's intent standard is nearly impossible to meet.

6

Even when a party can prove that he was profiled, the Court has made it very difficult to obtain a remedy that addresses the practice of profiling systemically. In *City of Los Angeles* v. *Lyons*, the Court ruled that victims of past police misconduct cannot obtain court injunctions against future misconduct unless they can prove that they will be *personally* subjected to the practice in the future. In 1994, a federal court in Florida dismissed a racial-profiling suit on these grounds even as it complained that the Supreme Court's *Lyons* decision "seemingly 'renders [the federal courts] impotent to order the cessation of a policy which may indeed be unconstitutional and may harm many persons.'"

7

An ACLU case now pending in Illinois illustrates just how difficult the courts have made it to challenge racial profiling. The Illinois State Police don't record the race of the drivers they stop, so the ACLU sought to obtain copies of ticketed motorists' license applications, from which they then planned to use Social Security or address information to develop racial data. The court ruled that the ACLU would have to pay Illinois $160,000 for that information.

8

Using last names as a rough proxy for ethnicity, the ACLU then showed that although Hispanics compose less than 8 percent of the state's population, they were 27 percent of those stopped and searched by a highway drug interdiction unit. The court replied that statistics aren't enough. The ACLU showed that the state police permit consideration of race, that their training materials focus on Hispanics as drug couriers and that state troopers admit they consider race. The court replied that the ACLU's claim still failed because the plaintiffs did not identify specific "similarly situated" white motorists who were not stopped and ticketed. When the ACLU pointed to a white lawyer who had been following a Latino motorist the day he was stopped, the court said the lawyer wasn't similarly situated, because her car was a different color and her license plate was from a different state.

9

Lawsuits have played an important role in the campaign against racial profiling, but not through any actions of the courts. The single most significant development to date on the profiling front was Robert Wilkins's decision in 1992 to sue when a Maryland state trooper illegally stopped and searched him and his family. Because Wilkins, a Harvard Law School graduate and prominent public defender, was such a sympathetic plaintiff, Maryland quickly settled, agreeing to record the race of those it stopped and to provide that data to the court and the ACLU. That led to the first systematic evidence of a problem that until then had been largely a matter of anecdotes.

10

Another settlement, in Philadelphia, was also crucial. In 1996, civil rights attorney David Rudovsky and the ACLU threatened the Philadelphia police with a lawsuit sparked by media revelations of rampant police abuse. The city settled before the suit was filed, allowing plaintiffs access to racial breakdowns of police stops. There, as in Maryland, the data have provided critical evidence for charges of racial profiling.   *11*

Despite the courts, more progress has been made on racial profiling than on any other issue of racial inequality in criminal law enforcement in the past decade. There are many reasons for this. The issue has tremendous organizing appeal and has captured the attention of mainstream civil rights groups, such as the NAACP and the Urban League, which have all too often shied away from criminal justice issues. Unlike most law enforcement victims, innocent victims of racial profiling elicit public sympathy. The practice targets not just the disfranchised poor but rich and middle-class minorities, who are much more likely to have their complaints taken seriously. Everyone who drives understands the ultimate arbitrariness of who gets pulled over. And because most people see the world to one degree or another through racial stereotypes, it is easy to believe that police officers act on these bases.   *12*

Equally important, the relief that activists have requested, at least at this stage, seems nonthreatening: They ask principally for the collection and reporting of data. How police departments and the public will respond when the results come in remains to be seen. Profiling is not the work of a few "bad apples" but a widespread, everyday phenomenon that will require systemic reform.   *13*

It also remains to be seen whether the advances made on racial profiling will prove to be a wedge for more deep-rooted and lasting reforms directed at racial disparity in criminal justice, or merely an exception to the rule of laissez-faire. But one thing is certain: The courts will not lead. At one time, one could have looked to the federal courts, protectors of individual rights and leaders in the fight against racial discrimination, to play a significant role in the battle. But today's courts are cut from a different cloth. Faced with stark evidence, they would rather deny than confront discrimination.   *14*

READING FOR INFORMATION

1. Paraphrase the position Cole states in paragraph 3.
2. Explain the two Supreme Court rulings that allow police to stop and search drivers without having to demonstrate probable cause.
3. Explain the various ways the Court hinders people from filing lawsuits against the practice of racial profiling.
4. Explain why so much progress has been made on racial profiling despite the courts.

READING FOR FORM, ORGANIZATION, AND FEATURES

1. Explain the function of paragraphs 1 and 2.
2. Review the list of organizational patterns on page 24. Which of these patterns does Cole use?
3. What types of evidence does Cole use to support his argument?

READING FOR RHETORICAL CONCERNS

1. What effect do you think this article had on readers of the liberal magazine, *The Nation*?
2. What is Cole's purpose in writing this article?

WRITING ASSIGNMENTS

1. For an audience who has not read Cole's article, write a 500-word summary explaining how the courts are protecting racial profiling, rather than helping end it.
2. In a 750-word essay, compare Patricia Williams's and David Cole's views of the justice system.
3. Is it likely that police officers will admit to racial profiling? Write a 750-word essay in which you draw on Jeffrey Goldberg's article "The Color of Suspicion" to respond to David Cole's argument in paragraph 6 that "unless the police admit to racial profiling, the Court's intent standard is nearly impossible to meet."

• • • • • • • • • • • • • • • •

WRITING ASSIGNMENTS FOR CHAPTER 13

1. Compose a 1,000-word comparison-and-contrast essay based on Alton Fitzgerald White's "Ragtime, My Time" and Patricia Williams's "Road Rage." Develop your own thesis and point of view on the topics you are comparing.
2. Select a specific controversial issue raised by Alton Fitzgerald White in "Ragtime, My Time," Patricia Williams in "Road Rage," and David Cole in "The Color of Suspicion," and write a 1,250-word essay synthesizing the three authors' views.
3. Write a 1,000-word argument essay defending your views about whether police should engage in any type of suspect profiling. Your position should be clearly stated and well supported with material from this chapter. Be sure to address and refute the opposing position.
4. Write a 1,000-word essay in which you explain how Alton Fitzgerald White's experiences in "Ragtime, My Time" illustrate the thesis of one of the other authors in this chapter.
5. Drawing on selections in this chapter and sources you have researched in the library and on the Web, write a 1,500-word paper in which you argue that in today's criminal justice system, both overt and covert racial discrimination does or does not exist.
6. Research one of the following topics, and write a paper in which you argue your position. Be sure to acknowledge and refute the opposing view.
   • Law enforcement in the black community
   • Racial disparities in imprisonment
   • Historical role of race in the United States criminal justice system
   • White crime versus black crime
   • Relationships between crime and drugs
   • Community policing

14

GENDER EQUITY IN SPORTS

Girls and women have long fought for the right to participate in sports on an equal footing with boys and men. It wasn't until the last third of the twentieth century, however, that attitudes toward women's participation in sports changed, resulting in mass participation of girls and women in the sporting arena. Much of the change was brought about by federal legislation, particularly Title IX of the Educational Amendments of 1972. Title IX states: "No person in the United States shall, on the basis of sex, be excluded from participation in, be denied the benefits of, or be subjected to discrimination under any education program or activity receiving Federal financial assistance." This government intervention requires secondary schools and colleges to provide equal opportunity to male and female athletes and to offer parity in overall athletic programs. In the years since this act was signed into law, new opportunities have been afforded to girls and women in school and college athletics, but not without conflict. The battle for equality has resulted in the gender equity debate.

In the opening selection, "Sport: Where Men Are Men and Women Are Trespassers," Pat Griffin discusses the social and cultural role sports play in developing masculinity. She argues that women are unwelcome in sports because traditionally they are man's territory. In "Gender Games: What about Men?" Douglas T. Putnam focuses on the controversy that has surrounded Title IX and discusses the concerns of the legislation's opponents and supporters.

Leslie Heywood, in "Satellite," relates her personal experiences as a champion runner who regularly worked out with the boys' cross-country team in high school. In the next selection, "Title IX from Outer Space," Walter Olson argues that Title IX is killing men's college sports. He claims that colleges have been forced to cut the number of men's teams to equalize participation. In contrast, Donald F. Sabo writes in support of Title IX and gender equity in "Different Stakes: Men's Pursuit of Gender Equity in Sports." In the next selection, "Unequal Opportunity," Laurie Tarkan discusses attempts to reassess the requirement of equal funding for men's and women's school sports, and in the final selection, "Title IX: Does Help for Women Come at the Expense of African Americans?" Craig T. Greenlee argues that the sports privileges given to women have had a negative effect on African American athletes.

Sport: Where Men Are Men and Women Are Trespassers

Pat Griffin

Pat Griffin is a professor in the social justice education program at the University of Massachusetts-Amherst. She is the coeditor of Teaching for Diversity and Social Justice: A Sourcebook for Teachers and Trainers *and the author of* Strong Women, Deep Closets: Lesbians and Homophobia in Sport.

Prereading ·

Examine Griffin's title. Does it indicate what the essay will be about? Speculate on the content of the essay.

· · · · · · · · · · · · · · · ·

Sport is more than games. As an institution, sport serves important social functions in supporting conventional social values. In particular, sport is a training ground where boys learn what it means to be men. Masculinity does not come naturally; it must be carefully taught. Specific rewards and punishments provide clear messages about acceptable and unacceptable behavior for boys. Boys who show an interest in "girl" activities, such as playing with dolls, dancing, or cooking, are teased by peers. Young boys learn at an early age that participation in athletics is an important, if not required, part of developing a masculine identity and gaining acceptance among peers.

Every Saturday morning in the fall little boys stagger up and down fields under the weight of full football drag, imitating the swagger and ritual they see in their professional sports heroes. Many fathers worry if their sons do not exhibit an interest in sports. They teach their sons to throw, catch, swing bats, shoot hoops. Adults comment on the size of young boys by predicting in which sports they will excel. Participation on school athletic teams, especially the big four (football, basketball, baseball, and ice hockey) ensure popularity and prestige among classmates and in the larger community. Young boys idolize professional and college team-sport athletes and coaches because of their physical size, strength, toughness, and competitiveness. Young boys and adult men wear caps, T-shirts, and jackets with their favorite professional or collegiate team mascot and colors.

Men's athletic events, especially the big four team sports, draw huge numbers of spectators. Men of all colors and social classes study team statistics and participate in intense postcontest analyses of strategy and performance. Cities spend millions of dollars building sports arenas with tax subsidies to woo men's professional teams to town or prevent them from moving to another city. The athletic equipment and clothing industries are multibillion-dollar enterprises that depend on the large number of boys and men who buy their increasingly sophisticated and specialized products.

The importance of sport in socializing men into traditional masculine gender roles also defines the sport experience for women. Because sport is identified with men and masculinity, women in sport become trespassers on male territory, and their access is

Reprinted, by permission, from Pat Griffin, 1998, *Strong Women, Deep Closets: Lesbians and Homophobia in Sport.* (Champaign, IL: Human Kinetics) 16–18.

limited or blocked entirely. Despite huge increases in women's sport participation, there is still tremendous resistance to an equitable distribution of resources between men's and women's athletics. *USA Today* reported that on the 25th anniversary of the passage of Title IX, the federal law prohibiting sex discrimination in education, 80 percent of college and university athletic programs in the United States are still not in compliance with the law.

Sometimes resistance to women's sport participation is more personal. In the spring of 1997 Melissa Raglin, 12, was the starting catcher for a Boca Raton Babe Ruth baseball team. During a game the plate umpire asked Melissa if she was wearing a protective cup. Melissa removed her helmet and catcher's mask and told him she was a girl. However, the Babe Ruth rules state that all players (assumed to be male) must wear a cup to protect their genitals. When Melissa, who had been playing in the Babe Ruth league for over two seasons, refused to comply with the rule, she was prohibited from playing catcher. She was allowed to play again only when she ordered a special cup designed for women, even though most doctors agree that there is no medical reason why a girl should wear a protective cup. This example shows the absurd lengths to which some men will go to try to humiliate a young girl to make sure she knows that she is trespassing on male turf. Male league officials' insistence that Melissa wear a cup, even at the risk of ridicule in news stories, demonstrates the seriousness and importance of protecting sport from female encroachment.

5

Women's presence in sport as serious participants dilutes the importance and exclusivity of sport as a training ground for learning about and accepting traditional male gender roles and the privileges that their adoption confers on (white, heterosexual) men. As a result, women's sport performance is trivialized and marginalized as an inferior version of the "real thing." These arguments ignore the overlap in sport performances among men and women in all sports and the growing interest among young girls in sport participation.

6

Sexism as a system of male privilege and female subordination is based on the acceptance of particular definitions of gender (what constitutes a man or a woman) and gender roles (what qualities, talents, and characteristics women and men are supposed to have). Women's serious participation in sport brings into question the "natural" and mutually exclusive nature of gender and gender roles. If women in sport can be tough minded, competitive, and muscular too, then sport loses its special place in the development of masculinity for men. If women can so easily develop these so-called masculine qualities, then what are the meanings of femininity and masculinity? What does it mean to be a man or a woman? These challenges threaten an acceptance of the traditional gender order in which men are privileged and women are subordinate. Thus, they account for much of the strong resistance to gender equity in sport and the need to marginalize and control the growth of women's athletics.

7

References

Brady, E. "Colleges Score Low on Gender-equity Test." *USA Today*, 3 March 1997, C1, C4.

Bryson, L. "Challenges to Male Hegemony in Sport." <u>Sport, Men and the Gender Order: Critical Feminist Perspectives</u>, eds. Donald F. Sabo and Michael A. Messner. Champaign, IL: Human Kinetics, 1990.

Sabo, Donald F., and Michael A. Messner, eds. <u>Sport, Men and the Gender Order: Critical Feminist Perspectives</u>. Champaign, IL: Human Kinetics, 1990.

READING FOR INFORMATION

1. Explain what Griffin means when she says, "Masculinity does not come naturally; it must be carefully taught" (paragraph 1).
2. According to Griffin, why are female athletes "trespassers on male territory"?
3. How does Griffin define "sexism"?

READING FOR FORM, ORGANIZATION, AND FEATURES

1. Explain the types of evidence (facts, statistics, references to experts, anecdotes, direct quotations, and so forth) Griffin uses to develop and support her position, and give examples of each type.
2. What is the effect of the rhetorical questions Griffin poses in paragraph 7?

READING FOR RHETORICAL CONCERNS

1. Explain Griffin's rhetorical purpose. Why has she written this piece, and what impact does she hope to have on her readers?
2. What is the effect of paragraph 5?

WRITING ASSIGNMENTS

1. In response to Griffin's reading selection, write a 750-word autobiographical essay about your participation in sports. Describe the role played by your family, peer group, and school (teachers and coaches).
2. Why do you think more males than females become involved in sport? Is it the result of biological differences or mechanisms of childhood socialization? Write a 750-word essay in which you argue either that children's play, toy selection, physical activity, and sport behavior are learned or that they are biologically determined.
3. Write a 750-word essay in which you investigate the extent to which "women's sport performance is trivialized and marginalized as an inferior version of the 'real thing'" (paragraph 6). Draw on your own experience and also examine press and TV coverage of women's sporting events. Be aware of the amount and quality of commentary, patronizing tone, sexual innuendo, and the quality of technical production.

• • • • • • • • • • • • • • • • •

Gender Games: What about Men?

Douglas T. Putnam

Douglas T. Putnam is an attorney who works for the County Commissioners Association of Ohio. He is a former contributing editor of The Lincoln Library of Sports Champions *and a member of the Professional Football Researchers Association. He is the author of* Controversies of the Sports World.

Prereading ●

Write your reaction to Title IX of the Educational Amendments of 1972 (see page 447). Then meet in small groups to discuss your ideas with your classmates. Appoint a spokesperson who will report the group's work to the class.

● ● ● ● ● ● ● ● ● ● ● ● ● ●

Emotional controversy . . . has surrounded Title IX since its passage: opponents vehemently contend that the law hurts boys' and men's sports programs by requiring a shifting of funds and resources to girls' and women's programs and by forcing the outright elimination of many male teams. There also are many who believe that Title IX has been used to force the sexual integration of the playing fields, to the detriment of males. "Over my dead body will girls ever play Little League baseball," fumed one male coach in the 1970s, before Congress revised the terms of the organization's federal charter and forced it to include females. "If one of them ever struck out a boy, he would be psychologically scarred for life" (Lipsyte 1997: H9). And despite the vast cultural changes that have occurred in the last quarter-century, there are still many who believe that it is inappropriate for women to be involved in athletics to as great a degree as men in any capacity—be it player, coach, referee, trainer, administrator, or even fan. "Young men today are swimming in a different sea," says Don Sabo, a former football player who is now a sports sociologist at D'Youville College in New York. "But I still have to tiptoe when I speak to male high school and college athletes . . . because when you start talking about gender issues, young men start feeling very put upon" (Lipsyte 1997: H9).

1

For many years, opponents of Title IX had a powerful ally in the NCAA. As an organization largely controlled by athletic directors and men's football and basketball coaches at the nation's major universities, the NCAA strongly supported a proposed amendment in 1974 that would have exempted college athletics from the law's requirements. Later the NCAA initiated a lawsuit that sought to render the law's administrative regulations invalid. Only after those two maneuvers failed did the NCAA soften its opposition and move toward compliance. It was not until 1991, ten years after it became the governing body for women's college athletics, that the NCAA's members formally adopted gender equity in athletics as a basic principle of the organization (Tarkan 1995: 26). Executive director Cedric Dempsey admits that progress has been slow. "We are trying to change a culture," he says. "It is more difficult than it might appear" (Chambers 1997: C10).

2

Concerns raised by Title IX opponents about reductions in men's programs are valid. In 1995, Congressman Dennis Hastert of Illinois chaired hearings in Washington on the issue of how Title IX affects opportunities for male athletes. The evidence shows that many men's programs in colleges and universities for sports other than basketball or football were discontinued between 1982 and 1996: thirty-two in gymnastics, twenty-seven in swimming, and forty-eight in wrestling (Wieberg 1997: 11C). Like many others, Hastert believes that the interest level of each gender should be considered when participation opportunities and resources are allocated. They maintain that males are more interested in playing sports than females and therefore should be given more chances to participate. In their view, it is ludicrous to enforce a law that compels females to participate in athletics as a matter of decree. Maureen Mahoney, one of the attorneys who represented Brown University in the *Cohen* case, shares those sentiments: "Are there substantially more men than women who have the desire and ability to compete on the varsity level? Because if there are, accomplished male athletes should not have to duke it out among themselves to get the slots that are left after all the women have been accommodated" (Mahoney 1997: 78).

The law's supporters counter those arguments with two points. First, they reject the notion that women are by their nature less interested in athletic competition than men. When Title IX passed in 1972, only 7 percent of the interscholastic athletes in high school were female. By 1992, that number had risen to 37 percent (Tarkan 1995: 26). To the law's supporters that does not indicate lack of interest. It indicates precisely the opposite. Once the doors of opportunity were opened and females were offered a chance to play, they did so by the millions.

Supporters also dismiss the claim that enforcement of Title IX necessarily leads to the elimination of men's programs. They contend that the true heart of the controversy is football, a sport played only by males and one that requires a huge allocation of resources for uniforms, equipment, liability insurance, field maintenance, travel expenses, and large coaching staffs. With Division I-A schools in the NCAA offering eighty-five football scholarships and often fielding teams with as many as 120 members, it is extremely difficult to achieve gender parity in terms of participation or financial aid. No single women's sport in the NCAA is allocated more than twenty scholarships (Wieberg 1997: 11C). If football expenses could be pared and the number of participants reduced, there would be considerably less need to eliminate smaller men's sports such as gymnastics, wrestling, and swimming.

Football supporters point to the fact that scholarship grants in the sport have been reduced steadily over the years and that other expenses have been cut significantly. Some question the second claim, especially when they read of the huge sums spent by a university to attract a coach. The same difficulty can arise when they read of the equally huge sum spent to buy out of the contract of the coach who has been fired because he could not produce the winning teams needed to keep the football program prominent and financially healthy.

On many campuses, football remains a virtually untouchable enterprise immune to significant change, backed by influential supporters, a century of rich tradition, and millions of vocal fans. Along with men's basketball, it also generates millions of dollars in revenue through the sale of game tickets and television broadcast rights. Only rarely does a school actually make the drastic move of discontinuing football, as Boston University did in 1997. It is one of only three Division I schools to drop the sport since 1992. In the words of David F. Salter, "College football's hierarchy has attacked gender equity with the tenacity of a blitzing linebacker facing fourth down at the one yard line" (Salter 1996: 49). Instead of confronting that linebacker, universities have chosen, in the view of Title IX advocates, to take the less painful course of eliminating other men's sports in order to level the playing field for women.

References

Chambers, Marcia. "For Women, 25 Years of Title IX Has Not Leveled the Playing Field." New York Times, June 16, 1997: A1, C10.

Lipsyte, Robert. "In the Gender Game, New Rules to Play By." New York Times, June 22, 1997: H9.

Mahoney, Maureen. "The Numbers Don't Add Up." Sports Illustrated, May 5, 1997: 78.

Salter, David F. Crashing the Old Boys' Networks: The Tragedies and Triumphs of Girls and Women in Sports. Westport: Praeger, 1996.

Tarkan, Laurie. "Unequal Opportunity." Women's Sports and Fitness, September 1995: 25–27.

Wieberg, Steve. "NCAA Finds Too Little Progress." USA Today, June 20, 1997: 11C.

READING FOR INFORMATION

1. What are some of the arguments of opponents of Title IX?
2. How do supporters of Title IX counter the arguments of opponents?
3. Why have small non-revenue-generating sports suffered as a result of Title IX?

READING FOR FORM, ORGANIZATION, AND FEATURES

1. Describe the different types of evidence (facts, statistics, references to experts, and so on) that Putnam uses to make his case.
2. Review the list of organizational patterns on page 24. Outline the selection, and explain which of these patterns Putnam uses.

READING FOR RHETORICAL CONCERNS

1. Is Putnam objective, or does he present only one side of the issue? Explain your answer.
2. Describe Putnam's tone.

WRITING ASSIGNMENTS

1. Design a questionnaire that will determine students' attitudes toward gender equity in sport, and administer it to a random sampling of men and women at your college. Then write a 750-word essay comparing and contrasting the views of the two groups.
2. Use a newspaper index such as the *New York Times Index* or the Internet newspaper index, NewsTracker, which you will find at http://nt.excite.com, to search for recent articles on the *Cohen* v. *Brown University* case mentioned in paragraph 3. Summarize developments in the case, and write your reaction. Your essay should be around 750 words long.
3. Interview your grandmother, mother, or older woman friends about their athletic experiences as schoolgirls. Write a 750-word essay in which you compare their experiences with your own.

Satellite

Leslie Heywood

Leslie Heywood is an assistant professor of English at Binghamton University in Binghamton, New York. She is the author of Dedication to Hunger: The Anorexic Aesthetic in Modern Culture, Bodymakers: A Cultural Anatomy of Women's Bodybuilding, *and* Pretty Good for a Girl. *Heywood is a former University of Arizona track star and cross-country runner.*

P r e r e a d i n g ....

"Satellite" is a chapter from Leslie Heywood's memoir, *Pretty Good for a Girl.* In high school, Heywood, a champion runner, regularly worked out with the boys' cross-country team. What do you think of this arrangement? Write your reaction.

. . . .

Amphitheater High School belongs to the sprinters, and to their coach, Coach Luke. The sprinters have pumped-up muscles, nicely feathered hair, standard handsome faces, butts that do much for their Levi's or the bright green running shorts we have to wear for every meet. Nice legs, nice chests, and they always run with their shirts off. Walk their lettermen jackets through the halls, all that. What is known from the female side as a catch, a privilege to snag them, to walk arm in arm with them a gift.

1

I am no gift. According to some of the sprinters, I am trouble. I yell too much. Stand out. I've dated a couple of them, and I've seemed to cross over some lines. Hank and a football player named Armando, until I finally settle on Vince. Vince has a broad smile and a soft voice, a guy who almost in spite of himself just happens to be sprinter-like too. Gentle hands. Perfectly feathered hair that isn't ever out of place, medium bod and a really sweet butt.

2

The sprinters own the weight room. The distance guys go in there with me, but they're really out of place. They're skinny and can't lift very much weight. Vince, like all the rest of the sprinters, can do lunges with a barbell stretched across his shoulders at 120 pounds; it brings out those thick rounds of hamstrings that bunch like a fist when he sprints. And if he can do 120, I've got to try it, too.

3

I'm not allowed to talk to any sprinters in the weight room while they're doing their sets. I'm the only girl in there, with the distance guys—no one worries about them—and the coaches, all men, always watch me to make sure I'm not distracting their guys, baseball, football, basketball, track. Sometimes, without looking, I can feel eyes cutting up on the tightness of my legs, my chest, so my skin burns a little bit red, but I learn early on to forget it and work. I work harder than anyone, the missing link between sprinters and distance runners, who are mostly fairly weak. The coaches don't like this. They look at me and the distance guys, the heavy plates on my bars and frown, but there's not a damn thing any one of them can say. Legally they have to let girls in here, and I lift what I lift. I can lunge Vince's 120, too, as long as someone, usually Victor or Jim, places it across my shoulders so I don't have to throw

4

it up over my head myself. Small under hulking iron plates, each lunge of the hamstring makes me larger, cutting up space. It's mine. I belong here. I always feel taller when I'm done.

I think I settle on Vince because of his eyes, which are very kind, always warm, not glinty like other sprinters. Christmas 1981, Vince and I stand in front of a blinking tree. I've got on a red velour shirt, hair curled up around my face. I'm holding a huge stuffed bear, red bow around his neck, his nose at my ear and big bear butt coming down to below my knees. Vince is holding me, one arm around my back and his other hand on the bear's left front foot. Vince's leg, substantial, nice, a muscular thigh tight in his pants, which run slim up his hip. White button-down shirt, the collar unbuttoned quite low, a V-necked lamb's wool pullover. Smiling and looking down. I look like someone who's been told she's a sweet, sweet thing. The Christmas lights spread over me, blinking. I have a boyfriend who has given me a bear. 5

But the bear is a rare moment of peace. I date Vince but hang with Kenny. Hang with the cross-country guys, not good, my white hair bouncing around in the midst of their pack, a pack I should not run with, according to the rules, either in practice or out of it. In the unspoken code that says if I date a sprinter I must only have eyes for them, I've transgressed a thousand times. I belong to Vince but snuggle with Kenny in the van or the pickup to and from the trails we run for practice. In his arms, smiling up. He makes me warm and laugh. I light up around him much as he does around me. We get lost on purpose on our morning runs, down some sidelong woods trail, in between silent groves of trees where not another foot turns over the leaves. We run, but we turn to each other, stop, too. Do we ever kiss? He has braces. I think we do, especially one Saturday on Mt. Lemmon, cool six a.m. air, calling birds and ferns and pines, endorphins from running the six-mile hill all mixed with the elixir of each other, arm to arm, mouth to mouth, sweat to sweat. Thinking his mouth the whole way up the hill. Lying in his arms the way home in the van most mornings, the other guys giving us a little quiet, space. They're all in my camp like the sprinters are not, for sprinters have boys in their camp and girls are just for one thing. 6

The sprinters shake their heads at me when I run by, say *trouble*, and Vince gets smaller and shrugs, "She's OK." And they jeer a little, call him by his nickname, "Lonzo," and give him a series of shoves. In this world, a football field ringed by this, our track, where we spend all our afternoon hours, the sprinters are big and I am a girl, not so big. Except when I win races, which somehow lets me grow. Then I'm big. But off the track, tucked under their arms, I am a shadow, a slow blow job in the desert, the back of a pickup weekend nights. 7

One day in early spring, I'm in the weight room. I'm sixteen, still the only girl in the place, again with my guys, the distance runners. Not the sprinters, who wear the flare of their hamstrings and biceps like some general's certificate that says the bench press and the squat racks belong to them. Rebel Barbie and her scarecrows carry not so much weight, we win races sometimes, but come on, men are men. There is only one incline bench and we are on it, pumping out sets and fair reps. A couple of sprinters start to circle in, drawing up their shoulders, flexing their pecs, and when that doesn't force us to give over our place, roll their eyes like they are saying, "little wimps." I look at them and snarl. I might be one of the guys with the long-distance men but to the sprinters we're nobody, just sawdust taking up some space. Invisible again. It won't happen. 8

The guys look over at me as I jump onto the bench, not even waiting to size up the right notches on the bar to place my fingers. I throw the weight up, quick and pissed. With twenty-five on each side and the bar forty-five, at ninety-five it isn't much, but it is more 9 than any girl in the school can do, and I am sure I belong to that bench. Six reps, seven, even ten, I'm into it cold, I'm not stopping, my face going red and my pecs beginning to sweat. I can feel Jim shift, kind of clearing his throat, and I throw in another couple, racking the weight with a clash.

I sit up and there he is: the sprinters' coach. He looks just like—*just like*—Luke Spencer on *General Hospital*, and this is Luke Spencer's year. A few months from now he will rape Laura [and] then marry her, and the whole country will tune in, whether they usually watch the soaps or not, the hype in the papers approaching that reserved for Prince Charles and Princess Di, whose wedding will also happen that month. Like Luke on TV, Coach Luke is gaunt and thin, skin really white, with unruly threads of albino-red hair fanning the air behind him,thinning a bit right on top. He moves quickly, and is sarcastic a lot like he's sarcastic right now, twisting that smile that says he knows it all and knows it right, your place in the universe nothing like his. I look up at him, ready for a fight. He looks at me like you'd look at a rooster who's strutting his stuff just before he's going to get cooked. Not this rooster, mister, not me. I look at him with his own look that says you don't even exist and you'd better get out of my way. His mouth turns up at one corner and he laughs, "Hey, my guys need this bench and you all should go do something else." I don't move. Ray looks at me, "Come on, Leslie." I sit. Coach Luke laughs again, turns away.   10

I'm really pissed now and this weight bench has never seen quite so much fervor and my voice rings out like nothing anyone would question: "Get me the thirty-fives." I throw off the twenty-fives like they were dimes. I've never done 115 but it's going up now, six times, eight times, I don't even falter until ten. I expand like I'm big enough to take on the whole gym and sit up like there's no way anyone could challenge my place. Jim and Ray are really nervous, say under their breaths, "Come on, let's go," but I ask for it, let him turn around, let him just come back here one more time.   11

Sure enough he does and he isn't laughing this time. He's got the voice of a parent who's been challenged. He draws himself to his rough six-foot height and thunders, "I told you my guys need this bench!" My ears sing and my face is hot and I place my feet as solid as I can and throw out some words like this gym's never heard. The clanging weights and the humming voices all stop. My words hang in the air like they're suspended, like time wound down: "Just what makes you think that your guys," I hiss, "have any more right to use this bench"—now I'm pounding it—"than we do? Why do you think this?"   12

I look at him, and first his eyes are quiet, kind of narrow, sitting toward the back of his head. Then they get brighter, as if in disbelief. As the voices stop and everyone listens he starts to move, in what seems like slow motion at first, but then he's on me in a second, so quickly I don't even have a chance to breathe. His white fingers are around my wrist and his face is an advanced shade of red. He jerks me off the bench so hard I think for a minute I'm flying, but then my head hits the wall behind me. I stand there, dazed, but his hands are on my hands again and I'm outside before I know it, backed up against the aluminum siding of that football-player gym, glowering like the bad girl whose father's yelling right up in her face.   13

His voice goes on and on and the words are like ice or the sound of faraway blows and I can just feel the echo as it rides off my skin and I have no idea what he is saying. I just know that it's all I can do to keep from screaming, that he's trying to tell me that I'm a ghost and he lives, and there's no way I'm going to take this. So he goes on and I don't   14 flinch and he keeps going until suddenly he's back inside and the sound of the weights start to clang like shots and I get the hell out and run home.

READING FOR INFORMATION

1. How do the male sprinters and their coaches react to a girl working out in the weight room?

2. Why do you think the sprinters have such a disparaging attitude toward Heywood and the other distance runners?

3. What is your reaction to Coach Luke's treatment of Heywood? How do you interpret her comment, "I just know that it's all I can do to keep from screaming, that he's trying to tell me that I'm a ghost and he lives, and there's no way I'm going to take this" (paragraph 14)?

READING FOR FORM, ORGANIZATION, AND FEATURES

1. Though a memoir is nonfiction, it has many of the characteristics of fiction. Examine "Satellite," and make a list of the characteristics you observe.

2. As you move through the selection, can you find details that prepare you for the ending? Make a list.

READING FOR RHETORICAL CONCERNS

1. Explain Heywood's rhetorical purpose. Why has she written the memoir, and what impact does she hope to have on her readers?

2. How does Heywood's voice engage the reader?

WRITING ASSIGNMENTS

1. Think of an event in your life involving participation in sport. Write a straightforward narrative of the event in the first person. Then draw some significance from the event. Delve beneath the surface. What did the event teach you? What did you discover about life? Rewrite the memoir, incorporating the significance. Your final draft should be around 750 words long.

2. Write a 750-word response to Heywood's memoir. Does the hostile climate Heywood describes still exist today? Have boys and men welcomed girls and women into sports, or do they simply tolerate the presence of girls and women? Are girls and women still subjected to discrimination and harassment?

3. Although the number of female athletes has increased since the passage of Title IX, the number of women coaches in high school and college sports has decreased significantly. Some analysts project that female coaches may be headed for extinction. Research this topic in the library and on the World Wide Web, and write a 750-word objective synthesis.

• • • • • • • • • • • • • • • •

Title IX from Outer Space

Walter Olson

Walter Olson works at the Manhattan Institute. He is a contributing editor to Reason *and the author of* The Excuse Factory.

Prereading ·

Meet in small groups to discuss what you know about Title IX (see page 447). Then speculate on Olson's title. Why would he refer to Title IX as "from outer space"? Appoint a spokesperson who will report each group's finding to the class.

· · · · · · · · · · · · · · · ·

"Giving Women a Sporting Chance: Cal State Plan Could Be a Template for Nation" jubilated a *Los Angeles Times* editorial. The month was October 1993, and the California State University system had just agreed to settle a National Organization for Women lawsuit by adopting a quota system for varsity sports participation, promising that women's share would come out within 5 percentage points of female enrollment at each of its 19 campuses.   *1*

According to the *Times*, this "welcome commitment" would put Cal State in the "vanguard of reform," for which its administration was "to be commended." "Gender fairness in sports is really not that difficult to comprehend," explained the *Times*, with that touch of condescension that so grates on non-feminist ears. "Too many athletic departments just don't"—can you tell where this sentence is headed?—"get it."   *2*

The settlement's compliance deadline was set for fall 1998, and by mid-1997 one of its results had become clear: massive cuts in men's sports throughout the Cal State system. In June, Cal State–Northridge dropped its baseball team, which had ranked among the nation's top 20, along with soccer, swimming, and volleyball. Cal State–Bakersfield drastically curtailed its outstanding wrestling program. San Francisco State, Fullerton, Hayward, Chico, Long Beach, and Sonoma all got out of football.   *3*

The Cal State men's sports massacre made news from coast to coast, and for good reason: As the *Times* headline predicted, it is going to serve as a model for the rest of the country. Last April, the U.S. Supreme Court declined to review a court decision against Brown University, leaving in place an interpretation of the federal Title IX law that has already begun to devastate such men's sports as track, wrestling, swimming, and diving nationwide. A survey by the National Collegiate Athletic Association found colleges have axed 200 men's teams in recent years, with 17,000 slots lost. Gymnastics teams, which numbered 133 as recently as 1975, are down to 32 overall. Even golf, a sport whose popularity in the outside world has soared, is hard hit.   *4*

The next targets for Title IX enforcers are elementary and secondary schools. Already, many high schoolers in Florida face a ban on all athletic competition because their schools haven't done well enough at equalizing sports participation. Armed with a 1992 Supreme Court decision which allows complainants to demand cash damages as well as lawyers' fees, litigators and regulators are swarming around the field house.   *5*

The premise of the gender-equity movement is simple: Women's sports should get just as much money, attention, and participation as men's. It's a lovely ambition, acceptable in the end to most college administrators as well as most social reformers. Only two obstacles remain: the fans and the participants.

College football, to begin with, is a huge business, generating fortunes in alumni donations, gate receipts, and broadcast fees. Yet it won't have a real female equivalent as long as women are free to avoid it. (Neither forced watching nor forced playing has yet arisen on the Title IX agenda.) Even aside from male-female differences in strength and stature, extremes of physical competition and the buzz of danger just don't play the same role in women's lives as in men's, either as players or as spectators. As *National Review*'s Kate O'Beime has pointed out, men made up a substantial majority of the television audience for the women's NCAA basketball finals.

In questionnaires of prospective Brown students, 50 percent of the men but only 30 percent of the women expressed interest in trying out for athletics. Intramural sports were open to all at Brown, but eight times as many men took part as women. Nor is it easy to argue that the dead hand of bygone male supremacy is the problem. Women at Vassar participate in varsity sports at a rate 13 percent lower than do men, even though Vassar was a women's college until 1969.

"Including football in counting the numbers is unreasonable," Olympic high jumper Amy Acuff told one reporter. "At my school [UCLA], they cut men's swimming and gymnastics so they could start water polo and soccer for women. It broke my heart because those men's teams were really good, and a lot of the women they brought into the new sports weren't serious athletes." (The defunct UCLA diving and swimming program had garnered 16 Olympic gold medals and 41 individual national titles.)

Tough, say the hard-liners at the U.S. Department of Education's Office of Civil Rights, which "has exhibited an astonishing indifference to the destruction of athletic opportunities for males," according to University of Chicago wrestling coach Leo Kocher. Anyone at all can file a complaint that triggers an OCR investigation, and such probes, as *Pittsburgh Post-Gazette* sportswriter Lori Shontz observes, are not always known for their sophistication and subtlety. Staffers who swooped down on Johns Hopkins University, for instance, demanded to know why the women's basketballs were smaller than the men's, not realizing that "women's basketballs are smaller by design to accommodate smaller hands."

As usual in Washington, the quota enforcers heatedly deny that quotas are actually mandatory, insisting that schools can comply by passing one of two other tests. They can show that women are satisfied with existing offerings—but then a complaint itself is apt to serve as evidence of dissatisfaction. Or schools can show a pattern of continued expansion of women's programs, which is to say continued progress toward proportionality. In practice, according to the American Football Coaches Association and other critics, proportionality is the "primary emphasis of enforcement," and the other two tests, though they may furnish the regulators some facade of deniability against quota charges, offer no enduring safe harbor of compliance.

In the *Brown* case, the federal court rebuffed the university's effort to offer evidence that men were more interested in athletics. Are women's teams undersubscribed and men's oversubscribed? Then a university must have fallen short in finding ways to make the women's programs attractive. Is it easier for women at a given level of achievement or commitment to obtain athletic scholarships than it is for men? Too bad: The university may lose anyway, unless it's brought the overall head count into line.

Nor can educators necessarily get off the hook by pointing to other demographic or   *13*
behavioral variables. The student body at Cal State–Bakersfield, reports Elizabeth Arens in
Policy Review, is 64 percent female and includes many women in their 40s and 50s who are
upgrading their education after launching families and disinclined to pursue varsity sports.

"The women's advocacy groups strongly oppose any effort to survey interest in athlet-   *14*
ics because they do not like the results," charges Chuck Neinas, executive director of the College
Football Association, who says the current state of legal interpretation "will make it difficult,
if not impossible, for those universities that sponsor football to comply with Title IX."

Feminist litigators make little secret of their animus toward football, many evidently   *15*
agreeing with University of Wisconsin–Milwaukee professor Margaret Carlisle Duncan that
it's "an institution that promotes male dominance." Where it can't be axed entirely, they
favor at least reducing the number of players on rosters, as Cal State–Fresno and other institutions have reluctantly done. College teams play with larger rosters than the pros, partly
because they can't rely on mid-season signups or trades to replace sidelined regular players.

Ironically, colleges with standout football teams, being flush with revenues for schol-   *16*
arships and equipment, have the easiest time expanding women's sports. Although top-
division football as a whole makes money, it is made unevenly, with some strong teams
raking in the receipts and others running deficits. Title IX activists urge colleges to boot
money-losing pigskin teams, though it seems unlikely that a conference whose cellar-
dwellers dropped out could for long achieve a Lake Wobegon effect and consist entirely of
teams with favorable win-lose records.

In any event, the head count, not money, is what's often really at legal issue. Wrestling   *17*
is among the least expensive sports to sustain. Princeton refused to accept a $2.3 million
alumni gift intended as an endowment to save its 90-year-old men's wrestling team, just as
the University of Southern California did when alumni tried to save its men's swimming
program. Roster cutbacks for "big" men's sports, a common feminist proposal, aid compliance efforts not so much because they save pots of money—the non-star "walk-ons"
dropped are typically already playing without scholarships, travel, or equipment subsidies—but because they keep down the number of male bodies.

Of course, the Equal Employment Opportunity Commission can't resist making   *18*
things worse. Last October, it put out new guidelines arm-twisting colleges to pay coaches
of women's teams as much as they do men's. The guidelines do start with a token conces-
sion that not every volleyball coach may be entitled to the salary of a Big Ten football
wizard, but from then on it's mostly bad news. Comparisons between dissimilar sports? No
problem. Offers based on market rates or current pay levels will be suspect: "Cultural and
social factors may have artificially inflated men's coaches' salaries."

The guidelines hint that if colleges can't show that they've advertised and promoted   *19*
men's and women's squads equally, women's coaches should win salary-dispute cases. Of
course, to hype a fanless team may be to throw good money after bad: In one well-known
case, the USC men's basketball program brought in 90 times as much revenue as the
women's. The agency also suggests a college may lose a case if it "sets up weekly media
interviews" for a red-hot men's team but not its languishing female equivalent.

In the whole Title IX controversy, incidentally, it appears next to impossible to find   *20*
anyone willing to criticize the law in principle. Sure, enforcement has gone haywire and the
results are crazy, but everyone hastens to add that of course they just adore the law itself.

As for the old idea that universities in a free society should be entitled to make their 21 own decisions—well, that notion, like so many men's track teams, is on its last lap.

READING FOR INFORMATION

1. List the evidence Olson gives for his claim that Title IX "is killing men's college sports."
2. According to Olson, what are the major obstacles to gender equity in sports?
3. Explain how colleges and universities can demonstrate that they are in compliance with the Title IX regulations, and describe Olson's attitude toward these tests.
4. According to Olson, what is feminists' attitude toward football? Do you think other people hold similar views?
5. What is Olson's attitude toward the new guidelines equalizing salaries of male and female coaches?

READING FOR FORM, ORGANIZATION, AND FEATURES

1. How does Olson use the introductory paragraphs to inform his readers of the direction he will take in the article?
2. Does Olson make concessions to the opposition before he refutes their views?
3. How would you describe Olson's tone?
4. What type of authorities does Olson cite to support his views?

READING FOR RHETORICAL CONCERNS

1. What impact does Olson want to have on his readers?
2. How effective is Olson's tone?
3. How does Olson view what others have said about Title IX and gender equity in sport?
4. What effect does Olson achieve by using each of the following words: *massacre* (paragraph 4), *devastate* (paragraph 4), *axed* (paragraph 4), *targets* (paragraph 5), *swarming* (paragraph 5), *lovely* (paragraph 6), *hard-liners* (paragraph 10), *swooped down* (paragraph 10), *quota enforcers* (paragraph 11), *facade* (paragraph 11) *too bad* (paragraph 12), *arm-twisting* (paragraph 18), *haywire* (paragraph 20), *crazy* (paragraph 20), *adore* (paragraph 20)?

WRITING ASSIGNMENTS

1. Claiming that he is one of the few critics of Title IX, Olson writes:

> In the whole Title IX controversy, incidentally, it appears next to impossible to find anyone willing to criticize the law in principle. Sure, enforcement has gone haywire and the results are crazy, but everyone hastens to add that of course they just adore the law itself. (paragraph 20)

Do some research in the library and on the World Wide Web to find articles and books by other critics of Title IX. Write an essay in which you synthesize their views. Your final draft should be around 750 words long.

2. Compare and contrast Olson's coverage of Title IX's effect on male athletes and men's sports programs with that of Douglas T. Putman in "Gender Games: What about Men?" Your final draft should be around 750 words long.

3. Undertake a collaborative writing project on gender equity in the sports programs at your college. Assign particular sports to each person in the group. Group members will investigate areas such as participation by men and women, expenditures, financial support by the college, qualifications and salaries of coaches, facilities, and practice times. Prepare a 750-word report, and present it to the class.

4. Write an evaluation of Olson's argument.

· · · · · · · · · · · · · · · · ·

Different Stakes: Men's Pursuit of Gender Equity in Sports

Donald F. Sabo

Donald F. Sabo is professor of social science at D'Youville College in Buffalo, New York. He is coauthor of Jock: Sports and Male Identity; Humanism in Sociology; Sport, Men, and the Gender Order: Critical Feminist Perspectives; *and* Sex, Violence, and Power in Sports: Rethinking Masculinity. *Sabo is a former NCAA Division I defensive football captain.*

P r e r e a d i n g ·

Read paragraphs 1–4. In small groups, brainstorm ways that nondiscriminatory athletics benefit male athletes. Appoint a group spokesperson who will report your findings to the class.

· · · · · · · · · · · · · · · · ·

I was returning home from the 1993 Women's Sports Foundation annual conference when the last leg of my flight was delayed by thunderstorms over La Guardia Airport. After being grounded for two hours, the passengers turned to one another for conversation and diversion. Two young men near me, having overheard me talking about women's sports, asked whether it is true that women's athletic programs benefit from the money that men's football programs generate. I explained that this idea is basically a myth; according to records maintained by the National Collegiate Athletic Association (NCAA), about 87 percent of all football programs (45 percent of NCAA Division I-A football teams and 94 percent of Division I-AA football teams) lose money (Raiborn 1990). Rather than being the goose that lays the golden egg, most big-time football programs siphon money away from women's athletic programs as well as lesser-status men's athletic programs.

In response to my comments, the young men explained that their intercollegiate sports (fencing and track and field) "are also getting screwed by the athletic department, which is

1

2

only interested in promoting football." The fencer lamented that "the women athletes have Title Six, or whatever it is, to help them fight for better treatment, but the guys in the smaller sports don't have anything working for us. Nobody is out there pitching for our interests."

"Hold your horses, guys," I retorted. "First of all, it's Title Nine not 'Six,' and it may   3
be more in your interest to support it than you might suspect."

I explained that Title IX was enacted by Congress in 1972 to stop discrimination on   4
the basis of sex in any program or activity receiving federal financial assistance. The male-dominated intercollegiate athletics establishment fought against the implementation of Title IX through a multimillion-dollar lobbying campaign during the 1970s. The forces against sex equity in sports won legal support in 1984 with the *Grove City* v. *Bell* case, which limited Title IX's ban on sexual discrimination to specific programs, rather than entire institutions, that receive federal funds. However, Congress put the legal bite back into Title IX with the passage of the Civil Rights Restoration Act in 1988. Since then, the legal and social forces seeking gender equity in sports have been getting stronger. I encouraged the two athletes to learn more about Title IX, because nondiscriminatory athletics will not only benefit female athletes, but most male athletes as well.

The Guises of Sexism in Sports

The struggle for Title IX in athletics is a struggle against sexism. Sexist ideology has taken   5
on many guises in the history and development of modern sports. In the nineteenth century and in much of the twentieth century, sexism helped men to keep women out of sports. Since men's aggression, strength, and competitiveness were believed to be biologically based, athletics seemed a natural activity for boys. Notions about women's physical frailty, emotional passivity, and nurturing proclivities helped keep sports an exclusively male domain. In this early phase of sports history, therefore, sexism served mainly to reinforce sex segregation.

Later, particularly after the 1972 passage of Title IX, sex segregation in sports began   6
to break down. Women's rapid development of their athletic skills chipped away at time-worn stereotypes of femininity and masculinity. Between the late 1960s and early 1980s, the number of women participating in college sports increased between 300 and 500 percent (Guttman 1991; Johnson and Frey 1985). Ironically, however, at the same time women were joining sport teams, men were taking over the coaching and leadership positions in women's sports. Whereas more than 90 percent of women's coaches were women before passage of Title IX, fewer than 50 percent of coaching jobs are held by women today. And women now hold fewer than one-third of the administrative positions in women's college athletics (Acosta and Carpenter 1993). The net professional result for women can be described as increased perspiration without political representation.

For the past twenty years or so, sexism has served in sports as an elitist ideology that   7
helps men to control the female athletes, coaches, and administrators who now occupy the corridors of what many men still consider a male domain. Elitist sexism assumes that men perform better in athletics than women do, that traditional male approaches to competition ought to be emulated by the female newcomers, and that the largest share of human and fiscal resources are best spent on men's games and men's health rather than women's games and women's health.

We seem to be entering a new era, though—one in which sexism is taking the form   *8*
of a wounded giant. Sexist remarks are usually unspoken, and the guardians of the patriarchal status quo no longer call for the exclusion of women from athletics. There is hardly
any public rhetoric, in fact, about preserving traditional masculinity or femininity. Instead,
opponents of gender equity say it will lead to the deterioration of competitive standards
and the erosion of athletic excellence. Woeful predictions are made about sagging support
from alumni and dwindling university public relations. Gender equity is equated with
organizational detumescence. Behind such assertions is the assumption that the existing
male-dominated system for organizing and defining sports is, after all, best for everybody.
To support gender equity, therefore, is to oppose sports. No one wants to do that, so the
institutionalized inequalities in elitist, male-dominated sports remain in place.

Wounded-giant sexism is divisive. Besides pitting men against women, it pits hetero-   *9*
sexuals against homosexuals. Have you ever wondered why you don't often read about or
hear whispers about gay men in sports although you may hear a lot of rumors about lesbian
athletes? It's not because there are no gay men in the locker room. It's because homophobia isn't being used to discredit and beat down men's sports the way it is being used against
women's sports. Wounded-giant sexism also pits coaches and administrators of elite men's
sports against coaches and administrators of women's sports and less prestigious men's
sports. My contacts in NCAA circles tell me that the gender-equity issue is increasingly
being framed as a struggle between so-called revenue-producing sports and lesser men's
sports. The opponents of gender equity are trying to divide and conquer.

Wounded-giant sexism also isolates and marginalizes those male coaches and male   *10*
administrators who lean toward adoption of more educational, inclusive, and equitable
athletics. Some men are paying a high personal and professional price for their activism on
behalf of gender equity in athletics. Rudy Suwara, a former volleyball coach at San Diego
State University, claims he was fired for insisting on equal treatment for female athletes. Jim
Huffman, a coach at California State University at Fullerton, has filed a lawsuit alleging that,
because he assisted his women's team in regaining the varsity status that was stripped away
from them, he was not retained when the department restored the team. I regard these men
as unsung heroes. Just as white men in the civil-rights movement learned there are knocks
to be taken for advocating racial equality, men who have allied with the forces of gender
equity have faced the political heat. Guts, vision, and commitment can help douse the flames.

And, finally, the key assumption behind wounded-giant sexism—that the system has   *11*
enough troubles already and that more reform will wreck all of sports—defuses the efforts of
racial and ethnic minorities to promote change. The message carried from the captains above
to the deckhands below is don't rock the boat—and it makes no difference whether the hands
on the oars are women's hands, black hands, brown hands, yellow hands, or red hands.

Whether in its separatist, elitist, or wounded-giant form, sexism benefits the elite men   *12*
who sit atop the administrative hierarchies that were formed in the historical heyday of
patriarchal sport. In the 1990s, sexism is thwarting the efforts of less advantaged groups in
sports to transform athletics into a more equitable, democratic, and healthful institution.

Men Are Discovering Title IX

The Women's Sports Foundation (WSF) operates as a clearinghouse for information about   *13*
women's sports and fitness. WSF also promotes greater opportunity for girls and women

in athletics, from the grass-roots level through school programs, Olympic sports, and professional sports. In over ten years of work with WSF, I've witnessed growing interest from men in achieving gender equity in sports. In the early 1980s, few men fought for the rights of female athletes. Today, however, more men are waking up to the fact that gender equity is their issue as well as women's. More men are beginning to realize that they have different stakes in the institution of sports than their dads or older brothers did in the male-dominated past. Men are not only gaining knowledge about Title IX and gender equity, they are acting on it as well. Many are organizing to get a fair shake for the girls in their schools and communities. Some are pursuing lawsuits on behalf of daughters, teams, or clients. Following are some examples, mostly from WSF files, of men's efforts to pursue equal opportunities for girls in sports.

- A maintenance man from Buffalo, New York, felt it was unfair that the local high school did not offer as many athletic programs for his daughters as it did for his sons. He gathered basic information about Title IX, composed a letter stating his concerns, and, along with several other parents, petitioned the school board for changes in policy.

- A male school board member got funding for a sex-equity evaluation of his Oregon school district. The evaluation saved the girls' field hockey team from dissolution and prompted improvements in the schedules for girls' sports events and in the girls' locker-room facilities.

- For the past three years, the members of the men's wrestling and rugby teams at a northeastern university have helped women to organize a recognition and awards breakfast in honor of National Girls and Women in Sports Day. Along with the women, they plan, decorate, sell tickets, wait on tables, and clap and cheer.

- When David Chapman, a mortgage loan officer and volunteer basketball coach from Dallas, Texas, first saw his nine-year-old daughter's gym, he was shocked by its poor condition. There were no bleachers, the flooring was worn linoleum tile, and the lighting was inadequate. The boys' gym, he discovered, was modern and well equipped. He joined forces with other parents, brought media attention to the inequities, and helped to teach the school board about matters pertaining to Title IX (Shuster 1993).

- A basketball coach in a southeastern Division II college is working with an attorney to redress apparent sex-based discrimination in the granting of athletic scholarships.

- The father of a soccer player approached a western school board about creating a girls' soccer team at his daughter's school. A survey of students revealed high interest in girls' soccer, yet the board voted down the request. The father has hired an attorney.

Katherine Reith, the assistant executive director of WSF, says that men can promote gender equity in athletics by being more aware of sexism in the sports pages. Men can phone or write newspaper and magazine editors, she suggests, to ask for more coverage of women's sports, or to complain about sports journalists who praise women's beauty rather than their athletic skills and accomplishments. She encourages men to show support for girls' and women's sports by attending games and events. Men can also donate funds to women's programs. When making a contribution to a former high school or college athlet-

14

ics department or alumni association, men might request that the funds be routed to women's athletics.

Finally, men can resist sexism in the locker room. Whether it's in the fitness center, the men's shower, a love relationship, or the workplace, personal behavior says a lot about gender politics. Men can quit going along with the tits-and-asses remarks that demean and evaluate women. Men can question comments that belittle women's athletic abilities and accomplishments. I recall watching the "regulars" playing basketball one day at the YMCA to which I belong. A tall, strong woman had joined the usually all-male lunchtime pickup game. She definitely knew her way around the court. Later, when the guys filed into the men's locker room sweating and puffing, I asked them what they thought of her play. A lawyer quickly replied, "She didn't have nice tits." Rather than laughing or remaining silent, I pushed him a bit: "Give me a break, Bill. Don't hand me that sexist bullshit. You know she was right in there with you guys." He then admitted that she played better than "a lot of guys can," and the guys talked for five minutes about how far women had come in basketball during the past ten years. This may seem like a small step to take in the face of the formidable foe of sexism, but, in my mind and heart, I sense that as long as we men allow stereotypes of femininity to go unchallenged, we will remain saddled with masculine stereotypes as well.

Men's Stake in Gender Equity

Friedrich Nietzsche announced in the nineteenth century that God is dead. Nietzsche did not mean that spirituality had ceased to exist or that God had keeled over with a brain aneurysm. Rather Nietzsche was observing that the traditional relationships between Western people and their God had been transformed by modernity. He recognized that the timeworn cultural representations of God didn't suit modern realities.

At the dawn of the twenty-first century, I am suggesting that masculinity is dead. Men's relationships to the icons of traditional masculinity have been transformed. The Marlboro man succumbed to lung cancer. Rock Hudson turned out to be gay. On some campuses, fraternity "brothers" are getting our daughters drunk and gang-raping them. Even Superman is six feet under the ground. Indeed, there is no one "masculinity" in American culture; there are only masculinities. Men are finding diverse ways to construct and explore their gender identities and personal relationships. Fewer and fewer men are protecting images of manhood that no longer fit the realities of their lives. They are slowly realizing that the old norms for manhood just aren't cutting it in the postmodern marriage and family, in the workplace, in government, or in sports. Traditional masculinity has become an imitation without an original (Butler 1989).

We're dealing with what sociologists call "cultural lag," which means that our conscious minds haven't caught up with changes in institutional realities. For example, the industrialization of American society had transformed the day-to-day relationships between the sexes, in marriage, family, and the workplace, long before feminists began to criticize patriarchy and reconsider what it means to be a woman or a man, a wife or a husband, a mother or a father. Feminist analyses of culture were, to a large extent, responses to institutional changes that had already occurred. Feminist politics and critiques also spurred social and political trends toward egalitarianism. In the same way, the old cultural equation of sports with masculinity no longer reflects the realities of sports in the 1990s. Women are no longer "entering" sports; they're already here. Women have already challenged the old patriarchal definitions of sports and competition. Men are changing, too. Mariah Burton Nelson, in her book *Are We Winning Yet?* (1991), observes that some men are helping to shape a "partnership model" in athletics that mixes cooperative values with competitive practices, strengthens the healthy body rather than putting it at risk for injury, and promotes respect and caring for teammates and opponents. Many female athletes and unknown numbers of their male counterparts are embracing this model and moving away from the traditional "military model" in athletes, in which sports are regimented, hierarchical, highly competitive struggles designed to facilitate domination and subjugation of others.

Increasingly, men are recognizing that the military model just doesn't work for them. *19* For me, twelve years of football led to seven years of lower back pain and a major surgery. I'm not alone. There is an invisible army of former athletes, now in their forties, fifties, and sixties, who deal with the pain and anguish of injured shoulders, knees, backs, and hips. There are the overworked coaches who've gained coronary thrombosis or broken families in exchange for winning records. There are guilt-ridden men who made injured athletes play so they themselves could win games, save jobs, or earn promotions. There are the millions of men and women who opted out of athletics by age fourteen or fifteen. Can you imagine creating and defending business practices that alienate 75–80 percent of your long-term customers? Think of the thousands of would-be coaches and administrators that would be working with these kids today if they had not been processed out of the elitist, hypercompetitive athletic model.

Finally, a growing number of antisexist men not only support gender equity but side *20* with women on issues such as men's violence against women, sexual harassment of women in the workplace, and the sexual abuse of women by male coaches. Some male coaches of women athletes use sexual tension or power to control their athletes. Male coaches need to look long and deep into their gender identities and sexualities and come up with answers to these problems. Indeed, within the military model of sport, traditional coaches rarely empower their athletes. Coaches arrange for the election of "captains" and extol the virtues of team leadership but, in the end, the coaches make all the decisions. Literally and figuratively, the coaches "call all the shots." The Marine Corps doesn't really build men as much as it manufactures conformists. Is there a parallel here with traditional coaching?

In summary, sexism is not a woman's problem or a man's problem. It is a social prob- *21* lem. It is a sports problem. Today much of the athletic experience is distorted or muted by sexist ideologies that hinder personal efforts to grow and change.

Whether separatist, elitist, or taking the guise of a wounded giant, sexism is gnaw- *22* ing away at the gut and soul of sports. Sexism belies the fundamental athletic ideal that everyone should become all that she or he is capable of being. Exposing sexism wherever it exists, and fighting for gender equity, will prove to be part of the cure for modern sports, not part of the illness.

Football continues to be the main roadblock stalling reform efforts in intercollegiate *23* sports. Ideologically, football epitomizes traditional masculinity and the military model in athletics. Football is also a major structural obstacle to reform. By providing many full-time scholarships, most college football teams commandeer exorbitant funds without returning profits on their investments. As Todd Crosset, a sports sociologist and a pro-equity NCAA swimming coach, has said, "What football scholarships are to athletics, nuclear arms are to the Cold War." The Berlin Wall has fallen, but efforts to scale back munitions production have been persistently opposed. Similarly, Title IX was passed more than twenty years ago, and yet the not-so-wounded giant of male-dominated sports lumbers forward. In the end, lesser-status men's sports as well as women's sports are being shortchanged.

Gender politics in sports no longer fit into the "we-men versus they-women" pattern.   *24*
Indeed, complex politics of masculinities are operating in athletics. Many men who make their livings from sports continue to fight to maintain the male-dominated status quo. They are angered or frightened by the threat of gender equity in sports. As one athletic director put it, "Everything I have worked for has been deemed unjust, and it's very, very hard for me to accept." A male coach confided, "I support the idea of equity, but I also have to live and work with guys who are not exactly in love with the idea of handing over more resources to the women." Other men, though, are struggling for gender equity in athletics because they feel it means fairness and a better life for them, the girls and women in their lives, and their institutions and communities. They are learning that the struggle to implement Title IX can be a vehicle for constructing modes of manliness that reach beyond sexism.

Today the stakes for changing sports and masculinity are higher than ever, and fewer   *25*
men are betting on the patriarchal past. They are not betting at all. They are busy envisioning and creating more equitable futures.

References

Acosta, R. Vivian, and Linda Jean Carpenter. "Women in Intercollegiate Sports: A Longitudinal Study—Fifteen Year Update, 1977–1992." Brooklyn, New York: Brooklyn College Department of Physical Education, 1993.

Butler, Judith. Gender Trouble: Feminism and the Subversion of Identity. New York: Routledge, 1989.

Carpenter, Linda Jean. "The Impact of Title IX on Women's Intercollegiate Sports." Government and Sport, ed. Arthur T. Johnson and James H. Frey. Totowa, NJ: Rowman and Allanheld, 1985. 62–78.

Guttman, Alan. Women's Sports: A History. New York: Columbia University Press, 1991.

Nelson, Mariah Burton. Are We Winning Yet? How Women Are Changing Sports and Sports Are Changing Women. New York: Random House, 1991.

Raiborn, Mitchell. Revenues and Expenses of Intercollegiate Athletics Programs. Overland Park: National Collegiate Athletic Association, 1990.

READING FOR INFORMATION

1. Explain what Sabo means when he says that "the net professional result [of Title IX] for women can be described as increased perspiration without political representation" (paragraph 6).
2. According to Sabo, what are the three assumptions of "elitist sexism"?
3. Summarize Sabo's discussion of "wounded-giant sexism."
4. Paraphrase what Sabo means when he suggests that masculinity is dead.
5. In athletics, what is the difference between the "partnership model" and the "military model"?

READING FOR FORM, ORGANIZATION, AND FEATURES

1. What function is served by the three opening paragraphs, besides being a lead that sets the tone of the article and tells the reader what it will be about?

2. How does Sabo bolster his argument with anecdotes, statistics, facts, and scholarly sources?

3. What is the function of the section of the article headed "Men Are Discovering Title IX"?

4. What is the function of paragraph 24?

5. Academic writers are bound by conventions that do not necessarily apply to writers of articles in popular periodicals such as the *New York Times Magazine*. Explain how Sabo's essay differs from a journalistic piece such as Jeffrey Goldberg's "The Color of Suspicion," in Chapter 13.

READING FOR RHETORICAL CONCERNS

1. For whom is Sabo writing?

2. What do you think Sabo expects his readers to do or think after reading his essay?

3. How do you think Sabo would react to Walter Olson's "Title IX from Outer Space"?

4. Would this essay be equally effective if it were written by a woman? Explain your answer.

WRITING ASSIGNMENTS

1. Write a 750-word essay in which you agree or disagree with Sabo's assertion that "sexism is thwarting the efforts of less advantaged groups in sports to transform athletics into a more equitable, democratic, and healthful institution" (paragraph 12).

2. Write a 750-word essay in which you respond to Sabo's recommendations for converting sport from the "military model" to the "partnership model."

3. Compare and contrast the views of Sabo and those of Walter Olson in "Title IX from Outer Space." Your final draft should be around 750 words long.

* * * * * * * * * * * * * * * *

Unequal Opportunity

Laurie Tarkan

Laurie Tarkan is a sportswriter and contributor to Women's Sports and Fitness *magazine.*

P r e r e a d i n g ···

Read paragraph 1; then write a response to Congressman Hastert's complaint that "young men are losing the opportunity to compete." Have you or young men you know lost the opportunity to compete in sports? Do you think men have more opportunities than women or vice versa?

·····················

Every group bound together by commonalities seems to have its nemesis. Female athletes who want a fair shake in school sports, it seems, have Congressman Dennis Hastert, an Illinois Republican and a former wrestling coach, who recently requested that a House subcommittee hearing be held to reassess the way Title IX is enforced. "Young men," he complained, "are losing the opportunity to compete."

To be fair, Hastert is only one of many critics accusing Title IX, the gender-equity law that requires that girls and women receive equal opportunity to play sports in school, of cutting into men's athletic programs. Ever since financially pinched schools began to eliminate men's teams in sports like swimming and wrestling, to reduce costs or (instead of adding women's teams) to achieve gender equity, guardians of men's athletics have been bounding up the steps of the Capitol and tossing out such voguish conservative buzzwords as reverse discrimination and quota, the latter from no less than Vartan Gregorian, president of Brown University.

With affirmative action already dangling over the precipice, Title IX seems on shaky ground. Yet the rising backlash against the 23-year-old law has appeared, coincidentally or not, at a time when the courts have finally started to put their judicial muscle behind it by finding that punitive damages can be awarded. What's more, schools are now being hit with a steady flow of lawsuits from women (and their parents and coaches) demanding their equal right to participate in sports. And ever since 1988, when Congress reaffirmed the obligation of campuses receiving federal funds to remain discrimination-free, women who've turned to the courts haven't lost a single case: The score stands at about 31 to 0.

Whether from fear of legal reprisal or out of a belief that it's the right thing to do, many colleges are improving their gender-equity records. Christine Grant, Ph.D., athletic director of the women's athletic department at the University of Iowa, who has studied gender equity in sports for more than two decades, reports that at least 800 women's teams have been added at the collegiate level since 1992. And sports associations are taking more of a leadership role. The NCAA voted in 1991 to support gender equity as a basic principle of the organization, and other conferences, such as the Big 10 and the Southeastern Conference, have voted to upgrade women's opportunities in their member schools.

1

2

3

4

Laurie Tarkan. "Unequal Opportunity." *Women's Sports and Fitness* Sept. 1995: 25–27.

The state of Illinois has come up with its own solution to the problem. As this issue   5
of *Women's Sports + Fitness* was going to press, observers expected Governor Jim Edgar to
sign off on a bill, already passed by the Illinois Senate, that would give state universities the
right to allocate more funds to athletics. The money would enable the schools to add
women's sports or more female athletes in existing sports. It would also keep men's teams
intact, thus helping to satisfy everyone including, undoubtedly, Illinois's own Congressman Hastert (but, perhaps, not those critics who fear that athletic harmony will be achieved
at the expense of academics).

Though all this sounds promising, now is no time to rest on our laurels. "During the   6
congressional hearings," says Grant, "there was a fair amount of sympathy for the men who
were losing their teams. Part of me was sitting there in disbelief, wondering, Where is all
the sympathy for the women who have never, ever had these opportunities?"

According to Donna Lopiano, executive director of the Women's Sports Foundation,   7
"It's all about football and not wanting to share money." As Mike Bohn, director of marketing at the College Football Association, sees it, "The law penalizes institutions that sponsor football because there's no matching sport for women in terms of participants." In
other words, why should women be given the 75 to 125 player spots that football requires
when no women's team needs that many players? "But those 75 to 125 player spots,"
contends Lopiano, "should be matched in sports of interest to women."

Although some football programs make a profit, the vast majority of them, contrary   8
to popular belief, actually lose money: This means that football drains athletic funds that
might otherwise be put to women's use. The Women's Sports Foundation and other organizations have offered suggestions of ways to reduce spending, the foremost being a reduction in football players' standard of living: Some schools put their teams up in a hotel
before home games and routinely give them an allowance of $25 for dinner and $15 for
breakfast. Most of these suggestions, Lopiano says, have fallen on deaf ears.

In some cases, though, Title IX violators have had no choice but to listen. The most   9
recent and highly celebrated case was one in which a federal judge ruled in favor of Brown
University's women's gymnastics and volleyball teams last spring, finding that the school's
athletic opportunities for women were not proportionate with its female enrollment (women
make up 51 percent of the undergraduates at Brown, but have only 38 percent of the opportunities to play). Gregorian listened up, all right, but has pledged to fight the decision.

For his part, Hastert maintains that the emphasis should be not on the proportion   10
of men and women in schools but on each gender's level of interest in athletics. Girls, he
argues, have historically been less interested in sports than boys. "Give a questionnaire to
students as they enter the school to find out what the real interest in sports is," he proposes.

That kind of assessment, however, doesn't necessarily reflect potential interest. "Girls   11
and women have been discriminated against over the years, and their interest in sports is
still developing," contends Arthur Bryant, who's the executive director of Trial Lawyers for
Public Justice, the nonprofit group that sued Brown on behalf of the school's women
athletes. In the 1970s only 7 percent of high-school athletes were female, but that 7 percent
exploded to 35 percent once girls and women were given the opportunity to play. "That
proves there's not a lack of interest."

Just imagine how interested we'd be if all schools really complied with Title IX.   12

READING FOR INFORMATION

1. In Greek mythology, Nemesis is the goddess of retributive justice or vengeance. In what way is Congressman Hastert the nemesis of female athletes?
2. According to Tarkan, what factors account for the recent rise in criticism of Title IX?
3. Explain why the contest over gender equity in sport is "all about football."
4. Explain what is wrong with Hastert's suggestion about surveying student interest in sport.

READING FOR FORM, ORGANIZATION, AND FEATURES

1. Describe the different types of evidence Tarkan uses to support her points.
2. What is Tarkan's closing strategy, and how effective is it?

READING FOR RHETORICAL CONCERNS

1. What prompted Tarkan to write this article?
2. To whom is the article addressed?

WRITING ASSIGNMENTS

1. Write a 750-word essay in which you agree or disagree with Congressman Hastert's argument that "emphasis should be not on the proportion of men and women in schools but on each gender's level of interest in athletics."
2. Conduct library research to determine the latest developments in the case of Amy Cohen, the gymnast who sued Brown University. Write up your findings as a 750-word objective synthesis.
3. Conduct library research to examine the extent to which schools and colleges are currently in compliance with Title IX. Begin with your own college or university. Write your research paper according to the guidelines presented in Chapter 8.

• • • • • • • • • • • • • • • •

Title IX: Does Help for Women Come at the Expense of African Americans?

Craig T. Greenlee

Craig T. Greenlee is a widely published sportswriter. He covers college football for the Mid-Eastern Athletic Conference for USA Today.

Craig T. Greenlee. "Title IX: Does Help for Women Come at the Expense of African Americans?" *Black Issues in Higher Education* 17 Apr. 1997: 24–27.

Prereading ....

Write a response to the title of the article. Speculate about how increased sports opportunities for women would have a negative effect on African Americans.

. . . .

Gender equity has created an intriguing set of circumstances in the world of college athletics. On the one hand, Title IX, the federal law which forbids sex discrimination in educational institutions receiving federal funds, has opened the window of opportunity for scores of female athletes.

1

The NCAA women's basketball tournament offers ample proof. The Women's Final has attracted a average of almost 50,000 fans over the past two years. And there are other examples. Soccer has blossomed as a premier women's sport in America. Colleges and universities are a major part of the feeder system that produced players for the 1996 Olympic gold-medal winning U.S. soccer team. Women's gymnastics and swimming are also on the rise as collegiate sports which feature top-caliber competition and widespread fan support.

2

But there is a down side. While there are now more women's sports programs on the collegiate scene, critics say that in general, women have benefited at the expense of men's sports.

3

It's All About Proportionality

In order for schools to comply with Title IX, schools have to provide opportunities for female athletes that are in line with the percentage of females on that campus. Put another way, if a school's student body is 55 percent women, 55 percent of its total athletic offerings must be geared toward women. The law doesn't mandate that schools treat men's and women's sports identically, but it does say that the benefits for both should be comparable. Few schools have yet met this test, according to recent surveys, but pressure to comply may increase after a landmark Title IX case against Brown University works its way through the Supreme Court. For many schools, adhering to Title IX means cutting men's sports to provide funding for women. In many instances, schools have had to eliminate some men's sports or reduce—sometimes dramatically—the number of scholarships and coaches in those sports.

4

"If you increase opportunities for one group, I'm not so sure that you don't wind up denying another group," says Alex Wood, head football coach at James Madison University and vice-president of the Black Coaches Association. "And because there's only so much money available to operate a college sports program, somebody will inevitably get the short end of the stick."

5

Football has become a main target for Title IX advocates because it eats up a large chunk of the athletic budget. The sport is expensive because of the large roster sizes (80–100 players), equipment, and recruiting costs.

6

Title IX supporters assert that schools can reduce football scholarships and still maintain a competitive program. They point to National Football League (NFL) teams which have roster limits of forty-five players. When compared to the eighty-five scholarship limit that the major college football programs have, they ask, "If the pros prosper with forty-five, why can't the colleges?" Decreasing the number of football scholarships, Title IX proponents explain, will free up sufficient money to finance women's sports.

7

Race versus Gender

This is where race and gender wind up on a collision course. "The race versus gender issue   *8*
is very real," says Wood. "In football, a large number of the players are Black. So when you
start cutting scholarships, you not only take away the opportunity to play, you take away
the opportunity to go to school. Playing football is the only way that a lot of Black players
get to go to college at all."

Black males aren't the only ones to feel the pinch. Black women, ironically, are also   *9*
caught in the crunch.

As a group, Black women have not benefited from Title IX because the expansion in   *10*
women's athletics involves sports where Black female participation is minimal. It is estimated that approximately 97 percent of the 4,000 Black female collegiate athletes participate in basketball or track and field. However, the so-called "emerging" or nontraditional
sports—gymnastics, swimming, crew, lacrosse and soccer, to name a few—are the ones
that many schools are opting to add to help meet Title IX guidelines.

"Women of color are hurt because they don't participate in those sports where all the   *11*
expansion is taking place," says Dee Todd, assistant commissioner of the Atlantic Coast
Conference. "Women of color have a double protected status [because of race and gender],
but they're still left out. Most play basketball or run track. You'll see a handful in volleyball, softball and soccer, but that's about it. As a result, Title IX doesn't do a whole lot for
women of color."

While Blacks don't participate in the nontraditional sports in large numbers, Todd   *12*
says there is one sport that many colleges and Black athletes have yet to look at as an alternative—team handball.

"I can't say why more schools aren't playing team handball," says Todd. "You don't   *13*
need a lot in terms of facilities, all you need is a wall. But the people who can do well in
this sport are athletes who've played basketball and volleyball—sports that require good
hand-to-eye coordination."

Broadening Athletic Horizons

In the long run, Black athletes—male and female—will have to broaden their athletic hori-   *14*
zons if they want to earn college athletic scholarships. In other words, Blacks will have to
begin taking up sports other than football, basketball and track because there won't be any
expansion in those sports. Todd feels Blacks can be steered toward other sports if they're
exposed at an early age. "I talk to youngsters all the time and I tell them if they want a
college scholarship, get a golf club and learn how to play, or take swim lessons, or get into
youth soccer. There's no reason why Black youngsters can't do well in those sports. It's all
a matter of exposure."

There are no easy solutions in the athletic competition between race and gender. In   *15*
too many instances, it seems that the two are always in direct conflict. But even when they
are not, problems can arise. For example, a school might add field hockey to its sports
menu to comply with Title IX, then discover that there is not sufficient interest among the
students to maintain it. In that scenario, the sport was added strictly because of Title IX,
not because the students wanted it.

In the short term, however, Wood contends that schools can individually do the right thing by choosing to allocate their athletic resources in a fair manner among men's and women's sports.   *16*

"Everybody should have the opportunity to play and have a good experience in doing so," Wood says. "The same kinds of opportunities should be provided for everybody, and nobody should feel like they're getting second-class treatment. Each school has to look at its own situation and make a decision based on what their individual needs are. Schools have to look at what their constituents want."   *17*

READING FOR INFORMATION

1. Summarize the positive and negative effects of Title IX.
2. Explain how supporters of Title IX view football.
3. Explain why black athletes have not benefited from Title IX.
4. Explain why black athletes need to broaden their athletic horizons.

READING FOR FORM, ORGANIZATION, AND FEATURES

1. Review the organizational patterns on page 24. Which pattern does Greenlee use?
2. What authorities does Greenlee cite to support his views?
3. What is the author's closing strategy?

READING FOR RHETORICAL CONCERNS

1. For whom is Greenlee writing?
2. What impact does Greenlee want to have on his readers?

WRITING ASSIGNMENTS

1. For an audience who has not read Greenlee's article, write a 500-word summary of the effects of Title IX legislation on black athletes in U.S. colleges and universities.
2. Write a 750-word essay in which you agree or disagree with Alex Wood's contention that increasing the athletic opportunities for one group inevitably results in denying them for another group.
3. Write a research paper on the external and internal barriers faced by African American women in sport. Investigate such topics as social acceptance, sex-role stereotyping, competence, self-esteem, role models, mentoring, and support networks.

• • • • • • • • • • • • • • •

WRITING ASSIGNMENTS FOR CHAPTER 14

1. Do you think large revenue-producing sports such as football should be funded at the expense of women's athletic programs? Write a 750-word essay in which you express your view. Draw on sources in this chapter.

2. Use Pat Griffin's "Sport: Where Men Are Men and Women Are Trespassers," Leslie Heywood's "Satellite," and, if you wish, your own experiences to write a 1,250-word synthesis essay on discrimination against girls and women in sport.

3. Write a 1,250-word essay in which you argue that the experiences of female athletes described in Pat Griffin's "Sport: Where Men Are Men and Women Are Trespassers," Leslie Heywood's "Satellite," and other selections in this chapter are the result of the "wounded-giant sexism" that Don Sabo discusses in "Different Stakes: Men's Pursuit of Gender Equity in Sports."

4. Compare and contrast the views of Walter Olson in "Title IX from Outer Space" and those of Laurie Tarkan in "Unequal Opportunity." Your essay should be around 1,000 words long.

5. Respond to claims stated in various readings in this chapter that football plays a key role in the controversy over gender equity in sports. Your essay should be around 1,250 words long.

6. Drawing on the reading selections in this chapter, write a 1,250-word essay in which you argue either for or against programs for attaining gender equality by cutting down the allocation for men's sports in favor of women's sports.

7. This is a collaborative writing assignment that requires you to conduct a survey of students on your campus to determine how knowledgeable they are about Title IX and the changes it has produced in men's and women's sports and to ascertain their views on gender equity in sports and athletics. First, break the class into three groups, given the following assignments: Group 1, Pat Griffin's "Sport: Where Men Are Men and Women Are Trespassers" and Leslie Heywood's "Satellite"; Group 2, Don Sabo's "Different Stakes: Men's Pursuit of Gender Equity in Sports"; and Group 3, Walter Olson's "Title IX from Outer Space," Laurie Tarkan's "Unequal Opportunity," and Craig T. Greenlee's "Title IX: Does Help for Women Come at the Expense of African Americans?" Each group will study the articles and draw up five major questions related to gender equity and sports. Then the groups will present and discuss the questions with the entire class and create a questionnaire of twenty questions. Each student in the class will administer the questionnaire to five students on campus. When you have your results, return to your groups and exchange questionnaires so that each group analyzes responses to the set of questions it created. Discuss your findings with the entire class. Then return to your groups and compose a four- to five-page essay describing the entire study and discussing the results. When you do collaborative writing, it is best to assign roles to each person involved—for example, planner and organizer, drafter, reviewer, editor. Each group will present its paper to the entire class. You might send the best one to the college newspaper.

8. Write a research essay on one of the following questions. Take a clear-cut position, and respond to individuals holding the opposing view.

   a. Have women left coaching, or are female coaches being discriminated against?

   b. Do the media present equal coverage of male and female athletes?

   c. What are other countries' attitudes toward women's ability to compete in sports?

   d. Are women of color at a disadvantage in U.S. sports?

   e. Does homophobia stigmatize women in sports?

A

DOCUMENTING SOURCES

MLA DOCUMENTATION STYLE

Parts I and II contain student essays written according to the Modern Language Association (MLA) rules for page format (margins, page numbering, titles, and so forth) and source documentation. In addition to providing many sample pages that illustrate MLA style, we describe how to type papers in MLA format (pages 316–318); use parenthetical documentation to cite sources that you summarize (pages 55–56, paraphrase (pages 62–63), or quote (pages 67–71); and construct a works cited list (pages 43–44). Some of our examples are based on the articles and book excerpts that are reprinted in Part III of this book. As a college student, you may need to document materials that follow a different format. You may need, for instance, to document a television newscast, a pamphlet, or a personal interview. The first section of this appendix explains how to document many types of sources. For an exhaustive discussion of MLA documentation style, see the *MLA Handbook for Writers of Research Papers*.

DOCUMENTATION MODELS FOR BOOKS

When documenting books, arrange the documentary information in the following order:

1. Author's name
2. Title of the part of the book (if you are referring to a section or chapter)
3. Title of the book
4. Name of the editor or translator
5. Edition
6. Number of volumes
7. Name of the series if the book is part of a series
8. City of publication
9. Abbreviated name of the publisher
10. Date of publication
11. Page numbers (if you are referring to a section or chapter)

Book with one author

> Kennedy, William J. <u>Rhetorical Norms in Renaissance Literature</u>. New
>
> Haven: Yale UP, 1978.

Two or more books by the same author (alphabetize by title)

Kennedy, William J. <u>Jacopo Sannazaro and the Uses of the Pastoral</u>. Hanover: UP of New England, 1983.

---. <u>Rhetorical Norms in Renaissance Literature</u>. New Haven: Yale UP, 1978.

Book with two authors

Lambert, William W., and Wallace E. Lambert. <u>Social Psychology</u>. Englewood Cliffs: Prentice, 1964.

Book with three authors

Kitch, Sally, Carol Knock, and Fran Majors. <u>The Source Book</u>. New York: Longman, 1981.

Book with more than three authors

Glock, Marvin D., et al. <u>Probe: College Developmental Reading</u>. 2nd ed. Columbus: Merrill, 1980.

Book with a corporate author

Boston Women's Health Book Collective. <u>Our Bodies, Ourselves: A Book by and for Women</u>. New York: Simon, 1971.

Book with an anonymous author

<u>Writers' and Artists' Yearbook, 1980</u>. London: Adam and Charles Black, 1980.

Book with an editor instead of an author

Bronfenbrenner, Urie, ed. <u>Influences on Human Development</u>. Hinsdale: Dryden, 1972.

Book with two or three editors

McQuade, Donald, and Robert Atwan, eds. <u>Popular Writing in America</u>. 3rd ed. New York: Oxford UP, 1985.

Book with more than three editors

Kermode, Frank, et al., eds. <u>The Oxford Anthology of English</u>
<u>Literature</u>. 2 vols. New York: Oxford UP, 1973.

Book with a translator

de Beauvoir, Simone. <u>Force of Circumstance</u>. Trans. Richard Howard.
Harmondsworth, Eng.: Penguin, 1968.

Book with more than one edition

Hodges, John C., and Mary E. Whitten. <u>Harbrace College Handbook</u>.
9th ed. New York: Harcourt, 1984.

Book that has been republished

Conroy, Frank. <u>Stop-Time</u>. 1967. New York: Penguin, 1977.

PARTS OF BOOKS

Section, chapter, article, or essay in a book with one author

Chomsky, Noam. "Psychology and Ideology." <u>For Reasons of State</u>. New
York: Vintage, 1973. 318-69.

Introduction, preface, or foreword written by someone other than book author

Piccone, Paul. General Introduction. <u>The Essential Frankfurt Reader</u>.
Eds. Andrew Arato and Eike Gebhardt. New York: Urizen, 1978.
xi-xxiii.

Essay or article reprinted in a book

Wimkoff, Meyer F., and Russell Middleton. "Type of Family and Type
of Enemy." <u>American Journal of Sociology</u> 66 (1960): 215-24.
Rpt. in <u>Man in Adaptation: The Cultural Present</u>. Ed. Yehudi A.
Cohen. Chicago: Aldine, 1968. 384-93.

Essay, article, short story, or poem in an anthology

Cornish, Sam. "To a Single Shadow without Pity." <u>The New Black</u>
<u>Poetry</u>. Ed. Clarence Major. New York: International, 1969. 39.

Novel or play in an anthology

> Gay, John. <u>The Beggar's Opera</u>. <u>Twelve Famous Plays of the</u>
>
> <u>Restoration and Eighteenth Century</u>. Ed. Cecil A. Moore. New
>
> York: Random, 1960. 573-650.

Signed article in a reference work

> Goris, Jan-Albert. "Belgian Literature." <u>Colliers Encyclopedia</u>. 1983
>
> ed.

Unsigned article in a reference work

> "Solar Energy." <u>The New Columbia Encyclopedia</u>. 4th ed. 1975.

DOCUMENTING A BOOK WITHOUT COMPLETE PUBLICATION INFORMATION OR PAGINATION

Supply as much of the missing information as you can, enclosing the information you supply in brackets to show your reader that the source did not contain this information. For example: Metropolis: U of Bigcity P, [1971]. Enclosing the date in brackets shows your reader that you found the date elsewhere: another source that quotes your source, the card catalog, your professor's lecture, and so on. If you are not certain of the date, add a question mark. For example: [1971?]. If you only know an approximate date, put the date after "c." (for *circa*, "around"). However, when you cannot find the necessary information, use one of the following abbreviation models to show this to your reader. These examples document material taken from page 42 of a source.

No date

> Metropolis: U of Bigcity P, n.d. 42.

No pagination

> Metropolis: U of Bigcity P, 1971. N. pag.

No place of publication

> N.p.: U of Bigcity P, 1971. 42.

No publisher

> Metropolis: n.p., 1971. 42.

Neither place nor publisher

```
N.p.: n.p., 1971. 42.
```

> *For example:* Photographic View Album of Cambridge. [England]:
>
> N.p., n.d. N. pag.

CROSS-REFERENCES

If you cite two or more articles from the same anthology, list the anthology itself with complete publication information and then cross-reference the individual articles. In the cross-reference, the anthology editor's last name and the page numbers follow the article author's name and the title of the article. In the following example, the first two entries are for articles reprinted in the third entry, the anthology edited by Kennedy, Kennedy, and Smith.

```
Duff, Raymond G., and A. G. M. Campbell. "Moral and Ethical

    Dilemmas in the Special-Care Nursery." Kennedy, Kennedy, and

    Smith 406-12.

Hentoff, Nat. "The Awful Privacy of Baby Doe." Kennedy, Kennedy,

    and Smith 417-24.

Kennedy, Mary Lynch, William J. Kennedy, and Hadley M. Smith, eds.

    Writing in the Disciplines. Englewood Cliffs: Prentice, 1987.
```

DOCUMENTATION MODELS FOR PERIODICALS

When documenting articles in a periodical, arrange the documentary information in the following order:

1. Author's name
2. Title of the article
3. Name of the periodical
4. Series number or name
5. Volume number (followed by a period and the issue number, if needed)
6. Date of publication
7. Page numbers

Article in a scholarly or professional journal; pages numbered separately in each issue

```
Maimon, Elaine P. "Cinderella to Hercules: Demythologizing Writing

    across the Curriculum." Journal of Basic Writing 2.4 (1980):

    3-11.
```

Article in a scholarly or professional journal; pages numbered consecutively through the entire volume

Callahan, Susan. "Conversations and Competence: How English Teachers

Fail to Connect." English Education 32 (2000): 182-93.

Signed article in a weekly or monthly magazine

Golden, Frederic. "Heat over Wood Burning: Pollution from Home

Stoves Is Nearing Crisis Proportions." Time 16 Jan. 1984: 67.

Unsigned article in a weekly or monthly magazine

"Planning Ahead: Proposals for Democratic Control of Investment."

Dollars and Sense Feb. 1983: 3-5.

Signed article in a newspaper (in an edition with lettered sections)

Miller, Marjorie. "Britain Urged to Legalize Cloning of Human

Tissue." Los Angeles Times 9 Dec. 1998: A1.

Unsigned article in a newspaper (in a daily without labeled sections)

"Breast Cancer Study to Begin on Long Island." Ithaca Journal 14

Jan. 1984: 2.

Editorial or special feature (in an identified edition with numbered sections)

"The Limits of Technology." Editorial. New York Times 3 Jan. 1999,

early ed., sec. 4: 8.

Review

Hoberman, J. "The Informer: Elia Kazan Spills His Guts." Rev. of

Elia Kazan: A Life, by Elia Kazan. Village Voice 17 May 1988:

58-60.

Article whose title contains a quotation

Nitzsche, Jane Chance. "'As swete as is the roote of lycorys, or

any cetewale': Herbal Imagery in Chaucer's Miller's Tale."

Chaucerian Newsletter 2.1 (1980): 6-8.

Article from *Dissertation Abstracts International (DAI)*

Webb, John Bryan. "Utopian Fantasy and Social Change, 1600–1660."
Diss. SUNY Buffalo, 1982. <u>DAI</u> 43 (1982): 8214250A.

DOCUMENTATION MODELS FOR OTHER WRITTEN SOURCES

Government publication

United States. Dept. of Energy. <u>Winter Survival: A Consumer's Guide
to Winter Preparedness</u>. Washington: GPO, 1980.

Congressional Record

<u>Cong. Rec</u>. 13 Apr. 1967: S505457.

Pamphlet

Hopper, Peggy, and Steve Soldz. <u>I Don't Want to Change My
Lifestyle--I Want to Change My Life</u>. Cambridge: Root and
Branch, 1971.

Dissertation

Boredin, Henry Morton. "The Ripple Effect in Classroom Management."
Diss. U of Michigan, 1970.

Personal letter

Siegele, Steven. Letter to the author. 13 Jan. 1983.

Published letter

Bloom, Ira Mark. Letter. <u>New York Times</u> 9 Oct. 1985: A22.

Public document

United States. Dept. of Agriculture. "Shipments and Unloads of
Certain Fruits and Vegetables, 1918–1923." <u>Statistical Bulletin</u>
7 Apr. 1925: 10–13.

Information service

Edmonds, Edward L., ed. <u>The Adult Student: University Challenge</u>.
Charlottetown: Prince Edward Island U, 1980. ERIC ED 190 008.

DOCUMENTATION MODELS FOR ONLINE SOURCES THAT ARE ALSO AVAILABLE IN PRINT

The World Wide Web offers electronic versions of many publications that are available in print, ranging from newspaper articles to full-length books. Entries for sources that have electronic addresses (URLs) should include as many of the following items as are available.

1. Author
2. Title of the source (article, poem, or other source type)
3. Editor, compiler, or translator (if relevant)
4. Complete publication information for the print version
5. Title of the Web site or database (if no title is given, provide a label such as "Home-page")
6. Web site editor or compiler (if relevant)
7. Version number of the source (if relevant)
8. Date of latest update
9. For sources from a subscription service, name of the service (if the subscriber is a library, provide the name, city, and state of the library)
10. Total number of pages, paragraphs, or sections (if available)
11. Organization or institution associated with the Web site
12. Date when the researcher collected the information from the Web site
13. Electronic address, or URL, of the source (enclosed in angle brackets)

Each of the elements should follow the format specifications on pages 477–85. For example, article titles should be placed in quotation marks, and book titles should be underlined. Web site names are underlined.

Book

> Shaw, George Bernard. <u>Pygmalion</u>. 1912. <u>Bartleby Archive</u>. 6 Mar. 1998
>
> > <http://www.columbia.edu/acis/bartleby/shaw/>.

Poem

> Carroll, Lewis. "Jabberwocky." 1872. 6 Mar. 1998
>
> > <http://www.jabberwocky.com/carroll/jabber/jabberwocky.html>.

Article in a journal

> Rehberger, Dean. "The Censoring of Project #17: Hypertext
>
> > Bodies and Censorship." <u>Kairos</u> 2.2 (Fall 1997): 14 sec. 6 Mar.
> >
> > 1998 <http://english.ttu.edu/kairos/2.2/index_f.html>.

Article in a magazine

```
Viagas, Robert, and David Lefkowitz. "Capeman Closing Mar. 28."

     Playbill 5 Mar. 1998. 6 Mar. 1998 <http://www.playbill.com/

     cgi-bin/plb/news?cmd=show&code=30763>.
```

Article obtained through library-based subscription service

```
Davidson, Margaret. "Do You Know Where Your Children Are?" Reason

     31.6 (Nov. 1999). Expanded Academic ASAP. Ithaca College

     Library, Ithaca. 8 Feb. 2000 <http://web6.infotrac.

     galegroup.com/itw/infomark/908/844/51266910w3/

     purl=rc 2_EA IM_1_Margaret+Davidson&dyn=sig!2?sw_aep=ithaca_lib>.
```

DOCUMENTATION MODELS FOR SOURCES THAT ARE AVAILABLE EXCLUSIVELY ONLINE

Certain electronic sources are available only online (on the World Wide Web, at Gopher sites, and so on). A myriad of organizations and individuals maintain Web sites that provide information that is not published in print form. For sources that do not appear in print, MLA works cited entries should include as many of the following items as possible.

1. Author
2. Title of the source (article, poem, or other source type) or title of a posting to an online discussion followed by the label "Online posting"
3. Editor, compiler, or translator (if relevant)
4. Title of the Web site or database (if no title is given, provide a label such as "Homepage")
5. Web site editor or compiler (if relevant)
6. Version number of the source (if available)
7. Date of latest update
8. For sources from a subscription service, name of the service (if the subscriber is a library, provide the name, city, and state of the library)
9. Name of discussion list of forum (for postings only)
10. Total number of pages, paragraphs, or sections (if available)
11. Organization or institution associated with the Web site
12. Date when the researcher collected the information from the Web site
13. Electronic address, or URL, of the source (enclosed in angle brackets)

All elements should follow the format guidelines presented on pages 477–85. For example, article titles should be placed in quotation marks, and book titles should be underlined. Web site names are underlined.

Posting to a discussion list

Grumman, Bob. "Shakespeare's Literacy." Online posting. 6 Mar. 1998.

Deja News. 13 Aug. 1998 <humanities.lit.author.>.

Scholarly project

Voice of the Shuttle: Web Page for Humanities Research. Ed. Alan

Liu. 3 March 1998. U. California, Santa Barbara. 8 Mar. 1998

<http://humanitas.ucsb.edu/>.

Professional site

Nobel Foundation Official Website. Nobel Foundation. Dec. 1998. 28

Feb. 1999 <http://www.nobel.se/>.

Personal site

Thiroux, Emily. Homepage. 7 Mar. 1998. 12 Jan. 1999

<http://academic.csubak.edu/home/acadpro/departments/english/

engthrx.htmlx>.

E-mail communication

Kennedy, Mary Lynch. "Re: Vygotsky." E-mail to Hadley M. Smith. 8

June 2000.

Synchronous communication (such as MOO, MUD, or IRC)

"Ghostly Presence." Group discussion. Telnet 16 Mar. 1997

<moo.du.org:8000/80anon/anonview/1_4036#focus>.

Gopher site

Banks, Vickie, and Joe Byers. "EDTECH." 18 Mar. 1997

<gopher://ericyr.syr.edu:70/00/Listervi/EDTECH/README>.

FTP (file transfer protocol) site

United States. Supreme Court directory. 6 Mar. 1998.

<ftp://<ftp.cwru.edu/U.S.Supreme.Court/>.

Some electronic sources are "portable"—CD-ROMs, for example—and may or may not
have print versions. Other electronic sources do not have URLs. In each case, use the style

that applies, listing the publication medium (CD-ROM, for example) and publisher and the computer network or service for an online source (for example, a computer database such as PsychINFO reached through CompuServe). Give the electronic publication information after the author, title, editor or compiler, and print publication information.

> Stucky, Nathan. "Performing Oral History: Storytelling and
>
> Pedagogy." Communication Education 44.1 (1995): 1-14.
>
> CommSearch 2nd ed. CD-ROM. Electronic Book Technologies, 1995.

DOCUMENTATION MODELS FOR NONPRINT SOURCES

Film

> Rebel without a Cause. Dir. Nichols Ray. With James Dean, Sal
>
> Mineo, and Natalie Wood. Warner, 1955.

Television or radio program

> Comet Halley. Prod. John L. Wilhelm. PBS. WNET, New York. 26 Nov. 1986.

Personal (face-to-face) interview

> Warren, Charles. Personal interview. 26 Apr. 1985.

Telephone interview

> Springsteen, Bruce. Telephone interview. 1 Oct. 1984.

Performance of music, dance, or drama

> Corea, Chick, dir. Chick Corea Electrik Band. Cornell U, Ithaca.
>
> 15 Oct. 1985.

Lecture

> Gebhard, Ann O. "New Developments in Young Adult Literature." New
>
> York State English Council. Buffalo. 15 Nov. 1984.

Recording: CD

> Green Day. Dookie. Reprise, 1994.

Recording: Cassette

> Tchaikovsky, Piotr Ilich. Violin Concerto in D, op. 35. Itzhak
>
> Perlman, violinist. Audiocassette. RCA, 1975.

Recording: LP

> Taylor, James. "You've Got a Friend." <u>Mud Slide Slim and the Blue</u>
>
> > <u>Horizon</u>. LP. Warner, 1971.

Videotape

> <u>The Nuclear Dilemma</u>. BBC-TV. Videocassette. Time-Life Multimedia, 1974.

Computer program

> <u>WordPerfect</u>. Vers. 5.1. Diskette. Orem: WordPerfect, 1990.

Work of art

> da Vinci, Leonardo. <u>The Virgin, the Child, and Saint Anne</u>. Louvre,
>
> > Paris.

Map or chart

> <u>Ireland</u>. Map. Chicago: Rand, 1984.

> <u>Adolescents and AIDS</u>. Chart. New York: Earth Science Graphics, 1988.

Cartoon

> Addams, Charles. Cartoon. <u>New Yorker</u> 16 May 1988: 41.

CONTENT ENDNOTES

In addition to a works cited list, MLA style provides for a list of comments, explanations, or facts that relate to the ideas discussed in the essay but do not fit into the actual text. You may occasionally need these *content endnotes* to provide information that is useful but must, for some reason, be separated from the rest of the essay. The most common uses of endnotes are as follows.

1. To provide additional references that go beyond the scope of the essay but help the reader understand issues in more depth
2. To discuss a source of information in more detail than is possible in a works cited list
3. To acknowledge help in preparing an essay
4. To give an opinion that does not fit into the text smoothly
5. To explain ideas more fully than is possible in the text
6. To mention concerns not directly related to the content of the essay
7. To provide additional *necessary* details that would clutter the text
8. To mention information contradictory to the view presented in the essay
9. To evaluate ideas explained in the essay

In MLA style, endnotes are listed on a separate page just before the Works Cited page. The endnote list is titled Notes. Notes are numbered sequentially (1, 2, 3, . . .) in the order in which they occur in the essay, and a corresponding number is included in the text of the essay, typed slightly above the line (in superscript), to indicate the material to which the endnote refers. Notice in the following example that the reference numeral (the endnote number) is placed in the text of the essay immediately after the material to which it refers. Usually, the reference numeral will appear at the end of a sentence. No space is left between the reference numeral and the word or punctuation mark that it follows. However, in the notes list, one space is left between the numeral and the first letter of the note.

Any source that you mention in an endnote must be fully documented in the works cited list. Do not include this complete documentation in the endnote itself. Never use endnotes as a substitute for the works cited list, and do not overuse endnotes. If possible, include all information in the text of your essay. For most essays you write, no endnotes will be necessary.

The following excerpts from the text of an essay and its list of endnotes illustrate MLA endnote format.

For example, in your text you would type

> For hundreds of years, scientists thought that the sun's energy came from the combustion of a solid fuel such as coal.[1] However, work in the early twentieth century convinced researchers that the sun sustains a continuous nuclear fusion reaction.[2] The sun's nuclear furnace maintains a temperature . . .

On the notes page, indent the first line of each note five spaces. One space separates the superscript note number and the first word.

> [1] Detailed accounts of pre-twentieth-century views of solar energy can be found in Banks and Rosen (141–55) and Burger (15–21).

> [2] In very recent years, some scientists have questioned whether or not the sun sustains a fusion reaction at all times. Experiments described by Salen (68–93) have failed to detect the neutrinos that should be the byproducts of the sun's fusion. This raises the possibility that the fusion reaction turns off and on periodically.

APA DOCUMENTATION STYLE

Just as MLA documentation style is an important standard in the humanities, American Psychological Association (APA) style is used widely in the social sciences. APA style differs from MLA style in many details, but both share the basic principles of including source names and page numbers (APA also adds the publication date) in parentheses within the text of the paper and of providing complete publication information for each source in an alphabetized list. We present here a point-by-point comparison of APA and MLA styles. For a complete explanation of APA style, see the *Publication Manual of the American Psychological Association*, (5th ed., 2001).

PARENTHETICAL DOCUMENTATION

MLA

Give the last name of the author and the page number when citing a specific part of the source. For example:

```
The question has been answered before (Sagan 140-43).

Sagan has already answered the question (140-43).
```

APA

Give the last name of the author, the publication date, and the page number when citing a specific part of the source. For example:

```
The question has been answered before (Sagan, 1980, pp. 140—143).

Sagan (1980) has already answered the question (pp. 140—143).
```

MLA

Use page numbers alone. Drop redundant hundreds digit in a range. For example:

```
Walsh discusses this "game theory" (212-47).
```

APA

Use the abbreviation "p." for *page* or "pp." for *pages*. Retain all digits in a range. For example:

```
Walsh (1979) discusses this "game theory" (pp. 212-247).
```

MLA

Use no commas in parenthetical references. For example:

```
The question has been answered before (Sagan 140-43).
```

APA

Use commas within parentheses. For example:

```
The question has been answered before (Sagan, 1980, pp. 140—143).
```

MLA

Use a shortened form of the title to distinguish between different works by the same author. For example:

```
Jones originally supported the single-factor theory (Investiga-
tions) but later realized that the phenomenon was more complex
(Theory).
```

APA

Use publication date to distinguish between different works by the same author. For example:

```
Jones originally supported the single-factor theory (1972) but
later realized that the phenomenon was more complex (1979).
```

LIST OF SOURCES

MLA

The title of the page listing the sources is Works Cited.

APA

The title of the page listing the sources is References.

MLA

Indent the second and subsequent lines five spaces, (call a "hanging indent").

APA

The 2001 APA *Publication Manual* recommends the same hanging indent.

MLA

Use the author's full name. For example:

```
Sagan, Carl.
```

APA

Use the author's last name, but only the initials of the author's first and middle names. For example:

```
Sagan, C.
```

MLA

Use the word *and* when listing more than one author.

APA

Use an ampersand *(&)* when listing more than one author.

MLA

When there are two or more authors, invert the first author's name, but give the other names in the usual order. Use *and* before the final name. For example:

```
Kennedy, Mary Lynch, and Hadley M. Smith.
```

APA

When there are two or more authors, invert all the names. Before the last author's name, use an ampersand *(&)*. For example:

```
Kennedy, M. L., & Smith, H. M.
```

MLA

Capitalize major words in the titles and subtitles of books and periodicals. For example:

```
The Beginner's Guide to Academic Writing and Reading: A New
Approach.

Reading Research Quarterly.
```

APA

Capitalize only the first word and all proper nouns in the titles and subtitles of books. Capitalize all major words in the titles of periodicals. Italicize titles of books and journals (underline if you cannot italicize) and include punctuation at the end.

```
The beginner's guide to academic writing and reading: A new
approach.

Reading Research Quarterly.
```

MLA

List book data in the following sequence: author, title of book, city of publication, shortened form of the publisher's name, date of publication. For example:

```
Fries, Charles C. Linguistics and Reading. New York: Holt, 1962.
```

APA

List book data in the following sequence: author, date of publication (in parentheses), title of the book, place of publication, publisher. For example:

```
Fries, C. C. (1962). Linguistics and reading. New York: Holt,
Rinehart and Winston.
```

MLA

List journal articles in the following sequence: *author, article, title,* journal, volume number, date of publication, inclusive pages. For example:

```
Booth, Wayne C. "The Limits of Pluralism." Critical Inquiry 3

     (1977): 407-23.
```

APA

List journal articles in this sequence: author, date of publication (in parentheses), *article, title,* journal and volume number inclusive pages. For example:

```
Booth, W. C. (1977). The limits of pluralism. Critical Inquiry, 3,

     407-423.
```

MLA

List the data for an article in an edited book in the following sequence: author of the article, title of the article, title of the book, editor of the book, place of publication, publisher, date of publication, inclusive pages. For example:

```
Donaldson, E. Talbot, "Briseis, Briseida, Criseyde, Cresseid,

     Cressid: Progress of a Heroine." Chaucerian Problems and

     Perspectives: Essays Presented to Paul E. Beichner, C.S.C. Ed.

     Edward Vasta and Zacharias P. Thundy. Notre Dame: Notre Dame

     UP, 1979. 3-12.
```

APA

List the data for an article in an edited book in the following sequence: author of the article, date (in parentheses), title of the article, name of the editor, title of the book, inclusive pages (in parentheses), place of publication, and publisher. For example:

```
Donaldson, E. T. (1979). Briseis, Briseida, Criseyde, Cresseid,

     Cressid: Progress of a heroine. In E. Vasta & Z. P. Thundy

     (Eds.), Chaucerian problems and perspectives: Essays presented

     to Paul E. Beichner, C.S.C. (pp. 3-12). Notre Dame, IN: Notre

     Dame University Press.
```

MLA

Use a shortened form of the publisher's name unless this would cause confusion. Abbreviate *University* and *Press* using U for *University* and P for *Press.* For publishers named for a person, use last name only. For publishers named for more than one person, use the name of the first person only.

APA

Use the briefest complete name for the publisher, but omit the terms *Publishers*, *Incorporated*, and *Company*. Retain *Books* or *Press*.

CONTENT ENDNOTES

MLA

Title the list of endnotes: Notes.

APA

Title the list of endnotes: Footnotes.

MLA

Place the endnote list immediately after the last page of text on a new page, but before the Works Cited page.

APA

Place the endnote list immediately after the References page. (and after the Author's Note page, if there is one).

MLA

Skip one space between the reference numeral and the endnote. For example:

```
 1 For more information, see Jones and Brown.
```

APA

Do not skip any space between the reference numeral and the endnote. For example:

```
1For more information, see Jones (1983) and Brown (1981).
```

Note: Both MLA and APA formats require that the firsline of a note be indented five full spaces. All subsequent lines are flush to the left margin.

B

WRITING ESSAY EXAMINATIONS

Strong essay examination answers have the characteristics of good writing that we have discussed throughout this textbook. They identify and support an interesting idea, develop according to a logical plan, draw on sources thoughtfully and accurately, use clear and appropriate language, and follow conventions for usage. That said, most students have difficulty producing their best writing when they are under time pressure and cannot refer to sources. As a result, professors usually do not apply to essay exam answers the high standards they set for out-of-class essays. For example, they do not expect elaborate introductions to topics or precise documentation of source material in essay examinations. The following factors have the greatest effect on professors' evaluation of essay exam answers.

ESSAY EXAM EVALUATION

When writing essay exams, students should be careful to do all of the following:

1. Answer the question fully.
2. Use clear language.
3. Organize the information so that key points stand out.
4. Include specific facts or concepts taught in the course.
5. Use the vocabulary of the discipline.

Since exams are written under time pressure, it is impossible to follow the writing process we have explained in this textbook. However, you can devote some time before the exam date to various planning activities that will prepare you to write.

PREPARATION STRATEGIES FOR ESSAY EXAMINATIONS

1. Try to anticipate topics that might appear on the test. Pick concepts that are central to the course and have been emphasized in class. Choose a maximum of ten topics that you will prepare. You might try running your list of topics past the professor for comments.
2. Use your course reading and notes to outline an essay for each of the topics you have chosen to prepare.
3. Memorize a basic outline for the essay. Use mnemonics as an aid to memory.

4. Memorize the organizational patterns that are often useful in exam situations:
   - List of reasons or examples
   - Comparison and contrast (block or point-by-point)
   - Negative versus positive (costs and benefits, problem and solution)

The preparation process takes time and requires you to memorize more than what will actually appear on the test, but it will pay off. If you prepare by just scanning your textbooks and notes, at the time of the exam, you will have to rely on your memory, to think through each question, and organize a response. Many people have trouble thinking and remembering while under stress, so they need to come into an essay exam with a notion of what they will say and how they will organize their thoughts.

When the exam begins, use your time efficiently. The following plan of attack will help you establish control over the exam.

WRITING ESSAY EXAMINATIONS

1. When you get the exam, note the number of questions and the points each is worth. Decide roughly how many minutes you can afford to spend on each question, and write this number next to it. Don't spend more than two minutes on this activity.

2. For each essay question on the test, take a few seconds to write a very general outline of the points you intend to make (a word or two for each point). Finish all the outlines before you begin answering any of the questions because as you become involved with the task of writing, it will become harder to remember what you have studied.

3. Tackle first the questions that carry the most points. If questions are of equal value, first do the ones that you feel you are best prepared for. Don't go beyond the time you have allotted for each question.

4. As you answer each essay question, stick with the organizational plan you chose initially.

5. If you don't know a precise answer to a question, present course content that has at least some relationship to the question, but don't spend too much time on questions for which you are unprepared.

Organization is key to a successful essay exam answer. A rambling, train-of-consciousness response will give the impression that you don't understand the material, even if your answer includes relevant information. Observe the following organizational principles as you develop your answer to each exam question.

ORGANIZING EXAM ANSWERS

1. Start with a direct answer to the question. Make this answer the first paragraph in your essay.

2. Organize the rest of the essay according to the organizational plan that is clearly indicated by the question, or use one of the following plans:
   - List of reasons or examples

- Comparison and contrast (block or point-by-point)
- Negative versus positive (costs and benefits, problem and solution)

3. Start a separate paragraph for each element in the organizational plan. Each paragraph should have only one major concept or example. Don't worry if paragraphs are short. Complex paragraphs that are composed quickly may seem incoherent.

4. Keep plans simple. Do not use elaborate structures.

Overly ornate language and unclear sentences will also give the impression that you don't know the material on the exam. As you write individual sentences, keep the following principles in mind.

WORD CHOICE FOR ESSAY EXAMINATIONS

1. Place sentence clarity ahead of all other stylistic considerations. If you find it particularly difficult to make yourself understood when you are writing under time pressure, use short declarative sentences.

2. Use the vocabulary of the discipline if you are confident with it, but do not force word choices in an attempt to sound "academic."

3. Don't devote substantial time to revision of word choices.

Works Cited*

Introduction

Scardamalia, Marlene, and Carl Bereiter. "Knowledge Telling and Knowledge Transforming in Written Composition." <u>Advances in Applied Psycholinguistics</u>. Ed. Sheldon Rosenberg, Boston, MA: Cambridge University Press, 1987. Vol. 2, 143.

Chapter 1

Haas, Christina, and Linda Flower. "Rhetorical Reading and the Construction of Meaning." <u>College Composition and Communication</u> 39 (1988): 167-83.

Kierkegaard, Søren. "Fear and Trembling." <u>Fear and Trembling and the Sickness unto Death</u>. Trans. Walter Lowrie. Princeton: Princeton UP, 1941.

Papalia, Diane, and Sally W. Olds. <u>Human Development</u>. New York: McGraw, 1978. Princeton: Princeton UP, 1968. 233.

Shaughnessy, Mina. <u>Errors and Expectations</u>. New York: Oxford UP, 1977.

Stein, Victoria. "Elaboration: Using What You Know." <u>Reading-to-Write: Exploring a Cognitive and Social Process</u>. Eds. Linda Flower et al. New York: Oxford UP, 1990. 144-48.

Wortman, Camille, B., Elizabeth F. Loftus, and Mary E. Marshall. <u>Psychology</u>. 2nd ed. New York: Knopf, 1985.

Chapter 2

Bambara, Toni Cade. "The Lesson." <u>Gorilla, My Love</u>. New York: Random, 1972. 87-96.

Dickens, Charles. <u>A Tale of Two Cities</u>. 1859. New York: Pocket, 1957.

Frude, Neil. <u>The Intimate Machine</u>. New York: New American Library, 1983.

Grant, Linda. "What Sexual Revolution?" <u>Sexing the Millennium: Women and the Sexual Revolution</u>. New York: Grove, 1994.

Heker, Liliana. "The Stolen Party." <u>Other Fires: Short Fiction by Latin American Women</u>. Ed. Alberta Manual. New York: Random, 1982. 152-58.

Laing, R. D. <u>The Politics of Experience</u>. New York: Ballantine, 1967.

Luckman, Joan, and Karen C. Sorensen. <u>Medical-Surgical Nursing</u>. Philadelphia: Saunders, 1974.

Moffatt, Michael. "College Life: Undergraduate Culture and Higher Education." <u>Journal of Higher Education</u> Jan.-Feb. 1991: 44-61.

Monaco, James. <u>How to Read a Film</u>. New York: Oxford UP, 1977.

Sagan, Carl. "In Defense of Robots." <u>Broca's Brain</u>. New York: Ballantine, 1980. 280-92.

Stephens, Gene. "High-Tech Crime Fighting: The Threat to Civil Liberties." <u>Futurist</u> July-Aug. 1990: 20-25.

Zuger, Abigail, and Steven H. Miles. "Physicians, AIDS, and Occupational Risk: Historical Traditions and Ethical Obligations." <u>Journal of the American Medical Association</u> 258 (1987): 1924-28.

Works cited are listed by chapter in which the first reference is made.

Chapter 3

Ehrenreich, Barbara. "The Economics of Cloning." <u>Time</u> 22 Nov. 1993: 86.

Flower, Linda. "Writer-Based Prose: A Cognitive Basis for Problems in Writing." <u>College English</u> Sept. 1979: 19-37.

Knowles, John. <u>A Separate Peace</u>. New York: Macmillan, 1969.

Las Casas, Bartolomé de. <u>Tears of the Indians</u>. Trans. J. Phillips. London, 1656.

Murray, Donald. <u>The Craft of Revision</u>. New York: Holt, 1991.

Chapter 4

Henley, Nancy, Mykol Hamilton, and Barrie Thorne. "Womanspeak and Manspeak: Sex Differences and Sexism in Communication, Verbal and Nonverbal." <u>Beyond Sex Roles</u>. Ed. Alice Sargent. 2nd ed. St. Paul: West, 1985. 168-85.

Chapter 5

August, Eugene. "Real Men Don't: Anti-Male Bias in English." <u>University of Dayton Review</u> Winter 1986-Spring 1987: 115-24.

Richardson, Laurel. "Gender Stereotyping in the English Language." <u>The Dynamics of Sex and Gender: A Sociological Perspective</u>. 3rd ed. New York: Harper, 1988. 19-26.

Chapter 6

Aristotle. <u>The Rhetoric</u>. Trans. W. Rhys Roberts. <u>The Rhetoric and Poetics of Aristotle</u>. Ed. Friedrich Solomon. New York: Modern Library, 1954.

Corbett, Edward. <u>Classical Rhetoric for the Modern Student</u>. 3rd ed. New York: Oxford UP, 1990.

Elbow, Peter. <u>Writing without Teachers</u>. New York: Oxford UP, 1973.

Messner, Michael A. "When Bodies Are Weapons." <u>Sex, Violence, and Power in Sports: Rethinking Masculinity</u>. By Michael A. Messner and Donald F. Sabo. Freedom: Crossing, 1994. 89-98.

Porter, Rosalie P. "The Newton Alternative to Bilingual Education." <u>Annals of the American Academy of Political and Social Science</u> Mar. 1990: 147-50.

Raspberry, William. "Racism in the Criminal Justice System Is Exaggerated." <u>Washington Post</u> natl. weekly ed. 15-21 Apr. 1996.

Chapter 7

Vidal, Gore. "The Four Generations of the Adams Family." <u>Matters of Fact and Fiction: Essays, 1973-1976</u>. New York: Random, 1978. 153-74.

Chapter 8

Gibaldi, Joseph. <u>MLA Handbook for Writers of Research Papers</u>. 5th ed. New York: Modern Language Association of America, 1999.

Weizenbaum, Joseph. "Technological Detoxification." <u>Technology Review</u> Feb. 1980: 10-11.

Index